Second Edition

Positive Behavioral Supports
for the Classroom

Brenda K. Scheuermann
Texas State University

Judy A. Hall

Boston   Columbus   Indianapolis   New York   San Francisco   Upper Saddle River
Amsterdam   Cape Town   Dubai   London   Madrid   Milan   Munich   Paris   Montreal   Toronto
Delhi   Mexico City   São Paulo   Sydney   Hong Kong   Seoul   Singapore   Taipei   Tokyo

Vice President and Editorial Director: Jeffery W. Johnston
Executive Editor: Ann Castel Davis
Editorial Assistant: Penny Burleson
Vice President, Director of Marketing: Margaret Waples
Marketing Manager: Joanna Sabella
Senior Managing Editor: Pamela D. Bennett
Production Manager: Laura Messerly
Senior Art Director: Jayne Conte
Cover Designer: Karen Salzbach
Cover Art: Fotosearch
Project Management: Munesh Kumar/Aptara®, Inc.
Composition: Aptara®, Inc.
Printer/Binder: Courier/Westford
Cover Printer: Courier/Moore Langen
Text Font: Garamond

Credits and acknowledgments for material borrowed from other sources and reproduced, with permission, in this textbook appear on the appropriate page within this text.

Every effort has been made to provide accurate and current Internet information in this textbook. However, the Internet and the information posted on it are constantly changing, so it is inevitable that some of the Internet addresses listed in this textbook will change.

Photo Credits: Anthony Magnacca/Merrill, pp. 2, 210, 232, 260, 340, 374; Todd Yarrington/Merrill, p. 36; Larry Hamill/Merrill, p. 70; Patrick White/Merrill, p. 144; Valerie Schultz/Merrill, pp. 172, 322; Superstock Royalty Free, p. 416.

Library of Congress Cataloging-in-Publication Data
Scheuermann, Brenda.
    Positive behavioral supports for the classroom / Brenda K. Scheuermann, Judy A. Hall.
      p. cm.
    ISBN-13: 978-0-13-214783-5
    ISBN-10: 0-13-214783-1
  1. Classroom management.   2. Behavioral assessment.   I. Hall, Judy A.   II. Title.
    LB3013.S34 2012
    371.102'4--dc22   2011003635

10 9 8 7 6 5 4 3 2

www.pearsonhighered.com

ISBN 10:   0-13-214783-1
ISBN 13: 978-0-13-214783-5

For Billy, from whom I have learned the most. For Dad, who taught me the power of teaching.

Brenda Scheuermann

I would like to dedicate my work to Wynette Barton. Her unfailing belief in my ability has always inspired me. I also want to give a special thank-you to Brenda Scheuermann for asking me to coauthor this text. I want to acknowledge all of my supervisors, professional peers, and students for their part in my career. Last, but certainly not least, I want to thank my parents, Roland and Frances Hall, and my brother, James Hall, for teaching me the importance of lifelong learning.

Judy Ann Hall

PREFACE

Virtually every educator takes classes on behavior management or classroom management, yet teachers consistently cite student discipline and classroom management as primary areas of concern. It is clear that many teachers are not sufficiently prepared to manage even the most minor behavioral challenges posed by today's students. The good news, however, is that the fields of classroom management, applied behavior analysis, and positive behavioral interventions and supports have powerful, evidence-based tools to help teachers effectively prevent most student behavioral problems and to intervene effectively and efficiently when behavioral difficulties develop.

In this book, we draw on this body of research as it has culminated in the field of positive behavioral supports. **Positive behavioral interventions and supports**, or **PBIS**, is an umbrella term that refers to a wide array of individual and systemic strategies to teach and strengthen appropriate behavior and to reduce challenging behavior. These techniques have abundant research to support their effectiveness with all types and ages of students in all types of situations. For the most part, these techniques are relatively easy to use, mesh seamlessly with instruction, and can be expected to produce desirable outcomes when used correctly.

To best prepare readers of this text to be able to apply the concepts and techniques presented, we focus on both the theoretical foundations of behavior and behavioral interventions, as well as the actual day-to-day application of strategies. Our goal is to help educators and educators-to-be bridge the gap between theory and practice. We believe that it is critical for educators to understand the theoretical explanations for behavioral problems and the many teacher-controlled factors that contribute to those problems, and then be able to design research-based interventions that reflect those theoretical underpinnings. Thus, the book not only describes *what to do* for behavior management purposes, but also explains *why*. This will help teachers and others be better prepared to assess challenging classroom and individual student behavioral problems, select evidence-based interventions, and problem-solve if those interventions fail to produce the desired effects.

The No Child Left Behind Act of 2001 placed unprecedented emphasis on the use of scientifically based educational practices. School discipline and behavior management, perhaps more than any other area in education, has often suffered from a lack of reliance on evidence-based practices. To change that, educators must understand evidence-based practices and how to apply them in real-life situations. To that end, the positive behavioral support strategies described in this book are based on extensive research that has evaluated their effectiveness for improving student behavior at the schoolwide, classroom, and individual student levels. We carefully explain the practices supported by this research base, but we also rely on our extensive experience in schools to give many real-life examples of PBIS concepts and strategies. Our personal experience enables us to provide realistic examples of how to apply the skills that we describe in this text, as well as deal with potential problems in their application.

The book explains how both undesirable behavior and desirable behavior are directly related to the contexts in which they occur. In addition, we also explain the many and varied functions that undesirable behaviors serve for students. And most importantly for the classroom teacher, we focus on how to use this information to design effective preventive and management interventions.

To the extent that we can prevent inappropriate behavior in the first place, we can direct more of our energies to classroom instruction. For this reason, we devote several chapters in this text to antecedent strategies, or strategies for preventing challenging behavior and encouraging appropriate behavior. However, despite the wealth of preventive strategies available, rarely can teachers establish a classroom where no behavioral problems ever occur. Consequently, we must also be proficient in planning and implementing effective management strategies for responding to those behavioral problems. These are not difficult skills to master, but they may require that educators learn to think differently about behavioral problems and perhaps change how they respond to student behavior. These efforts will ultimately result in the saving of many hours of teacher time because the ineffective strategies that many teachers currently use to respond to challenging behavior often fail to work and, in fact, frequently exacerbate the very behavior that they are trying to manage.

We were motivated to develop this book because, in our opinion, many classroom management books are insufficient for several reasons. Some texts describe effective strategies but do not provide the theoretical foundation needed to enable teachers to develop problem-solving skills for when those strategies do not work. Other books provide descriptions of effective strategies that are too sketchy for readers to generalize to actual classroom use. Many texts present a wide range of strategies without distinguishing which strategies have strong research support for schoolwide, classroom, or individual student behavioral interventions. Few books address the critical relationship between student learning and behavior and the role of the instructional environment on classroom behavior. And although many classroom management texts describe functional behavioral assessment as a behavioral assessment tool, few texts extensively explain how to use functional assessment data to develop hypotheses and how to develop interventions that directly reflect these hypotheses. This book is our attempt to help remedy the problem of why teachers *still* cite discipline as a major concern, despite all that is known about keeping schools and classrooms safe, orderly, positive, and productive.

NEW TO THIS EDITION

- **A new emphasis on a three-tier PBIS or response-to-intervention model** reflects the rapidly developing field of positive behavior interventions and supports.
- **Chapter 1 has been revised to include a stronger, more comprehensive introduction to PBIS and the 3-tier PBIS model,** giving readers a stronger understanding of why PBIS is so critical for today's educators.
- **New introductions to Parts 2, 3, and 4** reinforce the focus on the 3-tier model and help the reader frame the information as it applies to a particular tier.
- **Chapter 2 includes a greater focus on the Biophysical Model, the Behavioral Model, and Applied Behavior Analysis,** allowing readers

to understand biological contributions to behavior as well as the importance of behavioral theory as it applies to education.

- **Chapter 4 now includes a description of how behavioral measurement relates to the 3-tier model,** helping readers appreciate why it is important for educators to understand behavioral measurement.

ORGANIZATION OF THE BOOK

This book is organized in a logical, sequential manner that mirrors how we approach classroom management and individual student behavior management. **Part I** provides introductory and background information that is relevant to positive behavioral interventions and supports and theoretical models to explain behavior. In this section, Chapter 1 delineates the types of student behavioral problems that teachers will likely encounter and describes the diversity of today's classrooms, the implications for teachers, and the problems associated with traditional approaches to school discipline. We also provide introductory explanations of positive behavioral interventions and supports (PBIS), and compare PBIS and response-to-intervention (RtI). Finally, we describe nine Guiding Principles that reflect PBIS and that serve as the foundation for the remainder of the book. Chapter 2 explains theoretical models of behavior. Focusing on biophysical and behavioral models, we explain the theoretical assumptions, describe the intervention methods associated with these models, and summarize research that is pertinent to the models. We also discuss the relevance and usefulness of the theories and associated interventions for educators.

In **Part II**, we focus on assessment and monitoring of behavior. Chapter 3 explains functional behavioral assessment (FBA), including the Individuals with Disabilities Education Act (IDEA) mandates regarding FBA, the differences between functional behavioral assessment and functional analysis, and step-by-step instructions for how to conduct a functional assessment. We provide many forms for this purpose. In addition, this chapter describes how to use FBA data to develop hypotheses about challenging behavior and then how to use those hypotheses to develop behavioral intervention plans (BIPs). We provide several sample FBAs and BIPs in the form of case studies that are based on actual students. In Chapter 4, we describe data collection techniques for assessing and monitoring student academic and behavioral performance. We explain the various data collection systems and how to use them in the context of busy classrooms.

Part III focuses on creating proactive learning environments through universal-level interventions, including schoolwide positive behavioral supports, and the critical elements of classroom management (i.e., structure, relationships, and instruction). Throughout this section, we provide many examples that reflect the application of the skills and concepts in elementary and secondary schools. Chapter 5 explains the application of positive behavioral interventions and supports at the schoolwide level. This is an exciting movement in school disciplinary practices, and it is one that is proving to be highly effective for improving student behavior. We define schoolwide positive behavioral interventions and supports (SW-PBIS), explain the essential components and specific practices of SW-PBIS, and discuss SW-PBIS research. We also describe steps in planning and implementing SW-PBIS and provide many examples from schools that have been successful in implementing SW-PBIS. Chapters 6 through 8 focus on the critical elements of classroom management. Chapter 6 explains the importance of rules and procedures and how to develop and teach rules and procedures. In Chapter 7, we explain how to design the classroom schedule and how to organize the classroom in order to prevent behavioral difficulties. We also describe the classroom climate and give examples of the elements of classroom climate that contribute to a positive learning environment. This discussion addresses the important element of teacher–student relationships, and the potential for positive relationships to serve as a protective factor for students who are at risk. The last chapter in this section, Chapter 8, describes the correlation between instruction and student behavior. We describe the characteristics of successful learners in comparison with students who have learning and behavioral difficulties. We also provide an overview of the stages of learning and the types of instructional arrangements and activities. Finally, we describe instructional strategies that are associated with academic achievement for students with learning and behavioral difficulties.

Part IV of the text addresses targeted-level interventions and supports to increase appropriate behavior and reduce inappropriate behavior in students who are not sufficiently responsive to universal-level supports. Chapter 9 explains social skills instruction, including types of socialization problems, how to teach social skills, and how to choose social skills curricula. Chapter 10 presents a discussion of reinforcement theory, including definitions, types of reinforcers, how to choose reinforcers, reinforcement schedules, and how to develop and implement reinforcement systems. Chapter 11 describes specific reinforcement applications and systems, including the Premack Principle, token systems, contracts, and group reinforcement systems. We also explain self-management systems (i.e., self-monitoring, self-evaluation, self-instruction, and self-reinforcement) and how to use them to increase students' self-control and independence. Finally, in **Part V**, Chapter 12 describes behavior reductive and punishment systems to reduce or eliminate challenging behavior. In this chapter, we emphasize that a PBIS approach minimizes the need for punishment. We provide definitions of behavior reduction and punishment, and we explain how to determine when a behavior reductive intervention is needed, citing IDEA disciplinary requirements and guidelines for the ethical use of behavior reductive procedures. Finally, we describe a hierarchy of interventions to reduce challenging behavior, including differential reinforcement, extinction, response cost, time-out, and presentation of aversive stimuli. Although we discuss aversive stimuli, we advise readers to avoid these techniques because of the problems associated with punishment and because other PBIS-based interventions should be sufficient for most behavior management needs.

FEATURES OF THE BOOK

To create a text that is user friendly and that readers are able to apply in the classroom, we have incorporated a variety of pedagogical features that are based on effective instruction. These features are designed to help readers organize material, translate theory into application, and get ideas for behavioral interventions for a wide range of purposes. Each chapter includes the following features designed for this purpose:

- "Big ideas" to introduce each chapter.
- Chapter objectives to guide the reader.
- Margin notes that summarize important concepts.
- Multiple vignettes in each chapter to illustrate the concepts being described. The vignettes include elementary, middle school, and high school applications.
- Dr. I.C. Everything, or Dr. ICE, is a consultant who helps educators improve their positive behavioral support techniques. Throughout the book, we present vignettes in which Dr. ICE works with one or more teachers to assess student behavioral problems and to design an intervention to address those problems. In addition, most chapters feature one or more substantial end-of-chapter vignettes featuring Dr. ICE that synthesize the concepts and skills from the chapter.
- Diagrams that illustrate many of the strategies presented.
- Tables or figures to illustrate and expand on content.
- Boxes that provide step-by-step instructions for implementing many of the techniques presented.
- End-of-chapter summaries that review how each chapter objective was addressed.
- End-of-chapter learning activities so that readers can extend and apply the concepts presented in each chapter.
- Resources for each chapter, including websites, books, journal articles, reports, curricula, and materials.
- A self-assessment for readers to evaluate their own skills and knowledge level pertinent to the concepts presented in each chapter.

A FINAL NOTE

Both of us are passionate about using effective, positive behavioral intervention strategies and teaching others to use better strategies. Too many children suffer because their teachers and administrators are not fluent in using the best tools available to prevent challenging behavior or to efficiently manage it in its earliest stages. It is a joy to visit a classroom taught by a skilled teacher. Such teachers make behavior management look easy! We believe that behavior management *is* easy, but only if you use the right tools and use them correctly. We hope that this book will provide those tools for many current and future teachers and that those individuals will then teach others what they know.

ACKNOWLEDGMENTS

Writing a book is a journey that is filled with both rewards and challenges. The most exciting professional benefits are the requisite careful examination of a broad literature base and learning from many other experts. The challenges are the incredible time commitment required and the seemingly endless details. In our case, many people helped us meet those challenges. Our editor, Ann Davis, quite artfully guided our planning for this second edition. The task seemed daunting at first, but through Ann's tactful and succinct questions and suggestions, it gradually unfolded into a manageable task. Thank you, Ann, for your enthusiasm for this project, for your wisdom, and especially for your patience when we seemed baffled by how to conceptualize the changes that we wanted to make.

In addition to Ann, many other professionals at Pearson Education contributed to bringing this project to fruition. We are indebted to the following individuals for their consummate professionalism and unfailing patience:

- Penny Burleson, who is unfailingly gracious and pleasant.
- Carol Sykes, who was incredibly insightful and helpful in working with us during the photo selection process.
- Sheryl Langner, senior project manager, who skillfully and patiently guided us through each step of the production process. We particularly appreciate her assistance with the tedious permissions process. Thank you, Sheryl, for your patience with our endless small changes.
- Pat Onufrak, of Write With, Inc., Damascus, Maryland, whose attention to detail and command of the written language we envy!
- Brian Mounts, marketing coordinator, who is always incredibly responsive to our marketing suggestions and who quickly provides the resources to help us market the book in our work with educators.

The work of many outstanding teachers also contributed to this text. Through their knowledge and expertise, they have provided us with a wealth of effective practices that we are happy to be able to share with readers. Although there are too many to name, we wish to acknowledge their influence. We have learned much from these master teachers.

The book benefited from invaluable feedback from many reviewers who undoubtedly spent long hours to help improve our book. Our reviewers gave us excellent suggestions, and our book is significantly better for their assistance. They are Hollie Cost, University of Montevallo; Anne Gross, St. Thomas Aquinas College; Mabel Rivera, University of Houston; and Christopher Schwilk, Shippensburg University.

BRIEF CONTENTS

CONTENTS

FOUNDATIONS OF BEHAVIOR MANAGEMENT AND POSITIVE BEHAVIORAL INTERVENTIONS AND SUPPORTS

After reading this chapter, you will be able to do the following:

1. Describe the common types and dimensions of school-based challenging behaviors.

2. Describe why the teacher may be the most important variable in students' classroom behaviors.

3. Describe the diversity found in today's classrooms and explain the implications of this diversity for behavior management.

4. Describe traditional disciplinary methods and concerns associated with those methods.

5. Define and explain *positive behavioral interventions and supports*.

6. Define *response to intervention* and how this concept relates to positive behavioral interventions and supports.

7. Explain the nine Guiding Principles for managing behavior in school settings.

Introduction to Behavior Management and Positive Behavioral Interventions and Supports

Big ideas in behavior management and positive behavioral interventions and supports:

- All children exhibit undesirable behavior at times. Most children learn quickly what is and what is not allowed in particular settings; other children need more assistance to learn to exhibit appropriate, rule-following behaviors.

- A graduated model of increasingly more intensive supports, as needed, is an effective and efficient approach to increasing appropriate behavior and reducing challenging behaviors across all students in schools or other settings.

- Years of psychotherapy—for students or the teacher—are not the best way to manage unacceptable classroom behaviors! The most effective behavior management approaches are those that emphasize teaching and supporting desired behaviors.

- Teachers' beliefs about student behavior may determine effectiveness in classroom management.

- Classroom management problems and challenging behaviors exhibited by individual students may result from teachers' practices rather than students' problems (i.e., something about the teacher's behavior may be contributing to the situation). This is actually good news!

- Positive behavioral interventions and supports represent the latest evolution in behavior management for individual student, classroom, and schoolwide applications.

- The extent to which all educators understand positive behavioral interventions and supports and know how to use them in all types of school situations will make behavioral interventions for all students more effective and efficient.

All children exhibit inappropriate behavior at times. Most undesirable behavior is a normal, expected part of growing up. Fortunately, most children learn fairly quickly which types of behaviors are tolerated and which are not, and when to stop inappropriate behaviors. They also learn that behavioral expectations vary among people, places, and circumstances, meaning that they know with whom and where they can be more rambunctious, silly, or noncompliant. By the time most children enter school, undesirable behavior is more or less controlled by traditional means: reminders to behave, relatively infrequent reinforcement, reprimands, time-outs, and parental contacts. Most children need to experience minor consequences once in awhile throughout their school years, but for the most part, their behavior is appropriate and acceptable.

These strategies work for most children. However, anywhere from 10% to 30% of school-age children may not respond to methods that work for other children (Martella & Nelson, 2003; Office of Special Education Programs, 2005). When faced with the behaviors of these children, educators often tend to view the child as the problem rather than view the behavior management system as failing to meet the needs of that child (Martella, Nelson, & Marchand-Martella, 2003). It is true that some children are less prepared than their peers to meet both the behavioral and academic demands of school. Various individual, family, and societal factors, which we discuss in Chapter 2, play a role in children's behavior. However, teachers have control over many other school-based factors that affect behavior, including the design of classroom management and instructional systems. In fact, most teachers (58%) and parents (60%) believe that teachers have the power to positively influence student behavior (Public Agenda, 2004). This perception is supported by research that indicates that teachers' actions in their classrooms are highly influential on student achievement—as much as or more than school administrative and leadership policies (Marzano, 2003b). To achieve this positive influence, teachers need to plan classroom and individual behavior management systems with the goal of creating a meaningful, active instructional environment where rules and expectations are clear; where more attention is given to desired behavior than to inappropriate behavior; and where inappropriate behavior is dealt with systematically, consistently, and equitably.

Most of this text is devoted to explaining how to develop positive, proactive behavioral intervention systems and plan instruction in ways that are most likely to produce the desired outcomes. The majority of the techniques that we describe for these purposes are based on the philosophy and practices of **positive behavioral interventions and supports (PBIS)**. According to the Office of Special Education Programs Technical Assistance Center on Positive Behavioral Interventions and Supports:

> A variety of factors can interfere with a child's school success. Teachers have control over many school-based factors that influence student behavior.

Positive behavioral support is a general term that refers to the application of positive behavioral interventions and systems to achieve socially important behavior change . . . Positive behavioral support is not a new intervention package, nor a new theory of behavior, but an application of a behaviorally-based systems approach to enhancing the capacity of schools, families, and communities to design effective environments that improve the fit or link between research-validated practices and the environments in which teaching and learning occur. Attention is focused on creating and sustaining school environments that improve lifestyle results (personal, health, social, family, work, recreation, etc.) for all children and youth by making problem behavior less effective, efficient, and relevant, and desired behavior more functional. In addition, the use of culturally appropriate interventions is emphasized. (Sugai, et al., 2000, pp. 133–134)

PBIS represents a fundamental shift in managing unacceptable behavior from reactive, punitive responses to challenging behavior to a proactive emphasis on the prevention of behavioral problems by using positive, instructional, research-based strategies to teach and encourage appropriate behavior and manage the learning environment. PBIS is the integrated application of (a) behavioral science, (b) practical interventions, (c) social values, and (d) a systems perspective (Technical Assistance Center on Positive Behavioral Interventions and Supports, 2004) to design interventions at the individual, classroom, and schoolwide levels for the purpose of increasing success for all students. The techniques presented in this book reflect PBIS methods for preventing inappropriate behavior, teaching and encouraging appropriate behavior, and managing challenging behavior in all students, but particularly in students with mild to moderate disabilities, at the individual, classroom, and schoolwide levels.

PBIS is a proactive, instructional, preventive approach for improving outcomes for all students.

The goal of encouraging appropriate behavior and preventing and managing inappropriate behavior is a demanding task because teachers are expected to successfully teach a wide range of students, including students who are not well prepared for the demands of school and students who are not highly motivated to behave appropriately and learn. The task is complicated by the fact that schools serve a diverse population of students from varied cultural, ethnic, and religious backgrounds who have a range of abilities and learning histories. But the good news is that teachers have the power to meet this challenge by using a wide array of research-based tools to support appropriate behavior, to prevent and manage behavioral problems, and to deliver instruction. We describe these tools, as well as the research to support their use with diverse populations of students, in the remaining chapters of this text.

To illustrate the many concepts and skills presented throughout this book, each chapter will include one or more classroom vignettes. These vignettes will illustrate common classroom management issues and concerns. Many of the vignettes will feature our expert behavior management consultant, Dr. I. C. Everything, known to his friends as Dr. ICE. Dr. ICE got his nickname because he stayed cool during times of crisis. Dr. ICE began his work in the early seventies, when special education was just beginning to be implemented in all public schools across the country. Until then, many children with all types of disabilities did not go to school. Dr. ICE's university training was focused on learning about the characteristics of major disabilities, with only a couple of classes on basic reading and mathematics instruction. He took one class in behavior theory. Unfortunately, many of today's teachers are equally unprepared for the demands of teaching and classroom management (Darling-Hammond, 2005), as we will discuss later in this chapter.

Dr. ICE found out by lunchtime on the first day of teaching that he was underprepared for classroom management. He was not able to make much progress in his lesson plans because his students controlled his classroom. He had a rocky first year, to say the least. He spent the summer researching the topic of classroom management and thinking of changes that he could make in his classroom to make it a better learning environment. The changes helped and the second year was better. Still, Dr. ICE realized that he needed more training if he was to stay in this challenging profession. His efforts in the area of behavior management interested him a great deal, and he wanted to learn more. He has spent the rest of his career going to school to learn about behavior, teaching and observing in classrooms, and training children and adults.

BEHAVIORS THAT TEACHERS MAY ENCOUNTER

During their training, future teachers envision their classrooms as happy, productive environments where students are interested in learning and where they eagerly participate in lively discussions and exciting activities. Seldom do preservice teachers imagine classrooms that include students who do not do the assigned work, who do not relate to what is being taught, who talk back to teachers or defy teachers' instructions, who have difficulty making friends or who are the target of peers' taunts and derisive comments, who talk or move too much, or who come from home environments where there is little support for the types of behaviors that are expected at school. These behaviors abound, however, and every teacher will encounter them. Failure to anticipate and prepare for such behaviors may leave teachers underprepared for the challenges of real-life classrooms.

The most common behavioral concerns reported by teachers reflect relatively minor inappropriate classroom behaviors.

The students just described are present in almost every classroom in every school in the nation. In one survey, teachers reported spending more time dealing with student behavioral problems than teaching (Public Agenda, 2003). Secondary teachers report that they spend too much time dealing with problems related to low student motivation, student disrespect toward one another, disregard for the school dress code, use of cell phones or other prohibited electronic devices, and argumentativeness (Public Agenda, 2007). A 2004 survey of teachers on disciplinary problems and policies indicates that schools have made progress in dealing with more serious disciplinary problems, such as drugs and guns, but that minor behavioral infractions continue to be problematic (Public Agenda, 2004). Table 1-1 lists the most commonly cited disciplinary concerns reported by teachers. The good news for teachers is that minor misbehavior is easily preventable and manageable using the techniques described throughout this book; more serious behaviors will need more intensive interventions, such as those described in Chapters 3, 4, 9, 10, 11, and 12 of this text.

TABLE 1-1   Most Frequently Reported Disciplinary Problems

Percentage of teachers who say that each behavior is a "very" or "somewhat" serious problem:

Disrupting class by talking out loud and horseplay	69
Students treating teachers with a lack of respect	60
Cheating	58
Students showing up late to class	57
Bullying and harassment	55
Rowdiness in common areas, such as hallways and lunchroom	51
Truancy and cutting class	45
Illegal drugs	41
Physical fighting	36

Source: Information from *Teaching Interrupted* (p. 36) by Public Agenda, 2004. Available from http://www.publicagenda.org/reports/teaching-interrupted.

Another way to view the types of behavioral concerns listed in Table 1-1 is to consider behaviors along several dimensions. Often, students exhibit behaviors that are not serious but become disciplinary problems because of one or more of the following characteristics:

Frequency of Behavior. A student who gets out of her seat once during a class period without permission does not present a problem, but a student who is out of her seat 15 times during that same period does. A student who complains or argues about an assignment once does not pose a challenge to the teacher, but a student who argues about every assignment does. A student who talks to his friends once or twice a month during the teacher's lesson may not cause the teacher much concern. However, a student who continually tries to talk to others despite repeated warnings will soon have the teacher searching for other, probably more punitive, ways of dealing with the behavior.

Duration of Behavior. Many students exhibit brief instances of disruptive, noncompliant, or inattentive behavior at times during their school career. It is not uncommon, for example, for a student to talk out loud, joke, make off-task comments, talk to a peer, fail to follow the teacher's instructions to line up after recess, or stare out of the window during independent work time. However, some students may continue these types of behaviors even after the teacher redirects the student to stop the behavior or prompts the student to comply. Sometimes behaviors become a target of concern not because the behavior is highly inappropriate but because the behavior continues significantly longer than what is considered acceptable.

Intensity of Behavior. Although most children sometimes argue, complain, or tease their peers, some children engage in this behavior with so much intensity that they stand out from their peers. Often the intensity of their behavior renders these children unable to respond to directives or other attempts at intervention. Because of this, these children may have difficulty calming down once the problem behavior begins. For example, a child whose peers exclude him from a game that he wants to play may become so angry that he is unable to deal with the situation in an acceptable manner. Or, a student who is doing independent work who encounters a task that she does not know how to do might become so frustrated that she is not receptive to receiving assistance from the teacher.

Latency of Behavior. When teachers give instructions, it is not only important for students to comply with those instructions, but to do so in a timely manner. Latency of behavior refers to how quickly a behavior occurs once cued. A student who takes 10 minutes to begin a task, or who dawdles during transitions, is displaying problems related to latency. Of course, another latency-based problem is when students respond too quickly. This type of problem is characterized by a child who blurts out answers before the teacher calls on her, or students who begin a task before the teacher is finished giving instructions.

Age Appropriateness of Behavior. Some children exhibit behaviors that are inappropriate only because of the age of the child. For example, a tantrum may be an age-appropriate, typical behavior for a 2-year-old but not for a 10-year-old; grabbing items from other children may be expected behavior for a 5-year-old but not for a 12-year-old.

Behaviors may escalate into problems along one or more dimensions: frequency, duration, intensity, latency, age appropriateness, or type.

Type of Behavior.   Of course, a few children exhibit behaviors that are seldom demonstrated by their peers, such as refusing to work, cursing, talking back to teachers and administrators, walking out of class without permission, coming to school under the influence of drugs or alcohol, bullying, or exhibiting aggression. These behaviors are considered inappropriate at any time, under any circumstances, regardless of the age of the student.

Emotional/Behavioral Disorders in Children and Youth.   Most student behavioral problems present relatively minor challenges for educators. However, in 1999, U.S. Surgeon General David Satcher released a report estimating that as many as 20% of children ages 9 to 17 may have diagnosable mental or addictive disorders. Approximately 11% of children may experience significant impairment from these disorders, and 5% may experience extreme impairment (U.S. Department of Health and Human Services, 1999). More recent estimates of the prevalence of mental health disorders in young people support the figures reported by the surgeon general (National Advisory Mental Health Council Workgroup on Child and Adolescent Mental Health Intervention Development and Deployment, 2001). For example, the National Alliance on Mental Illness (NAMI) reports that 3 to 5 million children ages 5 to 17 (or 5% to 9% of this population) in the United States are affected by serious mental disorders (NAMI, n.d.). Researchers from the National Institute of Mental Health report that 20% of children and youth are affected by a mental disorder that interferes with functioning and 40% of those young people have more than one disorder (Merikangas et al., 2010). Many reports on the prevalence of childhood behavioral disorders state that 12% to 22% of children under age 18 are in need of services for emotional, mental, or behavioral problems (Center for Mental Health in Schools, 2003).

A comprehensive 2009 report from the Institute of Medicine of the United States National Academies estimated that between 14% and 20% of young people have an emotional or behavioral disorder (National Research Council and the Institute of Medicine, 2009). These disorders include both diagnosable disorders, such as anxiety disorders or depressive disorders, as well as behavioral difficulties that may not meet formal diagnostic criteria. More children and youth are identified with externalizing disorders than internalizing disorders. An **externalizing disorder** is one in which the behavioral manifestations are readily apparent to observers and include symptoms such as poor self-control or emotional regulation, hyperactivity, aggression, noncompliance, and so forth. An **internalizing disorder** is one in which symptoms are manifested more internally, such as excessive worry, a need for reassurance, or perseveration on a particular topic. According to the National Research Council's report, more children and youth are reported to have internalizing disorders than externalizing disorders. An estimated 8% of children and youth are diagnosed with some type of anxiety disorder or phobia, and a little over 5% have depression. In contrast, 6.1% of young people are reported to have some type of disruptive behavioral disorder and 4.5% are diagnosed with attention-deficit hyperactivity disorder.

Furthermore, children of all ages appear to be equally affected by mental health disorders, including preschool-age children (U.S. Public Health Service, 2000). Table 1-2 lists mental health disorders that affect children, the prevalence of each, and the corresponding behavioral characteristics that may interfere with

TABLE 1-2 Mental Health Disorders in Children, Including Prevalence and Behavioral Characteristics

Disorder	Prevalence (percentage of the school-age population)	Behavioral Characteristics
Attention-Deficit Hyperactivity Disorder	3% to 5% 8.6%	• High level of physical or verbal activity, excessive fidgeting • Difficulty concentrating or focusing attention • Easily distracted • High level of impulsivity
Depressive Disorders		
Major Depressive Disorder	At any one time, between 10% and 15% of the child and adolescent population has *some* symptoms of depression	• Extreme and pervasive sadness • Self-critical • Pessimistic • Problems concentrating • Lethargic • Irritable or hostile
Dysthymic Disorder	3%; after age 15, depression is twice as common in girls and women as in boys and men	• Same as major depressive disorder, but more chronic, with fewer symptoms
Anxiety Disorders		
Generalized Anxiety Disorder	3%	• Excessive worry • Perfectionism • Constantly seeking approval or reassurance
Social Phobia	3% to 13%	• Extreme fear of social situations (such as talking in class) • Tantrums or excessive timidness
Disruptive Disorders		
Oppositional Defiant Disorder	1% to 6%	• Persistent disobedience, defiance, or hostility toward authority figures • Argumentative • Easily loses temper

(Continued)

TABLE 1-2 *(Continued)*

Disorder	Prevalence (percentage of the school-age population)	Behavioral Characteristics
Conduct Disorder	1% to 4%	• Fights, intimidates, bullies others • Cruel to people or animals • Vandalism • Substance abuse
Substance Abuse Disorders	Of adolescents who take substances, 6% to 10% become chronic abusers (Newcomb & Richardson, 1995)	• Alcohol abuse • Drug use • Often appearing in conjunction with other mental disorders
Eating Disorders	3% of young women	
Anorexia	.1%	• Low body weight • Intense fear of gaining weight • Inaccurate perception of body shape or weight
Bulimia		• Episodic, uncontrolled eating followed by self-induced vomiting
Binge Eating		• Episodic, uncontrolled eating

Source: Unless otherwise indicated, U.S. Department of Health and Human Services. *Mental Health: A Report of the Surgeon General—Executive Summary.* Rockville, MD: U.S. Department of Health and Human Services, Substance Abuse and Mental Health Services Administration, Center for Mental Health Services, National Institutes of Health, National Institute of Mental Health, 1999.

school performance, as defined by the U.S. Office of the Surgeon General. Although the behaviors described in Table 1-2 pose significant challenges to educators, the techniques presented in this book will positively affect these student behaviors as well (Kerr & Nelson, 2006; National Research Council and the Institute of Medicine, 2009; U.S. Department of Health and Human Services, 1999). In fact, the best hope for students with behavioral difficulties may well be a consistent, proactive, positive school environment that maximizes students' academic and social success.

DIVERSITY IN THE CLASSROOM

Teachers must have a good understanding of their students' varied cultures and life experiences.

Schools serve richly diverse student populations from varied ethnic, cultural, religious, linguistic, and socioeconomic backgrounds. Approximately 42% of the students in public schools are members of minority groups (Miller, 2003/2004), yet only a small minority—approximately 16%—of teachers are from cultural or ethnic minority groups, and almost half of our nation's schools have no minority teachers at all (Strizek, Pittsonberger, Riordon, Lyter, & Orlofsky, 2006). This means that most minority students will be taught by a teacher from a different cultural or ethnic group. This fact has implications for teacher–student relationships, teacher–family relationships, and behavior management. Teachers must take special care to understand the values, priorities, beliefs, and behavioral styles of all of the diverse groups represented in their classrooms. Teachers also need to understand the subtle behavioral characteristics that may be typical of particular cultural or ethnic groups and not interpret these behaviors as "problems." A few examples of these characteristics are as follows:

- Asian American students may be reluctant to ask questions of teachers, participate in class discussions, or state opinions because of family teachings to respect older people and to be modest, polite, and quiet. Asian American students may feel uncomfortable with American teachers' friendliness and directness, may at first avoid eye contact (believing eye contact to be a sign of disrespect), and may view reprimands given to a student as shameful for the family (Cheng, 1998; Grossman, 1995; Zhang & Carrasquillo, 1995).
- African American students are often raised with an emphasis on family and community, with community concerns possibly superceding individual accomplishments and independence (Okun, Fried, & Okun, 1999). African American students may also exhibit specific behaviors that may conflict with school expectations, such as lack of direct eye contact when listening, maintaining closer physical proximity than other students, and reticence about discussing family problems and relationships (Randall-David, 1989). Franklin (1992) lists certain family practices among African Americans that may affect children's school behavior. These practices include high levels of family interactions in high-energy home environments, early lessons about racism, expectations that children should be assertive, and expectations that even young children may take on family responsibilities. Research indicates that instruction for African American students should address issues of race and racism (Schwartz, 2001).
- African American and Hispanic students cite teachers' encouragement rather than teachers' demands as a powerful motivational factor that is consistent across socioeconomic levels, family composition, and amount of schooling attained by the mother (Ferguson, 2002). Teachers' behaviors that were cited by students as being indicative of encouragement included providing thorough explanations, providing extra help to students outside of class time, and providing reassurance that the student has the ability to succeed.
- Students from extreme poverty may exhibit certain behaviors that teachers find unacceptable unless considered within the context of an impoverished home life. For example, the authors of this text have worked with students who did not flush the toilet after each use and who did not wash their hands after using the restroom or before eating. These students were not being forgetful or lazy; they had either been taught at home not to flush or wash their hands because those activities use water and water is expensive, or they

came from homes that had no running water. Another student hoarded food from the cafeteria to take home; the child's family was extremely poor, and there seldom was enough food. The child was simply trying to ensure that her brothers and sister had something to eat.

• The senior author of this text works with schools that serve large numbers of students whose families have emigrated from different Pacific Rim countries. Administrators and teachers from these schools cite particular behaviors exhibited by these students as problematic in the American school environment, including fighting (and being very quick to resort to fighting) and spitting as way to insult someone.

To be effective with students from all backgrounds, teachers must understand their students' lives. In terms of behavior management, teachers should always consider possible cultural explanations for behaviors. This does not necessarily mean that teachers must overlook certain behaviors that are culturally influenced, but are unacceptable at school (e.g., not flushing the toilet). This information should be used to guide the teacher in dealing with the behavior.

THE CRITICAL ROLE OF THE TEACHER

Polls of teachers, parents, and the public consistently cite discipline as a major concern (e.g., Langdon, 1999; Rose & Gallup, 2002, 2004). Unfortunately, most teachers receive insufficient training in research-based behavioral strategies that help prevent inappropriate behaviors or that allow educators to respond to challenging behaviors using positive educational approaches (American Federation of Teachers, 2003; Public Agenda, 2004). In a 2008 survey of first-year teachers, only 34% of the respondents reported that their teacher training coursework covered positive behavioral interventions as a method for classroom management (Public Agenda, 2008). Fortunately, as discussed in the previous section, most classroom behavioral problems are not serious, yet 85% of the teachers surveyed reported that, as new teachers, they felt completely unprepared to deal with student behavior (Public Agenda, 2004). Secondary teachers, in particular, report that their teacher training did not prepare them for the realities of adolescent behavior (Public Agenda, 2007). Reports in the popular media echo these findings, often highlighting teachers' lack of preparation for the day-to-day demands of classroom management (e.g., Wingert, March 6, 2010).

The limited classroom management training provided in teacher preparatory programs may give teachers the basic tools needed to manage minor disciplinary issues but not chronic or serious behavioral challenges. Given ongoing reports that teachers feel unprepared for managing student behavior, it appears that new teachers may not be taught research-based, positive behavioral support methods for managing classroom and individual student behavior. This is unfortunate because, as you will learn from reading this text, we have the technology for preventing behavioral problems and for managing all types of problems that do arise, from the minor to the more severe or chronic misbehaviors. Also, as you will learn in Chapter 8, the better managed the classroom, the more time teachers have to teach and the more students are likely to learn. Finally, the teacher's role in classroom management is critical. Other factors, such as students who have learning and behavioral difficulties or teaching in impoverished areas, may make the task more demanding, but the teacher remains the most critical element in the overall management and organization of the classroom. Simply put, a teacher who is fluent in classroom and behavior management techniques will encounter fewer behavioral problems than one who is not.

Perhaps the most important component of any behavior management program is prevention. It is critical for educators to know and to be able to implement proactive strategies to prevent misbehavior. To illustrate the importance of prevention, consider the following areas of our society and how the practices listed for each area serve a preventive function:

Public Health

- Prenatal care for expectant mothers
- Well-baby checkups
- Vaccinations
- Annual physicals for adults
- Healthy diet and exercise

Sports

- Helmets, pads, and other protective gear
- Training and diet
- Clear rules and procedures for group sports

Restaurants

- Laws governing food storage and handling
- Regular inspections

The Law

- Contracts
- Prenuptial agreements
- Leases

Airports

- Public address system announcements about rules and consequences for violating those rules
- Clearly designated areas for lining up for security inspection and flight check-in
- Clear procedures, posted and announced (e.g., for moving through security, for arriving at the gate prior to departure, the number of bags allowed to be checked, and the number of pieces of carry-on luggage)

Prevention is important for classroom management in several ways. First, the less time teachers spend on disciplinary problems, the more time they have to teach (Public Agenda, 2004). Second, sometimes "untreated" minor disciplinary problems escalate to more serious forms. The works of Alan Kazdin (e.g., Kazdin, 1987), Hill Walker (e.g., Walker, Ramsey, & Gresham, 2004), Kenneth Dodge

When teachers know and use positive, preventive behavior management strategies, many of the commonly reported minor inappropriate classroom behaviors can be avoided.

(e.g., Dodge, 1993), Shep Kellam (e.g., Kellam, 2002), Gerald Patterson (e.g., Patterson, DeBaryshe, & Ramsey, 1989; Patterson, Reid, & Dishion, 1992), and many others have provided a clear picture of the development of antisocial behavior. Serious antisocial behavior in teenagers (e.g., chronic truancy, academic underachievement, chronic problem behavior) usually begins with low-level rule breaking (e.g., noncompliance). Left untreated or treated with ineffective interventions, these low-level challenges may gradually escalate over time to more problematic behaviors.

One particularly persuasive series of studies examined the effects of well-managed versus weakly managed first- and second-grade classrooms on a variety of long-term undesirable behaviors (Dolan et al., 1993; Kellam, Ling, Merisca, Brown, & Ialongo, 1998). First graders in the 18 schools involved in the Baltimore Prevention Program studies were rated in terms of several behavioral characteristics, including aggressiveness and shyness. Next, students were randomly assigned to one of two types of classrooms: (a) either those where teachers implemented a systematic management system called the Good Behavior Game (we describe the Good Behavior Game in Chapter 10), or (b) classrooms where no systematic classroom management system was in place. Students from these classrooms were then followed into middle school, where they were again evaluated in terms of aggression, shyness, and antisocial behaviors (e.g., smoking, substance abuse).

The Good Behavior Game shows the importance of effective classroom management for young children.

Children who ranked in the top 25% of the group in terms of aggression fared poorly as they got older if their first-grade classrooms were disorderly. Aggressive children from disorderly first-grade classrooms were *59 times more likely to exhibit aggressive behavior* than the average child by the sixth grade! In comparison, other students from that top quartile who began school in first-grade classrooms where the Good Behavior Game was used were only 2.7 times more likely than other children to act out in the sixth grade. Other long-term benefits of the structured first- and second-grade classrooms were evident as well. Students from these classrooms who originally were rated as shy, based on social interactions, were significantly less shy in middle school and were significantly less likely to show symptoms of depression than their peers (Kellam, Rebok, Mayer, Ialongo, & Kalodner, 1994), and had reduced mental health problems in early adulthood (Petras, Kellam, Brown, Muthén, Ialongo, & Poduska, 2008). In addition, students from the Good Behavior Game classes had reduced risk for tobacco, alcohol, and illicit drug use (Ialongo et al., 1999; Kellam & Anthony, 1998). All of these studies show that early exposure to positive, proactive classroom management plays an important role in preventing and managing immediate problem behaviors and has a positive effect on long-term outcomes as well. The results of this study are astounding and clearly underscore the power of teachers and schools in preventing serious behavioral problems.

Also, as you will learn in Chapter 5, approximately 80% to 90% of all students will respond successfully to a positive, proactive school environment that emphasizes teaching students how to behave and ensuring that attention is paid to appropriate behaviors rather than simply punishing inappropriate behavior (Office of Special Education Programs, 2010). Another 5% to 15% of students will need more intensive, individualized interventions, such as those described in Chapters 9 through 12. Finally, approximately 1% to 7% of all students will need individualized, integrated services from multiple agencies. These compelling statistics should convince you of the importance of the teacher in preventing minor misbehaviors from becoming significant problems and managing behaviors effectively so that they do not escalate or become chronic problems.

CONCERNS REGARDING TRADITIONAL APPROACHES TO DISCIPLINE

Traditionally, educators have dealt with student misbehavior by responding to instances of challenging behavior with punishment (Gushee, 1984; Sugai & Horner, 2002). The term *discipline* has acquired the connotation of "punishment" because punishment has traditionally been the primary component of discipline. In fact, punishment and exclusion are the most common responses to challenging behavior, despite the fact that reactive responses such as reprimands, detention, and exclusion are unproductive behavioral change methods (Heumann & Warlick, 2001) and may even reinforce undesirable behaviors, as you will see in Chapter 3. Of course, traditional approaches also include a few proactive measures. Teachers are expected to establish classroom rules, most schools have designated consequences for breaking classroom or schoolwide rules, and most schools clearly define prohibited behaviors and consequences for those behaviors. However, a system consisting simply of rules and consequences for breaking those rules is apparently insufficient, given the widespread concerns about discipline and the fact that a relatively minor problem such as talking out during class is one of the most often cited disciplinary problems (see Table 1-1). Unfortunately, not only are traditional methods largely ineffective for the students who exhibit chronic behavioral problems, but these methods pose other problems as well, including the following issues:

1. ***Traditional disciplinary methods are disproportionately applied to certain minority students.*** One of the most pressing concerns with traditional, reactive approaches to discipline is that research has documented significant gender, racial, ability, and socioeconomic disparities in school discipline. Of particular interest is the fact that exclusionary disciplinary consequences are applied more often to minority students; particularly African American students, than any other students. In 1975, a landmark study conducted by the Children's Defense Fund produced several important findings. First, rates of suspension for Black students were two to three times higher than for White students at all grade levels. Second, a majority of the states suspended more than 5% of their Black student population but only four states suspended an equivalent number of White students. Finally, African American students were more likely than White students to be suspended more than once (Children's Defense Fund, 1975).

   These findings have remained consistent in the decades following that 1975 study: African American students continue to receive disproportionately more exclusionary and more punitive disciplinary consequences than other students, especially White students (Leone et al., 2003; Opportunities Suspended, 2000; Skiba, Michael, Nardo, & Peterson, 2000; Townsend, 2000).

> There are concerns related to traditional approaches to school disciplinary methods.

Furthermore, the National Longitudinal Transition Study-2 (2006) revealed that African American students with disabilities are suspended or expelled at disproportionately higher rates than White or Hispanic students with disabilities. Almost half of African American secondary students with disabilities have been suspended or expelled from school, compared to less than 30% of White students and 28% of Hispanic students.

Other groups are also disproportionately affected by traditional disciplinary policies. Research shows that, in addition to minority students, low-income students, and students with disabilities are more likely to receive exclusionary and more punitive consequences (e.g., corporal punishment, public reprimands) than are White, middle-class, or upper-class students (Leone et al., 2003; Skiba et al., 2000). Furthermore, within low-income subgroups, students of color still face more disciplinary consequences than do White students (Darensbourg, Perez, & Blake, 2010; Skiba et al., 2000; Taylor & Foster et al., 1986). Despite the disproportionate number of suspensions for minority students, no objective evidence suggests that students of color act out more or are more disruptive than other students. In fact, some evidence suggests that African American students are referred to the principal's office for more minor infractions than White students, are punished more severely for the same offenses, and receive more office referrals for subjectively determined behaviors (e.g., disrespect; see Leone et al., 2003; Opportunities Suspended, 2000; Skiba et al., 2000).

Skiba et al. (2000), Townsend (2000), and others recommend that one way to address the problem of disproportionate discipline of minority students is teacher training in effective, culturally competent methods of classroom management. This is especially critical given the fact that minority student enrollment in public schools was between 38% (Strizek, et al., 2006) and 42% (National Center for Educational Statistics, 2005) in the 2003–2004 school year; whereas most teachers are White and female. Only 16% of teachers are from cultural or ethnic minority groups (Strizek et al., 2006), and 42% of public schools have no minority teachers (National Education Association, 2004). Twenty-five percent of all teachers and only 16% of elementary school teachers are male (Strizek et al., 2006). Minorities are also underrepresented among school principals, who typically provide leadership in school disciplinary policy and decision making. In the 2003–2004 school year, only 16% of school principals were members of minority groups (Strizek et al., 2006).

> Traditional disciplinary methods tend to be disproportionately applied to certain minority students.

2. ***Most traditional disciplinary methods are reactive.*** Most traditional approaches to discipline, such as office referrals, detention, or calls to parents, are applied only after a problem behavior occurs. This means that the problem behavior must occur before an intervention is used to address that behavior. It is preferable to prevent misbehavior from occurring in the first place. Of course, some might argue that the threat of detention, office referral, or other interventions is preventive. This assumption, however, is not supported with data. In fact, most of the students who are the recipients of these disciplinary measures are "repeat offenders" (Public Agenda, 2004), indicating that, for these students, the discipline that they received did not prevent

future occurrences of misbehavior. Consider this analogy: Drivers who exceed the speed limit do so, in part, because the *potential* for receiving a speeding ticket is an insufficient consequence to control their speed. Once they receive a ticket, people generally slow down for a while, but then they gradually resume their previous driving patterns. Likewise, the *potential* for receiving a jail sentence or hefty fines is insufficient to prevent some individuals from committing crimes.

3. ***Reactive measures are often time—and resource—intensive.*** Teachers and administrators spend an inordinate amount of time dealing with problems related to student behavior (Heumann & Warlick, 2001; Public Agenda, 2004; University of Vermont, 1999). Such resources would be better spent providing positive, supportive environments and effective instruction.

   Consider the time spent on office referrals alone. According to one source, each office disciplinary referral requires approximately 10 minutes of an administrator's time and 20 minutes of a student's time (Illinois PBIS Network, 2005). The teacher must first write the referral, often during class time. Then the assistant principal, or the designated administrator who handles disciplinary matters, must call the student to the office, wait for the student to arrive, talk with the student, determine a consequence (e.g., detention, home call), and then inform the teacher of the action taken. Then there is paperwork to be completed in order to document the referral and the outcome. Finally, the actual consequence must be carried out, which may involve time from other school personnel (e.g., a detention teacher) and more paperwork. Multiply this process by the number of students who receive office referrals, and you can see the excessive amount of time spent responding to behavioral problems. Again, this time could be spent more productively on instruction and implementation of proactive, preventive behavior management strategies.

4. ***Many disciplinary methods put educators in a position with students that is contrary to their reasons for entering the profession.*** Educators enter the field to teach, guide, and mentor students. These are very positive and optimistic goals. The ineffective aspects of traditional disciplinary methods, at best, create an environment that is unpleasant for all involved and is, at worst, hostile and adversarial (Public Agenda, 2004).

5. ***Studies show that the disciplining of students continues to be at the forefront of teachers' concerns and is one of the major reasons that teachers leave the profession.*** Teachers often cite lack of training in dealing with the realities of teaching as a factor that influences their decision to leave teaching (Hardy, 1999; McCreight, 2000; Public Agenda, 2004). When well-trained, experienced teachers leave the field, it is not only a significant loss for the field but also a waste of valuable resources.

> Concerns related to classroom management are often cited as a reason that teachers leave the teaching profession.

The concepts and skills presented throughout this book are based on research related to effective behavioral interventions. To set the stage for these concepts and skills, in the next section we describe Guiding Principles, or ways of thinking about behavior. These Guiding Principles provide an important foundation for preventing and managing disciplinary problems.

MAKING SCHOOLS MORE EFFECTIVE FOR ALL STUDENTS

Positive behavioral interventions and supports refer to both a philosophy and an array of research-based practices that emerged as a result of concerns about aversive, punitive approaches for coping with challenging behaviors. The term *positive behavior support* is used in reference to practices that rely on "educational and systems change methods (environmental redesign) to enhance quality of life and minimize problem behavior" (Carr et al., 2002, p. 4). PBIS is conceptualized as a continuum of intervention levels that range from proactive, preventive strategies applied throughout a school or facility to comprehensive, intensive interventions developed for and applied to individuals who have significant behavioral needs (Walker et al., 1996). The overarching goal is prevention: preventing behavioral problems from developing, and preventing negative outcomes from those problems that do develop.

Walker and his colleagues (1996) proposed a three-tiered model of prevention/intervention approaches that reflect a public health model of prevention and intervention. In the public health model, **primary prevention** refers to universal strategies that are designed to prevent health problems (e.g., fluoridation of the public water supply to prevent cavities, recommendations to exercise and maintain a healthy diet in order to avoid heart problems). **Secondary prevention** strategies are designed to quickly and effectively respond to problems that develop despite primary prevention efforts. The goal is to catch problems early to prevent more severe problems. Public health examples include filling cavities to prevent further tooth decay and treating high blood pressure or high cholesterol levels to prevent heart disease. Finally, despite our best efforts at prevention, some serious health problems will occur. Treatment for such cases involves **tertiary interventions** that are designed to minimize the negative effects of problems. In the health field, tertiary treatments include root canals and other extensive dental repairs, and bypass and other surgeries to repair heart damage.

Educational applications of this three-tiered model address both academic and behavioral systems (see Figure 1-1). Primary prevention, also called **universal-level** academic approaches, includes reliance on evidence-based instructional methods and curricula for teaching reading, mathematics, and other academic subjects, and periodic screening to identify students who are not making the expected academic progress. Universal-level behavioral approaches include establishing and teaching schoolwide expectations, acknowledging rule-following behavior, and monitoring behavioral indicators to quickly identify students who are not responding to the universal-level strategies. Evidence suggests that when we implement comprehensive universal-level interventions, about 80% to 90% of the students will be successful. This means that we can expect universal interventions to result in about 80% to 90% of any student population—elementary or secondary—meeting academic and behavioral expectations.

Secondary-level academic interventions, also called **targeted-level** prevention, might include small-group instruction in areas of deficit (e.g., reading fluency or writing), along with more frequent progress monitoring. Secondary-level

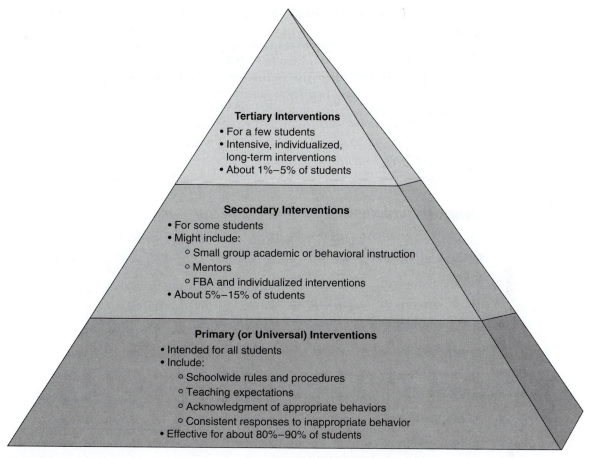

FIGURE 1-1   Three-Tier Model of Prevention   *Source:* Technical Assistance Center on Positive Behavioral Interventions and Supports. Available from www.pbis.org. Reprinted with permission.

behavioral interventions might include social skills instruction for identified students, or frequent reminders and feedback about expected behaviors. Approximately 10% to 15% of the students will be successful with these additional targeted interventions.

The remaining 1% to 5% of any given student population may need additional, more intensive, individualized supports, which are called **tertiary-level supports**. Tertiary-level academic interventions might involve individualized reading or mathematics instruction using a separate curriculum and specialized instructional methods. Tertiary-level behavioral interventions involve careful assessment of behavior, and comprehensive, individualized interventions that may include social services and/or mental health services in addition to school-based interventions.

Schools throughout the United States, and in other countries as well, are implementing academic and behavioral systems that are reflective of this tiered prevention model. Various terms are used to refer to these systems. The model, as it applies to academic interventions, is generally referred to as **response to intervention**, or **RtI**. The behavioral three-tiered prevention model is often referred to simply as **positive behavioral supports**, **positive behavioral interventions and supports (PBIS)**, **schoolwide PBIS (SW-PBIS)**, and more recently, **response to intervention for behavior**, or **behavior RtI**. We will use the phrase *positive behavioral interventions and supports*, or the acronym *PBIS*. As the title implies, this text focuses on the behavioral model, and will focus primarily on the application of PBIS principles and practices to classroom management and management of individual student behavior. The organization of the text generally reflects the three tiers of prevention and support: Part 2 reflects universal-level supports; Part 3, targeted-level supports; and Part 4, tertiary-level interventions.

GUIDING PRINCIPLES

Adherence to the Guiding Principles will help teachers become more independent problem solvers when faced with behavioral challenges.

The material in this text is based on several basic assumptions that we call **Guiding Principles** (see Table 1-3). A *principle* is defined as a "a comprehensive and fundamental law, doctrine, or assumption" (Merriam-Webster Online, n.d.). Our Guiding Principles have been culled from the large body of behavioral research (discussed throughout the text), as well as from our own experiences as teachers of children with challenging behaviors. Adherence to these Guiding Principles is an important step toward the ability to solve problems independently when faced with chronic behavioral problems.

TABLE 1-3   Guiding Principles

Guiding Principle 1: Changing inappropriate student behavior requires changing the teacher's behavior.

Guiding Principle 2: Some students require more time, attention, and structure than others.

Guiding Principle 3: Students exhibit both desirable and undesirable behaviors for a reason.

Guiding Principle 4: Many behavioral challenges reflect learning difficulties.

Guiding Principle 5: Most inappropriate behavior is predictably linked to specific contexts and activities.

Guiding Principle 6: It is more efficient and more effective to change student behavior by using positive strategies rather than punitive strategies.

Guiding Principle 7: It is more efficient and effective to use proactive, preventive strategies rather than relying on reactive strategies after a behavioral problem has already developed.

Guiding Principle 8: Students benefit when general educators and special educators work together to meet the needs of all students.

Guiding Principle 9: Students benefit when educators maintain close communication with parents in order to share information and collaboratively plan educational and home programs.

Guiding Principle 1: Changing Inappropriate Student Behavior Requires Changing the Teacher's Behavior

Typically, teachers respond to challenging behaviors by blaming the student or looking for student-centered explanations (Walker, 1995). For example, teachers may attribute a student's noncompliance to the student's family not enforcing limits or the family not teaching the student that he or she must follow teachers' instructions. Given this attitude, it may be sobering to many of us to realize that we are often the catalyst for the escalation of undesirable classroom behavior. Of course, the opposite is also true: A teacher's behavior facilitates appropriate behavior as well. The little things that we say to our students (or do not say), what we acknowledge (or ignore), the behaviors we smile at (or frown at), how we encourage (or discourage), and so on—all of these things have an impact on student behavior. A central premise of positive behavioral interventions and supports is that a teacher's behavior plays a central role in shaping a student's response: To achieve the goal of increasing appropriate student behavior, we must change aspects of our own behavior in the classroom.

> Sometimes, even small changes in a teacher's behavior will have a positive effect on student behavior.

This is both good news and bad news. The bad news is that it is likely that a teacher's actions are contributing directly in some way to student misbehavior. That is, teachers often do things, typically with good intentions, that actually serve to foster and reinforce undesirable behavior. But the good news is that the knowledge that the undesirable behavior is related to something that we are doing is far preferable to learning that the misbehavior lies somewhere outside of our control. Perhaps most significant is the understanding that if we can identify our behaviors that contribute to the escalation of problem behavior, we can change it—and that is good news.

This principle is nicely illustrated in the experiences of Ms. Valadez, who taught biology at Winters High School. She knew her subject well and her lesson plans were an excellent reflection of the state's curriculum. She had high expectations for her students in their academic endeavors and in their behavior, and she trusted that her students had been prepared for her class by their prior educational experiences. She also expected that students in the 10th grade would know how to behave in her classroom. The students who chose to act out were not welcome in her classroom. Ms. Valadez's classroom management system consisted entirely of sending students to the office for any behavioral infraction. Unfortunately, Ms. Valadez had the highest rate of office referral of all the teachers on that campus. Several of her students were repeatedly sent to the office for minor infractions.

Dr. ICE became involved when the leadership of the high school changed, as did the philosophy of the school district. Positive preventive approaches to classroom management were now expected at all levels. Teachers would be trained to implement these changes. Ms. Valadez was having a hard time buying into this new way of doing things.

Dr. ICE convinced her that if she made an effort to change her behavior, she would see dramatic changes in the behavior of her students. She agreed to make such an effort. First, Ms. Valadez worked with her students to develop rules for the classroom (we discuss in Chapter 6 how to use student input in developing rules). She designed the organization of the room so that she had better access to all of her students. She made it a point to praise her students and to give gentle corrections when she saw minor acting out.

When Ms. Valadez met with Dr. ICE six weeks later, she was smiling. She said that she smiled often these days. Her students followed her procedures and her classes were well behaved. She seldom sent students to the office because she was able to stop poor behavioral choices before they got out of hand. She told Dr. ICE that she felt a new power in herself. In past years, she had no idea that she could have such a positive influence on her students' behavior. She was inspired to learn more and asked Dr. ICE to help her do so.

Guiding Principle 2: Some Students Require More Time, Attention, and Structure Than Others

Children are different! Because of this, some children require considerably more resources than others. Some students need more time and attention from their teacher than their peers. Some students need more in the way of external control and support, more structure, or more frequent feedback about their behavior in order to regulate their behavior. What this all means is really quite simple: What works for most students is often not effective or is insufficient for students who exhibit chronic behavioral challenges.

We define students with behavioral challenges as those students who require differential behavior management techniques, more structure, and possibly more individualized instruction, above and beyond what is effective for the majority of students, in order to bring their behavior into compliance with school or classroom rules and in order for them to achieve academic and social success. In the three-tiered model of positive behavioral interventions and supports described previously, these would be the students who need targeted or tertiary supports and interventions. Of course, within that group, some students may need very little in the way of additional support in order to be successful, while others will need more intensive supports. To minimize the number of students who need the most intensive supports, educators are well advised to rely on the research-based practices described in this text.

To illustrate this principle, consider the experiences of Ms. Peacock, who teaches an after-school arts and crafts class at Albert Elementary School. She wants her students to enjoy her class and has created rules and procedures so that all of the materials can be used safely. All of her students have chosen to be in this extracurricular class. Ms. Peacock's students are an energetic group, and most of them listen and behave well with gentle verbal reminders. There are, however, three students who disrupt the class on a regular basis. Either they do not listen to directions and then ask endless questions about their project, or they succeed in getting everyone at their table off task. Ms. Peacock has worked with Dr. ICE on other occasions. She has asked him to help her identify strategies for assisting these three students in being more successful in her class.

At this point, we wish to differentiate between classroom management and behavioral interventions for individual students. Effective teachers need to understand and know how to use both types of management systems. For most situations, especially for students with high-incidence disabilities, positive, proactive classroom management systems will be sufficient for maintaining an orderly, safe, and productive classroom environment. The strategies that we describe in Chapters 5 through 8 address behavior management of groups of students. However, some students need more intensive, individualized interventions above and beyond what is used for the group. For these students, the group system is insufficient to encourage appropriate behavior and discourage inappropriate behavior. For these situations, we describe strategies that are most appropriate for individual students, such as those presented in Chapters 3, 4, and 9 through 12.

> Both desirable and undesirable behaviors occur for a reason.

Guiding Principle 3: Students Exhibit Both Desirable and Undesirable Behaviors for a Reason

There are usually one or more reasons for a child's undesirable behavior (Martella et al., 2003). If you are able to ascertain the reason(s) for the behavior, you are more likely to design intervention strategies to address that reason, increasing the likelihood of an effective intervention. This concept is a basic premise of positive behavioral support. In Chapter 2, we describe how factors in a child's immediate environment contribute to most challenging behaviors, and in Chapter 3, we explain how to determine those environmental factors that exacerbate problem behaviors, as well as other causes of unacceptable behaviors.

> Being alert to the environmental variables that may be contributing to a student's misbehavior can be an important first step in designing interventions to change that misbehavior.

As a simple illustration of the principle that behavior occurs for a reason, let's consider Mikey, a fourth grader who made noises during transition times as if he were passing gas. Every time that he made these sounds, his classmates laughed. Mikey's teacher had told him numerous times to "stop making those sounds" and had even sent him to the principal's office on two occasions. However, Mikey persisted in exhibiting the misbehavior, largely because he liked being the center of attention. The laughter of his peers was reinforcing his behavior, and because of this, he would continue making the passing-gas sounds as long as his peers continued to laugh, despite the other negative consequences that the teacher used in an attempt to eliminate the behavior. A more suitable intervention for Mikey might be to teach him other more appropriate ways to make his peers laugh at more appropriate times.

Or consider Sam, a second-grade student at Random Elementary School. He often comes to school with a story about hurting himself while playing or getting into trouble at home and having his toys taken from him. He does not have any friends in class. In fact, he regularly makes other students angry by tattling or by calling them names. He continues to annoy others until they threaten him. His outbursts often bring the learning process to a grinding halt. Sam and his younger brother and sister live with their grandparents. His mother left the family when Sam was 4 years old. His grandparents reported that he seems to go out of his way to get into trouble at home. His grandmother says that Sam's grandfather works two jobs and she works in a nursing home 4 days a week. She says that she is tired and that raising three young children at her age is hard enough without Sam taking up most of her free time. Dr. ICE, understanding the principle that behaviors occur for a reason, assessed Sam's behavior (using the methods that we describe in Chapter 3) and concluded that much of Sam's behavior is to get attention from adults and peers. Dr. ICE is now working with Sam's educational team to plan interventions that will allow Sam to obtain attention through more appropriate means.

Guiding Principle 4: Many Behavioral Challenges Reflect Learning Difficulties

When faced with a student who exhibits high rates of misbehavior, educators should determine whether academic skill deficits might be a contributing factor to that misbehavior.

Most students want to please, and they generally do the best that they can. Research has clearly shown that students who exhibit high levels of challenging behavior respond positively when provided with appropriate interventions, including interventions designed to aggressively remedy deficits in basic academic skills and interventions to teach students more appropriate alternatives to misbehavior (Kauffman, Mostert, Trent, & Hallahan, 2002; Walker et al., 2004). It is important for educators to understand that the more academic failure that exists in any given classroom, the greater the likelihood of undesirable behavior in that class (Kerr & Nelson, 2006; Martella et al., 2003; Scott, Nelson, & Liaupsin, 2001). Of course, the reverse is also true: The greater the level of academic success, the fewer undesirable behaviors will appear. A PBIS approach to managing behavioral problems requires that we consider all possible contributing factors to a student's behavioral difficulties, including curricular and instructional variables. This is why we devote an entire chapter in this text to the discussion of effective instructional methods.

Vance's situation illustrates this principle nicely. Vance is an 11th-grade student at Western High School. He reads on a fourth-grade level and is in a special education resource class. His teacher, Mr. Brice, is organized and consistent in both academics and classroom management. Mr. Brice has to choose the tasks that he gives Vance very carefully. A task that is too easy is quickly finished and then Vance usually disrupts the learning environment by telling jokes and pulling as many peers off task as possible. When Mr. Brice gives Vance a consequence, he often talks back and announces that all he gets is baby work. When Vance is given a task that he determines is too hard, he puts his head down and refuses to work or to talk to Mr. Brice.

Mr. Brice has reported that he has several students in each of his resource classes who present challenging behaviors. He has asked Dr. ICE to observe and to help him develop specific academic and behavioral plans for these students.

Guiding Principle 5: Most Inappropriate Behavior is Predictably Linked to Specific Contexts and Activities

Students seldom misbehave "out of the blue." Challenging behavior is not a random act that just happens: It typically occurs in the presence of certain predictable environmental events. These events may be external to the student (e.g., working in small groups, transitions, working independently) or internal to the student (e.g., hunger, fatigue, illness). Like Guiding Principle 3, the concept that behavior is influenced by the context in which it occurs is a critical element of positive behavioral interventions and supports. In Chapter 2, we explain this concept more thoroughly, and in Chapter 3, we describe data collection procedures to help identify when and where problem behavior is likely to occur and why. These data then assume a major role in the subsequent development of preventive behavior management strategies. For example, one of our former students was generally pleasant and cooperative until he was given a task that involved extensive writing, which he disliked. At that point, he usually responded by complaining about the task, saying that it was too hard. From there, he typically escalated to refusing to do the work, usually accompanied by cursing and sweeping the materials off of his desk. This behavior occurred under the very specific circumstances of being given a writing task. Knowing this, we were able to design interventions to target both the conditions under which the behavior was likely to occur and the reasons for the behavior.

Another example of this principle is Juan, who is an eighth grader at Wilcher Middle School. He receives language arts instruction in a special education resource class. His reading is almost at grade level, but his writing is several grade levels below his grade placement. Juan has been getting into trouble in his general education history class. His friends are into passing notes, but he will not do this because of his low writing ability. His friends have begun to tease him for not joining in. They do not know that he cannot write well, however, and he is afraid that they will soon find out. In order to draw their attention away from the notes, he has begun to entertain them by making jokes about Ms. Newsom, their history teacher. When they are laughing at their teacher, they are not thinking about his writing or teasing him. Ms. Newsom is becoming more and more frustrated because she is losing control of this class. Juan seems to "have it in for her." He makes fun of her, and the other students laugh. She does not understand why he has made her his target.

> Positive strategies are more effective and efficient than punishment.

Guiding Principle 6: It is More Efficient and More Effective to Change Student Behavior by Using Positive Strategies Rather than Punitive Strategies

The results of research indicate that focusing on school and classroom management strategies that promote positive social behavior and academic success for all students is essential to preventing disciplinary problems (Nelson, 1996; Nelson, Martella, &

Marchand-Martella, 2002). As we have indicated, responding to inappropriate behavior requires much teacher time. The extent to which inappropriate behavior can be prevented gives teachers more time to teach and students more time to learn.

Relying on proactive behavior management approaches is not yet the norm for all schools (Martella et al., 2003; Sprague, 2002). There are several explanations for why educators tend to overuse punitive approaches, particularly for students with chronic patterns of undesirable behavior. Maag (2001) offers reasons for widespread reliance on punishment for disciplinary purposes in schools, including the fact that punishment is easy to use, usually works quickly for students who do not exhibit high levels of challenging behaviors, and is reinforcing to teachers. Another explanation for punishment-oriented school discipline lies in zero-tolerance policies and rules. The term **zero tolerance** originally referred to applying uniform suspension and expulsion policies for serious school-based disciplinary infractions involving weapons, drugs, or violence (National Association of School Psychologists [NASP], 2001). However, over the years, zero-tolerance policies have been expanded to mandate harsh punishments for a wide range of rule infractions, sometimes even encompassing minor behaviors that are clearly not dangerous (NASP, 2001; Skiba, 2000). Zero-tolerance laws and policies require educators to administer these prescribed consequences regardless of their effectiveness in remedying the problem. We discuss punishment, including zero tolerance and problems with this approach, in Chapter 12.

> SW-PBIS is the application of PBIS philosophies and practices to whole-school environments.

As discussed earlier, given the ever-increasing knowledge base about the efficacy of positive, proactive approaches, there is a steady trend toward greater reliance on positive behavioral interventions and supports as the preferred method for school discipline. The 1997 reauthorization of the Individuals with Disabilities Education Act (IDEA '97) increased awareness of the concept of positive behavioral intervention and supports by requiring that behavioral intervention plans based on positive behavioral supports be developed for students who exhibit behaviors that interfere with their own learning or the learning of others. Prior to IDEA '97, PBIS was primarily viewed as a comprehensive array of interventions for individuals with developmental disabilities and severe behavioral challenges (Carr et al., 1999; Sugai & Horner, 2002). As discussed previously, PBIS has moved beyond its original concept as a tool for individual student application to use with entire schools—even entire school districts—in the form of schoolwide positive behavioral supports. Research has demonstrated the efficacy of PBIS for students of all ages and ability levels, and for schoolwide use as well as individual student applications. We describe schoolwide PBIS in Chapter 5.

Guiding Principle 7: It is More Efficient and Effective to Use Proactive, Preventive Strategies Rather Than Relying on Reactive Strategies After a Behavioral Problem Has Already Developed

> Preventing a problem is generally easier than dealing with the problem once it appears.

As you learned in our discussion earlier, most of our classroom and behavior management efforts should be geared toward preventing behavioral problems. Some educators may think that they shouldn't have to do anything special to prevent disciplinary problems; they may think that a teacher's job is simply to teach and not worry about behavior management, and that students who do not behave should be removed from the classroom.

While this may be a tempting attitude, it is nonetheless an unrealistic and ineffective one. As you have learned from our discussion of disciplinary concerns reported by teachers, all teachers must be prepared to deal with disciplinary problems. Teachers and other educators have two choices: they can wait until those problems develop and then use traditional, reactive, usually punitive responses, or they can anticipate problems and implement proactive strategies in an effort to prevent those problems. The former approach is seldom effective for students who exhibit chronic or challenging behaviors. The latter approach is not only an effective approach for most students, but is also associated with higher levels of teacher satisfaction, teachers' perceptions of efficacy, and improved school climate (Center for PBS at the University of Missouri–Columbia, 2009; Rentz, 2007).

The schoolwide model of positive behavioral interventions and supports—and, by extension, the application of this model to classroom management—is based on a preventive approach to discipline. As you have learned, this approach can prevent significant behavioral difficulties in the majority of the student population.

Guiding Principle 8: Students Benefit When General Educators and Special Educators Work Together to Meet the Needs of All Students

By definition, special education teachers are expected to work with other educators on individualized educational program (IEP) teams to conduct functional behavioral assessments (FBAs), develop behavior intervention plans (BIPs) (see Chapter 3), and plan and implement inclusive educational programs for students. A special education teacher who teaches in isolation will not be as effective for his or her students as a teacher who is part of the mainstream of the school setting and who interacts regularly with other teachers and students in the school. Research shows that all students, both students with disabilities and their peers without disabilities, benefit when special and general education teachers collaborate (Ripley, 1997). Special education teachers are professionals who have much to offer general education teachers and other educators (e.g., administrators, counselors, social workers); they also can learn much from these individuals. To be effective in collaboration with other professionals, we offer the suggestions listed in Box 1-1.

> Collaboration among special educators and general educators leads to more effective educational programs for students who exhibit challenging behaviors.

Guiding Principle 9: Students Benefit When Educators Maintain Close Communication With Parents in Order to Share Information and Collaboratively Plan Educational and Home Programs

> Parental involvement is important for students' school success.

Individuals who are preparing for a career as a teacher undoubtedly give much thought to the appeal of working in the school environment, helping students

Box 1-1

Suggestions for Effective Collaboration

- Embrace the belief that you can learn from other professionals.
- Develop behavioral interventions collaboratively with the general education teachers who will be implementing the interventions. Special education teachers may have more knowledge about behavioral interventions, but general education teachers will be able to help develop systems that are manageable within a busy general education classroom. In the process of designing behavioral or academic interventions, special education teachers should ensure that general educators fully understand the interventions and how they are to be implemented. For example, a BIP intervention to "provide frequent praise" might mean something very different to a high school English teacher than it does to a special education teacher. The special education teacher should be very specific about how frequently praise should be provided, for what types of behaviors, and how that praise should be given. As part of developing interventions, the team should also discuss how the special education teacher will provide support for the general education teacher with regard to implementing academic and behavioral interventions in the general education classroom.
- Listen carefully to general educators' concerns and then take steps to address those concerns. Remember that general education teachers are under pressure to cover required content. When developing behavioral interventions that will be implemented in general education classes, try to streamline those interventions as much as possi-

ble to make them easy for general education teachers to manage. Collaboration in developing interventions will help to accomplish this.

Sometimes special educators may have to take extra steps to ensure that they are viewed as part of the mainstream school faculty. To accomplish this, we recommend that special education teachers do the following:

- Be an active member of any school group or committee to which you are assigned. Follow through on tasks that you are given or for which you volunteer, attend meetings unless you have a conflict, and be a positive contributor in those meetings (as opposed to complaining or griping).
- Be willing to step outside of your assigned duties in order to experience new groups and school activities. For example, volunteer to be a chaperone at school dances or a sponsor for school clubs. Attend grade-level team meetings as much as possible for the grades of the students you teach; you will learn much about the curriculum, teacher expectations, and student behavior in those meetings. Go to the teachers' lounge regularly. Visit other teachers' classrooms. Attend extracurricular activities.
- Volunteer to share behavior management ideas with your peers, perhaps during faculty meetings or at other professional development venues. Offer your services to teachers who are experiencing classroom management problems; for these teachers, you will want to observe, ask the teacher about specific problems, make suggestions for specific strategies to address those problems, and possibly even volunteer to model some of the strategies that you describe.

succeed academically and socially, acting as a mentor and role model for youngsters, and simply being a part of one of the most significant aspects of children's development—education. However, being a teacher, especially a special education teacher, also involves another important role that new teachers are often underprepared for—that is, working collaboratively with families. Both IDEA and No Child Left Behind mandate specific types of family involvement in their children's school experiences. So it could be said that knowing how to facilitate collaborative relationships with families is important because it is required by law. However, family involvement is also important because having parents work closely with school personnel increases the effectiveness of educational programs for children with disabilities. For example, parental involvement has been shown to positively affect grades (Keith et al., 1998), attendance (Kube & Ratigan, 1991), and challenging behavior (Morrison, Olivos, Dominguez, Gomez, & Lena, 1993). Attaining these positive outcomes requires careful attention to developing relationships with parents and other primary caregivers to involve them in every aspect of their child's education. Attendance at the annual IEP meeting is important, but close collaboration with parents should also involve more frequent contact. In this section, we provide ideas for maintaining close contact with parents and focusing on strategies for collaborating with parents in areas related to behavior management.

It is important for teachers and future teachers to understand the impact of a child with special needs on the family, and the many roles that parents of children with disabilities play. While a thorough discussion of this topic is beyond the scope of this text, many excellent publications are devoted to that subject (see "Resources," p. 34). However, without a basic understanding of the factors that impact families of children with disabilities, teachers may find it difficult to have empathy, and possibly even respect, in their relationship with parents. For this reason, we present a brief overview of the important dynamics of families of children with disabilities, particularly as these dynamics potentially affect behavior management in the classroom.

Many parents of children with disabilities describe having experienced various stages of emotional reaction to having a child with a disability that are similar to the stages of mourning associated with death (Blacher, 1984; Ferguson, 2003). The stages most commonly reported are listed in Table 1-4, along with possible behaviors that may be indicative of each. Please note that these stages are simply what parents have reported experiencing and are not intended to be used by teachers to "diagnose" parents. Furthermore, is it not a given that all parents will experience these stages as listed; individuals may experience these stages at different times, with different intensity, or not at all.

Effective collaboration with families requires awareness of the diversity represented by students and their families. Antunez (2000) describes possible barriers that teachers may face in attempts to collaborate with families from diverse backgrounds, including language skills, work schedules, lack of trust in the school system, and the belief that educators are the experts and do not need parental involvement. Teachers must understand potential barriers and take steps to ensure that they do not prevent collaboration with families.

Not only do strong parent–teacher relationships contribute to more positive outcomes for students, collaborative relationships with parents can make your job as a teacher easier, and more pleasant. Like most aspects of classroom and behavior management, your relationships with parents should not be left to chance. Rather, you should actively implement strategies that are designed to encourage strong, collaborative relationships with parents. We present some of these strategies in Box 1-2. Of course, there are teacher behaviors that potentially interfere with productive relationships with families. Some of these are as follows:

- Acting authoritatively with parents, always providing information and recommendations without listening or soliciting information or the parents' ideas.

TABLE 1-4   Emotional Responses to Having a Child with a Disability

Stage	Characteristics
Shock, denial, disbelief upon learning that the child has a disability—For many children with disabilities (e.g., learning disabilities, behavioral disorders), identification of the disability may not occur until middle childhood. At first, parents may deny that there is a problem or feel that the problem stems from something that can be fixed (e.g., giving the child more attention, identifying a medical problem).	Searching for a definitive answer to questions about the child's problems; visiting many different types of professionals in search of answers and help. Parents may refuse services because, in their mind, there is no problem.
Guilt, anger, depression, rejection, or overprotectiveness of the child—Parents believe that they are responsible for their child's problems (e.g., mother drank a few glasses of wine during pregnancy), and/or if they work hard enough, they can fix the problem.	Parents may take extreme measures to correct the "mistakes" they believe that they've made. They may spend inordinate amounts of time and money to "fix" their child, sometimes to the point of neglecting other family members or family obligations.
They want someone to be held responsible for their child's problems; anger or blame may be directed at family members (perhaps at a spouse), doctors, or teachers. They may experience immense sadness over the realization that the child is not going to be cured and may be pessimistic about the future.	Ongoing dissatisfaction with the child's educational program; multiple complaints about the school and teacher that seem to have no solution; nonspecific complaints; inability to come to agreement on IEPs or BIPs.
	Lack of involvement with the school; apparent disinterest in the child's program.
Acceptance or coping—Parents have a realistic understanding of their child's disability, strengths, needs, and future.	Actively involved in the child's educational program; works collaboratively with educators.

- Avoiding contacting parents because of lack of time, a dislike for parents, a dislike for parent–teacher conferences, or other reasons.
- Failing to make parents feel welcome at school and/or failing to make it easy for parents to contact the teacher.
- Contacting parents only when there is a problem.
- Regularly sending students home because of behavioral problems at school. We strongly believe that school problems should be handled at school, although in collaboration with the parents. If school personnel do not know how to manage a behavioral problem, they have access to many available resources. We believe that sending students home as a consequence for challenging behavior is problematic for several reasons. First, if the function of the challenging behavior is avoidance, sending the student home may actually cause the behavior to get worse (see Chapter 3). Also, sending students home does not teach appropriate replacement behaviors. Finally, sending students home

Take specific steps to facilitate collaborative relationships with parents.

Box 1-2

Strategies for Facilitating Positive, Collaborative Teacher–Parent Relationships

- Initiate early contact with parents before the first day of school, if possible. Introduce yourself and provide information about your classroom (e.g., rules, expectations, procedures), behavior management system, how you will communicate with parents, how and when to reach you, and so on.
- Provide daily or weekly reports about behavior when that behavior is of concern. These reports will keep parents informed about the student's performance and will help the teacher and parents stay focused on important issues. This information can be in the form of behavior charts, notes, home–school notebooks, e-mails, or telephone calls.
- Take steps to ensure that parents feel welcome in the educational setting. Schedule meetings at times that are convenient to parents, allow sufficient time for meetings so that you can provide parents with your undivided attention, provide toys or activities for siblings while you talk with parents, provide adult-size furniture, hold conferences at a table rather than at your desk, and welcome other family members who wish to attend school functions.
- Use active listening to address parents' concerns. Our first response when parents voice concerns is often to either act reassuringly or become defensive. Neither response is productive. On the other hand, if you listen carefully and ask questions to be sure that you understand the parents' real concerns, you are more likely to be able to address those concerns objectively.
- Use lay terminology rather than educational jargon. Parents who hear, "Your child met the criterion in Phase Two of our differential reinforcement of zero levels of behavioral intervention" are probably not going to be inclined to ask too many questions!
- Rather than feeling intimidated by parents who are knowledgeable about special education law and practices, view these parents as a great resource for you! Take advantage of parents' expertise.
- Ask for parents' help when needed, but be specific in your requests. For example, you might provide parents with specific suggestions about how to most effectively review the child's weekly behavior folder with the child. Or you might ask

parents for information about the youngster's social relationships—whom he plays with, how frequently, how well they get along, and so on.
- Model effective practices. Explain your behavioral systems in simple terms. If you wish for parents to reinforce a particular behavior at home (e.g., completing homework on time, remembering to bring needed materials from home), give parents specific ideas for how to do this. You might even provide a simple behavior chart for parents to use (see Chapters 10 and 11 for ideas about reinforcement systems). Likewise, if you wish for parents to provide a consequence for something that happened at school, you might provide specific recommendations for that consequence.
- Understand that parents who speak a different language, are very poor, or are of a different race or ethnicity have much to offer. They are rich sources of information about their child and can be valuable partners in efforts to help the child succeed.
- Try to get to know a little about the family (e.g., brothers and sisters, grandparents, or others who might live in the home; where the parents work; family interests).
- Contact parents to share positive information more often than negative information. Too often, parents' only experience with schools is when school personnel call because of a problem. Make it a regular practice to let parents know about their child's successes and to share positive information about the student's school performance.

Working with parents can also enhance behavior management. To this end, teachers will need to communicate with families for the following reasons:

- Obtain information for functional behavioral assessments.
- Collaboratively develop behavioral intervention plans.
- Provide frequent information about students' behavioral and academic performance.
- Solicit information to determine whether changes in the home environment may be affecting a child's behavior in situations where the child's behavior changes significantly.
- Inform parents about disciplinary decisions for seriously inappropriate behavior.

means that students lose instructional time. As discussed previously, because behavioral problems often go hand in hand with learning problems, students who exhibit chronic challenging behavior can ill afford to miss school. In fact, students' instructional needs should be examined as a possible factor in the problem behavior.

Summary

These are interesting times for educators. We are under intense public scrutiny to raise academic standards and improve student outcomes. Yet, at the same time, teachers and administrators are challenged to serve children with multiple and complex needs: children who come to school ill prepared for even basic learning tasks, children with significant behavioral problems and learning disabilities, children with serious but untreated emotional conditions, and children from diverse backgrounds and family situations. These children respond positively to clear, predictable, and well-planned environments. But studies consistently reveal teachers' opinions that they do not have the training needed to address these students' disciplinary and behavior management needs. Teachers and administrators quickly exhaust all of their traditional tools with these students but to no avail.

But there is hope! Research over the past 40 years has produced a wealth of knowledge about effective prevention and intervention strategies for even the most difficult-to-manage students. The challenge now is to apply this knowledge, on a large scale, to ensure that every teacher and administrator has knowledge of effective behavioral prevention and intervention strategies, knows how to apply these strategies under varying conditions, and can use systematic problem solving to adjust techniques when needed.

The objectives for this chapter and how they were addressed are as follows:

1. Describe the common types and dimensions of school-based challenging behaviors. Students exhibit a variety of unacceptable behaviors. Most of these are minor, but a few are serious and can result in significant impediments to learning. Often these behaviors can be described along a continuum of dimensions such as frequency, duration, intensity, age appropriateness, and type of behavior.

2. Describe why the teacher may be the most important variable in students' classroom behaviors.

Research shows that teachers' behaviors are predictive of student behavior: Teachers who exhibit certain preventive behaviors (e.g., recognizing appropriate student behavior) and engage in preventive practices (e.g., scheduling to ensure high levels of student engagement) typically have fewer classroom management problems than teachers who do not do so.

3. Describe the diversity found in today's classrooms and explain the implications of this diversity for behavior management.

We presented data that document the rich diversity of today's classrooms. Given that the majority of teachers are White and female, we explained the implications for teachers, and the impact of this discrepancy on behavior management and discipline. It is critical for teachers to understand students' cultural, ethnic, religious, and other areas of diversity, and to engage in culturally competent methods of classroom management.

4. Describe traditional disciplinary methods and the concerns associated with those methods.

In this chapter, you learned that a major problem with traditional disciplinary methods is that some students, particularly minority students, male students, and students of low socioeconomic status, are more likely to be the recipients of exclusionary disciplinary practices and other punitive forms of discipline. Traditional disciplinary methods are also reactive rather than proactive and, for this reason, are not as effective at preventing behavior management problems. In addition, traditional disciplinary approaches are time intensive, especially for the outcomes produced, and such approaches appear to leave teachers underprepared for the demands of classroom management.

5. Define and explain *positive behavioral interventions and supports.*

The term *positive behavioral interventions and supports* (PBIS) refers to a proactive instructional approach to behavior management for individuals, groups, and entire schools. PBIS emphasizes on prevention, environmental clarity and predictability, the teaching of desired behaviors, and reliance on research-based methods in a tiered model of increasingly more intensive and individualized supports.

6. Define *response to intervention* and how this concept relates to positive behavioral interventions and supports.

Response to intervention, or RtI, is the term used to refer to a tiered system of academic interventions. Schoolwide PBIS is sometimes referred to as "RtI for behavior."

7. Explain the nine Guiding Principles for managing behavior in school settings.

We described nine Guiding Principles that summarize much of the knowledge base in the area of behavioral research. We suggested that adopting these Guiding Principles as the foundation for thinking about student behavior will better prepare teachers to solve the problems associated with classroom or individual behaviors by using interventions.

Learning Activities

1. Interview one novice and one experienced teacher. Ask each what types of behavioral challenges students exhibit in their classrooms and how they are expected to deal with problems related to those challenges. Ask the novice teacher if classroom management is easier or more difficult than he or she imagined and why. Ask the experienced teacher how classroom management needs have changed since he or she began teaching.

2. In small groups, discuss the effects of higher academic standards and public scrutiny of school performance on discipline.

3. In this chapter, we argue that changing student behavior usually requires that teachers change something about their own behavior. How do you feel about this? If you knew that this would improve student behavior, would you be willing to make changes in your interactions with students? Discuss these questions with a classmate.

4. In a small group, discuss primary prevention, secondary prevention, and tertiary interventions as they relate to managing student behavior. Give examples of each term.

5. Find examples from your own experiences or the experiences of friends or family members for each of the Guiding Principles presented in this chapter.

6. Describe how you will begin to establish a positive relationship with the following individuals:
- Administrators
- Office staff
- Teachers
- Paraprofessionals
- Custodians
- Cafeteria workers
- Bus drivers

7. Read the cases that follow. Then describe the problems and how you will address them with all of the individuals involved.

CASE STUDY OF AN ELEMENTARY SCHOOL STUDENT

Sam is a fourth-grade student in your class. He has stopped turning in his homework, but he is passing his tests. He does not really act out, but he is not as involved in class activities as he has been in the past. Now that you think about it, Sam has worn the same clothes for the past 3 days. In addition, when he looks at you, his face shows almost no emotion. You have talked briefly with his mother in the past, but only to convey information about field trips, needed supplies, or other minor topics. You have never had a face-to-face conference about Sam's school performance. You also know very little about Sam's home life.

CASE STUDY OF A SECONDARY SCHOOL STUDENT

Mary is in the seventh grade. She often acts very silly in class. She seldom takes responsibility for her behavior but instead offers excuses or blames others. Recently, she has been cursing in class, a

behavior that is new for Mary. Your first step in dealing with the problem is to talk to Mary. She giggles and says that the adults on her bus (the bus driver, other drivers who talk to that driver, and monitors) curse. You ask, "Do they curse at you or when they speak to one another?" She says that they often use bad words when they talk to each other.

8. What are your greatest concerns regarding discipline and classroom management?

Resources

BOOKS

Ban, J. (1999). *Parents Assuring Student Success (PASS)*. Bloomington, IN: National Educational Services.

Focuses on helping parents teach students effective study skills at home.

> National Educational Services
> Bloomington, IN
> (800) 733-6786 or (812) 336-7700
> Available on Amazon.com

Corner, J. P., & National PTA. (2000). *Building successful partnerships: A guide for developing parent and family involvement programs*. Bloomington, IN: National Educational Services.

Discusses why family partnerships are important and provides strategies to increase parental involvement.

> National Educational Services
> Bloomington, IN
> (888) 763-9045 or (812) 336-7700

Payne, R. (2001). *A framework for understanding poverty*. Highlands, TX: aha!Process, Inc.

An excellent primer on the culture of poverty.
http://www.ahaprocess.com/store/Family_
Framework.html

JOURNAL ARTICLE

Merikangas, K. R., He, J., Burstein, M., Swanson, S. A, Avenevoli S., Cui, L., Benjet, C., Georgiades, K., & Swendsen, J. Lifetime prevalence of mental disorders in U.S. adolescents: Results from the National Comorbidity Study-Adolescent Supplement (NCS-A). *Journal of the American Academy of Child and Adolescent Psychiatry*. 2010 Oct. 49(10):980–989.

OTHER

Association for Positive Behavior Support Standards of Practice—Individual Level (2007): This document delineates the skills and knowledge necessary for individuals who are responsible for implementing positive behavioral supports. The document may be downloaded from the Website of the Association for Positive Behavior Support, listed next.

WEBSITES

www.apbs.org Association for Positive Behavior Support: Provides information about conferences, state PBIS networks, PBIS information, and the Standards of Practice referenced above.

www.ncpie.org/resources National Coalition for Parent Involvement in Education: Provides resources for educators and families to enhance collaborative relationships.

www.pbis.org The Office of Special Education Programs, U.S. Department of Education, Technical Assistance Center on Positive Behavioral Interventions and Supports: Provides a comprehensive array of information about PBIS, including resources, links to other sites, research, examples of PBIS applications, and much more.

www.mentalhealth.org The Substance Abuse and Mental Health Services Administration (SAMHSA), a branch of the U.S. Department of Health and Human Services: Provides a comprehensive array of information pertaining to mental health, including treatment, promising programs, locating services, and a mental health hotline.

www.rti4success.org National Center on Response to Intervention: Provides information, resources, training, and tools related to response to intervention; funded by the Office of Special Education Programs, U.S. Department of Education.

http://cecp.air.org Center for Effective Collaboration and Practice: Provides information related to all aspects of emotional and behavioral problems in areas such as education, families, mental health, juvenile justice, child welfare, early intervention, school safety, and legislation. Includes downloadable booklets, manuals, and other materials; PowerPoint® presentations; case studies; training modules; interactive discussions; and much more.

www.indiana.edu/~safeschl The Safe and Responsive Schools Framework is a model demonstration and technical assistance project funded by the U.S. Department of Education. Provides publications, fact sheets, and resources related to school safety and violence prevention that stresses comprehensive planning, prevention, and parent–community involvement.

www.ccbd.net The Council for Children with Behavioral Disorders, a division of the Council for Exceptional Children: Provides information related to advocacy, intervention, and conferences.

www.chadd.org Children and Adults with Attention Deficit/Hyperactivity Disorder, a nonprofit organization for children and adults with ADHD and their families: Provides resources, information on research and public policy, online discussions, and "Ask the Expert" sessions.

www.iris.peabody.vanderbilt.edu/resources.html The IRIS Resource Locator on the Website of the IRIS Center for Training Enhancements provides case studies, an online dictionary, training modules, and other materials on the following topics: accommodations, behavior, collaboration, diversity, response to intervention, differentiated instruction, and disability.

www.secretservice.gov/ntac_ssi.shtml The National Threat Assessment Center, United States Secret Service, 2002 Secret Service Safe School Initiative provides information and tools related to school safety.

After reading this chapter, you will be able to do the following:

1. Describe the major theories of behavior and the research base and the usefulness of each theory for teachers.

2. Describe the basic assumptions and principles of the behavioral model.

3. Describe applied behavior analysis (ABA) and the relationship between ABA and positive behavioral interventions and supports.

4. Describe the antecedent, skill deficit, and the consequential explanations for inappropriate behavior.

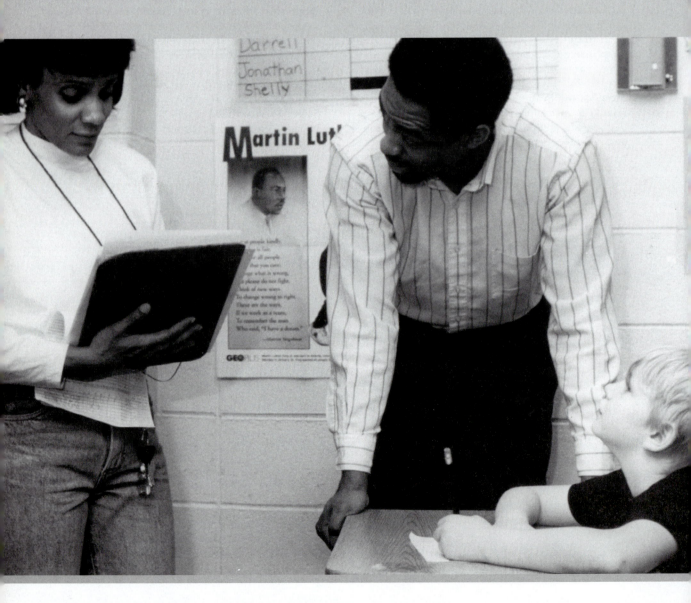

Theoretical Models to Explain Challenging Behavior

CHAPTER 2

Big ideas in theories about challenging behavior:

- Insisting on research-based practices will improve your effectiveness as a teacher and will help you better meet the expectations of the Elementary and Secondary Education Act of 1965 (its current reauthorization is the No Child Left Behind Act of 2001) and the Individuals with Disabilities Education Act of 2004.

- Many theories have been proposed to explain challenging behaviors but only a few of these theories offer interventions that are immediately useful, efficient, and effective for use in educational settings.

- The teacher's theoretical perspective will drive decisions about assessment and interventions.

- Most behavioral challenges occur in consistent patterns (i.e., educators can often predict when a certain challenging behavior will occur, under what circumstances it will occur, and where it will occur). This is valuable information!

- Inappropriate behavior occurs for a reason. This means that inappropriate behavior serves a purpose or meets a need for the student. Often, the inappropriate behavior is the most efficient and effective way for the student to satisfy that need, given the present conditions and the consequences.

One of the most common questions that educators and parents have when faced with a challenging behavior is, "Why does he (or she) do that?" Most of us, perhaps without even realizing it, have formed opinions about the driving forces behind atypical behavior. The authors of this text often encounter comments from concerned teachers, parents, and others about children who exhibit challenging behavior. We hear comments such as the following:

- MS. HUNTER: "I'm so frustrated with Kayla's behavior. I just can't get her to pay attention. I think that she might need medication."
- MR. WHEELER: "I just don't know what to do when Ben tries to avoid work. Getting him to do his independent work is a major struggle: He does everything that he can to avoid it."

- MS. LONG: "I don't see how I can make any headway with Terry—I get no support from his parents!"
- MR. WAYNE: "A.J. is so distrustful—his family has abandoned him, and he is just not able to form attachments at school. How can I help him?"

These comments reveal much about the speaker's perspective on what has caused those behavioral concerns. One's beliefs with regard to the causes of challenging behavior will influence decisions about interventions. It is important that educators understand their own beliefs about the causes of challenging behaviors; acknowledge how those beliefs influence decisions made in the classroom; and know whether those beliefs are, in fact, supported by research on the etiology of challenging behavior. This chapter will provide an overview of major explanatory theories for challenging behavior, a brief review of the research base for each, and a summary of the usefulness of each for classroom teachers. Because it is well beyond the scope of this text to present a thorough discussion of each theory, the majority of the attention will be paid to the biophysical and behavioral models for explaining challenging behavior. Our rationale for focusing on these two models is that the biophysical model offers documented evidence of biological causes and medical treatments for behavioral disorders. The field of positive behavioral supports acknowledges the role of biological factors in behavior (Center on Positive Behavioral Interventions and Supports, 2004). However, the biological model is limited in terms of utility for educators, unlike the behavioral model. Behavioral interventions have a long history of well-documented effectiveness with a wide range of behaviors, for all ages of students, and in all types of environments, as you will discover when we discuss strategies in later chapters. Furthermore, behavioral interventions are the most practical, available, and expedient options for educators. Used correctly, these interventions have a high probability of reducing many of the inappropriate behaviors that interfere with student success and establishing new, more adaptive behaviors. Finally, positive behavioral interventions and supports grew out of, and draw heavily on, behavioral strategies and procedures. The behavioral model provides the core technology for positive behavioral interventions and supports.

MAJOR THEORIES OF BEHAVIOR AND THEIR USEFULNESS IN EDUCATIONAL SETTINGS

Theories of behavior attempt to explain human behavior.

"What makes individuals behave in certain ways?" is one of the most intriguing questions for professionals in education and human services. The beliefs that we hold about behavior affect how we respond to behavior and the interventions that we choose for addressing atypical behavior (Fogt & Piripaval, 2002; Wood, 1978). Over the years, numerous theories that explain the origins of behavioral patterns have been put forth. These theories of behavior are known as **theoretical models of behavior** or philosophical belief systems about atypical behavior. In this text, we are primarily concerned with the science of behavior and scientifically proven behavioral interventions. For this reason, it is important to take into account the extent to which the assumptions and interventions associated with different theoretical models are supported by scientifically based evidence. Furthermore, because this text is designed for educators, we must consider the usefulness of each model for educators. In this chapter, we present a brief explanation of the basic principles, scientific validation, interventions, and the usefulness of five theoretical models that have widely influenced practitioners who work with individuals who exhibit atypical behavior.

WHAT CONSTITUTES "SCIENTIFIC EVIDENCE"

Marketing companies have long used phrases such as "scientifically based," "research based," and "proven" as a promotional tool to convince consumers that a particular product is superior to others. Unfortunately, these phrases are also widely used to convince educators to buy certain products or services, or to adopt certain techniques for use in schools. But are all products that claim to be "research based" truly so? That depends on your definition of *research*. Lembke and Stormont (2005) refer to research-based practices as

> those strategies, interventions, programs, or curricula that are sup-
> ported by rigorous substantiation of effectiveness (U.S. Department
> of Education, 2003). Educational practices that are research-based,
> evidence-based, promising, or proven are those that have been demon-
> strated to be effective for a group of students as compared to a group
> of students who did not get the intervention. Research-based practices
> have been examined in a variety of settings, replicated over time, and
> utilized with a variety of learners, which increases the generalizability
> of the practice. (p. 271)

The question of what constitutes research took on new importance with the passage of the No Child Left Behind Act of 2001 (P.L. 107–110; hereinafter referred to as NCLB). Originally the Elementary and Secondary Education Act of 1965, NCLB requires that schools adopt practices that are backed by "scientifically based research" (*Report on Scientifically Based Research Supported by U.S. Department of Education*, 2002). Table 2-1 gives an expanded definition of *scientifically based evidence* according to NCLB, which defines *scientifically based evidence* as ". . . research that involves the application of rigorous, systematic, and objective procedures to obtain reliable and valid knowledge relevant to education activities and programs" (U.S. Department of Education, 2002).

We support the high standard for evaluating research claims that is established by this definition because, too often, education has been vulnerable to adopting unproven interventions based on current fads or whims (Scheuermann & Evans, 1997). As much as possible, we have tried to adhere to this standard in choosing interventions to be included in this text.

The goal of research is to demonstrate a functional relationship between **independent variables** (e.g., the intervention) and **dependent variables** (e.g., the behavior that is the target of the intervention). To evaluate whether a functional relationship exists, researchers must design a research study to evaluate whether the independent variable does, in fact, produce a change in the dependent variable. There are two major types of research design for this purpose: group design and single-subject design. **Group designs** evaluate the effectiveness of an intervention on a group of individuals (e.g., a class of students, all fifth graders in

NCLB provides a definition of what constitutes scientific evidence in education.

TABLE 2-1   U.S. Department of Education Definition of *Scientifically Based Evidence*

As defined by the No Child Left Behind Act, *scientifically based research*

- employs systematic, empirical methods that draw on observation or experiment;

- involves rigorous data analysis that are adequate to test the stated hypotheses and justify the general conclusions drawn;

- relies on measurements or observational methods that provide reliable and valid data across evaluators and observers, across multiple measurements and observations, and across studies by the same or different investigators;

- is evaluated using experimental or quasi-experimental designs in which individuals, entities, programs, or activities are assigned to different conditions and with appropriate controls to evaluate the effects of the condition of interest, with a preference for random-assignment experiments, or other designs to the extent that those designs contain within-condition or across-condition controls;

- ensures that experimental studies are presented in sufficient detail and with sufficient clarity to allow for replication or, at a minimum, to offer the opportunity to build systematically on their findings; and

- has been accepted by a peer-reviewed journal or approved by a panel of independent experts through a comparably rigorous, objective, and scientific review.

Source: Guidance for the Reading First Program, April 1, 2002, U.S. Department of Education. Available online at www.ed.gov/programs/readingfirst/guidance.doc

a district, a sample of students with learning disabilities), often comparing the performance of individuals within the group who received a particular intervention with the performance of those in a similar group who did not receive the intervention. **Single-subject designs** evaluate the effects of the independent variables on individual students. Conducting group design research for educational purposes is not always feasible, particularly when evaluating interventions with individuals with autism, developmental disabilities, or other disabilities. For this reason, many researchers rely on single-subject designs to evaluate educational and behavioral interventions. The U.S. Department of Education accepts single-subject designs for research that focuses on special populations (*Scientifically Based Evaluation Methods*, 2005). Either group or single-subject design research was the basis for evaluating most of the techniques described in this text.

MAJOR THEORETICAL MODELS

The origins of atypical behavior have long been of interest to researchers, academicians, physicians, psychologists, and others who study human behavior. Of course, interest in the etiology of atypical behavior isn't restricted to professionals who pursue formal study in this area. Anyone who has encountered an individual who exhibits unusual or out-of-the-ordinary behavior has probably wondered, "What causes him/her to behave that way?" Whether an individual exhibits mildly atypical behavior, such as a child who is mildly noncompliant or who has unusual interests that set him apart from his peers, or seriously abnormal behavior, such as self-injurious behavior, aggression, or psychotic talk, we wonder how such unusual behaviors develop.

Over the years, various theoretical models have been developed to explain the origins of atypical behavior and the factors that maintain such behavior over time. These models vary dramatically in their proposed origins of unusual behavior, and each model uses unique terminology, concepts, assessment methods, and treatment procedures. While a study of the origins of abnormal behavior would reveal numerous theoretical models, the most common models are those identified by Rhodes and Tracy (1974) in their classic text, *A Study of Child Variance, Volume 1: Conceptual Models.* In this seminal work, Rhodes and Tracy discuss six models that explain emotional disturbances in children: the biophysical, behavioral, psychodynamic, sociological, ecological, and counter theory models. The first five models have remained the most common models used to explain abnormal behavior. In this chapter, we discuss the biophysical and behavioral models, and highlight the critical elements of the psychodynamic and ecological models, as well as another model that offers interventions sometimes used by educators: the cognitive model.

While the etiology of atypical behavior is interesting, it is important to distinguish between the following two questions: (a) What are the *origins* of atypical behavior (i.e., what causes such behavior to develop in the first place?), and (b) What maintains atypical behavior over time? Some of the models presented in this chapter focus on the origins of atypical behavior, while some focus primarily on factors that maintain the behavior. Even a cursory study of the etiology of abnormal behavior will lead one to conclude that there are no simple explanations for something as complex as human behavior; abnormal behavior most likely originates as a result of the complex interplay of multiple factors, including biological, environmental, developmental, and sociological factors. However, in our opinion, the *origins* of atypical behavior are not terribly important for us as educators. Even if we could identify one or more causes of atypical behavior, that information is of little use in fixing the problems that result from the atypical behavior.

The more significant question to us as educators is the second question that we posed: What maintains atypical behavior over time? What are the ongoing environmental or other factors that cause a student to exhibit continued noncompliance, or that cause a student to repeatedly engage in self-injurious behavior, for example? As educators, a theoretical model that helps us identify the ongoing contributors to problematic behavior is by far the most useful. Behavioral research provides the technology for identifying current environmental and other factors that maintain problematic behavior, and for using that information to develop effective interventions to expand an individual's repertoire of socially appropriate and functional behaviors and to minimize behaviors that interfere with the individual's academic, social, and vocational success.

Table 2-2 provides a summary of the main points of the psychodynamic, ecological, and cognitive models. The remainder of this chapter is devoted to discussion of the biophysical and behavioral models.

TABLE 2-2   Summary of Psychodynamic and Ecological Models

Model	Basic Assumptions	Interventions and Treatments	Research Support	Usefulness for Teachers
Psychodynamic Model	• Atypical behavior results from internal psychological events and motivational forces. • Psychological disturbances and behavioral problems result from an individual's failure to successfully complete developmental stages, or resolve the psychological conflicts that accompany each stage. • The best-known psychodynamic theory is Freud's psychoanalytic theory.	• Counseling, psychotherapy, psychoanalysis, play therapy, dream interpretation, or other forms of therapy. • Providing supportive environments (including classrooms) that place few demands on the child. • **Life Space Interview**, a therapeutic approach that uses verbal mediations (the Life Space Interview) to guide individuals through emotional/behavioral crises with the short-term goal of "emotional first aid on the spot" or the long-term goal of "clinical exploitation of life events" (Morse, 1963; Redl, 1959b).	• There is no scientific verification for the existence of psychological stages and conflicts. • Some research suggests that psychotherapy for children and youth is more effective than no treatment (Casey & Berman, 1985; Kazdin, 1993; Prout & DeMartino, 1986). • Research consists primarily of clinical impressions and case studies (Wicks-Nelson & Israel, 1984), which are less convincing than controlled studies. • LSI has been questioned because of lack of research and concerns such as disproportionate attention being paid to unacceptable behavior, and the time-intensive nature of LSI (Coleman & Webber, 2002; Gardner, 1990).	• Low, because teachers are not usually trained in psychodynamic techniques. • Accountability for student academic performance and demands on teachers' time may preclude the use of time-intensive psychodynamic techniques. • Psychodynamically oriented thinking (e.g., behavioral problems are attributed to negative early life experiences) may interfere with teachers' use of immediately useful assessment and intervention methods (e.g., the methods described in this text).
Ecological Model	• Atypical behavior is the result of an interaction between the individual and the environmental influences (e.g., family violence, neglect, transient family members, poor-quality educational programs, troubled neighborhoods) present in the various **ecosystems** in which the individual functions.	• **Ecological assessment**, the process of gathering information about a child's behaviors and the ecosystems in which the child functions. • Match students to teachers who have a high tolerance for the student's behavioral characteristics (Algozzine, Serna, & Patton, 2001).	• Studies have shown positive results for youth who received Project Re-ED services (Weinstein, 1974), and short-term (Lewis, 1988) and long-term (Hooper, Murphy, Devaney, & Hultman, 2000) maintenance of treatment outcomes.	• Low, unless teachers have access to the type of interagency (e.g., mental health, social services) collaborative efforts found in ecological programs (Center for Effective Collaboration and Practice, 1998; Duchnowski, Johnson, Hall, Kutash, & Friedman, 1993).

Model	Basic Assumptions	Interventions and Treatments	Research Support	Usefulness for Teachers
		• Project Re-ED (Re-Education of Emotionally Disturbed Children and Adolescents), a network of schools and facilities for students with emotional/ behavioral disorders based on an ecological model (Hobbs, 1966).		
Cognitive Model	• Reality therapy (Glasser, 1965): therapeutic interactions between adults and children with behavior problems are designed to help the child identify errors in thinking, and engage in more reality-based thinking. • Choice theory (Glasser, 1998a): the basis for Glasser's schoolwide program, Quality Schools (1998b); behavior is voluntary, but driven by basic needs for survival, love, belonging, power, freedom, and fun. * Rational emotive behavior therapy (REBT; Ellis, 1962): problem behavior stems from irrational thinking in response to antecedent stimuli.	• Interventions focus on verbal interactions, designed to help the child identify thinking errors or irrational thoughts, and learn new, reality-based thinking.	• Reality therapy and choice theory rely primarily on case studies and testimonials. • A meta-analysis of REBT research found positive outcomes for students involved in REBT interventions (Gonzalez et al., 2001).	• In our opinion, reality therapy and choice theory are based on appealing philosophies, but offer little in the way of effective day-to-day tools for preventing and managing problem behavior in busy classroom environments. • Zionts (1996) suggests REBT may be used as part of a school-based mental health or counseling program. Kaplan and Carter (1995) provide interesting REBT applications for teachers, but also recommend behavioral interventions as part of an overall management plan.

THE BIOPHYSICAL MODEL

The biophysical model, also called the medical model, is based on the assumption that atypical behavior is a result of either biological makeup or some type of organic dysfunction that is inherent in the individual (Sagor, 1974). There is much evidence to support the biological bases of such human behavior, despite the fact that this is a young and emerging field (Human Genome Project, n.d.). Although many categories of biophysical causation have been proposed, we will focus on five in particular.

Genetic Disorders

Advances in genetic research have revealed that some behavioral disorders may be partly caused by some form of genetic influence, either heredity or genetic abnormalities. For example, the results of studies have suggested that heredity plays a role in schizophrenia (Kallman & Roth, 1956; National Institute of Mental Health, 2009), autism (National Research Council, 2001), attention-deficit hyperactivity disorder (ADHD) (Goodman & Stevenson, 1989; National Institute of Mental Health, 2003), depression (Klein & Last, 1989), reading disorders (Olson, Wise, Conners, Rack, & Fulker, 1989), and bipolar disorder (National Institute of Mental Health, 2009; Rice et al., 1987). Chromosome abnormalities such as Trisomy 21, which results in Down syndrome because of the presence of an extra copy of chromosome 21, or Trisomy 18 or Trisomy 5, may also influence behavior. Some evidence suggests that the presence of genetic abnormalities is one explanation for antisocial behavior (Rosenhan & Seligman, 1989). However, the results of these studies also showed that genetics alone could not account for the antisocial behavior in the subjects studied; environmental influences also played a role. Recently, the work of the Human Genome Project has shed additional light on the role of genes in human behavior, including both how genetics and the interaction of genetic and environmental factors influence personality (Human Genome Project, n.d.).

Neurochemical and Biochemical Disorders

Biochemicals, particularly neurotransmitters such as serotonin and dopamine, have long been suspected in the etiology of various forms of behavioral disorders. Much of this speculation stems either from studies showing elevated levels of neurotransmitters in children with certain conditions or from the fact that certain conditions improve with the use of medication that affects neurotransmitter levels. For example, studies of self-injurious behavior in children with autism and developmental disabilities have indicated that self-injurious behavior results in the release of neurochemical transmitters and modulators that bind to certain receptors in the brain (National Research Council, 2001). Other biochemicals besides neurotransmitters have been identified as possibly influencing challenging behaviors. Endogenous opiates, a natural, morphine-like substance produced in the body, may also play a role in self-injurious behaviors (Crews, Rhodes, Bonaventura, Rowe, & Goering, 1999).

Temperament

Temperament, which refers to a basic disposition or personality style, appears to be both biologically based and also susceptible to influences from the environment (Coleman & Webber, 2002). Although the etiology of individual personality styles is still uncertain, landmark studies in the 1960s have taught us much about personality. In an attempt to explain the development of challenging behavior, Thomas, Chess, and Birch (1969) studied a large sample of children, starting in infancy

TABLE 2-3	**Thomas and Chess's Indicators of Temperament and the Three Temperaments**

Indicators of Temperament

1. Activity level
2. Regularity of biological functioning (e.g., eating, sleeping)
3. Style of responsiveness to new stimuli (e.g., positive or negative responses)
4. Adaptability
5. Amount of stimulation required to provoke a response
6. Intensity of the reaction
7. Quality of the mood (e.g., pleasant, irritable)
8. Distractibility
9. Attention span and persistence

The Three Temperaments

1. The easy child
2. The difficult child
3. The "slow to warm up" child

and continuing throughout adulthood. In this sample of children, the researchers identified nine indicators of temperament that were present at birth and were stable throughout the children's lives. From these nine indicators, Thomas and his colleagues then documented three basic temperaments (see Table 2-3) (Thomas & Chess, 1977, 1984). These three categories accounted for the majority, but not all, of the temperaments of the children studied. Also, the three temperaments were not perfectly predictive of behavioral problems. For example, children in the "difficult child" category were more likely to develop behavioral problems, but not all children in this category did so. Thus, Thomas and Chess hypothesized that certain personality traits are biological and are present at birth, but these personality traits are also responsive to environmental influences. In particular, Thomas and his colleagues believed that parent–child interactions and parenting styles were important variables in the eventual development of undesirable behavior (or lack thereof).

Prenatal, Perinatal, and Postnatal Influences

Various events before, during, and after birth can affect neurological development, potentially resulting in emotional or behavioral disorders later in childhood. Known and suspected prenatal risk factors for emotional and behavioral development range from the more familiar such as maternal substance abuse, nutrition, viral infections, and exposure to toxic substances (Alberto & Troutman, 2006) to maternal stress (Niederhofer & Reiter, 2004) and maternal emotional problems (Allen, Lewinsohn, & Seeley, 1998). Perinatal influences on child development include low birth weight, **anoxia** (oxygen deprivation), and brain hemorrhage during birth (Cullinan, 2003). Postnatal influences are discussed in the next section.

The biophysical model includes genetic; neurochemical; temperament; environmental; and prenatal, perinatal, and postnatal experiences as explanations for behavior.

Environmental Contributions

Research has identified possible environmental factors that negatively impact biological makeup and, ultimately, behavior, learning, and other areas of functioning. Although no studies have definitively proven that environmental factors cause aberrant behavior, much research has identified possible contributing environmental factors for a wide range of atypical conditions. For example, environmental factors have been associated with schizophrenia (National Institute of Mental Health, 2009), ADHD (National Institute of Mental Health, 2003), autism (Centers for Disease Control and Prevention, 2006), and general learning and behavioral disabilities (Healthy Children Project, n.d.). Generally, environmental factors include environmental toxins such as heavy metals (e.g., lead, mercury), chemicals (e.g., dioxins, flame retardants), solvents (e.g., benzene), pesticides (e.g., Dursban, lindane), molds, carbon monoxide, and air pollution (Environmental Protection Agency, 2003).

Interventions Derived from the Biophysical Model

The prescribing of medication is a primary treatment derived from the biophysical model. It is a generally accepted treatment for a wide range of challenging behaviors and behavioral conditions, including hyperactivity, inattention, aggression, self-injurious behavior, depression, bipolar disorder, anxiety disorders, and Tourette syndrome (McClellan & Werry, 2003; MTA Cooperative Group, 1999; National Institute of Mental Health, 2002). Treatment of ADHD, particularly with **stimulant medications**, is the most common reason that behavioral medications are prescribed for children. The use of medication as an intervention for behavioral concerns in children increased sharply from 1987 to 1997 for a number of reasons, including greater awareness of ADHD and other conditions on the part of physicians, the availability of a wider variety of medications designed to treat the symptoms of ADHD, and an increase in pharmaceutical marketing and promotion (Zito, 2000).

Since 1997, the use of stimulant medications in children has leveled off. An estimated 2.2 million children and adolescents (2.9% of the childhood population) take stimulant medications (e.g., Ritalin, Adderall, Concerta, Focalin, Dexedrine, Cylert) (Zuvekas, Vitiello, & Norquist, 2006). However, stimulant medications are only one class of medications administered to juveniles for behavioral purposes. Other types of medications, generally referred to as psychotropic medications, are used as well. **Psychotropic medications**, used to treat mental health disorders, include antidepressants (e.g., Prozac, Paxil, Luvox, Zoloft, Wellbutrin, Effexor), antipsychotics (e.g., Clozaril, Zyprexa, Seroquel, Risperdal), and antianxiety medications (e.g., Xanax, BuSpar, Librium). Unlike stimulant medications, very few psychotropic medications are approved for pediatric use (McClellan & Werry, 2003; Thomas, Conrad, Cassler, & Goodman, 2006). Despite this fact, psychotropic medications are increasingly prescribed for young people (Thomas et al., 2006). Vitiello and colleagues estimated that 1.4 million children and adolescents received antidepressant medications in 2002 (Vitiello, Zuvekas, & Norquist, 2006). Use of antipsychotic drugs in children ages 19 and younger increased 73% between 2001 and 2005, compared with a 37% increase in adults (Medco, 2006). In 2005, approximately 7 of every 1,000 children were taking an antipsychotic medication. From 2001 to 2005, there was a 103% increase in prescriptions of antipsychotics for girls and a 61% increase for boys.

Among students with disabilities, the highest usage of psychotropic medications is among students ages 10 to 14 years (Office of Special Education Programs, 2003). As in the general population of children, stimulant medications are the most commonly prescribed behavioral medications for children and youth with disabilities. Antidepressants and antianxiety medications are used in all age groups but are most common in adolescents (Office of Special Education Programs, 2003). ADHD and behavioral disorders are found in some students in every Individuals with Disabilities Education Act (IDEA) disability category, and the prescribing of medication for behavior control purposes is found among students in every IDEA disability category (Office of Special Education Programs, 2003).

The use of stimulant and psychotropic medications for the treatment of behavioral disorders in children and adolescents has generated much controversy. In the past few years, questions have been raised about the safety of certain types of antidepressants for children (Brent, 2004; Vitiello & Swedo, 2004). In 2003, the United Kingdom issued a warning strongly advising against the use of any antidepressant except for fluoxetine (Prozac). In 2004, the U.S. Food and Drug Administration (FDA) issued a warning about certain types of antidepressants possibly contributing to a worsening of symptoms in both children and adults with major depressive disorder (Bostwick, 2006; U.S. Food and Drug Administration, 2004). However, it appears that those concerns were the result of confusing misinformation rather than any scientific evidence of risk (Bostwick, 2006). In 2004, the FDA also asked drug manufacturers to add a warning to antipsychotic medications that describes an increased risk of hyperglycemia and diabetes in patients taking those medications (U.S. Food and Drug Administration, 2004). Although the prescribing of medications as a treatment for serious behavioral disturbances in children is a legitimate intervention, it must be closely monitored by the child's physician, mental health professionals, and educators. Professionals must stay abreast of the latest research and information about the indications and contraindications of medications, the potential side effects, and overall safety.

Other interventions derived from the biophysical model target prenatal maternal risk factors and postnatal environmental influences on child development. The David Olds' Nurse Home Visitation Program is an example of a comprehensive program designed to reduce prenatal risk factors (Olds et al., 1999). Registered public health nurses visit participating mothers-to-be regularly; visits continue until the infant reaches 2 years of age. During this time, the nurses provide a range of instructional, support, and case management services. The program has demonstrated strong, positive results in terms of improving the desired long-term outcomes for both the children and families involved in the program, as well as a substantial long-term cost–benefit savings (Olds et al., 1999).

This medical model, perhaps more so than any other theoretical model, also includes many interventions that are touted to improve or eliminate behavioral disorders or learning problems but that have little or no scientific evidence that those claims are valid. Examples of unproven interventions are as follows:

- *Dietary interventions*—One well-known example is the Feingold Diet. Dr. Benjamin Feingold, a medical doctor who specialized in pediatric allergies, speculated that ADHD was the result of food allergies (Feingold, 1975). As treatment, he recommended a highly restrictive diet that was designed to eliminate artificial food color-ings and flavorings, food preservatives, and naturally occurring salicylates (Feingold, 1976). However, a large body of research has failed to support either the theory of food allergies as a cause of behavioral difficulties or the Feingold Diet as an effective treat-ment for ADHD (Pescara-Kovach & Alexander, 1994).

- *Biofeedback*—Biofeedback involves the use of biological meas-ures of muscle tension or brain wave activity as indicators of arousal levels; children are taught self-calming techniques and are instructed to use those techniques to maintain levels of brain wave activity or muscle tension within a predetermined low range (Xu, Reid, & Steckelberg, 2002). Often promoted as an in-tervention for ADHD (Baron-Faust, 2000), the studies supporting the use of biofeedback for educational purposes are methodolog-ically flawed to the point that it is premature to recommend biofeedback as an intervention (Xu et al., 2002).

- *Sensory integration therapy*—The neurobiological theory be-hind this therapy postulates that the challenging behaviors associ-ated with autism, ADHD, learning disabilities, and other conditions are a result of the failure of the central nervous system to organ-ize and integrate the sensory feedback that typically occurs as part of a normal developmental process (Ayers, 1972). Interventions are designed to restructure and integrate sensory input using techniques targeted to specific sensory systems, such as proprio-ceptive or vestibular systems (through the use of swings, scooters, or weighted vests and blankets) and tactile systems (through the use of deep skin brushing) (Shaw, 2002). Although there are many case studies and testimonials about the effectiveness of sen-sory integration training, no scientific studies have proven that it is an effective intervention for challenging behaviors (Shaw, 2002; Werry, Scaletti, & Mills, 1990).

Research Support and Usefulness for Teachers

Educators should understand that not all therapies and interventions have independent verification of their effectiveness.

According to McClellan and Werry (2003), the efficacy of stimulant medications for the treatment of ADHD is well documented and is considered an acceptable form of treatment. Only a few other types of medications have empirical evidence that supports their use with children, although this evidence is limited in quantity. These include selective serotonin reuptake inhibitors (SSRIs) for obsessive-compulsive disorder, major depression, and anxiety disorders, and lithium for ado-lescent males with explosive behaviors. The use of medications as a treatment for behavioral issues in autism spectrum disorders and developmental disabilities has also been shown to be effective, especially risperidone (Risperdal) for aggression and self-injury (Gordon, 2002, 2003; McClellan & Werry, 2003).

One of the most comprehensive studies of the relative effectiveness of med-ications versus other treatments for children with ADHD was the Multimodal Treatment Study of Children with Attention Deficit Hyperactivity Disorder (MTA

Cooperative Group, 1999). This rigorous study randomly assigned approximately 600 children, ages 7 to 9, to one of four treatment groups: (a) medication alone, (b) behavioral interventions alone, (c) combined medication and behavioral interventions, and (d) no treatment; these children were referred to local mental health providers, where they received whatever treatment those professionals prescribed, which may have included medication. Over the 14 months of the study, the symptomology of ADHD showed signs of reduction in all four groups. However, the two groups that experienced significantly greater improvements were the medication alone group and the combined medication and behavioral interventions group. Children in these groups showed substantially greater improvement in all areas of functioning, including academic performance, compliance, parent–child relationships, and social skills. This study and others suggest that medications should be considered to be only one component of a comprehensive treatment regimen for children who exhibit challenging behavior. Medications for behavior control should always be combined with the types of behavioral interventions and positive behavioral supports that are described in this text (Forness & Kavale, 2001; MTA Cooperative Group, 1999).

For the most part, the biophysical model has limited direct usefulness for teachers beyond providing a better understanding of challenging behavior. Of course, this is an important benefit. The more educators understand the possible biological predispositions for challenging behavior, the more likely it is that they will be motivated to provide environments that are designed to help the student overcome these biological influences. Research shows that even when behavioral disorders are attributable to biological influences, the most effective treatment programs are those that include interventions beyond medically based treatments.

THE BEHAVIORAL MODEL

The behavioral approach is based on the fundamental assumption that all voluntary behavior, both typical and atypical, is learned as a result of the consequences associated with various behaviors. The behaviorist is concerned with observable, measurable behaviors, not underlying psychological causes, for the simple reason that such constructs cannot be observed. In addition, behaviorists are concerned with antecedents, environmental influences on behavior, and how environmental events can be manipulated to effect changes in behavior.

> The seven principles of the behavioral model form the foundation for all behavioral interventions.

Behavioral interventions are based on one or more of the seven basic principles of the applied behavior analysis model. These are as follows:

1. ***Positive reinforcement*** is a procedure that maintains or increases a behavior as the result of consequences experienced following the behavior. A child who screams and cries for a toy in a checkout line of the supermarket, and who then gets that toy, is likely to continue to exhibit that behavior each time that she wants a toy while waiting in the checkout line. Furthermore, this child may learn to use this technique anytime that she wants something, since it works so well in the supermarket! Likewise, a teacher who is praised for her good paperwork will likely continue to take care to produce neat, accurate documents. When your caller identification function shows a friend's

name, you answer the phone; because you like talking to your friend, you are reinforced by answering the phone and will likely to do so again.

2. ***Negative reinforcement*** is a procedure that maintains or increases behavior because the individual avoids or escapes negative conditions as a result of the behavior. A student may learn that being disruptive during independent seatwork results in being sent to the office, thus escaping the disliked seatwork. A teacher may choose not to go to the teacher's lounge at a certain time of day because he wishes to avoid another teacher who likes to complain about "those ill-behaved, disrespectful kids" in her classes. Using our previous phone example, when your phone displays the name of someone to whom you do not wish to speak, you might not answer. The reinforcing aspect of avoiding the call increases the likelihood that you will often ignore this person's call in the future.

3. ***Punishment*** is a process by which a behavior is weakened, reduced, or eliminated because of a consequence that follows the behavior. If peers laugh when a student answers a question incorrectly, and if this is embarrassing to the student, she may not volunteer an answer in the future. A principal's reprimand to a teacher who is habitually late to school may result in the teacher arriving on time in the future. If your cell phone bill is extraordinarily high because you vastly exceeded your allotted minutes, the punishing consequence of having to pay a lot of money may prompt you to make fewer calls and keep your calls shorter!

4. ***Extinction*** is a condition by which a behavior is weakened, reduced, or eliminated because it is no longer reinforced. A child whose silly noises no longer make his friends laugh may stop making those noises. A teacher whose attempts to initiate a collaborative project with a colleague are continually rebuffed will soon give up. A college student who repeatedly asks a young woman for a date and is turned down every time will eventually stop asking!

5. ***Stimulus control*** is a predictive relationship between a specific antecedent or class of antecedents and a specific behavior or class of behaviors. An **antecedent** is a stimulus (e.g., a request, activity, task, event) that immediately precedes a particular behavior and that may cue that behavior. Stimulus control means that a specific behavior is likely to occur in the presence of a particular antecedent. This relationship is established because that behavior has been reinforced when it followed the specific antecedent, whereas other behaviors have not. Driving offers many examples of stimulus control: When you approach a red light, you stop. Yet if you encountered a similarly placed purple light, you would do nothing, or at least you would not stop. "Stopping" is negatively reinforced (you avoid an accident or a ticket), but because you have no experience with purple lights, you have learned no associated behavior. When your cell phone rings, you answer it. You typically only open the phone and say "hello" when it rings. A student may behave well in your class but exhibit inappropriate behavior in other classes. That student apparently has learned that appropriate behavior is reinforced in one class but not in other classes. In fact, perhaps he has learned that *inappropriate behavior* is reinforced in other classes. Thus, other teachers or

perhaps peers or academic activities in those other classes are antecedents for inappropriate behavior from this student.

6. ***Modeling*** is demonstrating a behavior for the purpose of encouraging others to imitate the behavior. Albert Bandura (1969) demonstrated that much behavior is learned through modeling, or imitating the behavior of others. Modeling is the basis for most academic and social instruction. Teachers wisely show students how to solve a math problem, correctly serve a volleyball, use a microscope, or pronounce a word; these models help to ensure that students will exhibit the correct behavior. Teachers also point out appropriate behavior as a way to encourage all students to exhibit that behavior. For example, if a student is talking during independent work time, the teacher might praise other students who are working quietly as a way to encourage the talker to return to work. The theory behind this action is that the talker will see other students receive reinforcement for working quietly and will imitate their work behavior in order to obtain that same reinforcement. Of course, children also learn inappropriate behavior through modeling (Kauffman, 2005; Walker et al., 2004). Aggression, in particular, may be partially attributable to exposure to aggression in others (e.g., family members, friends, media portrayal of violence). One of the earliest demonstrations of aggression as a learned behavior was offered by Bandura (1973), who demonstrated that children will imitate aggression after observing a model exhibiting aggressive behavior.

7. ***Shaping*** is the teaching of a new behavior by reinforcing increasingly more accurate attempts at the behavior. Teachers praise young children's large, uneven letters when they first learn to write. However, by sixth grade, such writing would undoubtedly be punished (e.g., the student would be asked to redo the work or would be given a lower grade). High school teachers may allow more leeway with regard to expectations for students early in the year; however, as the year progresses, expectations are higher: Students are expected to remember rules and procedures with regard to homework, daily work, required materials, and so forth.

It is critical to note that these principles apply to all forms of behavior, both appropriate and inappropriate. That is, careless, unsystematic application of positive reinforcement can increase *undesirable* behavior, as well as desirable behavior. Extinction can eliminate both appropriate and inappropriate behaviors; this means that teachers must take care not to inadvertently cause the extinction of desirable student behaviors. Children may learn both correct and incorrect forms of behavior through modeling. This fact is both good and bad news: Inappropriate behavior is repeated because it is, in some way, reinforced; however, knowing this, if we can identify and control the source of the reinforcement, we may be able to reduce or eliminate the behavior. This is a crucial concept that we will discuss in later chapters.

The specialized application of behavioral principles is known as **applied behavior analysis (ABA)**. ABA is a more scientific approach to behavior change than the behavior change approaches that were formerly known as **behavior modification**, in part because ABA requires proof that behavior change interventions are responsible for behavior change—that observed changes are not simply coincidence

> Applied behavior analysis is the science of behavior change.

or a result of other variables (Alberto & Troutman, 2006). ABA was first defined by Baer, Wolf, and Risley (1968) as "the process of applying sometimes tentative principles of behavior to the improvement of specific behaviors and simultaneously evaluating whether or not any changes noted are indeed attributable to the process of application" (p. 91). The word *applied* in *applied behavior analysis* means that the behaviors that are targeted for intervention are socially significant behaviors or are behaviors that are critical to success in school and in other environments, such as at home, in the community, or at work (Cooper, Heron, & Heward, 2007). ABA relies on single-subject design research to demonstrate the effectiveness of interventions.

ABA is built on several basic assumptions as described in Table 2-4. The Guiding Principles presented in Chapter 1, although based on these assumptions, are broader in that they describe a general philosophy of behavior. These assumptions are more specific to behavior change efforts. As is true for any complex subject, there are many misconceptions about ABA. Generally, these misconceptions, a few of which are explained in Table 2-5, reflect an overly narrow understanding of ABA.

TABLE 2-4   The Assumptions of Applied Behavior Analysis (ABA)

1. **A person's past learning and biological makeup affect current behavior.** "Past learning" refers to what a child has learned to do in order to satisfy his or her needs (e.g., gets what he or she wants by screaming or avoids disliked tasks by biting). "Biological makeup" means that some children are genetically, biochemically, or neurologically predisposed to certain conditions such as hyperactivity, inattention, and self-stimulatory or self-abusive behavior. However, ABA procedures are effective, even when a child exhibits well-established patterns of behavior as a result of past learning or biological conditions.

2. **All voluntary behavior, both appropriate behavior and inappropriate behavior, is governed by the same principles.** *All* behavior can be explained in terms of one or more of the basic principles that we describe in this chapter (e.g., stimulus control, reinforcement, punishment). Being able to identify the principle(s) at work when inappropriate behavior occurs will help you to more effectively manage that behavior. For example, consider a child who dislikes sitting close to other children and is allowed to move away from peers because she hits herself when peers sit next to her. Understanding that the basic principle at work here is negative reinforcement (i.e., she is reinforced by being allowed to escape the disliked situation) will help you to design an intervention to effectively reduce this behavior and increase her tolerance for sitting close to peers.

3. **Behavior serves a purpose.** Most children learn appropriate ways in which to meet their needs, such as using words to express wants and dislikes. Children who have a limited repertoire of appropriate behaviors, especially communicative behaviors, must rely on inappropriate behaviors in order to meet their needs. **Functional behavioral assessment** (see Chapter 3) is used for deciphering the *purpose* that an inappropriate behavior serves for a student; FBA is an important step in developing interventions to address that behavior.

4. **Behavior is related to the environment in which it occurs.** The environment is one of the **antecedents** to behavior and can be external (e.g., a crowded room, a room that is too cold or too hot, being presented with a task that is disliked, experiencing social initiations by a teacher or peer) or internal (e.g., physical states such as hunger, discomfort, illness, sleepiness). For example, a student may exhibit self-stimulatory behavior as a response to the high noise levels of the cafeteria, bus-loading area, or hallways. Simply applying a behavior reduction strategy to eliminate that self-stimulatory behavior probably would not be very effective. Effective behavior intervention plans always consider the role of environmental antecedents and whether those antecedents can be modified in a way that will positively affect the target behavior.

TABLE 2-5 Misconceptions About Applied Behavior Analysis

Applied behavior analysis is a program for students with autism

The effectiveness of ABA in producing the desired outcomes for students with autism (National Research Council, 2001) and the fact that ABA is widely recommended as the basis for treatment interventions for individuals with autism (National Institute of Mental Health, 2008) have led to the common misconception that ABA was "invented for," or is only used for, children with autism. Actually, ABA originated in clinical settings with the work of John B. Watson, B. F. Skinner, and others (Cooper, Heron, & Heward, 2007). Ivar Lovaas was one of the first researchers to demonstrate the effectiveness of ABA techniques for students with autism (Lovaas, Koegel, Simmons, & Long, 1973), and his work has served as the foundation for ABA-based autism interventions. However, the field of ABA extends far beyond autism. For example, the Association for Behavior Analysis International (ABAI) includes more than 30 special interest groups that focus on areas for the application of ABA, ranging from animal behavior to sports and fitness.

ABA is a curriculum.

ABA is a scientific approach to changing behavior that relies on empirically proven techniques and procedures. These techniques and procedures can be used to teach or strengthen, or reduce or eliminate, virtually any voluntary behavior. It is **not** a prescribed curriculum or set of skills that must be taught. In fact, ABA methods may be used in almost any curriculum (e.g., mathematics, life skills, vocational skills, writing, language arts, behavior).

Only ABA "therapists" can provide ABA interventions

The field of ABA offers a credentialing process for certifying that individuals have completed a formal course of study in ABA and have demonstrated specific ABA competencies. However, certification as a behavior analyst is not required for implementing the ABA techniques. However, we strongly urge anyone who will be using ABA techniques to take courses or other forms of advanced training in ABA. ABA techniques are easily implemented by educators, but they must be implemented correctly.

ABA involves only individual work with the student in isolated settings, teaching discrete nonfunctional skills such as touching the nose, clapping the hands, or pointing to objects

While ABA techniques are often used to establish basic learning skills in one-on-one teaching sessions, they can also be applied in groups, and in natural settings, such as classrooms, hallways, buses, cafeterias, playgrounds, and vocational settings. In fact, as you will learn in Chapter 5, many of the schoolwide PBIS interventions that are applied to all students in a school, in all areas of the school, are practices that are rooted in ABA.

ABA works only with young children

ABA-based interventions can effectively change behavior in adults as well as in children. In fact, one of the special interest groups within ABA is Behavioral Gerontology, the application of ABA in elderly populations.

Positive behavioral interventions and supports (PBIS), as discussed in Chapter 1, are founded on behavioral principles, including ABA. PBIS extends behavioral science to broader applications for all types of behaviors and environments, from individualized interventions to systems-change strategies (Sugai & Horner, 2002).

As you can see, behaviorists acknowledge biological influences on behavior. Behaviorists do not, however, use these influences as justification for providing no intervention. Because behaviorists also believe that behavior serves a purpose, one of the first steps in developing an intervention plan for a challenging behavior is to attempt to determine the environmental influences on the behavior and the function (i.e., the purpose) that the behavior may serve for the child. This information is determined through a process called **functional behavioral assessment (FBA)**. We explain how to conduct an FBA in Chapter 3.

The A-B-C Model (The Three-Term Contingency)

All of the instructional and behavior management strategies of applied behavior analysis can be categorized in an easy-to-understand format called the **A-B-C model** or the **three-term contingency** (Cooper, Heron, & Heward, 2007), which is illustrated as follows:

Antecedents ◄———► Behavior ◄———► Consequences

Antecedents (A) are events that occur before behaviors that may cue or set the stage for certain behaviors; the **behavior** (B) is the behavior of concern (or a deficit in an adaptive behavior that is reflected in a problem behavior); and **consequences** (C) are the events that follow a behavior that determine whether the behavior will be repeated (i.e., reinforced) or not (i.e., punished). The arrows indicate that both antecedents and consequences affect behavior. This is an important concept; it means that we need to assess how antecedents may be contributing to behavior, and we should consider modifying antecedents in order to increase the desired behavior and reduce the inappropriate behavior. Many of the chapters in this text are devoted to managing antecedents, such as rules and procedures, classroom organization, and instruction. Table 2-6 presents sample antecedent and consequence interventions that are described later in this text.

Research Base and Usefulness for Teachers

The three-term contingency provides a framework for all behavioral interventions.

Behaviorism, by definition, is the science of behavior (Baum, 1994). Behavioral techniques are well-founded in decades of scientific proof, which means that, used correctly in behavior change programs, such techniques have a high probability of success. Behavioral techniques are also highly teacher friendly. Because behavioral strategies can be applied to any form of behavior (e.g., social, academic, language), the behavioral model is especially appropriate for educational applications. In fact, the instructional strategies that we present in Chapter 8 are founded on behavioral theory and practice. Furthermore, behavioral techniques are familiar to teachers: Most teachers have some concept of how to use positive reinforcement or modeling, for example. The goal is to ensure that educators understand behavioral theory sufficiently so that they correctly apply behavior change techniques.

Unfortunately, and perhaps because many behavioral strategies are widely used, they sometimes are used incorrectly and, thus, may not produce the desired changes. A good example of this is the time-out: The time-out is often recommended for use by teachers and parents as a consequence for a child's inappropriate behavior. Used correctly, the time-out is an effective behavior reduction

---

TABLE 2-6   Sample Antecedent and Consequence Interventions

Antecedent Interventions

- Setting rules and expectations.
- Implementing procedures.
- Ensuring successful engagement in academic tasks.
- Developing positive teacher–student and peer relationships.
- Providing meaningful and interesting academic tasks.
- Teaching appropriate behaviors.
- Teaching appropriate communication skills.

Consequence Interventions

- Providing positive reinforcement for desired behaviors:
  - Praise and social attention
  - Token economy
  - Contract
- Using differential reinforcement to increase desired behaviors while reducing undesirable behaviors.
- Using punishment to reduce undesirable behaviors:
  - Reprimand
  - Time out
  - Response cost

---

technique. Used incorrectly, it may actually *increase* the challenging behavior for which it is used. In any case, the time-out should be used only after other more proactive approaches have been proven to be insufficient for controlling an inappropriate behavior, and it should only be used in conjunction with other, more proactive approaches.

This text is based on the behavioral model, and the techniques presented throughout the book reflect behavioral theory and principles. In explaining the techniques, and in our examples, we always try to illustrate the underlying theory behind the technique. The extent to which educators are well versed in theory will help to ensure the correct use of the techniques and will facilitate problem solving if a strategy does not produce the desired outcome.

BEHAVIORAL EXPLANATIONS FOR CHALLENGING BEHAVIORS

As the title implies, the purpose of this chapter is to explain different theories as to why children exhibit problem behavior. In the behavioral model, functional behavioral assessment is the tool that helps professionals to determine the reasons for misbehavior. Grounded in behavioral theory, FBA is based on the assumptions that (a) antecedents affect behavior; some antecedents, called *setting events*, are distant in time and place from the behavior, and some antecedents immediately precede the behavior of concern; (b) sometimes problem behavior reflects a failure to learn a more appropriate alternative way in which to behave; and (c) behavior serves a purpose. In the remainder of this chapter, we explain each of these assumptions and give examples to illustrate their application in school settings.

Antecedents

The *A* in the A-B-C model refers to **antecedents**, or the environmental events that might set the stage for specific behaviors. The following is a list of common setting events and immediate antecedents for problem behaviors in the classroom.

SETTING EVENTS   Sometimes events or conditions that are not immediately connected in time and place to the behavior in question may affect the behavior; such conditions are known as **setting events**. Gardner and Sovner (1994) propose three categories of setting events: physical, biological, and social. Physical setting events are environmental conditions, such as high levels of classroom noise, a long bus ride, a room that is too hot or too cold, improperly sized furniture, or a flickering bulb in the overhead lights. Biological setting events are internal to the child and might include illness, allergies, hunger, and fatigue. Social setting events refer to the social environment, such as the presence or absence of certain people, a crowded classroom, or the quality of the teacher–student relationship. These conditions set the stage for undesirable behavior, but do not necessarily *cause* the behavior. For example, a student who has a cold may be more irritable and less compliant than usual. You may be able to intervene with regard to some setting events (e.g., you may establish a plan to reinforce students for appropriate behavior when a substitute is in your class) but not with others (e.g., there may be little you can do when a student is ill). The following are descriptions of a few setting events that teachers can control.

Lack of Clarity and Predictability in Expectations.   In classrooms that are chaotic, the behaviors that are expected or allowed, as well as those which are not allowed, are seldom clearly defined, and this lack of clarity invites unacceptable behavior. Just as it is easier for adults to perform well on a new job when the expectations for the job are made clear, children behave more appropriately when the rules and expectations are well defined and clearly communicated. When behavior problems occur, one of the first steps is to ensure that students know and understand what is expected of them and how they can meet those expectations.

Many classroom practices can be antecedents for challenging behaviors.

Low Levels of Task Engagement, Successful Academic Performance, or Lack of Meaningful and Dynamic Instruction.   Most people, children especially, will choose to have fun rather than be bored. Children who are actively participating in meaningful learning tasks should not be bored. Thus, it is important that teachers plan and deliver interesting lessons that keep all students engaged in learning activities most of the time.

Mr. Silsby's biology class illustrates the importance of task engagement. Mr. Silsby teaches chemistry and physics. However, this year, he has also been asked to teach a biology class, a class that he has never taught. It has been difficult for Mr. Silsby to add preparation for another class to his already busy schedule, plus it is difficult to get his lab ready for the one biology class each day. As a result, Mr. Silsby is often poorly prepared for class and ends up having students simply read and then answer questions from their text for most of the class period. This is causing problems because students often use this class to catch up on assignments from other classes, talk, or even sleep.

Likewise, the extent to which students are successful in academic tasks may correlate to challenging behaviors (Sutherland & Wehby, 2001). Students who are successful most of the time have little need to exhibit inappropriate behavior. However, students who frequently fail at academic tasks, or who are often frustrated with academic work that is too difficult, may communicate this frustration through their behavior. A signal that this may be an issue is if the student is exhibiting misbehavior that is associated with certain academic subjects or tasks (e.g., the student disrupts the class during reading, or when asked to write, or during independent work).

Poor Teacher–Student Relationships.   Most students want to please their teachers, and they want their teachers to like and take an interest in them. Positive teacher–student relationships are one important factor in motivating children to behave appropriately. When this relationship is not yet well established, or when the teacher–student relationship is mostly negative, students may be less motivated to follow the rules and do what is expected of them. In fact, if the relationship is characterized by high rates of negative comments, reprimands, or other forms of punishment, students may even skip class or exhibit inappropriate behavior in the hope that they will be removed from class.

As an example of the importance of the teacher–student relationship, consider Sam and his 11th-grade English teacher. Sam is the first person in his family to go this far in school. His mother died when he was 8 years old, and his father has worked two jobs to keep Sam and his sisters fed and sheltered. Because of his father's work schedule, Sam is often in charge of taking care of his sisters. He is frequently sleepy (because he sometimes doesn't get to start on his homework until quite late) when he gets to Mr. Anderson's last period English class; sometimes, he even falls asleep in class. Mr. Anderson thinks that Sam is just lazy. Yesterday, Mr. Anderson confronted Sam, accusing Sam of staying out all night and asking Sam if his mother and father knew what he was up to. Sam, who was hurt by this accusation, just said, "Man, you don't know what you're talkin' about," and walked out of the classroom. Mr. Anderson was not upset to see him go and simply continued teaching the class. Clearly, if Mr. Anderson had followed even a few of the recommendations that we present in Chapter 7 for establishing good teacher–student relationships, he would have known more about how Sam's difficult home life affects his school performance. Of course, we do not mean to imply that Mr. Anderson should simply overlook Sam's sleepiness; however, if Mr. Anderson had a good relationship with Sam, he might better be able to identify the source of the problem and help Sam identify ways in which to address the problem.

IMMEDIATE ANTECEDENTS   Some antecedent stimuli may predictably result in a particular behavior (e.g., a student argues each time that he is told to correct his work). Table 2-7 includes some of the potential antecedents for students who exhibit inappropriate behavior.

Behavior

The *B* in the A-B-C model refers to **behavior**. Sometimes, undesirable behavior occurs because the student has not yet learned a more appropriate way in which to behave or to satisfy his or her needs. This failure to learn more adaptive behaviors

---

TABLE 2-7   Potential Antecedents to Inappropriate Behavior

Some students, particularly students who exhibit higher levels of challenging behavior, may exhibit challenging behaviors when

- asked to do something that they do not want to do or something that is difficult, especially academic tasks;
- asked to do certain forms of work, such as written work or oral reading;
- expected to work with certain peers with whom they have a conflict;
- asked to correct errors on assignments;
- asked to stop doing a preferred activity (especially if that activity is followed by a less preferred activity);
- expected to transition from one activity or place to another;
- participating in activities with low levels of structure;
- participating in activities that are highly exciting or stimulating; or
- feeling frustrated, angry, or upset.

---

creates a setting event condition that increases the likelihood that undesirable behaviors will occur. Common skill deficits that are related to problem behaviors include the following:

Deficits in Academic Skills.   Students who lack the academic skills to fully engage in the learning tasks of a classroom will often choose to misbehave rather than ask for help or admit that they do not know how to do the work. Think about how you felt at a time when you were put on the spot to perform a task that you did not feel fully prepared to do, such as answer a question for which you were uncertain of the correct response. Deficits in academic skills may not be readily apparent, but it is a factor that should be considered, especially when undesirable behavior predictably occurs in conjunction with specific academic tasks or subjects.

An eighth-grade student we once worked with engaged in off-task or disruptive behavior every time that he was asked to write more than a couple of sentences. This student was on grade level in all subjects except language arts. Writing was difficult for him, almost painful to watch. He struggled with both the mechanics (e.g., spelling, punctuation, sentence formation) and the content, and his handwriting was almost illegible. However, when we suggested a few modifications, such as using voice recognition software to get his thoughts into a word-processing program, providing him with a personal spelling dictionary (Scheuermann, McCall, Jacobs, & Knies, 1994) to help him spell the words he frequently used, providing him with an editing checklist, and using a timer to delineate work periods interspersed with short breaks, his off-task behavior during this time decreased dramatically.

Some challenging behavior reflects skill deficits.

Deficits in Self-Control and Self-Management Skills.   Some students, especially young students, lack the self-control skills demanded of them in social and classroom settings in school. School demands much from students in the way of self-control: walk, do not run, in the hallways; raise your hand before answering; take turns when drinking from the water fountain or when using playground equipment or classroom materials; get to class on time by resisting distractions; and refrain from physical expressions of anger or frustration. Much of what we adults take for granted in terms of controlling impulsive behaviors are actually newly learned and, as of yet, imperfect skills for children. And, of course, there are some children who are biologically predisposed to have more difficulty learning self-control (e.g., children who have ADHD). Even with medication, these students must be taught self-control skills (see Chapters 9 and 11 for how to teach self-management and self-control skills).

Deficits in Social Skills.   For many reasons, some children fail to learn the basic social skills that will enable them to get along well with peers and adults or participate successfully in classroom and school activities. Deficits in social skills are particularly troubling because of the negative immediate and long-term ramifications of poor social skills. Children who have poor peer relationships, few friendships, and who do not adjust well to school are at significant risk for antisocial behavior, delinquency, and problems with adult emotional health and social situations (Hersh & Walker, 1983; Kupersmidt, Coie, & Dodge, 1990; Parker & Asher, 1987).

School demands much in the way of social skills in order to interact effectively with adults and peers. Most children learn these skills informally from observing behavior modeled at home and in other environments and through trial and error (e.g., parents scold their child for exhibiting a socially inappropriate behavior and, thus, the child learns not to engage in that behavior). When children fail to learn these skills from modeling, they must be taught, which we discuss in Chapter 9.

To illustrate the need for students to know how to use peer-related social skills, consider Ms. Stocks' class. Ms. Stocks has structured her class to include time each day for student study groups to meet and work on group projects. Jake moved to this school during the middle of the semester. Working with a group toward a common goal involved social skills that Ms. Stocks had been teaching since the first day of class. She assumed that Jake would catch on by watching the other students in his group. She was wrong. Jake was often not prepared with regard to his part of the project, and lately he had picked fights with other group members. He talked too loudly and often interrupted others. Because of Jake, his group was in danger of not finishing their project on time. Ms. Stocks now has a decision to make: She can continue the group work with no changes, which will be problematic for all of the students in Jake's group. She can allow Jake to work independently, which does nothing to help Jake. Her other choice is to assess why Jake is often unprepared, teach Jake the skills that he needs in order to participate in the group activities, and reinforce him for applying those skills during group tasks. We explain how to teach new skills in Chapters 8 and 9.

Deficits in Communication Skills.   Challenging behavior may sometimes serve as a form of communication, particularly for students with low cognition, autism, or other developmental disabilities (Carr & Durand, 1985; Ostrosky, Drasgow, & Halle, 1999; Prizant & Wetherby, 1987). When students lack adaptive ways of communicating wants, needs, and emotions, maladaptive behavior may serve that purpose. For example, if a student with autism is tired of working but has no appropriate way in which to express that feeling, she may begin hitting her head, screaming, or trying to bite the teacher as a way of saying, "I'm tired. I don't want to work anymore." Of course, if it is suspected that the behavior is for the purpose of communication, intervention should involve teaching appropriate forms of communication and reinforcing the student when she uses the alternative communicative method. For example, our student with autism might be taught to point to a picture card that represents "I am tired. No more work." When she points to this card, she may stop working. Other students may need to be taught more adaptive ways of expressing feelings or asking for assistance.

Consequences

The *C* in the A-B-C model refers to the consequences that follow inappropriate behavior, which can be examined in order to identify the **functions**, or purposes, for the behavior. Given the assumption that behavior serves a purpose (i.e., the function), we can evaluate what happens when those behaviors occur in order to develop hypotheses about the purposes that the behaviors might be serving for the student. Common purposes are to get something or to avoid something, as discussed in the following section.

The purpose of a challenging behavior may be to enable the student to get something or avoid something.

TO GET SOMETHING   Some inappropriate behavior results in the student getting something that he or she desires: attention, control, status, sensory stimulation, and so forth. This is **positive reinforcement**, which means that the inappropriate behavior will continue unless we provide the child with an alternative, appropriate way of obtaining the same outcome. We discuss positive reinforcement and its application in school settings in Chapters 10 and 11.

   Attention.   Research shows that teacher attention is a powerful tool that will increase a given behavior (Gunter & Jack, 1993; Sutherland, 2000). Of course, if more attention is paid to a challenging behavior than to an appropriate behavior, the likely outcome is that the challenging behavior will continue at a high rate. Likewise, students with behavior problems who receive low levels of positive teacher attention are less likely to exhibit the desired behaviors (Alber, Heward, & Hippler, 1999; Van Acker, Grant, & Henry, 1996).

   An example of how inappropriate behavior may be related to teacher attention is seen in the case of Juan, a 4-year-old prekindergarten student. Each morning, Mr. Harris conducted a group lesson with the students as they sat in rows on the carpet. Juan was in the last row, on the corner, far away from Mr. Harris. Juan enthusiastically waved his hand when Mr. Harris asked questions, but he was seldom called on. After about 10 minutes, Juan would begin scooting closer to Mr. Harris or even standing up. Mr. Harris still didn't call on him, but when Juan began turning somersaults, Mr. Harris took him by the hand to the time-out chair. Sadly, this individual attention from Mr. Harris only after high levels of misbehavior ensured that Juan would continue turning somersaults!

   Of course, peer attention may also be a source of positive reinforcement for inappropriate behavior. One of the authors once worked with a teacher regarding a second-grade student who was disrupting class with barking noises. The student had no medical condition that might cause this behavior. However, when the student barked, his peers laughed. Observations of the behavior suggested that the barking was positively reinforced by his peers' laughter. Based on this hypothesis, the intervention consisted of two parts: The student could earn time to tell the class a joke or an animal story (using joke books and other materials that he found in the library) *if* he completed his work during the day with no barking. In addition, at the end of the week, the entire class could participate in a fun activity if this student had less than a certain number of barks during the week (thus encouraging his peers not to laugh at the barks). The barking disappeared, supporting our hypothesis of peer attention as the maintaining factor.

Power and Control.   Some students may feel power when they control interactions with teachers and peers through their inappropriate behavior. Students who exhibit high levels of misbehavior such as noncompliance or intimidation influence the behavior of others, often in negative ways (Coie & Kupersmidt, 1983; Walker et al., 2004). When faced with a student who challenges a teacher's authority, the teacher with little training in effective strategies for managing difficult behavior may respond with frustration or exasperation. Pushing a teacher to this point may elicit very powerful feelings in some students. Students who use misbehavior (e.g., rude noises, off-task talking, inappropriate comments to peers) to stop the progress of learning in the classroom may feel more personal control in that type of situation than in other situations.

It is our experience that many children who exhibit high levels of inappropriate behavior are, in fact, children who have strong personalities. They are often assertive, often forceful, with an air of self-confidence. They may not be easily intimidated by authority figures or social conventions. Unfortunately, these children come to our attention because they lack the essential adaptive behavior and self-control skills, which exacerbates their strong-willed behavior. They also have not learned to use their strong personalities in positive, socially acceptable ways. For these students, the intervention plan should include strategies for teaching prosocial ways of expressing those strong personality traits, such as appropriate assertiveness skills or acceptable ways of influencing the behavior of others.

Over the last two decades, much attention has been paid to the concept of **resiliency**, or the mediating effect of protective traits on risk factors (Garmezy, 1985; Leone et al., 2003). Resiliency may explain why some children prevail over difficult life circumstances (e.g., poverty, abuse, poor parenting practices, family alcohol or drug abuse) that place them at high risk for developing antisocial behaviors. Interest in resiliency factors has led to an emphasis on the assessment of strengths in order to identify student traits that may help to reduce the risk factors in a child's life (Epstein & Sharma, 1998; Leone et al., 2003). Inherent protective traits may be targets for interventions designed to enhance and strengthen those traits, in addition to reducing and remediating maladaptive behaviors. We believe that the strong personalities of many children with challenging behaviors can be a protective factor; interventions should teach students how to use their strong personalities in positive ways, perhaps even in leadership roles.

TO AVOID SOMETHING   Sometimes misbehavior serves a **negative reinforcement** function: As a result of the misbehavior, the student escapes or avoids an unpleasant situation or task (Carr, Newsom, & Binkoff, 1980; Nelson & Rutherford, 1983) (see Chapter 3 for further explanation). Unless the reason for the avoidance or escape is addressed, the inappropriate behavior is likely to continue.

Work or Disliked Situations or Tasks.   Sometimes misbehavior occurs predictably during a specific class (e.g., physical education, algebra, language arts), academic task (e.g., oral reading, writing), or situation (e.g., independent work or group work, during transitions, lunchtime, recess). When this is the case, the context that is associated with the misbehavior should be careful assessed to identify why it might be more reinforcing for the student to escape or avoid that situation: Is the work too difficult or too easy? Does the student have the prerequisite academic and/or social skills to successfully handle the situation? Is the class boring? Does the class lack clear structure and organization? Chandler and Dahlquist (2002) recommend considering the student's perspective in these situations: Just because teachers think that it is punitive to be sent to the principal's office does not necessarily make it so. It may be that going to the office, where the student receives individual attention from office staff and administrators, is preferable to whatever is happening in the classroom. Likewise, a student who lacks the self-control and peer interaction skills to successfully manage the rather chaotic playground environment (and continually gets into trouble on the playground) may be happier to sit and watch or remain in the classroom and read a book; missing recess may seem to be punitive to teachers, but to this student, it is reinforcing.

People.   Sometimes students misbehave in order to avoid people, either teachers or peers. As you will see in Chapter 7, positive relationships are an important factor in preventing behavior problems. A neutral, or worse, a negative relationship with a teacher may predispose a student to behavior problems in that class. Students who lack the maturity and skills to confront someone with whom they do not get along may resort to misbehavior in order to avoid that person.

Embarrassment, Frustration, Fear of Failure.   Students who have lower academic skills than their peers may misbehave in order to avoid the academic demands of the classroom, especially public demands like reading in front of the group. When the problem behavior is frequently associated with academic situations, it is important to assess both the academic demands of the situation (e.g., the reading level of the materials, how long the student is expected to work independently, the type of materials used, how much and what type of help is available) and the skills of the student that are relevant to those demands.

Physical Discomfort.   As you have learned, students who exhibit chronic behavior problems may lack important social and self-control skills. These skill deficits may be especially evident when the student is hungry, does not feel well, or is tired. Most of us find it harder to concentrate, perform difficult tasks, pay attention, or do work we dislike when we are in physical discomfort. But we typically have the skills to either communicate our needs or take care of them ourselves. There may be little teachers can do if they suspect physical discomfort as an antecedent or setting event for problem behavior, especially if the problem is medically based (e.g., illness, allergies, injury), aside from temporarily reducing the demands on the student. However, an awareness of the situation is important, as is teaching the student self-awareness and self-advocacy skills in order to handle these conditions.

LACK OF CONSEQUENCES FOR MISBEHAVIOR   Sometimes misbehavior occurs because students are allowed to get away with it: There are either no effective consequences for misbehavior, or consequences are applied sporadically. Consider your own behavior as an example: Most of us occasionally exceed the speed limit when we drive, and we do so, in part, because we can get away with it. When we receive a speeding ticket, we usually slow down afterwards (or at least when we are driving in the area where we received the speeding ticket!). Undoubtedly, if we were ticketed *every time* that we exceeded the speed limit, we would be much more diligent about adhering to the speed limit.

> Consistency in responding to both appropriate and inappropriate behaviors is important to ensure effective classroom management.

Consider a classroom that has the rules and procedures posted (which is important, as you will see in Chapter 6). As the teacher conducts the lesson, he is often interrupted by off-task comments. In addition, a few students are passing notes, and one is sleeping. The teacher sometimes responds conversationally to the off-task comments and ignores the note-passing and sleeping. Compare this with a classroom in which all students are on task and are participating in the lesson. What is the difference? Most likely, the difference is that students in the second class have learned what is and is not allowed because the teacher consistently applies meaningful consequences to off-task behaviors like passing notes, making off-task comments, and sleeping. Students quickly learn the allowable limits for behavior from one class to the next by how teachers respond to unacceptable behavior.

For example, Ms. Cohen teaches eighth-grade art. Her classes are loud and unfocused, largely because Ms. Cohen is not well organized, and her students often have to wait for 10 minutes or more with nothing to do while Ms. Cohen gathers the needed materials. She feels guilty about wasting the students' time, so she allows them to talk and leave their tables, even though she has posted rules that instruct them to quietly wait in their assigned seats. Although students like Ms. Cohen's class, they do little work.

Thus, an important consideration when assessing problem behavior is to consider to what extent consequences have been consistently and effectively applied in the past. If consequences have been lacking or have been applied inconsistently, the first step is to develop fair and logical consequences and apply them consistently.

Summary

As the title implies, the purpose of this chapter is to explain various theories as to why children exhibit problem behavior. The objectives for this chapter and how they were addressed are as follows:

1. Describe the major theories of behavior and the research base and usefulness of each theory for teachers.

We discussed two theories of behavior: the biophysical and behavioral theories, and provided an overview of three additional models: the psychodynamic, ecological, and cognitive models. Of these, the behavioral model offers the greatest research support and the most usable tools for educators. Most of this text is devoted to behavioral interventions.

2. Describe the basic assumptions and principles of the behavioral model.

We described seven principles of the behavioral model that serve as the basis for understanding all typical and atypical forms of voluntary behavior. In addition, these principles are the foundation for positive behavioral support-based interventions such as those described throughout this text.

3. Describe applied behavior analysis (ABA) and the relationship between ABA and positive behavioral supports.

ABA is the scientific application of behavioral principles to change socially significant behavior. We described the four assumptions that are the foundation for ABA, as well as misconceptions about ABA. ABA is the basis for many of the practices and procedures used in positive behavioral supports.

4. Describe the antecedent, skill deficit, and consequence explanations for inappropriate behavior.

We described how antecedents, skill deficits, and consequences affect behavior and introduced the practice of functional behavioral assessment as a tool to pinpoint the environmental influences on behavior.

The conceptual models described in this chapter are illustrated in the following classroom vignettes. The Learning Activities for this chapter will help you to better understand the model depicted in each vignette.

Mr. Perry's Inclusion Kindergarten Class

Mr. Perry was a veteran special education teacher in a very new teaching assignment—an inclusion kindergarten class, co-taught by a general education teacher. Of the 22 students in the class, 8 were receiving special education. These students had varying degrees of disability. Two students had Down syndrome, two had autism, three had moderate speech impairments, and one had Smith–Magenis syndrome.

Mr. Perry used what spare time he had to learn about the disabilities of his young students. He remembered the biophysical model from his college courses and chose to read in that area, given the medical nature of some of his students' conditions. But as he read about genetics and biochemicals, he didn't think that this would help when his students became upset and self-abused or lashed out at other students.

Mr. Perry finally called in an old friend who specialized in classroom management, Dr. I. C. Everything, or Dr. ICE to his friends. Dr. ICE reminded him that a consistent environment is important for most students, especially students with behavioral problems, even if those problems have an organic basis. This was a helpful reminder for Mr. Perry. And even though Mr. Perry's readings did not help him much in terms of day-to-day interventions in the classroom, he acquired the vocabulary that was used for each disability, and he knew what medical treatments his students might be receiving. It meant a great deal to the parents of Mr. Perry's students, who had read everything that they could find regarding their child's condition, to know that the teacher was knowledgeable about their child's condition as well.

Mr. Ace's Behavior Class

Dr. ICE was called to USA High School to work with a special education behavior class teacher who was in contractual difficulty. This teacher, Mr. Ace, had been told that the law requires him to ensure that his students have access to general education classes and activities and that he needs to follow the general education curriculum as much as possible. To prepare his students for success in general education environments, Mr. Ace was told to teach the appropriate social and academic behaviors and to work on reducing his students' disruptive behaviors.

Mr. Ace believed that his students had suffered so much abuse in their early lives that they were incapable of changing their behavior until they learned to express their true feelings. In order to help them, Mr. Ace held many small group sessions for sharing feelings. Then the students were given a choice of creative assignments to help express their feelings. These activities took up much of their academic day.

Dr. ICE could tell that Mr. Ace cared about his students. However, he reminded him that his job was to teach the academic subjects and the behaviors that would prepare the students for their adult lives. Dr. ICE commended Mr. Ace for wanting to understand his students. He told Mr. Ace that he could use his knowledge to create a positive, consistent learning environment where his students would feel safe taking risks in learning academic and behavioral skills. In addition, Dr. ICE recommended that Mr. Ace visit a classroom where the behavioral model was being used.

Mr. Ace promised to think about what Dr. ICE had said. Dr. ICE hoped that Mr. Ace would make the changes because NCLB leaves little room for teachers to use a psychodynamic approach as the focus of their teaching.

Ms. Scott's Behavior Class

Ms. Scott taught in a self-contained classroom for students with behavioral and social skill problems. Her students had many types of disabilities. Ms. Scott used strategies that were based on a behavioral approach to successfully address each student's needs.

Ms. Scott's classroom was a model of consistency. Her students had been taught classroom rules and procedures and could explain them to a visitor. Ms. Scott modeled the behaviors that she expected from her students, such as using polite words, giving compliments, and apologizing. Their academic day was carefully planned, and the schedule was clearly posted. The students knew when a certain activity would happen because they knew the classroom routines. They knew what activities were allowed in each area of the room because each area was assigned one or more specific activities and no others.

There were individual reinforcement systems targeted toward each student's behaviors that needed to be improved, plus there was a group reinforcement system to encourage the class to work together. Each student could tell you what reward he or she was working toward and the behavior that was expected in order to earn it.

Ms. Scott used positive reinforcement as the basis for her behavioral intervention program. This was evident not only in the reward system, but also in the praise given and in the positive teacher–student interactions. Sometimes, however, she would also use negative reinforcement. This was especially helpful for increasing the homework completion rate. The students did their work in order to avoid weekend homework. In the past, one student had come in each morning with an excuse as to why his homework was not completed. Ms. Scott calmly told him that any homework that was not turned in by 8:00 A.M. must be completed during the morning break. As soon as the homework was completed, the student could join in on the break activities if there was any time left. Of course, after missing morning break 2 days in a row, that student began doing his homework at night and proudly turned it in first thing in the morning.

Ms. Scott made a point at the beginning of the year of telling her students that her classroom was a safe place—there was to be no violence! She enforced this rule by awarding points for verbal and physical composure and for exhibiting appropriate ways of expressing feelings, and by enforcing negative consequences if a violent behavior occurred.

Ms. Scott had learned much about behavior over the years. Some of what she learned was obvious, and some was not. For example, early in her career, she had awarded points for exhibiting appropriate behavior during math. One student would often ask to go to the restroom during this class, but it took a while for Ms. Scott to recognize the pattern. This student was earning enough points to obtain a reinforcer while avoiding 10 to 15 minutes of math class on most days. Ms. Scott decided to gradually reduce the time allowed in the restroom and added reinforcement for completed and correct math class work. In time, the student was taking a restroom break before math class, staying in the classroom for the entire period, and completing more of his math assignments on time.

Ms. Scott enjoyed the success that she experienced while using behavioral techniques. The techniques were easy to learn. It was her students who were complex, and so she had to use good problem-solving skills to assess and modify the interventions that were not working. Her work was challenging but interesting and very rewarding.

Learning Activities

1. Read each classroom vignette and then identify the conceptual model depicted in each. Discuss the cues that led you to your conclusions.
2. Choose an educational product that claims to be research based. Examine some of this research and decide whether it meets the NCLB standards for scientifically based evidence. Was this product evaluated with group design or single-subject design research?
3. Read medical information on conditions such as depression, ADHD, Rett syndrome, or others. What information did you learn that would be helpful for the classroom teacher?
4. Discuss in small groups ways that the applied behavior analysis method can be used to teach writing as well as behavior.

5. Read "Ms. Scott's Behavior Class," the scenario that illustrates the behavioral model. List the techniques that Ms. Scott used that reflect the seven principles of the behavioral model.
6. Write an example of how you could use each of the seven principles of the behavioral model in your classroom.
7. Discuss in small groups the relationship between ABA and positive behavioral supports.
8. Interview an educator about his or her perceptions about the causes of student behavioral problems. Next, identify the theoretical model or models reflected in the educator's response.

Resources

www.abainternational.org   The Association for Behavior Analysis International® is a professional organization for individuals interested in ABA.

www.cecdr.org   The Council for Exceptional Children's Division for Research: Provides Practice Alerts, which are concise summaries of research on popular topics/practices. Each Practice Alert is rated as "Go For It" or "Use Caution," according to the quality and quantity of the related research.

http://www2.ed.gov/rschstat/research/pubs/rigorousevid/index.html   Excellence in Government: Provides several publications to help consumers evaluate claims of product effectiveness, including *Identifying and Implementing Educational Practices Supported by Rigorous Evidence: A User-Friendly Guide*.

www.healthyplace.com   HealthyPlace, America's Mental Health Channel: Provides consumer information on mental health, including conditions, treatment, medication, and more. Includes interactive tutorials.

http://ies.ed.gov/ncee/wwc   The What Works Clearinghouse, a division of the Institute for Education Sciences, U.S. Department of Education: This site is a clearinghouse for educational research that meets the NCLB definition of "scientific evidence." Provides reviews of research on curricula and interventions for academic content areas (e.g., reading, math), behav-

ioral issues, and other areas. This site is continually updated as new reviews are completed.

www.naspcenter.org   The National Association of School Psychologists (NASP) Center: Provides a variety of resources related to school success in the areas of behavior, social skills, mental health, discipline, reading, assessment, diversity, and more.

www.nichcy.org/research   National Dissemination Center for Children with Disabilities: Provides a wide variety of information related to research-to-practice issues. Of particular interest are the articles on how to decipher and evaluate research.

www.nlm.nih.gov/medlineplus/druginformation.html   MedlinePlus, a service of the U.S. National Library of Medicine, National Institutes of Health: Provides a comprehensive array of information about medical conditions, medication, medical terminology, clinical trials, health resources, and more.

www.ornl.gov/sci/techresources/Human_Genome/project/about.shtml   Human Genome Project Information is a Website that provides information on all aspects of the comprehensive effort to map human genes and identify the behavior associated with a specific gene.

www.psyweb.com   PSYweb.com: Provides information on mental health conditions, diagnosis, treatment, medication, brain functioning, studies, and more.

www.re-ed.org American Re-EDucation Association is an organization that is dedicated to the principles and practices of Re-ED.

www.rebt.org The Albert Ellis Institute: Provides information on rational emotive behavior therapy, training, research, publications, a chat room, referral services, and more.

http://seab.envmed.rochester.edu/jaba *Journal of Applied Behavior Analysis* is the flagship research journal for the field of behavior analysis.

www.surgeongeneral.gov Office of the U.S. Surgeon General: Provides information about all aspects of physical and mental health, access to the surgeon general's reports, and links to resources.

www.wglasser.com The William Glasser Institute: Provides information about training and consultation in choice theory, quality schools, reality therapy, and other programs.

Two

ASSESSMENT AND MONITORING

After reading this chapter, you will be able to do the following:

1. Explain functional behavioral assessment (FBA) and the legal requirements for FBA.
2. Distinguish between functional analysis and functional assessment.
3. Describe indirect and direct assessment methods of data collection to help identify when, where, and why challenging behavior occurs.
4. Use the results of FBA to develop behavioral intervention plans (BIPs).
5. Describe the potential problems with and cautions regarding FBA.

Determining the Reasons for Challenging Behavior Through Functional Assessment

Big ideas in determining why challenging behavior occurs:

- Challenging behavior is usually predictable in terms of when and where it occurs.
- Challenging behavior occurs for a reason (i.e., it meets a need for the student).
- The process of determining when, where, and why challenging behavior occurs is called functional behavioral assessment (FBA) or functional assessment; a more scientific application of FBA is known as functional analysis.
- Interventions that are founded on FBA data have a greater potential to be effective than interventions that are developed without that information.
- Identifying when, where, and why a challenging behavior occurs is not difficult if you follow the procedures described in this chapter.

In Chapter 2, you learned that although a number of different theories have been proposed to explain human behavior, behavioral theory has the most comprehensive research to back both the theoretical foundation of behavioral theory and the methods used for behavioral assessment and intervention. You also learned that functional behavioral assessment (FBA), also referred to as functional assessment, is a behavioral approach used to identify when and where problem behavior is likely to occur and the purpose(s) or function(s) that behavior serves for a student.

> Functional assessment helps to identify the environmental contributions to challenging behavior and its functions.

Most teachers and other caregivers continually use informal variations of FBA to make decisions about how to address challenging behavior. Parents know, for example, that certain situations are especially difficult for their young children (e.g., long car rides, trips to the grocery store, or eating at certain restaurants) and, therefore, take steps to reduce the behavioral problems associated with those situations (e.g., plan activities for during the car ride, allow the child to help find grocery items from the shopping list, and provide a pencil and paper for the child to draw with while waiting for food to arrive). Teachers know that certain students should not sit next to one another because they talk or annoy one another, or that particular areas of the playground have a high probability for behavioral problems because of the activities that children engage in or because those areas are not well supervised. Teachers then use this information to take steps to prevent behavior management problems.

In our tiered model for meeting the needs of all students, as discussed in Chapter 1, formal FBA is most likely to be used for students who have been unresponsive to the interventions and supports provided at Tiers 1 and 2. As a Tier 3 procedure, FBA typically is used for only a small percentage of students: those students who exhibit the most serious or persistent behavioral problems and whose behaviors are the most disruptive to their own learning or the learning of others. For this reason, functional assessments typically are conducted by persons who have specialized training and expertise in this area, such as special education teachers, behavior specialists, or school psychologists. The information presented in this chapter will provide those individuals with the knowledge needed to conduct FBAs and to use FBA data to develop intervention plans to manage problem behaviors. However, we believe that all educators will be more effective in classroom and individual student management if they adhere to the principles discussed in this chapter (i.e., if they view all behavior as being functional and predictable, and if they are alert to the antecedents that precede problematic behavior and the consequences that may be maintaining such behavior).

FUNCTIONAL BEHAVIORAL ASSESSMENT VERSUS FUNCTIONAL BEHAVIORAL ANALYSIS

Behavioral assessment is often referred to by two similar phrases: functional assessment and functional analysis. Both phrases refer to similar processes that are founded on evidence. There are, however, important differences in these two terms. *Functional assessment* refers to the process of identifying the conditions and probable functions associated with a particular challenging behavior through direct and indirect assessment methods. Assessment data are then used to develop hypotheses about the conditions that are likely to produce the challenging behavior and the function(s) of the challenging behavior. Interventions are then developed on the basis of those hypotheses. *Functional analysis* involves at least one additional step before developing an intervention: the creation of conditions to scientifically manipulate the antecedents and consequences that were identified through functional assessment and then observing the target behavior under each condition. This allows for the verification or falsification of the hypotheses that were derived from the functional assessment (Kansas Institute for Positive Behavior Support, n.d.; Repp & Horner, 1999).

Functional Analysis

Functional analysis involves manipulating the environmental conditions and observing the effects of each condition on students' target behaviors; it is sometimes conducted when interventions founded on functional assessment data are ineffective. For example, Ms. Price had a student, Charlie, who frequently attempted to hurt himself by scratching, biting, or hitting himself. Previous interventions had been ineffective in eliminating this behavior, so Ms. Price used functional analysis to pinpoint the conditions under which the self-injurious behavior would likely occur and the function of that behavior. Using previous functional assessment data, Ms. Price specified four conditions under which she counted the number of times that Charlie attempted to injure himself. Under the first condition, Charlie was given easy tasks and no attention from the teacher if he attempted to injure himself. Under the second condition, Charlie was given easy tasks and high levels of attention following each self-injury attempt. The third condition consisted of difficult tasks and no attention for self-injury, and the last condition included difficult tasks and attention for self-injury. The different conditions lasted 30 minutes each, for 4 consecutive days, during independent work in mathematics. Charlie's frequency of self-injury attempts during the 30-minute work sessions were as follows:

Condition 1 (easy/no attention):   5, 1, 3, 2 (average = 2.75)
Condition 2 (easy/attention):   6, 11, 9, 10 (average = 9)
Condition 3 (difficult/no attention):   8, 12, 13, 9 (average = 10.5)
Condition 4 (difficult/attention):   10, 15, 14, 16 (average = 13.75)

From these data, Ms. Price hypothesized that Charlie's self-injurious behavior serves two functions: He receives attention and he escapes difficult tasks. This information will enable Ms. Price to design an intervention plan to provide Charlie with more attention for exhibiting appropriate behavior (i.e., completing tasks without resorting to self-injury) and to address the problem of Charlie wanting to escape difficult tasks (e.g., make the tasks more appealing, require shorter work periods during difficult tasks, provide choices, ensure that Charlie has the skills needed to complete difficult tasks, teach Charlie to request a break).

Ms. Price also used functional analysis to pinpoint the conditions associated with a challenging behavior exhibited by another student, Alicia. Typically, when Ms. Price gave a transition direction to Alicia (e.g., "Alicia, come to the table," "Alicia, go sit on the carpet"), Alicia failed to respond until she was given several additional prompts. However, at times, Alicia quickly followed directions with regard to changing activities or moving to another location, so Ms. Price was uncertain about the function of this behavior. She used functional analysis to better determine the function: For several days, Ms. Price and her paraprofessionals gave Alicia many prompts if she did not comply immediately. Then, for the next few days, no prompts were given after the initial instruction. Ms. Price and her assistants gave no further attention to Alicia and instead focused on the next activity and the students who had complied quickly. In addition, Alicia was given high levels of attention as soon as she complied. The timeliness of Alicia's compliance increased dramatically under the second condition, suggesting to Ms. Price that Alicia's noncompliance was for the purpose of getting attention.

> Functional analysis is a systematic approach to pinpointing the environmental variables that maintain challenging behaviors.

Research has clearly demonstrated the value of functional analysis in assessing challenging behaviors for the purpose of designing effective interventions (Hanley, Iwata, & McCord, 2003), including the viability of functional analysis in school settings (Broussard & Northup, 1995; Meyer, 1999; Northup et al., 1994). Functional analysis may be warranted for identifying the behavioral functions and potential interventions for students who exhibit serious misbehavior that has been resistant to previous attempts at intervention. However, for most students who have behavioral difficulties, functional assessment will usually yield sufficient data for developing effective interventions.

Functional assessment

Functional assessment involves interviewing and observing students to gather data about the conditions under which challenging behaviors are likely to occur (Kansas Institute for Positive Behavior Support, n.d.). These data are then used to formulate hypotheses about the function(s) of the problem behavior. Sometimes, especially in clinical settings or for students with extremely serious behavioral challenges, functional assessment is used first to formulate hypotheses about the function(s) of the problem behavior, then functional analysis is used to test those hypotheses (O'Neill et al., 1997). Functional assessment is most widely used in educational settings prior to the development of behavioral interventions, to problem-solve ineffective interventions, and as required by law as part of certain disciplinary procedures. (We will discuss this later in the chapter.)

The Advantages and Limitations of Functional Analysis and Functional Assessment

One distinct disadvantage of functional analysis is that the demands and complexities of the classroom setting may make functional analysis impractical, if not infeasible. Fortunately, functional assessment may provide sufficient data from which to develop effective behavioral intervention plans (BIPs), unless a function cannot be determined from interviews and observations (Dunlap & Kern, 1993). If functional assessment fails to yield clear hypotheses, or if the interventions founded on functional assessment are not effective, a subsequent functional analysis can be performed to verify the initial hypotheses or to identify new hypotheses (O'Neill et al., 1997).

Teachers and others who use these tools should be aware of the advantages and limitations of functional assessment and functional analysis as summarized in Table 3-1. If the interventions developed from the data gathered through functional assessment or functional analysis do not produce the desired changes in behavior, the teacher or others on the planning team may need to develop new interventions that are founded on the original hypotheses, develop new hypotheses that are founded on the existing data, or collect additional data to expand the functional assessment.

TABLE 3-1   The Advantages and Limitations of Functional Assessment and Functional Analysis

	Advantages	Limitations
Functional Assessment	• Is easy to conduct in school settings. • Can provide relevant data for developing effective interventions.	• The most commonly used approach to summarize observations, writing a narrative description, may be insufficient for generating hypotheses about the function(s) (Repp & Horner, 1999).
Functional Analysis	• Can more definitively pinpoint the functions of the problem behavior or rule out possible functions.	• May be difficult to conduct in classroom settings. • May not address the complexity or interplay of multiple antecedent stimuli that are present in the classroom.
Both Functional Assessment and Functional Analysis	• Tend to lead to more effective interventions than when interventions are developed without preliminary functional assessment or analysis.	• Problem behavior often serves multiple purposes, depending on the situation (e.g., a student may exhibit off-task behaviors to escape a boring task or to get attention in group settings). • Multiple behaviors may serve the same function (e.g., a student may refuse to work, run out of the classroom, or exhibit aggression toward the teacher, all for the purpose of escaping disliked tasks). • Setting events may have a strong influence on behavior, yet may be difficult to identify and/or control.

THE FUNCTIONAL BEHAVIORAL ASSESSMENT REQUIREMENTS OF THE INDIVIDUALS WITH DISABILITIES EDUCATION ACT

The Individuals with Disabilities Education Act (IDEA) amendments of 1997 require that school personnel conduct a functional behavioral assessment under certain circumstances related to placing a student in an interim alternative educational setting (IAES). Specifically, an FBA was required within 10 days of placing a student in an IAES if no FBA had been completed prior to the placement; an existing FBA had to be reviewed within 10 days of placement. The IAES was introduced in the 1994 Jeffords amendments to IDEA as a way to balance the right of students with disabilities to an appropriate education with the right of all students to a safe school environment (Bear, Quinn, & Burkholder, 2001). Students with disabilities who exhibit behaviors that fall under zero-tolerance rules (as discussed in Chapter 1) may not be expelled, but rather are to be placed in an IAES pending a review of the incident. Part of that review involves conducting an FBA of the behaviors that led to the student being placed in an IAES. An IAES is usually one or more classrooms in a separate building or separate area of the school. Most school districts have either one IAES that serves the entire district or one IAES for secondary school students (including middle school students) and one for elementary school students.

The 2004 reauthorization of IDEA modified the 1997 requirements, removing the 10-day deadline and stipulating that a child be placed in an IAES to continue to receive educational services, including FBA, as appropriate (Individuals with Disabilities Education Act, 2004). At the time that this text was being written, the regulations for this revised law were being developed. Therefore, the details of this requirement are unknown at this time. We encourage special education teachers and other personnel to inform themselves about this requirement. However, at the very least, the FBA must meet the technical requirements for assessment as specified by IDEA, including the use of multiple sources of data [20 U.S.C. 1414(b)(2)(A)].

Despite the rather limited requirements for FBA as mandated by IDEA, hearing officers and the courts have been clear about when FBAs are necessary and what should be included in a functional assessment. The hearing officer in the case of El Paso (Texas) Independent School District (2003) ruled that the obligation to conduct an FBA was not limited to only those disciplinary actions which resulted in a change in placement. In Independent School District No. 2310, MN (1998), the hearing officer made it clear that a 1-hour observation and teacher interview did not constitute an FBA. In still another case (Ingram Independent School District, TX 2001), the hearing officer ruled that the FBA must be sufficiently detailed and must address the functions of the challenging behavior.

We believe that functional assessment is a valuable tool for both teachers and individualized educational program (IEP) teams and that this tool is appropriately used under broader circumstances than just sending a student to an IAES. We regularly use FBA to assess difficult or unusual behaviors (e.g., a middle school student who was defecating in his pants during the school day) or behaviors that are resistant to intervention (e.g., a student whose behavior does not improve when she is placed on a contract or a point system or who does not respond to a group reinforcement system [see Chapters 9 and 10]). As we will discuss later in this chapter, FBA is not a perfect tool, and there are instances in which functional assessment may not yield information that will help in intervention planning. However, it is sufficiently beneficial, and sufficiently supported by research, to justify our recommendation that special education teachers should be highly skilled in understanding, planning, and completing functional assessments on a regular basis in order to assist with planning interventions.

USING FBA AS AN ASSESSMENT AND PLANNING TOOL

On the basis of research that supports the efficacy of FBA, this technique should be used whenever educators are faced with serious and/or chronic challenging behavior. For example, research demonstrates that interventions which are founded on functional assessment are more likely to be effective in changing behavior than are interventions which are not founded on FBA (Ingram, Lewis-Palmer, & Sugai, 2005; Newcomer & Lewis, 2004). Also, O'Neill and his colleagues (1997) suggest that developing interventions without prior functional assessment may actually worsen problems related to undesirable behaviors. Consider a student who is sent to the office for cursing and damaging materials during

IDEA requires FBA under restricted circumstances; the parameters of FBA have been delineated through the decisions of hearing officers.

Interventions founded on FBA data tend to be more effective than interventions developed in the absence of an FBA.

independent work. If the function of these behaviors is to avoid work, sending the student to the office would probably either maintain the problem or make it worse. For these reasons, we recommend that special education teachers (or other members of the IEP team) conduct a functional assessment prior to developing BIPs for students with chronic challenging behaviors. We also urge educators to use FBA when an intervention plan is not producing the desired outcomes, especially if an FBA was not done before developing the intervention plan.

On the other hand, because functional assessment requires some time and resources, teachers and others should be judicious in determining when it should be used. Minor behavioral problems (e.g., tattling, complaining about work, teasing) or behavioral problems that are responsive to existing interventions probably do not require functional assessment. Functional assessment typically should be used prior to interventions for serious misbehavior (e.g., aggression, high levels of noncompliance, self-injurious behaviors, highly disruptive behaviors), when there are chronic patterns of challenging behaviors for which previous interventions have been ineffective, or perhaps for usually atypical behaviors (e.g., making animal noises, talking to imaginary people, engaging in repetitive rituals). Used correctly, FBA can be an effective tool for assessing challenging behaviors and planning interventions to remediate those behaviors.

THE FUNCTIONAL BEHAVIORAL ASSESSMENT PROCESS

In this section, we describe the steps for conducting a functional assessment. First, however, is the issue of *who* should be responsible for this task. Every school district handles this matter somewhat differently. In some districts, assessment personnel (e.g., educational diagnosticians or school psychologists) are assigned the responsibility for conducting FBAs. Behavior specialists may have this responsibility in other districts. And in some districts, special education teachers take the lead in conducting FBAs. Regardless of who is in charge, two facts are important: First, teachers are fully capable of conducting a functional assessment. No specialized assessment training is needed, as long as the teacher has been instructed in the proper procedures for gathering and analyzing FBA data. Teachers will need assistance from others for various parts of the process, as you will see, but special education teachers are often the logical choice to take the lead in conducting FBAs because they know their students better than anyone else in the school. Second, the FBA process, especially analyzing the data and formulating hypotheses, should be a team effort. Each student's IEP team should collaborate in gathering and analyzing FBA data and then develop an intervention plan founded on the data, or the school may have another team that will take on this responsibility (e.g., prereferral teams or behavior management teams).

How to Conduct a Functional Assessment

Functional assessment is a *process,* not a single event or a matter of filling out a single form. It may take anywhere from 2 or 3 days to weeks, depending on the frequency of the target behaviors. Furthermore, it is our experience that analyzing FBA data often raises questions that require additional data to be collected before hypotheses are developed. In this section, we describe how to conduct a functional

FBA is a *process* that consists of multiple steps.

assessment using interviews and observations, provide sample forms for these purposes, and explain how to use FBA data to develop hypotheses about conditions under which the behavior is likely to occur and the functions of the problem behavior. We will not formally address functional analysis for the reasons stated earlier. At the end of this chapter, we provide two case studies that illustrate FBAs and BIPs for two actual students, Brock and Micah. Brock was a first grader when his FBA was completed, and Micah was 14 years old and in the ninth grade. In addition, we provide FBA data for you to analyze in Renée's case study. As you learn about the steps involved in the functional assessment process, we encourage you to study how these steps were applied in the case studies presented.

Functional assessment and intervention planning together consist of the following five steps:

1. Gather data both indirectly and directly. Indirect data collection involves gathering information from people who know the child well or who work with the child in educational settings. This is accomplished by conducting interviews and using rating scales and checklists. Direct data collection involves observing the student in the contexts associated with occurrences of the challenging behavior. The data collection step is used to determine the conditions under which the behavior does and does not occur and to begin to identify the potential function(s) of the inappropriate behavior (Repp, 1999). Note that the assessment process should identify the conditions under which the behavior of concern *does not* occur, as well as the conditions associated with the occurrence of the behavior. Knowing the antecedents of the appropriate behavior, as well as the inappropriate behavior, will help in the development of an intervention plan.

2. Analyze all sources of data, looking for consistent patterns.

3. Formulate hypotheses about the conditions under which the challenging behavior does and does not occur and about the function(s) of the behavior.

4. Develop an intervention plan to modify the antecedents for the target behavior, teach new behaviors to better enable the student to manage those antecedents, and describe strategies to enable the student to access desirable consequences through appropriate behavior rather than resorting to inappropriate behavior.

5. Monitor and adjust the intervention plan as needed.

Steps 1 through 4 are explained in the remainder of this chapter. Strategies for step 5, monitoring target behaviors, are described in Chapter 4.

Step 1: Gather Data—Indirect Methods.   The first step in the data-gathering process is to gather information indirectly. Indirect data collection is the gathering of data about the student and his or her behaviors while not actually observing the student. One form of indirect data collection is reviewing school records to identify the relevant educational, behavioral, social, and health information. Social histories are typically conducted when students enter special education, and these may provide useful information. Each year's annual IEP meeting summaries might also yield relevant information, particularly about recent behavioral changes, medications, home concerns, and so forth. For example, it would be helpful to know what medications a child is taking, how long the behavioral and/or educational problems have been occurring, previous strategies that have been attempted, and home status

The first step in the FBA process is to gather indirect and direct data.

(e.g., Does the child live with one or two parents? Has the child changed schools frequently? Have the parents expressed concern about the child's behavior?).

Another aspect of indirect data collection involves soliciting information about the child's behavior from teachers, paraprofessionals, parents, and others who know the student well using rating scales or structured interviews. Numerous forms for this purpose are available online, in various FBA workbooks, and in journal articles. Most school districts have one or more indirect data forms that are preferred for use in the district, either commercial forms that have been purchased for this purpose or forms that were developed by the district. Although the format and specifics vary, most indirect data forms have questions that direct the respondent to identify (a) the challenging behavior(s), (b) the frequency or intensity of each challenging behavior, (c) the possible setting events that contribute to each behavior, (d) the antecedents for each challenging behavior, and (e) the possible functions of each challenging behavior. Most of the forms also ask respondents to develop a summary statement or diagram that shows the relationship of specific antecedents and consequences to the behaviors of concern. It should be noted that indirect FBA assessment instruments have been criticized for insufficient technical adequacy, including test–retest reliability (i.e., the extent to which the results are similar from one administration to another over time), interobserver agreement (i.e., the extent to which two raters produce similar results), and convergent validity (i.e., the extent to which indirect assessment methods produce information that is consistent with the data from direct observation) (McIntosh et al., 2008; Rutherford, Quinn, & Mathur, 2004). While technical substantiation of indirect assessment methods is beginning to appear in research journals, there is still much to be learned. Because of concerns about the technical adequacy of FBA measures, we urge educators to rely on indirect assessment instruments that have at least minimal validity and reliability data, and not to rely on any single method for assessment purposes.

In this chapter, we have chosen two indirect data assessment forms as samples of the type of instruments that are available for this purpose. Remember that there are many others from which to choose. (See "Resources" at the end of this chapter.) The two indirect assessments that we describe include one checklist, the *Functional Assessment Checklist: Teachers and Staff (FACTS)*, and one structured interview form, the *Teacher Team Questionnaire*. These instruments are described next.

The ***Functional Assessment Checklist: Teachers and Staff (FACTS)*** (March et al., 2000) consists of two parts (see Figure 3-1). Part A asks the respondent to identify the child's strengths, the problem behaviors, and the conditions (referred to as *routines* on the FACTS) under which those behaviors are most likely to occur. In Part B, the respondent identifies one to three routines for further assessment to identify more details about the problem behaviors, suspected antecedents, typical consequences, and previous strategies that have been used to control the behavior. A summary statement is then developed (Step 6 of the FACTS), which is intended to serve as the basis for developing interventions.

Checklists such as the FACTS are quick, easy, and efficient tools to help identify the potential functions of problem behavior. However, checklists should be chosen with care. For example, some checklists or rating scales address the function(s) of the problem behavior but not the specific antecedents

Functional Assessment Checklist for Teachers and Staff (FACTS–Part A)

Step 1   Student/Grade: _____   Date: _____

Interviewer: _____   Respondent(s): _____

Step 2   **Student Profile: Please identify at least three strengths or contributions the student brings to school.**
_____

Step 3   **Problem Behavior(s): Identify problem behaviors.**

___Tardy	___Fight/physical Aggression	___Disruptive	___Theft
___Unresponsive	___Inappropriate Language	___Insubordination	___Vandalism
___Withdrawn	___Verbal Harassment	___Work not done	_Other _____
	___Verbally Inappropriate	___Self-injury	

Describe problem behavior: _____

Step 4   **Identifying Routines: Where, when, and with whom problem behaviors are most likely to occur.**

Schedule (Times)	Activity	Likelihood of Problem Behavior						Specific Problem Behavior
	Before School	Low 1	2	3	4	5	High 6	
	Math	1	2	3	4	5	6	
	Transition	1	2	3	4	5	6	
	Language Arts	1	2	3	4	5	6	
	Recess	1	2	3	4	5	6	
	Reading	1	2	3	4	5	6	
	Lunch	1	2	3	4	5	6	
	Science	1	2	3	4	5	6	
	Transition	1	2	3	4	5	6	
	Block Studies	1	2	3	4	5	6	
	Art	1	2	3	4	5	6	

Step 5   **Select 1–3 Routines for further assessment: Select routines based on (a) similarity of activities (conditions) with ratings of 4, 5, or 6, and (b) similarity of problem behavior(s). Complete the FACTS–Part B for each routine identified.**

(Continued)

FIGURE 3–1   Functional Assessment Checklist for Teachers and Staff (FACTS)

Functional Assessment Checklist for Teachers & Staff (FACTS–Part B)

Step 1 Student/Grade: _____   Date: _____

Interviewer: _____   Respondent(s): _____

Step 2 **Routine/Activities/Context: Which routine (only one) from the FACTS–Part A is assessed?**

Routine/Activities/Context	Problem Behavior(s)

Step 3 **Provide more detail about the problem behavior(s):**

What does the problem behavior(s) look like?

How often does the problem behavior(s) occur?

How long does the problem behavior(s) last when it does occur?

What is the intensity/level of danger of the problem behavior(s)?

Step 4 **What are the events that predict when the problem behavior(s) will occur? (Predictors)**

Related Issues (setting events)		Environmental Features	
_____ Illness Other: _____		_____ reprimand/correction	__ structured activity
_____ drug use _____		_____ physical demands	__ unstructured time
_____ negative social _____		_____ socially isolated	__ tasks too boring
_____ conflict at home _____		_____ with peers	__ activity too long
_____ academic failure _____		_____ Other	__ tasks too difficult

Step 5 **What consequences appear most likely to maintain the problem behavior(s)?**

Things that are Obtained	Things Avoided or Escaped From
_____ adult attention Other: _____	_____ hard tasks Other: _____
_____ peer attention _____	_____ reprimands _____
_____ preferred activity _____	_____ peer negatives _____
_____ money/things _____	_____ physical effort _____
	_____ adult attention _____

SUMMARY OF BEHAVIOR
Identify the summary that will be used to build a plan of behavior support.

Step 6

Setting Events & Predictors	Problem Behavior(s)	Maintaining Consequence(s)

(Continued)

FIGURE 3–1   (Continued)

Step 7	How confident are you that the Summary of Behavior is accurate?

Not very confident					Very Confident
1	2	3	4	5	6

Step 8	What current efforts have been used to control the problem behavior?

Strategies for Preventing problem behavior	Strategies for responding to problem behavior
____schedule change Other:____None_____ ____seating change _____ ____curriculum change _____	____reprimand Other:_____None_____ ____office referral _____ ____detention _____

Source: From *Functional Assessment Checklist for Teachers and Staff (FACTS)*, by R. March, R. H. Horner, T. Lewis-Palmer, D. Brown, D. Crone, A. W. Todd, and E. Carr, 2000, Department of Educational and Community Supports, Eugene, OR: University of Oregon. Reprinted with permission.

FIGURE 3–1   (Continued)

that may trigger the behavior. In addition, some potential functions may not be addressed in some checklists (e.g., control, escape from a variety of conditions). The FACTS is fairly comprehensive, addressing the setting events, specific antecedents, and several possible functions. The FACTS provides more functions as options for selection by the respondent than other forms, as well as space in which to indicate functions that may explain the behavior but that are not listed on the form. The FACTS also instructs the respondent to diagram the behavior chain, including the setting events and antecedents, problem behavior, and maintaining consequences. Thus, rating scales or checklists are quick methods for gathering indirect information. They can help to identify the possible functions or can be used to corroborate the functions identified via other methods. However, rating scales should be used in conjunction with interviews in order to obtain additional needed information.

Interviews with teachers, paraprofessionals, parents, and others who work with the student regularly are another form of indirect data collection. Interviews should be structured (i.e., should address a predetermined set of questions) to ensure that the needed information is obtained. In some cases, the target student should also be interviewed. O'Neill and his colleagues (1997) recommend interviewing a student if he or she can provide reliable information. O'Neill and his colleagues suggest that the purpose of the interview is to describe the behaviors of concern, identify the environmental factors associated with the occurrence and nonoccurrence of the problem behavior, and identify the consequences that may be maintaining the problem behavior. Several interview protocols are available to guide the interview process.

The ***Teacher Team Questionnaire*** (Murdock, O'Neill, & Cunningham, 2005) can be used to solicit the needed information from respondents, either during a structured interview or for the respondents to complete on their own. This form, shown in Figure 3-2, asks respondents to describe up to five problem behaviors,

Teacher Team Functional Assessment Questionnaire

Teachers' Names:_____

Student's Name: _____

Date: _____

Descriptions of Behavior(s) _____

What do the problem behaviors look like? Please describe one at a time.

1.
2.
3.
4.
5.

Things That Set Off the Behavior(s)

For each of the behaviors, describe what appears to set off the problem behavior. Please describe the conditions below in the same order as you have listed the behaviors above.

1.
2.
3.
4.
5.

Reinforcement for the Behavior(s)

From your observation, what does the student gain from the problem behaviors?

1.
2.
3.
4.
5.

Summary Statements

From the information above on this student, write a brief summary statement that includes what sets off the behavior, the behavior itself, and what the student gains from the behavior. For example: When Jason is given an assignment, he will throw his pencil across the room in order to obtain attention from the teacher.

1.
2.
3.
4.
5.

(Continued)

FIGURE 3–2   Teacher Team Functional Assessment Questionnaire

For each of the summary statements above, how confident are you that these are the reasons the student engages in this behavior? Please rate each with a number between 1 and 4.

1 = not at all confident
2 = somewhat confident
3 = confident
4 = very confident

1.

2.

3.

4.

5.

Rank the summary statements above from those that cause the most problems to the least problems. Begin with the statement that causes the biggest problems.

Source: From "A Comparison of Results and Acceptability of Functional Behavioral Assessment Procedures with a Group of Middle School Students with Emotional/Behavioral Disorders (E/BD)," by S. G. Murdock, R. E. O'Neill, and E. Cunningham, 2005, *Journal of Behavioral Education, 14,* 5–18. Form reprinted with permission.

FIGURE 3–2 (Continued)

the antecedents that set off each behavior, and the reinforcers for each behavior. Respondents are then asked to write a summary statement to describe the antecedent–behavior–reinforcement relationship for each behavior and to rate their level of confidence that each statement reflects actual events.

If the process of indirect data collection includes interviewing the target student, two instruments that are available to guide this process are the *Student-Directed Functional Assessment Interview* developed by O'Neill and his colleagues (1997) and the *Student-Assisted Functional Assessment Interview* (Kern, Dunlap, Clarke, & Childs, 1994). As you can see in Figure 3-3, the **Student-Directed Functional Assessment Interview** form asks for the student's perceptions about the behaviors that are a problem, specific information about when those problems are likely to occur during the school day, the setting events for and antecedents to those behaviors, and the possible functions of the problem behaviors. Next, the student assists in identifying strategies to reduce inappropriate behaviors and increase appropriate behaviors. We particularly like this feature for two reasons. First, soliciting student input into the intervention plan may help the student "buy into" the plan. Second, in our experience, students' ideas about interventions are often insightful and sometimes relatively simple to implement.

The **Student-Assisted Functional Assessment Interview** form (see Figure 3-4; see also Renée's case study at the end of this chapter) focuses on the features of academic work and the classroom environment that the student considers to be relevant to the appropriate and inappropriate behaviors. Given the close relationship between challenging behavior and academic tasks (see Chapters 1 and 8 for further discussion of this relationship), a careful examination of this variable is important. Soliciting the student's perception of his or

Student-Directed Functional Assessment Interview

Student Name: _____   Interviewer: _____

Referring Teacher: _____   Date: _____

I.   **Opening.** *"We are meeting today to find ways to change school so that you like it more. This interview will take about 30 minutes. I can help you best if you answer honestly. You will not be asked anything that might get you in trouble."*

Assist the student to identify specific behaviors that are resulting in problems in the school or classroom. Making suggestions or paraphrasing statements can help the student to clarify his or her ideas. You should have a list of behaviors nominated by the referring teacher.

II. **Define the behaviors of concern.** * *"What are the things you do that get you in trouble or are a problem?"* (Prompts: Late to class? Talk out in class? Don't get work done? Fighting?)

  Behavior   *Comment*

  1.

  2.

  3.

  4.

  5.

III. **Complete student schedule.** Use the "Student Daily Schedule" matrix to identify the times and classes in which the student performs problem behavior. Focus the interview on those times that are **most likely** to result in problem behavior.

* You will use the numbers to the left as codes for the identified behaviors as you complete the rest of the interview.

(Continued)

FIGURE 3–3   Student-Directed Functional Assessment Interview Form

Student Daily Schedule

Please place an "X" in each column to show the times and classes where you have difficulty with the behaviors we talked about. If you have a lot of difficulty during a period, place an "X" on or near the 6. If you have a little difficulty during the class or hall time, place the "X" on or near the 1. We can practice on a couple together before we start.

	Before School	1st Period	Hall	2nd Period	Hall	3rd Period	Hall	4th Period	Lunch	5th Period	Hall	6th Period	Hall	7th Period	Hall	8th Period	After School
Subject																	
Teacher																	
Model Difficult																	
6																	
5																	
4																	
3																	
2																	
Least Difficult 1																	

(Continued)

FIGURE 3-3 (Continued)

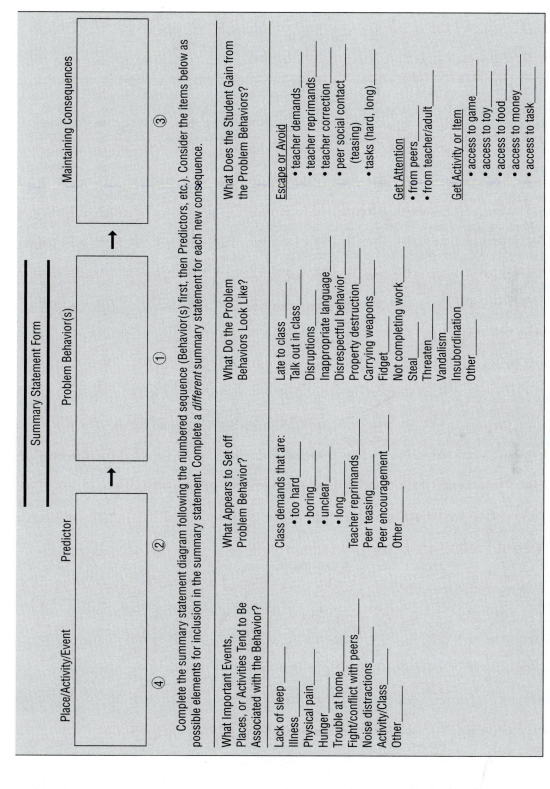

Summary Statement Form

Place/Activity/Event	Predictor	Problem Behavior(s)	Maintaining Consequences
④	②	①	③

Complete the summary statement diagram following the numbered sequence (Behavior(s) first, then Predictors, etc.). Consider the items below as possible elements for inclusion in the summary statement. Complete a *different* summary statement for each new consequence.

What Important Events, Places, or Activities Tend to Be Associated with the Behavior?

Lack of sleep ____
Illness ____
Physical pain ____
Hunger ____
Trouble at home ____
Fight/conflict with peers ____
Noise distractions ____
Activity/Class ____
Other ____

What Appears to Set off Problem Behavior?

Class demands that are:
- too hard ____
- boring ____
- unclear ____
- long ____

Teacher reprimands ____
Peer teasing ____
Peer encouragement ____
Other ____

What Do the Problem Behaviors Look Like?

Late to class ____
Talk out in class ____
Disruptions ____
Inappropriate language ____
Disrespectful behavior ____
Property destruction ____
Carrying weapons ____
Fidget ____
Not completing work ____
Steal ____
Threaten ____
Vandalism ____
Insubordination ____
Other ____

What Does the Student Gain from the Problem Behaviors?

Escape or Avoid
- teacher demands ____
- teacher reprimands ____
- teacher correction ____
- peer social contact (teasing) ____
- tasks (hard, long) ____

Get Attention
- from peers ____
- from teacher/adult ____

Get Activity or Item
- access to game ____
- access to toy ____
- access to food ____
- access to money ____
- access to task ____

Source: From *Functional Assessment and Program Development for Problem Behavior, A Practical Handbook*, 2nd edition, by R.E. O'Neill, R.H. Horner, R.W. Albin, J.R. Sprague, K. Storey, and J.S. Newton. © 1997 Wadsworth, a part of Cengage Learning, Inc. Reproduced by permission. www.cengage.com/permissions

FIGURE 3-3 (Continued)

87

Student: _____
Date: _____
Interviewer: _____

SECTION I

1.	In general, is your work too hard for you?	Always	Sometimes	Never
2.	In general, is your work too easy for you?	Always	Sometimes	Never
3.	When you ask for help appropriately, do you get it?	Always	Sometimes	Never
4.	Do you think work periods for each subject are too long?	Always	Sometimes	Never
5.	Do you think work periods for each subject are too short?	Always	Sometimes	Never
6.	When you do seatwork, do you do better when someone works with you?	Always	Sometimes	Never
7.	Do you think people notice when you do a good job?	Always	Sometimes	Never
8.	Do you think you get the points or rewards you deserve when you do good work?	Always	Sometimes	Never
9.	Do you think you would do better in school if you received more rewards?	Always	Sometimes	Never
10.	In general, do you find your work interesting?	Always	Sometimes	Never
11.	Are there things in the classroom that distract you?	Always	Sometimes	Never
12.	Is your work challenging enough for you?	Always	Sometimes	Never

SECTION II

1. When do you think you have the fewest problems with _____ in school?
   (largest behavior)

   Why do you not have problems during this/these time(s)?
2. When do you think you have the most problems with _____ in school?
   (largest behavior)

   Why do you have problems during this/these time(s)?
3. What changes could be made so you would have fewer problems with _____?
   (largest behavior)
4. What kind of rewards would you like to earn for good behavior or good schoolwork?
5. What are your favorite activities at school?
6. What are your hobbies or interests?
7. If you had the chance, what activities would you like to do that you don't have the opportunity to do now?

SECTION III

Rate how much you like the following subjects:

	Not at all		Fair		Very much
Reading	1	2	3	4	5
Math	1	2	3	4	5
Spelling	1	2	3	4	5
Handwriting	1	2	3	4	5
Science	1	2	3	4	5
Social Studies	1	2	3	4	5

(Continued)

FIGURE 3-4 Student-Assisted Functional Assessment Interview

English	1	2	3	4	5
Music	1	2	3	4	5
P.E.	1	2	3	4	5
Computers	1	2	3	4	5
Art	1	2	3	4	5

SECTION IV

What do you like about Reading?
What don't you like about Reading?
What do you like about Math?
What don't you like about Math?
What do you like about Spelling?
What don't you like about Spelling?
What do you like about Handwriting?
What don't you like about Handwriting?
What do you like about Science?
What don't you like about Science?
What do you like about Social Studies?
What don't you like about Social Studies?
What do you like about English?
What don't you like about English?
What do you like about Music?
What don't you like about Music?
What do you like about P.E.?
What don't you like about P.E.?
What do you like about Computers?
What don't you like about Computers?
What do you like about Art?
What don't you like about Art?

Source: From "Student-Assisted Functional Assessment Interview," by L. Kern, G. Dunlap, S. Clarke, and K. E. Childs, 1994, *Diagnostique*, *19*, 29–39. © 1994 PRO-ED, Inc. Reprinted with permission.

FIGURE 3–4   (Continued)

her academic work may provide insights that are not otherwise readily apparent to observers.

A word of caution from our own experiences: It is important to gather sufficient information from individuals who know the student well while keeping the amount of data manageable. Our rule of thumb is to start by collecting information from those who know the student best (e.g., teachers, paraprofessionals, and parents) and/or who supervise the student in areas where the problem behavior occurs (e.g., general education teachers, cafeteria monitors, administrators). If the information from these individuals is insufficient to contribute to the development of hypotheses or is vastly inconsistent, additional data can be collected from other persons.

Step 1: Gather Data—Direct Methods.   Before we explain how to gather direct data, it is important to understand why obtaining direct data is an important part of the data collection process. First, IDEA requires that FBAs include multiple sources of data. Also, hearing officers have ruled that FBA data should be drawn from multiple sources, should be current, and should be more than "cursory" (Etscheidt, 2006a). Second, research shows that information obtained through indirect assessment may not be valid; it is, after all, subjective in that indirect assessment relies on informants to provide information about the child's behavior (Cunningham & O'Neill, 2000). Third, direct observation typically generates more highly detailed information about the environmental events that are contributing to the challenging behavior than does indirect assessment (Carr, Langdon, & Yarbrough, 1999). Sometimes, observations will reveal antecedent or consequence factors that were not identified by analyzing the indirect data.

We have conducted many FBAs. The following are a few common findings from our FBAs for students who exhibit chronic behavioral problems. These findings support the importance of direct observation as part of the FBA process:

- These students usually exhibit more appropriate behavior than inappropriate behavior during the observation period. And, overall, their behavior is typically more appropriate than inappropriate. Often, however, we receive little information in indirect assessments about a student's appropriate behavior (unless we specifically direct the respondent to describe appropriate behaviors).
- These students typically receive little attention of any kind following the exhibiting of appropriate behavior. Most of the time, the exhibiting of appropriate behavior receives no response, particularly appropriate social behaviors (e.g., working on assignments, talking appropriately to peers, asking appropriate questions, following directions). Unfortunately, teachers often overestimate the attention that they give for a children's appropriate behavior (see Chapter 10). As an example, one of us (BKS) recently consulted with a middle school special education teacher about a student who was exhibiting high rates of disruptive behaviors. The teacher said that he is very positive with his students and gives "lots of praise." However, during a 4-hour observation of the classroom, the teacher gave only one statement of praise to the target student and none to the other students in the class, despite multiple opportunities for praise to be given (e.g., multiple instances of appropriate behaviors exhibited by all of the students).
- There are often predictable patterns in the teacher's responses to the student's inappropriate behavior. For example, the following is a common pattern: The first few instances of inappropriate behavior are ignored. If the behavior persists, many teachers respond by using ineffective strategies to control it (e.g., numerous redirections or talking to the student about the behavior) until, at some point, the student is sent out of the classroom (e.g., given an office referral or a time-out outside of the classroom). As you will see in Chapter 12, withholding attention for a behavior (i.e., ignoring it) can be an effective practice for some low-level challenging behaviors if used systematically and in conjunction with other strategies. Too often, however, the ignoring of misbehavior occurs spontaneously and is not part of a predetermined intervention plan. Also, it often seems that the student is sent out of the classroom when the teacher loses patience with the student's behavior rather than as a planned response.

If the student's behavior serves the function of gaining attention, talking to the student about the behavior will probably just make the problem worse; if the behavior serves the function of avoidance, sending the student out of the classroom will probably ensure that the inappropriate behavior is repeated in the future! Direct assessment data provide a wealth of information about teacher responses, such as giving attention or removing the student from class, which may be maintaining the inappropriate behavior. This information is critical for developing effective intervention plans.

For all of these reasons, direct observation is a critical component of functional assessment. Information from checklists and interviews will guide decisions about when and where to observe the student. That is, you will want to observe in those situations where problem behavior is most likely to occur. Of course, if time and other resources allow, we also recommend that you observe in situations that are not typically associated with the challenging behavior, which may provide information about the environmental conditions associated with appropriate behavior.

Many formats for structuring observations are available, including anecdotal reports, A-B-C descriptive analysis, and a modified narrative format described by Carr and his colleagues (1999).

An **anecdotal report** (also called an **A-B-C report** or **A-B-C recording**) is a simple data recording method in which the observer maintains a written description of events during an observation period using an antecedent–behavior–consequence (A-B-C) format. This report provides a written description of everything that happens with regard to the student during a specific period that is associated with direct antecedents and consequences (Bijou & Baer, 1961). A sample anecdotal report is shown in Figure 3-5. Note that the *A* on the report refers to the antecedents observed; *B* is the target student's observable behaviors; and *C* refers to the consequences, or events, that follow the behavior(s). To obtain an anecdotal report, observe the student during a time when the challenging behavior is likely to occur. First make note of the environmental conditions on the report (e.g., who is present; the activities that occur during the observation; any unusual circumstances that are potential setting events, such as the fact that the student has a cold or a new student is present; the time that you start and finish the observation). As you observe, make a written record of everything that you see, along with the time you record each entry. You should simply write what you see: Do not interpret, form conclusions, or make assumptions. Minimally, your observation should cover one activity and the transitions before and after that activity, although a longer observation may be needed to get an adequate sample of the behavior and the related contextual variables. In addition, you may need to observe the student over several days in order to get a complete picture of the student's behavior as it relates to all of the different environmental variables.

After the observations, review the completed anecdotal reports, looking for (a) what the student is doing that is inappropriate; (b) how frequently this inappropriate behavior occurs; (c) consistent patterns of reinforcement or punishment of that inappropriate behavior; (d) identifiable antecedents to the inappropriate behavior; (e) patterns in the antecedents; (f) recurring chains of specific antecedents, behaviors, and consequences; and (g) possibilities for intervention (Alberto & Troutman, 2006).

An A-B-C report is often used for gathering data through observation.

A-B-C Report Form

Name: _____ Date/Time of observation: _____

Place observation occurred: _____

Environmental conditions (number of students, arrangement, number of adults, etc.): _____

Activities observed during observation: _____

Unusual or potentially influential conditions: _____

Time	Antecedent	Behavior	Consequence

FIGURE 3–5   Anecdotal (A-B-C) Report

The **A-B-C descriptive analysis** format (Alberto & Troutman, 2006; Smith & Heflin, 2001) expands on the simple anecdotal format to allow for a greater level of detail in recording the events surrounding the identified undesirable behaviors (see Figure 3-6). It also prompts the observer to record the perceived functions of each target behavior. Originally referred to as a behavioral assessment form (Smith & Heflin, 2001), an A-B-C descriptive analysis data sheet uses codes rather than a narrative format to refer to the data categories (i.e., contexts/activities, antecedents, target behaviors, consequences, and student reactions). For example, in the "antecedents" column of the data form, the observer might note the antecedent(s) that precede a behavior by entering "1" to indicate that the teacher gave the child a direction, "2" to indicate that a peer made a comment to the child, "3" to indicate that the child was given an academic task, and so forth. Coding allows data to be recorded faster than if a narrative format is used, which means that the observer can potentially capture more information about the behavior and the related contextual events.

Prior to the observation session, the observer should prepare the data form by noting the codes for each column (i.e., contexts, antecedents, target behaviors, etc.). These codes will be different from observation to observation, depending on the student and the activities observed. The codes should be derived from the indirect data gathered from the rating scales and the interviews and from at least one practice observation using the form to observe the target student (Alberto & Troutman, 2006). Alberto and Troutman also recommend including operational definitions for each identified target behavior. An **operational definition** is an unambiguous, objective definition of a target behavior, which often includes examples of the presence or absence of the behavior. Operational definitions are important because they help to minimize confusion with regard to what constitutes an instance of a particular behavior, thereby increasing the consistency of the response to the behavior. A behavior is operationally defined if two or more people agree on the definition and on examples of the target behavior (Alberto & Troutman, 2006). Operational definitions are further discussed in Chapter 4, but, for now, remember that using precise action verbs (e.g., hits head with open palm, stands within 12 inches of another person, pushes, throws, kicks) rather than adjectives (e.g., self-abusive, intrusive, aggressive) to describe the behavior increases the operational value.

At this point, the A-B-C descriptive analysis form is similar to that used for an anecdotal report. During the observation period, the observer notes the times that the target behaviors occur and records the appropriate codes for the contexts, antecedents, consequences, and student reaction for each behavior. Each instance of behavior is recorded on a separate line. Note that each behavior may be associated with more than one antecedent, consequence, and student reaction.

The A-B-C descriptive analysis form should then be studied, looking for antecedents that consistently trigger challenging behaviors and the consequences that may be maintaining those behaviors. If these patterns are unclear, more data (both indirect and direct) should be gathered.

To avoid a potential problem with both anecdotal reports and A-B-C descriptive analysis, if the data are collected during real-time observations, someone other than the teacher or paraprofessional should conduct the observation. Because the

Student: _____   Date: _____   Page ____

Time	Context/Activity	Antecedent/Setting Events	Identified Target Behavior	Consequence/Outcome	Student Reaction	Comments
Begin and End	The student's environmental surroundings (people, places, events)	Describe exactly what happened in the environment just before the target behavior was exhibited.	List types of behavior displayed during the incident.	What happened in the environment immediately after the behavior was exhibited?	How did the student react immediately after the initial consequence was delivered?	
Describe keys for each column:	1. 2. 3. 4. 5. 6. 7. 8.	1. 2. 3. 4. 5. 6. 7. 8.	1. 2. 3. 4. 5. 6. 7. 8.	1. 2. 3. 4. 5. 6. 7. 8.	1. 2. 3. 4. 5. 6. 7. 8.	

FIGURE 3-6 A-B-C Descriptive Analysis   *Source:* From "Supporting Positive Behavior in Public Schools: An Intervention Program in Georgia," by M. L. Smith and L. J. Heflin, 2001, *Journal of Positive Behavior Interventions, 3*(1), p. 41. © 2001 PRO-ED, Inc. Adapted by permission.

adults in the classroom have a significant impact on the behavior exhibited by the students, the behavior of the adults may be serving as antecedents (e.g., giving directions, asking the student to correct his or her work, attending or not attending to the student) of problem behavior and the consequences that they provide may be maintaining the problem behavior (e.g., by giving or not giving attention, by withdrawing requests or tasks). Thus, the behavior of the adults in the classroom is critical and must be observed as part of the data collection process. The teacher cannot do this and teach at the same time, so another adult must conduct the observation. Fortunately, all of the observation forms that we have described can be easily used by other teachers, paraprofessionals, behavior specialists, school social workers, counselors, or other school personnel. Alternatively, the teacher (and possibly others) can conduct the A-B-C observations after class by viewing a videotape of the class activities.

> In classes where inappropriate behaviors occur, someone other than the teacher should conduct the observations.

Sometimes, an anecdotal report or A-B-C descriptive analysis may not be the best observation format to use. For example, if a target behavior occurs infrequently, or if no adult is available to conduct the observation, a different observation format is needed, such as an index card narrative format. An **index card narrative format** for recording direct observation data was described by Carr and his colleagues (Carr et al., 1994). Rather than observing all of the activities occurring during a designated observation period; this method involves recording the same information throughout the day as a target problem behavior occurs. Carr and his colleagues used index cards instead of data sheets (see the sample index card narratives in Micah's case study in the chapter appendix) to describe the following information for each incidence of a problem behavior: the interpersonal context (antecedents), the behavioral problem, and the social reaction (consequences). To avoid the problem of subjective judgment affecting what is recorded, the observer should take care to use only objective statements about the incident, just as in anecdotal reports.

Periodically during the data collection period, one or more members of the BIP team should sort the completed cards into categories of similar antecedents (e.g., was given a written task, was given a direction, was asked to put toys away, was asked to make a transition) and consequences (e.g., received the teacher's attention, received attention from peers, was able to avoid a task). Because both of these elements are recorded on the same card, more than one sorting may be needed. For example, you might first sort the cards according to similar antecedents, noting the different categories and the categories that contain the most cards, as well as the behaviors that those antecedents tend to trigger. Next, you would sort the cards according to consequence patterns, again noting the categories and the behaviors associated with each consequence or type of consequence.

> The index card narrative format is useful for collecting data on low-frequency behaviors.

There are several advantages to using the index card narrative system. First, the teacher or paraprofessional may be able to complete the index card record following a behavioral incident, avoiding the need for another person to conduct an observation. Second, the completed index cards can be sorted into categories of similar antecedents (e.g., asked to participate in a group activity, asked to transition) and consequences or functions (e.g., gets the teacher's attention, gets attention from peers, avoids task, avoids a particular situation). This concrete method of identifying patterns is easy to use and might be an efficient way to help the planning team recognize antecedent or functional patterns. Another advantage to the index card narrative system is that, unlike anecdotal reports that might not provide useful information for low-frequency behaviors, the index card narrative format allows for data collection on problem behaviors that occur infrequently. Finally, because the system is easy for classroom personnel to use and does not interrupt instruction, extensive data can be collected that can increase the validity of hypotheses.

Technology is also being used to facilitate the observation and data analysis process. Anecdotal reports can be developed using spreadsheet software that will produce quantitative analyses and graphs of the data entered on the spreadsheet during observations. Individuals who are fluent in developing spreadsheets can devise observation systems that are customized to the needs of a classroom or a school. In the "Resources" section at the end of this chapter, we list two Websites from which observation spreadsheets can be downloaded.

The second step in the FBA process is to analyze the data.

Step 2: Analyze the Data.   After each piece of data is collected, one or more persons should analyze the data to look for patterns in terms of when the problem behavior occurs (suggesting the antecedents and/or setting events for the behavior) and the consequences that follow the behavior (indicating the function(s) of the behaviors). We find it helpful to analyze the data in multiple ways. First, compare the indirect assessments (e.g., interviews, checklists) from all respondents and make notes about antecedents and possible functions. The more agreement that exists among the respondents, the more valid the data can be considered. For example, when all three respondents agree that Brock is likely to respond with threats or by calling his peers names when asked to do something that he does not want to do, such agreement indicates valid data. Data from one respondent that are not supported by other respondents may not be as strong. For instance, if Ms. Keller speculates that Brock acts out in order to obtain attention from his peers, but no other data support peer attention as a function, either peer attention is not a strong motivator for Brock or that function is unique to Brock's behavior in Ms. Keller's class.

Next, carefully review all direct assessments, looking for patterns in how the student responds to different antecedents and what happens after each instance of appropriate and inappropriate behavior. How does the teacher respond? How do his or her peers respond? Again, look for patterns in the antecedents and consequences. Similar patterns across multiple observations suggest that the antecedents and/or consequences involved may play a role in the student's behavior.

Finally, compare direct observation data against the indirect assessments. Are the speculations found in the indirect assessments supported by the direct observation data? If so, that suggests a strong explanation for the student's behavior. For example, if multiple respondents indicate that oral reading is an antecedent for Micah's problem behavior, and the direct assessment data show that Micah responds with inappropriate behavior when asked to read aloud, we can confidently conclude that oral reading is likely to predict unacceptable behavior from Micah. If the data from the indirect assessments are not corroborated by the data gathered in the direct assessments, it does not necessarily mean that the indirect assessment data are invalid. However, in these cases, we suggest further observation, if possible, trying to make careful observations during those times and conditions that are reported in the indirect assessments as being predictive of inappropriate behaviors.

Once all of the data have been analyzed, the next step is to develop hypotheses founded on the data.

Step 3: Formulate Hypotheses.   Using the results of the data analysis, the next step is to develop hypotheses. These hypotheses will guide the development of the BIP. In formulating the hypotheses, consider the range of setting events, antecedents, and functions associated with each behavior of concern. A useful format for organizing hypotheses for each behavior is the Competing Behavior Model form shown in Figure 3-7 (O'Neill et al., 1997). The competing behavior model provides a simple, clear approach to organizing FBA data for desired behaviors and problem behaviors. The competing behavior diagram plainly shows the setting events and antecedents associated with the problem behaviors; descriptions of the problem behaviors and the consequences that seem to be maintaining those problem behaviors; the desired behaviors and the consequences that currently follow those behaviors; and possible alternative replacement behaviors. As you can see in the sample Competing Behavior Model forms in the appendix to this chapter, the consequences for the desired behavior are usually not as intense, appealing, or immediate as the consequences for inappropriate behavior, which is one reason the inappropriate behavior occurs.

> The third step in the FBA process is to develop hypotheses.

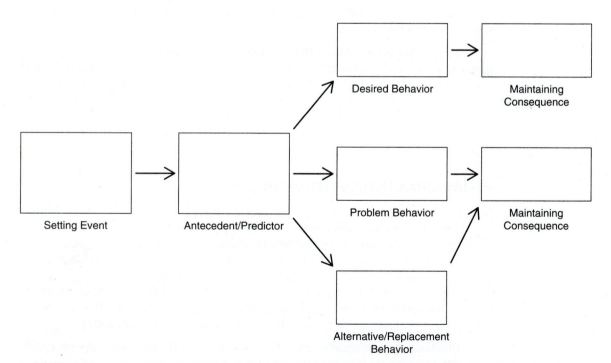

FIGURE 3-7 Competing Behavior Model   *Source:* From *Functional Assessment and Program Development for Problem Behavior, A Practical Handbook,* 2nd edition, by O'Neill/Horner/Albin/Sprague/Storey/Newton. © 1997 Wadsworth, a part of Cengage Learning, Inc. Reproduced by permission. www.cengage.com/permissions

Step 4: Develop a Behavioral Intervention Plan. A BIP describes strategies that adults in the school setting will implement to increase appropriate behavior and reduce or eliminate inappropriate behavior. The strategies listed in the BIP should directly reflect the results of the functional assessment. In other words, the BIP should describe strategies for addressing antecedents for problem be-havior, for teaching new replacement behaviors, and for enabling the student to gain access more appropriately to the consequences that are maintaining the challenging behaviors. It is imperative to carefully choose replacement behaviors and intervention strategies that will make those replacement behaviors work as well for the student as the challenging behavior (i.e., that will make the replace-ment behaviors *functional* for the student). The importance of choosing replace-ment behaviors is reflected in the **matching law,** described by Hernstein (1974), which states that the rate of any behavior is determined by the rate of reinforce-ment for that behavior. If the challenging behavior produces reinforcement every time it occurs but the desired alternative is only reinforced once in awhile, the unacceptable behavior will continue at a high rate, whereas the desired alterna-tive will occur infrequently. O'Neill and his colleagues (O'Neill et al., 1997) refer to this as **behavioral efficiency**: Students tend to use behaviors, whether appropriate behaviors or inappropriate behaviors, that require the least effort to produce the desired results and that require the least amount of instances to pro-duce the desired results. O'Neill and his colleagues also emphasize that inappro-priate behaviors must become ineffective (i.e., the inappropriate behaviors will no longer produce reinforcement, whereas the desired behaviors consistently will produce reinforcement).

Step 5: Monitor and Adjust the Intervention Plan as Needed. Target behaviors must be monitored to ensure that interventions are, in fact, producing the desired changes (Drasgow & Yell, 2001; Etscheidt, 2006a). In our experiences, because classrooms are busy and complex environments, and teachers have many demands on their time, data collection can be easy to overlook. We discuss be-havior monitoring later in this chapter and describe data collection techniques in Chapter 4.

BEHAVIORAL INTERVENTION PLANS

In this section, we present a model format for BIPs. However, most school districts expect teachers to use either a district-developed or state-developed BIP form. If this is the case, we strongly recommend that the planning team ensure that the fol-lowing components, at a minimum, are included on the form and that information for the missing components be added, as needed. These components reflect the current literature on best practices in the development of BIPs, which are informed by research and the decisions of hearing officers (Drasgow & Yell, 2001; Etscheidt, 2006a; Scott et al., 2005; Van Acker, Boreson, Gable, & Potterton, 2005):

- Challenging behavior(s) and target replacement behavior(s), operationally defined
- Setting events for each behavior
- Antecedents for each behavior

- Maintaining consequences (functions) for each challenging behavior
- Setting event strategies
- Antecedent strategies
- Teaching strategies
- Consequence strategies

Along with the information just listed, we are including additional helpful material on the BIP. The following is a description of other types of information that we believe are needed on the BIP, along with the rationale for each:

- *Criteria for each challenging behavior and target replacement behavior.* Just as for academic objectives, criteria are important for setting the standard by which to determine when a behavior has been mastered. In addition, attaining the criterion level that is set for a behavior allows the teacher to determine when the interventions for that behavior might be stopped or reduced (i.e., used less intensively).
- *Persons responsible for implementing the interventions.* In our experience, sometimes interventions are listed on a BIP without clear guidance as to who is responsible for implementation. This can be particularly problematic when the student who has a BIP is in general education classes for much of the day. For example, one of us (BKS) was asked to consult on a case where middle school administrators wanted to place a special education student in a more restrictive setting because of behavioral problems that occurred in the general education classes where the student received all of his instruction. The student's parents opposed a more restrictive setting and were prepared to request a due process hearing on the matter. The student had a BIP to address his behavioral problems. However, as the author reviewed the BIP with the special education teacher, it became clear that many of the provisions of the BIP were not being implemented. The most egregious oversight was that the BIP specified that the student receive social skills training; however, there was no time in the general education schedule to accommodate this stipulation and, therefore, it was never provided. Had the IEP planning team addressed the question "Who will be responsible for providing social skills training?" the problem of when and where to provide social skills instruction may have been anticipated and planned for in advance.
- *How each behavior will be monitored.* Just as with academic objectives, it is important to monitor the behaviors targeted for change in the BIP using objective measurement systems (Drasgow & Yell, 2001; Etscheidt, 2006a, b). To facilitate data collection on the target behaviors, we support Etscheidt's (2006b) recommendation that the planning team address when and how target behaviors will be monitored, who will be responsible for monitoring them, and how data will be reported. To facilitate maintenance and generalization of skills, we encourage IEP teams to plan for monitoring the behaviors over time and in environments other than where the skill will initially be taught. In Chapter 4, we will explain data collection methods that are manageable within the busy classroom setting and that provide useful information from which to judge the effectiveness of interventions.

> The components of the BIP have been delineated through research and the decisions of hearing officers.

The steps for developing a BIP using this format follow. Each step refers to the corresponding numbered column in the blank BIP form shown in Figure 3-8.

1. In the "Behavior of Concern" column, list (in operational terms) the behaviors to be reduced or eliminated.
2. List the criteria for each of these behaviors.
3. List hypotheses from the FBA that relate to each behavior of concern.
4. Identify a target replacement behavior for each behavior to be reduced. One or more replacement behaviors that will serve the same function as the behavior of concern should be identified. As O'Neill and his colleagues (1997) state, "A fundamental rule of effective behavioral support is that you should not propose to reduce a problem behavior without also identifying the alternative, desired behaviors [that] the person should perform instead of the problem behavior" (p. 71). These replacement behaviors must be functional for the student.
5. List a criterion for each replacement behavior.
6. List antecedent interventions that will be used to prevent problem behaviors and encourage replacement behaviors. A list of possible antecedent interventions is provided in Table 3-2; additional antecedent interventions are

---

TABLE 3-2 Sample Antecedent Interventions

- Teach the rules and procedures for the specific environment.
- Provide clear, concise directions.
- Use timers to delineate the required length of the tasks.
- Provide shorter tasks.
- Provide choices of materials, the order of the tasks, or where the work will be done as part of the academic tasks.
- Change the form of the task (e.g., have the student tape-record a report rather than write it, have the student develop a story map rather than write a book report).
- Ensure that the student has the skills needed to perform the assigned academic tasks.
- Increase the interest level of the tasks.
- Increase the structure inherent in the situation (especially during transitions).
- Provide reminders about expected behavior.
- Modify the physical environment (e.g., reduce crowding, separate students, reduce distractions).
- Increase the levels of task engagement by making the tasks more appealing or more interesting.
- Change the seating.
- Provide proximity control (e.g., maintain close physical proximity to the student).
- Provide physical reminders (e.g., tape a square on the floor to indicate the area where the student's desk is to remain; use orange cones to mark the boundaries of the play area).
- Use self-management interventions (see Chapter 11).
- Teach the needed social, self-control, and self-management skills.

Behavior Intervention Plan

Student: _____   Age: _____   Date: _____

Behavior of Concern	Target Criterion	Hypotheses	Replacement Behavior(s)	Target Criterion	Antecedent Interventions	Reinforcement Plan	Consequence Strategies for Reducing Behaviors of Concern	Monitoring Plan
1.								
2.								
3.								
4.								

FIGURE 3-8   Blank Behavior Intervention Plan

discussed in Chapters 5 through 8. Note that each behavior and the corresponding intervention information are numbered because, although some of the interventions will be unique to a particular behavior, if an intervention will be used for multiple behaviors, you may simply write "See #_" to refer the reader to an intervention that is listed previously on the form.

7. Identify reinforcement contingencies to reinforce the replacement behaviors. Remember that the desired behaviors should produce the same (or similar) consequences as those that have been maintaining the problem behaviors. In other words, the desired behaviors should address the same function as the problem behaviors. A discussion of reinforcement strategies for common behavioral functions, along with several unique reinforcement ideas, is provided in Chapters 10 and 11. Furthermore, the reinforcement strategies should enable the student to access reinforcement *as frequently* and *as intensely* as is currently given for the inappropriate behavior (Sprague & Horner, 1999). Otherwise, the problem behavior is likely to continue because it produces the desired consequences more easily, more frequently, or more predictably than the appropriate behavior. This is related to the concepts of matching law and behavioral efficiency as described previously in this chapter.

8. Behavior reduction interventions, if needed, should be included. We recommend that behavior reduction interventions be used only for behaviors that are dangerous, that significantly interfere with the child's school success, or that persist despite antecedent interventions. We describe behavior reduction strategies in Chapter 12 and provide the criteria for determining when the behavior reduction interventions are needed.

9. Describe how and when each behavior will be monitored. This section should describe which data collection technique will be used (see Chapter 4), when it will be used (e.g., during science class, 3 days per week), and by whom (e.g., the special education teacher and the paraprofessional).

Regardless of the format of the BIP, consistent, correct implementation is essential to the success of the plan. Gable, Quinn, Rutherford, and Howell (1998) identified a variety of factors that can reduce the effectiveness of the intervention plans. Among these factors are the following:

- Vague definitions of the behaviors of concern
- Insufficient data collection
- Incorrect interpretation of the data
- Insufficient intervention in dealing with the behavior
- Inconsistent application of the intervention plan
- Incorrect application of the intervention plan
- Failure to monitor implementation of the plan
- Failure to evaluate the effectiveness of the plan

Thus, functional assessment and the development of the BIP are just the beginning of the behavior change process. Each step, from the functional assessment to the data collection and analysis during the intervention, is critical for producing the desired results.

PROBLEMS AND LIMITATIONS OF FUNCTIONAL BEHAVIORAL ASSESSMENT

FBA is an important tool for educators; it is one that can make intervention planning more efficient and effective. It is not a perfect tool, however, and anyone who uses functional assessment should be aware of the following potential problems and limitations of the technique.

> Educators should be aware of the limitations of FBA.

First, functional assessment may not be helpful for high-intensity, low-frequency behaviors, or covert behaviors such as arson, stealing, vandalism, drug use, or cruelty to animals (Walker et al., 2004). Second, a single problem behavior or class of behaviors may serve many purposes (Carr et al., 1999). A student may spit, hit, kick, or punch to avoid a disliked activity, to escape a disliked peer, or because he cannot have something that he wants. A single intervention for this student's aggressive behavior is likely to be ineffective because the behavior serves multiple functions. Different interventions are needed to address the different functions of the behavior. On the other hand, multiple forms of behavior may serve the same function (Horner, 1994), requiring that the intervention be applied to all forms of the behavior. For example, sleeping, laying one's head on the desk, and writing notes may all be forms of avoidance behavior and would all be subject to the same intervention. Another caution is that the same behavior or class of behaviors may serve different functions for different students (Derby et al., 2000). Running out of the classroom without permission, for example, may reflect an escape function for some students or an attention-getting function for others. Thus, what works for one student may not work for another. This is one reason that we argue against relying on "recipes" for problem behavior or pat solutions for specific behaviors. Unfortunately, behavioral problems are seldom that simplistic. Finally, remember that FBA is not a one-time event. Children, their behaviors, and the contexts change over time. An FBA completed in October may not address new challenging behaviors that develop in February. Another FBA may be needed at that time to identify the environmental conditions associated with those new behaviors and the functions of those new behaviors.

Summary

In this chapter, we explained the technique of functional behavioral assessment, which is the process of gathering and analyzing data for the purpose of determining the conditions under which problem behavior is likely to occur and the functions of that problem behavior. This enables IEP teams or other planning teams to develop BIPs that have a higher probability of desired behavior change outcomes than intervention plans developed without functional assessment data. The objectives for this chapter and how they were addressed are as follows:

1. Explain functional behavioral assessment (FBA) and the legal requirements for FBA.

You learned that IDEA requires FBA only under limited circumstances, but because FBA is an effective practice founded on research, we recommend that it be used under far broader circumstances. Any intervention plan for severe, chronic, challenging behavior should be founded on functional assessment.

2. Distinguish between functional analysis and functional assessment.

These methods each have advantages and disadvantages. For most school-based behavior planning, functional assessment will suffice. However, for severe behaviors, chronic behaviors, or behaviors that have been resistant to previous interventions, functional analysis may provide more precise data.

3. Describe indirect and direct assessment methods of data collection to help identify when, where, and why challenging behavior occurs.

   Indirect assessment involves gathering information from individuals who know the student's behavior well, using interviews and/or checklists. Direct assessment follows indirect assessment and requires direct observation of the student in the contexts associated with the problem behavior.

4. Use the results of FBA to develop behavioral intervention plans (BIPs).

   The hypotheses formulated from FBA data serve as a template for developing an intervention plan. Interventions should address the possible setting events that set the stage for problem behavior, antecedents to the problem behavior, replacement behaviors that will enable the student to achieve

the desired consequences in more socially acceptable ways, and consequences that directly address the functions of the problem behavior. The formats for BIPs vary, but teams should ensure that the content always contains the elements described in this chapter.

5. Describe the potential problems with and cautions regarding FBA.

   If an intervention plan fails to produce the desired results, the planning team may need to consider whether this failure is a result of one or more of the limitations of FBA described in this chapter. If so, the BIP may need to be modified or additional FBA data may be needed.

   Functional assessment is an essential tool for educators who work with students who exhibit challenging behaviors. To help monitor your own use of FBA procedures, we provide an FBA Self-Assessment in Table 3-3. Additional self-assessments are provided in

TABLE 3-3   FBA Self-Assessment Form

Never	Seldom	Sometimes	Often	Always
1	2	3	4	5

Use numbers from the scale above to rate the following statements.

1. I define target behaviors by using operational definitions.   _____

2. I can determine when a student's behavior requires a functional assessment.   _____

3. I know how to apply the steps in a functional assessment.   _____

4. I conduct interviews with other teachers if needed.   _____

5. I use direct observation methods to gather data about the student's performance in the environments associated with the challenging behavior.   _____

6. I analyze all data, looking for patterns in the antecedents and consequences related to the challenging behavior.   _____

7. I work with others to formulate hypotheses about the conditions under which the challenging behavior does and does not occur and about the function(s) of the behavior.   _____

8. I use functional analysis to test the hypotheses formulated in the functional assessment.   _____

9. I work with my student's IEP team to develop a behavioral intervention plan.   _____

10. My students' BIPs include all of the components recommended in this chapter.   _____

11. I monitor BIPs regularly and adjust the plans as needed.   _____

Chapters 4 through 12 for the topics covered in each chapter. To use the self-assessments, respond to each statement by indicating the frequency with which you engage in the behavior described. Any statements rated as less than 4 may suggest a practice that, if incorporated to become a more regular part of your teaching repertoire, may enhance the effectiveness of your classroom management and teaching efforts.

Learning Activities

1. Explain the IDEA requirements for an FBA and why it might be beneficial for teachers to conduct assessments more often than required.
2. Explain examples of when an FBA might not be required.
3. Divide into small groups and discuss the usefulness of each FBA assessment tool and how teachers could efficiently use each tool as part of the FBA process.
4. Choose either Micah's or Brock's case study, which is presented in the appendix to this chapter. Write a 3-month outcome report that addresses the following scenarios:
   a. Success (i.e., Assuming that the interventions worked, how is the student performing now? How are the interventions being used now?)
   b. Little or no success (i.e., How would you change the program? What else would you do?)

5. Read Renée's FBA data, presented in the appendix to this chapter, and then do the following:
   a. Divide into small groups.
   b. Analyze the data provided for Renée.
   c. Formulate hypotheses about the conditions under which problem behaviors does and does not occur and the possible function(s) of the behavior.
   d. Develop one or more competing behavior charts for Renée.
   e. Develop an intervention plan using the BIP form presented in the appendix to this chapter.
   f. Prepare a role-play for the class that demonstrates the thinking processes that the team used to develop the BIP.

Resources

FUNCTIONAL BEHAVIORAL ASSESSMENT INSTRUMENTS

- The Functional Assessment Interview Form (O'Neill et al., 1997)
- The Student-Assisted Interview Form (O'Neill et al., 1997)
- The Functional Analysis Screening Tool (Iwata & DeLeon, 1996)
- The Motivation Assessment Scale (Durand & Crimmins, 1988, 1992)
- The Problem Behavior Questionnaire (Lewis, Scott, & Sugai, 1994)
- Questions About Behavioral Function (Matson & Vollmer, 1995; Paclawskyj, Matson, Rush, Smalls, & Vollmer, 2000)
- The Functional Analysis Observation Form (O'Neill et al., 1997)
- The Eco-Behavioral Observation System (Gable, Hendrickson, & Sealander, 1998)
- The State-Event Classroom Observation System (Slate & Saudargas, 1986)
- The Classroom Ecobehavioral Assessment Instrument (Scott & Sugai, 1994)

BOOKS

Crone, D. A., & Horner, R. H. (2003). *Building positive behavior support systems in schools.* New York: Guilford Press.

Nelson, C. M., Roberts, M. L., & Smith, D. J. (1998). *Conducting functional behavioral assessments.* Longmont, CO: Sopris West.

O'Neill, R. E., Horner, R. H., Albin, R. W., Sprague, J. R., Storey, K., & Newton, J. S. (1997). *Functional assessment and program development for problem behavior: A practical handbook* (2nd ed.). Pacific Grove, CA: Brooks/Cole.

Repp, A. C., & Horner, R. H. (Eds.) (1999). *Functional analysis of problem behavior: From effective assessment to effective support.* Belmont, CA: Wadsworth.

Watson, T. A., & Steege, M. W. (2003). *Conducting school-based functional behavioral assessments: A practitioner's guide.* New York: Guilford Press.

CHAPTERS

Fox, J. J., & Gable, R. A. (2004). Functional behavioral assessment. In R. B. Rutherford, M. M. Quinn, & S. R. Mathur (Eds.), *Handbook of Research in Emotional and Behavioral Disorders* (pp. 143–162). New York: Guilford Press.

SOFTWARE

Hofmeister, A., Morgan, D. P., Reavis, H. K., Likins, M., Althouse, B., & Jenson, W. R. (1999). Functional Assessment Intervention Program. This software analyzes responses to functional assessment questions and suggests strategies. Longmont, CO: Sopris West.

WEBSITES

www.pbis.org The Office of Special Education Programs, U.S. Department of Education, Technical Assistance Center on Positive Behavioral Interventions and Supports: Provides a variety of tools for and information about FBA. The FACTS can be downloaded from the Tools tab in the Resources box of the School, Tertiary Level section.

http://darkwing.uoregon.edu/%7Ettobin/ enufhtml.htm Function-Based Support at School: Summaries of Research Examples: Provides multiple cases from research studies that illustrate functional assessment and function-based interventions.

http://cecp.air.org/fba The Center for Effective Collaboration and Practice: Provides extensive resources and information on conducting a functional behavioral assessment and planning function-based interventions.

www.coe.ufl.edu/Faculty/Scott/terrys/tscott.html Home page of Terrance M. Scott, Ph.D., Associate Professor, Emotional and Behavioral Disorders, Department of Special Education, University of Florida: A School Data Collection Template, which is an anecdotal report in spreadsheet format, can be downloaded.

www.kipbs.org Kansas Institute for Positive Behavior Support: Provides a comprehensive collection of information and tools related to positive behavior support in home and at school. The online library includes extensive information about FBA, including FBA forms.

Appendix: Case Studies

CASE STUDY #1

Brock

Brock is a first grader who has just begun to receive special education services. He lives with foster parents because his mother is serving a jail sentence. Brock's teachers reported to Dr. ICE that he so frequently disrupts the class that the learning process for Brock and the other students stops. They stated that his problem behaviors are as follows:

- Leaves his seat without permission.
- Has tantrums (curses/screams).
- Invades the body space of other students in class and on the playground.
- Pushes/shoves the other students.
- Refuses to work by putting his head on his desk.

Assessment tools used for the FBA:

Indirect

- Functional Assessment Checklist: Teachers and Staff (FACTS)
- Teacher Team Functional Assessment Questionnaire

Direct

A-B-C Report Forms:

1. Resource Room, 3/24, 8:45–9:25
   Behaviors Observed

   - Exhibited off-task behaviors (did not look at his work; left his seat).
   - Screamed.
   - Left the room.
   - Taking a time-out incorrectly; also, he had to be guided to the time-out area.
   - Took a second time-out the right way.

   Important Information

   - His refusal to take a time-out resulted in a major consequence of losing 1 week of free-choice time.
   - The second time he was asked to go to time-out, he did so and waited quietly in the time-out area. However, the assistant principal came into the room during this time-out and escorted Brock out of the room, even though Brock was quiet at the time.

2. General Education: Social Studies, 3/28, 10:35–10:42
   Behaviors Observed

   - Refused to follow teacher's directions.
   - Exhibited a verbal tantrum.
   - Ran from the room.

   Important Information

   - Teacher responded quickly to his misbehavior (i.e., she said that she would call the office).

3. Playground: Free play, 3/31, 11:35–11:54
   Behaviors Observed

   - Played an appropriate game of chase.
   - Cut in on the line to the water fountain.
   - Shoved a student who complained about his cutting in on the line.
   - Refused to go to the office with the general education teacher.
   - Talked with the special education teacher.
   - Walked appropriately with the special education teacher.

   Important Information

   - Brock shoved the student who complained about his misbehavior.
   - Teacher was quick to demand that he go to the office.
   - Brock listened to and followed directions from the special education teacher.

All of the behaviors that were reported by his teachers were observed by Dr. ICE. In order to understand this student, Dr. ICE spent some one-on-one time with him. He came away from that meeting with the following impressions:

- Brock expressed many frustrations about his living arrangements and said that he was "mad at his mom," who is in jail.
- Normal school stresses, combined with Brock's emotional state, may result in the tantrums that are exhibited at school.
- When asked who cares about him, Brock put his head down.

This information tells us about the life experiences that Brock brings to school each day. However, the school staff cannot let sympathy for his situation become an excuse for his behavior. Brock's foster parents care about Brock and are very willing to work with the school.

Brock's team gathered on April 5 to analyze his FBA data and to develop his BIP. Brock's teachers, the school administrators, and his foster parents were present. The team summarized the FBA data in the competing behavior model; they included the following information:

Setting Event

- Experiences general anger about his living arrangements and his mother being in jail.

Antecedent/Predictor

- Brock is asked to do something that he does not want to do or to give up something that he wants to keep.

Problem Behavior

- Does not comply with the teacher's instructions.
- Exhibits tantrums, which include screaming, cursing, and shoving items or people.

Maintaining Consequences

- Receives attention from his teachers and peers.
- Experiences a sense of being in control.

Alternative Replacement Behaviors

1. Teach Brock to use a cool-down technique to help him regain self-control.
2. Teach Brock to negotiate.

Maintaining Consequences

- Receives positive attention.
- Experiences a sense of being in control.

Desired Behavior

- Follows directions.

Maintaining Consequences

- Currently, Brock receives virtually no attention or experiences no sense of being in control when he exhibits appropriate behaviors.

Functional Assessment Checklist for Teachers and Staff (FACTS–Part A)

Step 1

Student/Grade: _Brock/1ˢᵗ_   Date: _3/22_

Interviewer: _Dr. ICE_   Respondent(s): _Mr. Wilcher_

Step 2

Student Profile: Please identify at least three strengths or contributions the student brings to school.

assertive, strong personality, can be very sweet

Step 3

Problem Behavior(s): Identify problem behaviors.

___Tardy	✓ Fight/physical	___Disruptive	___Theft
___Unresponsive	✓ Inappropriate Language	___Insubordination	___Vandalism
___Withdrawn	✓ Verbal Harassment	___Work not done	_ Other: _____
	✓ Verbally Inappropriate	___Self-injury	

Describe problem behavior: _overall noncompliance_

Step 4

Identifying Routines: Where, When And With Whom Problem Behaviors Are Most Likely to occur.

Schedule (Times)	Activity	Likelihood of Problem Behavior	Specific Problem Behavior
7:45	Before School	Low 1 2 ③ 4 5 High 6	
9:45–10:45	Math	1 2 3 4 5 ⑥	aggression
	Transition	1 2 3 ④ 5 6	grabbing items from peers
	Language Arts	1 2 3 4 5 6	
	Recess	1 2 3 ④ 5 6	pushing
8:00–9:30	Reading	1 2 3 4 5 ⑥	
11:15–11:35	Lunch	1 2 ③ 4 5 6	
1:00–1:45	Science	1 2 3 ④ 5 6	verbal, physical aggression
	Transition	1 2 3 4 5 6	
12:10–1:50	Social Studies	1 2 3 ④ 5 6	
	Art	1 2 ③ 4 5 6	

Step 5

Select 1–3 Routines for further assessment: Select routines based on (a) similarity of activities (conditions) with ratings of 4, 5, or 6, and (b) similarity of problem behavior(s). Complete the FACTS–Part B for each routine identified.

Functional Assessment Checklist for Teachers & Staff (FACTS–Part B)

Step 1

Student/Grade: _Brock/1ˢᵗ_   Date: _3-22_

Interviewer: _Dr. ICE_   Respondent(s): _____

Step 2   **Routine/Activities/Context: Which routine (only one) from the FACTS–Part A is assessed?**

Routine/Activities/Context	Problem Behavior(s)
Any time Brock is asked to do something he doesn't want to do	–verbal, physical aggression

Step 3   **Provide more detail about the problem behavior(s):**

What does the problem behavior(s) look like?	–noncompliance –making threats –pushing
How often does the problem behavior(s) occur?	– one or more times per academic period
How long does the problem behavior(s) last when it does occur?	–anywhere from a minute to several minutes
What is the intensity/level of danger of the problem behavior(s)?	–often escalates to severe

Step 4   **What are the events that predict when the problem behavior(s) will occur? (Predictors)**

Related Issues (setting events)		Environmental Features	
____ Illness	Other: _____	✓ reprimand/correction	✓ structured activity
____ drug use	Mother in jail,	____ physical demands	✓ unstructured time
	Brock is in foster care		
____ negative social	_____	____ socially isolated	____ Tasks too boring
✓ conflict at home	_____	✓ with peers	✓ activity too long
____ academic failure	_____	____ Other:	✓ tasks too difficult

Step 5   **What consequences appear most likely to maintain the problem behavior(s)?**

Things that are Obtained		Things Avoided or Escaped From	
✓ adult attention	Other: Power control	✓ hard tasks	Other:_____
✓ peer attention	_____	✓ reprimands	_____
____ preferred activity	_____	✓ peer negatives	_____
✓ Money/things	_____	____ physical effort	_____
		____ adult attention	_____

(Continued)

(Continued)

SUMMARY OF BEHAVIOR
Identify the summary that will be used to build a plan of behavior support.

Step 6

Setting Events & Predictors	Problem Behavior(s)	Maintaining Consequence(s)
anger about mother, foster home, asked to do disliked activity	noncompliance verbal/physical aggression	attention control

Step 7

How confident are you that the Summary of Behavior is accurate?

Not very confident					Very Confident
1	2	3	4	5	⑥

Step 8

What current efforts have been used to control the problem behavior?

Strategies for Preventing problem behavior	Strategies for responding to problem behavior
____schedule change Other:____None____ ____seating change _redirection_ ____curriculum change	✓ reprimand Other: ✓ None____ _____ office referral _all home_ _____ detention

Source: From *Functional Assessment Checklist for Teachers and Staff (FACTS)*, by R. March, R. H. Horner, T. Lewis-Palmer, D. Brown, D. Crone, A.W. Todd, and E. Carr, 2000, Department of Educational and Community Supports, Eugene, OR: University of Oregon. Form reprinted with permission, shown here with case study details.

Teacher Team Functional Assessment Questionnaire

Teachers' Names: Wilcher

Student's Name: Brock

Date: 3/21

Descriptions of Behavior(s)

What do the problem behaviors look like? Please describe one at a time.

1. Noncompliance with teacher instructions

2. Verbal aggression: makes threats ("Get away from me or else"), curses, screams

3. Physical aggression: pushes, shoves other students

4. Grabbing, taking things from peers

5.

Things That Set Off the Behavior(s)

For each of the behaviors, describe what appears to set off the problem behavior. Please describe the conditions below in the same order as you have listed the behaviors above.

1. Teacher gives him a direction. He is especially noncompliant when the teacher is addressing him about his inappropriate behavior.

2. When asked to do something that he doesn't want to do or give up something that he wants, Brock is likely to scream, curse, or make threats.

3. When he sees something that he wants which another student has, Brock may push the student out of the way.

4. Brock grabs items that he wants.

5.

Reinforcement for the Behavior(s)

From your observation, what does the student gain from the problem behaviors?

1. Avoidance of task, control

2. Attention from teachers and peers

3. Control, power

4. Tangible objects

5.

(Continued)

(Continued)

Summary Statements

From the information above on this student, write a brief summary statement that includes what sets off the behavior, the behavior itself, and what the student gains from the behavior. For example: When Jason is given an assignment, he will throw his pencil across the room in order to obtain attention from the teacher.

1. When the teacher gives Brock a direction, he is likely to be noncompliant. He gets attention and control for this behavior.

2. Brock often makes threats to his peers, or screams and curses when the teacher asks him to do something he doesn't want to do. He gets attention from teachers and peers, and control.

3. Brock often pushes peers, especially during transitions or on the playground. He gets attention from peers and control.

4. If Brock sees something that he wants which a peer has, he often grabs it from the peer, resulting in Brock gaining access to the desired object.

5.

For each of the summary statements above, how confident are you that these are the reasons the student engages in this behavior? Please rate each with a number between 1 and 4.

1 = not at all confident
2 = somewhat confident
3 = confident
4 = very confident

1. 4

2. 4

3. 3

4. 3

5.

Rank the summary statements above from those that cause the most problems to the least problems. Begin with the statement that causes the biggest problems.

1, 2

3

4

Source: From "A Comparison of Results and Acceptability of Functional Behavioral Assessment Procedures with a Group of Middle School Students with Emotional/Behavioral Disorders (E/BD)," by S. G. Murdock, R. E. O'Neill, and E. Cunningham, 2005, *Journal of Behavioral Education, 14*, 5–18. Form reprinted with permission, shown here with case study details.

A-B-C Report Form

Name: _Brock_ _____   Date/Time of observation: _3/24, 8:45 AM_ _____

Place observation occurred: _Classroom_ _____

Environmental conditions (number of students, arrangement, number of adults, etc.): _Primary Resource Room, 1 adult_
8 students, Language Arts _____

Activities observed during observation: _Oral Reading by Teacher - Journals and Independent Work, sm gp - 3(S) W/T_

Unusual or potentially influential conditions: _One student came in late_ _____

Time	Antecedent	Behavior	Consequence
8:45	1. Teacher reads. One student comes in late.	2. Teacher asks group open-ended questions and praises answers.	3. Brock listens
8:58	4. Student comes in late.	5. Brock puts his head on his desk.	6. No attention is given to Brock by teacher or students.
9:00	Teacher stops reading and gives students a short (2-sentence) writing assignment for their journals. Begins to pass out journals.		
9:03	7. Teacher walks over to Brock and asks what he has written.	8. Brock shoves an empty journal page toward her.	9. Teacher says "You have 10 minutes for this assignment. You have 7 minutes remaining." (This is said to the entire class.)
9:04	10. Teacher is with a student in the back of the room.	11. Brock leaves his seat - goes to the student who came in late - screams "Your whole family is fat!"	12. Other student cries. Teacher tells Brock that he needs to go to the time-out area.
9:05	13. Brock shoves the student who is crying.	14. Teacher leads Brock to the time-out area - tells him that he has lost free choice time for the week.	15. Brock goes with the teacher, remains active in time-out (stands up, sits down, looks around the room).
9:07	16. Teacher says "Sit down and be quiet!"	17. Brock says "I hate this school!" as he runs from the room.	18. Teacher phones the office.
9:18	19. Principal leads a silent Brock into the classroom.	20. Brock walks to his desk.	21. Two students laugh.

A-B-C Report Form

Name: Brock _____ Date/Time of observation: _____

Place observation occurred: _____

Environmental conditions (number of students, arrangement, number of adults, etc.): _____

Activities observed during observation: _____

Unusual or potentially influential conditions: _____

Time	Antecedent	Behavior	Consequence
9:19	22. Teacher is working with three students.	23. Brock jumps up, screaming at the two students who had laughed, "I hate you and I hate this school!"	24. (1) Two students leave their seats and quickly move to the teacher. (2) Teacher takes Brock by the arm and walks to the phone to call for an administrator to come get him.
9:20	25. (1) Teacher asks the class to get back to work. (2) Teacher quietly talks to Brock.	26. Brock appears to have calmed down.	27. Teacher continues to quietly talk to Brock.
9:21	28. Teacher takes Brock to time-out area.	29. Brock sits and puts his head on the time-out desk.	30. Teacher quietly works with other students.
9:25	31. Assistant Principal comes to take Brock to the office.	32. Brock cries and tries to pull away.	33. AP continues to walk out of the room with Brock in tow.

A-B-C Report Form

Name: _Brock_   Date/Time of observation: _3/28 10:35_

Place observation occurred: _General Education Classroom_

Environmental conditions (number of students, arrangement, number of adults, etc.): _1 teacher, 22 students_

Activities observed during observation: _Social Studies-Paired activity_

Unusual or potentially influential conditions: _Brock enters classroom from Resource setting – lunch is at 11_

Time	Antecedent	Behavior	Consequence
10:35	1. Teacher had asked students to pick a partner for an activity. No one picked Brock, so teacher picked a partner for him.	2. Brock screams at her - "I want to pick my own partner!"	3. Teacher says "Brock, calm down and lets see what you and Sam remember to draw from yesterday's lesson." Students all stare at Brock.
10:37	4. Teacher tells Brock to get to work or she will call the office.	5. Brock runs from the room, gets under a desk thats just outside the door.	6. Teacher calls the office for help. Students laugh.
10:42	7. Principal arrives and talks a crying Brock out from under the desk.	8. Brock cries out that he does not want his aunt to be called.	9. Principal leads Brock down the hallway, teacher directs class to get back to work.

General Education teacher reports that this happens 3–4 times a week.

A-B-C Report Form

Name: _Brock_ _____ Date/Time of observation: _11:35 3/31_ _____

Place observation occurred: _Playground_ _____

Environmental conditions (number of students, arrangement, number of adults, etc.): _1 teacher, 22 students_ _____

Activities observed during observation: _Free play on playscape_ _____

Unusual or potentially influential conditions: _____

Time	Antecedent	Behavior	Consequence
11:35	1. Boys, including Brock, are chasing one another.	2. Brock is engaged, smiling.	3. Chase game continues.
11:48	4. Chase game ends as boys stop to get water from the fountain.	5. Brock cuts into the line for the water fountain.	6. Boys in back complain.
	7. Teacher calls for Brock to come over.	8. Brock shoves a boy to the ground.	9. Teacher runs over and demands that Brock go with her to the office.
11:52	10. Special Ed. teacher walks by and is asked by Gen. Ed. teacher to help with Brock.	11. Brock (now curled into a ball on the ground) screams "No, I don't want to go! I didn't do nothing; they lied on me."	12. Special Ed. teacher talks quietly to Brock.
11:54	13. Special Ed. teacher stands and offers her hand to Brock.	14. Brock takes her hand, still crying.	15. Special Ed. teacher and Brock walk to the building.

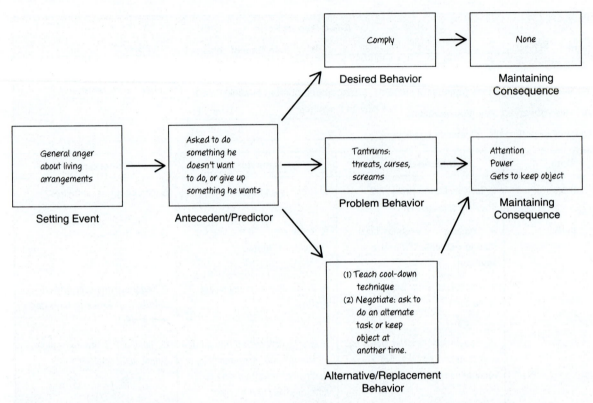

Behavior Intervention Plan

Student: _Brock_   Age: _6_   Date: _3-20_

Behavior of Concern	Target Criterion	Hypotheses	Replacement Behavior(s)	Target Criterion	Antecedent Interventions	Reinforcement Plan	Consequence Strategies for Reducing Behaviors of Concern	Monitoring Plan
1. Noncompliance	No more than one instance per period	-Avoidance of work -Control	Follow teacher directions	90%	-Teach compliance -Use precorrection -Provide choices -Give high-probability requests before low-probability demands	Stars for compliance, to be exchanged for time to help teacher	N/A	Count instances of compliance during reading
2. Verbal and Physical aggression	Zero instances per day	-Avoidance of work -Peer and teacher attention -Control	-Use words to express feelings -Ask for a break	100%	-Precorrection -Visual reminders -Self-monitor -Teach self-control procedure -Teach strategies for ignoring teasing or other inappropriate behaviors of peers	Stars for self-control to be exchanged for privileges with peers	N/A	Paraprofessional to monitor aggressive instances during reading and math
3.								
4.								

CASE STUDY #2

Micah

Micah is a 14-year-old boy who has been in special education classes since he was 9 years old. He is currently in the ninth grade at Wabash High School. Mr. Greer is his special education teacher for English and reading. Ms. Reinholt is his special education teacher for history and mathematics. Micah exhibits a pattern of behavioral problems in both Mr. Greer's classes and in Ms. Reinholt history class. The following behaviors have been noted:

- Makes fun of his peers.
- Curses.
- Always has an excuse for not having finished his work.
- Displays verbal aggression.
- Displays physical aggression.
- Is late to class.

Assessment tools used for the FBA:

Indirect
- Functional Assessment Checklist: Teachers and Staff (FACTS)
- Teacher Team Functional Assessment Questionnaire
- Student-Directed Functional Assessment Interview

Direct
1. A-B-C Report: 4/13, English, 8:30–9:30

   Behaviors Observed
   - Exhibited off-task behavior.
   - Became angry when his teacher questioned his behavior.
   - Left class without permission.

2. A-B-C Descriptive Analysis: 4/14, English, 8:30–9:30

   Behaviors Observed
   - Distracted his peers.
   - Laughed at the off-task behavior of his peers.
   - Refused to work.

3. Index Card Narrative Format: 4/15, English, 8:30–9:30

   Behaviors Observed
   - Cursed.
   - Called his peers names.

Micah's team met on April 17. Micah's mother, his teachers, and Dr. ICE agreed that in order for a plan to work with a student of Micah's age and abilities, Micah would have to be involved in creating the plan. The team summarized Micah's FBA data in the competing behavior model; they included the following information:

Setting Event

- Micah's problem behavior occurs most often in classes that require reading as the primary instructional vehicle. To determine whether deficits in reading skills are playing a role in Micah's behaviors, the team requested Micah's most recent reading assessment scores and then further questioned Micah's teachers about his reading skills.

Antecedent/Predictor

- Micah's problem behavior occurs when he is expected to read or to do tasks that involve reading, either in a group or independently.
- The problem behavior occurs whenever Micah perceives that his peers are looking at him or are laughing at him.

Problem Behavior

- Exhibits off-task behavior.
- Talks out in class.
- Laughs inappropriately.
- Distracts other students.

Micah's behavior has begun to escalate into physically aggressive behavior. The planning team agreed that the off-task behaviors occurred at the beginning of every severe episode of acting-out, although, at times, they were the only problem behaviors. Micah agreed that when he is engaging in these behaviors, he is not learning.

Maintaining Consequences

- Receives attention from his teachers and his peers.
- Experiences a sense of being in control.

Alternative Replacement Behaviors

1. Teach Micah to use a cool-down technique.
2. Teach Micah to negotiate.

Maintaining Consequences

- Receives attention from his teacher.
- Receives attention from his peers.

Desired Behavior

- Completes tasks, both independently and with his peers, without engaging in behaviors that distract his peers.

Maintaining Consequences

- Currently, Micah receives virtually no attention when he exhibits appropriate behaviors.

Functional Assessment Checklist for Teachers and Staff (FACTS–Part A)

Step 1

Student/Grade: Micah/9th

Date: 4/11

Interviewer: Dr. ICE

Respondent(s): Mr. G and Ms. R

Step 2

Student Profile: Please identify at least three strengths or contributions the student brings to school.

Micah makes friends. / He likes Math. / He has shown interest in problem solving in Science.

Step 3

Problem Behavior(s): Identify problem behaviors.

___Tardy	___Fight/physical Aggression	✓Disruptive	___Theft
___Unresponsive	✓Inappropriate Language	✓Insubordination	___Vandalism
___Withdrawn	___Verbal Harassment	✓Work not done	__Other: _____
	___Verbally Inappropriate	___Self-injury	

Describe problem behavior: _____

Step 4

Identifying Routines: Where, When, and With Whom oroblem Behaviors are Most Likely to Occur.

Schedule (Times)	Activity	Likelihood of Problem Behavior	Specific Problem Behavior
Rides Bus	Before School	Low ① 2 3 4 5 High 6	
9:30-10:20	Math	1 2 ③ 4 5 6	Laughs at/with peers, sometimes off-task
	Transition	1 2 3 4 5 6	
8:30-9:20	Language Arts Resource	1 2 3 4 5 ⑥	Talks out, laughs, distracts others
	Recess	1 2 3 4 5 6	
10:30-11:30	Reading Resource	1 2 3 4 5 ⑥	Talks out, laughs, distracts others
	Lunch	① 2 3 4 5 6	
	Science	1 2 3 4 5 6	
	Transition	1 2 3 4 5 6	
1:10–2:00	Social Studies	1 2 3 4 5 ⑥	Talks out, laughs, distracts others
	Art	1 ② 3 4 5 6	Distracts others at times

Step 5

Select 1–3 Routines for further assessment: Select routines based on (a) similarity of activities (conditions) with ratings of 4, 5, or 6, and (b) similarity of problem behavior(s). Complete the FACTS–Part B for each routine identified.

Functional Assessment Checklist for Teachers & Staff (FACTS–Part B)

Step 1 Student/Grade: _Micah/9th_   Date: _4/11_

Interviewer: _Dr. ICE_   Respondent(s): _Mr. G & Ms. R_

Step 2 **Routine/Activities/Context: Which routine (only one) from the FACTS–Part A is assessed?**

Routine/Activities/Context	Problem Behavior(s)
Any class in which reading is the primary delivery system of instruction.	Talking out, laughing, distracts others

Step 3 **Provide more detail about the problem behavior(s):**

What does the problem behavior(s) look like?   Talking out to teachers and/or peers, loud laughing — both will distract others

How often does the problem behavior(s) occur?   At least once per period — the duration can range from a few minutes to until he is sent to the office.

How long does the problem behavior(s) last when it does occur?   As long as he is given attention.

What is the intensity/level of danger of the problem behavior(s)?   These behaviors occasionally escalate into physically harming others.

Step 4 **What are the events that predict when the problem behavior(s) will occur? (Predictors)**

Related Issues (setting events)		Environmental Features	
____ illness	Other: ____	____ reprimand/correction	__ structured activity
____ drug use	____	____ physical demands	__ unstructured time
✓ negative social	____	____ socially isolated	__ tasks too boring
____ conflict at home	____	✓ with peers	__ activity too long
✓ academic failure	_academic failure of peers_	____ Other	✓ tasks too difficult for peers

Step 5 **What consequences appear most likely to maintain the problem behavior(s)?**

Things that Are Obtained		Things Avoided or Escaped From	
____ Adult attention	Other: ____	✓ Hard tasks	Other: _Tasks that are viewed_
✓ Peer attention	____	____ Reprimands	_as too hard by Micah or his_
____ Preferred activity	____	____ Peer negatives	_peers_
____ Money/things	____	____ Physical effort	____
		____ Adult attention	____

(Continued)

(Continued)

SUMMARY OF BEHAVIOR
Identify the summary that will be used to build a plan of behavior support.

Step 6	Setting Events & Predictors	Problem Behavior(s)	Maintaining Consequence(s)
	Micah is given a task that requires reading and his circle of peers are giving him attention.	Off task: Talks out, laughs, distracts others	Peer attention Teacher attention

Step 7   **How confident are you that the Summary of Behavior is accurate?**

Not very confident					Very Confident
1	2	3	4	5	⑥

Step 8   **What current efforts have been used to control the problem behavior?**

Strategies for Preventing problem behavior	Strategies for responding to problem behavior
____schedule change Other:____None ✓	✓ reprimand Other: ✓ None ✓
____seating change _____	✓ office referral suspension
____curriculum change _____	✓ detention _____

Source: From *Functional Assessment Checklist for Teachers and Staff (FACTS)*, by R. March, R. H. Horner, T. Lewis-Palmer, D. Brown, D. Crone, A. W. Todd, and E. Carr, 2000, Department of Educational and Community Supports, Eugene, OR: University of Oregon. Form reprinted with permission, shown here with case study details.

Teacher Team Functional Assessment Questionnaire

Teachers' Names: *Mr. Greer*

Student's Name: *Micah*

Date: *4-08*

Descriptions of Behavior(s)

What do the problem behaviors look like? Please describe one at a time.

1. *Off-task behavior: Laughs or makes inappropriate gestures or comments to peers to try to engage them in off-task, inappropriate behavior. Sometimes he makes mean, negative comments to peers, or laughs at them and makes fun of them.*

2.

3.

4.

5.

Things That Set Off the Behavior(s)

For each of the behaviors, describe what appears to set off the problem behavior. Please describe the conditions below in the same order as you have listed the behaviors above.

1. *Independent work, especially any task that involves reading.*

2.

3.

4.

5.

Reinforcement for the Behavior(s)

From your observation, what does the student gain from the problem behaviors?

1. *Peer attention, teacher attention, task avoidance*

2.

3.

4.

5.

(Continued)

(Continued)

Summary Statements

From the information above on this student, write a brief summary statement that includes what sets off the behavior, the behavior itself, and what the student gains from the behavior. For example: When Jason is given an assignment, he will throw his pencil across the room in order to obtain attention from the teacher.

1. When Micah is expected to do independent work that involves reading, he is likely to create a disruption by directing inappropriate (mean, taunting) comments to peers, or making inappropriate comments to teachers about the class or work.

2.

3.

4.

5.

For each of the summary statements above, how confident are you that these are the reasons that the student engages in this behavior? Please rate each with a number between 1 and 4.

1 = not at all confident

2 = somewhat confident

3 = confident

4 = very confident

1. 4

2.

3.

4.

5.

Rank the summary statements above from those that cause the most problems to the least problems. Begin with the statement that causes the biggest problems. 4

Source: From "A Comparison of Results and Acceptability of Functional Behavioral Assessment Procedures with a Group of Middle School Students with Emotional/Behavioral Disorders (E/BD)," by S. G. Murdock, R. E. O'Neill, and E. Cunningham, 2005, *Journal of Behavioral Education, 14*, 5–18. Form reprinted with permission, shown here with case study details.

Student-Directed Functional Assessment Interview

Student Name: _Micah_

Referring Teacher: _Mr. S_

Interviewer: _Dr. I. C. Everything_

Date: _4-12_

I. **Opening.** *"We are meeting today to find ways to change school so that you like it more. This interview will take about 30 minutes. I can help you best if you answer honestly. You will not be asked anything that might get you in trouble."*

Assist the student to identify specific behaviors that are resulting in problems in the school or classroom. Making suggestions or paraphrasing statements can help the student to clarify his or her ideas. You should have a list of behaviors nominated by the referring teacher.

II. **Define the behaviors of concern.*** *"What are the things you do that get you in trouble or are a problem?" (Prompts: Late to class? Talk out in class? Don't get work done? Fighting?)*

Behavior   Comment

1. Talking Out – I like to laugh with my friends.
2. I curse sometimes.
3. I fight when they do something first.
4. Sometimes I don't do my work.
5.

III. **Complete student schedule.** Use the *"Student Daily Schedule"* matrix to identify the times and classes in which the student performs problem behavior. Focus the interview on those times that are **most likely** to result in problem behavior. You will use the numbers to the left as codes for the identified behaviors as you complete the rest of the interview.

*You will use the numbers to the left as codes for the identified behaviors as you complete the rest of the interview.

Student Daily Schedule

Please place an "X" in each column to show the times and classes where you have difficulty with the behaviors we talked about. If you have a lot of difficulty during a period, place an "X" on or near the 6. If you have a little difficulty during the class or hall time, place the "X" on or near the 1. We can practice on a couple together before we start.

Subject / Teacher	Before School / Rides Bus	1st Period / English / Mr. G	Hall	2nd Period / Math / Ms.R	Hall	3rd Period / Biology / Ms. T	Hall	4th Period / Reading	Lunch	5th Period / P.E. / Mr.C	Hall	6th Period / Social Studies / Ms. R	Hall	7th Period / Art / Mr. P	Hall	After School
Most Difficult 6		X						X				X				
5																
4																
3				X		X				X						
2														X		
Least Difficult 1																

128

Summary Statement Form

④ Place/Activity/Event	② Predictor	① Problem Behavior(s)	③ Maintaining Consequences
Any class in which reading is the primary delivery system of learning.	Attention of peer group is focused on Micah.	Talking out, playing, laughing	Attention of his circle of peers

Complete the summary statement diagram following the numbered sequence (Behavior(s) first, then Predictors, etc.). Consider the items below as possible elements for inclusion in the summary statement. Complete a *different* summary statement for each new consequence.

What Important Events, Places, or Activities Tend to Be Associated with the Behavior?

Lack of sleep _____
Illness _____
Physical pain _____
Hunger _____
Trouble at home _____
Fight/conflict with peers _____
Noise distractions _____
Activity/Class ✓
Other: _____

Class demands that are:
• too hard ✓
• boring _____
• unclear _____
• long _____
Teacher reprimands _____
Peer teasing ✓
Peer encouragement ✓ ★
Other: _____

What Do the Problem Behaviors Look Like?

Late to class _____
Talk out in class ✓
Disruptions _____
Inappropriate language ✓
Disrespectful behavior _____
Property destruction _____
Carrying weapons _____
Fidget _____
Not completing work _____
Steal _____
Threaten _____
Vandalism _____
Insubordination ✓
Other _____

What Does the Student Gain from the Problem Behaviors?

Escape or Avoid
• Teacher demands _____
• Teacher reprimands ✓
• Teacher correction _____
• Peer social contact (teasing) _____
• Tasks (hard, long) _____

Get Attention
• From peers ✓
• From teacher/adult ✓

Get Activity or Item
• Access to game _____
• Access to toy _____
• Access to food _____
• Access to money _____
• Access to task _____

Source: From *Functional Assessment and Program Development for Problem Behavior, A Practical Handbook,* 2nd edition by R.E. O'Neill, R.H. Horner, R.W. Albin, J.R. Sprague, K. Storey, and J.S. Newton. © 1997 Wadsworth, a part of Cengage Learning, Inc. Reproduced by permission. www.cengage.com/permissions

A-B-C Report Form

Name: _Micah_____   Date/Time of observation: _4/13_____

Place observation occurred: _English class_____

Environmental conditions (number of students, arrangement, number of adults, etc.): _7 students, teacher,_____ _paraprofessional (teacher's assistant)_____

Activities observed during observation: _Independent work_____

Unusual or potentially influential conditions: _____

TA – Teacher's assistant

Time	Antecedent	Behavior	Consequence
8:55	1. TA checks on Micah and he has been working.	2. Micah slowly looks at his peers who are not attending to him.	3. Micah continues to work.
9:00	4. One of Micah's peers shoots a spitwad toward students at the front of the room.	5. Micah looks up at the movement and smiles.	6. The back of the room explodes in laughter.
9:12	7. Teacher asks, "What's going on?"	8. Micah sits still with a smile on his face.	9. Teacher asks, "Micah, what did you do?"
		10. Micah jumps up and screams, "I didn't do nothing."	11. Teacher says, "Sit Down."
		12. Micah slams his body into his desk.	13. Teacher says, "Everyone, get back to work."
9:16	14. Teacher talks with Micah.	15. Micah sits with hands curled into fists.	16. Students are quiet.
9:30	17. Class dismissal.	18. Micah slowly walks out of class with his peers.	19. TA follows them out of the classroom.

Time	Context/Activity	Antecedent/Setting Events	Identified Target Behavior	Consequence/Outcome	Student Reaction	Comments
Begin and End	The student's environmental surroundings (people, places, events)	Describe exactly what happened in the the environment just before the target behavior was exhibited.	List types of behavior displayed during the incident.	What happened in the environment immediately after the behavior was exhibited?	How did the student react immediately after the initial consequence being delivered?	
8:30	1,3	2,3	5	1	–	
8:35	2	1,3	3	2,3	–	
8:45	2	1,4	5	2	1	
8:55	1,3	4	–	–	–	
9:00	2	2	2	1,2,3	1,3	
9:15	2	2	2	1,2,3	1,3	
9:16	1	4	5	3	1	
9:30	4	4	–	2	–	

(Continued)

Continued

Time	Context/Activity	Antecedent/Setting Events	Identified Target Behavior	Consequence/Outcome	Student Reaction	Comments
Begin and End	The student's environmental surroundings (people, places, events)	Describe exactly what happened in the the environment just before the target behavior was exhibited.	List types of behavior displayed during the incident.	What happened in the environment immediately after the behavior was exhibited?	How did the student react immediately after the initial consequence being delivered	
Describe keys for each column:	1. Independent work	1. Sitting near his friends	1. Talks out	1. Verbal prompt	1. Defensive "I didn't do it."	
	2. Peer encouragement	2. Friends act out	2. Laughs	2. Proximity control	2. Laughs	
	3. Reading task	3. Peer attention	3. Distracts others	3. Redirection	3. Disrespectful	
	4. Dismissal	4. Teacher attention	4. Refuses to work	4. Removed from classroom	4.	
	5.	5.	5. Off task	5.	5.	
	6.	6.	6.	6.	6.	
	7.	7.	7.	7.	7.	
	8.	8.	8.	8.	8.	

Source: From "Supporting Positive Behavior in Public Schools: An Intervention Program in Georgia," by M. L. Smith and L. J. Heflin, 2001, *Journal of Positive Behavior Interventions, 3*(1), 41. © 2001 PRO-ED, Inc. Adapted by permission, shown here with case study details.

Index Card Narrative for Micah

Name: Micah   Observer: Mr. Greer   Date: 4-15

General Context: Resource English. Students have finished reading play and are now working in groups on projects related to the play. Micah's group is to research American family life in the early 1800s and create a collage representing work, recreation, homes, and communities for that time.

Interpersonal Context: Micah is doing Internet research with two other students. They are having problems with the computer. Micah loses patience and curses. The other students tell him to calm down and that they can go to another computer. Micah jumps up and tells them that they're stupid and to shut up.

Social Reaction: Students say, "Forget you," and move to the other computer. Micah stands by himself for a short time, then joins them. Students ignore him for a while, then gradually they begin to talk to him and include him in the activity.

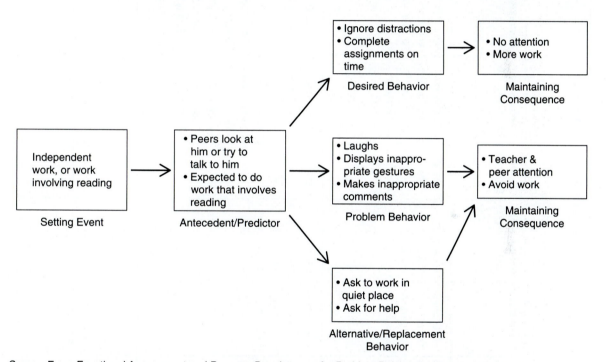

Source: From *Functional Assessment and Program Development for Problem Behavior, A Practical Handbook,* 2nd edition, by O'Neill/Horner/Albin/Sprague/Storey/Newton. © 1997 Wadsworth, a part of Cengage Learning, Inc. Reproduced by permission. www.cengage.com/permissions

Behavior Intervention Plan

Student: Micah   Age: 14   Date: 5/10

Behavior of Concern	Target Criterion	Hypotheses	Replacement Behavior(s)	Target Criterion	Antecedent Interventions	Reinforcement Plan	Consequence Strategies for Reducing Behaviors of Concern	Monitoring Plan
1. Off-task talking, laughing	No more than three instances per day	–Peer attention is a maintaining function	1. Complete tasks on time	90% of tasks	–Self-monitor on-task behavior –Timer for independent work	–Points for completed on time (may be used for peer activities)	N/A	Number of assignments completed on time (Micah will graph daily)
2. Distracting peers during work time or responding to peer's attempts to distract him	No more than three instances per day	–Peer attention is a maintaining function	1. Ignore distractions during work time 2. Ask to work in quiet area	90%	–Teach rules for independent work to whole group –Provide quiet area, away from peers, where Micah may work if he asks	–Group reinforcement plan for minding own business during work time. –Four days of following rules – group (academic) game on Friday	N/A	Number of assignments completed on time (Micah will graph daily)
3.								
4.								

CASE STUDY #3

Renée

Renée is a fourth-grade student living with her sister and brother with relatives while her parents are in jail. She is functioning academically about 2 years below grade level. Her teachers report that when Renée is given tasks that she does not like, she will engage in disruptive behaviors. The following behaviors were reported to Dr. ICE:

- Cursing.
- Throwing objects.
- Refusing to work.
- Talking back to teachers.

Teacher Team Functional Assessment Questionnaire

Teachers' Names: _Ms. Hall_

Student's Name: _Renée J._

Date: _4-4_

Descriptions of Behavior(s)

What do the problem behaviors look like? Please describe one at a time.

1. Tantrums: Screaming at teacher, making mild threats, refusing to comply

2. Distracting peers: She throws objects at them, makes unkind comments

3. Cursing

4.

5.

Things That Set Off the Behavior(s)

For each of the behaviors, describe what appears to set off the problem behavior. Please describe the conditions below in the same order as you have listed the behaviors above.

1. When asked to do something that she does not want to do

2. During group instruction

3. When things don't go her way, or when she does not get to do something that she wants to do

4.

5.

(Continued)

(Continued)

Reinforcement for the Behavior(s)

From your observation, what does the student gain from the problem behaviors?

1. *Teacher attention*

2. *Task avoidance*

3. *Peer attention*

4.

5.

Summary Statements

From the information above on this student, write a brief summary statement that includes what sets off the behavior, the behavior itself, and what the student gains from the behavior. For example: When Jason is given an assignment, he will throw his pencil across the room in order to obtain attention from the teacher.

1. *When Renée is asked to do something she doesn't want to do, she often screams, "I hate you" or "I hate school," refusing to comply. The teacher talks to her individually or calls the Assistant Principal to take her out of class (attention and avoidance).*

2. *During group work, Renée attempts to distract peers by throwing small objects at them or saying mean things to them (e.g., "Roberto, you're stupid. You do baby work."). Teacher tells her to stop; peers laugh, ignore her, or tell her to shut up.*

3. *When any small thing happens (e.g., she makes a mistake, someone says something to her that she doesn't like), Renée curses. Teacher tells her, "Don't say those words." Peers sometimes laugh.*

4.

5.

For each of the summary statements above, how confident are you that these are the reasons that the student engages in this behavior? Please rate each with a number between 1 and 4.

1 = not at all confident
2 = somewhat confident
3 = confident
4 = very confident

1. *3*
2. *3*
3. *4*
4.
5.

Rank the summary statements above from those that cause the most problems to the least problems. Begin with the statement that causes the biggest problems.

1, 3, 2

Source: From "A Comparison of Results and Acceptability of Functional Behavioral Assessment Procedures with a Group of Middle School Students with Emotional/Behavioral Disorders (E/BD)," by S. G. Murdock, R. E. O'Neill, and E. Cunningham, 2005, *Journal of Behavioral Education, 14,* 5–18. Form reprinted with permission, shown here with case study details.

Student-Assisted Functional Assessment Interview

Student: *Renée*
Date: *4/06*
Interviewer: *Dr. ICE*

SECTION I

1.	In general, is your work too hard for you?	Always	(Sometimes)	Never
2.	In general, is your work too easy for you?	Always	(Sometimes)	Never
3.	When you ask for help appropriately, do you get it?	Always	(Sometimes)	Never
4.	Do you think work periods for each subject are too long?	(Always)	Sometimes	Never
5.	Do you think work periods for each subject are too short?	Always	Sometimes	(Never)
6.	When you do seatwork, do you do better when someone works with you?	Always	(Sometimes)	Never
7.	Do you think people notice when you do a good job?	Always	(Sometimes)	Never
8.	Do you think you get the points or rewards you deserve when you do good work?	Always	(Sometimes)	Never
9.	Do you think you would do better in school if you received more rewards?	(Always)	Sometimes	Never
10.	In general, do you find your work interesting?	Always	(Sometimes)	Never
11.	Are there things in the classroom that distract you?	Always	(Sometimes)	Never
12.	Is your work challenging enough for you?	Always	(Sometimes)	Never

SECTION II

1. When do you think you have the fewest problems with *class disruptions* _____
   in school? *Math, P.E.*
   Why do you not have problems during this/these times? *I don't know.*
2. When do you think you have the most problems with *class disruption* _____
   in school? *Language Arts, Science, Social Studies*
   Why do you have problems during this/these times? *I don't know.*
3. What changes could be made so you would have fewer problems with *class disruption* ?
   I don't know.
4. What kind of rewards would you like to earn for good behavior or good
   school work? *Time with my friends*
5. What are your favorite activities at school? *Recess*
6. What are your hobbies or interests? *Kickball*
7. If you had the chance, what activities would you like to do that you don't have the opportunity
   to do now? *I don't know.*

(Continued)

(Continued)

SECTION III

Rate how much you like the following subjects:

	Not at all		Fair		Very much
Reading	1	2	3	④	5
Math	1	2	3	④	5
Spelling	①	2	3	4	5
Handwriting	①	2	3	4	5
Science	1	2	③	4	5
Social studies	1	②	3	4	5
English	①	2	3	4	5
Music	1	2	③	4	5
P.E.	1	2	3	4	⑤
Computers	1	2	③	4	5
Art	1	②	3	4	5

SECTION IV

What do you like about Reading?   long stories

What don't you like about Reading?   book reports

What do you like about Math?   I'm good at math

What don't you like about Math?   (shoulder shrug)

What do you like about Spelling?   nothing, boring

What don't you like about Spelling?   everything, boring

What do you like about Handwriting?   Same as spelling

What don't you like about Handwriting?   Same as spelling

What do you like about Science?   experiments

What don't you like about Science?   writing reports

What do you like about Social Studies?   stories

What don't you like about Social Studies?   copying

What do you like about English?   boring

What don't you like about English?   boring

What do you like about Music?   I like to sing!

What don't you like about Music?   reports

What do you like about P.E.?   games

What don't you like about P.E.?   nothing

What do you like about Computers?   games

What don't you like about Computers?   Type to learn

What do you like about Art?   clay and papier-m âché

What don't you like about Art?   drawing, painting

Source: From "Student-Assisted Functional Assessment Interview," by L. Kern, G. Dunlap, S. Clarke, and K. E. Childs, 1994, *Diagnostique, 19*, 29–39. © 1994 PRO-ED, Inc. Reprinted with permission, shown here with case study details.

A-B-C Report Form

Name: _Renée J,_ _____ Date/Time of observation: _4/8, 9:15 AM_ _____

Place observation occurred: _General Ed. Classroom_ _____

Environmental conditions (number of students, arrangement, number of adults, etc.): _1 teacher, 22 students_ _____

Activities observed during observation: _Science – direct teach leading into a hands-on learning experience_ _____

Unusual or potentially influential conditions: _Renée sits three seats from the back of the room_ _____

Time	Antecedent	Behavior	Consequence
9:15	1. Teacher asks for students to look at her.	2. Renée stops talking and looks at the teacher.	3. No attention is given to Renée.
9:18	4. Teacher tells the students that they will need to copy an outline from the board in order to complete an experiment later.	5. Renée launches a pencil eraser at the student in front of her.	6. Student turns and laughs as she throws the eraser back at Renée.
9:22–9:30	7. Teacher tells the girls to stop playing and get to work, then turns to talk with another group of students.	8. Renée smiles and launches the pencil eraser at the teacher's back.	9. Students laugh. Teacher looks directly at Renée and says, "Go to time-out."
	10. Renée goes to time-out.	11. Renée screams, "I want to do my work. You have to let me do my work! I'll have you fired." (Renée stays at her desk, making no movement toward the time-out area.)	12. Students stare silently at Renée. Teacher walks to the phone and calls the office.
9:37	13. Assistant Principal arrives and walks over to Renée, talks quietly with her.	14. Renée gets up. Walks with the AP to the door, turns and yells, "I hate you."	15. Some students laugh; the teacher turns to write on the board.

A-B-C Report Form

Name: _Renée_   Date/Time of observation: _4/9, 7:55 AM_

Place observation occurred: _Resource Room_

Environmental conditions (number of students, arrangement, number of adults, etc.): _1 teacher, 10 students_

Activities observed during observation: _Language Arts - Spelling_

Unusual or potentially influential conditions: _None_

Time	Antecedent	Behavior	Consequence
7:55	1. Teacher asks a student to pass out spelling notebooks.	2. Renée looks at the teacher, then asks to sharpen her pencil.	3. Teacher tells her to go ahead.
7:40-7:55	4. Teacher is working with each student in turn.	5. Renée looks at the board and writes the date (very large writing, not much control).	6. The student sitting next to Renée looks at her paper, laughs, and says, "You write like a baby!"
		7. Renée hits the student with her spelling notebook.	8. Student yells at Renée. Teacher goes to them and stays until they are back on task.
8:00	9. Teacher reminds the class that appropriate behavior earns credit toward the school's fun day.	10. Renée looks at the teacher and smiles.	11. All students go back on task.
8:05	12. The lead in Renée's pencil breaks.	13. Renée yells, "Damn it! I hate school!"	14. Students laugh. Teacher says, "Do not use ugly words!"
8:07	15. Teacher asks Renée to get back to work, as she gives her a new pencil.	16. Renée is quiet, and sits with hands clenched.	17. No attention is given.
8:20	18. Teacher says, "Spelling is over; please get out your readers."	19. Renée smiles as she puts away her spelling (unfinished?).	20. Teacher praises students for following directions.
9:00	21. Reneé stays on task and follows directions.		
9:40	22. She stays in her seat and reads her book.		

A-B-C Report Form

Name: _Renée_ Date/Time of observation: _4/10, 1:45–2:07_

Place observation occurred: _Art class_

Environmental conditions (number of students, arrangement, number of adults, etc.): _1 teacher,_
34 students (11/2 classes)

Activities observed during observation: _drawing and clay sculpting_

Unusual or potentially influential conditions: _____

Time	Antecedent	Behavior	Consequence
1:45	1. Teacher says, "I want to start by saying that I'm very proud of your papier mâché projects."	2. Renée smiles and looks at her smiling classmates.	3. No attention is given.
	"Today we are going to start work on our clay projects. First, I want you to make a sketch of what you want to sculpt. Your materials are on your tables."	4. Renée's smile fades and she looks down.	5. Classmate elbows her and says, "Come on, this will be fun!"
1:50	6. Teacher says, "Renée get started. I know you have many great ideas!"	7. Renée says, "I can't. I don't know. I hate school!"	8. Teacher says, "Renée, maybe you just need to start with the clay. Shut your eyes and feel it in your hand. Just try it."
1:53	9. Teacher moves around the room.	10. Renée reaches for the clay.	11. No attention is given.
2:05	12. Teacher asks Renée what she is making.	13. Renée says, "I don't know."	14. Teacher says, "Well, just keep on working and see what happens. Remember anything you make will be good!"
		15. Renée smiles.	16. Teacher smiles back.
2:07	17. Teacher says, "We have about 10 more minutes to work until cleanup!"	18. Renée appears to be concentrating on her clay.	19. All attention is on student work.

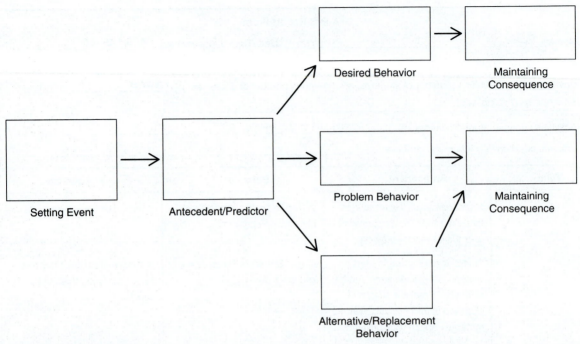

Source: From *Functional Assessment and Program Development for Problem Behavior, A Practical Handbook,* 2nd edition, by O'Neill/Horner/Albin/Sprague/Storey/Newton. © 1997 Wadsworth, a part of Cengage Learning, Inc. Reproduced by permission. www.cengage.com/permissions

Behavior Intervention Plan

Student: _____   Age: _____   Date: _____

Behavior of Concern	Target Criterion	Hypotheses	Replacement Behavior(s)	Target Criterion	Antecedent Interventions	Reinforcement Plan	Consequence Strategies for Reducing Behaviors of Concern	Monitoring Plan
1.								
2.								
3.								
4.								

After reading this chapter, you will be able to do the following:

1. Describe the strategies for collecting six types of data: event, interval, time sampling, duration, latency, and permanent products.

2. Describe how to collect data to monitor target behaviors and replacement behaviors.

3. Convert the raw data when necessary.

4. Construct a graph to provide a visual display of the data.

5. Interpret the data and make intervention decisions founded on the data.

Prevention of Challenging Behavior Through Behavioral Monitoring

Big ideas in monitoring behavior:

- Monitoring behavior is an important proactive technique.

- Monitoring progress toward both academic and behavioral goals is required by the Individuals with Disabilities Education Act (IDEA).

- Teachers who use objective, systematic methods for monitoring behavior are usually more effective than the teachers who do not use such methods.

- Most classroom behaviors can be monitored by counting how often they occur or how long they occur within a specified period.

- Behavioral monitoring should be a dynamic process: Gather data, plot the data on a graph, analyze the data, make a decision about which interventions should be implemented, adjust the interventions if necessary, and continue data collection for ongoing monitoring.

- Collecting data for behavioral monitoring can be structured to be a seamless component of instruction and behavior management.

Measurement and monitoring are used in all areas of society to assess whether a problem exists, to provide ongoing monitoring, and to signal when changes occur in order to prevent the development of more serious or costly conditions. Medicine, in particular, relies on measurement to determine an individual's state of health and to alert physicians to changes in key wellness indicators. Blood pressure, weight, cholesterol, and head circumference in infants are just a few of the many measurements used to monitor health. Dramatic changes, gradual but sustained changes, or measurements that deviate significantly from what is considered to be within normal bounds may heighten the concern of physicians. Sociologists and epidemiologists monitor the prevalence (i.e., the total number of individuals with a given condition) and incidence (i.e., the number of new cases of a given condition per predefined number of the population) for a wide range of disorders, diseases, illnesses, and injuries to assess whether potentially dangerous or harmful conditions are increasing. If so, steps may be taken to address the problem (e.g., recommendations for preventive actions, early testing, treatment). Meteorologists and environmental scientists monitor various aspects of the health of our planet (e.g. ozone depletion, the size of ice caps, earth temperatures, seismic activity) to determine whether

> Data collection is an important tool in most disciplines.

recommendations for action are warranted on the basis of either dramatic changes in certain measurements or a gradual pattern of change.

WHY BEHAVIORAL MEASUREMENT AND MONITORING IS IMPORTANT

Objective measurement of behavior will facilitate greater improvement in students by documenting the true effect of an intervention; casual observation may not accurately capture changes in behavior.

Without objective measures, it may be impossible for physicians, scientists, and others to identify problem situations. This is also true for student behavior. A teacher may be unable to detect the difference between 34 call-outs per class and 23 call-outs without objective measurement of that target behavior. Consider this example from the experience of one of the authors (BKS) when instructing a student named Michael, who exhibited high rates of off-task behavior during individual work sessions with her. Michael's off-task behavior consisted of covering his face; putting his head on the chair, table, or his lap; and pulling his shirt up over his face. Therefore, we operationally defined *off-task behavior* as any time that Michael's face touched anything (e.g., hands, shoulder, shirt, table). Prior to the implementation of the intervention, Michael averaged 139 face touches per 20-minute work session, which significantly interfered with instruction. Once an intervention to reduce face touching was initiated, the rate of Michael's face-touching behavior dropped to an average of 130 face touches per session, decreasing to 120 touches, then 108 touches, and eventually reaching the criterion of no more than 10 touches per session. Had we not been counting face touches, it would have been difficult, if not impossible, to detect that the intervention was, in fact, producing the desired change in his face-touching behavior. We may have even ended the intervention, complaining that it didn't work. Only because we had those objective measures of Michael's face touching did we know that his behavior was changing in the desired direction and would eventually reach the criterion of no more than 10 face touches per session.

Gathering objective data on student behavior, which we refer to as *data collection, behavioral monitoring,* or *behavioral measurement,* allows teachers to determine the effectiveness of interventions and whether those interventions should be continued without change, adjusted, or changed completely. This type of decision making on the basis of the data is a defining component of positive behavioral interventions and supports (PBIS) (Office of Special Education Programs, Technical Assistance Center on Positive Behavioral Interventions and Supports, 2004) and differentiates PBIS and applied behavioral analysis from other approaches to behavior management. Unfortunately, in our experiences, objective behavioral monitoring is not widely embraced by teachers. We hear many objections from teachers about behavioral monitoring: They are too busy; they do not see the value; they can determine improvement through simple observation. Our goals for this chapter are to state reasons that behavioral monitoring is important, to simplify behavioral monitoring for use in busy classrooms, and to illustrate how to use behavioral data to make decisions about interventions. The first goal is easy. The following are a few reasons special education teachers should make data collection for behavioral monitoring purposes a part of their daily routine:

The Individuals with Disabilities Education Act (IDEA) Requires the Monitoring of Behavioral Progress. IDEA requires that student progress toward academic and behavioral goals be monitored and reported to parents on a regular basis [20 U.S.C.

1414(d)(1)(A)(i)(III)]. Individualized educational programs (IEPs) and behavioral intervention plans (BIPs) should describe a plan for monitoring progress that includes who will be responsible for collecting the behavioral data, how the data will be collected, and when the data will be collected (Etscheidt, 2006a). Behavioral monitoring will also enable you to determine when a target behavior has been mastered according to the criteria described in either the IEP or the BIP. Data collection for monitoring both progress and the attainment of goals is important for providing objective documentation of progress or completion of a goal. Providing objective data during IEP meetings is considerably more valid and more professional than simply saying, "I think that Stuart has mastered this behavior. He isn't jumping out of his seat nearly as much as he used to."

Objective Data Can Be Used to Determine Present Levels of Functioning.   Measuring behavior enables teachers to determine current levels of functioning, from which goals for behavioral improvement can be determined. You must know how many minutes or seconds that a student currently plays cooperatively with peers before setting a goal to increase interactive play time, or the percentage of tasks that a student completes on time before being able to determine a criterion that will indicate improvement. In other words, you must know the starting point before you can determine the desired end point.

> There are many good reasons to collect data, including the fact that IDEA requires documentation of student progress.

Objective Measurement Provides a Basis for Evaluating Interventions.   Measuring behavior is the most reliable method for determining the effectiveness of an intervention. As you have seen from the examples given so far, simple observation will probably not detect subtle changes in behavior. Only through objective counts can you make decisions about whether an intervention should be maintained, adjusted, or changed entirely. Consider the following objective: "During academic classes, Marcy will raise her hand and wait to be called on 90% of the time." Let's say that on Monday, Marcy spoke 17 times during history class and raised her hand 10 times (59% of the time). On Tuesday, she spoke 23 times and raised her hand 17 times (74% of the time), and on Wednesday, she spoke 18 times, 14 of which she raised her hand (78% of the time). The intervention appears to be working (i.e., her percentage of call-outs is decreasing and hand raising is increasing), but it is doubtful that a teacher, who is busy with instruction and classroom management, would know this without counting the number of call-outs and hand raising.

Objective Measuring Helps to Meet the Requirements for Using Scientifically Based Practices.   Finally, in this age of educational accountability, data collection is more important than ever. The No Child Left Behind Act (P.L. 107-110) focused new attention on using scientifically based practices and results in schools (U.S. Department of Education, 2002). Unfortunately, there appears to be a disconnection between research and widespread application in school settings (Lewis, Hudson, Richter, & Johnson, 2004; Whelan, 2005). We believe, and special education hearing officers and courts have affirmed, that the burden is on teachers and administrators to document the effectiveness of interventions. In the absence of scientifically based evidence to support the use of a particular strategy, data for individual students are needed to document improved academic or behavioral performance as a result of the strategy. Data collection will provide evidence that interventions are effective and that students are making progress toward target goals and objectives.

Data for Behavioral Measurement and Monitoring in the Three-Tiered Model of PBIS

Data collection is a critical element in all tiers of positive behavioral interventions and supports. There are, however, differences in the purposes for the data at each tier and in the types of data needed at each tier. Universal-level data are used to identify needs for schoolwide PBIS programs, to monitor the impact of those programs on student behavior, and to assess the fidelity of implementation of those programs. **Fidelity** refers to the degree to which interventions are implemented correctly—in the manner in which they were originally designed and intended to be used. Data commonly used for these purposes will be discussed in Chapter 5.

Targeted-level data are used to monitor the effect of Tier 2 interventions on the social and/or academic behaviors of students who are receiving those interventions. While some of the behavioral measurement systems described in this chapter may be used for this purpose, most of the systems presented here will be used to monitor the behavior of students who are receiving tertiary-level interventions. That makes sense, given that these behavioral measurement systems are designed primarily for use with individual students, and tertiary supports are individualized for each student.

However, even though the behavioral measurement systems discussed in this chapter will be used mostly to monitor the effects of tertiary interventions, it will benefit educators who are responsible for designing and implementing data collection systems for universal and targeted levels to understand the concepts presented in this chapter. For example, the knowledge that different forms of behavior require different approaches (e.g., frequency versus duration, or latency versus intensity) to monitoring those behaviors will help educators develop meaningful systems for monitoring the behaviors of students who are receiving targeted-level supports. Likewise, classroom teachers who have even a rudimentary knowledge of how to count behavior can more reliably determine specific classroom behavioral problems that need to be addressed, and can more accurately monitor the effectiveness of interventions for those problems.

So, now that you are convinced of the importance of measuring and monitoring behavior, and the importance of data collection at all tiers of support, the next step is to learn how to collect meaningful data in an efficient manner and how to use the data for the purpose of making decisions. These tasks are described in the sections that follow.

HOW TO MEASURE BEHAVIOR

Measuring and monitoring behavior using objective data is easy if you use the seven steps presented next. These steps are listed in Table 4-1 and are described next.

Step 1: Operationally Define the Target Behavior

An operational definition is a definition that is precise and that would enable two people to agree on when the behavior is occurring. Examples and nonexamples of operational definitions are provided in Table 4-2. Remember that we can and should collect data on both academic and social behaviors. Therefore, target behaviors can be academic behaviors (e.g., the number of words spelled correctly, the number of

TABLE 4-1   Steps in Monitoring Behavior

Step 1:	Operationally define the target behavior.
Step 2:	Choose the behavioral measurement system to be implemented.
	Event recording
	Interval recording
	Time sampling
	Duration recording
	Latency recording
	Permanent product recording
Step 3:	Determine the data collection periods.
Step 4:	Collect the baseline data first and then collect the intervention data.
Step 5:	Convert the data if necessary.
Step 6:	Plot the data in a graphic display.
Step 7:	Interpret the data.

TABLE 4-2   Examples and Nonexamples of Operationally Defined Behaviors

Nonexamples	Examples
Rude	Says "Shut up"; calls other students names (e.g., gorilla, peanut-head, idiot, stinko).
Aggressive	Shoves peers with both hands; kicks peers; pinches peers; spits on peers.
On task	Writes with regard to the assigned task; looks at work; answers the teacher's questions.
Polite	Says "please" and "thank you" at the appropriate times.
Compliant	Follows directions within 10 seconds of receiving the request; does what the teacher requested with no more than one additional prompt.
Oppositional	When given a direction, says, "I don't have to" or "You can't make me," and does not do what the teacher requested.
Reads fluently	Reads 70 words per minute [for a second grader], with the correct intonation and response to punctuation.
Works hard	Maintains on-task behavior (see earlier description for "On task") for 15 consecutive minutes; asks for help when necessary, rather than complaining (e.g., "This is too hard" or "Why do I have to do this?") or putting his or her head on the desk.
Mean to peers	Pushes or trips other students during transitions; calls peers names (fat-head).
Talks back to teacher	Says "NO!" or "Don't tell me what to do."
Shy	On average, initiates less than one interaction with peers during each recess; sits quietly at lunch without conversing with peers.

words read correctly, the number of mathematical problems solved correctly, the number of correctly written sentences completed), classroom behaviors (e.g., calling out without permission, turning in assignments, following class rules), and social behaviors (e.g., taking turns during a game, standing in line, initiating greetings).

You may choose to focus on a student's inappropriate behavior as the target behavior. However, as you learned in Chapter 3, you should also identify **replacement behaviors** as a target for intervention (O'Neill et al., 1997). Focusing on replacement behaviors helps to ensure that the intervention will focus on reinforcement and positive support instead of simply punishing the challenging behavior (Vargas, 2009). This raises the issue of what should be measured: the challenging behavior or the replacement behavior? We recommend measuring the challenging behavior if that behavior is dangerous or is so disruptive that it threatens the student's ability to remain in a less restrictive placement and/or if engaging in the replacement behavior does not necessarily ensure that the challenging behavior will not occur. For example, if the challenging behavior is noncompliance, you can easily measure compliance, because it is impossible to be noncompliant and compliant simultaneously. As compliance increases, noncompliance automatically decreases. On the other hand, using appropriate words to express feelings does not necessarily ensure that hitting or pushing will not occur. Therefore, the teacher may choose to monitor instances of hitting or pushing.

Step 2: Choose the Behavior Measurement System to be Implemented

Selecting the correct measurement system is a critical step in data collection. Using the wrong system will result in irrelevant data.

This is critical, because using the wrong system will result in meaningless data. Each of the six measurement systems that we describe is appropriately used for certain types of behaviors. A good way to determine the correct behavior measurement system is to ask: What information do you wish the data to provide? For example, if you wish to know how many times a student engages in a particular behavior, the correct measurement system would be event recording. If you need to know how long it takes a student to begin a task, you should use latency recording. The six measurement systems and the types of behaviors for which each is used are described next. Please note that anecdotal reports, which we described in Chapter 3, are also a form of data collection.

Event Recording.   **Event recording** (also known as **frequency recording**) is used for behaviors that

- have a clearly observable beginning and end (e.g., writing words, reading words, saying "thank you," raising one's hand, completing a written assignment). These are known as **discrete behaviors**.
- occur briefly rather than for long periods of time. Behaviors that occur for long periods of time (e.g., sleeping, out-of-seat behavior, writing, playing a computer game) should not be measured using event recording because the data may show only one or two instances of the behavior, and not reveal that each instance lasted for 20 minutes.
- are not so fast that they cannot be counted. For example, pencil tapping is discrete and occurs briefly (usually), but the taps may be so fast that

each instance cannot be counted. Likewise, it may be difficult to count each instance of a curse word being used by a student who rattles off a long string of curse words embedded in other choice phrases!

A good rule of thumb is that event recording is appropriate when the goal is to increase or decrease the *number of times* that a behavior occurs. Each instance of the target behavior is recorded in some way. Tally marks are one easy way to record event data. Another solution is to use handheld mechanical counters, which are available through Amazon.com (search for "tally counters" on the Amazon Website). These inexpensive counters can be held, carried on a lanyard around your neck, or clipped to your belt or clipboard. Mechanical counters are useful when the teacher is engaged in an activity that precludes using a pencil and paper for making tally marks. Digital counters allow the teacher to count target behaviors effortlessly while attending to students. Because these counters are inexpensive and easily available, you might wish to keep one or more counters in each location where you will be collecting data, as well as provide counters to your paraprofessionals or other teachers who are responsible for data collection.

Once you determine that event recording is the correct measurement system to use, you must determine next which form of event recording is appropriate, either restricted event recording or unrestricted event recording (Scheuermann & Webber, 2002). **Restricted events** (also known as **restricted operants**) are those events which occur only in response to a specific stimulus (e.g., reading a word, responding to mathematics flash cards, answering a question, following a direction, correctly placing a certain number of story pictures in sequence). For such behaviors, you must count two things: the antecedent stimulus and the responding behavior. For example, you would need to count the number of questions asked and the number of questions answered correctly, the number of directions given and the number of directions followed, the number of pictures available and the number of pictures correctly placed in sequence. Figure 4-1 shows several examples of data recording formats for restricted event recording.

Unrestricted events (also known as **free operants**) are behaviors that can occur at any time, rather than only in the presence of a particular stimulus. Examples of unrestricted event behavior include initiating a social interaction, asking a question, hitting, screaming, grabbing a toy from a peer, or running out of the classroom. There are two options for collecting data for unrestricted events. One is to simply record the number of times the behavior occurs and plot that number on a graph. This option would be appropriate for behaviors that occur infrequently (e.g., running out of the classroom, initiating a fight) or if the length of the observation period is constant. Think about the earlier example of Michael, who engaged in frequent face touching. Michael's data collection periods (the one-on-one work periods) were always 20 minutes long; thus, we could simply count how many face touches occurred during that 20-minute period. The second option is to record the length of time during which data were collected and then convert the data to a rate (i.e., the number of instances of the behavior divided by the number of minutes in the observation period), which is explained in Step 5. This option is appropriate if the length of the observation periods varies (Alberto

> The two types of event recording are restricted event and unrestricted event recording.

Example 1
| = Direction given + = Direction followed
Data collection period: Morning group, 8:20–8:40

Monday	| | | + | | + + | |
Tuesday	+ + | | | + + +

Example 2		
Date	**Number of questions asked during mathematics direct teaching**	**Number of questions answered correctly**
Monday	✓ ✓ ✓ ✓ ✓ ✓	✓ ✓
Tuesday	✓ ✓ ✓ ✓	✓ ✓ ✓ ✓
Wednesday	✓ ✓ ✓ ✓ ✓ ✓ ✓	✓ ✓ ✓ ✓

Example 3
✓ = Number of greetings directed toward the student during the morning walk from the bus to the classroom and during breakfast ⊘ = Number of responses to those greetings ("Good morning," "Good," "OK," "Fine," "Hi")
Tuesday, 9-10   ⊘   ⊘   ⊘   ✓   ✓   ⊘
Thursday, 9-11   ✓   ✓   ✓   ✓
Tuesday, 9-16   ✓   ⊘   ⊘   ⊘   ⊘
Thursday, 9-18   ⊘   ⊘   ✓   ⊘   ⊘   ⊘   ⊘

FIGURE 4-1 Data Recording Formats for Restricted Event Behaviors

& Troutman, 2006). Figure 4-2 provides examples of unrestricted event recording formats, including formats for recording the length of the observation period.

Interval Recording.   **Interval recording** is used to measure continuous or high-frequency behaviors—behaviors that would not be appropriately measured using event recording. To use interval recording, determine a length of time during which the target behavior will be measured. This should be done when the behavior is most likely to occur. A short observation period (e.g., 5 or 10 minutes) is usually feasible for teachers. Remember, the purpose of data collection is to gather *samples* of the target behavior, not to measure all occurrences of the behavior. Then divide this period into equal intervals. These intervals can be anywhere from 6 to 15 seconds (Cooper et al., 1987); intervals should not be longer than 30 seconds (Cooper, 1981). Shorter intervals will provide a more accurate reflection of the amount of behavior that actually occurs. Next, observe the student for the predetermined time. As you observe, indicate on your data collection form whether the target behavior did or did not occur at any time during each interval. Occurrences can be indicated by a + or another symbol. Intervals during which the behavior did not occur are typically marked with a —. See Figures 4-3 and 4-4 for sample interval data forms.

Example 1			
✓ = Hitting head with open palm			
Activity	**Length**	**Occurrences**	**Rate**
Monday, morning centers	8:00–8:17	✓ ✓ ✓ ✓ ✓ ✓ ✓ ✓ ✓ ✓ ✓ ✓ ✓ ✓ ✓	0.88 hits per minute
Monday, lunch	11:30–11:55	✓ ✓ ✓ ✓ ✓ ✓ ✓	0.28 hits per minute
Monday, afternoon work session	2:05–2:25	✓ ✓ ✓ ✓ ✓ ✓ ✓ ✓ ✓ ✓ ✓ ✓ ✓ ✓ ✓ ✓ ✓ ✓	0.9 hits per minute

Example 2
Number of play initiations during morning recess (10:00–10:20 each day). (*Play initiation* is asking a peer to play, asking to join an activity, etc.) Monday   0 Tuesday   + + Wednesday   + + Thursday   + + + + Friday   + + +

FIGURE 4-2   Sample Formats for Recording Unrestricted Event Behaviors

Behavior: Sharing blocks in the play center (defined as building with blocks at the same time that another student is using the block center). Noninstance: Taking a block away from another student, grabbing a block as another student is reaching for it.

Date/Time: 11/08, 9:40–9:45

Format: Whole-interval recording

+ = Sharing

− = Not sharing

	15 seconds	**30 seconds**	**45 seconds**	**1 minute**
1 minute	+	+	−	+
2 minutes	−	+	−	+
3 minutes	+	+	+	+
4 minutes	+	−	−	+
5 minutes	−	+	−	+

Sharing occurred during 13 intervals (65% of the observation time).
Sharing was not exhibited during 7 intervals (35% of the observation time).

FIGURE 4-3   Sample Whole-Interval Recording Form

Behavior: On task during mathematics independent work (defined as writing, or eyes oriented toward book or paper).

Date/Time: 11/10, 1:30–1:40

Format: Partial-interval recording

✓ = On task

— = Off task

	10 seconds	20 seconds	30 seconds	40 seconds	50 seconds	60 seconds
1 minute	✓	✓	—	—	—	—
2 minute	✓	✓	✓	✓	✓	✓
3 minute	✓	—	—	—	✓	✓
4 minute	—	—	—	—	—	—
5 minute	—	✓	✓	✓	✓	✓
6 minute	✓	✓	✓	✓	—	—
7 minute	✓	—	✓	✓	✓	✓
8 minute	✓	✓	—	✓	✓	✓
9 minute	—	✓	✓	✓	✓	—
10 minute	✓	✓	✓	✓	✓	✓

Total on-task intervals: 40/60 intervals (67%).
Total off-task intervals: 20/60 intervals (33%).

FIGURE 4-4 Sample Partial-Interval Recording Data Collection Form

Interval recording can be either whole-interval or partial-interval recording.

One of the disadvantages of interval recording is that it does not reveal how much of the behavior occurs during each interval. Even if the behavior occurs only briefly during an interval, an occurrence is noted on the data form, in which case the data may indicate a higher rate of behavior than is actually occurring. Likewise, if a behavior occurs throughout the interval, the interval is marked only once. One way to increase the accuracy of interval data is to use either whole-interval recording or partial-interval recording. With **whole-interval recording**, before you begin collecting data, you decide that only occurrences of the target behavior that last *throughout the interval* will be counted as an occurrence. For example, Mr. Miller uses whole-interval recording to monitor Derrick's on-task behavior. Mr. Miller observes Derrick during the first 10 minutes of independent work twice a week. This 10-minute period is divided into 15-second intervals. If Derrick is on task (e.g., looking at his work, writing) during an entire 15-second interval, Mr. Miller records a plus sign (+) on his data form. If Derrick looks away from his work or leaves his seat at any time during the interval, a minus sign (−) is recorded. Because whole-interval recording sets a higher standard for the amount of behavior that must occur, it may provide a more accurate reflection of the behavior.

However, whole-interval recording requires high levels of teacher's attention during the observation period. In a busy classroom, a teacher may be unable to use this type of measurement system. An alternative approach is **partial-interval recording**, in which a positive occurrence is recorded if the behavior occurs at any time during the interval. Using this approach, the teacher would not need to watch the student for the duration of each interval; once the behavior occurs, the appropriate code is recorded on the data form and the teacher can attend to other tasks until the start of the next interval. For example, during reading group, Ms. Wallace uses partial-interval recording with 15-second intervals to monitor Anna's on-task behavior. As soon as Ms. Wallace observes Anna using on-task behavior during the interval, Ms. Wallace scores that interval as positive for on-task behavior; no further action is needed until the next interval begins, at which time Ms. Wallace again watches Anna closely for on-task behavior.

Time Sampling.   **Time sampling** is a variation of interval recording in which the data collector is interested in whether the target behavior is occurring at the end of each interval. Time sampling, like interval recording, is done by determining a length of time during which to observe and then dividing that time into intervals of equal length. However, the observation period for time sampling can be much longer (e.g., hours, an entire day) and the intervals can be longer (e.g., several minutes or longer). Mr. Carson used time sampling to determine how many students were using a particular learning center during the learning center period. At the end of 10-minute intervals during the 45-minute learning center period, he recorded whether there were any students in that center. Ms. Dillon taught students with autism. A goal for each of her students was to reduce the amount of **stereotypic behaviors** (i.e., repetitive behaviors such as hand-flapping, rocking, twirling objects, or monotone humming that appear to be for the purpose of self-stimulation). Ms. Dillon taught each student an appropriate replacement behavior and then used time sampling to measure the students' stereotypic behaviors. During the morning (8:00–11:20), she observed each student at the end of 20-minute intervals and recorded which students were engaging in stereotypic behaviors at that moment. The form shown in Figure 4-5 depicts Ms. Dillon's data for 2 days. Note that Ms. Dillon used time sampling to monitor the behavior of multiple students simultaneously. We discuss this later in this section.

> In time sampling, behavior is measured at the end of each interval.

Time sampling is appropriate for the same types of behaviors as interval recording, but may be more user friendly for the teachers because it does not require extended periods of observation with continuous data recording. Of course, a certain amount of accuracy may be sacrificed for this convenience. Because positive occurrences are noted only if the target behavior is occurring at the end of an interval, the data may underreport or overreport how much of the target behavior actually occurred. For example, if Moira is on task for the entire 20-minute interval but then puts her head down just as the timer rings to cue the teacher to observe, the teacher must record that Moira was off task at that moment. Her extended on-task behavior prior to the moment of observation does not count.

> Duration recording measures how long a behavior occurs; latency recording measures how long it takes for a behavior to begin.

Duration Recording.   This technique is used when the goal is to increase or decrease how long a behavior occurs. **Duration recording** involves measuring the length of time that a behavior is exhibited; it is appropriate for behaviors that

	Paul	Jason	Michael	Rana
Behavior: Stereotypic behaviors Paul = Hand-flapping Jason = Spinning objects Michael = Humming Rana = Rocking + = Occurrence of the target behavior – = Nonoccurrence of the target behavior		Date/Time: 4/08, 8:00–11:20		
8:00	–	+	+	–
8:20	–	+	–	–
8:40	–	+	–	+
9:00	–	+	–	+
9:20	–	–	–	–
9:40	–	+	+	–
10:00	+	–	+	–
10:20	+	+	–	–
10:40	–	+	–	–
11:00	–	–	+	+
11:20	–	+	+	–
TOTALS	2/11 intervals 18%	8/11 intervals 73%	5/11 intervals 45%	3/11 intervals 27%

FIGURE 4-5 Example of Time-Sampling Data

have a clearly identifiable beginning and end. Behaviors that may be appropriately measured using duration recording include the following:

- How long it takes a student to complete an assigned task (with the beginning of the task defined as when the teacher says, "OK, begin," and the end of the task defined as when the student signals that he or she is finished).
- How long a student remains in his or her seat.
- How long a student shares a toy with a peer (defined as both children sitting within 5 feet of one another and looking at or using the same toy).
- How long it takes a student to finish lunch (defined as the elapsed time from when lunch is placed in front of the student until the student leaves the table).
- How long a student spends in the bathroom (defined as the elapsed time from when the student leaves the classroom until he or she returns).

Duration behaviors may be recorded by simply noting start and stop times, or by using a stopwatch, which is more convenient and more accurate.

Latency Recording. Sometimes the goal is to increase or decrease how long it takes for a behavior to begin. In such cases, **latency recording** is the measurement system of choice. Latency refers to the time elapsed between when a stimulus (e.g., instruction, academic task) is given and when the response to that stimulus begins (e.g., student begins to comply, student begins to work on task). To collect latency data, simply note when the stimulus is given and when the response begins. The number of minutes and/or seconds between those two instances is the latency period. The following are a few examples of goals for which latency recording would be the appropriate measurement tool:

- Decrease the amount of time that it takes for a student to sit down once the bell rings.
- Decrease the amount of time required for students to begin working once instructed to do so.
- Increase the amount of time that a student thinks about a response before answering.

Permanent Product Recording.   By far the most widely used method of data collection, **permanent product recording** indicates the concrete, tangible results or outcomes of a behavior (Alberto & Troutman, 2006). Permanent products can take many forms, but the most common is written work completed by students. Other types of permanent products are listed in Table 4-3. Permanent products are useful tools for teachers because it is not necessary to actually observe the behavior that

> Permanent product recording provides an easy way for busy teachers to monitor behaviors that result in tangible evidence that the behavior occurred.

TABLE 4-3 Permanent Products

Permanent Products	Measurement Systems
Academic worksheets	Restricted event recording
Assembling, collating, or other vocational tasks	
number of pages collated or number of completed packets	Restricted event recording
number of packets sealed	Restricted event recording
number of items of clothing folded	Restricted event recording
number of items shelved	Restricted or unrestricted event recording
Number of dishes washed	Restricted event recording
Puzzle pieces correctly placed	Restricted event recording
Homework assignments completed and placed in correct folder	Restricted event recording
Number of words written in essays	Unrestricted event recording
Instances of vandalism	Unrestricted event recording
Trash left in cafeteria after lunch	Unrestricted event recording
Personal items (e.g., jacket, books) left on the playground	Unrestricted event recording
Number of Internet references located and printed	Unrestricted event recording
Audiotaped recordings	
words read aloud	Restricted or unrestricted event recording
curse words used during the observation period	Unrestricted event recording
off-task comments made during direct teaching	Unrestricted event recording
tantrums	Duration recording
Videotaped recordings (almost any observable behavior)	Any of the measurement systems, depending on the target behavior

produced the permanent product in order to monitor it. Thus, teachers can attend to other classroom duties and record data at a later time.

Permanent products alone are not data. Event or duration data must be recorded from the permanent product and then converted, if necessary, and plotted. Table 4-3 lists the measurement system that might be used for each permanent product.

Remember that using the correct system for measuring behavior is essential in order to produce valid data. In this chapter, we described six approaches to measuring behavior. Each system is appropriate for certain types of behaviors. Table 4-4 presents a list of common classroom behaviors and the measurement system that would be most appropriate for each.

Step 3: Determine the Data Collection Periods

One of the misunderstandings about collecting data for monitoring behavior is that data must be gathered continuously throughout the day. Because such a task would be unmanageable, many teachers don't gather objective data in order to monitor behavior. A more manageable—and correct—approach is to gather samples of data about target behaviors for brief periods of data collection spread out over the course of the day.

The length of the data collection period depends on the behavior being monitored. For low-frequency behaviors (e.g., those that occur only a few times during the day or week), the data collection period could easily be an entire day. For high-frequency behaviors, data collection could occur during a single period or part of a period, such as only during independent work or during several brief observation periods throughout the day (e.g., 15 minutes in the morning and in the afternoon). It is not necessary to monitor target behaviors constantly throughout the day. You can collect data for part of one period, for one period, or several times throughout the day. For example, Ms. Sperry monitors Jamal's appropriate use of toys by using duration recording to measure how long he uses a toy correctly during the first play period of the day, 2 days per week. Ms. Harris evaluates an intervention to reduce the number of copying errors that Lee makes by randomly selecting 10 papers each week on which he has been required to copy material from his text or from the blackboard. Mr. Coleman counts how many assignments two of his students complete on time during one morning and one afternoon period, 2 days per week. The goal of data collection is not necessarily to count every occurrence of a behavior for the entire day, but rather to gather representative samples of the behavior on a regular basis.

Data collection should always occur during times of the day when the target behavior is most likely to occur. This information can probably be determined from functional behavioral assessment data. To help ensure that data reflect meaningful, consistent information about the behavior being measured, data collection should occur at the same time, and in the same place, from one data collection period to the next.

Step 4: Collect the Baseline Data First and Then Collect the Intervention Data

The actual process of monitoring behavior should begin by collecting **baseline data** on the target behavior, which means measuring the behavior for three to five

TABLE 4-4   Measurement Systems for Classroom Behaviors

Following are some measurement systems that can be used to monitor each of the target behaviors listed. For some behaviors, more than one measurement system could be used. In such cases, the most appropriate system is listed first. Not all of the behaviors listed are operationally defined, which would be necessary before beginning data collection.

Desired Behaviors	Measurement System
Assignments completed	Restricted event recording
Number of directions followed	Restricted event recording
Number of mathematics problems solved correctly	Restricted event recording
Number of puzzle pieces correctly placed	Restricted event recording
Number of times that the student initiates requests for assistance during independent work	Unrestricted event recording
Number of social initiations toward peers	Unrestricted event recording
Number of packets assembled and stapled	Unrestricted event recording
Number of words written in daily journal	Unrestricted event recording
Number of bites of food taken without spitting	Restricted or unrestricted event recording
Number of times that the student raises his or her hand without calling out	Unrestricted event recording
Amount of time spent sharing a toy	Duration recording Interval recording Time sampling
How long it takes the student to go to the restroom and return to class	Duration recording
Length of time on task	Duration recording Interval recording Time sampling
Amount of time spent interacting with peers on the playground	Duration recording Interval recording Time sampling
How long the student sits next to peers without hitting	Duration recording
How long the student keeps eyeglasses on his or her face	Duration recording Interval recording Time sampling
How long the student participates in a group game	Duration recording
How long the student waits before calling out the answer to a question	Latency recording
How long it takes the student to take his or her seat after the bell rings	Latency recording

(continued)

TABLE 4-4 Measurement Systems for Classroom Behaviors (*Continued*)

Inappropriate Behaviors	Measurement System
How long it takes the student to begin working once he or she is told to do so	Latency recording
Noncompliance	Restricted event recording
Hitting the teacher in response to receiving directions	Restricted event recording
Being late	Restricted event recording
Cutting in line at lunchtime	Restricted event recording
Biting self or others	Unrestricted event recording
Grabbing materials	Unrestricted event recording
Screaming	Unrestricted event recording (or duration recording for extended screaming)
Cursing	Unrestricted event recording
Tantrums	Event recording (restricted or unrestricted, depending on the situation) or duration recording (for extended tantrums)
Name-calling	Unrestricted event recording
Sleeping during class	Duration recording
	Interval recording
	Time sampling
Calling out an answer before the teacher is finished asking the question	Restricted event recording

observation periods before beginning the intervention. This allows you to ascertain the current level of functioning, which facilitates determining the mastery criteria and provides a standard against which to judge the effectiveness of the intervention. Consider Tony, a 7-year-old with significant cognitive delays. Tony often spits out his food during mealtimes, sometimes picking up what he has spit out and eating it again. Before beginning the intervention, Tony's teacher counted how many times Tony spit out his food during a 30-minute lunch period for 1 week. The frequency and rate of Tony's food spitting during the baseline period were as follows:

Monday   15 times (0.5 times per minute)

Tuesday   17 times (0.6 times per minute)

Wednesday   12 times (0.4 times per minute)

Thursday   20 times (0.7 times per minute)

Friday   18 times (0.6 times per minute)

The baseline data reflect the level of the behavior prior to implementation of the intervention.

Knowing how many times Tony currently spits out his food and at what rate this behavior occurs enables Tony's teacher to better determine where to set the criterion for reinforcement during the first phase of the intervention. In Tony's case, his teacher implemented a system in which Tony earned a token for each minute that he kept food in his mouth without spitting; the intervals were noted by using a timer. After lunch, Tony could exchange the tokens for his favorite activity: playing with his puzzles. As Tony became successful at controlling his food spitting, the teacher increased the length of the interval required in order to earn a token. Eventually, Tony ate his entire lunch with zero instances of food spitting.

An exception to the rule of collecting baseline data first is that, in classroom situations, you do not collect baseline data for target behaviors that are dangerous to the child or others, or that are highly disruptive. Dangerous behaviors might include hitting, kicking, spitting, throwing objects, or running out of the classroom. Highly disruptive behaviors could include behaviors that interrupt the class to the point where instruction cannot continue or that result in the student losing significant instructional time (e.g., a student who is sent to in-school suspension for yelling and running in the cafeteria). One of us (JAH) once helped a teacher who was concerned about one of her early childhood students. This student engaged in high rates of aggressive behavior toward his peers (i.e., biting, pinching, kicking). This was a dangerous behavior that we had to get under control quickly; we could not justify taking the time to obtain baseline data in this situation. Instead, we began collecting data on the first day of the intervention, and we judged the effectiveness of the intervention by comparing the data against our goal of zero instances of aggressive behavior per day. When you are dealing with dangerous or extremely disruptive behaviors, begin the intervention immediately after the functional assessment has been completed and continue to measure the behavior to verify that it is decreasing.

After obtaining approximately three to five baseline data points, begin the intervention and continue to collect the data. It may not be necessary, or possible, to collect the data daily. Some target behaviors, especially academic behaviors (e.g., the number of words read correctly per minute, the number of mathematics problems solved correctly, the number of mathematics facts given correctly, the number of words spelled correctly), are best monitored only two or three times per week. Severe problem behaviors like aggression or extremely disruptive behaviors should probably be monitored daily, and the data analyzed frequently to determine the effectiveness of the intervention.

Step 5: Convert the Data if Necessary

Some raw data may not be in a form that can be used for valid comparisons across data collection sessions as our previous examples have shown. For this reason, a decision must be made about whether to convert the raw data. Restricted event raw data require conversion to a percentage (i.e., the number of instances of the target behavior divided by the total number of opportunities to respond) prior to plotting the data, unless the opportunities to respond are controlled (e.g., the number of opportunities to respond are consistent across sessions). For example, a teacher may decide to direct 10 questions to a student during each math period to monitor the target behavior of responding appropriately to questions. Because the number of opportunities to respond is always the same (i.e., 10 in this case), the teacher needs only to record how many questions the student answered correctly.

Unrestricted event data may be reported as raw data if the length of the observation period is always the same or if the behavior occurs infrequently. If the

> Conversion of the data may be needed in order for the data to be meaningful.

length of the observation period varies, conversion to rate allows for a standardized format by which to compare data. For example, Javier called out off-task comments during independent work, which varied in length from period to period and day to day. On Wednesday, he called out eight times during the 20-minute work period in science, which means that the behavior occurred at a rate of 0.4 times per minute (8 divided by 20). During journal writing, he called out only four times, but that work period was only 10 minutes long, resulting in a rate of 0.4 behaviors per minute (4 divided by 10). At first glance, it looks as if he called out fewer times during journal writing, but the rate of the behavior is actually the same across both periods. Rate is a widely used method of reporting event data.

Interval data and time-sampling data should be converted to percentages. To calculate a percentage, count the total number of intervals. Next, count the number of intervals in which the target behavior occurred. Divide the number of intervals in which the behavior occurred by the total number of intervals to obtain the percentage of occurrences of the target behavior. Figures 4-3 through 4-5 show examples of whole-interval data, partial-interval data, and time-sampling data converted to percentages.

No conversion is needed for duration data or latency data. For duration data, simply plot the number of minutes and/or seconds that the target behavior occurred. For latency data, plot the number of minutes and/or seconds between the antecedent and the onset of the target behavior.

Step 6: Plot the Data

Plotting of the data on a graph allows for visual inspection of the data.

Plotting the data on a graph allows quick and easy visual inspection of the data, which facilitates decision making and communicating with others about the behavior. Plotting data is easy, takes very little time, and can be rewarding for both teachers and students. Instructions for plotting data on a graph are provided in Table 4-5, along with sample graphs to illustrate each step.

Step 7: Interpret the Data

There are formal methods for interpreting data that are beyond the scope of this text. We will focus on simple, visual approaches to interpret data for decision-making purposes. Examine the plotted data for **trends,** or three consecutive data points in the same direction (Barlow & Hersen, 1984). If the plotted data indicate a trend in the desired direction (i.e., ascending for behaviors to be increased, descending for behaviors to be decreased), continue the intervention until the student reaches the criterion. At that point, the behavior does not need to be monitored regularly; however, it is good practice to monitor the behavior periodically (e.g., once per week, once per month, once every other month) to ensure that it is being maintained at the desired level.

If the data line is erratic or inconsistent, is moving opposite to the desired direction, or is flat for more than three data points (thus indicating no progress), you should consider the following: First, examine the intervention to make sure that it is being implemented consistently and correctly (i.e., with fidelity). If the intervention is being implemented with fidelity, yet data indicate no progress, it may be necessary to modify the intervention slightly. For example, you may need to reinforce

TABLE 4-5

1. **Set up a graph for each target behavior using graph paper.**
   a. Draw the vertical line (this is called the **y-axis**, or **ordinate)** and label it to reflect the target behavior that was measured (e.g., Number of initiations during recess, Number of questions asked during independent math work, Time spent brushing teeth, or Percentage of directions followed within 1 minute).
   b. Draw the horizontal line (called the **x-axis**, or **abscissa)** and label it to reflect the observation periods (e.g., Daily recesses, Independent math work).

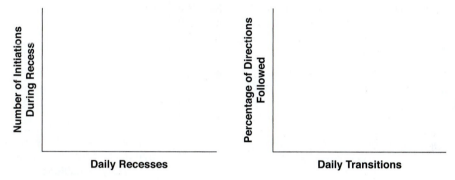

   c. Divide the y-axis into *equal* increments (it is usually easiest to use the squares of the graph paper as the increments), and label each increment to show the number, percentage, or minutes and/or seconds, depending on the form of the converted data. The intersection of the vertical and horizontal lines is always zero, and numbering begins from that point. For example, to set up a graph for percentage data, the increments could be labeled 10%, 20%, 30%, 40%, and so on. For duration data, the increments might be labeled 15 s; 30 s; 45 s; 1 min; 1 min, 15 s; 1 min, 30 s; and so on.
   d. If data are clustered among high values or divided between high and low values, the graph can be condensed to allow all data points to be plotted on the same page. This is done by inserting a **scale break**, or two short lines, across the y-axis at the point where the increments on the scale are omitted. In our sample graphs, a scale break is inserted on the graph on the right.

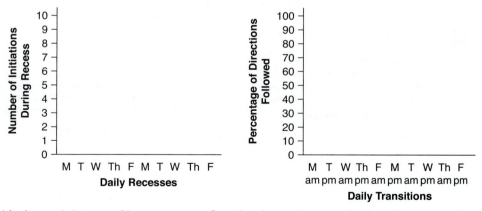

   e. Divide the x-axis into equal increments to reflect the observation periods when data were collected. Each vertical line will represent one observation period.

(continued)

TABLE 4-5   *(Continued)*

2. **Plot the baseline data.** Data from each observation session are plotted on the intersections of the vertical and horizontal lines. These points are called **data points**. No data points are plotted on the ordinate and the abscissa. Also, data points are plotted on consecutive lines: There should be no skipped lines.

3. **Connect the data points with straight lines.**

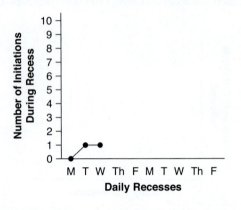

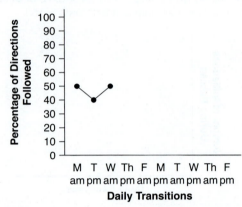

4. **Once you have finished plotting the baseline data, draw a vertical dotted line next to the last baseline data point.** This line separates the baseline data from the intervention data. When plotting behavioral measurements, vertical dotted lines signal that something has changed. In this case, the baseline has ended and the intervention has begun.

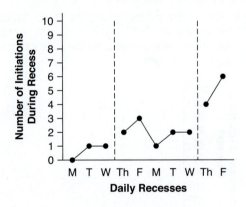

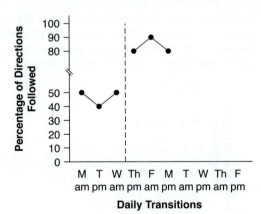

(continued)

TABLE 4-5 *(Continued)*

5. **Begin the intervention and continue collecting and plotting the data, one data point on each vertical line.** The sample graph on the left shows that a change was made in the intervention after Day 5 of the intervention.

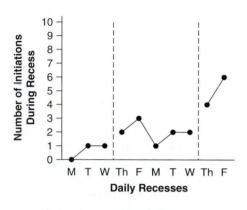 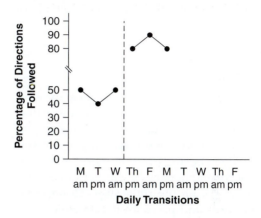

6. **If any change is made in the intervention, indicate that change with a vertical dotted line.** These lines are known as **condition change lines.** Do not connect the data points across the condition change lines.

7. **If the student is absent for a day or if data are not collected during an observation session, skip that vertical line.** Record a code to indicate the reason for the skipped line and do not connect the data points across this space.

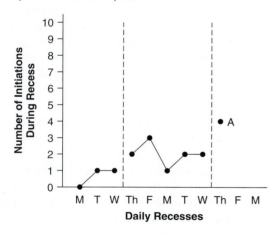 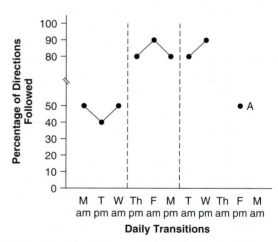

more frequently, use a different reinforcer, or add additional practice activities (in the case of academic tasks). If the target behavior is a challenging behavior, the hypotheses developed from the functional assessment should be reexamined; new hypotheses may be needed. Another option is to implement a new intervention (e.g., use a different instructional technique or add a behavior reduction technique to the antecedent and reinforcement interventions already in place).

Summary

Measuring behavior may not be the most exciting task that you do as a teacher, or the most dramatic, or even the most fun. It may, however, be one of the most important tasks that you do. The data that you collect in order to monitor key social and academic behaviors will help to ensure that you are taking the right steps to improve those behaviors and prevent unacceptable alternatives to those behaviors from occurring. Without data, teachers run the risk of continuing ineffective interventions, thus wasting valuable time or discontinuing effective interventions too soon. Effective teachers make data collection and analysis a regular part of their daily routine. In this chapter, we explained the importance of monitoring behavior and how to incorporate various types of behavior measurement into your daily teaching routine. The objectives for this chapter and how they were addressed are as follows:

1. Describe strategies for collecting six types of data: event, interval, time sampling, duration, latency, and permanent products.

   We described these methods for monitoring behavior and the types of behaviors appropriate for each method. Selecting the correct method is an important step in the monitoring process. Using the wrong system (i.e., a system that does not accurately reflect the target behavior) will result in incorrect, misleading data.

2. Describe how to collect data to monitor target behaviors and replacement behaviors.

   We presented a few strategies for using behavioral measurement systems to monitor various types of target behaviors. You can develop your own strategies as well. Behavioral

measurement methods that are unobtrusive and easy to use are more likely to be used!

3. Convert the raw data when necessary.

   Raw data are not always in a form that is meaningful for decision-making purposes. It may be necessary to convert the raw data into a standardized form from which valid conclusions can be drawn and decisions made about an intervention. The most common conversion formats are percentage and rate.

4. Construct a graph to provide a visual display of the data.

   This is a very rewarding part of monitoring behavior! Plotting the data provides a picture of how the behavior is changing over time. Examining the graphs regularly can facilitate timely decision making. Graphs can also enhance communication about behavior. We presented rules for plotting data to ensure consistency in graphing.

5. Interpret the data and make intervention decisions founded on the data.

   A simple approach to analyzing plotted data is to visually inspect the data for trends by looking for three consecutive data points that move in the desired direction. A trend indicates that the intervention is producing the desired results and should be continued. The absence of a trend may suggest that the intervention should be modified.

We provide a self-assessment form for behavioral monitoring in Table 4-6. Use this form periodically during the school year to help ensure that you are using objective data to monitor behavior and to guide decision making about instructional and behavioral interventions.

TABLE 4-6   Behavioral Monitoring of Self-Assessment Form

Never	Seldom	Sometimes	Often	Always
1	2	3	4	5

Use the numbers from the preceding scale to rate the following statements:

1. I monitor my students' behavior as a preventive technique. _____
2. I use objective, systematic methods of monitoring both academic and social behaviors. _____
3. I develop operational definitions for behaviors to be monitored. _____
4. I determine the appropriate measurement system on the basis of the nature of the target behavior. _____
5. I identify times for data collection when the target behavior is most likely to occur. _____
6. I plot and analyze the data that I have collected in order to make decisions and adjust interventions when necessary. _____
7. I convert the raw data when necessary. _____
8. I take the baseline data before I begin an intervention. _____
9. I plot and analyze data on a regular basis. _____
10. I use data on target behaviors as the basis for decision-making about interventions for those target behaviors. _____

Learning Activities

1. Select five behaviors and write an operational definition for each one. Mime the behavior for a partner. That person will then write a definition for the behavior. Compare and discuss the two definitions.
2. Make a list of five excuses why a teacher might choose to not collect data and counter each with a professional reason as to why it is essential to collect behavioral and academic data.
3. Discuss how measuring behavior will help you to justify the program decisions that you make for your class.
4. In small groups, discuss organizational techniques that will make measuring behavior a part of your daily routine.
5. Observe the instructor of this class. Choose a behavior exhibited by this person and follow the six steps listed in Table 4-1. Share your graph with the class.
6. Complete the teacher survey and justify your answers.
7. Read the case study that follows, and then plot the data for Brandon's off-task talking.

Dr. Ice Behavioral Monitoring Case Study

Dr. I. C. Everything often consulted with teachers at Anderson Middle School. At this time, Ms. Proctor, a special education teacher, was having problems with one of her students being off task more than he was on task and thus disturbing the other students. Brandon was observed and several data samples were collected. When Brandon's team met to review the data, they determined that the first target behavior should be "off-task talking," which seemed to be a precursor to other unacceptable behaviors. When this behavior was under control, they would assess and work on other target behaviors.

Dr. ICE had taken baseline data during his initial observations, and a plan was developed to decrease the off-task talking and increase the on-task behavior. Ms. Proctor agreed that she would implement the plan and measure the off-task talking with unrestricted event recording for 3 weeks. At that time, the team would meet to analyze the results.

At the end of the first week, Dr. ICE checked in with Ms. Proctor to review the data. He was dismayed when he checked the data notebook and found that it was incomplete. Ms. Proctor gave him an

	Warm-Up	Direct Teach	Guided Practice	Independent Practice	Total for Period
BASELINE					
Monday	3	2	2	5	12
Tuesday	4	3	3	4	14
Wednesday	2	2	4	4	12
INTERVENTION (Earning game time)					
Thursday	0	1	3	5	9
Friday	1	1	2	6	10
Monday	0	0	2	5	7
Tuesday	0	0	1	6	7
INTERVENTION (Peer buddy system during independent work)					
Monday	0	0	1	3	4
Tuesday	0	0	0	2	2
Wednesday	0	1	0	1	2

FIGURE 4-6   Data Collection Chart for Brandon's Off-Task Talking

angry response when he asked about the missing data. She said that she had not realized how time consuming the data collection process would be and that she did not believe that the intervention was working anyway! Dr. ICE asked her how she had been collecting the data and she said that she had used a small notepad and had made a mark each time Brandon made an off-task comment. Dr. ICE asked about the chart that had been suggested at the meeting. Ms. Proctor replied that she had lost it and that she had decided to obtain daily totals instead of collecting data for each academic period. She said that sometimes she got too busy and forgot to make the tally marks. She wondered if Dr. ICE realized how hard it was to teach a class!

Dr. ICE said that he thought he could devise a system that would help her gather the data that would be needed to determine whether the intervention (i.e., earning time to play an instructional game with a friend if all assignments were completed on time) was working. He purchased a handheld mechanical counter and created a notebook with a data recording chart for each day. Informal observation indicated that Brandon exhibited the highest levels of off-task talking during mathematics, language arts, and social studies. To make data collection more manageable for Ms. Proctor, Dr. ICE determined that the data should be collected only during mathematics instruction. On the data recording chart, each mathematics period was divided into spaces representing the academic activities that occurred during the period (see Figure 4-6).

Dr. ICE explained to Ms. Proctor that she could keep the counter in her pocket and click it each time that Brandon made an off-task comment during mathematics instruction. Then, after each math period, she should record the total number of comments for that day. He also encouraged Ms. Proctor to record the total number of comments associated with each activity, saying that this would enable them to identify the activities that were most likely to be associated with off-task talking. Dr. ICE felt that once Ms. Proctor became more comfortable with data collection, she would be able to record more individual activity data. Dr. ICE told her that he had included the baseline data on the chart and that he would check back at the end of the week. Ms. Proctor agreed to try to keep good data.

Friday afternoon, Dr. ICE returned to Ms. Proctor's classroom. He was pleased to see a complete week's worth of data. Ms. Proctor was also impressed with the ease with which she had been able to collect the data. The counter was a great help. It also did not interfere with her teaching, because she could click it without her students' knowledge. She had, on occasion, been able to note the tally after several activities in one academic time block. She said that she could see how this would yield useful information for assessing the intervention plan. She said that she thought that she would use this technique from this point forward. Dr. ICE told her that he would be back in 2 weeks to review the data.

After 2 weeks, Dr. ICE returned to Anderson Middle School to visit Ms. Proctor. He was pleased to see that the data notebook contained entries for each academic period every day. Ms. Proctor was enthusiastic about using the intervention with Brandon. She said that the data showed a decline in his off-task talking behavior. This was also evident in that she was finding the class easier to teach. She was not spending as much time correcting Brandon; thus, she had more time for the rest of her students.

Three weeks later, Brandon's team met to analyze the data that had been collected. The data showed that the intervention was working and that Brandon's off-task talking had been significantly reduced during most periods. However, it did show that he had a higher rate of off-task talking during independent math work than during any other activity. The team decided to modify the behavior plan to include Brandon working with a partner during independent work. Dr. ICE told Ms. Proctor that he would check in with her in another 2 weeks to see if the plan was working.

Resources

WEBSITES

**www.jimwrightonline.com/php/chartdog_2_0/
    chartdog.php**   ChartDog 2.0: This application allows you to create your own progress-monitoring time-series charts using behavioral data.

CREATING A PROACTIVE LEARNING ENVIRONMENT THROUGH UNIVERSAL-LEVEL SUPPORTS AND INTERVENTIONS

After reading this chapter, you will be able to do the following:

1. Explain schoolwide positive behavioral interventions and supports (SW-PBIS), including the rationale for schoolwide PBIS and its philosophy.

2. Describe the critical attributes of SW-PBIS systems.

3. Describe research support for SW-PBIS.

4. Describe and give examples of the essential features of SW-PBIS programs.

5. Describe the steps for planning and implementing an SW-PBIS program.

6. Describe the assessment and monitoring methods for universal and targeted levels.

Prevention of Challenging Behavior Through Schoolwide Positive Behavioral Interventions and Supports

CHAPTER 5

Big ideas in schoolwide positive behavioral interventions and supports:

- Traditional "get tough" responses to school violence are not the most effective ways to make schools safer and more effective.

- Positive behavioral interventions and supports (PBIS), described throughout this text for use with groups and individual students, are also effective beyond the classroom for the entire school.

- Schoolwide PBIS is not a quick-fix solution. Long-term success requires long-term commitment to systems change.

- To begin to address the challenges of students who exhibit highly problematic, chronic behavioral problems, it is important to improve the school climate for all students.

- Schoolwide PBIS is a data-driven process that relies on data to assess needs, to monitor the fidelity of the implementation of the interventions, and to monitor impact.

In the late 1990s, a series of school shootings carried out by students in those schools changed how schools are managed. Suddenly, national attention was focused on school safety, how to prevent dangerous and severely disruptive behavior, and how to identify and meet the needs of students who might be at risk for dangerous behavior. In addition to high-profile school shootings, the 1990s also brought increased criticism of schools for lack of discipline and problems with drug and alcohol use among students (Sugai & Horner, 2002).

Initially, schools responded to this negative attention by tightening security and adopting "get tough" disciplinary policies that stipulated mandatory responses to a wide range of misbehavior, in some cases, even including behaviors that occur outside of school (Skiba, 2000). Actions taken by schools have included adopting zero-tolerance policies, installing metal detectors or conducting random security checks, conducting random locker searches, placing school safety officers (e.g., law enforcement personnel) on campuses, requiring identification badges for everyone at school, requiring clear book bags for students, requiring all visitors to sign in, and requiring students to remain on campus during lunch periods (Hoffman & Sable, 2006; Skiba, 2000; U.S. Department of Education, 1998).

Despite widespread use, there is no credible evidence to support the belief that zero-tolerance practices produce safer, more orderly schools.

These punitive, controlling responses were intended to make schools safer and more disciplined. However, no credible evidence exists which indicates that these approaches achieve those outcomes (Leone et al., 2003; Skiba, 2000). Furthermore, when used in isolation, without the corresponding efforts to teach and support appropriate behavior, highly punitive approaches are actually associated with increases in the very behaviors that they are intended to eliminate (Horner, Sugai, & Horner, 2000).

As the trend toward more negative, security-oriented disciplinary policies gained momentum, professionals concerned with child welfare, education, and mental health argued that making schools more punitive was unproductive and contrary to the mission of schools and the goals of education. Zero-tolerance polices, in particular, were questioned, with studies showing that harsh, exclusionary punishments are disproportionately applied to males, minority students, and students with disabilities (Leone et al., 2003; Skiba, 2000; Skiba & Knesting, 2002; Skiba, Michael, Nardo, & Peterson, 2000). Furthermore, more than 15 years of data on the effectiveness of zero-tolerance policies have provided no evidence that "get tough" approaches improve student behavior or increase school safety (Leone et al., 2003; Skiba, 2000). It was clear that educators needed more effective tools to prevent and manage disruptive behavior and to identify students who were at risk for dangerous or violent behavior without resorting to the questionable practices of zero tolerance. Also, during this time, as discussed in previous chapters, the 1997 reauthorization of the Individuals with Disabilities Education Act (IDEA) mandated the use of PBIS and functional behavioral assessment for students with disabilities who exhibited chronic challenging behaviors. Requiring PBIS for students with disabilities whose behavior interfered with learning was an important step toward changing our perspectives on discipline and behavior management for all students.

In response to the school shootings in the 1990s, the U.S. Departments of Education and Justice published *Early Warning, Timely Response* (Dwyer, Osher, & Warger, 1998), the first major guide for helping administrators keep schools safe through prevention and early intervention for at-risk students. In 2000, a follow-up guide was published to provide more comprehensive and detailed information on research-based strategies for improving school safety (Dwyer & Osher, 2000). These two publications emphasized prevention and early intervention, organized around a three-tiered approach to improving the school climate for all students and identifying students who require more intensive, individualized supports for challenging behavior. All of these factors have led to the expansion and continuing evolution of PBIS for schoolwide application. There is much support for this new approach to school discipline in large part, because of the growing research base that demonstrates the effectiveness of schoolwide PBIS for improving student behavior and school climate (Bradshaw, Mitchell, & Leaf, 2010; Horner, Sugai, Smolkowski, Eber, Nakasato, & Todd, 2009). In this chapter, we will describe schoolwide PBIS and its research base, explain how to plan and implement schoolwide PBIS, and give examples of elements of schoolwide PBIS.

WHAT ARE SCHOOLWIDE POSITIVE BEHAVIORAL INTERVENTIONS AND SUPPORTS?

Throughout this text, we describe the concepts and practices associated with positive behavioral interventions and supports (PBIS) for preventing and managing challenging behaviors in classrooms and with individual students. As discussed in Chapters 1 and 2, PBIS draws on the principles of applied behavior analysis to achieve socially important changes at the schoolwide and individual student levels. According to the *PBS Implementation Blueprint* (Office of Special Education Programs [OSEP] Center on Positive Behavioral Interventions and Supports, 2004),

> Schoolwide positive behavior support (SW-PBIS) is comprised of a broad range of systemic and individualized strategies for achieving important social and learning outcomes while preventing problem behavior with all students. SW-PBIS is the integration of four theoretical elements:
>
> - Operationally defined and valued outcomes,
> - Behavioral and biomedical science[s],
> - Research-validated practices, and
> - Systems change to both enhance the broad quality with which all students are living/learning, and reduce problem behaviors. (p. 8)

Operationally defined and valued outcomes are specific, measurable indicators of behavior and learning outcomes that are selected and evaluated by using multiple sources of data. In addition, valued outcomes focus on improvement in the quality of life as determined by individual or school preferences and needs.

The **behavioral and biomedical sciences** basis for SW-PBIS refers to the assumptions of applied behavior analysis, which are presented in Table 2-4 of Chapter 2. Overall, these assumptions reflect the fact that behavior is lawful and predictable, is governed by interaction between environmental and physiological factors, and can be changed by manipulating environmental variables.

Reliance on **research-validated practices** is a hallmark of SW-PBIS. Research-validated practices are founded on intervention strategies that have documented evidence of effectiveness, according to the definition of scientifically based evidence presented in Chapter 2. Individual or schoolwide data are used for making decisions about intervention needs and strategies, and for evaluating intervention practices.

Finally, SW-PBIS emphasizes **systems change**, which refers to the reshaping of organizational policies, administrative leadership, operational routines, and resources to facilitate sustained reliance on effective, efficient school management practices (e.g., behavior management at the schoolwide and individual student levels). This systems change approach is a critical feature of SW-PBIS because it focuses on increasing the capacity of schools to solve their own problems. When educators move from responding reactively to challenging behavior to thinking proactively and preventively on a broad scale, they increase their effectiveness and efficiency at improving both the academic and behavioral outcomes of their students.

Four essential theoretical elements differentiate PBIS from other disciplinary approaches: (a) operationally defined outcomes, (b) a foundation in behavioral and biomedical sciences, (c) research-validated practices, and (d) an emphasis on systems change.

TABLE 5-1 Critical Attributes of Schoolwide Positive Behavioral Supports

---

1. A focus on all systems within the school.
2. Attention to the needs of all students through a three-tiered prevention model.
3. Widespread commitment to participating in and supporting SW-PBIS activities.
4. Intervention strategies that are designed to meet the unique needs of each campus.
5. Team-based planning and decision making.
6. An emphasis on an instructional approach to discipline and behavior management.
7. Data-based decision making.
8. Long-term commitment to systems change and implementation of SW-PBIS practices.
9. Continual evaluation and refinement of SW-PBIS interventions.

Critical Attributes of Schoolwide Positive Behavioral Interventions and Supports

A number of critical elements characterize SW-PBIS and differentiate it from most commercial school disciplinary programs and other efforts to improve school safety and student performance. These elements are listed in Table 5-1 and are explained next.

A FOCUS ON ALL SYSTEMS WITHIN THE SCHOOL SW-PBIS focuses not only on the school as a whole, but also on student performance within each subsystem of the school environment. These interconnected systems include classrooms, nonclassroom settings (e.g., cafeteria, bus-loading areas, hallways, parking lots), the school as a whole, and individual students. SW-PBIS involves evaluating student performance in each of these areas and designing interventions to improve student success if needed. Evaluation of each system means considering the extent to which students (both groups and individuals) are successful (both academically and behaviorally) and follow the rules. If problems in any of the systems are identified, interventions are developed to remediate those problems and to prevent future problems.

ATTENTION TO THE NEEDS OF ALL STUDENTS THROUGH A THREE-TIERED PREVENTION MODEL As discussed in Chapter 1, a defining characteristic of SW-PBIS is its fundamental three-tiered prevention and intervention approach. This three-tiered model includes three levels of prevention and intervention that are distinguished by the number of students affected and the intensity of the support services provided (Turnbull et al., 2002). The three levels in this model serve as a structure through which school personnel provide proactive, preventive interventions for all students, while designing timely, efficient, and effective interventions for students who need more intensive services. Because the proactive and preventive elements of SW-PBIS meet the needs of most students, school personnel are able to better focus resources on students who are unresponsive to other schoolwide strategies.

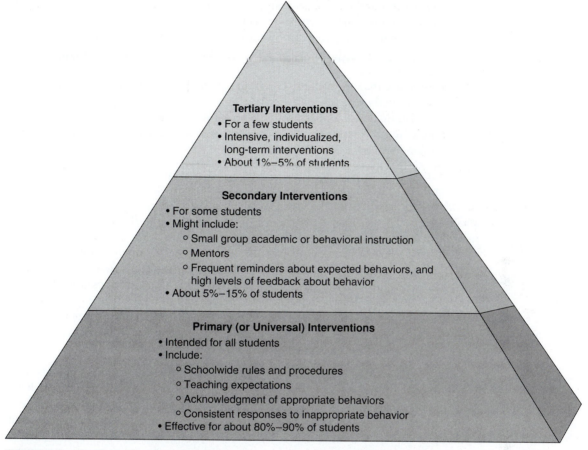

Tertiary Interventions
- For a few students
- Intensive, individualized, long-term interventions
- About 1%–5% of students

Secondary Interventions
- For some students
- Might include:
  ◦ Small group academic or behavioral instruction
  ◦ Mentors
  ◦ Frequent reminders about expected behaviors, and high levels of feedback about behavior
- About 5%–15% of students

Primary (or Universal) Interventions
- Intended for all students
- Include:
  ◦ Schoolwide rules and procedures
  ◦ Teaching expectations
  ◦ Acknowledgment of appropriate behaviors
  ◦ Consistent responses to inappropriate behavior
- Effective for about 80%–90% of students

FIGURE 5-1 The Three-Tiered Model of Prevention *Source:* National Technical Assistance Center on Positive Behavioral Interventions and Supports. Available from www.pbis.org. Reprinted with permission.

Figure 5-1 illustrates the three tiers of prevention and the associated interventions that follow.

- ***Primary-level prevention.*** At the primary level (also referred to as the universal level), universal interventions are used that incorporate strategies to help ensure that all students exhibit appropriate behavior and to reduce the number of new cases of problem behavior and academic difficulties (Ausdemore, Martella, & Marchand-Martella, n.d.). Universal interventions focus on all students and are used by all staff in all settings (OSEP Center on Positive Behavioral Interventions and Supports, 2004). Universal interventions include the following:
  - Establishing schoolwide rules for all areas of the school.
  - Teaching all students the rules and how to follow those rules in all areas of the school.
  - Identifying and modifying antecedent factors associated with problem behavior, including reconfiguring physical environments to reduce

The three-tiered prevention model on which PBIS is founded ensures efficiency in meeting the needs of all students and can minimize the number of students who require the most intensive services.

crowding and congestion, and using visual cues (e.g., signs, clearly delineated boundaries, picture cues) to prompt desired behaviors.

- Using one or more acknowledgment systems to ensure that students receive more attention for appropriate behavior than for inappropriate behavior.
- Ensuring that all teachers use high-quality curricular materials and instructional methods.
- Providing consistent consequences for unacceptable behavior.
- Relying on various forms of data for identifying needs and monitoring implementation of SW-PBIS systems.

According to the Technical Assistance Center on Positive Behavioral Interventions and Supports, primary-level prevention should be effective for 80% to 90% of the population of any given school (OSEP, n.d.). In this chapter, we focus primarily on universal-level supports. However, adherence to the three-tiered model of supports means that schools should provide effective supports for all students, not just those who successfully respond to universal-level systems. Often, schools focus on universal-level systems during their first year or two of SW-PBIS, with the goal of developing positive, proactive practices for addressing the behavior of all students in the school. The extent to which this important foundation is in place, and to which universal systems are dynamic and responsive to changing disciplinary needs, should reduce the number of students who require more intensive supports because of behavioral difficulties.

- *Secondary-level prevention.* Referred to as the **targeted level**, this level relies on interventions for target students who are considered at risk for chronic or serious problem behavior or academic failure, or who continue to exhibit high levels of inappropriate behavior or academic skill deficits despite exposure to universal interventions. The goal of the procedures and interventions at this level is to identify problems early and to provide intensive, targeted supports to remediate those problems. Targeted interventions might include the following:
  - Mentors who meet regularly with identified students.
  - Frequent reminders and feedback about expected behaviors. This type of support can be provided through the use of programs created for targeted-level supports, such as Check In Check Out (Filter, McKenna, Benedict, Horner, Todd, & Watson, 2007; Hawken & Horner, 2003; Todd, Campbell, Meyer, & Horner, 2008); the Behavior Education Program (Crone, Hawken, & Horner, 2010); and Check, Connect, and Expect (Cheney, Stage, Hawken, Lynass, Mielenz, & Waugh, 2009). Most of these programs include regularly scheduled contacts with specific adults for the purpose of providing behavioral reminders and support; some type of daily behavior rating card on which teachers evaluate students' rule-following behaviors throughout the day by using a point system based on schoolwide expectations; and, finally, systematic reinforcement, in which students earn desired reinforcers contingent on earning a minimum number of points on the behavioral rating card.
  - Behavioral contracts for individual students, such as those we describe in Chapter 11.

- Small-group instruction in social, self-control, or anger management skills. We discuss this type of instruction in Chapter 9.
- Small-group instruction to remediate academic skill deficits.
- Close monitoring of student progress to determine the effectiveness of interventions. The data used for monitoring purposes should target the behaviors for which the student was originally referred for targeted-level supports and therefore are more individualized than universal-level monitoring data. At the targeted level, student progress might be tracked through office disciplinary referrals (ODRs), attendance, points earned on daily behavior cards, or behavioral rating scales or checklists completed by teachers.

Approximately 5% to 15% of a school's population will require targeted interventions, and approximately 67% of those students will benefit from these interventions (OSEP Technical Assistance Center on Positive Behavioral Interventions and Supports, n.d.).

- ***Tertiary-level interventions.*** This level focuses on the needs of individual students who require the most intensive, individualized, and long-term interventions, approximately 1% to 5% of a school's population (OSEP Technical Assistance Center on Positive Behavioral Interventions and Supports, n.d.). The goal of tertiary-level supports is to reduce the frequency and intensity of challenging behavior while increasing the student's repertoire of functional, appropriate behaviors. Tertiary-level interventions include the following:
  - Functional behavioral assessment, functional behavioral analysis, and/or structural analysis (i.e., assessment to determine those antecedent events which have the strongest effect on behavior) (Stichter & Conroy, 2005).
  - Individualized behavioral intervention and support plans.
  - Close monitoring of target behaviors to assess the effectiveness of interventions and to facilitate timely problem solving. Direct measurement systems, such as those described in Chapter 4, are often used for this purpose.
  - A team-based approach to developing interventions and problem solving. Teams include not only school personnel and family members, but also the student, when appropriate, and representatives of other service providers who are or may be providing intervention and supports for the child and/or family. Three important concepts are fundamental to tertiary-level PBIS planning: (a) person-centered planning, (b) quality of life, and (c) self-determination. These concepts emphasize the importance of developing goals and designing supports that reflect the individual's preferences, interests, and quality of life. Planning is driven by what the needs and preferences of the individual are more than which services are immediately or conveniently available (Association for Positive Behavior Support, 2007).
  - Wraparound services, or facilitating access for the student and his or her family to local, community, or state services that are needed to help achieve maximum independence, the highest quality of life, and personal satisfaction (OSEP Technical Assistance Center on Positive Behavioral Interventions and Supports, 2010).

> The goal of tertiary-level prevention is to increase individual students' skills with regard to appropriate functional behaviors and to reduce the severity and frequency of challenging behaviors.

WIDESPREAD COMMITMENT TO PARTICIPATING IN AND SUPPORTING SW-PBIS ACTIVITIES   According to the Technical Assistance Center on Positive Behavioral Interventions and Supports (OSEP, 2010), 80% of the school staff should agree that discipline is a concern and a priority, and commit to participating in activities to improve student performance and school climate before beginning an SW-PBIS program. This widespread buy-in is critical to the short-term success and long-term sustainability of SW-PBIS programs and differentiates SW-PBIS from commercial disciplinary programs.

We have witnessed many attempts to improve school climate through the use of one commercial disciplinary program or another, only to have the program gradually disappear because of disuse. A common scenario that we encounter is as follows: The principal (or a staff member) attends a workshop or conference presentation that promotes a particular program. The program sounds good and a decision to purchase it is made. Staff members receive brief in-service training in the program and then are expected to use it. Gradually, staff attention becomes focused elsewhere, the program is used less and less, and eventually it fades away completely. An SW-PBIS approach avoids this problem not only by incorporating the critical attributes described in this section, but also by ensuring that the majority of a school's staff view discipline as an important concern and by obtaining a commitment from the majority of the staff to support the goals of improving school climate and the students' social and academic performance.

INTERVENTION STRATEGIES THAT ARE DESIGNED TO MEET THE UNIQUE NEEDS OF EACH CAMPUS   Every school has unique needs and resources. Multiple variables define a school: student population, staff, location, ethnic and cultural diversity, size, grades served, and community values and expectations, among others. Because of inherent and often significant differences across schools, it is doubtful that any single program that offers a "one size fits all" approach to improving discipline will meet the needs of every school (Horner et al., 2000). SW-PBIS is not a package program. Rather, it is a model for educators to follow in designing disciplinary systems that directly meet the needs and match the personality of each campus. Furthermore, as a school changes over time (e.g., as the student population changes), the features of that school's SW-PBIS program can be adjusted to meet new challenges. Although many SW-PBIS programs share similar features, each school's PBIS program is distinctly its own. No two schools use exactly the same SW-PBIS program. It is individualization and flexibility that make PBIS effective and sustainable and that also make PBIS appealing to the school personnel.

> SW-PBIS is responsive to the unique culture and needs of each individual campus.

TEAM-BASED PLANNING AND DECISION MAKING   A team that represents the key stakeholders of the school should make decisions about SW-PBIS interventions. Often referred to as the PBIS leadership team, school PBIS teams typically include the following individuals:

- Administrator: Administrative leadership is critical to the sustainability of SW-PBIS; for this reason, the school principal or an assistant principal must be a part of the leadership team (Horner et al., 2004). One of us (BKS)once provided training and implementation guidance for SW-PBIS teams from several schools. One of the teams included enthusiastic team members but no administrator.

During the course of the year, this team struggled to keep PBIS at the forefront of the school's activities, in large part because the principal was not closely involved and, therefore, did not provide the support and leadership needed by the team. For example, the team had a difficult time obtaining ODR data from the office, and team members were seldom given time to provide status reports to the school faculty during meetings. Because of a lack of administrative leadership, school staff simply viewed PBIS as another committee that had little to do with the day-to-day activities of the school. This school had virtually no improvement in the problems that originally led the principal to apply for her school's participation in the SW-PBIS training project (e.g., a high number of student behavioral problems). Administrative participation on the leadership team communicates commitment and support for SW-PBIS activities and ensures that administrators understand which resources are needed to successfully implement the program.

- Teacher from each grade level for elementary teams, and broad representation of content areas for secondary teams.
- Special education teacher.
- Representatives from support personnel (e.g., counselor, speech teacher, gym teacher).
- Staff representative (e.g., lunchroom monitor, playground monitor, bus driver, cafeteria worker, office worker).
- Parent: Sometimes, parents are ad hoc members of the team, attending some, but not all, meetings to provide input and to facilitate communication about PBIS systems with parent and/or community groups.
- Student, if appropriate: Some teams, particularly in secondary schools, invite student input into certain aspects of the PBIS system by having one or more student representatives attend some team meetings. We recommend that student team members be representative of the population of students who are "consumers" of the school disciplinary system (i.e., students who have experienced ODRs, detention, or other disciplinary actions). Their input can be valuable in terms of identifying factors that will increase the effectiveness of universal systems for these students.

The leadership team is responsible for reviewing data to identify disciplinary needs, collecting data on a regular basis for decision making, soliciting input from school faculty and staff about all aspects of the SW-PBIS program, designing universal interventions, training faculty and staff, keeping school faculty informed about SW-PBIS activities and progress, and developing SW-PBIS materials and activities (or assigning these tasks to others). These duties are accomplished through regular team meetings and by ensuring high levels of structure during team meetings. In the first stages of planning and implementation, teams may need to meet frequently (e.g., weekly or biweekly). As systems become established, the team should be able to meet less frequently, but should continue meeting on a regular basis in order to monitor data and address new problems that may emerge as the year progresses. Leadership teams are most productive when they have an agenda for each meeting, assign responsibilities to team members for completing various tasks, and have systematic procedures for providing updates on activities. Finally, the leadership team must maintain close communication with the rest of the school faculty and should publicize meeting schedules and encourage others to attend.

SW-PBIS emphasizes *teaching* the expected behaviors and views behavioral challenges as skill deficits.

AN EMPHASIS ON AN INSTRUCTIONAL APPROACH TO DISCIPLINE AND BEHAVIOR MANAGEMENT   Under a schoolwide PBIS approach, students are taught appropriate behavioral skills in the same manner that they are taught academic skills. Likewise, challenging behaviors are viewed as skill deficits (i.e., the student has not learned a more appropriate way of getting his or her needs met), and an important part of intervention is teaching the student appropriate functional behaviors.

Schools that successfully implement SW-PBIS devote much effort to teaching students how to behave and how to follow the rules. Typically, time is devoted at the beginning of the school year for this instruction, complete with schedules for teaching the rules (i.e., who will be teaching, when, and where), and lesson plans developed by individual teachers, teams of teachers, or the school's SW-PBIS team. Every school uses a slightly different approach to teaching expectations, but the common denominator is that students are actively taught the rules and expected behaviors. We do not simply assume that the students will know what to do. In addition, expectations are retaught throughout the year, as needed. For example, one school's ODR data indicated that referrals increased after standardized statewide tests were administered in April. The PBIS leadership team at this school developed a plan for reteaching the schoolwide expectations on a regular basis from April until the end of the school year. This reteaching reminds the students about the expected behaviors, but may also help the staff be more consistent in acknowledging rule-following behavior and responding to rule violations.

An instructional approach to discipline means that when students make behavioral errors (i.e., when they misbehave), one intervention is to reteach the rule that was violated. At one elementary school that is implementing SW-PBIS, the fifth-grade teachers established a procedure for responding to minor rule violations. First, each teacher created a laminated set of sentence strips on which were written the schoolwide expectations and how those expectations apply in the classroom. These laminated rule reminders were posted prominently in the room. When a student exhibited a minor misbehavior, the first response was to retrieve the sentence strip showing the rule that the student had violated and review that rule with the student. These teachers clearly understood the concept of an instructional approach to discipline, and their classroom management procedures reflected that concept.

DATA-BASED DECISION MAKING   Most schools recognize when problems exist within the school (e.g., high levels of problem behavior and/or low levels of academic success), and most schools take steps to fix those problems. A distinguishing characteristic of SW-PBIS schools, however, is their reliance on objective and multiple sources of data to identify needs and evaluate the effectiveness of interventions. Each level of support relies on somewhat different data to identify needs and monitor the effectiveness of interventions. We discuss data types and purposes later in this chapter.

LONG-TERM COMMITMENT TO SYSTEMS CHANGE AND IMPLEMENTATION OF PBIS PRACTICES   Because of their frustration with challenging behavior and their need to "fix the problem," school and district administrators often take one of two steps. They might purchase a commercial disciplinary program with the expectation that the program will produce the desired changes, or they may adopt a "get tough" approach in an attempt to crack down on and, therefore, solve the discipline problem. Unfortunately, as we have discussed previously, these approaches seldom result in long-term desired changes because neither approach addresses the underlying reasons why discipline is a problem in the first place. A more permanent solution to the problem of challenging behavior requires a different philosophy about challenging behavior and a different approach to discipline, one that focuses on preventing challenging behavior and creating more effective school environments for all students. These types of changes will not occur in a single school year. In fact, the Technical Assistance Center on Positive Behavioral Interventions and Supports recommends a 3- to 5-year commitment to implementing schoolwide PBIS. Long-term commitment is necessary to achieve the systemic changes required in an SW-PBIS model and to fully plan and implement the three tiers of prevention practices.

> SW-PBIS requires a long-term commitment to systems change, during which the school's PBIS programs are continually evaluated and refined to reflect the changing needs of the school population.

CONTINUAL EVALUATION AND REFINEMENT OF SW-PBIS INTERVENTIONS   Any SW-PBIS program is a work in progress. SW-PBIS teams must never stop evaluating their PBIS systems (by analyzing ODR data) and fine-tuning those systems. Schools are dynamic entities that have ever-changing student and staff populations and needs. Any disciplinary program that is unable to adapt to reflect these changes will probably fail. The dynamic nature of SW-PBIS means that interventions will always be responsive to the unique needs of any school population. This will help ensure long-term durability and success.

RESEARCH SUPPORT FOR SCHOOLWIDE PRIMARY-LEVEL PREVENTION

The research support for primary-level prevention is encouraging. Over the past decade, numerous studies have been published in peer-reviewed journals that document the effectiveness of schoolwide PBIS. Researchers and teams of school personnel have reported up to 60% reductions in ODRs because of SW-PBIS programs (Horner et al., 2004; Sprague et al., 2001; Taylor-Greene et al., 1997). In addition, SW-PBIS interventions have a record of documented effectiveness in improving student behavior in specific areas of the school. Studies have shown reductions in problem behavior during recess (Lewis, Powers, & Kelk, 2002; Todd, Haugen, Anderson, & Spriggs, 2002), on school buses (Putnam, Handler, Ramirez-Platt, & Luiselli, 2003), in hallways (Oswald, Safran, & Johanson, 2005), in cafeterias (Kartub, Taylor-Greene, March, & Horner, 2000), and during morning arrivals (Nelson, Colvin, & Smith, 1996).

The use of PBIS, particularly universal-level supports, in alternative educational and treatment settings is a relatively new extension of schoolwide PBIS. Emerging research suggests positive outcomes of universal-level PBIS in various types of alternative settings. For example, the implementation of universal-level

A broad research base supports SW-PBIS as an efficacious approach to improving student performance in a wide range of academic and social areas.

PBIS in juvenile correctional facilities has produced reductions in serious behavioral incidents, the use of physical restraint, and classroom removals (Jolivette & Nelson, 2010; Nelson, Sugai, & Smith, 2005; OSEP, n.d.). A 3-year case study of the effects of universal-level PBIS in a disciplinary alternative school showed reductions in both serious behavioral incidents and the number of students who exhibited aggressive behaviors (Simonsen, Britton, & Young, 2010). Finally, Miller and his colleagues reported reductions in the use of physical restraints and seclusionary time-outs for students with emotional/behavioral disorders at an alternative school (Miller, George, & Fogt, 2005). Researchers continue to explore the application of PBIS in alternative settings. For example, Jolivette and Sprague recently began a multistate examination of PBIS in juvenile correctional settings (K. Jolivette, personal communication, October, 2010). In 2009, Texas passed a law mandating the implementation of PBIS in all 10 of the state's secure juvenile correctional facilities. Brenda Scheuermann, C. M. Nelson, Eugene Wang, and Michael Turner began guiding and overseeing the implementation of this mandate in the summer of 2010, and analyses of outcomes of this initiative will begin in spring 2011. Researchers have just begun to examine universal-level PBIS in disciplinary and treatment settings; however, only the most rudimentary applications and analyses have been used for this purpose. Future research will apply more sophisticated research designs to continue to define effective universal-level practices in disciplinary settings. That research should examine specific design elements, valid and reliable assessment methods, and outcome variables. In particular, we need to know more about the most efficacious design of universal-level components in various types of alternative settings, as well as about both immediate effects on behavior and other areas of performance and long-term effects on behavior, academic performance, recidivism, graduation rates, and other variables.

Finally, PBIS has also been associated with improvements in academic achievement as measured by student performance on standardized achievement tests (Lassen, Steele, & Sailor, 2006; Luiselli, Putnam, Handler, & Feinberg, 2005). These findings are particularly important given the fact that student performance on standardized achievement tests is the main indicator used by the public to judge school effectiveness. Other researchers are examining the amount of time associated with administering disciplinary procedures, working under the hypothesis that interventions that improve student behavior will result in students remaining in the classroom, which should improve academic achievement. Scott and Barrett (2004) examined the amount of student instruction time that was lost because of ODRs and suspensions, and the amount of time that was gained after SW-PBIS was implemented. Calculating that a student loses an average of 20 minutes of instructional time for every ODR, these researchers reported a gain of 27.7 days for students during Year 1 of a schoolwide PBIS intervention and a gain of 31.2 days in Year 2. They also reported a gain of 45 and 55 student-instruction days, respectively, in the first 2 years of SW-PBIS implementation as a result of fewer disciplinary suspensions.

In all, the data supporting schoolwide PBIS are strong and convincing. Research continues to examine specific elements of schoolwide PBIS (e.g., interventions for classroom and nonclassroom areas and for various types of behavioral concerns) and the efficacy of specific interventions at the primary, secondary, and tertiary levels.

FEATURES AND EXAMPLES OF UNIVERSAL INTERVENTIONS

As discussed in the previous section, every school's PBIS program is slightly different, reflecting the unique needs and character of each school. However, several features are recommended as essential components in primary-level prevention (OSEP Technical Assistance Center on Positive Behavioral Interventions and Supports, 2004; Horner et al., 2004). In general, these features reflect antecedent, teaching, and consequential interventions. Antecedent interventions include strategies for ensuring that the expectations are clear and for helping students remember those expectations. Teaching interventions include making sure that students know what is expected by teaching the school rules as they apply in all areas of the school. Finally, consequence interventions include strategies for acknowledging appropriate behavior and providing consistent responses for inappropriate behavior. In this section, we describe these features and provide examples of each feature from schools across the country. These features are listed in Table 5-2.

THREE TO FIVE SCHOOLWIDE RULES ARE DEVELOPED. As we will discuss in Chapter 6, classroom rules should be limited to a few positively stated expectations; the same is true for schoolwide rules. Because one underlying assumption of SW-PBIS is that disciplinary problems sometimes reflect a lack of clarity about what is expected, the first step in developing universal-level interventions is for the staff to agree on three to five positively stated expectations. Table 5-3 shows examples of school expectations from schools using SW-PBIS. Although each set of expectations differs slightly, note the commonalities: All include no more than five rules; all rules are stated positively; and many address safety, respect, and responsibility. Also, note that many schools tailor the rules to reflect their school motto or school mascot.

Once school rules have been established, signs and other reminders are provided throughout the school to remind students (and staff) about the expectations. For example, Figures 5-2 and 5-3 show examples of signs used by two different schools to remind students of schoolwide expectations. One of us (BKS) works with several schools, guiding the development and implementation

> Three to five schoolwide rules form the basis for SW-PBIS programs.

TABLE 5-2 • Features of Schoolwide Positive Behavioral Support Systems

1. Three to five schoolwide rules are developed, and reminders of those rules are provided throughout the school (e.g., signs, announcements, posters).

2. There is a rule matrix in which each rule is defined for each area of the school.

3. Systematic, planned instruction is provided to all students in order to teach the school rules and to reteach as needed.

4. Acknowledgment systems provide feedback to students with regard to rule-following behaviors.

5. There is differentiation between classroom-managed and office-managed behavioral infractions.

6. There is a system of predetermined, consistent consequences for use in correcting problem behaviors.

TABLE 5-3 Examples of Schoolwide Rules

Elementary

**Parkway Elementary School*, Frederick County Public Schools, Frederick, Maryland

- Respect Ourselves
- Respect Others
- Respect Property

**Stevens Forest Elementary School*, Howard County Public School System, Columbia, Maryland

- Be Respectful
- Be Responsible
- Be Ready

▲*Maplebrook Elementary School*, Humble Independent School District, Humble, Texas

Mascot: Maplebrook Bears (Note: Rules, reinforcement systems, reminder signs, and other aspects of their SW-PBIS system are designed around a "bee" theme, reflecting that bears like honey, and bees make honey.)

- Bee Respectful
- Bee Safe
- Bee Ready

Middle Schools

**Governor Thomas Johnson Middle School*, Frederick County Public Schools, Frederick, Maryland

Motto: Respect T.O.S.

- **T**ask
- **O**thers
- **S**elf

▲*El Campo Middle School*, El Campo Independent School District, El Campo, Texas

Motto: Show your RICEBIRD PRIDE

- Be **P**repared
- Show **R**espect
- Be **I**nformed
- Follow **D**irections
- Be Saf**E** at School

▲*Fannin Middle School*, Amarillo Independent School District, Amarillo, Texas

Motto: The Fannin Four

- Responsible
- Respectful
- Successful
- Safe

▲*Mann Middle School*, Amarillo Independent School District, Amarillo, Texas

- Be Safe
- Be Prepared
- Be Respectful
- Be Involved

High Schools

*Kenwood High School, Baltimore County Public Schools, Essex, Maryland

Motto: Kenwood Pride

- Be There and Prepared
- Live Responsibly
- Uphold Integrity
- Earn and Give Respect

Lansdowne High School, Baltimore County Public Schools, Baltimore, Maryland

- Be Respectful
- Be Responsible
- Be Ready

▲*El Campo High School*, El Campo Independent School District, El Campo, Texas

- **E**arn and give respect
- **C**ommit to excellence
- **H**onor yourself and others, and
- **S**uccess will follow

Sources: ▲Information from the various schools listed; Reprinted with permission. * PBIS Maryland: School Examples. Available online at http://www.pbismaryland.org/. Reprinted with permission.

of SW-PBIS programs. In one middle school, students created a video about the school's SW-PBIS program, including explanations of the schoolwide expectations and role-plays of students demonstrating the rules. The video plays on a monitor in the lobby of the school, providing an interesting reminder of the SW-PBIS system and school rules for students, staff, and all visitors to the school. In an elementary school, lines were painted down the center of each hallway to help students remember that they are to walk on the right side of the hallway. In addition, large stop signs were painted on the floor at each intersection to prompt students to stop and look before crossing the hallway intersection. Several schools include reminders about the schoolwide rules in the morning announcements.

THERE IS A RULE MATRIX IN WHICH EACH RULE IS DEFINED FOR EACH AREA OF THE SCHOOL.   As you can see from Table 5-3, schoolwide rules are broadly stated. These expectations must be operationally defined according to specific behaviors that reflect each rule in all areas of the school. Typically, this is done by developing a rule matrix that lists each rule and the behaviors associated with each rule in all

RESPECT During Arrival

TASK

- Remove your hats when you come in the building
- Do not use vending machines
- Remember not to eat or drink in the gym/cafeteria

OTHERS

- Find a seat quickly and sit down
- Do not yell
- Listen for announcements

SELF

- Go directly to gym/cafeteria
- Ask permission if you need to leave
- Walk when you enter and exit the gym/cafeteria

FIGURE 5-2 Sign from Governor Thomas Johnson Middle School, Frederick, Maryland *Source:* PBIS Maryland: School Examples. Available online at www.pbismaryland.org/schoolexamples.htm. Reprinted with permission.

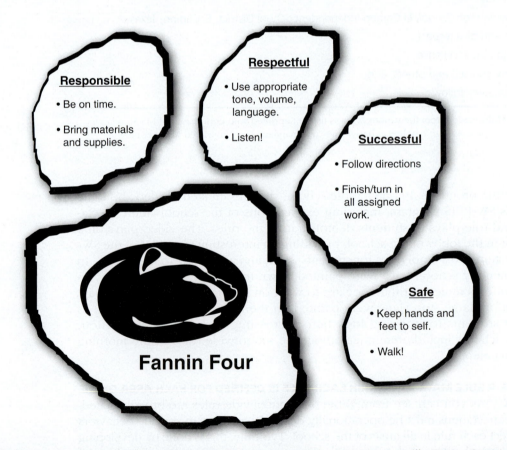

Responsible
- Be on time.
- Bring materials and supplies.

Respectful
- Use appropriate tone, volume, language.
- Listen!

Successful
- Follow directions
- Finish/turn in all assigned work.

Safe
- Keep hands and feet to self.
- Walk!

Fannin Four

FIGURE 5-3 Sign from Fannin Middle School, Amarillo Independent School District, Amarillo, Texas *Source:* Fannin Middle School PBIS program, Amarillo Independent School District, Amarillo, Texas. Reprinted with permission.

TABLE 5-4   Rule Matrix for Parkway Elementary School, Frederick, Maryland

BEHAVIORAL EXPECTATIONS
Parkway Elementary

School Expectations	Respect Ourselves	Respect Others	Respect Property
All Settings	Be on task. Always do your best. Work cooperatively.	Follow adult directions. Be kind. Keep hands, feet, and other objects to yourselves. Share/Help others. Use inside voice.	Recycle. Clean up after yourself. Use only what you need to use. Take care of your own belongings.
Hallways	Walk quietly. Maintain personal space.	Walk to the right in the hallways. Travel without talking.	Keep hallways clean. Pick up trash.
Playground	Choose a game or activity with school equipment.	Play safely. Include others. Share equipment. Take turns. Encourage others.	Pick up litter. Use equipment properly. Return equipment to its proper place.
Bathrooms	Take the pass. Flush the toilet. Wash your hands.	Respect privacy. Use soft voices.	Keep the bathroom clean.
Lunchroom	Eat your own food. Come prepared.	Practice good table manners. Use quiet voices.	Pick up and clean floor and around your table. Stay seated; get up only with permission.
Library and Computer Lab	Return books on time. Come prepared.	Use whisper voices.	Take care of books, magazines, and computers. Push in chairs.
Assembly	Sit in one spot. Stay in your space.	Sit quietly. Eyes on speaker. Appropriate applause.	Sit in chairs correctly.
Buses	Walk to seat. Remain seated. Keep hands and feet in your own space. Enter and exit quietly and orderly.	Quiet voices. Keep hands and feet to yourselves.	Eat at appropriate time. Keep bus clean. Pick up trash.

Source: PBIS Maryland: School Examples. Available online at www.pbismaryland.org/schoolexamples.htm. Reprinted with permission.

areas of the school. Table 5-4 shows an example of a rule matrix from one elementary school. Maplebrook Elementary School in Humble, Texas, uses colorful flip charts to help teachers and other staff members remember the schoolwide expectations (see Figure 5-4). Each page of the flip chart lists a different area of the school (e.g., hallways, playground, morning arrival, cafeteria, restrooms) and

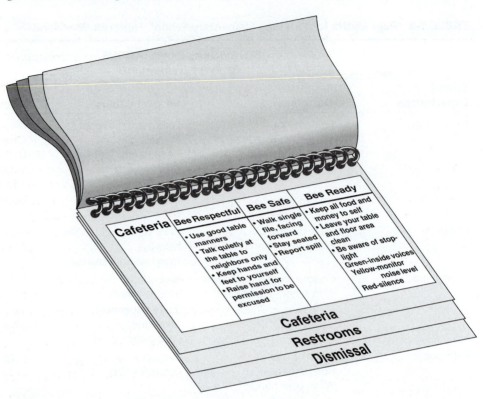

FIGURE 5-4 Maplebrook Elementary School Rule Flip Chart *Source:* Maplebrook Elementary School PBIS program. Humble Independent School District, Humble, Texas. Adapted with permission.

operationally defines the three schoolwide rules (i.e., Bee Respectful, Bee Safe, Bee Ready) for that particular area. The flip charts are simple, attractive, and easy for teachers to use as a quick reference tool.

Defining the broadly stated expectations for all areas of the school is an important step in developing universal systems. In essence, these specific expectations become the behavioral curriculum for the school: the skills that students are expected to learn and that all teachers and staff are expected to teach. This helps facilitate consistency in behavioral expectations across environments and across staff members; lack of consistency in expected student behaviors and adult response to student behavior is a common concern among teachers and staff. These behavioral definitions also provide a common language for all adults in a school to use when prompting students for particular behaviors, or when correcting behavioral infractions.

> Schoolwide rules should be directly and explicitly taught in all areas of the school.

SYSTEMATIC, PLANNED INSTRUCTION IS PROVIDED TO ALL STUDENTS IN ORDER TO TEACH THE SCHOOL RULES, AND TO RETEACH AS NEEDED. As discussed earlier in this chapter, instruction in appropriate behavioral skills is a fundamental principle of SW-PBIS. Teachers and administrators in SW-PBIS schools do not simply assume that setting rules is sufficient to change behavior. They also ensure that every student understands those rules by actively teaching the rules, usually during the first few days of school.

For example, Fern Ridge Middle School in Elmira, Oregon, has been using SW-PBIS since 1995. In the first years of their PBIS efforts, two full days at the beginning of the school year were spent teaching students the school rules and expectations (Fern Ridge Middle School, 1999). After that first year, minor changes were made so that all students participate on the first day, and only the sixth graders participate on the second day. During these teaching days, groups of students follow a schedule in which they rotate through all of the training areas in the school (e.g., hallway, gym, main office, media and technology center, bus-loading area). Teaching activities in each training area are planned and presented by groups of teachers and staff, approximately six to eight staff members per training area. Teaching activities include explaining the rules for each area, conducting skits to demonstrate examples and nonexamples of rule-following behaviors, and having each student practice the expected behaviors. Substitute teachers and volunteers are invited to participate in the activities, and students earn high levels of reinforcement for their participation in the role-plays. It is clear that this level of attention toward teaching students the expected behaviors should increase the likelihood of everyone (staff and students) remembering and following the rules!

ACKNOWLEDGMENT SYSTEMS PROVIDE FEEDBACK TO STUDENTS WITH REGARD TO RULE-FOLLOWING BEHAVIORS.   An important component of SW-PBIS programs is ensuring that students receive more attention for appropriate behavior than inappropriate behavior. This is accomplished by both teaching staff to provide high levels of praise and verbal acknowledgment of rule-following behavior and by using schoolwide token systems. It is important to remember that a schoolwide reinforcement plan is just one component of PBIS. Reinforcement alone *does not* constitute SW-PBIS. It is easy to focus on this at the expense of other less exciting components (e.g., team decision making, data-based decision making). We often talk with teachers who tell us that they teach at an SW-PBIS school because their school uses a schoolwide reinforcement system. However, when questioned, these teachers are sometimes unable to describe any other component of their SW-PBIS system (e.g., schoolwide rules, procedures for teaching those rules).

We discuss how to develop reinforcement systems for individuals and groups in Chapters 10 and 11. The steps listed in those chapters also will help you design a schoolwide reinforcement plan, which will include identifying target behaviors (which will probably be the schoolwide expectations), tokens (typically school theme-based tickets, cards, or other items that are given when a desired behavior is exhibited), reinforcers, and structured times and procedures for students to exchange tokens for reinforcers. For most universal-level acknowledgment systems, students spend their tokens in a school store to purchase school supplies or other desired items or activities, or they turn in tokens in order to participate in a school drawing for desired reinforcers. In addition to a schoolwide acknowledgment system, many schools implement reinforcement systems that target specific behavioral concerns, such as dress code, tardies, or texting, or specific problem areas, such as the playground, cafeteria, or parking lot. The following are a few examples of schoolwide reinforcement plans that reflect these formats.

The reinforcement program at Fern Ridge Middle School includes multiple components (Fern Ridge Middle School, 1999). First, students earn "High Five" tickets for exhibiting rule-following behaviors. The school rules (the High Fives) are written on each ticket, and the rule that the student was observed following is circled when the ticket is given to the student. The student writes his or her name on the ticket, which can be used for a variety of reinforcer options, including participation in raffles and obtaining High Five buttons. High Five buttons are numbered, and from time to time, random numbers are called over the intercom. Students who are wearing buttons with those numbers may go to the office for a special treat. Still another component of the Fern Ridge reinforcement program is the Gold Card. All students are given a Gold Card, which entitles them to special privileges (e.g., being allowed to eat popcorn at lunch, being allowed in the hallway without a pass, getting out early to go to lunch or the bus, attending a Gold Card game night at the school). Students lose their Gold Card if they receive detention, an ODR, or a bus citation. Gold Cards are reissued quarterly. The last component of the High Five program is the Sub-Five program. Substitute teachers are taught the High Five program and are given Sub-Five tickets to use while they are substituting. Any Sub-Five ticket that a student receives may be exchanged for five High Fives from their regular teacher. As a result, students are highly motivated to cooperate with substitutes! This is an excellent example of developing a PBIS intervention to address a specific problem.

In Amarillo, Texas, Mesa Verde Elementary School uses a multicomponent reinforcement program. One interesting program is Thunderbird Feathers (the Thunderbird is the school mascot), which are given by administrators to classes that are observed following the school rules. The teacher's name and the rule that was being followed are written on the ticket and posted on a large Thunderbird. At the end of each grading period, the class with the most tickets is recognized and earns a reinforcer (e.g., free gym time, flying kites, a popcorn party). Another Amarillo school, Puckett Elementary, home of the Puckett Panthers, uses a similar program. Classes earn Pawsitive Behavior Paws for following school rules. Paws are color-coded by grade level and posted in the hallway. When a grade level's Paws reach designated points in the hallway, classes at that grade level earn a reinforcer.

> Schoolwide reinforcement plans should address specific needs as determined by the data.

The staff at Kenwood High School in Essex, Maryland, recognize appropriate student behavior by giving "Gotcha" coupons (see Figure 5-5). Gotcha coupons are entered in drawings for weekly, monthly, and quarterly reinforcers. Students at Governor Thomas Johnson Middle School can earn "TJs" for rule-following behaviors. TJs may be entered in raffles, used in the school store, or used in classrooms for reinforcers determined by the teacher (e.g., the teacher might allow a student to use TJs to obtain materials if the student has forgotten his or her book or other materials).

Data should drive the reinforcement plan. For example, the PBIS leadership team at Maplebrook Elementary School in Humble, Texas, became aware of increasing behavioral problems in the cafeteria because the number of ODRs from the cafeteria gradually increased over several months. In response, the team developed a reinforcement plan for the cafeteria. Their plan consisted of Cafeteria Coupons, which were filled out by the cafeteria monitor or teacher on an intermittent basis when students were observed following the cafeteria rules.

Gotcha!

Presented to: _____ Room_____

Location	**Be there and prepared**
☐ Classroom	☐ On time
☐ Cafeteria	☐ Materials
☐ Hallway	☐ Drill ☐ Other
☐ Bus	☐ Homework
☐ Other	

Steps

Live responsibly

1. Name behavior and
   expectation.
2. Fill out slip.
3. Give positive verbal/social
   acknowledgment.
4. Give slip to student.
5. Remind student to place
   in folder.

☐ Planner   ☐ Pride
☐ Effort   ☐ Other
☐ Organization

Uphold integrity
☐ Honesty   ☐ Other
☐ Good Citizenship
☐ Accountability

Earn and give respect
☐ Dress
☐ Self-Control
☐ Kindness   ☐ Other
☐ Courtesy

Given by:_____

Date:_____   Time:_____

FIGURE 5-5 Kenwood High School Gotcha Coupon *Source:* PBIS Maryland: School Examples. Available online at www.pbismaryland.org/schoolexamples.htm. Reprinted with permission.

Cafeteria Coupons (see Figure 5-6) were printed on 3-sheet carbonless paper; one copy was sent home with the student, and one copy was placed in a Prize Patrol box. There was one Prize Patrol box in the cafeteria for each grade level. During monthly drawings, one coupon was drawn from each box and the students whose names were drawn earned a reinforcer. As a result of the intervention, cafeteria behavior improved so dramatically that Cafeteria Coupons are no longer used.

In Chapter 1, we made the case that to change children's behavior, teachers must change their own behavior. In Chapter 10, you will learn that praise is an underused, but important, behavior change technique. Many SW-PBIS programs include components to reinforce teachers for desired changes in behavior (i.e., to reinforce teachers for acknowledging appropriate student behavior and adhering to the school's SW-PBIS plan). For example, teachers at Kenwood High School in Essex, Maryland, enter their name on the Gotcha coupons given to students. In the raffles, teachers whose names are on the Gotcha coupons that are

SW-PBIS plans should include reinforcement contingencies for staff, as well as for students!

FIGURE 5-6 Maplebrook Elementary School Cafeteria Coupons
Source: Maplebrook Elementary School PBIS program, Humble Independent School District, Humble, Texas. Reprinted with permission.

drawn earn a reinforcer. At Mesa Verde Elementary in Amarillo, Texas, administrators award Thunderbird Bucks to teachers who are observed implementing the school SW-PBIS plan. Thunderbird Bucks may be exchanged for various reinforcers, such as special treats, wearing jeans for a day, or having an extended lunch period.

THERE IS DIFFERENTIATION BETWEEN CLASSROOM-MANAGED AND OFFICE-MANAGED BEHAVIORAL INFRACTIONS. To ensure consistency in responding to disciplinary infractions and to minimize the instructional time lost as a result of disciplinary consequences, SW-PBIS leadership teams are advised to determine which behavioral problems should be managed in the classroom by the teacher, and which problems should result in ODRs for administrative intervention. These two categories are referred to as either "minor" and "major" behavioral problems or "classroom-managed" or "teacher-managed" and "office-managed" problems. A common practice is for leadership teams to develop a flowchart for teachers and staff to follow in managing inappropriate behavior. Figure 5-7 shows a disciplinary flowchart used by Kenwood High School in Essex, Maryland.

To ensure consistency, school staff should clearly describe the types of behaviors that constitute minor infractions and those which are considered major infractions. The forms shown in Figures 5-8 and 5-9 provide an interesting and detailed description of the levels of problem behavior and the associated consequences. These comprehensive documents clarify the types of behavioral infractions and possible and required consequences for different levels of problem behavior, all of which should increase consistency in the responses to problem behaviors.

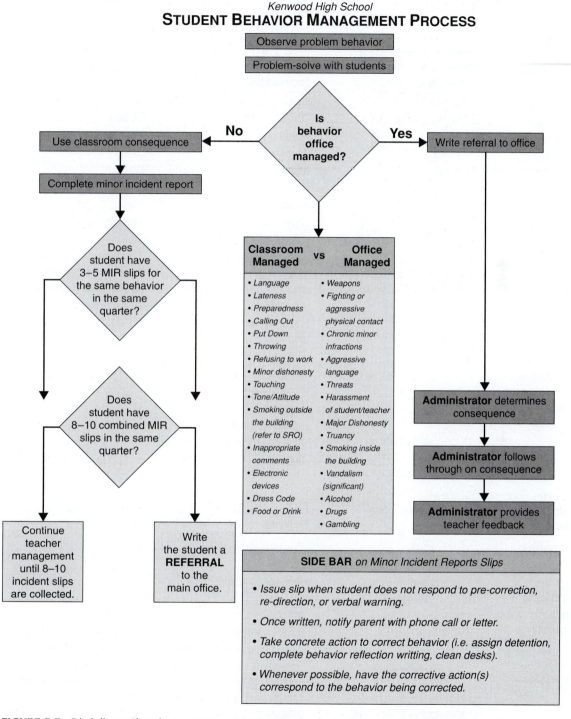

FIGURE 5-7 Disciplinary Flowchart   *Source:* PBIS Maryland: School Examples. Available online at www.pbismaryland.org/schoolexamples.htm. Reprinted with permission.

	Consequences		
Level 1: Behaviors that Impact Only the Student	**Level 2: Behaviors that Interfere with the Learning of Others**	**Level 3: Behaviors that Affect an Orderly Environment**	**Level 4: Harmful/Illegal Behaviors**
-Not prepared -Out of seat -Breaking pencils -Not following directions -Whining -Playing in desk -Not doing class-work -Not in line -Sleeping -Copying behaviors -Not listening -Leaning in chair -Refusing to work -Crawling on floor -Not taking responsibility for action -No homework -Not having a pencil	-Talking out -Visiting/talking -Inappropriate noises -Tattling -Touching -Poking -Standing on furniture -Constant talking -Out of seat and interfering with others' learning -Crawling on floor and interfering with others' learning -Inappropriate chair manners -Consistently not following directions	-Talking back to adult -Throwing things -Teasing -Lying -Cheating -Forgery -Inappropriate language -Tantrums -Climbing in bathroom -Looking under bathroom stalls -Pushing -Disrespect to others -Leaving room without permission -Hallway behaviors -Banging on window -Profane hand gestures -Pinching -Vandalizing school property -Spitting on others -Bullying	-Actions that cause harm -Stealing -Fighting -Drugs -Weapons -Punching -Biting -Throwing furniture -Stealing -Threatening to do injury to person or property -Sexual harassment -Sexual behaviors
Ideas for Controlling Behavior	**Ideas for Controlling Behavior**	**Ideas for Controlling Behavior**	**Ideas for Controlling Behavior**
-Eye contact -Proximity -High levels of supervision -Discussion about expectations -Verbal warning -Preteaching of expectations	-Eye contact -Proximity -High level of supervision -Discussion about expectations -Verbal warning -Preteaching of expectations -Reteaching of school rules/expected behaviors -Link rewards to appropriate behaviors	-Eye contact -Proximity -High level of supervision -Discussion about expectations -Verbal warning -Preteaching of expectations -Reteaching of school rules/expected behaviors -Link rewards to appropriate behaviors	-Eye contact -Proximity -High level of supervision -Discussion about expectations -Preteaching of expectations -Reteaching of school rules/expected behaviors -Link rewards to appropriate behaviors

FIGURE 5-8   Behavioral Definitions from General John Stricker Middle School, Baltimore, Maryland   *Source:* PBIS Maryland: School Examples. Available online at www.pbismaryland.org/schoolexamples.htm. Reprinted with permission.

-Reteaching of school rules/ expected behaviors -Link rewards to appropriate behaviors	-Consultation with grade-level teams/school counselor/ school psychologist/for classroom/individual behavior management ideas	-Consultation with grade-level teams/school counselor/ school psychologist for classroom/individual behavior management ideas	-Consultation with grade-level teams/school counselor/ school psychologist for classroom/individual behavior management ideas
Consequences May Include	**Consequences May Include**	**Consequences May Include**	**Consequences May Include**
-Time-out in room -Parent contact -Detention -Loss of privileges -Moving seat *Students should only receive refer- rals at this level AFTER at least 3 reteaching oppor- tunities have occurred unsuccessfully and 3 conse- quences have been applied with no results.*	-Time-out in room -Time-out in team leader's room -Parent contact -Loss of privileges -Behavior contract -Admin/parent/student/ teacher conference -Referral to team leader *Students should receive referrals to the team leader if ideas for controlling behaviors have not been successful.*	-Time-out in room -Time-out in team leader's room -Parent contact -Loss of privileges -Behavior contract -Office referral -Admin/parent/student/ teacher conference -Referral to team leader -Suspension *Students should be referred to the team leader and/or office at the referring teacher's discretion.*	-As per Board of Education discipline policies *IMMEDIATE office referrals should occur with this level of infraction.*

FIGURE 5-8 Behavioral Definitions from General John Stricker Middle School, Baltimore, Maryland *(Continued)*

THERE IS A SYSTEM OF PREDETERMINED, CONSISTENT CONSEQUENCES FOR USE IN CORRECTING PROBLEM BEHAVIORS. PBIS does not mean that there are no conse-quences for inappropriate behavior. The difference between an SW-PBIS approach and a traditional approach is that, in an SW-PBIS approach, the first response to a minor inappropriate behavior is to reteach the expected behavior (i.e., behavioral infractions are viewed as problems of learning). For minor (or teacher-managed) offenses, the first response should be to reteach the rule or expectation that the student violated. Note that reteaching the rule is a more focused, instructional ap-proach than simply "talking to the student" about the misbehavior. Reteaching the rule means explaining the rule, describing or showing examples and perhaps nonexamples of following the rule, having the student role-play following the rule, and soliciting a commitment from the student to follow the rule in the future. If the minor misbehavior occurs again, the teacher may administer a consequence. The behavior reduction techniques we describe in Chapter 12 are appropriate for teacher-managed behaviors. For example, the first time a minor behavioral prob-lem occurs, the teacher should reteach the rule. If the problem continues, the teacher might implement a differential reinforcement system, a response cost (e.g., taking away tokens or a privilege), or a time-out in the classroom.

SW-PBIS plans should differentiate between classroom and office-managed behavioral problems and provide staff with strategies for responding to unacceptable behaviors.

TEACHER INITIATED TIER 1 BEHAVIOR FORM ECHS

LEVEL 1:	**LEVEL 2:**	**LEVEL 3:**
Students should only receive office referrals at this level AFTER at least 3 different re-teaching opportunities have occurred unsuccessfully and 3 consequences have been applied with no results:	*Students should be referred to the office at the referring teacher's discretion.*	*IMMEDIATE office referrals should occur with this level of infraction.*
Behaviors that impact only the student and/or that interfere with the learning of others	**Behaviors that affect an orderly environment**	**Behaviors that affect an orderly environment**

Level 1	Level 2	Level 3

Date of Occurrence
____-Not Prepared   ____-Out of seat
____-Sleeping   ____-Teasing
____-Not doing   ____-Not following
  class work   directions
____-Not listening   ____-Lying
____-No homework ____-Talking out
____-Not having a   ____-Refusing to
  pencil   work.
____-Visiting/talking ____-Inappropriate/
  during instruction   noises
____-Consistently not following directions
____-Not taking responsibility for action
____-Out of seat & interfering with
  others learning
____-OTHER
  Describe:_____
	Date of Occurrence
	____-Talking back to adult
	____-Throwing things
	____-Cheating
	____-Stealing
	____- Forgery
	____-Inappropriate language
	____-Disrespect to others
	____-Leaving room without permission
	____-Hallway behaviors
	____-Profane or Gang related hand gestures
	____-Vandalizing school property
	____-Bullying
	____-OTHER
	  Describe:_____
		Date Of Occurrence
		____-Actions that cause harm
		Describe:_____
		____-Fighting
		____-Drugs
		____-Weapons
		____-Throwing furniture
		____-Threatening to do injury to person
		  or property
		____-Sexual harassment
		____-Sexual behaviors
		____-Gang related writing
		____-OTHER
		  Describe:_____

Ideas for controlling behavior
Making eye contact and maintaining proximity is expected of all teachers; in addition, documentation is required for:
 	
Initial & date each as you apply.
____-Positive Parent Contact
____-High-levels of supervision
____-Discussion about expectations
____-Verbal warning
____-Pre-teaching of expectations
____-Re-teaching of school rules/
  expected behaviors
____-Link rewards to appropriate
  Behaviors
____-Consultation with guidance
  counselor
	Ideas for controlling behavior
	Making eye contact and maintaining proximity is expected of all teachers; in addition, documentation is required for:
	
	Initial & date each as you apply.
	____-Positive Parent Contact
	____-High-levels of supervision
	____-Discussion about expectations
	____-Verbal warning
	____-Pre-teaching of expectations
	____-Re-teaching of school rules/
	  expected behaviors
	____-Link rewards to appropriate
	  behaviors
	____-Consultation with guidance
	  counselor
		Student Name — Date(s) of Discipline Referral:

Initial & date each as you apply.
Consequences must include:
____-Parent Contact (at least 3 documented attempts by letter, email or phone, then if still not able to contact then contact Parent Liaison)
 	
Consequences may include:
____-Loss of Privileges
____-Moving Seat
____-Behavior Contract
____-Admin./parent/student/teacher
  conference
	Initial & date each as you apply.
	Consequences must include:
	____-Parent Contact (at least 3 documented attempts by letter, email or phone, then if still not able to contact then contact Parent Liaison)
	
	Consequences may include:
	____-Loss of Privileges
	____-Behavior Contract
	____-Office Referral
	____-Admin./parent/student/teacher
	  conference
	____-Suspension
		Consequences may include:
		____-As per Board of Education discipline Policies
		
		For extended interventions please visit
		www.interventioncentral.org
		www.theteachingzone.com

FIGURE 5-9 Major–Minor Infractions Form Used at El Campo High School, El Campo Independent School District, El Campo, Texas. Reprinted with permission.

For behaviors that warrant an ODR, administrators should have a clearly identified hierarchy of consequences for responding to behaviors according to the severity of the behavioral problem. Administrative consequences might include a telephone call to the student's parents, detention, loss of privileges, in-school suspension, or Saturday school (e.g., student is required to attend a disciplinary class at school on Saturday). The goal is to provide consistent, predictable consequences for behavioral infractions. Of course, administrators and leadership teams must balance consistent consequences with flexibility in responding to chronic behavioral problems. Clearly, as we have discussed in this and previous chapters, if a student receives repeated ODRs, simply increasing the severity of the punishment will not be effective. Repeated ODRs should trigger intervention by the student support team to evaluate the student for secondary-level interventions; these interventions should include individualizing both the reinforcement and the punishment consequences for the student in order to reflect the functions of the problem behaviors.

Data Sources for the Universal Level

At the universal level, data are needed for four general purposes: (a) to determine the need and readiness for SW-PBIS, (b) to monitor the effectiveness of the universal-level interventions, (c) to monitor the fidelity of the implementation of the universal-level interventions, and (d) to identify students who are not responding to universal-level supports. In addition, the leadership team typically uses data to identify students who are not responding sufficiently to universal-level supports. The following are explanations of these purposes and sources of data for each.

Determine the Need and Readiness for SW-PBIS. Evidence indicates that it is important for 80% of the faculty and staff on a campus to agree that discipline is a concern and that SW-PBIS is needed (OSEP Technical Assistance Center on Positive Behavioral Interventions and Supports, 2010). With this level of commitment, SW-PBIS is more likely to be implemented with fidelity. If there is less than an 80% buy-in, one of the first steps taken by the leadership team should be to communicate to all staff the need for SW-PBIS, perhaps sharing objective indicators such as the number of ODRs, the number of in-school or out-of-school suspension days, academic test scores, attendance, or other data that reflect the overall functioning of the school.

One source of data for determining the need and readiness is the Effective Behavior Support (EBS) Survey (Sugai, Horner, & Todd, 2000). This survey is used before implementing SW-PBIS and then annually to determine all staff members' perceptions of the status of specific features of four PBIS systems (i.e., schoolwide, nonclassroom, classroom, and individual student) and the priority for improvement of each feature. Survey results are summarized, charted, and used to develop an SW-PBIS action plan. Prior to beginning SW-PBIS, the leadership team can use this survey to determine whether 80% of the school's personnel agree that discipline is a concern and a priority, and to identify staff perceptions regarding priorities for SW-PBIS systems (i.e., schoolwide, nonclassroom, classroom, or individual) and features.

Using the EBS Survey may not be feasible because of time constraints. For this reason, some leadership teams instead use a simple two- to five-question survey, often administered electronically. Such a survey might ask simple questions such as "Do you think that discipline is a concern on our campus?" and "Should improving our disciplinary systems be a priority for our campus?" This approach is certainly not as comprehensive as the EBS Survey, and, of course, it lacks the technical adequacy of the EBS Survey (Safran, 2006). It can, however, provide leadership teams with an approximate assessment of staff perceptions regarding the need to improve discipline.

ODR data are used for various decision-making purposes in SW-PBIS systems.

Monitor the Effectiveness of the Universal-level Interventions.   The standard measure for determining the impact of universal-level systems is ODRs (Sugai, Sprague, Horner, & Walker, 2000). ODRs are a valid and reliable indicator of overall discipline (Irvin et al., 2006), and are particularly convenient because most schools maintain records of ODRs as standard practice (Sugai et al., 2000). ODRs as a source of data are used for multiple purposes in schoolwide PBIS systems. First, ODRs are considered a main indicator of the overall effectiveness of SW-PBIS systems (Irvin, Tobin, Sprague, Sugai, & Vincent, 2004; Nelson, Benner, Reid, Epstein, & Curran, 2002; Sugai et al., 2000). The total number of ODRs before and during SW-PBIS implementation is generally used to monitor the overall effectiveness of the SW-PBIS program. ODR data are also used to identify specific problems within the school. For example, ODR data might indicate an increase in ODRs before vacations or might reveal that most disciplinary referrals originate from one particular area of the school. The school's leadership team can then develop interventions to target those specific problems. ODRs are examined regularly (at least monthly) to monitor the effectiveness of SW-PBIS systems and to identify the areas that need attention. Typically, ODRs are disaggregated, which means that total ODRs are broken down into subcategories, such as specific infractions, locations, teachers, grade level, time of day, and time of year. Disaggregating ODRs allows leadership teams to identify specific patterns of behavioral difficulties or specific areas of need, and to evaluate the effectiveness of interventions for those areas. The extent to which data are available in a user-friendly format will influence the extent to which leadership teams and administrators use those data regularly to guide decision making. For this reason, many schools use the School-wide Information System (SWIS™), a Web-based data management system (see the "Resources" section at the end of this chapter).

For consistency in reporting across schools, or across periods when the student population in a given school may vary, ODRs can be reported as ODRs per school day per 100 students. The calculation is

$$\text{Total ODR} \div \text{Total School Days} \div (\text{Total Enrollment} \div 100)$$

ODRs are just one indicator of need and effectiveness. Other types of data that may be used include number of in-school and/or out-of-school suspension days; attendance; measures of school climate or school safety; and even academic performance indicators, such as statewide test scores. One interesting source of data is to report staff and administrator time spent dealing with ODRs, as discussed previously in this chapter. This information can make a compelling case for the need for a more effective approach to discipline, especially when multiplied by hundreds of ODRs processed by administrators, or numerous referrals accumulated by individual students.

Monitor the Fidelity of the Implementation of the Universal-level Interventions.   Two tools are widely used for evaluating the fidelity of implementation; schools choose one of these (or other similar measures) to annually assess the extent to which a campus has the essential features of SW-PBIS in place. The first is the Schoolwide Evaluation Tool (SET; Todd et al., 2005). The SET relies on multiple sources of information to assess the extent to which the essential features of SW-PBIS are in place. An external evaluator conducts the SET by gathering information through interviews with administrators, teachers, and students; a review of disciplinary materials; and observations. The SET provides percentage scores in seven areas that reflect the essential features of SW-PBIS, as well as an overall score. Implementation of universal-level systems with fidelity is indicated by a total SET score of 80% on the total score plus a score of 80% on the teaching expectations sub-scale (Todd, Lewis-Palmer, Horner, Sugai, Sampson, & Phillips, 2003).

Another tool for assessing the fidelity of implementation is the Benchmarks of Quality (BoQ; Kincaid, Childs, & George, 2010). This tool relies on observations of SW-PBIS features conducted by an SW-PBIS coach and ratings completed by members of the leadership team. A total score is calculated, on the basis of a possible 100 points. The results from the SET or the BoQ can then be used for developing annual action plans to identify the steps needed for improving PBIS systems.

Identify Students Who are Not Responding to Universal-level Supports. Fundamental to PBIS is a philosophy of early intervention and rapid response to behavioral difficulties. In order to provide early intervention, however, we must first identify those students who are at risk for behavioral difficulties. Consistent with the goal of early intervention, it is important to identify students who are not responding to universal-level supports. Perhaps the most widely used method for identifying students who need targeted-level supports is to track the number of ODRs: A student who acquires a second ODR should be considered for targeted-level supports (Sugai et al., 2000). In addition, many schools use some type of universal screening system in which all students are screened for behavioral issues. Typically, these screeners rely on teacher ratings of individual student behavior using a standardized behavior rating instrument, such as the Systematic Screening for Behavioral Disorders (Walker and Severson, 1992). Another promising method identified by Burke and his colleagues is to use teacher evaluations of student behavior relative to schoolwide expectations (Burke et al., 2010). Other methods may be used as well, including tracking teacher disciplinary referrals, automatic disciplinary referrals for major offenses, accumulation of multiple absences or tardies, or academic concerns.

STEPS IN PLANNING AND IMPLEMENTING SCHOOLWIDE SW-PBIS

The critical attributes and essential features of SW-PBIS systems described so far should provide a general idea of how to develop SW-PBIS programs. However, for clarity, the steps for designing and implementing SW-PBIS are presented in Table 5-5. Although most of these steps have been discussed in this chapter, we provide additional clarification for those steps that have not been addressed. We encourage educators who are interested in SW-PBIS for their school to read further and to attend workshops or conferences to expand their knowledge in this area. The more knowledgeable the team members are about the theoretical and conceptual bases of PBIS, the better they will be able to design effective SW-PBIS programs and resolve problems that arise during planning and implementation. The resources listed at the end of the chapter can help.

One or more members of the school PBIS team should become well informed about the theoretical foundations of PBIS and the full range of PBIS applications.

TABLE 5-5   Steps in Designing and Implementing SW-PBIS

1. **Establish the need for SW-PBIS.**

   There should be a need for SW-PBIS. The need may be because of obvious disciplinary concerns, such as high levels of disruptive, aggressive, or disrespectful behaviors; problems with truancy or attendance; or high levels of ODRs, suspensions, or placement in alternative schools. The need might be less obvious, such as low student and/or teacher morale, weak academic performance, or concern about the consistency of disciplinary responses.

2. **Organize an SW-PBIS leadership team.**

   The team should be representative of the stakeholders in the school, as discussed previously.

3. **Ensure administrative leadership and commitment.**

   For SW-PBIS to be successful and sustained, school administrators must be fully committed to ongoing support of PBIS efforts (e.g., providing time for the leadership team to meet, allowing the team to provide updates at faculty meetings, attending leadership team meetings) and resources (e.g., access to ODR data; funds for SW-PBIS materials, such as signs, tokens, and reinforcers).

4. **Obtain the commitment of the staff.**

   This is typically accomplished by informing the staff about PBIS and using the EBS Survey to assess staff perceptions about the need and priorities for intervention. Throughout the SW-PBIS planning process, staff should be kept informed about SW-PBIS activities and should be allowed input into each aspect of the program.

5. **Gather data.**

   The need that led to the program will determine the data that should be gathered. Data will be used to identify the priorities for intervention; evaluate the effectiveness of the interventions; and, once universal-level interventions are well established, identify the students who need more intensive supports.

6. **Develop a long-term plan for the SW-PBIS program.**

   Remember that SW-PBIS is a long-term commitment to systems change. Leadership teams should prioritize the needs and develop a timeline for addressing those needs. For example, most schools focus their first-year efforts on primary-level prevention, and only then do they focus on secondary- and tertiary-level supports after the universal systems are well established. In addition, in our experiences, teams sometimes try to accomplish too much, too quickly, leading to frustration and possibly burnout. Prioritizing the needs and the intervention targets will help the teams to pace themselves and to stay focused on the critical elements.

7. **Develop three to five school rules.**

   Existing rules should be evaluated with respect to the guidelines that we provided for setting school rules. If no school rules currently exist, new rules should be developed that reflect the school's needs.

8. **Develop a rule matrix to define the rules for all areas of the school.**

   This activity should be done with input from all staff. It is important to involve nonteaching staff, such as cafeteria monitors, playground supervisors, hall monitors, bus drivers, and custodians. These individuals often have a unique perspective about the problems that occur in their areas of the school and can provide valuable input about desired behaviors in those areas.

9. **Assess the environmental factors that may contribute to problem behavior and design antecedent interventions to address those factors.**

   For example, the leadership team, with input from others, may determine that one reason the cafeteria is so messy after lunch is that there are not enough trash cans, or the trash cans are not located in places that encourage students to use them after lunch when they are in a hurry. One solution to this problem is to add more trash cans at logical locations, making them easier for students to use. Another example of an antecedent intervention would be to clearly mark the boundaries of the playground where students are allowed in order to avoid the problem of students migrating to areas where they are not easily supervised. Another relatively simple antecedent intervention is to teach all staff how to actively supervise students at all times. Teachers should be in the halls during transition periods and should be instructed to actively supervise all students in the area around their classrooms. Playground supervisors should be taught to circulate throughout the playground during recess; there should be no adults standing in groups at the edges of the playground talking during recess.

   As discussed in this chapter, antecedent interventions also involve the use of signs, banners, announcements, and other reminders to help students remember the school rules and how they are applied in all areas of the school.

10. **Develop a plan for teaching the school rules to all students.**

    The PBIS leadership team should decide when and how this will be done and then develop lesson plans (or have all teachers assist with this task) for teaching the rules and expectations. All teachers and staff should be taught how to teach the rules before beginning the instructional activities with students.

11. **Develop an acknowledgment system to provide all students with positive reinforcement for exhibiting appropriate, rule-following behaviors.**

    Like any reinforcement system, schoolwide reinforcement systems should be easy to use and maintain and should be appealing to students.

12. **Develop an acknowledgment system for teachers.**

    In most cases, adhering to the various elements of an SW-PBIS program will require that teachers change certain aspects of their behavior (e.g., providing more attention to appropriate behavior than to inappropriate behavior, providing active supervision). This is hard work and is difficult for some teachers. To encourage teachers and staff to follow the SW-PBIS program, the leadership team should develop a reinforcement system for the teachers and staff, as well as the students.

13. **Teach the system to the school staff.**

    Remember that the SW-PBIS components that staff will be expected to use are new concepts and new skills for many. Teaching school personnel how to provide careful supervision and how to use the reinforcement system and strategies for classroom-managed versus office-managed behavioral problems should be done through a direct instructional approach (e.g., explain, model, have staff practice through role-plays). The leadership team will probably be responsible for informing others about PBIS and teaching the SW-PBIS components. It may not be possible to teach all of these new skills at once, so the team should develop a plan for systematically teaching the skills over the first few weeks of school. Remember that reinforcing the staff for using SW-PBIS techniques is important for generalization and maintenance of the SW-PBIS program.

    In addition, all teachers and staff should be given an SW-PBIS notebook that was developed by the team. The notebook should explain all aspects of the

(Continued)

TABLE 5-5 *(Continued)*

---

universal system, including procedures such as how to obtain more tokens and ideas for storing the tokens. A "Frequently Asked Questions" section is also a nice addition for SW-PBIS notebooks in order to answer questions such as "What if a student loses his or her tokens?" or "How do I make suggestions to the PBIS team?"

14. **Meet regularly to evaluate progress and identify needs.**

The PBIS team should plan to meet at least monthly, perhaps even more frequently at first. Meetings should be structured, with an agenda and specific team member responsibilities. In particular, one or more persons should be assigned the responsibility of obtaining ODR data and bringing the data to the leadership team meeting. ODR data should be examined and discussed at each meeting.

15. **Provide regular updates to all staff.**

This can be done at faculty meetings, through faculty newsletters or bulletin boards, or through electronic communication. This update process should also include provisions for obtaining feedback from the staff about all elements of the SW-PBIS program.

16. **Inform others about the SW-PBIS program.**

Parents, substitute teachers, volunteers, and district administrators should be kept informed about the SW-PBIS program. Some of these individuals may be expected to participate in portions of the universal-level program. Others will hear students and teachers talking about it. The SW-PBIS program should be kept at the forefront of the school's communication efforts. This can be done by posting information about the program on the school's Website, having a PBIS column in the school newsletter, making presentations at parent–teacher association meetings, and making presentations at district-level administrator meetings or school board meetings. As positive data emerge from the program, the PBIS team should also consider publicizing those successes through the local news media.

Summary

Schoolwide PBIS is an exciting and effective response to the problems of school violence, disruptive behavior, high levels of disciplinary actions, and poor school climate. SW-PBIS extends and expands the successes of behavioral science, especially applied behavior analysis, to making schools more effective for all students. The objectives for this chapter and how they were addressed are as follows:

1. Explain schoolwide positive behavioral interventions and supports (SW-PBIS), in-cluding the rationale for schoolwide PBIS and its philosophy.

We defined SW-PBIS and described the evolution of PBIS as an efficacious approach to school discipline. We discussed the fact that zero-tolerance and "get tough" approaches have produced no evidence of effectiveness and are associated with a wide range of ethical and educational concerns. SW-PBIS provides an effective, positive response to concerns about school safety and effectiveness.

2. Describe the critical attributes of SW-PBIS systems.

SW-PBIS is characterized by multiple critical attributes that differentiate SW-PBIS from other disciplinary approaches. These critical attributes include an emphasis on the following: (a) systems change, (b) a three-tiered approach to matching interventions and supports to the intensity of the students' needs, (c) broad staff commitment to improving student performance, (d) programs tailored to each school, (e) team-based decision making, (f) an emphasis on teaching appropriate behaviors and viewing behavioral problems as problems of learning, (g) decision making founded on data, (h) long-term commitment to systems change, and (i) ongoing refinement of the SW-PBIS universal-level systems and processes.

3. Describe research support for SW-PBIS.

We provided a brief overview of the large and growing body of evidence that SW-PBIS can improve student academic and social performance. Numerous studies have shown the effectiveness of SW-PBIS interventions for improving student behavior in all areas of the school (e.g., classrooms, playground, cafeteria, buses), for all grade levels, and all types of schools (e.g., rural, urban). In addition, research is beginning to demonstrate a positive correlation between SW-PBIS and improved academic performance, and, in addition, positive effects on student behavior in disciplinary alternative settings and mental health treatment programs.

4. Describe and give examples of the essential features of SW-PBIS programs.

We described the antecedent, instructional, and consequential elements that make up most of the primary-level interventions in SW-PBIS programs. These elements vary in design, but generally include a few positively stated school rules; instructions for how those rules are to be applied in all areas of the school; systematic instruction in the school rules for all students; one or more systems for acknowledging appropriate behavior; differentiation between classroom-managed and office-managed behaviors; and clear, consistent consequences for infractions of the rules.

5. Describe the steps for planning and implementing an SW-PBIS program.

We provided a step-by-step summary of how to begin an SW-PBIS program. We believe that it is important for school personnel to have a good understanding of the conceptual bases for PBIS and why each element of the universal-level system is important. This underlying theoretical knowledge will help teams plan and implement more effective, comprehensive programs and will enable them to problem solve when they encounter obstacles in implementation.

6. Describe assessment and monitoring methods for universal and targeted levels..

We described four types of universal-level data needs and data sources for each. The four needs are to determine the need and readiness for PBIS, to monitor effectiveness, to monitor fidelity, and to identify students who need more intensive supports. In addition, we described methods for monitoring students who are receiving targeted-level supports. Two such methods are tracking daily points earned on daily behavior cards and using behavioral rating scales or checklists.

In our experience, teachers are often the catalyst for a school's move to the PBIS model. One or more teachers learn about SW-PBIS through university courses or at a conference or workshop and then bring that information back to their school. For this reason, teachers should be knowledgeable about the basic elements of SW-PBIS. To test your understanding of SW-PBIS, we provide a self-assessment in Table 5-6.

TABLE 5-6 SW-PBIS Self-Assessment

Never	Seldom	Sometimes	Often	Always
1	2	3	4	5

Use the numbers above to rate the following statements.

1. I can define and explain the theoretical elements of PBIS to my professional peers. _____
2. I can explain and give examples of the critical attributes of SW-PBIS. _____
3. I can give examples of primary-level prevention (i.e., universal interventions). _____
4. I can give examples of secondary-level prevention (i.e., targeted interventions). _____
5. I can give examples of tertiary-level interventions. _____
6. I can describe the purposes of data collection in SW-PBIS systems and can give examples of _____ types of data that are commonly used and the purposes of each.
7. I know how to critically evaluate commercial school improvement or school disciplinary _____ programs.
8. I can explain the essential features of SW-PBIS and can give examples of each feature. _____
9. I can describe the steps involved in beginning an SW-PBIS program. _____
10. I have the ability to widen the focus of my thinking about managing student behavior from _____ my classroom and my students to the entire student body and every area of the school.

Dr. ICE Helps a School District with PBIS

NOTE: In these Dr. ICE vignettes, we describe problems that are sometimes encountered as a school begins an SW-PBIS program. Because of those problems, the schools described in these vignettes approach SW-PBIS in a slightly more limited way than we described in this chapter. We present these vignettes to illustrate that SW-PBIS plans should be responsive to the needs and capacity of each school. For example, if a school is not ready for schoolwide rules and acknowledgment systems (e.g., perhaps the staff does not view this as a need) or does not need such systems to improve general schoolwide behavior, SW-PBIS interventions may be focused on specific problems or areas of the school. This approach is still consistent with SW-PBIS principles.

Another problem illustrated in the following vignettes is when one or more elements of the SW-PBIS plan fail to produce the desired results. The elementary school vignette described here shows how a PBIS leadership team addressed this problem.

Dr. ICE agreed to work with a large urban school district to train staff to use PBIS throughout all of the schools in the upcoming year. The superintendent asked Dr. ICE to train teams, composed of administrators and

teachers from district schools, in SW-PBIS in a large-group setting. These teams will then go back to their schools and train the entire school staff in SW-PBIS. Prior to the large-group training, the staff of each school will be asked to fill out a questionnaire to determine their priorities regarding discipline as a target for improvement. At least 80% of each school's staff will need to agree that improving discipline and school climate are important needs at their school in order for that school to participate.

Once the schools are chosen, each school will then select the members of the PBIS leadership team. The team will need a representative from the administration; a teacher from each grade level; a special education teacher; a representative from student support services, the paraprofessional staff, and the nonteaching staff (e.g., clerical staff, custodial staff, or lunchroom staff); a parent representative; and a student.

As the schools began to plan for the next year, Dr. ICE is asked to follow the progress of an elementary school, a middle school, and a high school. In this way, he can monitor how well the training is being implemented and observe the problems that develop and how the teams address those problems. The following vignettes describe some problems that the teams faced and how they arrived at solutions.

ELEMENTARY SCHOOL

The elementary school, for the most part, had few general disciplinary problems, but staff recognized that there were problems in specific areas of the school (e.g., the playground, bus-loading area, restrooms). The elementary school team decided to begin by using SW-PBIS in only one of those areas. The team surveyed the staff and parents, and examined ODRs to determine the common area where PBIS interventions would first be applied.

The cafeteria was chosen as the area that had the most significant disciplinary problems. The behavior of the students in the lunchroom had been a problem for years, so the administration was very pleased with this choice.

The team members then determined the behaviors that they wanted from the students (e.g., the rules for the cafeteria). In addition, procedures for using the cafeteria (e.g., how to enter, how to leave, what behaviors are acceptable while eating) were created and taught to the school staff. The PBIS team leader agreed to train the lunchroom monitors.

The PBIS team also developed a reinforcement system for the cafeteria. After lunch, the students went to recess. In the new PBIS system, students would wear a clothespin with their name on it to lunch. If a student exhibited inappropriate behavior during lunch, the monitor would take the clothespin and the student would lose recess.

The problems began within the first week. On rainy days with no recess, students' behavior in the cafeteria deteriorated. On days when the weather allowed recess, many of the students who missed recess because of their cafeteria behavior then had behavioral problems in their afternoon classes. Some teachers did not provide clothespins for their students. It was evident that some teachers had not taught their students the new lunchroom procedures.

The PBIS team met to solve these problems. The team members agreed that the cafeteria procedures were good. They did, however, realize that they had made a mistake in using recess as a reinforcer. They decided on a new reinforcement system that would work for the students and their teachers. In the new system, students would earn points each day: 4 points if every student kept their clothespin during lunch, 3 points if one student lost his or her clothespin, 2 points if two students lost clothespins, and 1 point if more

than two students lost clothespins. Cafeteria monitors would record the points on class charts that were posted on the wall in the cafeteria. At the end of the week, the three classes that earned the most points would earn a reinforcer: an end-of-the-day popcorn party on Friday. To reinforce the teachers, an administrator or counselor would come into the classroom to conduct the party and take care of dismissal, and the teacher could leave 30 minutes early that day. The PBIS team also asked each class to create posters about the new lunchroom procedures that would be displayed in the hallways.

The teachers had almost 100% immediate buy-in. Teachers used the hallway posters to remind their students about the procedures. They kept charts of lunch points in their classrooms. They praised the class for earning points every day when they picked their students up from lunch.

The PBIS team learned a big lesson: An appropriate reinforcement system for both students and adults is important. The team would apply this lesson as it developed PBIS interventions for the next area of the school.

MIDDLE SCHOOL

The middle school PBIS team knew that it needed an SW-PBIS plan to address student behavior throughout the school, but hallway behavior was particularly problematic, and there were many safety issues to be addressed.

The team developed a plan that included schoolwide rules, antecedent interventions, and a reinforcement plan. Unfortunately, over the summer, new school attendance lines were drawn, teacher assignments were changed, and the school was assigned a new principal. As soon as possible, the PBIS team leader (who was to remain at the school) contacted the new administrator, who had been hired from another district and who had not been trained by Dr. ICE and was only vaguely aware of PBIS. Furthermore, there were questions about how the new staff would feel about the SW-PBIS program that had been developed.

The PBIS team leader arranged for the team to meet with the new principal to provide her with information about SW-PBIS and the school's SW-PBIS plan. The team members arrived with all of their data, their SW-PBIS training guide, and general information about PBIS. The team gave a general overview of SW-PBIS and the school's need for PBIS (using the data).

Then each team member explained his or her responsibility and how it was important for implementing the plan. The administrator was impressed with the team's knowledge and commitment to SW-PBIS and agreed to continue the focus on the initiative. Next, the team and the new administrator developed a plan to train the new staff in their school before the students arrived.

Dr. ICE and the superintendent were so pleased with the professionalism, communication skills, and commitment to SW-PBIS shown by this team that they asked the team to train new administrators in the future.

HIGH SCHOOL

This large school had a diverse population of students and staff. There was low faculty support for SW-PBIS, but the principal was certain that support would increase with the success of SW-PBIS. This was the first problem: The principal ignored what he had been taught in PBIS training: Staff commitment is very important to the success of SW-PBIS.

The principal knew that student behavior needed to be addressed, so he asked staff members who shared this concern to be a part of the PBIS team. The team knew that it needed to address a problem that affected the most teachers. With that in mind, the team chose tardiness as the first student behavior to be addressed in its SW-PBIS plan. Like the team in the elementary school, this team needed to make the intervention plan reinforcing to both students and teachers.

Teachers had one duty period (e.g., supervision of a nonclassroom area, study hall, or other student activity) and one planning period each day. Each week, the names of teachers who had three or fewer students who were late to class were put into a drawing. The winner was relieved of his or her duty period on Monday (administrators, paraprofessionals, or other nonclassroom staff took over for the teacher). In addition, each week, the names of all teachers who had three or fewer tardies were noted. At the end of the year, the 10 teachers who had the fewest tardies would be given first priority in checking in books and completing their end-of-year checklist.

The PBIS team then developed a reinforcement plan to help students get to class on time. The plan was simple: First, all teachers were given a laminated picture of the school mascot (a Viking). Next, during the first 2 days of school, students were taught the schoolwide expectation that students are to be in their assigned classroom or area when the bell rings. Each day that all students are on time to class, the teacher simply places the Viking picture on the clip outside the classroom door. Administrators, office staff, and counselors randomly roam the halls during classes, noting the classes that have the Viking posted. Those teachers' names and class periods (e.g., Mr. Austin's first period English, Ms. Rogers' sixth-period gym) are placed in a drawing, and every Friday 10 names are drawn. Students in those classes earn a reinforcer (e.g., an ice cream sandwich, passes to a school event, a voucher for the school store, passes to go to lunch 5 minutes early). Administrators visit the winning classes on Monday to deliver the reinforcers.

When the team presented this plan to the staff, the response was enthusiastic, and teachers were eager to begin. Within 2 weeks, the number of tardies dropped dramatically. The intervention for tardies was so successful that the school faculty was now convinced of the power of PBIS and was ready to develop SW-PBIS components (e.g., schoolwide rules) to address other student behavioral problems.

Learning Activities

1. In small groups, discuss the four theoretical elements of SW-PBIS. Next, develop a lesson plan for teaching them to a school faculty and staff. Remember that not all of your audience will be trained educators.
2. In a large group, discuss how ODRs are used for evaluating SW-PBIS systems.
3. Using the critical attributes of SW-PBIS and what you know about punitive approaches to discipline, develop a model for choosing school disciplinary programs and making decisions about them.
4. In small groups, discuss ways to help a PBIS leadership team maintain a long-term commitment to the SW-PBIS process. Share your findings with the larger group.
5. Write three to five schoolwide rules. Then divide into small groups; each group should define those rules for one or more areas of the school and develop reminders that will help students to remember the expectations.
6. Using the rules developed in the preceding activity, work in small groups to develop an

acknowledgment system to reinforce students for following the rules.

7. Working individually, or in small groups, choose a commercial school improvement/school discipli-nary program and evaluate that program according to how it reflects the critical attributes of SW-PBIS. Assess the research on which the program is based.

Resources

WEBSITES

www.pbis.org The Office of Special Education Programs, U.S. Department of Education, Technical Assistance Center on Positive Behavioral Interventions and Supports: Provides a wealth of information about PBIS and tools for implementation.

www.apbs.org Association for Positive Behavior Support: Provides information about conferences, state PBIS networks, PBIS information, and the Standards of Practice. Membership in APBS includes subscriptions to *The Journal on Positive Behavior Interventions* and the quarterly *APBS Newsletter*.

Many states have Websites for state PBIS initiatives. In general, these Websites provide a wealth of information about PBIS, tools for implementation and evaluation of SW-PBIS, links, publications, and examples from schools that are using SW-PBIS. A few of these state Websites are listed here. Also, an Internet search on "positive behavioral interventions and supports" or "PBIS" will provide links to school district or campus PBIS Websites, many of which provide examples of their PBIS elements.

Arizona: **http://www.pbisaz.org/**
Colorado: **www.cde.state.co.us/pbs**
Florida: **http://flpbs.fmhi.usf.edu**
Illinois: **www.pbisillinois.org**
Kansas: **www.kipbs.org**

Maryland: **www.pbismaryland.org**
New Hampshire: **http://www.nhcebis.seresc.net/**
New York: **www.emsc.nysed.gov/sss/MentalHealth/ PBIS-short.html**
North Carolina: **www.ncpublicschools.org/ec/ supportprograms**
www.swis.org Schoolwide Information System: SWIS is a Web-based software system for collecting and summarizing ODRs in schools. School personnel enter ODR data into SWIS and then produce a variety of data summary reports. For example, ODR data can be summarized by total number, location, students, grade level, teacher, type of infraction, time of year, time of day, and many other variables.

http://e-dbrc.tamu.edu Electronic Daily Behavior Report Card: e-DBRC is a Web-based program for monitoring a student's behavior throughout the day. The program can generate multiple types of graphs and reports that may be useful for monitoring purposes.

JOURNALS

The Journal of Positive Behavior Interventions. Publishes articles related to the field of PBIS, including SW-PBIS. This journal is available to members of the Association for Positive Behavior Support, but it can also be purchased by individual subscription.

After reading this chapter, you should be able to do the following:

1. Provide a rationale for having clear rules and procedures for your classroom.
2. Develop rules and procedures for your classroom.
3. Give examples of types of reminders.
4. Describe how to teach rules and procedures.
5. Describe strategies for communicating with families regarding classroom management.

Prevention of Challenging Behavior Through Rules and Procedures

Big ideas in rules, procedures, and reminders:

- We can learn a lot about classroom management by studying our country's road system, airports, and theme parks!
- *Developing* rules is just the first step; *teaching* rules and being consistent and fair in the enforcement of rules are also essential.
- Procedures are important in the classroom, even in our personal lives. Many of us rely on our daily procedures to keep us organized, effective, and efficient.

Imagine a roadway system that has no rules: no speed limits, no rules about where you can and cannot drive, and no rules about when and where you must stop. Consider what a professional football game would be like if the rules were not consistently enforced. Would you travel on commercial airliners if there were no rules about passenger behavior or procedures for boarding or if the rules for pilot behavior were not consistently enforced?

Rules and procedures are critical elements of virtually every sector of our society. We have rules and procedures about where we are to stand in line in banks, when we must pay bills, how long we are allowed to keep library books, how much we must pay in taxes, and who can receive services from various social service agencies. Rules and procedures govern our behavior in almost every environment, including at work, at home, at play, and while traveling. Furthermore, most rules are consistently enforced and most procedures are consistently followed. You have to pay a late charge if you don't pay your bills on time. You may get fired if you break certain rules at work. Perhaps most importantly, we can predict that those rules which are not consistently enforced are the ones that you most often violate. For example, how many of you regularly exceed the speed limit when driving? A society without rules that are consistently enforced could not survive. A society without common procedures would be chaotic.

In this chapter, we describe the first three aspects of preventive management practices: rules, procedures, and reminders. Although developing rules, procedures, and reminders is not difficult, it does require some time and consideration.

WHY RULES ARE IMPORTANT

In a society that depends so heavily on rules and procedures, it is ironic how often teachers fail to employ these most basic elements of preventive management consistently and systematically in their own classrooms. In any business, recreational activity, or transportation system, the clearer the rules and procedures are, and the more consistently those rules are enforced and the procedures are followed, the better will be the behavior of the people involved. The same is true for classrooms. The extent to which students know the rules and know how to follow them is positively correlated with appropriate behavior (Brophy & Good, 1986; Emmer, Evertson, & Anderson, 1980; Emmer, Sanford, Clements, & Martin, 1983). Likewise, when there are no clear rules, or when those rules are not enforced, students tend to exhibit more problematic behaviors. This is especially true for students who have difficulty adjusting to the demands of school.

Just as the rules for football, basketball, or soccer set the boundaries for behavior on the field or court, the rules for the classroom establish the boundaries for behavior in class. And just as the rules for driving are preventive in nature (i.e., they help to prevent accidents), developing rules for the classroom is also preventive. In fact, it is the first step in preventing behavioral problems.

> Rules form the foundation for effective classroom management.

Developing Rules for the Classroom

Developing the rules for your classroom requires some deliberation. First, you must consider the rules of the district and the school in which you work. Just as township and city rules must be consistent with state constitutions, and state laws must not violate the parameters of the U.S. Constitution, your classroom rules must align with the rules of your local campus and school district. Although your classroom rules will be slightly different from the school rules, you must not establish rules that violate the policies of the higher authority. For example, if your school has a rule that students must not chew gum, this rule should apply in your classroom as well. This consistency will make it easier for your students to remember expected behaviors from one class to another and will keep you out of the uncomfortable position of having to explain to your administrator why you "let students get by with" breaking rules that are enforced in other areas of the school.

Once you are clear with regard to the rules of the school, the next step is to decide what rules you will set for your classroom. To help you determine what rules you need, we recommend that you engage in a little fantasy: Sit back, relax, and imagine your classroom running perfectly. Envision your students energetically doing their assignments and being highly engaged in different types of activities in all areas of the classroom. Specifically, take note of your students' positive behaviors. Remember, at this moment, we are envisioning the "perfect" classroom.

Next, list the positive behaviors you see when you imagine your perfect classroom. What are your students doing that makes this your dream classroom? Are they working cooperatively in small groups? Are they raising their hands when they have questions? Are they self-starting their assignments? Are they in their seats when the bell rings? Do they leave when they hear the bell or when you dismiss them? How do your students interact with one another? This is your classroom, so it should reflect your expectations and what you need to ensure that you can teach, that your students can learn, and that they are safe and happy in your classroom.

According to the Institute on Violence and Destructive Behavior (1999) at the University of Oregon, rules should address safety, respect, and responsibility. So, as you are imagining your perfect classroom, consider what you see (or do not see) that helps to ensure student safety. For example, are students allowed to engage in minor horseplay, or is this not allowed because it easily escalates into fights? What do you see as you visualize your perfect classroom that reflects respectful behavior? For example, do the students say "Ma'am" or "Sir," as is expected in many schools in southern states? Finally, what are the students responsible for in your imaginary classroom? Do they have their materials with them, ready to begin each class? Do they return the materials to the proper place? Do they take care of classroom furnishings? Do they behave appropriately when outside the classroom and away from the teacher?

Now, group these positive behaviors that you envision in your imaginary classroom into categories. Your categories might be safety, respect, and responsibility, plus you might have other categories, such as work-related behaviors or social behaviors. Grouping similar behaviors together will help you to develop rules that address more than one desired behavior.

> Rules should address safety, respect, and responsibility.

Next, from your list of positive behaviors, develop rules that will help to ensure that your real classroom reflects your imaginary classroom as closely as possible. There are some basic guidelines to consider in developing your rules. These "rules for rule making," also listed in Box 6-1, are as follows:

State the rules in positive terms. We recommend that the rules be stated in a form that tells your students *what you want them to do*, instead of stating the rules in a negative form by telling them *what you do not want them to do*. For example, if one of your rules is designed to ensure that students walk rather than run in the hall, the rule should state, "Walk in the classroom and halls" as opposed to "No running in the classroom or halls." There are two reasons for stating rules in positive terms. First, a negative statement identifies only one disallowed behavior (in this case, no running). You can count on some creative students to test this rule by

Box 6-1

The Rules for Making Rules

State the rules in positive terms.

Keep the number of rules to a minimum.

Set rules that cover multiple situations.

Make sure that the rules are appropriate for the students' ages and developmental levels.

Teach your students the rules.

Set an example for rule-following behavior.

Be consistent in enforcing the rules.

skipping, turning cartwheels, or crawling, leaving teachers in the unenviable position of having to explain that those behaviors also are not allowed, despite the fact that the rule addresses only running. The second reason is that, as you may remember from Chapters 1 and 2, students who exhibit chronic behavioral problems often suffer from a failure to learn more appropriate alternatives. Also, remember our mantra: "Never assume." Never assume that if you tell students what not to do, they automatically will know what to do instead! Stating the rules positively simply makes them clearer for students and teachers.

Set only a few rules and state them positively.

Keep the number of rules to a minimum. Choose only the most important behaviors from your list to translate into rules. The significance of your rules will diminish if you overload your students with too many rules. Also, too many rules make it difficult for the students and the teacher to remember them. We see both of these problems in the many rules for driving. How many of you remember the distance at which you are required to dim your headlights when approaching an oncoming car at night? Also, we suspect that this is a rule that seldom gets enforced. When there are too many rules, both students and teachers begin to ignore them, and all of the rules begin to lose their significance. The age, maturity level, and behavioral characteristics of your students will determine how many rules are appropriate. However, we agree with Babkie's (2006) recommendation that there should be no more than five rules.

Set rules that cover multiple situations. One way to cover the many behaviors you want students to exhibit without having too many rules is to develop rules that are sufficiently general to address multiple situations. For example, if your rule is "Have your pencil, paper, and book ready when class begins," what if some subjects, at times, require other materials? A better rule is "Be prepared for class," which covers a broader range of situations. Of course, "Be prepared" must then be **operationalized**, or specifically defined, for each class period to ensure that the students know exactly what the rule means. For example, the rule "Be nice to others" addresses a wide range of both desired (e.g., be polite, help others, share) and undesired behaviors (e.g., do not fight, do not engage in name-calling). Students will learn what each rule means under a variety of circumstances when you teach the rules, as we discuss later in this chapter.

Make sure that the rules are appropriate for the students' ages and developmental levels. As students mature, the rules need to reflect age-appropriate levels of responsibility. Otherwise, the following simple axiom will come to pass: Students will rebel against rules that they have outgrown. For example, teachers may rightfully expect second-graders to raise their hands before talking during a lesson, because 8-year-olds may not have the impulse control needed to take turns during discussions without the structure of a hand-raising rule. However, such a rule may be inappropriate for juniors and seniors in high school, who by this time have sufficient self-control to patiently take turns and listen without interrupting others during a discussion. Requiring these older students to raise their hands for permission to speak may actually have a negative effect on participation. The rules may even change over the course of the school year. For example, in the beginning of the year, the teacher may start with fairly strict rules and then gradually relax those rules as students learn sufficient levels of self-control. The rules should evolve over time as students consistently meet the specific behavioral expectations and, consequently, require a different set of behavioral priorities.

Teach your students the rules. We often make the mistake of assuming that simply verbally reviewing the rules on the first day of class, along with posting the rules on the classroom wall, is going to create a class full of "rule followers." Unfortunately, this approach may be insufficient. We must teach our students the rules that we expect them to follow. In fact, it is essential that we communicate to students the significance that we place on classroom rules by using class time to teach both the classroom and the schoolwide rules and then reviewing them frequently. Remember: Never assume that students know the expectations for rule-following behavior, even secondary students, until you show them and they are able to demonstrate the behavior. We describe how to teach rules later in this chapter.

Set an example for rule-following behavior. It is also important that we demonstrate our classroom rules by modeling them ourselves. It is unrealistic to expect students to respect rules that we do not follow ourselves. For example, if a middle school teacher has a rule stating, "Students will turn in assignments on time," the teacher would be sending her students a mixed message if she failed to return their graded assignments to them on the day promised. A primary-grade teacher would be giving his students an inappropriate message if he engaged in casual conversation with them while walking in line if the classroom rule stated, "Students will have quiet mouths and bodies when walking in line."

| Rules must be taught. |

Be consistent in enforcing the rules. Rules are only effective to the extent that they are enforced. For example, those who sometimes exceed the speed limit probably do so, in part, because they get away with it! We predict that if you received a fine *every time that you exceeded the speed limit,* it would not take many fines for you to always drive the speed limit. Too often, it seems to us that teachers develop rules because someone told them that they should have rules. Those rules are dutifully posted and then not enforced. Or, another problem that we observe is that the rules are enforced only when student behavior starts to become unmanageable. For example, perhaps the rule is "Raise your hand for permission to speak or leave your seat," but that rule is not enforced during class discussions. Instead, the teacher allows students to make comments without permission until the noise level gets too high. Then the teacher says something like "OK, OK, you're getting too loud! You need to start raising your hands if you want to talk." This is not a very effective way to run your classroom, and it makes your job harder, not easier. The message that is being communicated to students is that you have rules, but they are not important, or they are enforced only when the teacher's patience is exhausted. In our opinion, it is not fair in such cases to then become frustrated with the students for misbehaving!

The first step in rule enforcement is to reinforce rule-following behavior. When students are praised or receive other reinforcement for following the rules, it helps them to learn what behaviors are expected. If they like the reinforcement that they receive for following the rules, they will be more likely to continue to follow those rules (see Chapter 10 for an explanation of reinforcement theory). Effective teachers use motivational systems, such as those we describe in Chapter 11, to encourage rule-following behavior.

Only set rules that you are willing to enforce at all times, or clearly communicate to students when a rule is in place and when it is not. For example, perhaps you want your students to participate in class discussions freely, without them having to raise their hands, but you want them to raise their hands if they have questions when working independently. It is acceptable to have the "raise your hand" rule only for independent seatwork. Just make sure that your students know when and where the rules apply. The chart presented in Table 6-1 shows an example of changing rules to cover talking and in-seat behavior in different contexts in the classroom. This chart allows the teacher to specify different rules for talking

TABLE 6-1   Talk/Movement Chart

	TALK	**MOVEMENT**
Level 1	**No talk**	**In seat**
Level 2	**Quiet talk**	**In seat**
Level 3	**Conversational talk**	**Movement allowed**

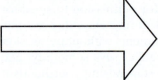

The arrow should be attached to a clothespin and then placed on the chart and moved as the Talk/Movement levels change during the day.

and in-seat behavior for different activities during the day. During independent work time, for example, the teacher would place the arrow on Level 1, but during small-group work, the arrow might be placed on Level 3.

Although it may seem that the steps we have outlined for developing and implementing the rules are time consuming, keep in mind that the time invested in developing the rules for the classroom is time saved in the long run. The more time you spend developing and implementing effective preventive strategies, such as rules, the less time you will have to spend responding to inappropriate behavior.

Table 6-2 shows examples of classroom rules for both elementary and secondary students. Note that we have labeled each rule "safety," "respect," or "responsibility" in order to identify which function(s) that rule serves.

Allowing the students to have input into rule development may be an appropriate way to give students a sense of ownership in the class, which may increase the likelihood that students will follow the rules (Emmer, Evertson, & Worsham, 2003; Martella, Nelson, Marchand-Martella, 2003; Salend & Sylvestre, 2005). Emmer and his colleagues also suggest seeking the students' input regarding the rationale for the rules as another strategy for soliciting student involvement (Emmer et al., 2003). We support student input into rule development, with the following cautions: First, as the teacher, you know best what types of student behaviors are needed to accomplish the desired learning and behavioral outcomes. Teachers will need to ensure that the rules adequately address these outcomes. Second, students tend to set too many rules, and their rules tend to be overly restrictive (Rhode, Jenson, & Reavis, 1993). Third, allowing the students to have input into setting the rules may place you in an awkward position if the students suggest rules that violate school policy. For example, let's say that you teach in a school which has a rule that "no hats are to be worn in school." On the first day of school, you meet your first period class and ask for their help in setting the rules for the classroom. The first rule that they suggest is "Hats may be worn in this classroom but must be removed before entering the hall." Now what do you do? Of course, you could define the limits for student-generated rules by not permitting rules that violate laws or school rules, but even this does not ensure that creative students will not come up with some idea that, although not in violation of laws or school rules, is still unacceptable (e.g., "You may sleep in class once you finish your work," "You may sit wherever you like"). Finally, we see potential ethical problems in requiring students to comply with rules set by peers, particularly if those rules are different from what the teacher would set and if students would receive punishment for breaking the rules.

Basically, the most important issue in setting, teaching, and enforcing rules is that the teacher is fair and reasonable. If students, especially middle school and high school students, perceive the teacher as autocratic, they are less likely to follow the rules unquestioningly. But if students believe that the teacher's rules are reasonable (i.e., the teacher has given a convincing rationale for his or her rules) and fairly enforced, they are more likely to adhere to those rules, even if they do not like them or do not agree with them.

In this section, we discussed establishing rules only for your classroom. Of course, your students participate in activities in many other school environments,

> Rules are meaningless unless they are enforced.

TABLE 6-2   Examples of Rules

Early Childhood

Say nice words. (Respect)

Put toys away. (Responsibility)

Keep hands to yourself. (Safety, respect)

Kindergarten

Do what the teacher tells you to do. (Responsibility, safety, respect)

Share toys and materials. (Responsibility)

Take turns. (Safety, responsibility)

Primary (Grades 1–3)

Be seated in your seat when the bell rings and begin warm-up activity. (Responsibility)

Raise your hand if you want to speak or leave your seat. (Respect, responsibility)

Keep quiet and behave appropriately when walking in line and working in groups. (Safety, responsibility)

Elementary

Do what the teacher tells you to do. (Safety, responsibility, respect)

Share materials and take turns. (Safety, responsibility)

Stop talking when you hear the signal to be quiet. (Safety, respect)

Intermediate (Grades 4–5)

Bring all necessary materials to class. (Responsibility)

Turn in completed homework when you enter the classroom. (Responsibility)

Raise your hand when you want to speak. (Respect, responsibility)

Only one person at a time may use the restroom. (Safety)

Keep your hands to yourself. (Safety)

Middle School or Junior High

Come to class prepared to work. (Responsibility)

Use a respectful tone of voice at all times. (Respect)

Turn in your homework during the first 10 minutes of class. (Responsibility)

Participate in group discussions and group work. (Responsibility)

Keep your hands, feet, and objects to yourself. (Safety)

High School (Grades 9–12)

Arrive on time (be in your seat when the bell rings). (Responsibility)

Arrive prepared (have all necessary materials). (Responsibility)

Take care of your materials. (Responsibility)

Take care of yourself (ask for help when needed, talk to the teacher if you have a problem). (Responsibility)

Use the appropriate words and tone of voice. (Respect)

and each of those environments should have clearly established rules. The rationale that we presented for implementing clear classroom rules also applies to other areas of the school: cafeteria, bus-loading area, halls, restrooms, and so forth, as discussed in Chapter 5. The extent to which schoolwide rules are clear and consistently enforced will also affect student behavior.

In examining the rule examples that we have provided, you may be wondering how you can maintain a well-managed classroom with so few rules. For instance, our rules do not specify many of the behaviors that you will have to manage as a teacher, including sharpening pencils, using the restroom, getting materials, and so forth. In setting your own rules, you will probably discover that it is difficult to choose just a few rules to designate as your classroom rules. Because of our rule about limiting the number of rules that you establish, it would be impossible to have rules to cover every expected student behavior. Rules set the basic framework and define the overall expectations. However, in order to achieve your well-managed classroom, you must also rely on the procedures that will cover the student behaviors that will enable your classroom to run smoothly, efficiently, and without problems.

PROCEDURES

When you begin to plan how you are going to teach your students the classroom rules, you will notice that most of the rules will require your students to learn several behaviors in order to comply with a single rule. Consider an example from your own life: Your employer may have a rule that you must be at work by 8:00 A.M. That rule simply defines the parameters of the expected behavior (i.e., when you must arrive at work). But there are many specific tasks that you must complete in order to comply with the rule: You must get up by a certain time, be dressed and ready to go by a certain time, go directly to work (or allow sufficient time if you need to make other stops), and so on. We refer to these tasks as **procedures**. Emmer and his colleagues (2003) offer this definition for *procedures*: "Procedures, like rules, are expectations for behavior . . . they usually apply to a *specific* activity, and they usually are directed at accomplishing something rather than at prohibiting some behavior or defining a general standard" (p. 19). Procedures are an important part of our everyday lives. We all follow a procedure in the morning to help us prepare for the day (e.g., we may take a shower, read the paper, drink a cup of coffee). Many of us have procedures that we follow at night to help us relax and prepare for sleep (e.g., reading, watching television, soaking in the bathtub). We follow a course of action that enables us to achieve a likely result. How significant are these procedures to us? Well, do you recall how you felt the last time that you overslept and had to rush to work without having had time to drink your coffee, read your newspaper, or take that all-important shower? It probably was not a good feeling. In fact, it may have affected your entire day! Even if you were lucky enough to make it through the traffic that you normally avoid because you leave early, you may still have felt "out-of-whack" the entire day. Procedures are significant. Society is filled with examples of well-established procedures that help to ensure that businesses, recreational activities, and even family events run smoothly.

Consider all of the procedures that we use in the following locations and what it would be like without well-established routines:

- Restaurants (procedures for being seated, ordering a meal, paying the tab)
- Airports (procedures for waiting in line, going through security, retrieving luggage)
- Home life (procedures for celebrating holidays and special occasions, cleaning house, preparing meals)

At school, it is important that we have procedures for everything we want the students to do. Whether it is entering the classroom, asking for help, sharpening pencils, turning in homework, using the restroom, or lining up for recess, we need procedures (Babkie, 2006). Research has shown that effective teachers establish procedures, teach them to their students, and expect the students to follow them (Brophy & Good, 1986; Evertson, 1985). Procedures save time, allow classrooms to run smoothly, and, most importantly, maximize the time available for instruction.

How to Develop Procedures

Deciding what procedures you need and then developing them so that they are clear and easy to follow will take some effort. You should begin thinking about what procedures you want to have in place in your classroom and start developing them during the summer, before the beginning of the school year. If you follow this approach, you will be miles ahead of your peers in terms of classroom management.

Developing good procedures for your classroom will require that you consider every task that students will need to do from the time they enter the classroom until they leave at the end of the day. Begin by making a list of everything that students are expected to do while in the classroom. Your list may include such activities as entering the classroom, preparing for work, turning in homework, working independently, participating in class discussions, asking for help, exiting the classroom, using the restroom, going to their lockers, and so forth. See Table 6-3 for examples of common procedures and Table 6-4 for sample procedures.

Once you determine what procedures are needed, the next step is to determine how students are to complete each task by breaking each procedure down into its component parts. To do this, first consider the desired outcome (e.g., homework is to be placed at the designated spot by the designated time) and then ask yourself, "What steps are necessary in order to achieve this outcome?" Remember: Never assume anything, especially if you are working with young children. It may help to role-play the procedure. Another helpful strategy for developing a procedure is to ask yourself, "What errors are students likely to make in performing this procedure?" For example, when developing the procedure for turning in homework, you may not think to have students check to make sure that their name is on their papers. However, forgetting to put one's name on an assignment is a common error that students make. Therefore, checking that the name is on the assignment should become a part of that procedure. The number of steps involved

TABLE 6-3 Common Procedures for the Classroom and Other School Areas

Elementary School

Waiting for the bus

Entering the classroom

Leaving the classroom

Getting the teacher's attention

Getting help when the teacher is busy

Transitioning from one activity to the next

Working in groups

Reading a book when you are finished with work

Sharpening pencils

Using the restroom and the water fountain

Passing out papers

Turning in work

Participating in classroom independent work activities (e.g., what activities are permissible, how the activities are to be selected, how many students may participate in any given activity)

Lining up and walking in lines

Maintaining the student folders (e.g., what should be in the folders, where the folders are to be kept, what is to be done with the folders during the day)

Learning position (i.e., how to sit)

Using the playground equipment

Using the restroom (e.g., knowing how many students are allowed in the restroom at one time, washing hands, flushing the toilet, disposing of trash)

Using the cafeteria (e.g., getting food, taking one's seat, talking, cleaning up)

Using the library (e.g., when students may go to the library, how many books may be checked out at one time)

Going to the office (e.g., reasons for going to the office, times that a student may request to go to the office)

Attending assemblies (e.g., how to enter the auditorium or gymnasium, how to exit)

Secondary School

Entering the classroom

Leaving the school after being dismissed

Turning in work (e.g., where work is to be placed, when work is to be turned in)

Participating in class discussions

Participating in small-group activities or projects

Maintaining folders or notebooks

Correcting work (e.g., timelines for making corrections, how corrections are to be made)

Taking tests (e.g., how to ask for help, where to put your name, what to do when you are finished, what to do with books and other materials while taking the test)

Waiting in the bus-loading area

Using the common areas of the school before and after school (e.g., where students are allowed to congregate, what behaviors are allowed)

Using the cafeteria

Walking in the halls, using the lockers

Going to the office

Using the library

Using the restroom

Attending assemblies

TABLE 6-4 Examples of Procedures

ELEMENTARY SCHOOL

Lining Up

1. Place books and materials neatly in your desk.
2. Sit quietly when you hear the "be quiet" signal.
3. Quietly stand up when your name (or row) is called.
4. Push your chair under your desk.
5. Quietly walk to the line.
6. Stand with your hands at your sides, facing forward; no talking.

Learning Position

1. Sit with your back against the back of your chair.
2. Sit with your legs under your desk.
3. Keep both feet on the floor.
4. Look at the teacher when he or she is talking to the class.
5. Keep your materials on top of your desk.

During Lessons

1. Sit in the learning position.
2. Raise your hand to talk unless the teacher calls on you.
3. Follow directions.
4. Read your book if you finish your work early.
5. Wait until independent work time to go to the restroom or the water fountain.

SECONDARY SCHOOL

Turning in Assignments

1. The last person in each row passes the assignment to the person in front of him or her.
2. The next person does the same until the assignments reach the first person in each row.
3. The first person in each row passes the assignments to the right.
4. The first person in the last row on the right places all assignments in the basket on the teacher's desk.

Class Discussions

1. Prepare for the discussion by reading the required assignment in advance.
2. Wait until the other person is finished speaking before you talk.
3. Stay on topic.
4. Respect others' opinions and contributions: Use appropriate expressions of disagreement.

Entering the Classroom

1. Enter the classroom before the bell rings.
2. Take your seat and get out the materials that you need for class.
3. Talk quietly until the bell rings.
4. Begin the morning assignment when the bell rings.

in your procedure will depend on the age of your students (e.g., young children typically need more detailed procedures), your students' learning histories (e.g., students who have previously been in classes where procedures were well established and consistently followed will probably learn new procedures more quickly), and your own needs. The procedures that you develop are just a start. You may find that steps need to be added (and taught) after you observe students actually following the procedures.

REMINDERS

Let's pretend for a moment that you are driving and you suddenly forget all of the rules for driving. You do not remember how fast you are allowed to go, where on the road you must drive, when you must stop, and so forth. Chances are that you would still be able to arrive safely at your destination *if* you paid careful attention to the many reminders that exist along our roadways. These reminders include signs (e.g., speed limit, stop, yield, one-way), road markings (e.g., lane dividers, roadway edge lines, warning bumps), lights (e.g., traffic signal, flashing lights), and more. Most drivers have a lot of experience, and they are supposed to know the rules for driving. (In fact, they probably had to pass a test about those rules before they received their driver's licenses.) They are also highly motivated to follow most of the rules in order to avoid tickets or accidents. Despite this, state departments of transportation spend millions of dollars installing many different types of reminders to help drivers remember the rules.

Once you develop your rules and procedures, you should next decide what forms of reminders you will use to help students remember those rules and procedures. Most of the time, the only reminder used is the posting of the rules somewhere in the classroom. We argue that reminders should be much more prominent if they are to be meaningful. In addition, those reminders should be actively incorporated into teaching and review activities, and possibly changed from time to time in order to keep them fresh in the students' minds. If highly motivated and experienced adult drivers need so many reminders, why would we expect students to remember complicated rules and procedures with only one poster?

Reminders can take many forms—the more creative, the better! See Table 6-5 for a few examples and Figure 6-1 for one example of a reminder to help students remember what to do when they need help in the classroom. We recommend that students help develop the reminders. Pose the question, "What can we do to help you remember to . . . ?" Once you provide several possible types of reminders as examples, you may be surprised to find that students often have good ideas for meaningful reminders.

Reminders are important for students of all ages.

IMPLEMENTING RULES AND PROCEDURES

Once you have determined your classroom rules and have developed your procedures, the next step is to plan lessons for teaching those rules and procedures. This should be your focus during the *first week* of class. Do not forget to

TABLE 6-5 Examples of Reminders

Visual Reminders

- Signs and posters (teacher made or computer generated), with pictures or icons associated with each rule.
- Student-drawn pictures that depict the rules.
- Digital pictures taken of students who are displaying rule-following behavior.
- Cartoons that depict the rules.
- Tape on the floor to designate where the students are to line up, where desks are to be placed, and where the students are to sit.
- Step-by-step pictorial guide (similar to those found in restrooms to explain hand-washing procedures).
- Footsteps on the floor to indicate where the students are to walk or line up.
- Index cards on the students' desks that list the rules.
- Icons or pictures posted in key places (e.g., a large clock that shows the time the bell rings each morning, which would be posted on the outside of the classroom door as a reminder to students to be in their seats before the bell rings; a cartoon of a student flushing the toilet posted inside each restroom stall).
- Questions posted in key places (e.g., a large sign, "Do you have your book, notebook, and calculator?" posted outside the door to the mathematics center; a small sign, "Have you logged out?" posted next to the computer).
- Arrows or other symbols.
- Hand signals or gestures.
- A video of students explaining and role-playing the rules for various environments in the school (The video can be used to explain the rules to new students.).

Auditory Reminders

- Timers to indicate the amount of time allowed for transitions, playtime, work time, and other activities.
- Hand claps or finger snaps (e.g., a special rhythmic clap that is a signal for students to get quiet).
- Music playing quietly during transitions that gradually gets louder as the transition time ends. The music is a reminder not to talk, and the gradual increase in volume is a signal that the transition is nearly finished.
- Music playing quietly during independent work time (a signal that no talking is allowed).
- A special word or phrase that is only used to get students' attention or signal a particular behavior (e.g., the teacher says, "Purple pumpernickel" to get students' e.g., the teacher says, "Purple pumpernickel"). To get the students' attention when they are working on other tasks; the teacher says, "Are you ready? Let's go!" to start the lesson at the beginning of class; students are not dismissed until the teacher says, "Now go, be great students").

I need help

- wait quietly for Ms. Preston to come help you
- Keep working or read your library book

I need help

FIGURE 6-1 Sample Reminder for a Rule: "When you need help, put up your help sign, then continue working or reading until I come to you."

Box 6-2

How to Teach Rules and Procedures

A. Introduction
1. State the rule or procedure.
2. Explain why you chose this rule or procedure. Giving a rationale for the rule or procedure shows students why the rule or procedure is important, thus helping to increase the students' motivation to follow the rule or the steps in the procedure.

B. Instruction
1. Describe behaviors that reflect the rule or procedure.
2. Describe behaviors that *do not* reflect the rule or procedure.
3. For elementary school students: Demonstrate the rule or procedure.
4. Ask for the students' feedback about your demonstration: Was this an appropriate example of following the rule? Did you exhibit all of the steps in the procedure?

C. Practice
1. Elementary school students: Have each student role-play the rule or procedure. This can be done in small groups.
2. Have other students provide feedback about whether the demonstration accurately reflected following the rule or procedure.

D. Feedback
1. Use various types of feedback systems, both formal and informal, to inform the students about their rule- and procedure-following behaviors.

include plans for teaching schoolwide rules and procedures along with your classroom rules. Explicit instructions in rules and procedures will help to ensure better behavior from your students. Therefore, an important preventive step is to teach the rules and procedures, and have the students practice them. Throughout the remainder of the school year, it is important to periodically review the rules and procedures, as needed (i.e., when instances of rule-breaking increase or the following of procedures breaks down). Box 6–2 describes how to teach rules and procedures.

The process of teaching the rules and procedures should begin on the first day of school because it allows teachers to set the expectations for learning and behavior from their first moments with the students. Research shows that starting off the year with effective classroom management, including clear rules and procedures, results in higher levels of appropriate behavior and higher academic performance later in the year (Emmer et al., 1980; Evertson & Emmer, 1982). We present a schedule for teaching rules and procedures in Table 6-6. We recommend that you devote much attention to teaching the rules and procedures early in the year and then fading this attention as students become more independent in exhibiting rule- and procedure-following behaviors. However, a clue that you need to reteach particular rules or procedures is when you find yourself reprimanding students or giving many reminders about expected behaviors.

Not only is it necessary to teach the rules and procedures directly through explanation, demonstration, and role-playing, but also it is important to provide high levels of reinforcement for rule-following behavior, particularly during the first weeks of school. Reinforcement will be discussed in detail in Chapters 10

TABLE 6-6 Schedule for Teaching Rules and Procedures

First Grading Period

- Teach the rules and procedures for all areas of the school during the first week of school. During this time, provide many opportunities for reviewing and practicing the rules and procedures. Provide frequent reinforcement for following the rules during this time.
- After the first week, review the rules two or three times per week. The following are ideas for reviewing the rules and procedures:
  - During the first or last few minutes of class, conduct rapid-paced oral reviews asking questions such as "What is the rule about sharpening your pencil?" or "How do you get ready to go home?"
  - Give surprise quizzes about the rules for extra-credit points.
  - Divide the class into two or more teams. Ask review questions about the rules and procedures for the teams to answer and award a point for each correct answer. The team with the most points at the end of the week (or month) earns a special privilege.

Second Grading Period

- Review the rules and procedures once per week.

Remainder of the Year

- Review the rules and procedures periodically, as needed.

and 11. The time that you spend teaching the rules and procedures during the first few weeks of school will pay large dividends in improved student behavior, increased learning time, and even greater academic achievement during the remainder of the school year. Occasional reinforcement should continue throughout the year as students follow the proper rules and procedures. In addition, it is important to respond to rule-breaking behaviors consistently, as it will be discussed in Chapter 12.

Two tests can help you to determine whether the rules and procedures in your class are clear and are understood by your students. The first test is that a visitor to your class should be able to discern the rules and procedures for your class on the basis of the students' behavior and teacher interactions with students about their behavior. The second test is that the visitor should be able to ask several randomly selected students about the rules and receive similar responses from each student.

In addition to teaching students the classroom and schoolwide rules, teachers should also consider how they will ensure that parents know and understand those rules. Typically, in the beginning of the year, you should communicate with parents regarding your rules, procedures, and other elements of your classroom management system. In addition, throughout the year, you should keep parents informed of any changes in your system. Box 6-3 presents ideas for communicating with parents about your rules and procedures.

Box 6-3

Ideas for Communicating with Parents Regarding Classroom Rules and Procedures

- Prepare a booklet of all pertinent classroom information to give to parents on the first day of school. This booklet might include the following:
  - ✓ **Who you are**—Provide a brief overview of your teaching career, your philosophy of teaching, your hobbies, or other information that you would like to share.
  - ✓ **Introduction to your classroom** —Present the rules and give examples. Include the expectations (e.g., students are expected to maintain a notebook, students will have homework three nights per week), an explanation of your behavior management system, and how you will communicate with parents.
  - ✓ **How parents can help at home** —Tell parents the expectations for parental assistance with homework, including providing help with academic tasks (e.g., reading, math facts, study skills). Provide suggestions for how they can help their children remember schoolwide and classroom rules. (This is especially important for young children.).
  - ✓ **Overview of the school year** —List important dates, class field trips, and other activities; include ways that parents can help with these activities.
  - ✓ **Contact information**—Provide your contact information and the times you will be available to meet with parents.
- Ensure that parents know your classroom rules and exactly what each rule means by providing examples and nonexamples of each rule.
- Provide parents with ideas for applying your classroom rules, or similar rules, in the home. For example, if one of your classroom rules is "Be responsible," you might provide parents with ideas for how this rule could be applied at home, such as the following: Pick up your toys before bedtime; put outside toys in the garage when you are finished playing with them; put your dishes in the dishwasher; put dirty clothes in the laundry basket.
- Provide parents with ideas about developing home procedures, such as procedures for preparing for school, completing homework, or preparing for bedtime.
- Provide parents with ideas for implementing home versions of other aspects of your classroom management system, such as reinforcement systems (see Chapters 10 and 11) and behavior reduction strategies (see Chapter 12).

Summary

A society without rules and procedures would fail. Likewise, a classroom without rules and procedures will have higher levels of inappropriate behavior than a classroom where the rules and procedures are clearly communicated and enforced. This is especially true when students with potentially high levels of problem behavior are present. Rules and procedures set the boundaries for expected behavior and, when consistently enforced, make the environment clear and predictable for all students.

In this chapter, we described the importance of rules, procedures, and reminders as preventive classroom management strategies. The following are the chapter objectives and how they were addressed:

1. Provide a rationale for having clear rules and procedures for your classroom.
2. Develop rules and procedures for your classroom.

We explained how to establish rules and procedures. Rules and procedures help to ensure an environment in which teachers can teach and students can learn. Because every teacher and every class is different, each teacher should determine what rules he or she needs in order to maximize learning time. Procedures help the class run smoothly, enabling students to complete routine tasks without assistance or reminders. Teachers who follow well-established procedures have classes that are more efficient and that have fewer behavioral problems than teachers who do not use procedures.

3. Give examples of types of reminders.

Reminders help students remember what behaviors are expected of them. Just as many signs, announcements, and other forms of reminders are provided to help us remember the rules of the road, rules in public places, and other expected behaviors, young people can benefit from creative cues about what teachers and administrators want the students to do.

4. Describe how to teach rules and procedures.

We not only explained why it is important to teach rules and procedures, but also provided suggestions for how to do this regularly throughout the school year. We emphasized that expecting students to follow rules and procedures should not be left to chance. Actively teaching students the expectations for behavior helps to ensure higher levels of appropriate behavior.

5. Describe the strategies for communicating with families regarding classroom management.

We described a few strategies for informing families about your classroom management system, including your rules and procedures, and for sharing ideas about the home application of this system for parents.

In Table 6-7, we provide a self-assessment form for teachers to evaluate their use of rules and procedures. This self-assessment form will help teachers determine whether their class rules and procedures reflect the guidelines for rules and procedures that we provided in this chapter.

TABLE 6-7   Rules and Procedures Self-Assessment Form

Never	Seldom	Sometimes	Often	Always
1	2	3	4	5

Use the numbers from the scale above to rate the following statements.

1. I have three to five positively stated classroom rules. _____

2. My classroom rules are consistent with school rules. _____

3. My classroom rules address behaviors related to safety, respect, and responsibility. _____

4. My rules are enforceable. _____

5. I developed my rules with the students' input. _____

6. I actively teach rules, particularly in the beginning of the school year or when new students enter my class. _____

7. I have procedures for every classroom task. _____

8. My procedures include step-by-step instructions for performing the desired task. _____

9. I use many and varied reminders to help the students remember class rules and procedures. _____

10. I have shared my rules and procedures with my students' parents or guardians. _____

Learning Activities

1. Describe some of our society's rules that influence school rules.
2. Discuss with your classmates the relationship between school rules and classroom rules.
3. List the rules that you would establish for your classroom and describe why you chose each rule.
4. List procedures that might be needed for areas outside of the classroom (e.g., bus loading area, cafeteria, halls).
5. Using the list developed in the preceding activity, develop steps for two of the procedures.
6. Role-play teaching elementary or secondary students a particular rule or procedure.
7. Read the vignettes that follow about Ms. Preston and Mr. Gonzalez. Develop rules and procedures for each teacher's situation that will address the problem areas.

Ms. Preston's Kindergarten

Ms. Preston, a new kindergarten teacher, came to you nearly in tears. She complained that her students are very energetic and rambunctious each morning. She finally gets them calmed down in the classroom, but then the same thing happens after recess. The students arrive at school between 7:10 and 7:35 every morning. The children who need to eat breakfast go to the cafeteria, which is crowded, loud, and chaotic. The students who do not eat breakfast go to the gym to play, where a monitor supervises them. There are many children of all ages in both the gym and the cafeteria.

To help Ms. Preston, you agree to observe her class and make recommendations to help her achieve order. On the day that you observe, Ms. Preston picks up her children from the two areas. She herds them together and attempts to get them to form a line. However, the line never really takes shape, and Ms. Preston continually scolds the children as they walk down the hall (e.g., "You need to be behind Emily," "Why are you walking next to Jamal?").

Once they reach the classroom, the children laugh and play as they put their coats and backpacks away. After a few minutes, the teacher claps her hands twice and says, "Circle time!" The children move to their assigned places and the lesson begins. After circle, the teacher again claps her hands two times, and when she says, "Go to your tables," the students walk to their tables and sit in their chairs. At 9:00 A.M., Ms. Preston instructs the students to line up for outside play. She calls students by their table numbers to get their coats and line up. They then walk in a line outside, where they are dismissed to play.

After 20 minutes of recess, Ms. Preston calls for her students to line up. Some children come immediately, but others either do not hear her or choose not to come. The teacher leaves those children who responded to her in order to go to the swings and gather the rest of the group. At the door, it takes several minutes for the children to calm down sufficiently so that they can enter the school; however, as they walk down the hall, the children become noisy and active. Again, the teacher scolds them. Back in the classroom, the students continue their rowdy behavior until the teacher claps her hands two times and says, "Time for reading circle," at which time the students move to their carpet squares for reading group.

Mr. Gonzalez's 10th-Grade American History Class

Mr. Gonzalez teaches history. His fifth-period 10th-grade American History class is always the low point of his day. The students in that class simply do not pay attention, and no matter how many office disciplinary referrals he makes, it doesn't seem to change anything. Let's look-in on this class:

All but two students arrive at the class before the tardy bell rings. Students talk and laugh as they make their way to their desks. Mr. Gonzalez has to ask them to be quiet and pay attention three times before everyone is seated and quiet for the taking of attendance. During attendance, about half of the 18 students pull out papers and begin to write, but it isn't clear whether they are working on class-related material.

After he finishes taking attendance, Mr. Gonzalez begins the day's lecture, which is on the topic of the

Townshend Act of 1767. After explaining the Townshend Act, Mr. Gonzalez makes comments and asks questions about the effect of this act on the development of the Revolutionary War. Some students take notes, but many continue to work on other material. Upon closer inspection, it appears that these students are working on last night's homework. They make little effort to attend to Mr. Gonzalez despite his many attempts to engage the entire class in the discussion. At the end of the class, Mr. Gonzalez reminds the class to pick up their homework packets. He also reminds students that the week's homework is due on Friday and that it will be 50% of their weekly grade.

Resources

WEBSITES

www.theteachingzone.com The Teaching Zone: Provides online training modules (approximately 1 hour each) on topics related to classroom management.

www.nwrel.org/scpd/sirs/5/cu9.html Education Northwest: Includes a comprehensive collection of easy-to-read articles that summarize research in various areas of classroom management, school discipline, and related topics.

www.education-world.com/a_curr/archives/ management_tips.shtml Education World®: Includes practical tips and information related to classroom management.

www.aft.org/teachers/jft/management.htm American Federation of Teachers: Includes tips on classroom management.

www.ldonline.org/indepth/classroom LD Online: Provides materials related to classroom management, including articles, books, and links to other Websites.

www.naset.org/?id=783 National Association of Special Education Teachers: Provides an in-depth series of articles on a variety of topics related to classroom management.

JOURNALS

Beyond Behavior (available online at www.ccbd.net)
Preventing School Failure
Teaching Exceptional Children (available online at http://www.cec.sped.org/Content/Navigation Menu/Publications2/TEACHINGExceptional Children/default.htm)
Each of these journals includes many articles related to teaching students with disabilities, including the issue of classroom management.

After reading this chapter, you will be able to do the following:

1. Explain the importance of careful attention to scheduling, climate, and organization as an essential component in preventing classroom behavior management problems.

2. Describe research that relates to scheduling, climate, and organization.

3. Describe the steps for developing your schedule and strategies for creating effective schedules.

4. Describe ideas for creating a classroom climate that is positive and conducive to learning.

5. Describe how to organize your classroom in order to address scheduling needs and climate.

Prevention of Challenging Behavior Through Effective Use of Scheduling, Climate, and Classroom Planning and Organization

CHAPTER 7

Big ideas in scheduling, climate, and organization:

- How do you schedule your classroom time is an important variable in classroom behavior management: The more students who are actively and successfully engaged in meaningful instructional activities, the fewer management problems you will have.

- Creating a safe and positive classroom climate that emphasizes learning and where students receive high levels of attention for appropriate behavior will increase the likelihood of appropriate student behavior.

- The organization of your classroom can function as a reminder of expected behaviors and can facilitate higher levels of appropriate student behavior.

Now that you have developed your rules and procedures, move your attention to other preventive aspects of planning: developing your schedule, planning your classroom climate (this refers to the overall appearance and feel of your room, not the temperature!), and organizing your classroom. Like rules and procedures, these facets of classroom behavior management are important for encouraging appropriate behavior and preventing inappropriate behavior. As an illustration, consider the following examples from public and professional life.

Most of us have attended long meetings or workshops. Which sessions were more productive? Those sessions which followed a clearly defined agenda with specific goals or tasks to be accomplished or those which included large amounts of off-task time and off-task talk without clearly defined goals or outcomes? We predict that you preferred the more structured meetings and found poorly structured meetings to be frustrating and a waste of time.

Also, think about businesses or other public places that you enjoy visiting. What is it about those environments that make doing business or visiting there pleasant? Our guess is that you like stores that are clean and well organized with a logical layout and clear signage so that finding products is easy. You probably like parks that are clean and perhaps that have specially designed areas for picnics, play, kite flying, and other activities. You may like to patronize businesses that make you feel welcome and relaxed, such as bookstores that offer comfortable couches and complimentary coffee, or hair salons that offer you a glass of wine and provide a nice scalp massage during your shampoo. Above all, you probably prefer establishments where the employees are polite, friendly, and efficient.

Most businesses and other public facilities take great care to make their environment pleasing and welcoming to the public. Planning the environment and preparing employees to work with the public are not left to chance. Business owners know that people are more likely to linger and return when the environment meets high standards for organization and climate. This chapter will describe how to address these important elements in your classroom. Granted, students do not really have a choice about "lingering" in your room or being a "return customer." However, happy students are more likely to be cooperative, and if your classroom is a place where students want to be, they will be less likely to exhibit inappropriate behavior in order to escape (as discussed in Chapters 2 and 3).

Scheduling, climate, and attention to classroom organization all seem like relatively simple tasks. However, each of these tasks requires careful attention. If not done correctly, management problems may arise because of inattention to one or more of these areas. For example, a classroom that has high levels of downtime (i.e., time when students are not engaged in meaningful tasks) is likely to have more management problems than classrooms where students are usually successfully engaged. Consider classrooms that are highly disorganized, where students receive little positive attention or where students are not treated with care and respect. Undoubtedly, these are classrooms where high levels of significant management problems are commonplace. A classroom that is crowded, has congested spots in high-traffic areas, or has furnishings that are not appropriate for students' physical and instructional needs is also a place that is ripe for a wide range of behavioral problems.

This chapter provides guidelines for developing the daily schedule, establishing a positive classroom climate, and organizing the room in a way that avoids predictable management problems. Done correctly, each of these strategies can help avoid common management problems.

> The places you enjoy visiting may give you a clue about how to make your classroom attractive to students.

THE DAILY SCHEDULE

The term *scheduling* refers to the time allocated during the school day for each activity that must occur. The times for some activities are predetermined (e.g., lunch, music, physical education, special services such as speech therapy or counseling). The teacher usually then schedules the remainder of the day. Although many aspects of the schedule depend on the instructional arrangement in which you are teaching (e.g., resource class, self-contained class, inclusion program), scheduling is still a complicated undertaking. Following certain basic steps, described later in this section, will facilitate this task. First, however, it is important both to clarify the terminology that is commonly used to refer to various aspects of scheduling and to list some facts about the significance of careful scheduling.

Research on the Relationship Between Scheduling and Student Performance

Beginning in the early 1970s, a number of large-scale research studies examined the correlation between teacher behaviors and student achievement (Berliner,

1978; Brophy & Evertson, 1976; Evertson, 1979, 1982; Evertson, Anderson, Anderson, & Brophy, 1980; Evertson, Anderson, & Brophy, 1978; Stallings, 1980; Tikunoff, Berliner, & Rist, 1975). Following these correlational studies, further research established that many of the variables identified were actually causal; in other words, the extent to which teachers demonstrated certain behaviors influenced student achievement and behavior (Anderson, Evertson, & Brophy, 1979; Brophy & Evertson, 1976). Some of these critical teacher behaviors included setting and teaching rules and procedures, as described in Chapter 6. Others are described in this chapter and pertain to scheduling, climate, and organization.

Generally, the body of literature pertaining to instructional time uses certain terms to refer to different aspects of the schedule. Some of these components of the schedule are predictors of student learning and behavior. Table 7-1 provides a summary of research on the relationship between the various levels of instructional time and student learning and behavior. In addition, a model that shows

---

TABLE 7-1 Summary of Research on Instructional Time

- Special education teachers spend approximately equal amounts of time on instructional activities and noninstructional activities (e.g., paperwork, support activities) (Vannest, Soares, Harrison, Brown, & Parker, 2010).

- Fisher (2009), in an observational study of 15 high school classes, reported that students spent the majority of the time (48% of the observed time) in "listening" activities, which did not necessarily require any type of active engagement. The next most frequent activity was waiting (17% of the observed time).

- Teachers spend an average of 23% of their time on noninstructional activities, such as arts and crafts, holiday parties, classroom behavior management issues, and even preparation for standardized tests (Metzker, 2003).

- Numerous studies have shown that improving students' academic success can produce concomitant improvements in classroom behavior (Cotton & Savard, 1982; Gettinger, 1988).

- Rosenshine (1980), in his landmark study of classroom instructional time, reported that 58% of the school day is allocated for instructional activities, 23% for nonacademic activities (e.g., music, art, story time), and 19% for noninstructional activities (e.g., lunch, transitions, housekeeping tasks). Hofmeister and Lubke (1990) reported that approximately 79% (4 hours, 44 minutes) of available time is allocated for instruction.

- Rosenshine (1980) also reported that allocating more time for instruction did not result in corresponding reductions in student attention. That is, scheduling longer periods of instruction did not increase student off-task behavior.

- Studies have reported varying percentages of engaged time:
  - 28% to 56% of the time spent in school in a given year (WestEd, 1998)
  - 42% (2 hours, 31 minutes) of the available time (Hofmeister & Lubke, 1990)
  - Hofmeister and Lubke (1990) reported academic learning time totals that range from 10% to 25%, with an average of 17% (approximately 1 hour, 1 minute of a 6-hour day!).

- Latham (1992) reported an average of 18% of the day spent in academic learning.

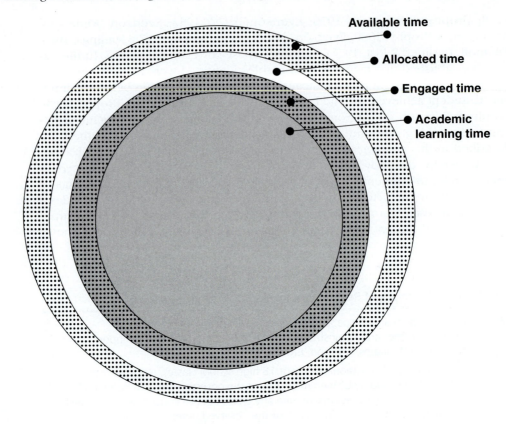

FIGURE 7-1 Scheduling Terminology

how these different components are related is provided in Figure 7-1. Definitions for each term follow.

AVAILABLE TIME OR OPPORTUNITIES TO LEARN Student learning is contingent on the content to which the students are exposed (e.g., how many chapters in a text are taught, how many skills are covered). The opportunity to learn is determined, in part, by the total number of hours in the school day that are available for instruction. For example, out of a 6-hour school day, it is possible that only $4\frac{1}{2}$ hours are devoted to academic classes. Nonacademic classes (e.g., music, art, physical education, lunch, and transitions may consume the remaining hour and a half.

ALLOCATED TIME   Allocated time (or scheduled time) refers to the amount of time that the teacher delegates for each instructional activity. Hofmeister and Lubke (1990) estimated that only approximately 79% of the available time is actually allocated for instruction (see Table 7-1).

Become familiar with scheduling terminology.

Allocating as much time as possible for academic instruction is important for both student learning and appropriate behavior (Brophy & Evertson, 1976; Hofmeister & Lubke, 1990). The following elementary class schedule illustrates high levels of allocated time:

8:00–9:00	Reading/language arts
9:00–9:05	Break
9:05–10:05	Math
10:05–10:10	Break
10:10–11:00	Reading/language arts
11:00–11:05	Break
11:05–11:50	Social studies
11:50–12:20	Peer tutoring/curriculum projects
12:20–12:40	Lunch
12:40–12:50	Recess
12:50–1:35	Science
1:35–2:10	Special area (e.g., P.E., music, art)
2:10–2:25	Reinforcement activities
2:25–2:30	Preparation to go home or to after-school activities
2:30	Class is dismissed

Total available time: 390 minutes

Time allocated for academic instruction and practice activities: 290 minutes (74% of the day)

Reading/language arts: 110 minutes (28%)

Math: 60 minutes (15%)

Social studies: 45 minutes (12%)

Science: 45 minutes (12%)

Breaks/recess: 25 minutes (6%)

Reinforcement activities: 15 minutes (3%)

Note that in this schedule, short breaks are planned throughout the day and that core curricular areas (e.g., language arts, math) are scheduled early in the day. Note also that more than one period is scheduled for language arts and that more time is allocated for language arts and math instruction than any other area. The reason for this is discussed later in this section, but basically, if students have significant deficits in basic skill areas, one instructional period per day may be insufficient to address students' many needs in these areas. Remember that student achievement is related to the opportunity to learn or to exposure to instructional content.

ENGAGED TIME, ACADEMIC ENGAGED TIME (AET), OR TIME ON TASK   Not all of the time that is allocated for instruction is actually spent on instruction. AET represents the percentage of allocated time that students actively participate in instructional activities: listening to instruction, answering questions, asking questions, writing, working in groups, and working on projects (Brophy & Evertson, 1981). High levels of engaged time is one of the most critical variables in both student learning and appropriate behavior (Berliner, 1978; Brophy & Evertson, 1976; Hofmeister & Lubke, 1990). Students do not learn unless they have the opportunity to learn through interaction with instructional stimuli. Furthermore, unengaged time (i.e., downtime) can lead to a vicious cycle of behavioral problems: When students are not meaningfully engaged in instructional activities, misbehavior is likely to occur. If not dealt with quickly and effectively, these behavioral problems can escalate to more serious forms of behavior that take even more of the teacher's time, potentially interfering with the next scheduled instructional activity (Martella, Nelson, & Marchand-Martella, 2003). Unfortunately, studies have shown disturbingly low levels of engaged time, as evidenced by the data presented in Table 7-1. Possible reasons for low levels of engaged time are implied in Table 7-1, including inefficient procedures for conducting transitions and other routine tasks, and inefficient scheduling.

ACADEMIC LEARNING TIME (SUCCESSFUL ENGAGED TIME)   High levels of engaged time is an insufficient goal in and of itself. If students have high levels of on-task time, but during that time they make many errors, they may be learning little more than how to do the work incorrectly. Students learn best when they respond correctly. Also, high levels of errors can lead to behavioral problems because of frustration or the desire to avoid a difficult task. Thus, one final level of learning is critical: academic learning time, or the amount of engaged time that students are successful in the academic responses. Academic learning time is significantly positively correlated with academic achievement and appropriate behavior (Fisher et al., 1978). Likewise, the more time that students are not engaged in instruction, the more likely the teacher is to have classroom behavior management problems (Martella et al., 2003).

Scheduling is an important step in preventive behavior management.

Thus, research shows that high levels of student learning and appropriate student behavior depend somewhat on the amount of time that is allocated for instruction and largely on the amount of time that students are successfully engaged in learning. Teachers can take specific steps, described in Box 7-1, to ensure that the instructional day includes high levels of allocated, engaged, and academic learning time. Some of the suggestions listed in Box 7-1 were described in Chapter 6; others are explained in this chapter and in later chapters of this text.

You can see that one of the recommendations listed in Box 7-1 cautions against the use of "rest time," "free time," or "reinforcement time." Rest time is only appropriate if you are teaching young children or children who have physical or health conditions that require rest periods during the day. It is not appropriate to schedule rest periods to allow for breaks for the teacher and/or paraprofessionals or to simply fill time during the day.

Box 7-1

Strategies for Increasing Engaged and Academic Learning Time

Establish and Use Rules and Procedures

- Establish and teach the rules for classroom behavior (see Chapter 6).
- Establish and teach the procedures for managing all classroom tasks and activities (see Chapter 6). Make sure that you have procedures in place that will minimize issues that detract from on-task behavior (e.g., procedures for passing out materials, getting needed supplies, turning in completed work, getting help while working, what to do when one has finished working).
- Reinforce students for following the rules and procedures (see Chapters 10 and 11). Reinforcement typically takes less time than responding to behavioral problems.

Be Prepared

- Have materials ready for each lesson that you will teach during the day: textbooks or other books, maps, films, DVDs, pictures, blank transparencies for the overhead projector, markers, chalk, erasers, or any other materials needed during each lesson.
- Have materials ready for each student activity that you have planned during the day: materials for cooperative groups or peer tutoring sessions, learning centers, independent work activities, games, computers (e.g., make sure that both the computer and the software work properly).
- Preview all materials that you plan to share with students by interacting with the material in the same manner that the students will. This means watch, read, or answer questions in the material from *start to finish*. Too often, teachers preview only the first few minutes of audiovisual media, the first few screens of a software program, or the first few items on a worksheet. Then, when the material is actually being used, the teacher discovers that it is inappropriate for some reason (e.g., too difficult, too easy, does not address target objectives, shifts focus midway). Many classroom behavior

management problems develop as a result of students encountering work that is too difficult or too easy (Gettinger & Seibert, 2002).
- Carefully plan what your paraprofessional will be doing during the day, and have a procedure in place for communicating these plans before the day begins.

Provide Effective Instruction

- Make sure that you allocate most of the day to instruction. This means that your schedule should not include large periods of free time, reinforcement time, or rest time.
- Develop detailed lesson plans for each period during the day, and then follow them! (See Chapter 8.)
- Provide interesting, relevant instruction that incorporates a variety of learning activities (Beyda, Zentall, & Ferko, 2002; Kern, Bambara, & Fogt, 2002; Miller, Gunter, Venn, Hummel, & Wiley, 2003; WestEd, 2001). When students are learning skills that are meaningful to their lives and when those skills are taught in ways that are motivating and fun, students are more likely to participate in classroom discussions and to complete their work.

Manage Interruptions

- Take steps to manage interruptions such as announcements or the presence of people who need to talk to you during class time. The following are a few ideas for doing this:
  - Inform colleagues and administrators that you prefer not to be interrupted while directly teaching lessons. If they need to talk with you, they should leave a note or talk with you when you are not teaching.
  - At the beginning of the year, communicate this same policy to parents. Let parents know how and when you can be reached. Of course, your intent is not to keep parents out of the classroom. Invite them to observe lessons with the understanding that you will be

(continued)

better able to talk with them after the lesson is over.

- If someone comes to your door to talk with you while you are teaching, remember that your first responsibility is to your students. Finish what you are doing, if possible, and make sure that the students are engaged in other tasks before you stop to talk with the visitor. It is important, but difficult, to be consistent with this policy. An excellent teacher with whom the authors once worked had asked those individuals who frequently came to his class (e.g., principal, behavior specialist, counselor) to wait until he finished teaching his lesson. He let them know that he could not talk with them until his students were working independently. Furthermore, he stuck to this policy, meaning that anyone who came to his class waited until the students were able to work on their own for a moment. This admirable policy communicated to the students that nothing was more important than their instruction! Interestingly, the students modeled their teacher's behavior:

The students paid no attention to visitors until their teacher did!

- Provide your school office staff with times when you are not teaching, and ask them to limit contact (e.g., phone calls, contact via the intercom) to those times.
- If your school uses the public announcement system indiscriminately (i.e., announcements are made at random times during the day), propose to your administrators or site-based school management team that announcements be limited to either the first few minutes of the day or the first few minutes of each class.
- Finally, teach your students a procedure that is to be followed in the event that you are faced with an unavoidable interruption (e.g., a student has a seizure, the school has a power outage and you are unable to use the audiovisual media, a serious behavioral problem develops). For example, you might make sure that students always keep a book or other reading material in their desks or in a central location in the room. Teach students to take out their reading material and read until further notice when you give a particular signal.

Free time or any unstructured time creates a situation that is high risk for encountering behavior management problems. Consider this scenario:

Ms. Ballard (to her fifth-grade class):	We have a few minutes until the bell rings. You may talk to your neighbors or read if you like.
	Spike turns sideways in his chair, leans back, and extends his legs out toward Rosario's desk, which is next to his.
Rosario:	Get out of my space. Keep your feet to yourself.
Spike (keeping his legs right where they are):	Hey, I don't want trouble! I'm just tryin' to relax and talk to you.
Rosario:	Ms. Ballard, tell Spike to keep his feet in his own space. He's bugging me.
Ms. Ballard:	Spike, sit up straight.
Spike:	But Ms. Ballard, you said that we could talk to our neighbors. I'm just trying to be neighborly with Rosario, but she won't talk to me!

And so, Ms. Ballard finds herself in the position of having to deal with Spike's behavior, which up until this point, has been on task. Many students, particularly students with behavioral difficulties, find it hard to self-direct and self-regulate during unstructured free time, particularly when this free time is not part of a regular routine and when rules or parameters for allowable behaviors are not clearly stated. These children may choose activities that are unacceptable (e.g., talking too loudly, making inappropriate comments, making spitwads, writing on themselves or on the materials or furniture, standing in the doorway to check out what is going on in the hall), particularly when the free time is given spontaneously with little guidance about what is and what is not acceptable. But this does not mean that free time is acceptable as long as it is given regularly and the expectations are explained. Few teachers can afford to squander valuable instructional time. Teachers are under significant pressure to cover required amounts of academic content, often while teaching a widely heterogeneous student population, as discussed in Chapter 1. Also, as you will learn in Chapter 8, there is a close relationship between students' behavior and academic performance. The more academic difficulties a student experiences, the more likely the student is to exhibit challenging behavior, and vice versa. Students who are experiencing academic difficulties cannot afford to lose valuable instructional time. Some teachers allow students to earn free time as a reinforcement activity for appropriate behavior. In Chapters 10 and 11, we will discuss how to provide reinforcement for appropriate behavior in ways that do not interfere with instruction. Thus, we see no reason for having free time as a regular part of the classroom schedule.

Of course, all students need breaks (and some need breaks more frequently than others), but breaks do not have to be unstructured in order to accomplish the goal of relaxing or relieving stress. In addition, for some students, especially students with autism or developmental disabilities, breaks and playtime provide opportunities for teaching critical play and leisure skills. For most students, providing structured breaks will help to avoid behavior management problems during those times and will make it easier for students to transition between breaks and instructional times. A few ideas for structuring breaks (including reinforcement time) are provided in Box 7-2. Remember that appropriate student behavior is most likely to occur when teachers carefully and systematically plan and implement specific strategies to accomplish that goal. Failure to plan proactively for appropriate behavior will increase the likelihood of classroom behavior management problems.

Scheduling High Levels of Allocated Time

One of the strategies recommended in Box 7-1 is to ensure that your schedule includes high levels of allocated time. Again, although your schedule will depend on the grade level that you are teaching and the subjects that you are expected to cover, the following guidelines will help you to allocate time for instruction during the school day:

1. List the school start and end times.
2. Block out times that are unavailable for instruction: lunch, teacher planning period, special area classes (e.g., P.E., music, art), or related services (e.g., speech therapy, counseling).
3. List all of the subjects that you must teach during the day. This may be determined by your teaching assignment (e.g., the schedule for a high school

Box 7-2

Strategies for Increasing Appropriate Behavior During Breaks

- Establish and teach the rules and procedures for breaks. One of these procedures should include reminders about the levels of talking and movement allowed during the break (as discussed in Chapter 6). Rules and procedures should also address where students are allowed to go and how, and what they are allowed to do during the break. For example, are students allowed to go to the restroom? If so, must they obtain permission before leaving the room? What materials, games, and equipment are students allowed to use? How many students may be in a particular area (e.g., the computer area) at a given time?
- Particularly for elementary school children, you should provide activities from which students can choose during breaks. Activities might include the following:
  - Games for pairs, small groups, or individual students
  - Art activities
  - Reading materials (or listening to audiobooks)
  - Outdoor physical activities such as basketball, races of various kinds, kickball, or scavenger hunts
  - Indoor physical activities such as stretching, isometrics, standing push-ups against the wall, or possibly the use of exercise equipment (perhaps parents, community members, or businesses will donate equipment)

teacher assigned to teach English/language arts will look significantly different than that of a teacher who must cover all subject areas) and your students' individualized educational program goals and objectives.

4. Identify the times, if any, that must be devoted to particular subjects. For example, a fifth-grade resource teacher may need to schedule math students during the same time that the general education fifth-grade classes have math instruction. A self-contained high school special education teacher may have to schedule social skills instruction when all of the students are available (e.g., they are not in general education classes).

5. Try to schedule the main language arts and math instructional periods in the morning, if possible.

6. Consider students' skill levels when developing the schedule. If you are teaching students who have significant deficits in any major skill areas (e.g., reading, writing, math), you may need to schedule more than one instructional period to address those subjects. For example, if you teach high school students who are reading on an elementary level, you may need to schedule two or more periods to address reading and writing, and either address English (age-appropriate content for high school students) within the context of reading instruction or schedule a separate period for English.

7. Try to alternate high-motivation subjects with low-motivation subjects. If your students have a low interest in history but love science, science should be scheduled after history if possible.

8. If you have a paraprofessional available, you may need to consider when you will schedule his or her breaks. This should be done during times when either you have fewer students in the classroom or when the subject is something that you can cover without assistance.

9. Consider how you will schedule breaks for students. If you teach in high school or middle school, these breaks might be in the form of the predetermined passing periods that all students in the school follow. If you teach in a self-contained class or at the elementary level, you may need to include breaks in the schedule.

10. Once you have the instructional periods scheduled for the day, begin planning what will happen during each of those periods. We discuss instructional planning in detail in Chapter 8. At this point, you may consider structuring each period with a consistent set of routine activities. Just as procedures tell us *how* to do basic classroom activities, **routines** tell us *when* those activities (and others) will occur. Most of us have a daily routine that we follow when we get up in the morning, when we arrive at work, when we get home after classes or work, or when we do our grocery shopping. Adherence to the same routines makes these activities go smoothly. When something happens to interfere with a routine (e.g., oversleeping), we may forget to do certain things, or we may feel a little out-of-kilter for the day.

Just as in our personal lives, establishing routines in a classroom helps to ensure that things run smoothly and efficiently. For example, each period in a high school class might follow a routine such as this one:

- Warm-up activity to allow the teacher to attend to administrative tasks and to allow students to turn in work and gather needed materials (5 minutes)
- Review of the material from the previous day's lesson (3–5 minutes)
- Direct teaching lesson for the day (large- and/or small-group instruction, 20–40 minutes)
- Practice activities (15–30 minutes)
- End-of-class activities such as assigning homework or reviewing ongoing assignments and upcoming events (3–5 minutes)

Establishing and maintaining a consistent routine for each period should help to prevent management problems because students have become accustomed to consistent routines. It may also make daily planning easier for the teacher: By having the basic framework for each period set in advance, all that the teacher needs to do is to determine what each activity will include or what content will be addressed.

These 10 steps provide a general template to be followed in developing your schedule. Although each teacher's situation will be slightly different, these basic steps should help to make planning your schedule a manageable task.

THE CLASSROOM CLIMATE

Climate refers to the overall atmosphere of the classroom environment. Businesses understand the importance of climate and invest time and resources to create a climate that reflects a particular atmosphere or feeling. For example, physicians may try to create a calm, relaxing environment for their waiting room. Retail businesses undoubtedly want their facilities to be clean and well organized, with friendly and knowledgeable staff. Like businesses, teachers should strive to create a classroom environment that is reflective and supportive of the business of a school: children's learning and socialization. Your classroom should look like a place where learning occurs, where learning is important, and where learning is celebrated. Your classroom should feel warm, inviting, and safe, without losing the overall ambience of a learning environment (see Box 7-3). Emmer and his colleagues (2003) summarize this goal nicely, saying that "students should look forward to the class" (p. 135). Just as businesses carefully plan all aspects of the environment, from customer service to store layout to color schemes, teachers should plan how they will achieve the desired elements of climate.

Borich (2004) describes classroom climate as the amalgamation of the social environment and the organizational environment. The social environment of the classroom refers to the style of interactions allowed and promoted by the teacher, including the following:

- how the teacher exercises his or her authority and power,
- the extent to which the teacher exhibits warmth and concern toward students, and
- the extent to which the teacher allows and encourages student input and choice.

Climate refers to the overall look and feel of the classroom.

The organizational environment refers to the physical climate of the classroom: arrangement, lighting, decorations, and amenities.

In large part, climate is determined by the style and nature of teacher interactions with students. Teacher–student relationships are the foundation of climate and are important to student success. Teacher–student relationships appear to influence student achievement, the dropout rate and delinquency, antisocial behavior in general, and even school safety issues.

Research suggests that teachers have a far broader role in the school setting than simply delivering academic content. For example, teachers can be a motivating factor in students' academic performance. Strong, positive relationships with one or more teachers have been associated with higher grades (Niebuhr, 1999), better performance on achievement tests (Green, 1998), increased student commitment to learning (Borich, 2003), fewer behavioral problems, greater social competence, and better school adjustment (Pianta, Hamre, & Stuhlman, 2003). A review by Marzano (2003a) revealed that teacher–student relationships are a critical factor in classroom behavior management: Teachers who had high-quality relationships with students had 31% fewer disciplinary problems than other teachers. Likewise, negative teacher–student interactions are associated with undesirable outcomes, including lower levels of achievement, antisocial behavior, poor school adjustment, and externalizing and internalizing behavioral problems (Ladd, Birch, & Buhs, 1999; Murray & Greenberg, 2006; Murray & Murray, 2004; Soar & Soar, 1979).

The potential for positive teacher influence is also seen in studies of dropouts and juvenile delinquency. In one major study of what causes students to drop out of school, Wehlage and Rutter (1986) followed approximately 30,000 students from more than 1,000 high schools. One commonly cited explanation among many of the students who eventually dropped out of school was the perception that teachers lacked interest in the students. In the late 1980s, three major studies began a long-term examination of the causes and correlates of delinquent behavior in children

Box 7-3

Strategies for Achieving a Positive Classroom Climate

Social Environment

- Stand at the door as students enter the classroom and greet each student by name as he or she enters.
- Provide high levels of appropriate, specific praise (see Chapter 10 for more information about providing praise).
- Display student work.
- Provide students with choices whenever possible.
- Provide opportunities for students to interact with peers through academic activities (e.g., classes, projects, peer tutoring) and social activities (e.g., lunch, recess, clubs).
- Provide amenities that increase the motivational aspects of the classroom and also are instructional (e.g., pets, plants, hobbies).
- Know your students' needs (e.g., physical, emotional, learning) and be as responsive as possible to those needs. This means that you may need to provide (or make arrangements) for students' basic physical needs (e.g., food, clothing, rest) if those needs are not fully met at home, emotional needs (e.g., a place to cool down, a way for the student to let the teacher know that a private conversation is needed), and, of course, learning needs (e.g., identify needs in all academic, social, and behavioral areas). However, knowing your students' needs also means paying close attention to students during lessons and adjusting instruction accordingly. Are students looking confused or starting to become distracted? You probably need to better describe the concepts or skills that you are teaching, provide more examples, reteach earlier concepts, or use other strategies to make the content clearer. Are students looking bored? You must do something to keep their attention (e.g., give them a short break, begin a hands-on activity).

Physical Environment

- Maintain a neat, orderly classroom with materials properly stored or ready for use, appropriate storage for student supplies and personal materials, and easily accessible instructional materials.
- Ensure that all materials, areas of the room, and equipment intended for student use are accessible for all students, including students who use special equipment for mobility.
- Arrange the classroom in a manner that facilitates specific activities in different areas of the room (e.g., reading area, group instruction area, peer tutoring area, learning centers).
- Arrange the classroom in a manner that reduces congestion at critical points (e.g., entrance, sink, pencil sharpener).
- Ensure that lighting, equipment, furniture, windows, walls, and so forth are all in good repair and good working order.
- Provide appropriately sized furniture that is well suited to students' instructional needs.

Instructional Environment

- Ensure that all materials needed for daily instructional activities are prepared and ready for use before the students arrive.
- Set high, but reasonable and attainable, expectations for student learning and behavior.
- Ensure that students have meaningful tasks to do at all times; tasks should reflect students' instructional goals.
- Provide a variety of instructional activities (e.g., large-group instruction, small-group instruction, independent work, peer tutoring, learning centers).
- When grading students' work, pay attention to what students do well, along with the errors made. Make comments on the paper about what each student did well, and where there are errors, briefly describe the error and what the student should do next time to improve (e.g., "You added here instead of subtracting"; "A comma is not necessary to separate a compound sentence"; "This fraction can be reduced further").
- Celebrate student successes and achievement: Post student work, have students set goals and frequently chart progress toward those goals, send positive notes to parents and/or contact parents by phone or e-mail in order to share positive news,

(continued)

and remind students of past successes when they are faced with a difficult task or situation.

Behavior Management Environment

- Post reminders of rules, procedures, and reinforcement systems, and be consistent in implementing and enforcing all of these.
- Develop class traditions. For example, your class might have a special way of acknowledging birthdays, a special routine for welcoming new students into the class, or a unique celebration when all students achieve a particular goal (e.g., homework turned in on time, an 80 or above on a test). Just as every family has its own traditions and customs, including such practices in your classroom will help students feel a sense of belonging.
- Teach the consequences for rule violations and review as needed.
- Respond to rule violations consistently, following predetermined consequences, in a matter-of-fact manner.
- Refrain from arguing with students about rule violations.
- Ensure that students earn reinforcement regularly and consistently.
- Engage in a systematic problem-solving process if students are not successful at earning reinforcers.
- Ensure that you have mechanisms in place for supporting students' emotional needs.
- Listen carefully to students and acknowledge student concerns and complaints.
- Ensure a safe, positive, learning climate. Learn the early warning signs of student behavioral problems, and intervene early and quickly when problems arise, in order to prevent escalation to more serious problems. Intervene in behavioral problems in ways that allow students to maintain dignity and respect without using embarrassment or ridicule to control behavior.

and youth. These studies and others indicate that school-based factors such as low achievement, lack of connection with and commitment to school, and feeling unsafe at school are all correlates of juvenile delinquency (Chibnall & Abbruzzese, 2004; Wyrick & Howell, 2004). Furthermore, students who exhibit high levels of inappropriate behavior and low levels of socially acceptable behavior are likely to experience school failure and peer rejection. Both of these are highly predictive of antisocial behavior and delinquency (Beebe-Frankenberger, Lane, Bocian, Gresham, & MacMillan, 2005; Walker, Ramsey, & Gresham, 2004).

The wave of school-based shootings in the 1980s and 1990s prompted a large-scale evaluation of conditions that fostered violent behavior in schools and how schools could identify warning signs and take preventive action. The U.S. Department of Education disseminated two documents to help school personnel recognize the early signs of potential violent behavior and create preventive, proactive school environments. The first document was titled *Early Warning, Timely Response*; the follow-up document was *Safeguarding Our Children: An Action Guide*. Both documents emphasize close, caring teacher–student relationships as an important element in identifying the early warning signs of potential violence (Dwyer & Osher, 2000; Dwyer, Osher, & Warger, 1998). When teachers know students well, they get to know students' needs and feelings, and are more likely to recognize changes in behavior patterns. Students who have a close relationship and frequent contact with one or more teachers or other school personnel may be more likely to disclose important personal feelings and problems (e.g., suicidal ideation, bullying or harassment, abuse, social isolation), and are more likely to feel a sense of connection to the school (Dwyer & Osher, 2000).

Some experts suggest that a positive, nurturing, caring relationship with an adult, including a teacher, may provide a protective buffer against the risk factors that increase the likelihood of learning and behavioral problems. Resiliency research has examined individual, family, school, and community factors that increase a child's risk for antisocial behavior and factors that provide protection against negative influences. Each arena (i.e., individual, family, school, community) has the potential for both risk and protective factors. School-based conditions that are risk factors for antisocial behavior include poor-quality schools, negative interactions with teachers, negative interactions with peers, and inappropriate peer models (Center for Mental Health in Schools, 2002). However, schools can also serve as buffers to negative individual, family, and neighborhood influences. Protective school-based conditions include positive relationships with one or more teachers; appropriate peer models; positive interactions with peers; school success; and a nurturing, caring school environment (Center for Mental Health in Schools, 2002; Werner, 1990). On the basis of her extensive study of resiliency, Werner notes that protective factors tend to be a more profound influence than specific risk factors, providing a mediating force for helping children overcome powerful negative life conditions (Werner & Smith, 2001).

Zionts (2005) presents an interesting discussion of teacher–student relationships as they relate to positive school adjustment. She examines the effects of students' primary relationships (i.e., relationships with parents or other primary caregivers) on school adjustment and how positive teacher–student relationships can be a mediating factor that affects current and future school adjustment. Zionts argues that a strong, positive teacher–student relationship provides a "secure base" that can ameliorate the potentially negative effects of poor primary relationships, increasing the likelihood that a student will successfully adjust to the demands of school.

Given the impact of positive, caring teacher–student relationships, it is important to examine the specific teacher behaviors that contribute to, or detract from, such a relationship. Furthermore, teachers should consider whether students have the skills that are critical to forming and maintaining relationships, and are able and motivated to use those skills in the appropriate contexts. Teachers, for example, expect students to pay attention and follow directions, accurately complete assigned tasks, effectively manage conflicts with peers and teachers, use self-control, and be cooperative (Beebe-Frankenberger et al., 2005; Hersh & Walker, 1983; Kerr & Zigmond, 1986). Students who lack these skills are at greater risk for exhibiting inappropriate behavior, which may interfere with the development of a positive teacher–student relationship. These skills must then be taught and/or reinforced. For example, we suggest that healthy relationships are built on empathy, integrity, interest, and respect. These concepts should be explained and discussed with students, and behaviors that are reflective of each concept should be identified and labeled.

Teacher behaviors and attitudes that show warmth and caring toward students, such as praise, soliciting and using student ideas, listening to students, respecting student contributions, and socializing with students, are indicators of positive teacher–student relationships (Evertson, Anderson, Anderson, & Brophy, 1980). Box 7-4 lists specific teacher behaviors that will facilitate good relationships with students.

Teacher–student relationships are the most basic element of the classroom climate.

Box 7-4

Strategies for Establishing Positive Relationships with Students

- Always model respectful and polite behavior with your students. Examples of this strategy seen in exemplary teachers over the years include the following:
  - ✓ Mr. Kircher always says "please" and "thank you" to his students and always maintains a calm, professional demeanor even in the face of serious misbehavior from his students. He calmly reminds students what their choices are, the consequences of those choices, and that he hopes that the students make good choices.
  - ✓ Ms. Ozar speaks to her elementary students in a way that sounds very grown up, yet is still on their level of understanding, and she always turns a problem into a learning opportunity. For example, in talking with a student who forgot his homework, she might say, "I can see that you're upset by this, and I understand that. You know that you'll need to do your homework before you go out to recess this morning. But let's think of a way in which we can help you avoid this problem in the future. What could you do to make sure that you remember your homework tomorrow?"
  - ✓ Mr. Pendergast always wears a tie to school because he knows that he is an important role model for his secondary students.
- Know your students. Find out what they like and dislike, what they find easy or challenging, and use this information to plan and adjust lessons accordingly. Talk to students about their lives. Ask questions about their interests, hobbies, families, and neighborhoods. Learn something about the things that interest your students, even if those things do not interest you! You should be able to carry on a conversation with students about the movies they watch, the music they listen to, the stars they admire, and the sports they play.
- Spend time interacting with your students. Although you will do this during class, you should also spend time outside of class: Greet your students when you see them in other areas of the school, talk to them, eat lunch with them, and go to their extracurricular activities (e.g., plays, academic competitions, sporting events).

Not only will you get to know your students better, but they will get to know you as well.

- Learn and use effective listening skills. Active listening will help you to identify the feelings that may be the impetus behind student behaviors and verbal messages (Brandt, 1988; Gordon, 1974). Active listening is especially important when a student is experiencing intense emotion (e.g., anger, frustration) and not only can help the teacher identify what is upsetting the student, but also can defuse the situation quickly. The following are two examples of active listening responses:

Example 1 (high school):

STUDENT: I hate Ms. Calvin's class! I'm not going back if she keeps disrespecting me that way.

TEACHER: Sounds like you're having some problems with Ms. Calvin.

STUDENT: *I'm* not having problems—*she* is! Nothing I do pleases her.

TEACHER: So you think that she's picking on you—maybe holding you to higher or different standards than the other students.

Example 2 (elementary):

STUDENT: (almost crying) I'm not doing my journal today, Mr. Kircher. You always make us write about what we did last night, and I didn't do anything. I don't have anything to write, so I'm not going to do my journal.

MR. KIRCHER: So you're telling me that you have nothing to say about your evening.

STUDENT: (crying) I don't want to write. I'm not doing my journal.

MR. KIRCHER: It seems that maybe something happened last night that you don't want to write about, something that was pretty upsetting for you.

- Use humor. Humor is a powerful tool that can help make students comfortable and relaxed, can defuse potentially problematic situations, and can help reduce the stress of undertaking difficult tasks. Of course, humor should never be at a student's expense, nor is sarcasm acceptable.
- Solicit student input about the class. When students feel that they have a say and, thus, a degree of control over their environment, they are less likely to misbehave in order to achieve that control. The following are a few ways to give students a voice in the classroom:
  ✓ Have students help with basic classroom tasks (e.g., pass out or collect papers, write assignments on the board, put away materials, straighten or organize shelves, deliver messages).
  ✓ Use peer tutoring (see Chapter 8).
  ✓ Give students choices ("You may do this by yourself or with your partner"; "You may either work on your spelling or your math review"; "Your product can be a skit, a debate, or a mural depicting the critical elements of your topic").
  ✓ Have group meetings to discuss students' concerns.
  ✓ Provide a classroom suggestion box. You might also provide forms for students to fill out when making a suggestion (e.g., "I like it when we _____; I do not like _____").
- Use positive, caring talk when speaking to other educators and parents about students. Negative comments are unproductive, and if those comments reach the student, the teacher–student relationship will suffer. The student will lose trust in the teacher and will be less likely to confide in the teacher and less likely to be motivated to behave appropriately.

Unfortunately, for many students, an overall positive school experience and positive teacher–student relationships are not the norm, particularly for students who act out or exhibit disruptive behaviors. Jenson and his colleagues (2004) describe the "sea of negativity" that characterizes the school experiences of students who have externalizing disorders. Negative teacher–student interactions or overly critical teachers contribute to this "sea of negativity." Beaman and Wheldall (2000) provide a comprehensive review of research on the frequency and manner in which teachers communicate approval and disapproval. Overwhelmingly, teachers communicate more disapproval, or "negativity," than approval. Other research suggests that teachers respond significantly more frequently to inappropriate behavior than to appropriate behavior, overlooking the majority of the appropriate student behavior (Alber, Heward, & Hippler, 1999; Shores, Gunter, & Jack, 1993; Van Acker, Grant, & Henry, 1996).

The field of psychology includes a rapidly growing area known as "positive psychology." Positive psychology is the "scientific study of the strengths and virtues that enable individuals and communities to thrive... . Positive [p]sychology has three central concerns: positive emotions, positive individual traits, and positive institutions" (Positive Psychology Center, University of Pennsylvania, 2007). The focus of positive psychology extends far beyond schools, but does provide a number of ways in which to make schools (and classrooms) more positive environments for students. A thorough discussion of positive psychology exceeds the focus of this text, but interested readers are referred to the "Resources" section at the end of this chapter.

At the core of a positive classroom climate is positive teacher–student interactions. To create a positive classroom climate, Martella and his colleagues (2003) recommend that teachers actively practice positive interactions with students.

Positive teacher–student relationships can have a powerful impact on students' lives.

Emmer and his colleagues (2003) suggest that teachers can create an environment where students want to be by

- communicating positive expectations,
- praising appropriate student performance, and
- using incentives or rewards.

Positive teacher language is just one small way in which teachers can achieve a positive classroom climate. Other strategies will also help achieve this desired outcome, such as communicating positive expectations (see Chapter 6), and using praise and incentives to enhance motivation (see Chapters 10 and 11). Providing high levels of praise for appropriate student behavior is essential for a positive classroom climate. In addition, teachers can do other things to contribute to a positive climate. Review the suggestions provided in Boxes 7-3 and 7-4, and then consider your own ideas for accomplishing this important element of preventive behavior management.

CLASSROOM ORGANIZATION

Research has demonstrated that classroom arrangement and organization can have a positive impact on student behavior. When teachers use the physical arrangement of their classrooms to support instructional and social expectations, student behavior tends to be more appropriate (Evans & Lowell, 1979; C. Weinstein, 1977; R. Weinstein, 1979). Many classroom management textbooks and other materials discuss classroom arrangement as one of the first steps in behavior management. As you can see, we discuss classroom organization as one of the last of our preventive strategies. It is tempting to begin yearly preparation activities by organizing the classroom, because this is such a tangible and immediately reinforcing endeavor. However, we maintain that organizing your classroom should be one of the last tasks that you do to prepare for your students, because everything that you do prior to this step will influence your classroom organization. The daily activities that are included on your schedule will help you to decide how the students' desks should be arranged (e.g., rows, clusters), what other instructional features that you will need (e.g., space for learning centers, computers, reading), and what materials and supplies you will need to have available for students. For example, after developing the schedule and routines for each class period, you may realize that you need space for large-group instruction and small-group instruction, as well as a place for students to do independent work and peer tutoring. The types of reinforcement systems that you decide to use will inform decisions about what charts, reinforcers, and other materials will be needed and where these materials should be stored or displayed. For example, if you decide that students will be able to earn time to play a group game each Friday, you will need to determine where this activity will take place.

Thus, we recommend that before you begin to arrange your classroom, you must first develop the following preventive elements:

Effective teachers are organized teachers.

- Rules, procedures (after you finish organizing the physical layout of the classroom, you may find that additional procedures may be needed for accessing the various areas of the classroom), and reminders (see Chapter 6)

- Group and individual reinforcement systems (see Chapters 10 and 11)
- Daily schedule
- Climate features

A few general guidelines will help you decide how to organize your classroom. First, visualize and then list the types of activities that you want students to experience and the type of arrangements that you will need for those activities. We recommend that you go through each period of your schedule to guide this effort. Table 7-2 provides examples of various activities for elementary and secondary school students. Consider what kind of space or configuration each activity listed in Table 7-2 would require. For example, some of the activities would require students to sit at desks, some would require students to be able to work together in small groups, and some would require an informal arrangement such as a carpet or beanbag chair. Given that space is a valuable commodity in many classrooms, think about whether more than one of the activities could take place in the same space. For example, a table could be used for small-group instruction, a cooperative group activity, or for playing instructional games.

Next, focus on each of those activities to identify more specifically the resources (e.g., materials, storage) that will be needed for each. The following questions can help guide this process:

1. What materials will need to be stored in this area?
2. How will the materials be stored and labeled?
3. What materials will students access on their own?
4. What materials will require adult supervision and access?
5. What type of cleanup will be necessary at the end of each activity?

Table 7-3 shows how these questions might be answered for the sample activities presented in Table 7-2.

Now you are ready to begin organizing your classroom. You may wish to make a scale model of your classroom on graph paper, or you can simply arrange (and rearrange) the classroom. In addition to accommodating the activities that you have already identified, your classroom arrangement should adhere to a few basic rules:

1. Plan independent work areas that avoid or minimize distractions or highly congested areas of the room (Evertson, Emmer, & Worsham, 2003). For example, independent work areas should not be next to the door, classroom pets, the pencil sharpener, or the area where small-group instruction will occur. Evertson and Poole (n.d.) offer two recommendations for avoiding distractions through careful arrangement: (a) identify possible distractions by sitting in each of the areas where students will be seated, and (b) minimize or hide (e.g., perhaps by using curtains or screens) distractions that are unavoidable.
2. Ensure that every student has a clear line of sight to the teacher, the chalkboard, and anything else that will be used during a lesson (Evertson & Poole, n.d.).
3. Ensure that the teacher and the paraprofessional have easy access to every student and that students can be seen at all times (Shores, Gunter, & Jack, 1993).

TABLE 7-2 Examples of Activities for Elementary and Secondary School Students

Elementary

1. Large-group activities
   a. Direct teaching using blackboard, overhead projector, document camera, or other equipment
   b. Discussions
   c. Independent work
2. Small-group activities
   a. Small-group instruction
   b. Discussions
   c. Cooperative groups
   d. Games
3. Learning centers
   a. Listening center
   b. Classroom library
   c. Games
   d. Math center
   e. Language arts center
   f. Computer stations
   g. Arts and crafts
   h. Educational toys and technology
4. Other
   a. Quiet area
   b. Reinforcement area
   c. Snack area
   d. Backpack storage
5. Storage of teaching materials
   a. Textbooks
   b. Workbooks
   c. Paper and pencils
   d. TV/VCR, smart boards, data projectors, augmentative or alternative communication devices
   e. Computer software, DVDs, CDs
   f. Art supplies
   g. Personal work materials (e.g., markers, chalk, pens)

Secondary

1. Large-group activities
   a. Direct teaching with blackboard and overhead projector
   b. Discussions
   c. Independent work activities

TABLE 7-2 *(continued)*

2. Small-group activities

   a. Instruction

   b. Discussions

   c. Cooperative groups

   d. Review activities (e.g., games)

3. Other

   a. Learning centers

   b. Computer stations

   c. Quiet area

   d. Reinforcement area

4. Storage of teaching materials

   a. Textbooks

   b. Workbooks

   c. Paper and pens/pencils

   d. TV/VCR, smart boards, data projectors, augmentative or alternative communication devices

   e. Computer software

   f. Personal work materials (e.g., markers, chalk, pens)

TABLE 7-3 Questions to Guide Planning

Elementary Classroom (math learning center area)

1. What materials will need to be used or stored in this area?

   a. Materials for two or three math centers. (This will depend on the skills being taught, but might include objects to be measured, rulers, scales, manipulatives for hands-on math, fact tables, problems, geometric shapes, geoboards, clay to be cut into fractional parts, and play money.)

2. How will the materials be stored and labeled?

   a. Each math learning center will be stored in a small, clear plastic box. Math centers will be labeled with a picture of dolphins, eels, or stingrays (to designate the student groups who are allowed to use each center). Other materials will be stored on shelves, labeled with small pictures to identify the appropriate place for each item.

   b. Remember that all materials that students will access must be accessible to children who use special equipment, such as wheelchairs or walkers, and that consideration must be given to students with physical impairments in order to allow these students easy and independent access to all materials.

3. What materials will students access on their own?

   a. Math center boxes during center time; other materials may be used with permission from the teacher

(continued)

TABLE 7-3 Questions to Guide Planning

---

4. What materials will require adult supervision and access?

   a. Clay (should not be used on the rug)

5. What type of cleanup will be necessary at the end of this activity?

   a. All center materials will need to be returned to the proper box.

   b. Other materials will need to be returned to the appropriate place on the shelf.

Secondary Classroom (history class)

1. What type of materials will need to be used or stored for this activity?

   a. Textbooks

   b. Computers

   c. Class library

2. How will the materials be stored or labeled?

   a. Textbooks are stored on a designated shelf.

   b. The library will include sections for reference, fiction, and nonfiction by author.

   c. Remember that all student materials must be accessible to children who use special equipment, such as wheelchairs or walkers, and that consideration must be given to students with physical impairments in order to allow these students easy and independent access to all materials.

3. What materials will students access on their own?

   a. All

4. What materials will require teacher's supervision and access?

   a. Teacher edition of texts

   b. Student use of the Internet while using computers

5. What type of cleanup will be necessary?

   a. Library books are to be returned to the proper place.

   b. Students must log off of the computers.

   c. Textbooks are to be returned to the proper place (unless the book is checked out to the student).

One of us (BKS) once visited a special education classroom where each student's desk was located behind a separate refrigerator box that had the back cut out. The teacher explained that she had been told that students should have their own "offices." Unfortunately, the result was that each student could only be seen when the teacher was standing almost directly behind the student. Students were, for the most part, hidden from view! Of course, this type of arrangement is unsatisfactory for many reasons, not the least of which is safety.

4. Furniture and equipment should be arranged to allow for easy movement through the classroom and easy access to materials (Evertson et al., 2003;

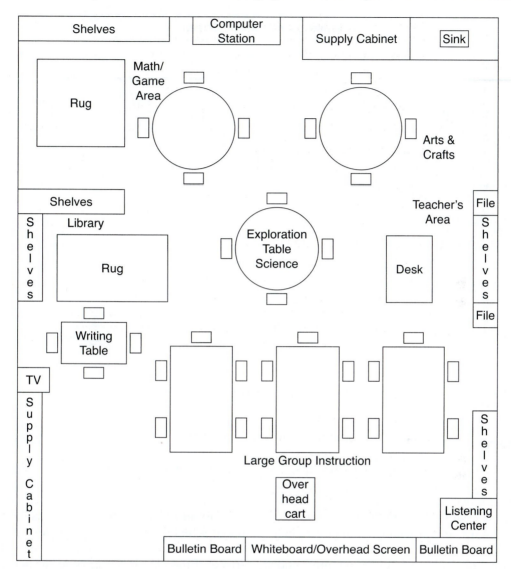

FIGURE 7-2   Sample Elementary School Classroom Arrangement

Shores et al., 1993). Unused furniture, equipment, or supplies should be removed from the classroom (Evertson & Poole, n.d.). Do not allow your room to become a depository for broken, discarded, or unwanted materials!

Figures 7-2 and 7-3 show sample classroom arrangements for elementary and secondary classes. Examine the classroom plans carefully to see how each reflects the guidelines described in this section.

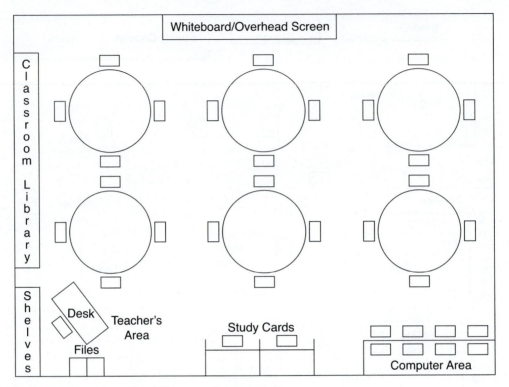

FIGURE 7-3　Sample Secondary School Classroom Arrangement

Summary

Throughout this text, we argue that prevention is the first step in classroom behavior management. In Chapter 6, we presented the basic preventive strategies of establishing and teaching clear rules and procedures, and providing reminders to help students remember those rules and procedures. This chapter presents three additional prevention techniques: classroom scheduling, climate, and organization.

The objectives for this chapter and how they were addressed are as follows:

1. Explain the importance of careful attention to scheduling, climate, and organization as an essential component in preventing classroom behavior management problems.

Students perform best, both behaviorally and academically, when they are provided with high levels of active learning time and when the learning environment is positive, clear of distractions and extraneous material, and organized to facilitate appropriate behavior. For this reason, teachers should carefully develop the daily instructional schedule, plan how to achieve a positive classroom climate, and organize the physical space of the classroom in order to achieve the desired behaviors.

2. Describe research that relates to scheduling, climate, and organization.

Much of the early research in the areas of effective teaching and classroom behavior management focused on the role of scheduling, climate, and organization, and documented the relationship of these elements to student behavior. Students tend to have fewer behavior problems when their teachers maintain high levels of student engagement in instructional activities, when they create a positive and welcoming atmosphere, and when they maintain a well-organized classroom.

3. Describe the steps for developing your schedule and strategies for creating effective schedules.

We described strategies for preventing student behavior problems. Among such strategies is carefully planning the class schedule and student breaks. Students are most likely to exhibit appropriate behavior when the class schedule allows for low levels of unengaged time and when breaks are structured and organized.

4. Describe ideas for creating a classroom climate that is positive and conducive to learning.

Classroom climate is a multidimensional concept, one critical component of which is the quality of the teacher–student relationships. We discussed the wide range of positive outcomes that come about through good teacher–student relation-

ships, and we described strategies for establishing such relationships.

5. Describe how to organize your classroom in order to address scheduling needs and climate.

This chapter provided specific ideas for organizing the classroom environment in a manner that facilitates desired behaviors. Conscientiously considering the desired outcomes before you begin to develop the instructional schedule or arrange the classroom and then following the steps that we described for doing so will help to ensure that your classroom is a positive, productive learning environment in which students exhibit high levels of appropriate behavior.

In Table 7-4, we provide a self-assessment form for teachers to use in evaluating their use of the preventive measures described in this chapter. The self-assessment addresses scheduling, climate, and organization in the classroom.

TABLE 7-4   Scheduling, Climate, and Organization Self-Assessment Form

Never	Seldom	Sometimes	Often	Always
1	2	3	4	5

Use the numbers from the scale above to rate the following statements.

1. My schedule includes high levels of allocated time. _____

2. I take proactive steps in order to maximize academic learning time. _____

3. I monitor the interactions between adults and students in my classroom in order to ensure that most interactions are positive. _____

4. I work to achieve a positive relationship with each of my students. _____

5. My classroom provides a positive, safe, learning environment. _____

6. My room is visually appealing. _____

7. Visitors to my classroom have complimented me on how attractive my room is. _____

8. I organize my classroom only after developing the schedule, rules, reinforcement systems, and instructional activities that will occur. _____

9. My classroom includes areas that are designated for specific activities. _____

10. I have effective systems for organizing materials in my classroom in order to keep them neat and easy to access. _____

11. My classroom is well organized and tidy. _____

Learning Activities

1. Consider businesses that you prefer to visit. What elements of climate and organization contribute to the appeal of this business for you?
2. Brainstorm ideas about how to organize a classroom in order to signal that specific activities are to occur in certain areas.
3. Discuss in small groups how you would develop a positive, caring climate in your classroom.
4. Read the vignettes, "Ms. Morgan's Elementary Class" and "Mr. Davis's Resource Math Class." What advice would you give to Ms. Morgan? To what do you attribute Mr. Davis's success?

Ms. Morgan's Elementary Class

Dr. I. C. Everything was called to Mango Elementary to work with Ms. Morgan, a veteran special education resource teacher, who had an excellent history of classroom behavior management. Lately, however, she was having problems with her afternoon class.

When Dr. ICE walked into Ms. Morgan's classroom, he was impressed with the physical organization of the room. Students' work was displayed along with posters of rules and procedures. The room had a warm, bright feel to it.

Dr. ICE stayed and observed Ms. Morgan's classes. Academic instruction progressed smoothly and according to the schedule. Dr. ICE and Ms. Morgan had lunch together and she discussed the afternoon class. She said that students came in the afternoon only if they needed help with their general education afternoon classes. She was very concerned because these same students, who had been well behaved in the morning, showed frustration and refused to work in the afternoon.

The afternoon schedule was determined by the general education class rather than by Ms. Morgan. Some students came every day, some only once a week. There did not seem to be any set routine. The students asked for the personal attention of their teacher more than in the morning session. She was not able to give them the one-on-one attention that they wanted and they acted out.

Dr. ICE met with Ms. Morgan to share his thoughts about her afternoon class. He suggested that she work on some routines for the afternoon that would make her classroom feel more predictable to her students. Then he asked her how she felt in her afternoon class. Looking surprised, she admitted that she was usually tired in the afternoon and that she often felt worn out by the end of the day. Dr. ICE told her that he noticed that her energy level dropped from the morning to the afternoon. In the afternoon, she did not smile as often and she seemed distracted. He told her that her low energy in the afternoon may be contributing to her interacting less often with the students. He reminded her that everything counts in the classroom: Scheduling, climate (including the teacher's energy level), and physical organization all work together. If one part is weak, the system will not work well.

Mr. Davis's Resource Math Class

Mr. Davis taught a resource math class for 9th and 10th graders. It was important to his students that this class resembles a general education class as much as possible. They did not want to be seen as special education students.

Mr. Davis liked this idea and decided to work with the general education teachers in order to accomplish the goal of making the resource classes as similar as possible in appearance and expectations to the general education classes. First, a survey of the classrooms in his school revealed that the majority of the teachers arranged the desks in small clusters. Mr. Davis organized his students' desks in this manner, with work tables for small-group lessons on one side of the room. He also placed equipment for large-group instruction (e.g., overhead and document camera) in the front of the room, near the large whiteboard. Mr. Davis used schedules and routines that were similar to those used in many of the general education classes (e.g., the roll was taken at the beginning of class, a warm-up activity was waiting for the students when they entered the classroom, a combination of independent work and group work was used). Mr. Davis found that many general education teachers required students to maintain portfolios of their best work, so he implemented this requirement in his math classes. Finally, he also had students chart their progress in their math folders, which was an idea that he borrowed from one of the general education math teachers. Mr. Davis's attention to his students' wishes and his carefully planned schedule and organization created a positive learning environment with few behavioral problems.

Resources

WEBSITES

http://cecp.air.org The Center for Effective Collaboration and Practice: Provides access to *Early Warning, Timely Response*, and *Safeguarding Our Children, An Action Guide*, as well as information related to violence prevention and creating a positive, healthy school environment.

www.state.ky.us/agencies/behave/homepage.html The Kentucky Department of Education and the University of Kentucky Department of Special Education and Rehabilitation Counseling Behavior Home Page: Addresses all facets of behavior management and discipline.

http://iris.peabody.vanderbilt.edu The Iris Center for Training Enhancements, Vanderbilt University: Offers course enhancements for university professors, as well as a number of tools that are useful for educators, including IRIS modules, case studies, activities, and information briefs.

http://smhp.psych.ucla.edu Center for Mental Health in Schools, part of the UCLA School Mental Health Project: Contains articles, information, presentations, training aids, and resources on a wide range of topics pertaining to children's mental health in schools (e.g., classroom climate, prevention and intervention strategies, comprehensive planning).

www.ppc.sas.upenn.edu/index.html Positive Psychology Center, University of Pennsylvania: Provides information about research, practices, and resources in positive psychology. Resources on learned helplessness and resiliency research in children are available, including information on a resiliency curriculum.

www.nasponline.org/about_nasp/ig_positive.aspx Positive School Psychology Interest Group, National Association of School Psychologists: Provides access to articles on positive psychology in schools and resilience.

JOURNALS

Communiqué Online, National Association of School Psychologists, available online at www.nasponline.org/publications/cq/cqmain.aspx

The Journal of Positive Psychology

Journal of School Psychology

School Psychology Quarterly

School Psychology Review, National Association of School Psychologists, available online at www.nasponline.org/publications/spr/sprmain.aspx

After reading this chapter, you will be able to do the following:

1. Describe the learning characteristics of successful students and students with learning and behavioral difficulties.

2. Define and sequence the stages of learning.

3. Explain the instructional arrangements and activities that are recommended for students with learning and behavioral disabilities.

4. Use the acronym SCORE CHAMPS to develop teaching practices that encourage higher levels of appropriate behavior and learning.

5. Describe the types of instructional activities that typically occur in classrooms, as well as common problems encountered and solutions for each.

Prevention of Challenging Behavior Through High-Quality Instruction

Big ideas in instruction for students with disabilities:

- Instruction may be the most critical antecedent for appropriate behavior.
- There is a well-established relationship between instruction and behavior.
- Everything related to instruction should be carefully and systematically planned; every decision that teachers make with regard to instruction is critical.
- Students with learning and behavioral difficulties benefit from an instructional environment that shares similar characteristics with successful classroom management: A well-managed classroom is structured, clear, and focused on student's success.

THE RELATIONSHIP BETWEEN BEHAVIOR AND INSTRUCTION

School plays a powerful role in children's lives and is second only to the family in terms of potential influence. School experiences shape a child's life beyond academic preparation; the quality of a child's school experience is an important predictor of success later in life. Children and youth who successfully manage the academic and social challenges of school typically have more positive post-school experiences than children who struggle academically or socially. As we discussed in Chapter 1, educators have a significant impact on students' lives. Our mind-sets about students, how we teach, how we relate to students, and how we deal with student's behavior can positively or negatively influence and shape students' lives both in and out of school. Perhaps the most obvious influence that educators have is in the area of academic instruction: the curriculum that educators present and the instructional strategies used to teach that curriculum. Most teachers are well aware of their role as purveyors of academic content. Less obvious, however, is the fact that instruction is a critical component in preventing behavioral problems. The relationships between instruction and behavior and between academic performance and behavior are clear. How teachers instruct influences not only student academic performance but social and behavioral performance as well.

The reciprocal relationship between learning and behavior is well established. Generally speaking, students who are academically deficient experience significantly more negative interactions, more punitive consequences, less demanding academic tasks, and less instructional time with the teacher because of a greater frequency of disciplinary actions that remove these students from the classroom (e.g., office disciplinary referrals) (Leone et al., 2003). High-achieving students typically experience greater behavioral and social success in school, whereas low-achieving students experience higher levels of behavioral and social failure (Caprara, Barbaranelli, Pastorelli, Bandura, & Zimbardo, 2000; Catalano, Loeber, & McKinney, 1999). What is unknown, however, is whether this relationship is causal: In other words, do learning problems *cause* behavioral problems? Do behavioral problems lead to learning problems? It appears that many children who exhibit high levels of inappropriate behavior enter school less prepared for the demands of school, both socially and academically, than their peers who exhibit more appropriate behavior (Kame'enui & Carnine, 1998; Sutherland & Wehby, 2001). This insufficient preparedness may be manifested in high levels of behavior that is considered unacceptable in school contexts, such as difficulties with attention and concentration, low levels of compliance, and inappropriate peer interactions. These unacceptable behaviors may set the stage for teacher and peer interactions that interfere with learning and may shape teachers behavior in negative ways. We know that teachers influence student's behavior, but it is also clear that students influence teacher behavior (Gunter, Denny, Jack, Shores, & Nelson, 1993; Gunter et al., 1994; Nelson & Roberts, 2000). This appears to be especially true for students who exhibit high levels of negative behaviors (or who have a history of such behavior) (Nelson & Roberts, 2000). Research has shown that these students receive less instruction from teachers than students who exhibit appropriate classroom behavior. Carr, Taylor, and Robinson (1991) and Wehby and his colleagues (1998) reported that teachers provide less instruction to students who exhibit disruptive behavior or students who are perceived as aggressive. These findings are significant in that they help explain the vicious cycle of school failure for students with chronic behavioral difficulties: Students exhibit challenging behavior, which leads to teachers responding negatively and with lowered academic expectations, which causes students' academic skill-deficits to become increasingly more pronounced while behavioral difficulties become more firmly established.

| A well-established relationship exists between challenging behavior and academic performance. |

Understanding the relationship between behavior and academic performance has led to research that examines whether improving academic performance produces a concomitant improvement in behavior. Evidence suggests that increasing academic engagement (i.e., the extent to which students are actively involved in academic responding) may result in increased on-task behavior and lower levels of inappropriate behavior (Sutherland & Wehby, 2001). This implies that instructions provided by teachers can improve both student learning and student behavior. When teachers use dynamic, structured, engaging instructional methods, students learn more and behave better.

In this chapter, we provide an overview of the instructional methods that are most effective for students with learning and behavioral difficulties. First, we compare the learning and social characteristics of typical or high-achieving students with students who have difficulties in the areas of learning and behavior. Next, we explain the types of instructional activities that typically occur in classrooms for students of all ages. Finally, we describe the characteristics of effective instruction that teachers must incorporate in order to meet students' complex learning needs. The extent to which teachers incorporate the instructional methods that we describe in this chapter can predict the extent of the student behavioral problems that the teachers will encounter. Teachers who rely on the methods that we describe will typically encounter fewer behavioral problems than teachers who use other approaches. Remember that a teacher's behavior influences students far beyond academic performance alone.

THE CHARACTERISTICS OF STUDENTS WITH LEARNING AND BEHAVIORAL PROBLEMS

Most students attend school, do their assignments, turn in homework, and generally handle the academic demands of school. As students mature, most develop strategies and adjust their learning activities to better meet the varying demands of school tasks. For example, in a difficult course, a student may take more detailed notes, read chapters more than once, make vocabulary cards, or study with friends in an effort to better ensure at least minimally satisfactory performance. Even young children adjust their behavior when faced with difficult tasks: A preschooler who is engaging in a new or challenging task (e.g., tying shoes, writing) will often focus more intensely on the task than when doing a familiar or easier task (e.g., coloring, playing).

Students with learning and behavioral difficulties, however, typically exhibit different, and usually less effective, learning behaviors. It is instructive for educators to know the characteristics of both typical successful students and students who have learning and behavioral difficulties. The discrepancies between the academic and social behaviors of these two populations can tell us much about what teachers should do to facilitate success for all students.

The Characteristics of Effective Learners

By effective learners, we are referring to students who are successful both academically (e.g., they do their work, make passing grades, pass statewide academic assessments, graduate) and socially (e.g., they have friends among their peers, they are liked by peers and teachers, they seldom behave in ways that are objectionable to peers or teachers).

According to research that has examined the relationship between behavior and academic performance, academically successful students, for the most part, are goal oriented, intrinsically motivated, use self-regulation and metacognitive skills to meet school demands, assume responsibility for learning, and exhibit prosocial behaviors (Caprara et al., 2000; Ellis, 1992; Ellis & Worthington, 1994; Grimes, 1981; Swift & Swift, 1968, 1969a, 1969b, 1973). Table 8-1 lists specific learning and behavioral characteristics of academically successful students.

> The characteristics of both effective students and students with learning and behavioral difficulties have implications for instruction.

Characteristics of Students with Learning and Behavioral Difficulties

Ellis (1992) states simply that students with learning and behavioral problems typically exhibit learning behaviors that are the opposite of effective students. This

---

TABLE 8-1   Characteristics of Academically Successful Students

---

Engagement in the Learning Process

Academically successful students typically do the following:

- Actively participate in class discussions.
- Ask relevant questions about content and assignments.
- Volunteer answers.
- Do more than the minimum required for academic tasks.
- Attend to detail on academic tasks.
- Interact with the teacher outside of class time. For example, engaged learners may talk to teachers about topics of interest, come to teachers for help with difficult material, and discuss assignments with teachers.
- Are appropriately independent in their work habits in and out of class. They may need a few verbal prompts or reminders, but overall, they start work and complete tasks with little supervision.
- Possess a broad general knowledge base because of active engagement in the learning process, interest in learning, and participation in learning activities beyond school. For example, engaged learners typically read for pleasure outside of school, participate in discussions with family members and friends about current and historical events, and explore areas of interest on the Internet.

Self-Regulation of Learning

Academically successful students typically do the following:

- Actively use strategies to connect new learning to previously learned knowledge and skills. These connections make new learning easier and more efficient.
- Actively use strategies to help memory, organization, studying, and task completion. For example, effective learners may use mnemonics to aid memory, organize their materials by subject, have a systematic method for studying (e.g., review vocabulary, make note cards for important information), and set a timeline for completion of major assignments.
- Use metacognitive skills to assess learning demands, self-monitor performance, and evaluate performance. For example, to complete a major project, effective learners might carefully review the requirements for the project, develop a rough draft, ask the teacher for feedback on the draft, attend to important details such as the appearance of the written product, and evaluate the finished product for completeness and accuracy before turning it in.
- Use a broad array of academic skills flexibly and fluently to effectively manage a wide range of academic demands. For example, effective learners know when they must read carefully (or even multiple times) in order to sufficiently learn content and when they can simply skim the material.

Attribution and Motivation

Academically successful students typically do the following:

- Expect to succeed.
- Attribute success and failure to their own level of effort. Assuming responsibility for success or failure is known as having an **internal locus of control.** An **external locus of control** refers to attributing success and failure to factors beyond the individual's control (e.g., luck, unfair treatment, being picked on by the teacher, an anomaly).

- Have sufficient levels of motivation to participate in school activities, complete academic work, and engage in learning behaviors. This motivation is, for the most part, intrinsic (e.g., students enjoy learning, they like getting good grades) and goal oriented (e.g., they want to graduate with honors, they want to go to college). Although some motivation is extrinsic (e.g., they like positive attention from teachers and parents), these students are able to function on thin reinforcement schedules (i.e., teachers and parents do not praise every successfully completed assignment or every good performance in class).

Prosocial Behaviors

Academically successful students typically do the following:

- Use peer-related prosocial behaviors (e.g., cooperating, sharing, helping) in school and classroom environments.
- Understand their own emotions and the emotions of others and use that information to adjust their behavior according to the demands of a situation.
- Follow the rules, both formal and informal, of social situations.

means that students who struggle behaviorally and/or academically probably do not possess or exhibit the characteristics listed in Table 8-1. Furthermore, research results indicate that students with learning problems use inefficient and ineffective strategies for acquiring and remembering information. For example, they may have problems distinguishing relevant versus irrelevant stimuli; they may not remember information as well as their nondisabled peers; they may not use active learning strategies to improve learning; and they may use ineffective metacognitive strategies for preparing for learning, for organizing and understanding information to be learned, and for problem solving (Deschler, Schumaker, Alley, Warner, & Clark, 1982; Hallahan & Kauffman, 2006; Hallahan & Reeve, 1980; Heward, 2009; Torgeson, 1977, 1980). In addition, these students often exhibit behaviors that actively interfere with learning (McKinney, Mason, Clifford, & Perkerson, 1975; Shinn, Ramsey, Walker, Stieber, & O'Neill, 1987; Walker & McConnell, 1988; Walker, Ramsey, & Gresham, 2004). Table 8-2 lists the specific characteristics of students who have learning and behavioral challenges. Teachers who understand the learning characteristics of these students may be more likely to implement instructional and management strategies that teach students to be more effective, independent learners.

Kauffman (2005), Walker and his colleagues (2004), and others argue convincingly about the potential role that school plays in contributing to students' learning and behavioral challenges. We believe that it is important for educators to be aware that schools can be the best hope for students with learning and behavioral difficulties, but that the potential also exists for schools to exacerbate problems. Teachers and administrators who understand this potential negative impact will, hopefully, be better skilled at recognizing when these factors may be at work and will be more vigilant in advocating for schools that are more effective for all the students.

The physical environment of schools, such as overcrowding and damaged or deteriorating facilities, has been associated with aggression and vandalism (McAfee, 1987; Rutter, Maughan, Mortimore, & Ouston, 1979). Systemic issues may

TABLE 8-2 Characteristics of Students with Learning and Behavioral Difficulties

Engagement in the Learning Process

Academically and behaviorally unsuccessful students tend to do the following:

- Participate minimally in instructional activities (e.g., ask fewer questions, volunteer less often).
- Have difficulty attending to the important aspects of information that is to be learned or the critical features of tasks that are to be completed.
- Exhibit negative behaviors during the instructions that require the teacher's intervention (e.g., off-task comments, inattention, disruptive behavior).
- Bring fewer materials to class.
- Produce work that is messy and includes careless mistakes.
- Work quickly with the goal of finishing rather than producing neat and accurate work.
- Be minimally self-directed in relation to schoolwork, often relying too much on teachers for guidance and assistance in initiating and completing tasks. For example, these students may ask more questions than needed, sometimes asking the same question repeatedly. They may request high levels of feedback from the teacher about their work, or they may simply not do what they have been instructed to do, requiring the teacher to repeat instructions and explanations.

Self-Regulation of Learning

Academically and behaviorally unsuccessful students tend to do the following:

- Not use strategies to organize new information or recognize how new information is related to previously learned material.
- Use few strategies or use inefficient strategies to facilitate learning. For example, to study for a test, a struggling student may simply flip through the pages of the chapter, whereas an effective learner will review notes, review vocabulary words, answer end-of-chapter questions, and engage in various self-check activities to assess his or her level of mastery of the content.
- Approach tasks with little planning or assessment of the demands of the task. Self-monitoring of performance during a task is weak or lacking. Upon completion of tasks, they tend not to edit or evaluate their work before turning it in. For example, a struggling learner may give little advance thought to the demands of an assignment, therefore failing to take home the materials necessary to complete the assignment.

Attribution and Motivation

Academically and behaviorally unsuccessful students tend to do the following:

- Expect failure.
- Attribute success and failure to factors beyond their control (i.e., external locus of control). When they do poorly on an assignment, they may attribute the poor grade to factors such as "That teacher hates me" or "I'm stupid."
- Have low motivation for learning, doing academic work, and participating in school life. Of course, their low motivation is understandable, given the fact that these students typically have learning histories of repeated failures, low levels of success, and high levels of negative feedback about behavior and academic performance.

Prosocial Behaviors

Academically and behaviorally unsuccessful students tend to do the following:

- Have low frustration tolerance and ineffective skills for coping with frustration. For example, where most students might ask the teacher for help when encountering something that they do not understand or know how to do, students with learning and behavioral difficulties might act out (e.g., curse, slam their books, crumple their paper), refuse to attempt the task, or just leave the classroom.

- Have little awareness of their own emotions or the emotions of others and, typically, have poor self-regulation skills for managing emotions (with regard to students with behavioral difficulties). This may be, in part, reflective of underlying language disorders, particularly with regard to **pragmatics** (i.e., the use of language for social purposes) (Getty & Summy, 2006; Sanger, Maag, & Shapera, 1994; Walker, Schwarz, Nippold, Irvin, & Noell, 1994). Pragmatic language problems may be reflected in inappropriate social behaviors, particularly with peers. For example, these students are often extremely opinionated and not open to others' ideas. They may use language to tease, intimidate, and coerce. For this reason, Kauffman (2005) recommends instruction in specific language-based social skills. We discussed social skills instruction in Chapter 9. In the classroom, these pragmatics problems may interfere with students' success in group activities or the give-and-take of group discussion.

- Violate formal and informal rules and social parameters in school. This includes behaviors that range from overt noncompliance to the more subtly inappropriate interpersonal behaviors described previously.

---

play a role as well. Kauffman (2005) identifies a number of ways in which schools may contribute to learning and behavioral difficulties, including being insensitive to students' individuality, inconsistently managing behavior, providing ineffective instruction in critical skills (e.g., reading, writing, math, social skills), and inappropriately using reinforcement contingencies (e.g., reinforcement for inappropriate behaviors, failure to reinforce appropriate behaviors, negative reinforcement contingencies). Certainly, these factors are not universal. However, substantial research exists that supports the contributing role these factors play in students' academic and social failure in school, particularly for students who enter school less prepared than their age peers for the demands of school (Kauffman, 2005; Keogh, 2003; Rylance, 1997; Walker et al., 2004). Educators who apply the techniques presented in this text will provide instructional environments that will help to ensure that these students experience success in the classroom and that schools are supportive environments for all students.

CHARACTERISTICS OF EFFECTIVE INSTRUCTION

The academic performance of our nation's students has been the subject of scrutiny over the past decade. Concerns about academic underachievement have led to increasingly higher standards for academic performance and mandatory statewide assessments to monitor academic progress. In fact, two major features of the No Child Left Behind Act (NCLB) of 2001 (P.L. 107-110, the Elementary and Secondary Education Act) are mandatory state content standards for reading/language arts, mathematics, and science, and annual testing in mathematics and language arts for all public and charter school students in grades 3–8 and once in grades 10–12 (No Child Left Behind, 2004). Of course, simply raising standards without examining how content is taught may not result in improved student performance. For this reason, NCLB requires that educational practices be founded on scientific research (U.S. Department of Education, 2006). What this means for schools is that teachers must be prepared to teach a rigorous curriculum, using proven methods, to ensure that most students are able to pass statewide assessments. We are strong supporters of the requirement that educators rely on proven practices and programs. This will benefit students with disabilities in particular. Special education teachers must rely on the best technology available to ensure that their students learn to read and write, are able to comprehend and apply mathematics and science, and can accomplish tasks ranging from basic memorization to problem-solving and critical-thinking skills, all while engaging in socially acceptable and functional behaviors.

> Requiring educators to use scientifically proven practices is a cornerstone of the No Child Left Behind Act.

The instructional methods described in this section are research-proven methods that have been shown to improve learning outcomes for students with learning and behavioral difficulties. Because these students struggle academically, every aspect of instruction should be designed with the students' learning characteristics and behavioral needs in mind. Every instructional decision that a teacher makes is critical: what words to use to explain a concept, what questions to ask (as well as when and how to ask them), how to give students feedback about their responses, and which examples to use to illustrate a concept or demonstrate a procedure. These decisions, and the hundreds of other decisions that teachers make daily, may determine whether students learn and whether their behavior is sufficiently appropriate to allow learning to occur. As you will see, most of the methods described in this chapter directly address the characteristics of students who lack academic and social proficiency.

In the following sections, we first describe stages of learning. Next, we explain common instructional arrangements, or formats for delivering instruction. We describe two effective approaches for teaching new content and briefly discuss other commonly used instructional activities. Finally, we describe effective teaching practices and explain how they apply to these various instructional activities. As you read these sections, keep in mind the characteristics of students with learning and behavioral difficulties as discussed previously and consider why the strategies presented would be effective with these students.

Stages of Learning and How They Relate to Instructional Arrangements and Activities

To better understand the various instructional arrangements and activities, teachers should fully comprehend the four stages of learning: acquisition, proficiency or fluency, maintenance, and generalization (Alberto & Troutman, 2006; Meese, 2001). These stages apply to all learners regardless of age or ability level.

Acquisition. *Acquisition* is the first step in learning a new task. At this point, learners are beginners at the task and usually need some level of teacher assistance. Learners in the acquisition stage typically perform tasks more slowly, clumsily, and with less accuracy than proficient learners. When young children first learn to count to 10, they count slowly, perhaps using their fingers, and they sometimes skip numbers. A youngster learning to ride a bike is wobbly at first and does not go far without falling. New drivers usually need to actively think about all of the things that they need to do before they start the car and as they drive (e.g., check the mirrors, watch for traffic, use the signals, monitor the speed, watch for signs).

How teachers teach new skills can make a difference in how well students learn those skills. Numerous studies clearly demonstrate that students with disabilities learn best with direct, teacher-led, explicit instruction that facilitates high levels of correct responding (Fuchs & Fuchs, 2001; National Institute of Child Health and Human Development, 2000). In later sections of this chapter, we describe how to provide explicit instruction and offer many examples of teacher behaviors that contribute to explicit instruction.

Teachers must understand that in the acquisition stage, learners may need higher levels of support and assistance than when they are more proficient. For example, a student who is just learning how to solve long-division problems may need to use a mnemonic device or a chart that lists the steps involved in the process. This need for support is true for both academic behaviors and social behaviors (e.g., learning to accept negative feedback, expressing complaints appropriately, sharing, raising one's hand to answer questions).

Proficiency or Fluency.   When learners reach **proficiency** or **fluency**, they are able to complete a task in a timely manner, efficiently, and with few errors. Fluency is important because if a task takes too long to complete or is too difficult, most learners will not voluntarily engage in that task, may exhibit inappropriate behavior as a way to avoid the task, or be less prepared to learn more advanced skills. For example, students who cannot read effortlessly are unlikely to choose reading as an activity to do on their own. Students who have trouble writing coherent, interesting passages that are neat and grammatically correct may try to avoid writing tasks. Students who are inconsistent in their recall of basic mathematics facts may find it hard to learn more advanced mathematics skills. Fluency does not just happen: It comes with repeated practice of new skills. For many functional skills, this practice is unplanned—it occurs because of a need to use the skill. For example, children who are learning to tie their shoes or put on clothing have multiple, naturally occurring opportunities to practice. New drivers have many opportunities to practice their new skills and are usually highly motivated to do so. However, teachers will need to systematically plan practice opportunities for most academic skills. These practice opportunities, as we discuss later, should be varied, interesting to students, and allow for the application of skills in meaningful contexts. Worksheets, although perhaps the most common form of practice, are not necessarily the most interesting or even the most appropriate for some skills. For example, students who are learning to write paragraphs might appropriately practice this skill in writing letters, stories, journals, or articles for the class newsletter. Peer tutoring might be the most appropriate form of practice for building fluency in spelling or vocabulary words, and structured play activities may help build fluency in peer-to-peer social skills.

Learners predictably pass through four stages of learning: acquisition, proficiency, maintenance, and generalization.

Maintenance.   **Maintenance** refers to the retention of skills over time (Meese, 2001). Failure to maintain essential "building block" skills (i.e., the basic skills that are required for later, more complex tasks) over time can mean exponential interferences in learning. For example, a student who cannot consistently, accurately, and quickly recall letter–sound relationships will never be a proficient reader. A student who has trouble remembering vocabulary words may struggle with content-area subjects, given the strong emphasis on vocabulary in many subjects (e.g., biology, physical science, English literature, health). A common problem for many students with disabilities is that they have problems with short- and long-term memory (Torgeson, 1988). Many students with learning disabilities and behavioral disorders may not use active memory-enhancing strategies that successful learners use, typically without specific instruction to do so (Mastropieri & Scruggs, 1998; Scruggs & Mastropieri, 2000).

Maintenance of skills must not be left to chance, but rather must be systematically developed from the beginning stages of instruction. One way to facilitate maintenance is to ensure the strong acquisition of new skills by using effective, efficient instructional methods for initial learning, such as those described later in this chapter. Another way to enhance maintenance is to teach students to use memory tools, such as mnemonics and other cognitive strategies, which have been shown to improve academic performance in students with and without disabilities in a variety of instructional settings (Deschler et al., 2001; Mastropieri, Sweda, & Scruggs, 2000; Scruggs & Mastropieri, 2000). Mnemonics are "a systematic procedure for enhancing memory" (Scruggs & Mastropieri, 2000, p. 202) For example, most of us who once took piano lessons still remember the familiar mnemonic "Every good boy does fine" (which represents the notes on the lines of the treble clef—E, G, B, D, F), even if we have not read music for many years. We may also remember all of the colors of the optical spectrum (red, orange, yellow, green, blue, indigo, violet) because we used the first-letter mnemonic "Roy G. Biv" to help us learn those colors initially.

Finally, intermittent practice is essential to the maintenance of skills. Perhaps the most effective practice is that which occurs within meaningful contexts. For example, once students reach fluency in reducing fractions, they do not need to practice this skill in isolation every day. However, using the skill in the context of other tasks (e.g., solving word problems, adding fractions) will help to ensure maintenance.

Generalization.   **Generalization** refers to being able to use a skill in different settings, with different people, or with different materials. This may be the most critical stage of learning because if a student is unable to generalize newly learned skills, those skills may be functionally meaningless. Generalization across settings means that the student can perform the skill in environments or under conditions other than where it was originally learned. For example, Joshua learned the phonemic awareness task of identifying the initial sound in objects in his preschool classroom. He now happily states the initial sound of almost every object he touches, no matter where he is. Generalization across persons means the student can use newly learned skills with individuals other than the teacher. For example, Mariel once had difficulty following directions. Her teacher implemented an intervention designed to improve Mariel's skills in following directions. Mariel now follows her teacher's directions most of the time, but still does not follow directions given by the paraprofessional, substitute teacher, or lunchroom monitor; she has failed to generalize compliance across individuals. Generalization with regard to new materials means that the student can perform the skill with materials other than those initially used for instruction. A child who has generalized bicycle-riding skills can ride any appropriately sized bike, even those that differ somewhat in size and shape from the bike on which he or she learned to ride.

For many of us, learning proceeds from acquisition to generalization with little systematic attention. For students with difficulties in learning academic and social skills, however, teachers must systematically plan for each stage of learning. Several instructional arrangements and activities can help with this. The most common instructional arrangements and activities, and the purposes for each, follow.

TYPES OF INSTRUCTIONAL ARRANGEMENTS AND ACTIVITIES

The term **instructional arrangement** refers to how the instructional environment is organized for teaching purposes. *Instructional activities* refers to what teachers and students do to promote learning. In any classroom, instructional arrangements and activities are typically for one of two general purposes: presenting new information or reviewing previously learned material. Many types of instructional arrangements and instructional activities are used to accomplish these tasks, each of which has specific purposes.

INSTRUCTIONAL ARRANGEMENTS

The most common types of instructional arrangements are large-group instruction, small-group instruction, and one-on-one instruction. Each instructional arrangement has a place in teaching students with learning and behavioral difficulties. In our three-tiered positive behavioral support model, the first instructional arrangement, large-group instruction, is most likely to be used in Tier 1 (the universal level); small-group instruction is most likely to be used at both the universal and targeted levels. One-on-one instruction is usually a tertiary-level instructional arrangement.

Large-Group Instruction

In **large-group instruction**, or **whole-group instruction**, new content is delivered to the entire class (the acquisition stage). Large-group instruction is typical in general education classes, particularly at the secondary level. Primary and intermediate general education classes may provide large-group instruction for certain content areas (e.g., science, social studies) and small-group instruction for core subjects such as reading and math.

Although large-group instruction is often not associated with special education, there are reasons why this arrangement is sometimes appropriate for special education classes, as well as for general education classes. First, research has shown that large-group instruction can be effective for students of varying ability levels, not just "typical" learners (Ellis & Worthington, 1994; Gersten, Carnine, & Woodward, 1987). Ellis and Worthington (1994) suggest that large-group instruction may be effective because it allows teachers to spend more time actually engaging in effective teaching behaviors than do other arrangements; in other words, the efficiency of large-group instruction may contribute to its effectiveness. This efficiency is another argument for large-group instruction. Large-group instruction can reduce the number of transitions and the amount of time that students must work independently, while at the same time increasing the amount of teacher supervision and the feedback that the students receive. In addition, because large-group instruction is common in general education, it should benefit students to be exposed to this arrangement in special education classes where the "large groups" may be smaller than in general education. Participating in large-group instruction in special education classes may help students learn the behaviors that are necessary for successful participation in general education classes, behaviors that are often weak or lacking in students with learning and behavioral difficulties (e.g., taking turns talking, focusing on the teacher).

Finally, special education teachers may be responsible for teaching multiple grades and subjects, sometimes even during a single period. For example, we visited a high school resource teacher who, in one period, had students in her class for basic algebra, integrated chemistry and physics, and biology! Another high school teacher in a self-contained class for students with behavioral disorders had five students in his class during one period. These five students were scheduled for three different subjects during that period: English, math, and social skills! Even though these may be extreme examples, without grouping of some kind, it may be impossible for teachers to incorporate the effective instructional behaviors that are essential for student learning.

One concern that we sometimes encounter is that large-group instruction for students with disabilities might mean that individualization is sacrificed for efficiency. Polloway, Cronin, and Patton (1986) define **individualized instruction** as an instruction that is appropriate for a specific individual, but they argue that individualized instruction does not have to mean one-on-one instruction. Individualization can occur as part of group instruction and during practice activities.

> Large-group instruction is compatible with individualized instruction.

Small-Group Instruction

In **small-group instruction**, the teacher divides the large group into two or more smaller groups and teaches each group separately. The small groups usually consist of two to six students with similar ability levels in the content area being taught (i.e., **homogeneous groups**) (Ysseldyke, Thurlow, Wotruba, & Nania, 1990). For example, groups might consist of students who have similar individualized educational program (IEP) objectives or students who are at the same grade level in reading or math. While the teacher works with one group, the remaining students work on other instructional activities (e.g., worksheets, computer-assisted instruction, peer tutoring), either independently or under the supervision of a paraprofessional or in a co-teaching arrangement. Like large-group instruction, small-group instruction is used to deliver new information during the acquisition stage.

Small-group instruction has been shown to be effective for students of varying abilities (Carnine, Silbert, Kame'enui, & Tarver, 2010); however, like any instructional arrangement, it requires that the teacher possess certain skills. To effectively and efficiently implement small-group instruction, the teacher must be proficient at (a) scheduling to ensure that all students have sufficient instructional time with the teacher; (b) classroom management to ensure efficient transitions from group activities to other tasks and to ensure that students who are not being directly supervised maintain appropriate behavior; (c) organization to ensure that all instructional materials are ready for use by each group and also to ensure that students have engaging and meaningful tasks to do when they are not working directly with the teacher; and (d) supervision to effectively monitor all student behavior in the classroom, even for the behavior of those students with whom the teacher is not directly working.

One-on-One Instruction

In **one-on-one instruction**, a teacher works individually with a student to deliver instruction. The advantage of one-on-one instruction is that the teacher can customize instructional language, examples, and explanations for a single student, which may help the student avoid frustration (Bloom, 1984). However, the teacher must ensure that one-on-one instruction includes the elements of effective instruction that are known to be correlated with higher levels of students' achievement, as discussed in later sections of this chapter. The teacher must also guard against one-on-one instruction being used only in informal, reactive, or unplanned ways (Evertson, 1979). For example, we are often called to consult with teachers, usually special education teachers, who are struggling because of the behavior of one or more students. In these situations, we often observe students being required to work independently (e.g., reading passages from textbooks, completing worksheets), with no direct instruction for teaching new concepts and with the teacher assisting the student only as needed. This *is not* one-on-one instruction, and it is not surprising that some students act out under these conditions. We understand that most teachers do not operate this way. However, our observations are consistent with research that suggests that the educational experiences of students with behavioral disorders are characterized by low levels of meaningful teacher-led instruction and low levels of academic engaged time (Knitzer, Steinberg, & Fleisch, 1990; Sutherland & Wehby, 2001; Wehby et al., 1998). For all of these reasons, we encourage teachers to use one-on-one instruction rarely, mainly to reteach or to teach new content to a student whose needs would not be met in group instruction because his or her learning objectives differ significantly from other students in the class. One-on-one instruction can be beneficial, but we believe that it should not be the primary form of instruction for most students.

> Teachers should rely on small-group instruction as the primary form of instruction for students with learning and behavioral difficulties, especially for instruction in the core academic areas.

INSTRUCTIONAL ACTIVITIES

In this section, we describe two instructional approaches that are used primarily for teaching new skills (i.e., the acquisition stage) to students with mild to moderate disabilities: (a) generic direct instruction (lowercase *d*, lowercase *i*) and (b)

Direct Instruction (capital *D*, capital *I*). These two approaches are similar in that both involve explicit, direct, teacher-led instruction, which has been associated with the strongest learning outcomes for students with learning and behavioral difficulties (Ellis & Worthington, 1994; Hallahan, Lloyd, Kauffman, Weiss, & Martinez, 2005; Heward, 2009). However, there are important qualitative differences between these two methods, as we will explain. Next, we briefly discuss other instructional methods for teaching new skills, including methods that are typically used for students with developmental disabilities or students with autism. Finally, we describe practice activities that are largely utilized for building fluency or enhancing maintenance and generalization of skills.

Generic Direct Instruction

Explicit, teacher-led instruction is often referred to as *direct instruction*.

The general teacher-led instructional approach, in which the teacher systematically follows a series of steps to explicitly teach new skills and concepts, is usually referred to as direct instruction. A highly versatile approach, direct instruction can be used to teach virtually any type of skill, is the most effective approach for teaching new content to students with learning and behavioral challenges, particularly in language arts and mathematics. However, the direct instruction approach is also used to teach social and behavioral skills. The coaching–modeling–behavioral rehearsal format described in Chapter 9 reflects a direct instruction approach. Direct instruction has a long history of proven effectiveness for all types of learners, including students with disabilities (Brophy & Good, 1986; Englert, 1984; Rosenshine, 1986). Direct instruction is also known as mastery teaching (Hunter, 1994, 2004), explicit instruction, and active teaching. All of these terms refer to teacher-led instruction that is characterized by

- the organization of instruction around specific instructional objectives;
- large-group or small-group instruction;
- structure, clarity, and repetition;
- explanation supported by demonstration;
- high levels of student engagement; and
- mastery learning, in which students are expected to practice skills independently only after they demonstrate a minimal level of mastery (e.g., accuracy in responding) in performing those tasks under teacher supervision.

These characteristics suggest why direct instruction is effective for students with learning and behavioral difficulties. The direct instruction model incorporates features that address the learning and behavioral characteristics necessary for learning that many students with disabilities lack.

The steps in a direct instruction approach are designed to provide structured, systematic instruction that reflects what is known about student learning and needs.

Although specific terminology and arrangement vary, the following steps are typically recommended in a direct instruction model:

1. ***Gain the attention of the learners.*** A common mistake that some teachers make is attempting to present instruction before the students are fully attentive. Teachers gain students' attention by using a consistent signal or procedure (remember our discussion of procedures from Chapter 6). For example, Ms. Gonzalez gets her third-grade students' attention for each lesson by saying, "Class, we will begin math [or whatever subject is scheduled

in 3 minutes. Please put away your materials, get out your books and pencils, and take care of any personal business. I will set the timer. If everyone is ready to go when the timer rings, our class gets a star on our "Ready to Go" chart." Mr. Todd starts his high school history classes immediately after taking attendance.

2. ***Review previously learned material that is relevant to the new information to be presented.*** This step includes checking for understanding to ensure that students remember previous material and reteaching if needed. This step addresses the fluency and maintenance stages of learning.

3. ***State the goal of the lesson.*** This includes stating the objectives for the day's lesson and providing the rationale for why the material is important or meaningful for students. This can accomplish two things: First, it helps students to know exactly what they will be held accountable for, and second, it can provide motivation for students to learn difficult or unfamiliar content.

4. ***Present new content in small steps.*** Because this step addresses the acquisition stage of learning, students will benefit from certain teacher behaviors designed to support new learning. We describe these later in this chapter. To ensure that skills and concepts are broken down into understandable steps, the teacher must be familiar with task analysis, which is described later in this chapter. Throughout the presentation of new material, the teacher should continually pose questions in order to monitor the students' understanding of the material. If, at any point, students are uncertain or incorrect in their responses, reteaching will be necessary.

5. ***Model the skill.*** Although we list this as a separate step to illustrate its importance, modeling actually occurs simultaneously with the presentation of information. As new content is being introduced, it should be accompanied by multiple examples of concepts or demonstrations of the skill. Later in this chapter, we discuss in greater detail the designing of instructional examples.

6. ***Provide prompted practice.*** This is sometimes referred to as **guided practice**. In this step, students either recite new information in unison with the teacher (e.g., count to 10, recite the formula for metric conversion, state the definition of a new vocabulary word) or practice new skills or concepts under the teacher's supervision with immediate feedback. Guided practice might be in the form of worksheets, activities at the blackboard, or written responses on individual dry erase boards. Guided practice can also be oral. The purpose of prompted practice is to ensure that students have acquisition-level mastery of the new material. As we discuss more extensively later in this chapter, research indicates that students should respond correctly at least 80% of the time during guided practice (Council for Exceptional Children, 1987; Rosenshine, 1983).

> It is important for teachers to ensure that students can perform the targeted skills with at least 80% accuracy before allowing students to practice the skills without teacher supervision.

7. ***Provide unprompted practice.*** The next step is to test students' mastery of the skill or concept by asking them to perform the task without teacher assistance. In this step, the teacher might call on individual students to count to 10, state a metric conversion formula, or recite the definition for a vocabulary word. The purpose of this step is to ensure that each student can perform the

new task independently before actually having students work on the skill without supervision.

8. ***Provide repeated opportunities for independent practice.*** During **independent practice**, students apply the newly learned skills or concepts in activities that are done with little teacher supervision, such as seatwork, homework, learning centers, computer-assisted instruction, or peer tutoring. The purpose of independent practice is to build mastery and automaticity (Rosenshine, 1983), and to move students from the acquisition stage to the fluency, maintenance, and generalization stages of learning. Remember, we assume that students know *how* to do the skill (e.g., write a paragraph, solve long-division problems, write the letters in their name, tie a shoe, read a passage) at this point, but that they need additional practice in order to become fluent in using the skill. Most students with disabilities will need multiple opportunities to practice newly learned skills. One worksheet will not provide sufficient practice for a student to become proficient in matching letter sounds to objects or reducing fractions. Students will need repeated and varied practice opportunities to ensure that skills are learned well enough to be remembered over time (i.e., **maintenance**) and to be used in new settings or applications (i.e., **generalization**). To achieve the level of mastery required for maintenance and generalization of skills, students should exhibit high levels of correct responding during independent work. The Council for Exceptional Children (1987) recommends setting the standard at 90% correct responding during independent practice activities; Rosenshine (1983) recommends 95% accuracy. Practically speaking, this means that a student who independently completes a worksheet, answers questions during a game, or gives responses during a peer tutoring activity should be able to answer at least 9 out of 10 questions correctly. If students are not exhibiting this level of proficiency in independent work, additional teaching or guided practice is needed.

The direct instruction model assumes that during each step, teachers exhibit certain behaviors that increase desired learning and behavioral outcomes. These effective teaching behaviors are explained later in this chapter.

> The direct instruction approach is an effective method for teaching academic skills to students with disabilities.

To present effective direct instruction lessons, teachers must devote time to planning what they will say and do during each step of the process. Usually, this planning is recorded in the form of a lesson plan. Most teachers will be expected to turn in lesson plans to their principal, although in our experience, what must be submitted for this purpose is never as detailed as is needed for effective teaching. Writing lesson plans is a good practice that should result in instruction that is more effective. Research indicates that teachers who write and follow lesson plans tend to be more effective than teachers who do not do so (Everhart, Oaks, Martin, & Sanders, 2004). Furthermore, the implementation of detailed lesson plans seems to be correlated with student achievement (Panasuk & Todd, 2005). In fact, research indicates that achievement and behavior are enhanced when teachers write scripts to delineate what the teacher will say when presenting information, what questions will be asked, and the correct responses to be expected from students. The results of studies have shown that teachers who develop and follow instructional scripts have students with higher levels of achievement and lower levels of off-task and disruptive behavior than teachers who do not do so (Gunter & Reed, 1997; Gunter, Shores, Jack, Denny, & DePaepe, 1994). This makes perfect sense: A builder would never begin building a home without a detailed plan. Most of us map out our route before driving in the car to a new destination. Even businesses develop business plans to guide decision making. It *is not* acceptable for teachers to "wing it." The authors of this text, despite many years of teaching experience, still develop lesson plans before we meet with our classes, whether they are elementary school students, college students, or in-service teachers! The more inexperienced the teacher or the more unfamiliar the content area, the more important it is to write a detailed lesson plan.

There are infinite variations for the format of lesson plans. We do not endorse any particular format, but we do insist that the lesson plan include information that follows the steps in the direct instruction model. Tables 8-3 through 8-5 provide three different examples of lesson plans, one each for elementary, middle school, and high school, respectively. As you review the lesson plans, note how each step of the direct instruction model is addressed.

Direct Instruction

Direct Instruction (capital *D,* capital *I*) is a highly systematic, organized, and comprehensive approach to instruction and curriculum design. In contrast to direct instruction (lowercase *d,* lowercase *i*), **Direct Instruction (DI)** refers to the model developed by Sigfried Engelmann, Douglas Carnine, and others at the University of Oregon in the mid-1960s. DI incorporates a highly structured set of specific teaching behaviors, coupled with carefully designed curricula that include scripted lessons for teachers (Association for Direct Instruction, 2003).

The following passage provides an explanation of Direct Instruction according to Gersten, Carnine, and Woodward (1987):

It is a complex way of looking at all aspects of instruction—from classroom organization and management to the quality of teacher–student interactions, the design of curriculum materials, and the nature of inservice teaching. . . .

The key principle in Direct Instruction is deceptively simple: For all students to learn, both the curriculum materials and teacher presentation of these materials must be clear and unambiguous. While many writers treat curriculum design and effective teaching research as separate strands, practitioners play them in concert.

Direct Instruction focuses on what many consider mundane decisions: the best wording for teachers to use in demonstrating a skill, the most effective way to correct students' errors, the number and range of examples necessary to ensure mastery of a new concept. (pp. 48–49)

Unlike many more widely used educational techniques, DI is well supported, with four decades of research proving its effectiveness for students of all ages, for students from diverse populations, and for teaching all types of academic and

TABLE 8-3 Sample Elementary Lesson Plan

Elementary Resource, Kindergarten/First-Grade

Instructional Objective

- Students will predict and complete the ending piece of an ABAB and ABBA pattern of colors with 90% accuracy.

  Type of learning: Problem-solving

Setting

- Large group sitting on the carpet.

Review

- Color identification.
- Pattern repetition ABAB and then ABBA.
- Present ABAB pattern using red/blue.
- Ask students to chant the pattern three times.
- Ask each student, one by one, to chant the pattern.
- Repeat until all of the students say the pattern correctly.
- Repeat the steps with the ABBA pattern.

Introduction

- Tell students that learning about patterns will help them as they learn to read, write, and do math. Get them excited by reminding them how successful they were in the review activity.
- Tell them about the new "big word" that will be in today's lesson: *prediction*. Define prediction as making an educated guess. You make that guess by using what you already know in determining your answer.
- Say, "I am going to show you a pattern that is missing the last piece. I want us to predict [define this as an educated guess] what this piece will be."
- Hold up a pattern card and ask the entire group to read it. Then hold up its mate with the last color covered.
- Ask for volunteers to make a prediction.
- Draw students' attention to the first pattern to help them in the decision-making process.
- Repeat this pattern card process until each student has answered correctly (even if you have to guide their answers).

Guided Practice

- Pass out bags of colored, differently shaped blocks used for making patterns.
- Pair off the students. Direct one student in each pair to make an ABAB pattern, leaving off the last piece.
- The student's partner will then choose the correct colored block to finish the pattern.
- Have the students switch roles and repeat the previous two steps.
- Monitor the groups closely to guide the predicting process if necessary.
- Repeat this process with the ABBA pattern.

Independent Practice

- When all of the students are able to complete the patterns with at least 80% accuracy, make bags of pattern blocks and pattern cards available for students to complete during center time.

TABLE 8-4   Sample Middle School Lesson Plan

Grade 7 Resource Mathematics

Instructional Objective

- Students will use regrouping in multiple-digit times single-digit multiplication problems with at least 90% accuracy.

  Types of learning: Procedural, Rules, Factual

Review

- Regrouping in addition problems.
- Basic multiplication tables (oral drill).

Introduction

- State the learning objective. Then ask the question: "When and why would you have to multiply numbers of more than one digit by using your brain?"

  Answer: If you do not have a calculator.

  Answer: Because you will need to know how to do this in order to work math problems that are more fun and complicated.

- Using the overhead projector/computer, present problems with easy-to-calculate numbers such as 22×5.
- Use the following task analysis to solve the problem:

  1. Multiply the 2 in the ones place by the multiplier 5.
  2. Record the answer: Write the 0 in the ones place in the answer section of the ones column.
  3. Write the 1 on top of the tens column of the problem.
  4. Multiply the 2 in the tens place by the multiplier 5 and then add the 1 to that answer.
  5. Record the answer: Write a 1 in the tens place in the answer section and another 1 in the hundreds place in the answer section.
  6. The answer is 110.

- Workout five more problems, asking students procedural (e.g., "What is the next step?") and factual (e.g., "What is 7×7?") questions to guide the work.

  87×7

  693×5

  $2,509 \times 8$

  324×6

  $2,732 \times 9$

Guided Practice

- Pass out a dry erase board, marker, and eraser to each student.
- Show one problem and ask the students to copy and solve it.
- Give students 15 to 30 seconds (or longer if needed) to solve their problems. Call out "Show me" as a signal for the students to raise their boards.
- Call on students to explain the process that they used in obtaining the answer.
- Continue this exercise until students are able to solve 80% of the problems correctly.

Independent Practice

- Five new problems on a worksheet.
- Multiplication game in the learning center (i.e., students solve problems and record their answers on answer sheets, self-correct their work by using the answer key, and then turn in their work to the teacher).

TABLE 8-5   Sample High School Lesson Plan

10th-Grade Resource Reading

Learning Objective

• Students will determine whether statements from reading selections are fact or opinion with 90% accuracy.

Type of learning: Conceptual, Rule

Review/Introduction

• This is the first time that this skill is being addressed in this class. However, it has been addressed in science class.

• Ask the students to recall that, in science, they had been asked if the answer that they gave was an observable, measurable fact or if it was their own opinion of what they thought to be true. Remind them about their success in using this skill in science.

• Provide definitions of "fact" and "opinion" and write them on the board.

• Provide examples of facts and opinions, and relate each example to the definitions.

• Give examples of fact and opinion statements and have students identify them as fact or opinion:

Fact: Seasons change.

Opinion: Summer is better than winter.

Fact: Music takes many forms and styles.

Opinion: Rap is great!

Fact: Football players are injured sometimes while playing football.

Opinion: Football is dangerous and should not be played at school.

• Ask students how to determine fact or opinion.

Fact includes information that can be verified.

Opinion may include personal beliefs or descriptive adjectives.

• Ask students to generate examples of facts and opinions.

Guided Practice

• While showing them the text on the overhead projector, read brief passages (no more than one short paragraph). Highlight each sentence consecutively, asking, "Is this a fact or an opinion?" "How do you know?"

• Repeat with new passages until each student is responding with at least 80% accuracy.

Independent Practice

• Homework: Have students read one newspaper or magazine article and find and label 10 fact and 10 opinion statements. During review tomorrow, the students must be prepared to justify their answers.

One reason that Direct Instruction programs are highly effective is that they include curricular and pedagogical elements that are designed to avoid common teaching errors that lead to unclear, ambiguous, or confusing instruction.

cognitive skills (Adams & Engelmann, 1996; Becker & Gersten, 2001; Gersten, Woodward, & Darch, 1986; Gersten et al., 1987), as well as social skills (Walker, Todis, Holmes, & Horton, 1988; Walker et al., 1988). The Walker social skills curricula ACCEPTS and ACCESS, described in Chapter 9, use a DI format.

Watkins and Slocum (2004) describe the major components that contribute to DI's effectiveness. Table 8-6 provides a brief explanation of these components. Table 8-7 provides a partial list of the many DI programs.

TABLE 8-6 Essential Components of Direct Instruction

Program Design

1. *Curricular content analysis:* The curricular sequences presented in DI programs are designed to address the ultimate purpose of learning: generalization of skills.

2. *Clarity in instructional language and formats:* DI programs provide scripts for teachers to ensure that all explanations, examples, questions, and feedback are communicated in ways that maximize clarity and minimize ambiguity.

3. *Sequence and continuity of skills:* Skills are carefully sequenced to ensure that students are never asked to give a response for which they have not learned all of the prerequisite skills needed for that response. Easier skills are presented first, and similar skills are separated in order to avoid confusion. In addition, after the skills are initially introduced, they will appear repeatedly in successive lessons to provide multiple opportunities to practice the skill over time (which enhances fluency, maintenance, and generalization).

Organization of Instruction

1. *Students are placed in flexible, homogeneous groups.* As students' skills change, they can be placed in different, more appropriate groups.

2. *DI procedures maximize active engaged time.* Students are highly engaged in instruction, which proceeds quickly but with much repetition.

3. *Teachers follow scripts for DI lessons.* Given the complexity of teaching and the many tasks required of teachers, it is better not to leave such things to chance. The scripts provided for teachers are scientifically based, incorporating those aspects of effective instruction known to be critical for student learning. Not having to plan these elements on their own gives teachers significant time to devote to other important areas of teaching (e.g., monitoring student performance, classroom management, planning practice activities).

4. *DI programs include a variety of ongoing assessments of student performance.* Assessment data are used to make decisions about grouping and instructional delivery and pace.

Teacher–Student Interactions

1. *Active student participation through signaled unison responding, accompanied by individual questions for monitoring purposes that follows a brisk pace.* DI programs incorporate the high levels of student response opportunities known to be correlated with learning. To ensure maximum student engagement, students respond chorally (in unison) much of the time. To provide structure for choral responses, students learn to respond when the teacher gives a particular signal. However, choral responses do not allow the teacher to adequately assess individual learning, so individual questions are also used. During a DI lesson, questions and other response opportunities are provided at a brisk pace, allowing for maximum student engagement.

2. *Correction procedures.* DI programs are designed to increase correct responding and minimize student errors. However, when errors occur, they are always corrected. Error correction is designed to help teachers assess the type of error that was made, correct it, and provide additional practice on similar items. Error correction is done immediately and efficiently.

3. *Provisions are included to enhance student motivation.* DI programs include a variety of motivational features, ranging from specific praise as feedback to having students graph daily performance.

Source: From *Introduction to Direct Instruction*, by N. Marchand-Martella, T. A. Slocum, & R. C. Martella, Boston: Allyn & Bacon. © 2004 Pearson Education. Adapted with permission from the publisher.

TABLE 8-7   Direct Instruction Programs

Reading/Language Arts

- Horizons—a core reading program for grades K–4.
- Reading Mastery—a core reading program for grades K–2 (Reading Mastery Classic) or K–6 (Reading Mastery Plus and Reading Mastery Rainbow Edition).
- Corrective Reading—an intensive reading program for struggling readers in grade 3–adult.
- Language for Learning 2008—an oral language program that teaches students the foundational language skills needed for success in school.
- ❖ REWARDS—a reading program for students in grades 4–12 that focuses on strategies for reading long words and improving fluency, especially in content areas. REWARDS Plus–Science and REWARDS Plus–Social Studies teach these reading skills using science and social studies content. REWARDS–Writing teaches critical writing skills.
- ❏ Teach Your Child to Read in 100 Easy Lessons—a beginning reading program for young children.

Spelling

- Spelling Mastery—a spelling program for grades K–6 that teaches phonemic, morphemic, and whole-word approaches to spelling.
- Spelling Through Morphographs—a spelling program for older students (grade 4–adult).

Math

- DISTAR® Arithmetic—a basic mathematics skills program for grades K–3 that emphasizes mastery learning and consistent, task-analyzed thinking processes.
- Connecting Math Concepts—a mathematics curriculum for grades K–8 that teaches not only specific mathematics strategies but also how mathematics concepts are connected.
- Corrective Math—an intensive mathematics program for grade 3–adult that focuses on critical skills and concepts that struggling students often lack.
- Essentials for Algebra, SRA—provides foundational skills to prepare students in grades 7–12 for beginning or advanced Algebra.

Language

- DISTAR® Language III—an oral and written language skills program for grades 2–4 that teaches vocabulary, sentence structure, grammar, meaning, and inferences.
- Language for Learning—a program to teach language and thinking skills to students in grades K–2 that teaches language rules and strategies, vocabulary, and concepts.
- Language for Thinking—for grades 1–3, extends the skills taught in Language for Learning.
- Language for Writing—a comprehensive writing program for grades 2–5 that focuses on word usage, syntax, vocabulary, grammar, punctuation, and fluency in writing.
- Language Through Literature—for grades K–6, uses a literature-based approach to develop skills as readers, speakers, and writers.
- Reasoning and Writing—teaches higher-order thinking skills as a foundation for writing skills for grades K–8.

Writing

- Language for Writing—a writing program for grades 2–5 that teaches writing skills, vocabulary, sentence formation, and organizational skills for good writing.
- Basic Writing Skills—a writing program for grades 6–12 that emphasizes basic mechanics and sentence formation.
- Expressive Writing 1 and 2—a program to help poor writers in grades 4–8 improve writing and editing skills.
- Cursive Writing Program—for teaching speed and accuracy in cursive writing for students in grades 2–4.

Other

- Your World of Facts—for students in grades 3–6; teaches important facts and factual relationships as it builds background knowledge that enables students to better understand science and social studies content.
- ➤ ACCEPTS and ACCESS—social skills curricula for elementary (ACCEPTS) and secondary (ACCESS) classes. Teaches classroom skills, peer interaction skills, skills for interacting with adults, and self-management skills.

- Available from McGraw Hill Education, www.mheonline.com
- ❖ Available from Sopris West Publishing Co., Longmont, CO, www.sopriswest.com
- ❏ Published by Simon & Schuster. Available in bookstores. Readers may view samples of the text on www.Amazon.com and www.barnesandnoble.com.
- ➤ Available from PRO-ED Inc., www.proedinc.com

One interesting feature of DI programs and a DI approach is the use of scripts for teachers to follow in delivering instruction. Regarding scripts, Marchand-Martella and her colleagues (2004) state the following:

> Scripts are tools designed to accomplish two goals: (1) to [ensure] that students access instruction that is extremely well designed, from the analysis of the content to the specific wording of explanations, and (2) to relieve teachers of the responsibility for designing, field-testing, and refining instruction in every subject that they teach. (p. 42)

Some teachers object to following scripts, saying that this approach stifles their creativity (Bessellieu, Kozloff, & Rice, n.d.). Rather than being concerned about creativity (there are many other, less critical outlets for creativity in any classroom), we encourage teachers to view scripted lessons as a way to deliver expert instruction in every lesson. Teachers using DI curricular materials can be confident that they are using highly sophisticated programs that have carefully juxtaposed curricular and pedagogical details to ensure effective, efficient instruction (American Federation of Teachers, 1998). Because of the success of DI programs, other instructional programs have attempted to duplicate some of the more salient features of DI. However, just because a program is scripted, for example, does not mean it includes all of the features of a true DI program.

Space precludes a thorough discussion of the sophistication and elegance of DI programs. Suffice it to say that DI not only incorporates all of the elements of effective teaching known to be essential for student learning, but DI programs also take the guesswork and potential for error out of teaching: Nothing is left to chance. Given the critical task facing many special education teachers—educating students who are underprepared for school, who lack essential skills for learning, and who have low motivation for academic work—we strongly urge teachers to rely on the expertise of DI programs to guide instruction, especially in the critical content areas of reading, language, and math. Teachers who use DI programs can feel confident that they are using the best technology research has to offer for teaching students with learning and behavioral needs.

Other Instructional Methods for Teaching New Skills

Our focus on direct instruction/Direct Instruction for teaching new skills does not mean that these are the only methods available. There are many other effective research-based methods for instruction during the acquisition stage; most of these methods are founded on applied behavioral analysis. Although many of the methods are typically used for students with developmental disabilities or autism, all could be used with any student, particularly for young students, or for teaching basic skills that students have not learned through other methods. Typically, the methods presented here are techniques that would be used at the tertiary level. While a thorough discussion of each of these methods is beyond the scope of this chapter, we want educators to be aware of these techniques. We urge all special educators to pursue training in these methods and to practice them so that they become a viable, functional part of their instructional repertoire.

> The extent to which teachers are skilled at task analyzing the skills and concepts that they teach will affect how easily students learn those skills and concepts.

Task Analysis.   While not an instructional technique per se, task analysis is critical for effective instruction. **Task analysis** is the process of identifying the specific, discrete cognitive and manual steps required to perform a task. Task analysis and an associated instructional technique known as chaining can facilitate learning for difficult, complex tasks. Effective teachers must be able to task-analyze anything that students are expected to do or learn. By task-analyzing complex behaviors, teachers can then use chaining to teach complex tasks or can identify where students are having difficulty with a skill. Table 8-8 shows several examples of task analysis used to break down complex tasks into their component steps. To conduct a task analysis, we recommend that you work through the task, noting each overt and covert step. Note that our task analyses are written in language which is appropriate for the teacher. The teacher would then translate these steps by using language that is appropriate for the students' developmental levels. Because we bring skills to tasks that students may not yet have, do not assume anything or omit any step. In our task-analysis examples, you can see several instances where we specified behaviors that may seem obvious but that might not be obvious to students.

Chaining.   **Chaining** refers to the process of joining discrete behaviors, or links, to form a longer, more complex behavior (Skinner, 1953). Most of the behaviors that make up our daily routines are sets of complex behavioral chains. Getting ready for work may consist of a behavioral chain that includes showering, washing hair, shaving or applying makeup, and dressing. Each of these links are, of course, accomplished by performing additional behavioral chains. Likewise, most academic tasks consist of multiple behavioral chains. For example,

TABLE 8-8 Sample Task Analyses

Tying Shoe

1. Pick up ends of laces.
2. Cross one lace over the other.
3. Pick up laces where they touch.
4. Grasp the end of the top lace.
5. Insert it through the opening and release.
6. Pick it up on the other side.
7. Pull gently.
8. Grasp the end of the other lace.
9. Pull firmly.
10. Pick up the lace that is closer to the dominant hand.
11. Place the index finger of the other hand against the lace.
12. Fold the lace over the index finger to form a loop.
13. Hold the two sides of the loop together at the base using a pincer grasp with the dominant hand.
14. Pick up the other lace with the other hand.
15. Circle the lace around the loop.
16. Using the index finger of the dominant hand, push the second lace against the thumb of the same hand and push it through the opening (follow the thumb through the opening).
17. Grasp the small loop with the nondominant hand.
18. Grasp the top of the larger loop with the dominant hand.
19. Pull firmly in opposite directions.

One-to-One Correspondence Counting

1. Line up the objects, one next to the other, horizontally.
2. Place the index finger on the first object on the left.
3. Say "1" as you touch that object.
4. Touch the next object.
5. Say "2" as you touch that object.
6. Continue until you have touched the last object.

Asking a Question

1. Think about what it is that you do not know or that you need help with.
2. Raise your hand.
3. Wait until the teacher calls on you or comes to your desk.
4. Tell the teacher your question.
5. Listen carefully to the teacher's answer.
6. Ask yourself: "Do I understand now?"
7. If so, say, "Thank you."
8. If not, ask another question.

TABLE 8-8   (Continued)

Writing a Short Story

1. Ask yourself, "What should my story be about?"
   a. Did the teacher assign a topic?
   b. Can you choose a topic? If so, choose a topic about which you are familiar and that interests you.
2. Jot down some notes about what you might include in your story (e.g., names, places, events).
3. Organize your notes using an outline, story map, or graphic organizer.
4. Using your notes, write the first draft of your story.
5. Read your story.
6. Ask yourself:
   a. Does the story make sense?
   b. Is the story interesting?
   c. Do I need to add anything?
   d. Do I need to take anything out?
7. Revise your story by making the following changes:
   a. Add more information as needed.
   b. Delete unnecessary information.
8. Rewrite the final draft of your story.

Looking Up a Word in the Dictionary

1. Check the first letter of your word.
2. Find the section of the dictionary that includes words beginning with that letter. Use the letters on top of the pages to guide you.
3. Check the second letter of your word.
4. Find the page that contains words beginning with those two letters.
5. Check the third letter of your word.
6. Scan the words from top to bottom in each column until you find your word.

completing a mathematics worksheet requires the student to gather materials, read the directions, solve each problem (using another set of behavioral chains), and turn in the paper.

Chaining is an efficient way to teach task-analyzed skills and concepts. There are three types of chaining: forward, backward, and total task presentation. **Forward chaining** means that the first step of the task analysis is taught until the student can perform it independently. Then the next step is added to the first step. When the student can perform both steps independently in sequence, the third step is added, and so forth, until the student can perform all of the steps of the task without assistance. Forward chaining is commonly used when it is difficult to **prompt** the student through a step (e.g., by giving verbal, gestural, or physical guidance). For example, children learn to play a musical selection on an instrument

Chaining is an instructional method for teaching task-analyzed skills and concepts.

by playing the first few measures or the first few lines; then, after they master those, additional measures or lines are slowly added until they can play the entire piece. Children learn to hit a baseball by first hitting a ball off of a tee, then hitting a ball that is tossed slowly from a short distance, and, finally, hitting balls that are pitched with ever-increasing speed. Table 8-9 provides examples of tasks that would be appropriately taught with the use of forward chaining.

Backward chaining, as the term implies, teaches a task-analyzed skill by starting with the last step in the task and teaching that step to mastery. Then, the next-to-last step is added. When the student can perform those last two steps independently, the third-to-last step is added, and so on, until the first step is reached. Backward chaining is often used to teach functional skills (e.g., dressing, eating, grooming, toileting) to students with cognitive disabilities. Backward chaining is most appropriate for those tasks in which the student can perform the steps with assistance or prompts (see Table 8-9 for examples). This assistance is then withdrawn on the last step, then the last two steps, then the last three steps, and so forth. One advantage to backward chaining is that the task is repeated numerous times during the backward chaining process. For complex tasks such as tying shoes or memorizing the prologue to *Romeo and Juliet*, for example, the student practices the task many times with assistance (e.g., for tying shoes, verbal prompts

---

TABLE 8-9 Chaining Formats for Various Tasks

Forward Chaining

Forward chaining would be an appropriate way to teach the following:

- How to play a musical instrument
- How to perform a dance
- How to shoot a lay-up in basketball
- Functional skills (e.g., dressing, eating, grooming, toileting)
- How to write an essay
- How to use the computer to search for library books
- How to write increasingly more complex sentences

Backward Chaining

Backward chaining would be an appropriate way to teach the following:

- Functional skills
- Rote memorization tasks (e.g., counting, the alphabet, an address, a telephone number, poems, the preamble to the Constitution, lines in a play)

Total Task Presentation

Total task presentation would be an appropriate way to teach the following:

- Functional skills
- Motor skills (e.g., hopping, riding a bicycle, dribbling a basketball)
- Many academic skills (e.g., making computations, following laboratory procedures, learning formulas)
- Social skills

and models are provided; for memorization of the prologue, written prompts are provided) before the student is expected to do the task independently. This makes backward chaining an excellent choice for teaching verbal chains.

The last type of chaining is **total task presentation**. In this format, the student is expected to perform all steps of the task-analyzed skill each time the task is presented, although assistance or prompts may be provided. For example, Ms. Price uses total task presentation when teaching her students with severe mental retardation to go through the cafeteria line. She verbally prompts students to stand in line, pick up their trays, place their trays on the rail, point to the foods that they want, and so forth. When her students are able to perform the steps independently, she gradually **fades** the prompts (i.e., provides fewer prompts or includes less information in the prompt). Total task presentation is commonly used to teach social skills, functional skills, motor skills (e.g., skipping, shooting a free throw, riding a bicycle, throwing a ball), and many forms of academic skills (e.g., factual associations, computations, computer skills, writing tasks; see Table 8-9).

Although some tasks naturally lend themselves to a particular type of chaining, deciding which chaining technique to use is largely a matter of personal preference. One teacher may use forward chaining to teach the steps for multiplying fractions, whereas another teacher may prefer total task presentation. For example, Mr. Campbell teaches his kindergarten students the days of the week using backward chaining: He says the days in unison with the students. After three or four days of practice at this level, he says "Monday—Tuesday—Wednesday—Thursday—Friday—Saturday" with students and allows them to recite "Sunday" independently. When they consistently say "Sunday" independently, he then lets them say "Saturday Sunday" without his assistance. Ms. Shipman, on the other hands, prefers total task presentation to teach this same skill. She says the days of the week with her students each time. Eventually, she allows students to say the days alone, prompting them as needed. This is one of the advantages of chaining: Teachers have access to three different types of chaining as instructional tools, and for the most part, they do not need to worry about using the wrong type.

Discrete Trial Instruction.   **Discrete trial instruction, or discrete trial training (DTT)**, is a highly structured method for teaching task-analyzed skills. DTT is widely considered to be the instructional method of choice for students with autism. However, because DTT incorporates the characteristics associated with effective instruction as discussed in this chapter (e.g., instructional clarity, structure, frequent opportunities to respond, redundancy, mastery learning), we believe that teachers who know how to use DTT will be more effective in their use of other instructional techniques.

> Discrete trial teaching and time delay are similar, highly structured methods for teaching new skills or building fluency in previously learned skills.

DTT involves presenting multiple trials, with each trial consisting of four steps: cue, prompt (if needed), student response, and feedback. After each trial, the teacher records data about the student's response (e.g., correct, incorrect, correct with prompt, incorrect with prompt, no response), and then presents another trial. A teaching session typically consists of multiple, rapidly paced trials.

DTT is a highly versatile, effective method for teaching all types of skills to individuals or groups of students. See the "Resources" section at the end of this chapter for more information on DTT.

Time Delay.   **Time delay** includes the same steps as DTT, except that it includes wait time, or time for the student to respond, between the delivery of the cue and the prompt. The two types of time delay are **constant time delay**, in which the time between the cue and the prompt is always the same, and **progressive time delay**, in which the time between the cue and the prompt is gradually increased as the student becomes more proficient in responding. Time delay has a substantial research base that supports its use with all types of learners and for teaching or developing fluency in a wide range of skills (Wolery et al., 1992).

PRACTICE ACTIVITIES FOR BUILDING FLUENCY AND FACILITATING MAINTENANCE AND GENERALIZATION

The two instructional delivery systems discussed previously are the most effective methods for teaching new academic content to students with learning and behavioral needs. However, teachers are also responsible for ensuring that students master new material beyond the acquisition stage. Although some components of direct instruction are for the purpose of building fluency or maintaining the skills, these stages of learning, along with generalization, are addressed primarily through other methods. There are many activities that teachers can design to provide students with opportunities to practice newly learned skills.

The activities that follow are often used to provide opportunities for students to practice newly learned skills. Note that not all of these activities are supported by research for use with students with disabilities. Despite this, we include them with the caveat that, in any learning activity, teachers incorporate the elements of effective instruction as described in this chapter. Above all, remember that a minimum of 90% accuracy in responding should be expected during instructional practice activities. To ensure that students meet this criterion, teachers must frequently, systematically, and objectively monitor the students' performance (using curriculum-based measurement on all practice activities.

Practice Activities That are Supported by Research

Response Cards.   According to Heward (2009), **response cards** are "cards, signs, or items simultaneously held up by all students to display their responses to a question or problem presented by the teacher. There are two types: preprinted and write-on" (p. 230). Response cards have been shown to increase student responding in comparison to teachers calling on individual students (Gardner, Heward, & Grossi, 1994) and to improve student behavior (Heward, 2009). Dry erase boards are available through teacher supply stores or online, or are easily made by having a home improvement store cut a large dry erase panel (ask for tileboard, also known as shower board) into small sections and then taping the edges with duct tape for safety. Individual chalkboards could also be used. During review, Mr. Colin poses questions pertaining to previous lessons (e.g., "List four states explored by Cabeza de Vaca"; "Who first explored New Mexico and Arizona?"; "List one important result of the expansion of railroads"). For example, Mr. Colin uses response cards during the review and guided practice portions of

> Response cards help to ensure high levels of student engagement and are a fun way for students to practice newly learned skills.

his social studies lessons. Each student has his or her own dry erase board, marker, and eraser. Later, during guided practice, Mr. Colin presents response opportunities related to the current lesson. Of course, prior to using the response cards, Mr. Colin taught his students the procedure for using them during lessons.

Peer Tutoring (Delquadri, Greenwood, Whorton, Carta, & Hall, 1986; Osguthorpe & Scruggs, 1986). During peer tutoring, students work in pairs in order to practice basic skills (e.g., spelling words, vocabulary, mathematics facts, oral reading, comprehension questions). The peer tutoring sessions are highly structured with specific procedures that students follow for taking turns, presenting information, recording responses, and giving feedback for responses. Peer tutoring enjoys strong research support for use with students who have learning and behavioral difficulties, with the benefits accruing for both the tutor and the tutee (Spencer, 2006). These benefits are undoubtedly due to the fact that peer tutoring reflects many of the elements of effective instruction that are critical for student learning: It is highly structured, provides high levels of student engagement and response opportunities, allows for the monitoring of student responses, and provides immediate feedback and error correction. Furthermore, it is an enjoyable way for students to practice skills while freeing the teacher to work with other students in small-group or one-on-one formats.

Several peer tutoring models intended for classwide use have been shown to be effective for all types of students, including students with disabilities. One of the first such programs was Class-Wide Peer Tutoring (CWPT), developed at the Juniper Gardens Children's Project in Kansas City, Kansas (Delquadri, Greenwood, Stretton, & Hall, 1983). CWPT involves four components: (a) weekly teams, (b) a structured peer tutoring procedure, (c) a daily point system and public posting of student performance, and (d) practice in meaningful instructional activities (Maheady, Harper, & Mallette, 2003). Teams (e.g., peer tutoring pairs) are randomly selected. Each day, teams spend 20 to 30 minutes in peer tutoring activities; one student acts as a tutor for approximately 10 minutes and then the other student becomes the tutor. The tutor's job is to present the instructional stimuli (e.g., words to be spelled or read, mathematics facts), provide feedback, and award points for both correct responses and for *corrected* responses (i.e., responses that are correct after the tutor provides corrective feedback and the tutee practices the correct response a few times). During the peer tutoring sessions, the teacher supervises the peer tutoring activity and awards bonus points to teams that are using correct peer tutoring procedures. At the end of the peer tutoring session, teams chart their points on a class chart. On Friday, each student is assessed individually; students can earn additional points for themselves and for their teams for each correct response on the assessment. The winning team (i.e., the team with the most points) is awarded a certificate that is posted in the classroom. Multiple studies have provided research support for CWPT, showing positive effects in reading, math, spelling, and writing for students in all grade levels and for all student populations (Maheady & Gard, 2010). Results of one longitudinal study of CWPT showed that students in the CWPT group had lower rates of referral for special education services and lower dropout rates (Greenwood, Maheady, & Delquadri, 2002). CWPT has also been shown to be successful in integrating students with autism into general education (Kamps, Barbetta, Leonard, & Delquadri, 1994) and in improving outcomes for English language learners (Greenwood, Arreaga-Mayer, et al., 2001).

A similar classwide peer tutoring format is **Peer Assisted Learning Strategies (PALS)**. In PALS, peer tutoring pairs are formed by pairing high-performing and low-performing students (Sayeski, 2006). Then each pair is assigned to one of two class teams. Pairs earn points during peer tutoring sessions, and these points are added to the team's points. The peer tutoring pairs remain in place for 4 weeks and then new teams are formed. Like CWPT, PALS has been shown to improve the academic performance of all populations of students, including students with and without disabilities (Fuchs, Fuchs, & Burish, 2000; Maheady et al., 2003). Newer applications of classwide peer tutoring models have shown that CWPT and PALS can also be used to address higher-order thinking skills (Fuchs, Fuchs, Hamlett, et al., 1997; King, Staffieri, & Adelgais, 1998).

Peer tutoring incorporates many of the features of effective instruction. In addition, the highly structured, systematic nature of peer tutoring may help to ensure high levels of on-task behavior and, therefore, lower levels of off-task behavior. Further, the point systems that are a part of peer tutoring formats should enhance students' motivation to participate, resulting in fewer challenging behaviors during peer tutoring sessions.

Computer-Assisted Instruction.   Various applications of **computer-assisted instruction (CAI)** have been shown to improve learning outcomes in students with disabilities (Silver-Pacuilla & Fleischman, 2006). In fact, research suggests that, for some students, CAI may be an effective approach to teaching new skills as well as building fluency in previously taught skills (Coleman-Martin, Heller, Cihak, & Irvine, 2005). CAI can provide high levels of response opportunities and immediate feedback, which are necessary components for learning as we explain later in this chapter. Furthermore, the entertaining aspects that are a part of most educational software programs can enhance student motivation for learning (Jerome & Barbetta, 2005).

Practice Activities with Questionable Research Support for Students with Disabilities

Homework.   *Homework* refers to practice activities that are related to previously learned skills that students complete outside of the instructional environment. For students in general education, homework appears to increase academic achievement (Cooper, 1989), but results are mixed for students with disabilities (Rivera & Smith, 1997). It appears that homework can be beneficial for students with learning and behavioral disabilities, but teachers must take care to ensure that students are able to do the work independently, that homework is reviewed with students, and that homework completion is reinforced. Above all, if students consistently respond with lower than 90% accuracy on homework, teachers must reassess homework procedures or use other forms of practice.

Of course, homework is required in most general education classes. For this reason, homework skills may be an important target of instruction for many students with mild or moderate disabilities. Although little research has focused on homework for students with disabilities, the results of some studies suggest that homework completion can be improved through the use of strategies designed specifically to increase homework completion, including reinforcement, use of homework planners, and involving parents in homework monitoring (Bryan & Burstein, 2004).

Homework is used in social skills and self-control instruction to facilitate generalization of newly learned skills. Most often, the homework is in the form of self-monitoring or self-assessment activities in which students evaluate their use of the targeted skill. Unlike other forms of homework, research has shown that social skills homework can facilitate generalization of skills (Goldstein et al., 1998; McGinnis & Goldstein, 1997b).

Independent Seatwork (Worksheets).   Worksheets are arguably the most widely used form of independent practice in both general and special education. Most instructional materials (e.g., textbooks, commercial curricula, and even computer programs) include worksheets for student practice. According to Engelmann and Carnine (1991), worksheets are for review, expansion, or integration of previously learned skills. Despite the ubiquitous use of worksheets, virtually no research exists on the efficacy of worksheets for instructional practice. Perhaps the most complete treatment of how worksheets should be designed is offered by Engelmann and Carnine (1991). They list several advantages of worksheets but acknowledge that a major disadvantage is that worksheets do not provide corrective feedback, which is an important element of effective instruction. Because of this, they recommend that worksheets should only be used when students are sufficiently proficient at the task that they can be expected to make few errors. This recommendation, of course, is consistent with the expectation that students should respond with 90% accuracy or better on independent work.

We are concerned about the use of worksheets for several reasons: First, we are concerned that, for many students, worksheets are a discriminative stimulus for negative behavior because of the students' learning histories with this type of activity. Second, in our experience, teachers too often select worksheets for the wrong reasons (e.g., they "look fun") rather than choosing or designing worksheets that accurately reflect the learning objectives and that provide carefully designed and sequenced practice items. Finally, when other forms of academic practice activities are lacking, worksheets too often appear to function as busywork to keep students occupied. This observation is supported by studies which show that students in special education spend the majority of their time in special education classes doing worksheets (Vaughn, Levy, Coleman, & Bos, 2002). We have been in numerous special education classrooms where students are given packets of worksheets to complete, one after another, on their own, with little teacher interaction. This is not instruction, nor is it even appropriate independent practice. We are not opposed to using worksheets; when used correctly, worksheets can provide appropriate practice for building fluency. We do, however, caution teachers to closely examine worksheets to identify the objective of the items presented on the worksheet, evaluate whether those objectives are appropriate for the given students, and provide feedback to the students about their performance on the worksheet as soon as possible.

Cooperative Learning. **Cooperative learning (CL)** occurs when students are placed in heterogeneous groups in order to complete a group task. Typically, CL addresses both academic and social goals through structured formats in which each team member has specific responsibilities and that holds both the group and individual students accountable for learning outcomes. Cooperative learning is widely recommended, and research has shown that it can enhance the academic performance of students with disabilities in inclusive settings (Slavin, 1991; Slavin, Stevens, & Madden, 1988). However, in a comprehensive review of research on the use of cooperative learning for students with learning disabilities, McMaster and Fuchs (2002) concluded that (a) many of the studies that support cooperative learning are poorly designed, (b) it is premature to conclude that cooperative learning is equally or more effective than other practice activities (e.g., peer tutoring), and (c) cooperative learning does not appear to benefit students with learning disabilities as much as their average-achieving peers. Overall, the authors advised that it is premature to recommend cooperative learning as a best practice for students with learning disabilities.

Learning Centers. **Learning centers** are instructional activities for students to complete individually or in small groups of two or three students. Typically, a learning center consists of (a) one or more activities in a single content area (e.g., reading, math, writing), (b) activities for multiple grade or ability levels, and (c) hands-on activities or activities that have high motivational value. Learning centers should reflect specific learning objectives and should include ways for the teacher to indirectly monitor students' performance on learning center tasks. Intuitively, we like well-designed learning centers; we believe that the motivational aspect is important. However, although widely recommended in educational methods textbooks, professional development trainings, and other sources, there is little or no research supporting the efficacy of learning centers for improving student achievement. Because of the lack of research, we caution teachers to design learning centers to address specific instructional and/or behavioral objectives and to systematically and objectively monitor students' performance on learning center tasks. Students should respond with 90% accuracy or better (Council for Exceptional Children, 1987) on these practice activities.

When designed correctly, learning centers can be a fun, creative way for students to practice skills that might be tedious under other conditions. As an illustration, consider the learning center developed by Andrea Scott, a special educator in Humble, Texas. Each of her resource students had reading and writing language objectives in their IEPs, but the students disliked writing. To encourage her students to write, Andrea developed an imaginative learning center called "Clues." In Clues, students play the role of detectives in finding answers to a mysterious situation; in their answers, they use various clues to form conclusions about the mystery. As detectives, students are required to present their findings in the form of a written report in which they must distinguish between the facts and their opinions (another IEP objective for these students) about the case that they are solving. Table 8-10 provides a description of the Clues learning center. This learning center is fun for students, and

TABLE 8-10 "Clues" Learning Center Activity

Needs

This learning center was designed for the following purposes:

1. Increase the amount of time that students are engaged in writing tasks without complaining.
2. Build student confidence in writing.
3. Address the following IEP objectives (each student had one or more of these objectives on his or her IEP):
   a. Use correct capitalization and punctuation at the beginning and end, respectively, of a sentence.
   b. Identify a fact.
   c. Identify an opinion.
   d. Use correct penmanship (e.g., letter formation, spacing).
   e. Write in complete sentences.
   f. Correctly spell high-frequency words.
   g. Use correctly formatted paragraphs in written work.

Description

Students listen to a prerecorded message from a detective asking for help in solving a mystery. The detective is swamped with cases and knows that Ms. Scott's students have learnt the difference between a fact and an opinion. The detective asks the students to look in their clue bags and write a report, using complete sentences, neat handwriting, and correct spelling. The detective cannot turn in messy work to the chief! The learning center contains a variety of clue bags and special paper on which the students are to write their reports. When the students are finished with their reports, they place them in a large, brown, legal-sized envelope. The teacher then writes comments back to students as if they had come from the detective. In her comments, Ms. Scott reinforces work that pertains to the IEP objectives and provides corrective feedback when needed.

Implementation

This learning center was introduced on Day 3 of a week-long unit on fact and opinion. Ms. Scott began by telling the class that a detective has contacted her in the hope that her class can help him out with his cases. The teacher played the prerecorded message from the detective and then led the class in a lesson on how to write a report. During this lesson, the teacher stated the criteria for the reports (e.g., the reports must contain three facts and three opinions, and must be edited for spelling and grammar). Materials were then made available to the students in the learning center. The students could use the learning center when they finished their assigned independent work. The students were limited to writing about one clue bag per day. When time allowed, the students read their reports to the class and the class identified the facts and opinions stated in the report.

Materials

- Digital recording of message from a detective.
- Miscellaneous items for the clue bags. Ms. Scott used anything that she could find (e.g., a pair of broken eyeglasses, an empty film container, a safety pin, a button, a ticket stub). Each bag contained three or four items.
- Zippered plastic bags to hold the clues.
- Storage containers to hold the clue bags, report paper, and other materials.
- Report paper.
- Writing implements.
- Envelopes in which to submit the finished reports.

students' assessment data indicate a dramatic increase in the quantity of their writing, as well as improvements in the quality of their writing (e.g., longer sentences, more complex sentence structures, improved mechanics). Complaints about writing also drop to zero when students can practice their writing in the context of this center. In fact, students ask to use the center; in other words, they ask to write!

Other Activities. There are many other types of instructional practice activities, such as projects, self-correcting learning materials, and instructional games. Of these, only self-correcting materials have been substantiated by research (Mercer, Mercer, & Bott, 1984), and even that research is limited. As with learning centers, the motivational aspects of games may warrant their use, but as we have repeatedly cautioned, teachers must carefully design activities and materials to reflect learning objectives and to allow for monitoring of student performance.

EFFECTIVE INSTRUCTIONAL PRACTICES

Up to this point, we have described various formats for teaching students. However, any discussion of effective instructional practices is incomplete without identifying specific teacher behaviors that are associated with higher levels of student achievement and lower levels of behavioral problems. One of the advantages of Direct Instruction programs is that these effective teaching behaviors are incorporated through the script and other elements of structure in the programs. This is not true for direct instruction lessons or even for the various practice activities (e.g., peer tutoring, learning centers). Teachers who are using these formats must actively plan these effective teaching behaviors and monitor to ensure that those practices are implemented in all activities.

The research base that documents the positive effect of these practices on student achievement is substantial. The earliest investigations of effective teaching focused on describing overt teacher behaviors that were positively correlated with student achievement (Ellis & Worthington, 1994). Recent attention has focused on those covert *student* behaviors that are prerequisites for learning, such as self-regulation and structuring and organizing information. Many of these behaviors were described in our previous discussion on the characteristics of successful learners. We understand that these cognitive behaviors are critical for learning. We also now know that teachers can help develop these skills in students for whom such skills are weak or lacking.

In this section, we describe teacher behaviors that reflect both overt teacher actions and covert student cognitive behaviors that enhance learning. To make this long list of recommended practices easier to remember, we have organized them using the mnemonic SCORE CHAMPS, which stands for Structure, Clarity, Opportunities to respond, Redundancy, Explicit instruction, CHoices, Assess the forms of knowledge, Monitor student learning, Practice, and Success. A discussion of these elements follows, along with specific strategies for each. Some elements are more complex than others and require multiple teacher actions in order to accomplish them. Others are simpler to explain and implement. Box 8-1 lists the steps of SCORE CHAMPS and specific recommended practices for each step.

Box 8-1

How to Implement Each Step of SCORE CHAMPS

S = Structure

- Write and follow lesson plans.
- State objectives.
- Use graphic organizers.
- Provide mediated scaffolding.
- Use effective classroom management techniques.

C = Clarity

- Provide explicit instruction.
- Prime background knowledge.
- Carefully design examples.
- Define vocabulary.
- Teach conspicuous strategies.
- Repeat important information.
- Use organization language (e.g., "First we are going to . . ., then we are going to,. . . .").

O = Opportunities to respond

- Provide high levels of opportunities to respond to instructional stimuli during new learning and practice.
- Ensure high levels of correct responding.
- Use a variety of response formats, including choral responding and response cards.

R = Redundancy

- Ensure repetition in teaching new skills.

E = Explicit instruction

- Provide direct, teacher-led instruction.
- Incorporate elements of structure, clarity, opportunities to respond, and redundancy.
- Provide clear feedback for student responses.

C = CHoices

- Provide choices before and during academic tasks.

A = Assess the forms of knowledge

- Determine whether instructional targets represent factual learning, rule learning, conceptual learning, procedural learning, or problem-solving learning.
- Use instructional methods that are appropriate for the form of knowledge being taught.

M = Monitor student learning

- Monitor students' academic progress using frequent, objective data.

P = Practice

- Provide sufficient practice opportunities that reflect the learning objectives, provide high levels of response opportunities, and provide immediate feedback.

S = Success

- Ensure high levels of success in academic tasks.

Structure

Remember SCORE CHAMPS for effective delivery of instruction!

Remember that effective learners actively use a variety of cognitive strategies to impose structure on learning tasks and self-regulate learning, but students with learning and behavioral difficulties tend to be deficient in these skills. There are multiple ways in which teachers can provide structure and help students learn to self-regulate instruction, including the practices that follow.

Write and follow lesson plans.　As we indicated previously, lesson plans are important for helping teachers ensure that all elements of effective instruction are provided. Gunter and his colleagues (1994) speculated that many disruptive student behaviors were motivated by a desire to escape a task that is too difficult because the student lacks the information needed to complete the task correctly. In their study, these authors found that more than 80% of the time students were asked to perform tasks without being given the necessary information to do so (e.g., read a word without being taught the phonetic skills for decoding the word, solve a word problem without knowing basic mathematics facts). New teachers, especially, are well advised to write detailed lesson plans, and even scripts, that include how they will explain skills or concepts, examples they will use for modeling, questions they will ask to assess student learning, expected students' responses, and how they will correct students' errors.

State Objectives.   By stating the objectives for the day's lesson during the introduction step of a direct instruction lesson, teachers alert students to what the students will be held accountable for later. Stating the objectives means indicating what students should be able *to do* by the end of the lesson, not just describing the teacher's plans for the day. Saying, "Today we will review c-v-c words and then learn a new pattern" is not stating the objective. For example, before Ms. Greer's ninth-grade biology class arrived, she wrote the following objectives on the blackboard: By the end of this lesson, students will be able to

1. Describe the essential characteristic of organisms in the kingdom Procaryota.
2. Give examples of five different organisms found in the kingdom Procaryota.
3. Describe three examples of the effects of the kingdom Procaryota on daily life.

In another classroom, Mr. Peterson introduced a vowel digraph to his first-grade class, saying, "Today you will learn how to pronounce /ea/, and you will read words spelled with /ea/."

Use Graphic Organizers.   **Graphic organizers** are diagrams that help organize information and show hierarchical, sequential, or comparative relationships. Graphic organizers can assist students in becoming more independent and self-regulated in their learning by helping them to make connections to previously learned material, distinguish between critical and noncritical content, and elaborate on topics in order to enhance learning. Graphic organizers can be introduced early in the lesson and completed as the teacher progresses through the lesson. For older students, the completed graphic organizer can serve as a useful study tool after the lesson.

Graphic organizers have been shown to positively affect students' achievement (Horton, Lovitt, & Bergerud, 1990; Ives & Hoy, 2003; Lovitt et al., 1990). The Faculty of the Institute for Academic Access, a partnership between faculty members at the University of Kansas and the University of Oregon to improve the educational outcomes of adolescents with disabilities, have developed a number of research-based tools designed to help students become more strategic, independent learners. One such tool is the **concept anchoring table** (Bulgren, Deschler, Schumaker, & Lenz, 2000), a graphic organizer designed to help students relate new information to previously learned content. Figure 8-1 shows an example of a concept anchoring table for helping students learn the new concept of "temperature control systems in warm-blooded animals" by comparing it with the known concept of "temperature control systems in modern buildings."

Provide Mediated Scaffolding.   According to a dictionary definition, *mediate* means to effect by action as an intermediary. *Scaffolding*, of course, refers to temporary support structures used in construction. In education, **mediated scaffolding**

Anchoring Table

Name: _____ Date: _____

Unit: _____

② Known Concept
Temperature control systems in modern buildings

① New Concept
Temperature control systems in warm-blooded animals

③ Known Information

- furnace
- air
- conditioner
- 72 degrees
- thermostat
- notices
- change
- set temp.
- anywhere
- electronic
- signals

④ Characteristics of Known Concept

Building temperature is set to stay the same (72 degrees).

Thermostats notice temperature changes.

When temperature changes, thermostat sends electronic signals.

Signals start action in furnace or air conditioner.

Furnace or air conditioner corrects building temperature to 72 degrees.

⑥ Characteristics Shared

Inside temperature is supposed to stay the same.

Something notices temperature changes.

When temperature changes, a sensor sends signals.

Signals start other systems.

System corrects temperature.

⑤ Characteristics of New Concept

Body temperature stays the same (98.6 degrees).

Nervous & endocrine systems notice temperature changes.

When temperature changes, nervous & endocrine systems send signals.

Signals start action in circulatory system or muscles.

Circulatory system & muscles correct body temperature.

⑦ **Understanding of the New Concept**

Temperature control systems in warm-blooded animals are like those in modern buildings because the temperature is supposed to stay the same, but when the temperature changes, something notices. A sensor sends signals to start other systems that correct the temperature.

ANCHORS Linking Steps:

1. Announce the New Concept
2. Name Known Concept
3. Collect Known Information
4. Highlight Characteristics of Known Concept
5. Observe Characteristics of New Concept
6. Reveal Characteristics Shared
7. State Understanding of New Concept

FIGURE 8-1 Concept Anchoring Table *Source:* Reprinted with permission from J. A. Bulgren, J. B. Schumaker, and D. D. Deshler, 1994. © Edge Enterprises, Inc. The Anchoring Table shown in Figure 8-1, which is part of the Content Enhancement Series, is a data-based teaching instrument that has been found to be effective when used with a planning routine and a teaching routine that combines cues about the instruction, specialized delivery of the content, involvement of the students in the cognitive processes, and a review of the learning process and content material. It has not been shown to be an effective tool if it is simply distributed to students. For more information on Content Enhancement Routines and associated professional development sessions, contact the director of professional development at the Center for Research on Learning, University of Kansas (phone: 785-864-4780; e-mail: crl@ku.edu).

is used to providing support during the early stages of learning to assist learners in performing new tasks that otherwise might be too difficult or complex. As students become more proficient in the targeted skills, the mediated scaffolding is gradually withdrawn. The goal of instruction is for learners to self-regulate their own learning in order to increase their independence as learners. Teachers can facilitate this process by anticipating the problems that students might have with learning a new concept or performing a new skill and then using mediated scaffolding to help students avoid those problems, thereby avoiding the frustration that accompanies "not getting it" (Kame'enui & Simmons, 1999).

Mediated scaffolding can take a variety of forms, depending on the individual needs of students and the types of problems that students might encounter in the early stages of acquisition. Many teachers use mediated scaffolding intuitively. For example, teachers provide models of cursive handwriting for students to refer to while writing, multiplication tables for students to use during math, or a list of formulas for students to use during physics lab. They teach students mnemonics to facilitate memory, such as "Please Excuse My Dear Aunt Sally" to remember the order of operations in mathematics (parentheses, exponents, multiplication, division, addition, subtraction), or "King Phillip's Class Ordered a Family of Gentle Species" to remember the classification system for living things: Kingdom, Phylum, Class, Order, Family, Genus, Species. All of these are good examples of mediated scaffolding; remember, the purpose of mediated scaffolding is not to make the content easier, but rather to provide the student with strategies to make the content easier to learn or use.

Mediated scaffolding may assist the student in using the cognitive strategies that effective learners tend to acquire without formal instruction. The self-management techniques described in Chapter 11 can be applied to academic tasks to help students better regulate their own learning through self-monitoring, self-evaluation, and self-instruction. For example, students may be given an editing checklist to follow to guide them in reviewing and editing their papers before turning them in. A teacher whom we know teaches her students a mnemonic to help them remember the steps of long division: "Drive My Super Cool Buggy, Check It Out," which stands for divide, multiply, subtract, compare, bring down, check by multiplying. The first long-division worksheets that students use are structured to prompt students to follow each step, as shown in Figure 8-2. Later worksheets fade the prompts by providing only the mnemonic at the top of the page, then no mnemonic at all. By this time, students have internalized the steps and can either do the problems without using the mnemonic or say the mnemonic without prompting.

Providing high levels of opportunities to respond is one of the most critical elements of instruction with implications for both achievement and behavior.

Prevention Through High-Quality.   In social skills instruction, mediated scaffolding may consist of posters with the skill steps listed or skill cards that students keep on their desks. Teacher prompts to use certain skills may also be a form of mediated scaffolding.

Use Effective Classroom Management Techniques.   One final aspect of structure is classroom management. Remember to follow all classroom management procedures while teaching. Rules are still in effect and must be enforced;

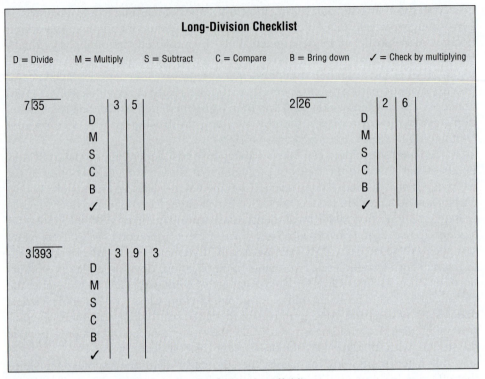

FIGURE 8-2   Worksheet That Illustrates Mediated Scaffolding

procedures for transitions, asking/answering questions, obtaining help, passing out materials, and turning in assignments must be established and followed; and reinforcement plans must be implemented while teaching. As we have discussed throughout the text, all of these steps will help provide the structure that is important for student learning.

Clarity

Instruction should be clear and easy to understand. Much has been written about features that contribute to or detract from clarity. According to Hiller, Fisher, and Kaess (1969) and Smith and Land (1981), the following problems detract from clarity:

- ***Vague instructional language***—the use of terms such as *about, not many, a few, sort of, and so forth, chances are,* and *probably.* In one consulting experience, one of the authors (BKS) demonstrated teaching a lesson on idioms to incarcerated adolescents. One of the idioms taught was "in a nutshell." This idiom was difficult for students to understand. Later that same day, while observing in another class in the same facility, the author heard a history teacher introduce a summary statement by saying, "So, in a nutshell, . . .". How many students in the class did not understand that comment?

- *Hesitant, dysfluent instructional speech*—instructional language that includes false starts, fillers (e.g., "uh," "um"), and sentence structures that are overly complex and hard to follow.
- *Discontinuity*—interrupting instruction with off-task, irrelevant comments or discussing unrelated content at inappropriate times (in the middle of a social studies lesson, the teacher says, "Oh, by the way, help me remember to send your reading project guidelines home with you today!").

Instructional clarity can be enhanced by doing the following:

- Make instructions explicit. We discuss how to accomplish this in a later section.
- Inform students how new information relates to previously learned material or existing knowledge. Kame'enui and his colleagues (Kame'enui & Carnine, 1998; Kame'enui & Simmons, 1999) refer to this as **priming background knowledge**. Successful learners actively make these connections, but some students need explicit guidance in order to do so. Informal assessment before teaching (or during review) will help teachers identify essential background knowledge that students may not possess, which then has implications for instruction. If students have this information, teachers should directly relate new learning to existing knowledge.
- Carefully design examples to highlight the salient aspects of skills or concepts being taught and to ensure that easier examples are presented before more difficult examples of the skill or concept.
- Define both content vocabulary and instructional words that students may not know.
- Teach **conspicuous strategies**, which means teaching new learners what experts know will make the task easier to perform or information easier to learn or remember (Kame'enui & Carnine, 1998). For successful learners, these strategies are internal and often subtle to the point that even skilled learners may not realize what strategies they are using in the learning process. However, the extent to which teachers can identify and articulate these strategies to unskilled learners may help them learn more efficiently. For example, teachers might instruct students to use mnemonics to aid memory, apply shortcuts for problem solving (e.g., if the last digit in the dividend is even, the number can be divided by 2), or employ other strategies that experts have found to promote successful learners (e.g., scan the chapter before reading it; recognize that the boldface words are important; use an outline or other organizational tool before writing; make a list of items to bring to school; check your test before you turn it in).
- Repeat important words, definitions, formulas, rules, or concepts.
- Use words and phrases to organize information (first, second, last; the most important point is . . .) and to cue students to important information (e.g., "this will be on the test," "you will need to remember this for the lab activity tomorrow," "write this definition on your vocabulary page").

Direct Instruction programs provide scripted lessons that incorporate carefully designed instructional explanations and examples to ensure maximum clarity in teaching the methodically organized curriculum. The attention to instructional detail that is inherent in DI programs is one reason these programs are effective. In terms of direct instruction lessons, it is easy to understand why preparing a script for a lesson, particularly a lesson that is new or difficult for the teacher, could enhance clarity. Taking the time to plan the details of the lesson (e.g., what words will be used, what examples will be provided and in what order) can make instruction clearer for students and, therefore, result in better learning outcomes.

Opportunities to respond

One of the most consistent recommendations regarding effective instruction for students with disabilities is to provide high levels of **opportunities to respond (OTR)** to instructional material. As you learned in Chapter 7, maintaining high levels of academic engaged time is critical for both learning and behavior. Academic engaged time can be measured in terms of OTR. An opportunity to respond occurs whenever the teacher provides an instructional stimulus (e.g., an oral question, a flash card, a passage to be read, a problem to be solved). During the acquisition stages of learning, each student should be provided with a minimum of four to six OTR per minute and students should be responding with at least 80% accuracy (Gunter, Coutinho, & Cade, 2002; Gunter & Denny, 1998; more about accurate responses later). Thus, during the instruction of new material, each student should respond correctly three or four times per minute, on average, during Step 1 and Steps 3 through 7 of the direct instruction model. Furthermore, during review activities for which the goal is building fluency (Steps 2 and 8 of the direct instruction model), each student should have 9 to 12 OTR per minute with a minimum of 90% accuracy. [Note: Rosenshine (1983) recommended 95% accuracy during review activities.] In other words, teachers should expect 8 to 10 correct responses per student per minute during review activities. It is expected that students will make some errors; errors, however, should be the exception, not the rule, during all stages of learning.

The relationship between high levels of correct responding and both achievement and appropriate behavior is significant. Unfortunately, research suggests that students who exhibit challenging behaviors are not provided with high levels of OTR as a routine part of instruction (Knitzer et al., 1990; Van Acker, Grant, & Henry, 1996). For example, Van Acker and his colleagues (1996) studied academic response rates in students considered to be at risk for aggression in grades 2, 3, and 5. They found that these students seldom made correct academic responses: The rates ranged from 0.014 to 0.021 correct responses per minute. Extrapolated to reflect the entire school day, this would indicate that these students responded correctly only 0.84 to 1.26 times per hour, or 5.04 to 7.56 correct responses per day!

High levels of correct responding relate to academic engaged time and academic learning time, both of which are positively correlated with student achievement and appropriate behavior. However, correct academic responding may also be important because correct academic responses are also more likely to result in teacher praise than correct behavioral responses (e.g., following

Providing high levels of opportunities to respond is one of the most critical elements of instruction and has implications for both achievement and behavior.

directions, completing work, raising one's hand) (Lewis et al., 2004; Van Acker et al., 1996). We discuss the importance of teacher praise in Chapter 10: Higher levels of teacher praise are associated with both greater academic achievement and higher levels of appropriate behavior. In the Van Acker study, for the group of students who were identified as being less aggressive, the probability that teacher praise would follow a correct academic response was 0.43. If we calculate this probability on the basis of the number of correct responses exhibited by this group (7.56×0.43), we find that these students have experienced only approximately 3.25 teacher praise statements per day for correct academic responses. In the same study, the probability that a correct academic response from a student in the group who was identified as being more aggressive would produce teacher praise did not even exceed that attributed to chance. Given this fact, it is likely that these students could attend school all day without receiving a single teacher praise statement for a correct academic response. Other studies support the findings of the Van Acker study with regard to praise (Lewis et al., 2004; Shores, Gunter, & Jack, 1993; Sutherland, 2000; Wehby, Symons, & Shores, 1995). It appears that students who exhibit challenging behaviors typically receive low levels of praise in both special education and general education classes. However, ensuring that students produce high levels of correct academic responses is perhaps the surest way to increase teacher praise.

Inexperienced teachers may be skeptical that it is possible for teachers to provide the high levels of OTR that we have described. It is most definitely possible by using the following techniques:

- Provide group OTR by having all students responding in unison. If you ask individual questions to students only one at a time, you will probably be unable to achieve the recommended levels of OTR. Most OTR should be in the form of questions posed to the group, with responses given in unison. Of course, individual OTR are also important in order to monitor individual student learning.
- Use a variety of forms of OTR. Not all OTR must be oral. You can also use signaled or written unison responses. Response cards, as discussed previously, are one way to provide high rates of OTR.
- Keep up a brisk pace during group instruction. A brisk pace is associated not only with higher achievement because teachers are able to cover more material (Brophy & Good, 1986), but also it facilitates student engagement and OTR. Englemann and Becker (1978) reported that when teachers provided approximately 12 questions per minute, students responded correctly 80% of the time and exhibited off-task behavior only 10% of the time. When the instructional pace dropped to four questions per minute, accurate responses dropped to 30%, while off-task behavior increased to 70% of the time.

One advantage of Direct Instruction programs is that they incorporate high levels of response opportunities. Teachers who use a direct instruction format can also achieve this, but are more likely to do so if they develop a script for lesson presentation. Gunter and his colleagues (1998) have designed a form (see Figure 8-3) for use by teachers to monitor students' correct academic responses. Correct

Teacher _____   Observer _____

Date _____   Starting time _____   Ending time _____

Length of observation in minutes _____ and seconds _____

$$\times\ 60$$

_____ plus   _____ = _____ seconds
                                                        /60

                                        = _____ time

Frequency of Correct Responses

Frequency of correct responses _____
            Divided by
Time _____
= Rate of correct responding _____

For instruction of new material, the rate of correct responses should be at least 3 per minute.
For drill-and-practice instruction, the rate of correct responses should be at least 8 per minute.

Teacher _MR. EFFECTIVE_____   Observer _SELF-OBSERVATION__

Date __0/100/y2k_____   Starting time _10:00_____   Ending time _____10:19:30_____

Length of observation in minutes ___19_____ and seconds ___30____

$$\times\ 60$$

___1140_____ plus   ___30_____ = __1170___ seconds
                                                /60

                                    = _19.5___ time

Frequency of Correct Responses

ɪɴ̸ ɪɴ̸ ɪɴ̸
ɪɴ̸ ɪɴ̸ ɪɴ̸
ɪɴ̸ ɪɴ̸ ɪɴ̸
ɪɴ̸ ɪɴ̸ ɪɴ̸
ɪɴ̸ ɪɴ̸ ‖‖

Frequency of correct responses _____73____
            Divided by
Time _19.5_ ◄
= Rate of correct responding ____3.74____

For instruction of new material, the rate of correct responses should be at least 3 per minute.
For drill and practice instruction, the rate of correct responses should be at least 8 per minute.

FIGURE 8-3   Protocol for Monitoring Students' Academic Responses   *Source*: From "Are Effective Academic Instructional Practices Used to Teach Students with Behavioral Disorders?" by P. Gunter, J. H. Hummel, and M. L. Venn, 1998, *Beyond Behavior, 9*(3), p. 9. © 1998 Council for Children with Behavioral Disorders. Reprinted with permission.

academic responses are tallied during the lesson; the total correct responses are then divided by the total observation time to produce the rate of correct responding. Of course, to achieve the recommended levels of correct responses, teachers must provide 4 to 6 OTR during new instruction and 9 to 12 OTR during review activities. In order to monitor correct responses while teaching, teachers can use a handheld tally counter as described in Chapter 4, noting the time when counting was begun and when it was ended. We encourage teachers to use this self-monitoring procedure frequently to ensure that they are meeting the recommended levels of OTR and that students are exhibiting the recommended levels of correct responses.

Redundancy

Most students need repeated exposures in order to learn instructional material. Most students do not learn a mathematics fact, a spelling word, a science formula, or the definition of a new vocabulary word the first time that they see it. Lyon (1998) stated that some students need more than 20 exposures to a word before they can read it fluently, and the average child requires between 4 and 14 repetitions to be able to reach proficiency with a new word. Swanson (1999) identified repetition as one critical component of instruction for students with learning disabilities. Redundancy can be achieved through high levels of OTR, daily review of previously learned information, and multiple and varied practice activities.

Explicit instruction

Whether students learn more effectively and efficiently through direct, explicit, teacher-led instruction or through implicit or discovery learning has been the topic of much debate in the field of education. The research, however, is clear: **Explicit instruction**, in which teachers make clear to students the instructional objectives, expectations, and content, is superior to other, less explicit forms of instruction (i.e., discovery learning) for producing high levels of achievement (Ellis & Worthington, 1994; Stevens & Rosenshine, 1981). As Rosenshine (1986) explains, explicit teaching can help students become more self-regulated learners. Many of the instructional recommendations provided up to this point can contribute to explicit instruction. Teachers should provide explicit instruction in the following ways:

- Clearly state the instructional objectives and specific learning expectations.
- Present new information in small steps and have students practice after each step.
- Provide clear and detailed instructions and explanations.
- Provide high levels of OTR to keep students engaged and to allow teachers to monitor students' progress.
- Provide immediate feedback and corrections for students' responses.
- Provide multiple opportunities to practice skills so that students will achieve fluency, maintenance, and generalization of skills.
- Teach conspicuous strategies, as described earlier, to make learning more explicit. If these are not identified in the curricular materials, teachers must ask

themselves, "How do I [insert the name of the task]?" For example, how do I remember which part of a fraction is the numerator and which part is the denominator? How do I identify the main idea in a passage? What strategies do I use to decipher a word that I do not know? How do I determine what I will need to know for a test? The extent to which teachers "let students in on the secrets" of experts will make learning more productive and enjoyable for students.

Explicit instruction is critical when teaching social skills, self-control skills, or other behavioral skills. Because such skills consist mostly of covert behaviors, teachers must be explicit about how to perform those behaviors. The guidelines for explicit instruction listed here also apply to teaching sociobehavioral skills.

> Explicit instruction is critical for student learning.

One of the recommendations for explicit instruction that warrants additional discussion is feedback about student responses. We have previously discussed the impact of teacher praise on student achievement and behavior. Teachers should inform students when their answers are correct, but error correction is even more important. Student errors should never go uncorrected. When students make an error, tell them in a matter-of-fact manner, provide them with the correct response, and then have them repeat the correct response. In the following example, Ms. MacMillan demonstrates this error correction procedure for Josh, a first-grader, during reading:

- JOSH: (reading) "The matter cat hopped down."
- MS. M: No, Josh, this word is "mother" [pointing to the word]; "The mother cat hopped down." Read it again.
- JOSH: "The mother cat hopped down."
- MS. M: Good, Josh.

In our experience, teachers hesitate to directly correct errors out of fear of hurting student's feelings or making the learning experience negative for the student. Often this results in teachers using encouraging but unclear responses to errors. For example, consider the following exchange between Leah and Ms. Ayala:

- MS. AYALA: Leah, what is the sum of 7 plus 9?
- LEAH: 15?
- MS. AYALA: Oh, almost, Leah: You are very close. Try again.
- LEAH: 16?

In this example, Ms. Ayala would not know whether Leah's second attempt is correct because she remembered the right answer or because she guessed the right answer. Note how much clearer and more efficient the first error correction procedure is. In the first example, José knows exactly what error he made and what the correct answer is. Table 8-11 provides additional examples and nonexamples of error correction. Note how the nonexamples fail to make clear to students what error they made and what the correct answer should be. Students are left to guess the correct responses, and in some cases they must even guess what their error was. Everything that is known about student responding indicates that correcting student errors will not make learning a negative experience for students. On the contrary, appropriate error correction will make learning easier because it is clearer.

TABLE 8-11 Examples and Nonexamples of Error Correction

Examples

Teacher (reviewing "Stacey, the first word in a the sentence should always be
Stacey's writing sample): capitalized. This letter needs to be capitalized."

Teacher: "Colin, what is the capital of New York?"
Colin: "Austin?"
Teacher: "No, Colin, the capital of New York is Albany. What is the capital of New York?"
Colin: "Albany."
Teacher: "That's correct."

Madison is attempting to tie her shoe. She performs one step incorrectly.
Teacher: "No, Madison, do it this way: Wrap the lace around the loop."
  Teacher then demonstrates as she instructs. Madison performs the step
  correctly.
Teacher: "Good job!"

Teacher, writing the fraction 4/8 on the board: "Jacob, is this fraction in lowest terms?"
Jacob: "Yes."
Teacher: "Remember that if both the numerator and denominator can be divided by the same
  number, the fraction is not in lowest terms. Can the numerator be divided by 4?"
Jacob: "Yes."
Teacher: "Can the denominator be divided by 4?"
Jacob: "Yes."
Teacher: "Is 4/8 in lowest terms?"
Jacob: "No."
Teacher: "Jacob, reduce 4/8 to lowest terms."
Jacob: "1/2."
Teacher: "Yes. Now look at this fraction: 6/18. Is this fraction in lowest terms?"
Jacob: "No, because both parts can be divided by 6."
Teacher: "Excellent, Jacob."

Nonexamples

Teacher (reviewing "Stacey, you missed something important in this sentence. What is
Stacey's writing sample): it?"
Stacey: "Uh, I misspelled this word?"
Teacher: "No, that word is spelled correctly. Look more closely. What else is wrong with
  this sentence?"

Teacher: "Colin, what is the capital of New York?"
Colin: "Austin?"
Teacher: "No, Colin. Think about it. We just talked about it yesterday."

(Continued)

TABLE 8-11   (Continued)

Colin: "Los Angeles?"

Teacher: Not quite. It starts with an *A*.

Colin: "Annapolis?"

Madison is attempting to tie her shoe. She performs one step incorrectly.

Teacher: "No, Madison, you forgot a step. What should you do after you make the loop?"

Madison: "Pull it tight?"

Teacher: "No, not exactly. Remember how we did it last time?"

Teacher, writing the fraction 4/8 on the board: "Jacob, is this fraction in lowest terms?"

Jacob: "Yes."

Teacher: "No, not exactly. Try again."

Jacob: "No?"

Teacher: "Good! Now look at this fraction: 6/18. Is this fraction in lowest terms?"

Jacob: "No?"

Teacher: "Good!"

(Of course, we do not know whether Jacob has learned the rule for determining whether fractions are in lowest terms or whether he is repeating the previous answer that was praised.)

CHoices

Providing students with the opportunity to make choices may not sound like an instructional practice. However, research indicates that allowing students to make choices, especially during academic tasks, not only can increase student engagement and reduce disruptive behavior, but it can also improve response accuracy (Cosden, Gannon, & Haring, 1995; Dunlap et al., 1994; Jolivette, Wehby, Canale, & Massey, 2001). This is an easy-to-use strategy that can produce desirable results. Jolivette and her colleagues (Jolivette, Stichter, McCormick, & Tice, 2002) suggest the following options for providing opportunities to make choices:

- **Provide choices before a task.** Teachers may allow students to choose when they will do a task (e.g., allow students to choose to do their assignment first or their classroom jobs first), what they will do after they complete the task (e.g., allow students to choose the reinforcer for completing the task), how long they will work before taking a break, or which materials they will use during the task (e.g., allow students to choose the writing implement, the eraser, the color of scratch paper, or the manipulatives).
- **Provide choices during the task.** Teachers may let students choose the order in which they will complete multiple tasks, which peers to work with, how they will get the teacher's attention while working, where they will do the task (e.g., students could choose to work in their seats, on the floor, or at the table), or the manner in which they will complete the task (e.g., students

could choose to do the last question first, work from the back of the page to the front, or work from bottom to top).

You can see from these examples that allowing students to make choices does not change either the amount of work that the students are expected to complete or the essential components of the tasks. Giving students choices does appear to provide students with an appropriate method for gaining control, which, as you learned in Chapter 3, could prevent one of the common causes of misbehavior in students who exhibit chronic behavioral problems.

Assess the forms of knowledge

One aspect of instruction that educators sometimes fail to consider is the type of knowledge being presented to students. Not all learning is the same. For example, learning how to tie your shoe is a very different form of learning than memorizing mathematics facts. Learning the steps for reducing fractions is a different type of learning than learning the reasons that the South wanted to secede from the Union and how the South's secession contributed to the Civil War. The form of knowledge that you are teaching has implications for instruction. Different forms require slightly different teaching techniques. A number of authors have proposed different terms and categories for these various forms of knowledge or types of learning (Ellis & Worthington, 1994; Kame'enui & Simmons, 1990; Mastropieri & Scruggs, 2002). The categories that we describe are based on the work of these authors. The forms of learning are not mutually exclusive. In fact, one form often depends on another.

> Different forms of learning may require different instructional techniques.

Factual Learning.   **Factual learning** is perhaps the most common form of learning and is essential to academic success (Mastropieri & Scruggs, 2002). Factual learning consists of the following:

- *Simple associations* of a specific stimulus with a specific response. Examples of simple associations include basic decoding skills (e.g., reading letters, words, sentences), mathematics facts, state capitals, telling time, measurement equivalencies, geographical locations and characteristics, historical dates, and so forth. As you can see, the list of simple associations that students are required to learn is almost endless!
- *Verbal chains* are facts that must be learned as part of a sequence. Examples include days of the week, months of the year, rote counting, skip counting, reciting the alphabet, and spelling.

Factual learning is taught with the use of the methods that we have described in this chapter. The most important work on factual learning, however, may occur during independent practice activities, during which students build fluency and automaticity in their response to factual stimuli. Fluency and automaticity are necessary for success in developing more complex skills. For example, being able to quickly produce answers to mathematics facts is critical for learning all later forms of computation (e.g., addition, subtraction, multiplication, division, fractions, measurement, time). Being able to read words effortlessly is essential for comprehension. For this reason, independent practice activities should focus on accurate, timely performance of factual learning tasks. An effective way to accomplish this is to have students do timed practice (e.g., timed mathematics facts drills, reading word drills), perhaps as a peer tutoring activity. Students can chart their performance and receive reinforcement for improvement in both accuracy and speed.

Rule Learning.   **Rule learning** refers to the connections between two sets of facts or concepts. Sometimes rules are stated as the defining characteristics of a set. For example, arthropods have exoskeletons (outer skeletons), segmented bodies, and jointed appendages. A trapezoid is a quadrilateral with two sides that are parallel. Other rules are stated as "if–then" propositions: If you miss school, then you must bring a note; if you finish all of your work, then you may use the computer; if a number is even, then it is divisible by two. One aspect that makes learning rules difficult is the inconsistency with which many rules are applied, especially in reading and spelling. For example, students learn certain phonetic rules but then encounter words such as *island, debt,* and *ski,* all of which illustrate exceptions to rules that they have learned. They learn that \th\ makes one sound in some words and a different sound in other words. Generally, rules should be taught until they are understood well, with exceptions introduced later.

Many sociobehavioral skills involve learning rules, as well as other forms of learning. Usually, these rules are the unwritten rules of our society. For example, students may need to learn that, when carrying on a conversation with a peer, they should stand no closer than approximately 2 feet. Students may also need to learn that, upon encountering a new acquaintance who extends his or her hand to be shaken, one responds by shaking the person's hand. Make unwritten rules clear to students. Do not assume that they know these rules.

All of the techniques that we have described in this chapter apply to teaching rules. Rules should be stated explicitly instead of having students try to discern the rules on their own, and examples should reflect the essential components of the rule while varying the nonessential components. Teaching the rule for trapezoids should involve presenting a variety of shapes, including squares and rectangles. The essential components are consistent in all of these examples, whereas the nonessential components (e.g., size, color, slant of the nonparallel sides) vary. Both examples and nonexamples should be presented with accompanying questions that reflect the rule. The teacher may first show a square and then a triangle, asking each time, "Is it a quadrilateral?" "Are two sides parallel?" "Is it a trapezoid?" Note that learning the rules involves both factual learning and conceptual learning.

Conceptual Learning.   Kame'enui and Simmons (1990) define a concept as "an object, event, action, or situation that is part of a class of objects, events, actions, or situations that are the same, based on a feature or set of features that is the same" (p. 70). Examples of concepts include colors, shapes, positions (e.g., on, under, above, in), number, quantity, democracy, equality, invertebrates, and inflation. You can see that concepts can be simple or quite complex.

Many concepts are taught through rule relationships in order to identify the essential characteristics, and then multiple examples and nonexamples are given to limit or expand the meaning (Kame'enui & Simmons, 1990; Mastropieri & Scruggs, 2002). For example, one of the authors (BKS) has a granddaughter who, at age 18 months, had "learned" that "dog" refers to anything with four legs. Using her concept of "dog," she happily labeled cats, bears, elephants, and any other mammal as "dog" (albeit using her pronunciation, "gog"). As she grew older, she further refined the concept to limit its meaning to the correct species. On the other hand, sometimes learners, especially learners with cognitive impairments and autism, learn overly narrow definitions for concepts. For example, we once worked with a student with autism for whom "red" meant only a particular red toy. He could not correctly identify any other form of "red."

For higher-functioning students, concepts are taught by teaching the rules that define the concept and then presenting both examples that illustrate the concept and examples that do not (nonexamples). Teachers must anticipate errors in conceptual learning and choose examples and nonexamples to address those errors. Errors can also be avoided by varying the nonessential components of examples of concepts. In teaching the positional concept of "under," Ms. Kahila uses a variety of objects in her examples (e.g., boxes, golf balls, dolls, trucks, chairs, tables). She wants her students to understand that "under" refers to the position of an object relative to another object and that the nature of the objects is irrelevant. On the other hand, Mr. Batson teaches his third-graders the concept of magnetism through explanation, examples, and nonexamples. He wants his students to learn that the type of material is essential to magnetism. Teachers present a variety of examples in teaching addition with regrouping to show that the same rules apply, regardless of the size of the numbers being added: The process for adding $16 + 7$ is the same as for adding $2,438 + 1,595$. Direct instruction mathematics curricula teach the concept of fractions by including examples of both proper (e.g., 1/2, 2/5, 15/18) and improper (e.g., 7/5, 4/2, 12/3) fractions because the *rule* (i.e., the top number represents the number of parts *under consideration* and the bottom number represents the *total* number of parts) stays the same regardless of the type of fraction.

Procedural Learning. **Procedural learning** involves the "execution of a series of behaviors in a specific sequence" (Mastropieri & Scruggs, 2002, p. 35). Many subject areas rely heavily on procedural learning. Mathematics, science, social skills, physical education, art, vocational skills, and functional skills all include tasks that must be completed by applying procedural learning. Many types of procedural learning tasks are efficiently taught using chaining. For example, teaching students how to use a sewing machine, how to conduct science laboratory tests, how to solve quadratic equations, and how to serve a volleyball are all procedures that could be taught using one of the chaining techniques. Of course, procedural learning often involves other forms of learning as well. To reduce a fraction, students must follow a series of steps while at the same time applying rules (e.g., a prime number is divisible only by itself and 1) and facts (e.g., $2 \times 2 = 4$; $2 \times 3 = 6$).

Problem Solving and Higher-Level Learning. Sometimes students are expected to perform tasks for which there is no immediately apparent or single solution. When faced with these tasks, students cannot rely exclusively on previously learned rules, facts, or concepts, but instead must use cognitive strategies drawing on one or more elements of each of these forms of learning and apply them in a systematic way. For example, for students to draw inferences from a passage, they may need to rely on factual knowledge, concepts, and rules. For students to assume the roles of Abraham Lincoln and Stephen A. Douglas in a simulation of the Lincoln–Douglas debates, students will have to draw on factual learning (e.g., in his first inaugural address, Lincoln stated that he was against federal interference in states that allowed slavery), concepts (e.g., slavery, the Union, Democrat, Republican), and rules (e.g., the rules that govern a simulated debate). It is important for students to engage in higher-level learning and problem solving. Teachers should expect this type of learning from their students, while understanding the forms of knowledge that are prerequisite to carrying out higher-level learning tasks. For example, Ms. Carver developed a learning center in which students must design a "new" arthropod. In doing so, students must generalize their factual and conceptual learning with regard to arthropods, which Ms. Carver has taught to mastery in a direct instruction lesson before introducing the learning center.

Why discuss forms of learning in a text about the prevention and management of behavioral problems? Because, as we have seen in this chapter, learning is inextricably related to behavior. For students with learning and behavioral difficulties, many behavioral concerns reflect frustrations that are related to learning. Also, as you have learned, teachers may need to teach students sociobehavioral skills. One way that teachers can help to reduce frustration and make instruction clearer is to identify the form of knowledge being taught, consider the other prerequisite forms required for this learning, and then teach students by using the techniques described throughout this chapter.

Monitor student learning

To ensure achievement, use curriculum-based measurements to monitor student learning.

Curriculum-based measurement (CBM) is a data-based approach for systematically and frequently monitoring academic progress. Frequent, systematic monitoring of academic performance using CBM is positively correlated with student achievement (Fuchs, Deno, & Mirkin, 1984). One reason that CBM produces higher levels of achievement is because studies indicate that teachers who use CBM adjust instruction more frequently in response to students' progress, or lack thereof, than teachers who do not use CBM (Fuchs, Fuchs, Hamlett, & Steecker, 1991). CBM may, therefore, be important for ensuring high levels of correct academic responding. For this reason, teachers should use CBM to monitor students' performance on basic academic skills. Space and focus preclude a thorough discussion of CBM in this text; however, readers can consult the "Resources" section at the end of this chapter for more information.

Practice

Moving from the acquisition stage of learning to fluency, maintenance, and generalization requires repeated practice of the targeted skills. Earlier, we described various types of academic practice activities. Effective teachers provide high levels of repeated, meaningful practice opportunities for students. Practice tasks, like initial instruction, should have the following characteristics:

- Relate directly to the original instructional objective. For example, if the objective is to write complete sentences, practice tasks should involve the students writing complete sentences. Worksheets that require students to circle the complete sentence from a list of sentences, or to write "C" or "IC" to label the sentences as complete or incomplete, do not address the same objective. Writing a complete sentence is a more difficult task than recognizing a complete sentence. A better practice activity would be for students to write a letter to a friend or write about their favorite game.

- Provide high levels of response opportunities. Remember, 9 to 12 OTR per minute is recommended.
- Provide immediate feedback for students' responses.

In addition, teachers must monitor students' performance during independent practice activities to ensure that students meet the 90% accuracy requirement, or 8 to 10 correct responses per minute. One way to monitor this is to note the time that students begin an independent task, the time that they finish, and the number of items completed correctly.

Success

The last thing that teachers must remember with regard to effective teaching practices is that students should be successful. We have provided specific criteria for successful responding during new learning and practice activities. Teachers should monitor students' responses to ensure that these criteria are met, reteaching or adjusting instruction if they are not. Successful student responding is not only critical to academic performance, but it also appears to be negatively correlated with disruptive, off-task behavior. To the extent that students are actively and successfully responding to instructional stimuli, they are *not* engaging in behaviors that interrupt and detract from learning.

In sum, a direct instruction approach to teaching is important, but insufficient. Teachers who follow a direct instruction format must also exhibit specific behaviors that are associated with higher levels of learning and appropriate behavior. We have referred to these behaviors by using the acronym SCORE CHAMPS. Again, we reiterate that every aspect of teaching requires meticulous planning to ensure that teachers remember to include all of the many elements that are so important for students' learning. Few teachers, especially novice teachers, will be able to incorporate these practices without thorough advance planning and much practice.

COMMON INSTRUCTIONAL PROBLEMS AND SUGGESTED SOLUTIONS

Even teachers who conscientiously plan and monitor instruction sometimes have problems. Effective teachers respond to these problems by adjusting what they are doing, how they are teaching, the management techniques that they are using, and so on. Ineffective teachers blame the students. In the sections that follow, we describe common instructional problems that teachers encounter and we offer possible solutions to each.

> Instructional problems will arise regardless of the skill level of the teacher; effective teachers will address those problems systematically by evaluating their instructional and management practices.

Problems During Large-Group Activities

1. One or more students are not paying attention.
   a. Remind the group about large-group procedures.
   b. Ask a student who is sitting close to the inattentive student(s) a question as an indirect way of communicating to the inattentive student(s) that you are aware of his or her behavior.
   c. Walk among the students as you talk and ask questions.
   d. Stand next to the student(s) who is not paying attention. (This tactic is known as **proximity control**.)
   e. Make sure that the student(s) has the skills needed to participate.

2. Planning and delivery are difficult in groups with multiple ages and/or abilities.

   a. Use large-group instruction for the general topic (e.g., addition, World War II, sentences). Much of the content in state curriculum guides and other curricula is spiral, which means that topics appear once and then are revisited in greater detail or difficulty levels in subsequent grades. For example, most school curricula introduce the topic of maps and globes in kindergarten and then again at each subsequent grade level, with increasingly more detail and expansion of the topic. This provides an excellent way in which to address mixed grade-level groups. The general topic is taught with more or less detailed instruction directed toward all students, depending on the expectations of their grade level or IEP objectives.

   b. Address individual students' specific instructional levels by using the appropriate level of questions, guided practice activities, and independent activities.

Problems During Small-Group Activities

1. One or more students are not on task while the teacher is working with one of the small groups.

   a. Reinforce on-task behavior (see Chapters 10 and 11 for ideas).

   b. Make sure that you have a procedure in place to deal with problems that might arise while you are occupied with the small group: how to get assistance, what the student should do when he or she has finished working, what to do if you need more materials, or any other possible problems. For example, a reasonable procedure for addressing the potential problem of a student who needs assistance while the teacher is busy with another group might be that the student should first ask his or her peer buddy for help. (Peer buddy pairs should be assigned in advance.) If the peer buddy is unable to help, the student should signal that help is needed (perhaps by using the "Help" sign shown in Chapter 6) and then work on another part of the task or another task (e.g., homework), or read a book until the teacher is able to offer help.

   c. Make sure that the assignment is one that addresses skills that have previously been taught directly and for which students have demonstrated 80% accuracy or better in responding during initial instruction.

2. Staying focused is difficult when the classroom is a little louder and more active than when students are working in a large group or individually.

   a. Use a system such as the "Talk/Movement" chart described in Chapter 6.

   b. Reinforce quiet working.

   c. Reinforce on-task behavior.

Individual Activities

1. Students refuse to work or interfere with other students' learning.

   a. Review the procedures for working independently.

   b. Make sure that you have reinforcement contingencies related to working independently and that you are consistently implementing the system. If

the problem lies primarily with one student, a contract may be appropriate. (See Chapter 11 for a discussion of contracts.)
   c. Check the student's ability level and the required skill level of the task.
   d. Schedule a brief review session before independent work begins.
   e. Make sure that you and your paraprofessional, if available, circulate among the students, checking on progress and accuracy.
   f. Arrange a conference with the student and the parents.
2. Students rush through their work, paying little attention to accuracy.
   a. Reinforce completing the task accurately, not just completing the task.
   b. Make sure that students have the skills needed to complete the task.
3. Students do not ask for help when needed or ask for help too frequently.
   a. Teach students how and when to ask for help.
   b. Make sure that you have a procedure in place by which students can ask for help.
   c. Check the correlation between the ability of the student and the demands of the task.
   d. Increase attention (i.e., praise or other reinforcement) for appropriate on-task behavior.
   e. Reinforce students for asking for help appropriately. A student who excessively asks for help might be given five popsicle sticks (or whatever number you think is appropriate). Each time a student asks for help, he or she turns in one of the sticks. When the student finishes the task, the student can earn additional reinforcement for each stick that remains on his or her desk. Also, consider one of the differential reinforcement strategies described in Chapter 12.

Summary

It is well beyond the scope of this chapter to provide an in-depth treatment of the design and delivery of effective instruction. However, by now, you should understand that behavior management cannot be separated from instruction and learning. When students are successful in their learning pursuits, their behavior tends to improve. Likewise, low levels of success in academics are associated with low levels of appropriate behavior.

The following are the objectives for this chapter and how each was addressed:

1. Describe the learning characteristics of successful students and students with learning and behavioral disabilities.

We discussed the characteristics of both typical effective students and students with learning and behavioral difficulties in terms of engagement in the learning process, self-regulation of learning, attribution and motivation, and prosocial behaviors. In general, successful students tend to be more active, motivated, and self-regulated than students who are having difficulties with learning and behavior. The learning characteristics of both populations have implications for instruction.

2. Define and sequence the stages of learning.

Learning occurs in stages. Acquisition is the initial stage of learning. As students practice newly learned skills, they reach fluency: The students can do tasks correctly and in a timely manner. Continued practice enables students to reach the maintenance stage, which is the ability to perform a skill long after the initial learning phase. In the generalization stage, students have the ability to use skills in new settings and under new conditions. There are specific steps that teachers can take to ensure that students reach the stages of fluency, maintenance, and generalization.

3. Explain the instructional arrangements and activities that are recommended for students with learning and behavioral disabilities.

Instruction can be provided in large groups, in small groups, or one-on-one. Each format can be effective for students with disabilities, but large groups and small groups may be more manageable in busy classrooms and may be more appropriate formats for effective instructional practices. Direct instruction is the recommended methods for teaching new content. After initial instruction, a variety of practice activities can be used for building fluency or addressing generalization.

4. Use the acronym SCORE CHAMPS to develop teaching practices that encourage higher levels of appropriate behavior and learning.

SCORE CHAMPS summarizes what is known about the types of teaching behaviors most strongly associated with student learning. SCORE CHAMPS stands for Structure, Clarity, Opportunities to respond, Redundancy, Explicit instruction, CHoices, Assess the forms of knowledge, Monitor student learning, Practice, and Success. Although complex, this set of teaching behaviors is important for achieving desired learning outcomes and appropriate behavior.

5. Describe the types of instructional activities that typically occur in classrooms, as well as common problems encountered and solutions to each of them.

Even the most skilled and best prepared teachers encounter problems related to instruction. We described some of these problems and offered possible solutions for each.

Given the critical role of instruction in behavior management, we encourage teachers to periodically self-evaluate their teaching behaviors using the self-rating scale provided in Table 8-12.

TABLE 8-12   Self-Assessment of Instructional Behaviors

Never	Seldom	Sometimes	Often	Always
1	2	3	4	5

Use the numbers from the scale above to rate the following statements.

1. I develop lesson plans for every lesson that I teach. _____
2. I know the learning characteristics of my students and address these characteristics in my lesson plans. _____
3. I plan for fluency, maintenance, and generalization of the skills that I teach. _____
4. I use task analysis for both academic and behavioral skills. _____
5. I know the different forms of learning and choose the correct teaching techniques that correspond to each one. _____
6. I actively plan for and use SCORE CHAMPS elements during instruction. _____
7. I provide high levels of response opportunities when teaching new skills or reviewing previously learned skills. _____
8. I build in students' choice when creating my lesson plans. _____
9. I immediately and clearly correct students' errors. _____
10. I monitor student responding to ensure that students are meeting the recommended criteria for correct responding.

Dr. ICE Helps Teachers Improve Instruction

ELEMENTARY RESOURCE: GRADES 3–5

Ms. Malloy asked Dr. ICE for help in designing an instructional system for her classroom. She said that from 8:00 to 10:00 she teaches 12 students in language arts/reading. The instructional levels of these students range from first grade to high third. Ms. Malloy has frequent management problems during this class; a situation that she acknowledges is mostly a result of her poor organization of instruction.

Dr. ICE visited the classroom and took these notes:

> The first eight students come in and sit in desks arranged in small clusters facing the front of the room. Ms. Malloy begins teaching. It is clear that rules and procedures are in place because the students' behavior appropriate during this time. About 20 minutes into her lesson, two additional students arrive, along with the paraprofessional, and then management problems begin. The paraprofessional leaves the room to make copies in the teacher's workroom. The two students who have just walked into the classroom begin talking and asking what they are to be doing. The students in the large group begin looking up from their guided practice activity and start talking to the new students. The learning process begins to unravel. Ms. Malloy leaves the large group to start the two new students on their task and asks her teaching assistant to stay with the large group. While she is working with these two students, another student comes into the classroom. He is so full of energy that it is contagious—in an instant, most of the students are totally off-task—laughing and talking. With 40 minutes to go in the class, some of the large group leave in order to return to their general education classrooms. Ms. Malloy tries to get the class back on track.

Dr. ICE met with Ms. Malloy during her planning time at the end of her day. They talked about his observations and she agreed that it was typical of her problems this semester. Her students' schedules have changed, so there is more coming and going, which is very disruptive. They decided to make the following changes:

- The first group of students will continue to be taught using the direct instruction model.

- The other students who enter the room while Ms. Malloy is teaching will be taught a procedure for entering the room and settling down to work. Their desks will be placed in another part of the room, and they will have a warm-up activity waiting for them on their desks when they enter. The paraprofessional will oversee this warm-up activity.

- When the first group of students (those who are being taught by Ms. Malloy) are ready for independent practice, the paraprofessional will move to their part of the room to assist those students, and Ms. Malloy will begin a direct instruction lesson with the other students.

- Ms. Malloy will add reinforcement contingencies for entering the room appropriately, working without disturbing others, and completing assignments.

Ms. Malloy agrees with Dr. ICE that she needs her paraprofessional to help her teach the class rather than to run errands and make copies. Dr. ICE suggested that Ms. Malloy use her planning period to give her paraprofessional specific instructions and guidance about the next day's lessons and activities.

Dr. ICE told Ms. Malloy that he will be back in 3 weeks. He will again observe the class, and then they will discuss how the changes are working.

LINCOLN MIDDLE SCHOOL— GRADE 7 RESOURCE

Mr. Howard told Dr. ICE that his instruction is often interrupted by students imitating another student, Carlos, who dresses and acts like a gang member "wannabe" and rarely works in class. Instead, Carlos jokes with other students, talks to Mr. Howard and the paraprofessional, or sleeps. He frequently tells Mr. Howard, "I don't need no school. My homies are waiting for me, and they have big plans." Mr. Howard has just about given up on him and is fearful that the students who are imitating him will also stop working.

Dr. ICE agreed to observe Mr. Howard's class. He already has his suspicions about what is needed in Mr. Howard's class, but he knows that he needs to observe the class before making any final decisions. Before observing, Dr. ICE asked Mr. Howard about each student's instructional level. Mr. Howard knows the least about Carlos's skills because he never does any work. After observing for two class periods, Dr. ICE made an appointment with Mr. Howard to meet the next day during his planning period.

Dr. ICE began the meeting by telling Mr. Howard that what he has to say might surprise him. He said that Mr. Howard should begin making changes in the classroom by addressing the academic needs of the gang member "wannabe" student. The significant point is that, although this student does not work, he does comes to class every day. Dr. ICE suggested the following actions:

- Mr. Howard needs to take steps to build a relationship with this student.
- At the same time, a meeting should be held to consider in-depth academic testing. (Dr. ICE suspects that this student cannot read.) The test results will help Mr. Howard choose an instructional approach and curriculum to address this student's specific needs. Carlos will need to experience a high rate of success in any instructional program, along with a rich reinforcement program.
- In order to help Carlos save face with his peers, Mr. Howard should start giving Carlos tasks that will provide him with status and power. Carlos is clearly a leader in this group; Mr. Howard must tap into those leadership skills in a positive way.
- Mr. Howard should design high-interest instructional tasks for Carlos. For example, Carlos is very talented in drawing and loves model cars, airplanes, and army tanks. Dr. ICE brainstormed with Mr. Howard about how this interest could be used as a basis for learning academic tasks. For example, after Mr. Howard learns more about Carlos's reading and mathematics levels, perhaps Carlos could use the World Wide Web to research specific types of cars or other vehicles (which would address the curricular objectives for research and planning), draw a scaled sketch of a car of his choosing (which would address the curricular objectives for measurement conversions and equivalencies), create a clay or wood model of the car (which could be a reinforcement activity), and write a news release about his vehicle (which would address the curricular objectives for writing).

Dr. ICE made plans with Mr. Howard to check back with him in a few weeks. He reminded Mr. Howard to take steps to ensure that he knows the exact nature of all of his students' strengths and weaknesses, including their specific skill levels in core academic areas. He stressed the importance of this knowledge when lessons are being designed and when a student's behavior seems to stop the learning process.

CARVER HIGH SCHOOL—RESOURCE HISTORY

Ms. Grant is a new teacher in special education. Previously, she taught high school English in a different school district. She asked for Dr. ICE's help with one of her classes. Her students often do not complete all of their in-class assignments. They are beginning to talk back to her and to act out. She also said that the Dean of Instruction has told her that parents of her students have called to complain about the amount of homework that she assigns each night.

Dr. ICE observed the class and looked over Ms. Grant's lesson plans. Then they met and looked at the instructional materials that Ms. Grant uses. All of her students can read, but most of them have problems with comprehension and writing. They also have difficulty with problem solving and higher-level thinking skills.

Ms. Grant admitted to Dr. ICE that her primary approach to teaching comprehension skills is to provide her students with a reading passage at the appropriate skill level and then have them answer comprehension questions. Dr. ICE pointed out that, unfortunately, this approach does not teach students *how* to perform the various comprehension tasks (e.g., stating the main idea, making inferences, predicting outcomes, drawing conclusions). Together, Dr. ICE and Ms. Grant took the following steps to address this problem:

- They identified specific comprehension and writing objectives for each student on the basis of formal and informal assessment data.
- They formed instructional groups on the basis of the similarities in those objectives.
- They developed an instructional schedule to allow Ms. Grant the opportunity to provide direct instruction to each group, each day.
- They task-analyzed each instructional objective so that Ms. Grant will know how to teach these skills to her students.
- They developed several model direct instruction lesson plans for various comprehension and

writing tasks, incorporating the elements of effective instruction.

- They brainstormed ideas for instructional practice activities for her students that would be age appropriate and interesting, and that would provide high levels of opportunities for successful responding. The two ideas that they agreed on are listed next:
  - *A learning center for writing*—Each student will have a box with writing materials, various writing tasks (e.g., write a sports column, write an ad to sell a car, write a letter about a job), and a checklist to use to review and edit his or her writing. (The tasks will be personalized to accommodate each student's objectives.) In addition, students will count and graph the various elements of their daily writing performance (e.g., number of sentences, number of adjectives or adverbs used, percentage of sentences capitalized or punctuated correctly).
  - *A peer tutoring activity for comprehension tasks*—In this activity, students will be paired for a partner reading activity. First, one student will read the passage, and then each student will ask his or her partner a set of comprehension questions. The questions, which will be based on each student's individual objectives, will be provided by Ms. Grant. In addition, an answer key will be provided, along with a scoring sheet. The students will record whether their partner's response is correct, partially correct, or incorrect. Of course, before implementing the peer tutoring activity, Ms. Grant will teach her students the skills needed for the activity, including how to give feedback, correct an incorrect response, and record the answers.

- They modified Ms. Grant's class reinforcement plan to address on-task behavior, task completion, and homework completion.

- Finally, Dr. ICE and Ms. Grant examined Ms. Grant's homework requirements. Not only are the students' homework assignments excessive, but also, the students are given tasks for which they lack the prerequisite skills. Together, Dr. ICE and Ms. Grant determined reasonable homework expectations and designed homework tasks that her students can do independently.

After a couple of weeks, Dr. ICE returned to Ms. Grant's class and found a totally different environment. Her students are concentrating intensely on tasks, are making on-task comments to one another, and generally appear to enjoy participating in Ms. Grant's direct instruction lessons and other activities. Ms. Grant also appears to be happier and more relaxed. Dr. ICE is satisfied that Ms. Grant is now meeting her students' instructional needs.

Learning Activities

1. In a small group, discuss the learning characteristics of students with learning and behavioral problems. Develop a role-play for the class that accurately depicts these characteristics.

2. Write about how your knowledge of the four stages of learning—acquisition, proficiency (fluency), maintenance, and generalization—will help you develop lesson plans for your students. Share your ideas with the class.

3. Write a lesson plan that includes all elements of effective instruction that are recommended for students with learning and behavioral disabilities. Come to class prepared to teach this lesson to your classmates.

4. In a small group, discuss how you will learn the practices associated with the acronym SCORE CHAMPS. Develop a short test. Trade tests with another small group and test your knowledge.

5. List different types of instructional activities; include instructional and/or behavioral problems that can occur during each activity. Discuss in small groups how you could prevent those problems.

6. Choose one academic skill and one behavioral skill; use task analysis to break those skills down into their most basic steps. Teach one skill to a partner.

7. Take what you have learned in this chapter and write a short vignette that describes how you would use this knowledge in your classroom.

Resources

BOOKS

Marchand-Martella, N. E., Slocum, T. A., & Martella, R. C. (2004). *Introduction to direct instruction.* Boston: Pearson Education, Inc.

Wright, J. *Curriculum-Based Measurement: A Manual for Teachers.* This comprehensive manual guides teachers in planning for and implementing CBM in reading, mathematics, written expression, and spelling. Available for downloading at www.jimwrightonline. com/pdfdocs/cbaManual.pdf

JOURNALS/ARTICLES

Beyond Behavior. The Fall 1998 and Spring 2000 special issues are devoted to topics related to effective instruction of students with behavioral disabilities. Available online at http://www.ccbd.net/ beyondbehavior/archive.cfm?categoryID=D646D2 93-C09F-1D6F-F9C4E203B21F5EB8&startRow=19

Jolivette, K., Stichter, J. P., & McCormick, K. M. (2002). Making choices—Improving behavior—Engaging in learning. *Teaching Exceptional Children, 34*(3), 24–29. Available online at www.casenex.com/ casenex/cecReadings/makingChoices.pdf

The Journal of Direct Instruction. Some issues are available online at http://www.adihome.org/index. php?option=com_content&view=article&id=135& Itemid=78

WEBSITES

www.adihome.org Association for Direct Instruction: Provides a variety of resources for Direct Instruction, including video clips of DI. This Website is a good starting point for those who are interested in learning more about DI.

www.cast.org/index.html Center for Applied Special Technology: CAST focuses on applying the principles of Universal Design for Learning. This Website is an excellent resource for anyone who is interested in learning more about virtually any aspect of instruction.

http://iris.peabody.vanderbilt.edu The Iris Center for Training Enhancements, Vanderbilt University: Provides case studies, online training modules, and numerous other resources for educators.

www.theteachingzone.com The Teaching Zone: Provides a variety of materials for helping teachers to learn better behavior management and instructional skills.

http://www.cehd.umn.edu/EdPsych/people/ Faculty/Deno.html Stanley Deno, professor of educational psychology, University of Minnesota: Provides references related to curriculum-based measurement and links to additional CBM materials.

www.aimsweb.com.omdex.php Provides online tools and assistance with CBM-based progress monitoring. Numerous tools are available for purchase for individual or schoolwide use.

www.interventioncentral.org/index.php/ cbm-warehouse Curriculum-Based Measurement Warehouse: Provides virtually all of the information and tools needed to implement CBM, including training manuals, worksheets, data sheets, ideas for computer-based CBM, and more.

Four

TARGETED AND TERTIARY-LEVEL INTERVENTIONS AND SUPPORTS

After reading this chapter, you will be able to do the following:

1. Describe the types of socialization problems and strategies for remediating each type of problem.

2. Describe social skills interventions for universal-level and targeted and/or tertiary levels of schoolwide positive behavioral interventions and supports (PBIS).

3. Describe criteria for choosing a social skills curriculum.

4. Describe how to facilitate the generalization of social skills.

Providing Support Through Social Skills Instruction

CHAPTER 9

Big ideas in social skills instruction:

- Students who exhibit challenging behaviors typically have difficulties with various aspects of social behavior.
- Social skills problems usually reflect skill deficits, performance deficits, or fluency deficits.
- Social skills are learned and can be taught, but the goal of generalizing the skills should guide all aspects of assessment and instruction.

Relationships are the basis of our society. Every element of society is, to a certain extent, characterized by relationships—from the most intimate family relationships to corporate relationships designed to increase productivity and profit. The importance of relationships can be seen in all areas of life. In health care, patients who do not feel like they have a good relationship with their physician are likely to find another doctor. At work, we tend to gravitate toward colleagues who share similar interests; who show an interest in us; and who are enjoyable to spend time with because of their sense of humor, caring nature, or other characteristics. In looking for caregivers for their child, parents are likely to look for individuals who not only have experience in child care but who also relate well to the child by talking to the child, expressing an interest in the child's activities, showing kindness and caring, and so forth. Many of our relationships are casual; others are deeper and more personal. Most relationships that we choose to maintain, however, are characterized by certain elements, such as empathy, integrity, respect, and mutual interest. Bookstores devote entire sections to self-help and advice books targeted at helping us to improve our relationships. In earlier chapters, we explored the importance of relationships between teachers and students, between teachers and parents, and between special education teachers and general education teachers. In this chapter, we discuss the skills required for successful relationships, an area of difficulty for many students who exhibit chronic challenging behaviors. These students often lack basic interpersonal skills, such as the use of appropriate topics of conversation or how to play with peers. These deficits place students at risk for poor peer relationships, with problems ranging from being the target of teasing to active avoidance by peers. As you will see, simply punishing students for misbehaviors related to social skills deficits (e.g., grabbing toys, using inappropriate language with peers) will not teach the child to use other, prosocial behaviors. They cannot use something that they have not learned.

In the three-tiered model of PBIS, attention to teaching social skills could be appropriate as part of systems at the universal level (Tier 1), the targeted level (Tier 2), or the tertiary level (Tier 3). At the universal level, social skills would consist of schoolwide instruction in prosocial behaviors for all students. Targeted-level social skills interventions would typically consist of small-group instruction for students who need additional supports beyond those supplied at the universal level. Social skills interventions at the tertiary level may include comprehensive, individualized instruction in social skills; self-control skills; or any area in which there is a social/behavioral deficit.

In this chapter, we discuss types of social skills problems and social skills interventions for students at the targeted or tertiary level of support. Next, we briefly discuss social skills interventions that might be included as part of universal-level systems. Finally, we provide an overview of social skills curricula and guidelines for selecting a curriculum.

Children's social behavior is closely correlated with both social success and academic success, and students who have problems in either of these areas may also exhibit behavioral difficulties. Murray and Greenberg (2006) show that students with mild disabilities who experience difficulties with peers are likely to exhibit conduct problems, delinquency, anxiety, and depression. Longitudinal research has demonstrated that children's prosocial behavior plays an important role in both current and later academic and social success (Caprara, Barbaranelli, Pastorellin Bandura, Zimbardo, et al., 2000; Coie & Krehbiel, 1984; Gresham, Sugai, & Horner, 2001; Malecki & Elliot, 2002; Morrison et al., 1993). The more socially skilled students are, the more likely they are to experience academic and social success throughout school and life. Without minimal competencies in social skills, students are not well prepared for the interpersonal demands of school, potentially leading to poor relationships with teachers and peers, and academic and behavioral difficulties (Beebe-Frankenberger et al., 2005).

According to Walker and his colleagues (2004), **social skills** are

> . . . a set of competencies that (1) facilitate the initiation and maintenance of positive social relationships, (2) that contribute to peer acceptance and friendship development, (3) that result in satisfactory school adjustment, and (4) that allow individuals to cope with and adjust to the demands of the social environment. (p. 179)

Types of Social Skills Problems

Recognize social skills problems as acquisition deficits, performance deficits, or fluency deficits.

Gresham (1981, 1995) describes social skills problems as acquisition deficits, performance deficits, or fluency deficits. **Acquisition deficits** are those skills which the student has never learned to use, use correctly, or use in the appropriate contexts. These are problems of learning or a problem of "can't": The student does not know how to use the skill and, therefore, cannot exhibit an expected skill even if he or she wanted to. Samantha, for example, never shares toys or materials; anytime that she is in a situation that requires sharing, she either hoards items or attempts to take them away from her peers. **Performance-deficits** are skills that the student knows how to perform but chooses not to because of motivational factors.

There may be insufficient motivation to exhibit a particular skill, or the student may receive stronger reinforcement for inappropriate behavior. Performance deficits are problems of "won't": The student can use the skill, but will not do so. For example, Hunter may ask for help appropriately during language arts class, which he likes, but not exhibit this critical behavior during science class, which he dislikes. When he encounters something that he does not understand in science class, he exhibits disruptive behavior (e.g., calling out loudly for help, complaining, refusing to work). The attention and task avoidance that he experiences as a result of this inappropriate behavior may compete with his motivation to exhibit the desired behavior (e.g., asking for help appropriately).

Finally, **fluency deficits** occur in situations where the student knows how to perform a needed skill and is sufficiently motivated to perform the skill, but the actual performance of the skill is awkward and ineffective. A fluency deficit may indicate that the student can use the skill in some situations but not in others. For example, a student may be able to ignore teasing by some peers but not by others. Another indicator of a fluency deficit is if the student attempts to use a skill, but his or her use of the skill does not produce effective outcomes. For example, Alicia tries to ignore teasing, but when the teasing continues, she is unable to continue to ignore it and resorts to inappropriate behavior. Veronica, a withdrawn, extremely shy high school student, attempts to initiate conversations with others but does so ineffectively (e.g., uses a weak or timid voice, is hesitant in her approach, doesn't use eye contact).

Each of these types of deficits has implications for intervention. Acquisition deficits require instructions in the skills that students need, but do not yet know how to do correctly. To correct performance deficits, the source of the motivation for the competing behavior must be identified and controlled, if possible, and a stronger reinforcer must be offered for the use of targeted social skills. Fluency deficits may require instruction in the use of the skill, as well as structured practice opportunities. According to Walker and his colleagues (2004), the majority of social skills problems are caused by performance or fluency deficits, a causal connection which indicates that teachers should carefully plan interventions to address student motivation to perform the necessary social skills and develop strategies for prompting and coaching the use of social skills in naturalistic contexts.

Social Skills versus Social Competence

In addition to considering the extent to which a student uses socially important skills, the student's overall effectiveness in social situations should also be assessed. These two areas are differentiated as **social skills** and **social competence.** According to McFall (1982), who first distinguished between these two concepts, social skills are the behaviors that individuals perform to carry out social tasks (e.g., making friends, dealing with stressful situations). Social competence refers to the overall effectiveness of those behaviors and others' evaluations of an individual's social behavior. The goal of socialization interventions must be not only to improve children's social skills, but also, more importantly, to enhance their social competence. Social skills interventions that focus on teaching skills in isolation will be less effective than programs that use strategies to improve the fluent use of socially appropriate behaviors in actual social environments. It may also be important to

Social skills are important; social competence is more important.

include peers as part of the socialization interventions, perhaps by addressing how others (both peers and adults) respond to the child's attempts to use socially appropriate behavior.

Interventions to Improve Social Skills

Interventions to improve students' social skills include strategies that are designed to address deficits in acquisition, performance, and fluency. In addition, as discussed previously, teachers may also need to take steps to improve social competence. One commonly recommended intervention for acquisition and possibly fluency deficits is social skills training, or direct instruction in specific social skills. In this model, social skills are taught using techniques that are similar to those used in teaching academic skills. Although this approach is widely recommended, many have also criticized social skills training as being ineffective in producing generalized or sustained changes in social behavior. These criticisms are usually based on comprehensive analyses of social skills research, analyses which often indicate that there is only modest remediation of social skills deficits (Lane, Wehby, & Barton-Atwood, 2005; Mathur, Kavale, Quinn, Forness, & Rutherford, 1998; Miller, Lane, & Wehby, 2005; Zaragoza, Vaughn, & McIntosh, 1991). However, recently, explanations for the limited success of social skills improvement efforts have been offered. Reasons for the modest outcomes produced by social skills training include failure to systematically assess social skills deficits prior to intervention (Gresham et al., 2001), failure to provide instruction in the specific skills that teachers and parents consider to be important (Lane, Givner, & Pierson, 2004), failure to implement the interventions within the classroom setting by teachers who are most familiar with the students' social needs (Lane et al., 2005), and failure to address the generalization of skills across settings and over time (Mathur et al., 1998). Therefore, it is essential that social skills interventions be carefully planned to address these issues, as they can undermine intervention efforts. In the sections that follow, we describe interventions for these purposes.

The assessment and intervention methods to be discussed are appropriate for both the targeted and tertiary levels of schoolwide PBIS. Interventions at each level may differ in intensity (e.g., the amount of time that students are exposed to social skills instruction each week), the duration of the individual sessions, and the types of skills taught.

Assessing Social Skills

It is important to determine which social skills students need to learn, just as we determine which academic skills they need to learn.

Before initiating any socialization intervention, teachers should assess a student's strengths and weaknesses in the area of social skills. The effectiveness of social skills interventions will be determined, in part, by the extent to which students are taught the skills that they lack, but which are needed for successful social functioning. Specifically, it is important to know which social skills the students exhibit regularly (i.e., the areas of strength for the students), the types of social skills deficits exhibited by the students (e.g., acquisition deficits, performance deficits, or fluency deficits), and whether competing problem behaviors are interfering with the use of social skills.

The first step in social skills assessment is to determine whether the student's behavioral problems represent acquisition deficits, performance deficits, or fluency deficits. Acquisition versus performance deficits are best determined by answering the following question: "Is the student ever observed using the skill effectively under the appropriate conditions?" A student who never uses a skill, even under neutral or positive conditions, probably does not know how to perform the skill and, thus, reflects an acquisition deficit. A positive response to this question may suggest either a performance or a fluency deficit.

Social skills assessment can be conducted either informally (e.g., observation, self-reports, checklists, office disciplinary referral data) or formally (i.e., using normative tests that were designed for that purpose). Collecting functional behavioral assessment (FBA) data is one approach to informal assessment that will provide much useful information about the student's strengths and needs with regard to social skills. FBA data may also help teachers and other professionals determine whether a student's problems reflect deficits in acquisition, performance, or fluency. In fact, those persons who are conducting FBAs should attempt to determine the type(s) of social skills deficit during the process of gathering the data by inquiring whether the student ever uses particular skills and, if so, under what circumstances. Patterns of appropriate social behaviors should be identified as part of the data analysis. If this information was not pinpointed as part of the FBA process, additional interviews and observations may need to be completed before initiating a social skills intervention program.

Another approach to the informal assessment of social skills is to use the rating scales or checklists that are included in many of the social skills curricula. We discuss these curricula later in this chapter and indicate those which include checklists or rating scales. All of the curriculum-based social skills rating scales can be completed by classroom teachers or others who know the student well. These tools take little time to complete, but can provide useful information about the skills that the student needs to learn, as well as the progress made on the skills that have been taught.

As discussed briefly in Chapter 5, campus PBIS leadership teams may use a variety of information to identify students for targeted-level supports. Some of this information may be useful in helping teams to identify general areas in which students have social deficits. For example, a teacher may refer a student for targeted-level supports because of extreme shyness and not having any friends. That information may suggest the general type of social skills interventions that the student needs. Another student may be referred for additional supports because he has accumulated a number of office disciplinary referrals for disruptive behavior. When the student's teachers are questioned further about that disruptive behavior, it is revealed that his disruptive behavior occurs during particular types of activities or situations (e.g., during group activities, during transitions, during activities when he is expected to work or play with other students). Again, this information may indicate certain social skills that the student needs to learn.

Social skills may also be assessed formally by using standardized instruments. A number of rating scales are available to help teachers and others identify areas of strength, as well as needs, in terms of the student's social skills. Many of these measures gather information from multiple sources, such as teachers, parents, and/or students, and assess the strengths and/or needs in several areas that are critical to social competence. A list of social skills rating scales, along with a brief summary of each, is provided in Table 9-1.

TABLE 9-1 Tests for Assessing Social/Behavioral/Emotional Strengths and Needs

---

The Behavioral and Emotional Rating Scale–Second Edition (BERS-2) (Epstein, 2001), Austin, TX: PRO-ED

- Can be completed by teachers, parents, and students.
- Is suitable for ages 5 through 18.
- Is a strengths-based assessment that addresses interpersonal strengths, involvement with family, intrapersonal strengths, functioning at school, affective strengths, and career strengths.

The Walker–McConnell Scale of Social Competence and Social Adjustment: Elementary Version (Walker & McConnell, 1995a) and *Secondary Version* (Walker & McConnell, 1995b), Florence, KY: Thompson Learning

- Can be completed by teachers and other school personnel.
- The elementary version is suitable for grades K–6; the secondary version is for grades 7–12.
- Items are rated on the Likert scale in terms of the frequency of occurrence.
- The elementary version has three subscales: Teacher-Preferred Social Skills, Peer-Preferred Social Skills, and School Adjustment; the secondary version has four subscales: Empathy, Self-Control, School Adjustment, and Peer Relations.

The Social Skills Rating System (SSRS) (Gresham & Elliot, 1990), Circle Pines, MN: American Guidance Service

- There are three versions of the SSRS: Preschool (ages 3–5), Elementary (grades K–6), and Secondary (grades 7–12).
- Can be completed by teachers and parents (Preschool) or teachers, parents, and students (Elementary and Secondary).
- Provides comprehensive assessment of social skills, competing problem behaviors (on teacher and parent forms only), and academic performance.
- Items are rated on the Likert scale in terms of the frequency of occurrence and the importance of the skill.
- Addresses social skills in five domains: Cooperation, Assertion, Responsibility, Empathy, and Self-Control.
- Addresses competing problem behaviors in three domains: Externalizing, Internalizing, and Hyperactivity.
- Assesses academic performance on the teacher form only and addresses reading and mathematics performance, overall achievement, motivation, and parental encouragement.
- Includes a system for compiling the results from each rater in order to generate a list of acquisition deficits, which then become the target skills for instruction.

School Social Behavior Scales (SSBS) (Merrell, 2002), Austin, TX: PRO-ED

- Contains 65 items that are completed by teachers.
- Items are rated on the Likert scale in terms of the frequency of occurrence.
- Addresses two domains: Social Competence and Antisocial Behavior.

Preschool and Kindergarten Behavior Scales (Merrell, 1994), Austin, TX: PRO-ED

- Contains 76 items that can be completed by teachers, parents, day care providers, and others.
- Suitable for children ages 3–6.
- Items are rated on the Likert scale in terms of the frequency of occurrence.
- Addresses two domains: Social Competence and Antisocial Behavior.

The Waksman Social Skills Rating System (WSSRS) (Waksman, 1985) Portland, Oregon: Enrichment Press. Republished by ASIEP Education Company, Portland, Oregon, 1984, Republished by Pro-Ed Publishers, Austin Texas, 1988. Republished by PAR Publishers, 1992. Republished by Enrichment Press, 1996

- Contains 21 items that are completed by teachers.
- Suitable for grades K–12.
- Addresses two domains: Aggressive and Passive.
- Also generates a total score.

The Matson Evaluation of Social Skills for Youngsters (MESSY), 2nd ed. (Matson, 1994), Worthington, Ohio: International Diagnostic Systems

- Contains a 64-item form that is completed by teachers and a 62-item form that is completed by students.
- The form for teachers addresses two areas: inappropriate assertiveness and appropriate skills.
- The self-rating form for students addresses five areas: appropriate social skills, inappropriate assertiveness, impulsive/recalcitrant, overconfident, and jealousy/withdrawal.
- The scores on the two forms can be compared.

Components of Socialization Interventions

According to Walker, Ramsey, and Gresham (2004), the four goals of socialization interventions are to (a) teach the skills that the student lacks, (b) enhance the fluency of the skills, (c) reduce or eliminate the challenging behaviors that may serve a social function for the student (while replacing those behaviors with more appropriate alternative behaviors), and (d) improve the use of the skills across settings and over time. The sections that follow describe strategies for accomplishing each goal.

> Use strategies to accomplish the four goals of social skills interventions.

Teach the Skills That Students Lack. When students do not know how to perform particular skills, these skills must be taught. When classroom behavior management or individual student behavioral problems arise, it is possible that those behavioral problems reflect one or more social skills that students have failed to learn. Teachers must be cognizant of students' behavior in all areas of the school, observing carefully for signs that students may lack the skills that are essential for successful relationships with peers and teachers.

Teaching social skills is very much like teaching academic skills: The skill must be task analyzed (i.e., broken down into specific steps), explained, and demonstrated, and then the students must practice the skill with supervision and feedback. Elliott and Gresham (1991) refer to these steps as coaching, modeling, and behavioral rehearsal (i.e., practice). The guidelines for teaching social skills using a coaching–modeling–behavioral rehearsal approach are listed in Box 9-1.

Box 9-1

How to Use Coaching, Modeling, and Behavioral Rehearsal to Remediate Social Skills Acquisition Deficits

Coaching

- Define the skill.
- Explain the importance of the skill, particularly in terms of students' daily lives.
- Discuss the consequences of using and not using the skill.
- Have students generate examples of situations in which the use of the skill could have improved the outcome of the situation.
- Describe each task-analyzed step for performing the skill. Some of these steps will be covert (e.g., self-talk, self-questions that others cannot hear or see), others will be overt (e.g., behaviors that are observable to others). As the steps are explained, they should be written on a chart for students to refer to throughout the lesson.
- For each step, describe examples and nonexamples of the correct use of the step.

Modeling

- Two or more persons should be involved in a demonstration of the skill. One of these is the main actor who will demonstrate the skill. The others are co-actors who will help to set up the situation where the skill is needed and who respond to the main actor after he or she models the skill. For example, if the target skill is "giving a compliment," the confederate(s) might enter the area and greet the main actor, providing an opportunity for the main actor to give a compliment. The co-actor(s) would then respond to the compliment appropriately (e.g., say "thank you").
- Prompt students to observe the modeling performance for evidence of each step in the skill. Covert steps should be spoken aloud. For example, if one step of a skill is, "Think about your choices," the person doing the modeling would quietly "think out loud" by verbalizing the choices.
- The person demonstrating the skill should also model the fact that certain skills will be somewhat difficult to perform. According to Bandura (1977) and McGinnis and Goldstein (1997b), observers are more likely to imitate a model

when a **coping model** is presented. A coping model is a model into which the struggles inherent in performing the skill correctly are incorporated. For example, the model could demonstrate that the student might wrestle in a low-key manner with making the right choice. If the modeling display appears to be effortless, students are less likely to attempt the skill under the stress of a real-life situation.

- The modeling display always turns out well or produces the desired outcomes in the social situation being modeled. Students are more likely to imitate a model that is reinforced (Bandura, 1977), in this case, by producing the desired outcomes or resolving the social situation satisfactorily.
- Keep the modeling display brief and to the point. It takes just a few minutes to complete the entire modeling sequence: Present the antecedent for the target skill, model the skill, and have the other actors in the modeling display react to the main actor's use of the skill.
- Following the modeling display, question students about whether each step was included, what the actors did for each step, and whether the overall display was correct and effective.

Behavioral Rehearsal

- Select the student who will practice the skill and choose one or more co-actors to assist the main actor in the rehearsal.
- Have the main actor describe a real-life situation in which he or she needs to use the skill. This situation will serve as the basis for the role-play. The role-play situation should imitate the real-life situation as much as possible to enhance generalization (Stokes and Baer, 1977).
- Instruct the students who are observing the rehearsal to look for each step in the skill sequence.
- Prompt the student, or refer the student to the chart that shows the steps in the skill if he or she forgets a step.
- After the student demonstrates the target skill, allow for a response from the co-actors. The co-actors should be encouraged to respond in

much the same way as they would expect their peers to respond in a real-world situation.
- Following the behavioral rehearsal, solicit feedback from the main actor, the co-actors, and the observers with regard to the main actor's use of the skill. The teacher should then give the main actor feedback about his performance.

- Ensure that each student in the group has the opportunity to practice the skill at least once. If a student has difficulty with a skill, he or she should be given additional practice opportunities.

Source: Goldstein and McGinnis (1988); Walker, Ramsey, and Gresham (2004).

Choosing a Social Skills Curriculum.   There is an abundance of commercial social skills curricula from which educators can choose. However, given the importance of social skills for students' overall success, we believe that it is important for educators to select a curriculum that is most likely to produce desirable outcomes. To this end, we propose the following criteria for selecting a social skills curriculum:

1. Choose a curriculum that is easy to use and easy to implement in the busy, complex environment of schools. This means that (a) the materials should be relatively simple and straightforward, (b) the curriculum should utilize terminology and teaching methods that are familiar to teachers, (c) the lesson should not require substantial amounts of time to prepare or implement, and (d) specialized training is not required to use the program. Curricula that meet these requirements are more likely to be implemented consistently.

2. Choose a curriculum that incorporates a coaching–modeling–behavioral rehearsal approach, which we know to be the most effective approach for teaching new social skills.

3. Choose a curriculum that teaches observable, task-analyzed skills rather than abstract constructs. As you learned in Chapter 8, students who struggle with learning and behavior benefit from direct instruction in skills. Simply encouraging students to "be kind," for example, or admonishing students to "show respect" does not mean that students know how to be kind or to show respect. Many of the steps involved in almost any social behavior are internal. For example, telling a student who responds easily to a provocation to "just ignore it" does not provide the student with the critical information needed to carry out that task. For any of us, "just ignoring it" means that we must first recognize that we are in a situation that should be ignored. Then we must do something to control our unacceptable responses (e.g., take a deep breath, remind oneself of the consequences, count to 10), and perhaps continue to engage in that self-control technique as long as the provocation continues. An observer probably would not be able to detect that we are engaged in the skill of "just ignoring it" because these are cognitive activities.

4. Choose a curriculum that has been field-tested in school settings with student populations similar to your students. Given the challenges involved in changing social behaviors, you will want a curriculum that is backed by evidence that it does, indeed, produce the desired outcomes. A curriculum or program that has fancy marketing and packaging may be appealing, but that does not equate to successful outcomes.

Table 9-2 presents a list of commercially available social skills training curricula that meet all or most of these criteria. All of these curricula are easy to use, rely on a coaching–modeling–behavioral rehearsal approach, and teach observable skills; most have been field-tested.

TABLE 9-2   Social Skills Curricula

Curriculum	Author(s), Publisher	Skills Taught	Assessment Included?
Aggression Replacement Training	Goldstein, Glick, and Gibbs (1998), Research Press	Teaches skill alternatives to aggression in three components: Skillstreaming (social skills), Anger Control Training (self-control training), and Moral Reasoning (social problem solving).	Yes, for social skills
ASSET: A Social Skills Program for Adolescents	Hazel, Schumaker, Sherman, and Sheldon (1995), Research Press	Uses videotaped modeling, discussions, and role-play to teach skills in eight areas: giving positive feedback, giving negative feedback, accepting negative feedback, resisting peer pressure, problem solving, negotiating, following instructions, and conversing.	No
The PREPARE® Curriculum: Teaching Prosocial Competencies	Goldstein (1999), Research Press	Designed for middle and high school students but may be adapted for use with younger children. Includes 10 interventions and 93 supplemental activities (e.g., games, role-plays, reading) for reducing aggression, stress, and prejudice.	No
Skillstreaming in Early Childhood Skillstreaming the Elementary School Child Skillstreaming the Adolescent	McGinnis and Goldstein (1997a), Research Press McGinnis and Goldstein (1997b), Research Press Goldstein, McGinnis, Sprafkin, Gershaw, and Klein (1997), Research Press	The three Skillstreaming curricula teach a variety of skills that are needed for classroom and social success. Each level uses a structured learning approach, including modeling, role-playing, feedback, and homework. Supplemental instructional materials are available.	Yes
Social Skills Intervention Guide	Elliott and Gresham (1991), American Guidance Service	Corresponds to the Social Skills Rating System. Addresses skill deficits in five domains: cooperation, assertion, responsibility, empathy, and self-control.	No, but the guide is designed to be used in conjunction with the Social Skills Rating System.

Curriculum	Author(s), Publisher	Skills Taught	Assessment Included?
Social Skills in the Classroom	Stephens and Arnold (1992), Psychological Assessment Resources	Uses scripted rehearsals and role-plays to remediate skill deficits and fluency deficits. Addresses skills in four categories: environmental behaviors, interpersonal behaviors, self-related behaviors, and task-related behaviors.	No
Stop and Think Social Skills Program	Knoff (2001), Sopris West	Available in four levels for preschool through middle school. Uses role-playing, group activities, and reinforcement contingencies to teach interpersonal, survival, problem-solving, and conflict resolution skills.	No
Tools for Getting Along	University of Florida	Includes 20 lessons, plus 6 booster lessons, that teach students how to recognize and manage anger, communicate effectively, and use social problem-solving skills. Uses a direct instruction approach, with a daily cumulative review, guided practice, and independent practice activities.	No
The Tough Kid Social Skills Book	Sheridan (2000), Sopris West	Includes activities for assessing, teaching, and reinforcing social entry skills; maintaining interactions; and problem solving.	Yes
The Walker Social Skills Curriculum: The ACCEPTS Program: A Curriculum for Children's Effective Peer and Teacher Skills The Walker Social Skills Curriculum: The ACCESS Program: Adolescent Curriculum for Communication and Effective Social Skills	Walker, McConnell, Holmes, Todis, Walker, and Golden (1988), PRO-ED Walker, Todis, Holmes, and Horton (1988), PRO-ED	Uses scripted lessons to teach skills in five areas (classroom skills, basic interaction skills, getting-along skills, making-friends skills, and coping skills) to children in elementary school (ACCEPTS) or skills in three areas (relating to peers, relating to adults, relating to yourself) to middle and high school students (ACCESS). The elementary school version is designed for students with or without disabilities; the secondary school version is designed for students with mild to moderate disabilities.	Yes
The Waksman Social Skills Curriculum for Adolescents, 4th ed.	Waksman and Waksman (1998), PRO-ED	Provides goals, objectives, worksheets, and homework for teaching assertive behavior in specific areas such as getting along with others, expressing feelings, accepting criticism, and anger management.	No, but the curriculum is intended for use with the Waksmans Social Skills Rating System.

Enhance the Use (Fluency) of the Skills. Fluency deficits may indicate that the student did not master a new skill during the initial teaching of that skill, that he or she is not yet sufficiently able to use the new skill effectively in real-life situations, or that naturalistic conditions are interfering with the student's ability to perform the skill (e.g., insufficient motivation in some or all environments, peers and others do not respond in a manner that encourages the student's efforts in using a new skill, competing problem behaviors). Intervention might then consist of the following: (a) reteaching the skill until the student can perform the skill effortlessly in the role-play (i.e., the behavioral rehearsal) and (b) providing reminders, encouragement, or other forms of support when the student is attempting to use a newly learned skill. These supports might include **precorrection**, a proactive strategy (see Box 9-2 for instructions on how to use precorrection); coaching when the student is actually attempting to use the skill; reinforcing use of the skill (see Chapters 10 and 11 for reinforcement ideas), or teaching self-management skills to help the student remember how and when to use the skill (see Chapter 11 for a discussion of self-management techniques).

Other supports may include one or more of the targeted-level interventions described in Chapter 5, such as Check-In Check-Out; Check, Connect, and Expect;

Box 9-2

How to Use Precorrection

1. Identify specific problem behaviors (e.g., cursing, pushing, noncompliance, grabbing).
2. Identify antecedents to the problem behavior(s). These might be specific activities (e.g., transitions, group work, independent work), situations (e.g., when given negative feedback about behavior, when asked to do something), times of the day (e.g., just before lunch, immediately upon entering the room after P.E.), or environments (e.g., hallway, cafeteria, general education class).
3. Identify the desired alternatives for each problem behavior. For example, instead of grabbing peers' toys during playtime, Ms. Carver wants Mark to share toys and take turns. Mr. Anderson expects Erica to walk into the classroom quietly and take a seat instead of entering the classroom noisily (e.g., calling out, bumping into peers' desks).
4. Practice those appropriate behaviors with the student in the actual contexts where they are needed (e.g., in the play area during playtime, entering the classroom). If any of the behavioral problems reflect acquisition deficits, those skills may first need to be taught and then practiced in the real-life situation.

5. Consider whether environmental modifications can help increase the likelihood of desired behaviors. For example, ensure that there are adequate toys or materials for all students or teach a specific routine for transitions.
6. Determine how appropriate behaviors will be reinforced (see Chapters 10 and 11 for a discussion of reinforcement).
7. Just before each antecedent associated with an inappropriate behavior, remind the student about the expected behavior and the consequences for exhibiting the expected behavior. For example, just before playtime, Ms. Carver reminds Mark about the rules for sharing and taking turns, and that he can earn extra playtime if he obeys the rules. Mr. Anderson greets Erica at the door and reminds her about the rules for coming into the classroom and that she can earn center time for the class if she follows the rules.

Source: Adapted from Colvin, G., Sugai, G., and Patching, B. (1993). Precorrection: An instructional approach for managing predictable problems behaviors. *Intervention in School and Clinic, 28*, 143–150.

or the Behavior Education Program. The social skills that the students have been taught might be listed on the students' daily behavior rating cards. Such a list should serve as a reminder to all staff who interact with a student that he or she is working on those skills and should be given prompts to use those skills, perhaps in the form of precorrection, as well as feedback about the use of the skills. This should help students build fluency in the newly learned social skills and should facilitate generalization of those skills to new settings. Also, because daily point cards are usually associated with some type of reinforcement system, these systems may also increase motivation to use the social skills.

Eliminate or Reduce Challenging Behaviors.   The more often that a student exhibits inappropriate behavior, the less likely it is that the student will exhibit regular, consistent use of socially acceptable behaviors. The reason for this may lie in the controlling functions of the problem behaviors, usually either negative reinforcement (e.g., the student avoids or escapes disliked events as a result of the inappropriate behavior) or positive reinforcement (e.g., the student gets attention, status, or control as a result of the inappropriate behavior) (Walker et al., 2004). The concept of behavioral efficiency was discussed in Chapter 3: The newly learned social skills that are intended to replace inappropriate behaviors must become more efficient for the student in terms of producing reinforcement than does engaging in the inappropriate behaviors.

Improve use of skills across settings and over time.   One of the major hurdles in social skills training is facilitating the generalization of newly learned skills to new situations and maintaining those skills over time. In fact, most experts agree that these tasks are far more difficult than teaching new skills (Goldstein & McGinnis, 1988; Walker et al., 2004). Because of this difficulty, a socialization intervention program must include specific, planned strategies for enhancing generalization and maintenance of skills. Box 9-3 describes such strategies.

Thus, focusing on the prevention of behavioral problems includes paying attention to the social abilities of the students. Problems with social skills may be at the heart of behavior management issues and, if so, should be addressed through direct instructions in prosocial behaviors.

SOCIALIZATION INTERVENTIONS AS PART OF UNIVERSAL-LEVEL SYSTEMS

Given the fact that universal-level system focus on preventive, instructional supports to encourage appropriate behavior and minimize unacceptable behavior, it is natural to consider instruction in social skills as one component of these systems. Many schools have adopted some type of schoolwide program for teaching and enhancing prosocial behaviors. A multitude of programs are available for this purpose. These programs vary in content, theoretical basis, and implementation methods, and include programs that target a specific problem area, such as the prevention of bullying, the prevention of drug use/abuse, or violence prevention programs, or programs that have as a goal the improvement of general traits related to character. A thorough discussion of schoolwide social–behavioral programs

Box 9-3

Strategies for Enhancing Generalization and Maintenance of Social Skills

- Ensure that the skills being taught are actually skills that the students need in generalized settings. Functional behavioral assessment can provide this information, as can ecological assessment. As discussed in Chapter 2, **ecological assessment** refers to the process of determining the expectations inherent in the environments in which students are expected to function. For example, when Mr. Burris was considering inclusion placements for several of his students, he first observed the general education classroom and the common areas (e.g., hallways, cafeteria, library) to identify the behaviors that students were expected to perform independently. He then asked the general education teachers in whose classes his students would be placed to describe their expectations for student behavior (e.g., what behaviors should be exhibited without the teacher's assistance, what behaviors the teacher will help the students learn, what behaviors are unacceptable). This information is then compared against the students' current skill levels; the areas in which there is a discrepancy become targets for instruction.
- Make the role-play (i.e., behavioral rehearsal) sessions as much as possible; like the real-life situations in which the students will be expected to use the skill (e.g., ask the students to carefully describe the setting in which they will use the skill, use peers as co-actors, encourage peers to behave much like the actual peers would behave in the situation).

- Provide structured opportunities for practicing the newly learned skills by assigning homework. One form of social skills homework might consist of having students first predict where they will need to use certain skills; then, they would self-monitor their use of those skills in generalized settings. Finally, they would self-evaluate how well they performed the skills and whether the use of the skill enabled them to more effectively manage the situation (see Chapter 11 for an explanation of self-monitoring and self-evaluation techniques).
- Ensure that reinforcement of the newly learned skills is sufficiently intense and frequent in order to compete with the reinforcing contingencies that may be maintaining the problem behaviors.
- Reinforce attempts to use the newly learned skills as part of the process of shaping these skills into socially competent forms.
- Reduce or eliminate competing behaviors.
- Prompt peers and teachers to respond appropriately to attempts to use the newly learned skills. For example, teachers may need reminders to provide specific, contingent praise when a student uses social skills. Peer confederates may need to be included as part of the intervention; peers would prompt the appropriate social skills and give feedback on the appropriate and inappropriate use of the social skills.

Sources: Center for Innovations in Education (2005); Goldstein and McGinnis (1988); Goldstein et al. (1997); McGinnis and Goldstein (1997b); Walker et al. (2004).

is beyond the scope of this text. However, for more information, refer to the resources listed at the end of this chapter. Included in these resources are the Websites of organizations that provide reviews and ratings of social–behavioral programs, such as the National Registry of Evidence-Based Programs and Practices and the What Works Clearinghouse.

In Chapter 5, we discussed the importance of establishing schoolwide expectations and then defining these expectations for all areas of the school. This set of specific behavioral expectations can function as a quasi-social–behavioral curriculum for the school, particularly if it is developed with the goal of teaching students the full range of expected social behaviors. For example, when defining the schoolwide expectation of "Be Respectful," the PBIS team might include behaviors that reflect peer-to-peer interactions, such as "Use kind words when talking to peers," "Offer to help peers," or "Take turns and share toys and equipment." This embedded social curriculum is then taught, and associated behaviors are prompted and reinforced.

Summary

In this chapter, we make the case that social skills are important to students' success and that social skills instruction should be considered as part of a comprehensive three-tiered approach to SW-PBIS and classroom management. We discussed types of social skills problems, methods for assessing social skills, curricula for teaching social skills, and strategies for ensuring that students acquire and use newly learned social skills. The following are the objectives for this chapter and how each was addressed:

1. Describe the types of socialization problems and strategies for remediating each type of problem.

Difficulties in getting along with peers are often at the heart of behavioral problems. Research has revealed important information about how to address these problems, including how to identify and assess socialization problems, strategies for remediating socialization problems, and strategies for ensuring that social skills are used in all environments and maintained over time.

2. Describe social skills interventions for universal level and targeted and/or tertiary levels of schoolwide positive behavioral interventions and supports (PBIS).

In this chapter, we focused primarily on social skills interventions for the targeted or tertiary level. Effective social skills interventions at either level involves assessing students' skill deficits, and remediating those deficits through a direct instruction approach that involves coaching, modeling, and behavioral rehearsal.

3. Describe criteria for choosing a social skills curriculum.

Social skills curricula should reflect best practices in teaching social skills, namely, a direct instruction approach. In addition, curricula should be easy to use and should have documented evidence of their effectiveness.

4. Describe how to facilitate the generalization of social skills.

Students might not generalize the use of newly learned social skills to real-world settings and activities. However, we can facilitate generalization through careful attention to the types of skills that are selected for instruction. In addition, generalization is also facilitated through particular elements of instructional design and by prompting and reinforcing students' attempts to use the newly learned skills.

Teaching social skills will not prevent or solve all behavior management problems. Social skills acquisition, particularly for students who exhibit challenging behaviors, should not be left to chance; rather, when students exhibit chronic behavioral difficulties, an assessment of those students' social skills should be conducted and skills that are weak or lacking should be explicitly taught. To help teachers monitor the extent to which they assess and teach social skills, we provide a social skills self-assessment in Table 9-3.

TABLE 9-3   Social Skills Self-Assessment Form

Never	Seldom	Sometimes	Often	Always
1	2	3	4	5

Use the numbers above to rate the following statements.

1. I view instruction in social skills for students who have challenging behaviors as being as important as their academic instruction.   _____

2. I understand the types of socialization problems.   _____

3. I know how to remediate each type of socialization problem.   _____

4. I know how to implement social skills interventions for the universal level of schoolwide PBIS.   _____

5. I know how to implement social skills intervention for the targeted and tertiary levels of schoolwide PBIS.   _____

6. I understand the criteria for choosing a social skills curriculum.   _____

7. I model social skills by using respectful, polite language with students, staff, and parents at school. .   _____

8. I know how to enhance students' fluency in using newly learned skills.   _____

9. I know assessment, instructional, prompting, and reinforcement strategies for facilitating the generalization of social skills.

10. I use prompting and reinforcement to encourage my students to practice the use of newly learned social skills.   _____

Learning Activities

1. In a small group, discuss the similarities and differences in teaching social skills on the universal and tertiary levels.
2. Explain why social skills are important to your students.
3. In a small group, discuss the use of coaching, modeling, and behavioral rehearsal in teaching social skills.
4. Task analyze the following social skills:
   - Accepting negative feedback from teachers
   - Controlling one's response to provocation by one's peers
   - Incorporating appropriate topics of conversation
   - Taking turns using materials
5. Using the direct instruction approach described in Chapter 8, and the coaching–modeling–behavioral rehearsal techniques described in this chapter, write a lesson plan for teaching one of the task-analyzed skills from activity 4 above.
6. Read the following cases that were first presented in Chapter 1, and then describe the problem and how you would address it using social skills instruction:

CASE STUDY OF AN ELEMENTARY SCHOOL STUDENT

Sam is a fourth-grade student in your class. He has stopped turning in his homework, but he is passing his tests. He does not really act out, but he is not as involved in class activities as he has been in the past. Now that you think about it, Sam has worn the same clothes for the past 3 days. In addition, when he looks at you, his face shows almost no emotion. You have talked briefly with his mother in the past, but only to convey information about field trips, needed supplies, or other minor topics. You have never had a face-to-face conference about Sam's school performance. You also know very little about Sam's home life.

CASE STUDY OF A SECONDARY SCHOOL STUDENT

Mary is in the seventh-grade. She often acts very silly in class. She seldom takes responsibility for her behavior but instead offers excuses or blames others. Recently, she has been cursing in class, a behavior that is new for Mary. Your first step in dealing with the problem is to talk to Mary. She giggles and says that the adults on her bus (i.e., the bus driver, the other drivers who talk to that driver, and the monitors) curse. You ask, "At you or when they speak to one another?" She says that they often use bad words when they talk to one another.

Resources

AUDIOVISUAL MATERIALS AND PROGRAMS

Amendola, M., Feindler, E., McGinnis, E., & Oliver, R. *Aggression Replacement Training.*

This video provides guidance for implementing the *Aggression Replacement Training* curriculum.

> Research Press
> Dept. 11W
> P.O. Box 9177
> Champaign, IL 61826
> (800) 519-2707
> www.researchpress.com

The Caring School Community.

A component of *The Child Development Project*, this program for grades K–6 is designed to strengthen students' connectedness to school through a variety of classroom and school activities.

> Child Development Project
> Development Studies Center
> 2000 Embarcadero, Suite 305
> Oakland, CA 94606
> Phone (510) 533-0213 or (800) 666-7270
> http://www.devstu.org/caring-school-community

Goldstein, A. *Teaching Prosocial Behavior to Antisocial Youth.*

This video provides instruction on how to implement the *Skillstreaming* social skills curricula.

> Research Press
> Dept. 11W
> P.O. Box 9177
> Champaign, IL 61826
> (800) 519-2707
> www.researchpress.com

WEBSITES

www.nrepp.samhsa.gov National Registry of Evidence-based Programs and Practices: This searchable database is offered by the Substance Abuse and Mental Health Services Administration, U.S. Department of Health and Human Services.

http://www.ies.ed.gov/ncee/wwc/reports/ What Works Clearinghouse: Established by the Institute of Education Sciences, U.S. Department of Education, the WWC provides a searchable review of character education curricula and programs.

www.promisingpractices.net Promising Practices Network on Children, Family, and Communities: Provides reviews of evidence-based programs, including social–behavioral curricula.

www.cfchildren.org Committee for Children: Publishes Second Step® and other violence prevention curricula.

http://csefel.uiuc.edu Center on the Social and Emotional Foundations for Early Learning: Provides training modules and other materials for improving the social competence of young children.

After reading this chapter, you will be able to do the following:

1. Define reinforcement terminology and give examples of positive reinforcement, primary reinforcer, secondary reinforcer, pairing, negative reinforcement, reinforcement schedules, and thinning.

2. Provide rationales for using reinforcement and for rebuttals of those who argue against the use of reinforcement in school.

3. Describe how to use reinforcement.

4. Describe the steps for problem solving when reinforcement contingencies fail to produce the desired outcomes.

Prevention of Challenging Behavior Through Reinforcement: Introduction to Reinforcement

Big ideas in reinforcement:

- Positive reinforcement is a naturally occurring process, not an arbitrary invention of behaviorists. Behaviorists simply named and systematized this process.

- Positive reinforcement is an important element in PBIS.

- Reinforcers can be determined only by the functional effects on behavior. A consequence that maintains, increases, or strengthens a behavior is a reinforcer, regardless of whether the consequence was *intended* as a reinforcer.

- Negative reinforcement is *not* punishment! Negative reinforcement is a reinforcement procedure that increases a behavior by removing a negative antecedent stimulus when the behavior occurs.

- Praise is an easy-to-use form of positive reinforcement.

During a brutally hot summer, one of the authors (BKS) had to run several errands. Traffic was unusually chaotic and the temperature was more than 100 degrees Fahrenheit. By the last stop on her list of errands, the author wanted nothing more than to finish those tasks, go home, and get a cool drink. As she entered the last store, she was greeted at the door by a smiling clerk who asked if she would like an ice-cold bottle of water. The small, family-owned store had decided to treat their customers that day. Nothing could have been more welcome on that searing day. Because of that friendly clerk and that cold water, the author is very likely to continue to shop regularly at that store.

Another author's (JAH) mother has an appointment each month to have her blood checked. The nurse who draws her blood always takes her time and compliments her clothes or jewelry. The blood is drawn while they are talking, and Mom is always surprised that the procedure is over so quickly. She looks forward to seeing that nurse each month.

A massage therapist comes to an elementary school on the first Wednesday of each month. He charges $15 for a 20-minute massage. However, if 15 time slots are taken, the price goes down to $10 for a 20-minute massage. Because he offers a price break for 15 time slots, the massage therapist almost always has all of the time slots booked.

The principal of a large urban elementary school expects her teachers to use high levels of praise with students. During the week, when the principal hears a teacher using particularly effective praise, she hands the teacher a "Jeans Day" coupon. The coupon allows the teacher to wear jeans to school for 1 day; on that day, the teacher simply turns in the coupon to the school office.

All of the scenarios just described are examples of positive reinforcement that occur in daily life. Life is full of examples of behavioral principles, including reinforcement. Once you better understand reinforcement and other behavioral principles, you will begin to recognize their role in shaping your own behavior and how you use these tools to affect the behavior of others. Of all of the tools available to behaviorists, positive reinforcement may be the most valuable for anyone who must manage the behavior of others, including teachers, administrators, paraprofessionals, parents, and child care workers. The ability to use positive reinforcement correctly and wisely will make teaching, classroom management, and management of school personnel much easier and more efficient. Furthermore, positive reinforcement is a critical component of PBIS. In Chapter 5, we described the use of positive reinforcement as a universal-level intervention to acknowledge appropriate rule-following behaviors in all students. In this chapter, we explain the behavioral principles of positive and negative reinforcement and describe how to use reinforcement as a management tool. The reinforcement applications discussed in this chapter and in Chapter 11 are appropriate for small groups or individual students, particularly those students who require targeted and tertiary supports. These reinforcement strategies are also appropriate for use as part of a classroom management system, to reinforce an entire class, small groups within the class, or individual students in the class.

WHAT IS REINFORCEMENT?

Reinforcement maintains or increases a behavior.

Reinforcement is a process in which a behavior is strengthened as a result of a consequence that follows the behavior. Reinforcement can increase the frequency, rate, intensity, duration, or form of a behavior. Whether or not a consequence is reinforcing can be determined only by monitoring the effect of that consequence on the targeted behavior. If a behavior occurs more frequently, is present in greater magnitude or intensity, lasts longer, or improves in form as a result of the consequence, reinforcement has occurred. If the behavior does not increase in frequency, rate, intensity, or duration, or improve in form, reinforcement has not occurred, even if that was the goal of using the consequence.

Reinforcement is not a strategy that was invented by behaviorists. Rather, it is a naturally occurring behavioral process that was observed and described by early behaviorists, who then learned to manipulate and apply the process in order to achieve desired behavioral outcomes. To illustrate naturally occurring applications of reinforcement, consider the following examples:

• Your dog quickly learns a new trick because each time that she does the trick, you give her a treat.

- You wear a new pair of jeans and receive lots of compliments. You begin wearing the new jeans more than any other pair that you own.
- Ben works particularly hard learning a new play during football practice. The team scores as a result of the play and wins the game. Ben keeps working extra hard during practices, and the coach continues to use the play in future games.
- Young Halle raises a fuss in the grocery store. She wants a particular brand of cereal, but her mother refuses to buy it. Halle's protests become louder and more intense until her frazzled mother says, "OK, but just this once." Halle, however, continues this behavior with great success every time that she goes to the store with her mother.
- You try a different study technique in order to prepare for an upcoming exam. Not only do you feel more confident during the exam, but also you receive the highest grade ever achieved by any student in that class. You continue to use that study technique for exams in all of your classes.
- A salesman puts in especially long hours during a particular sales period. The result is that his sales totals are the highest of all the members of the sales force, an achievement that increases his pay and earns him a nice bonus. As a result, he continues to work harder than ever before.

Natural reinforcement is at work in each of these examples and, as a result, has influenced the behaviors of these individuals. Reinforcement is a powerful force for shaping behavior. Effective teachers will use reinforcement to teach and encourage appropriate, prosocial behavior.

Positive reinforcement is the contingent delivery of a consequence stimulus immediately following a behavior that maintains or increases the frequency, rate, intensity, latency, or duration of the behavior, or improves the form of the behavior. The behavioral shorthand for positive reinforcement is S^{R+}. The consequence that has this effect is called a **reinforcer** (S^R), or **positive reinforcer**. Note the difference between these terms: *Reinforcer* refers to the *consequence*, and *reinforcement* refers to the *process* or *relationship* between the behavior and the consequence.

Recall from Chapter 2 that one of the assumptions of applied behavior analysis is that all voluntary behaviors are governed by the same principles. This means that positive reinforcement has the potential to maintain or increase inappropriate behavior, as well as appropriate behavior. In our previous list of examples, young Halle's fervent demands for a particular brand of cereal were reinforced when her mother gave in and, therefore, Halle continued her demanding behavior each time that she was in the grocery store. In another example, Lee repeatedly asks his teacher questions about a task, even though the teacher has explained the task well. Each time that Lee asks a question, the teacher goes to him and gently encourages him to try it on his own. The teacher's attention may be maintaining Lee's undesirable behavior of asking too many questions.

Furthermore, if a behavior continues or increases, reinforcement has occurred, regardless of what the consequence was intended to do. For example, Enrique, a quiet student, volunteers an answer in class. The teacher praises him (i.e., attempts to reinforce his participation), but his peers covertly laugh at him and call him "schoolboy." Enrique stops volunteering in class or even answering

> **Reinforcers** are earned through the process of **reinforcement**.

questions when called on. The teacher intended to reinforce Enrique's participation in class. However, the teacher's praise was overpowered by the peers' negative response and, therefore, reinforcement did not occur. In another example, a student disrupts his algebra class and is sent to the office. The disruptive behavior continues on subsequent days, each time resulting in the student being sent to the office. We can only conclude that something about the office disciplinary referral is reinforcing to the student. Perhaps he is glad to escape a difficult, disliked class, or perhaps he likes the attention that he receives from his peers for this behavior.

When a student exhibits a high rate of inappropriate behavior, you must ask yourself how the behavior is being reinforced. Does the student get something that he wants or likes as a result of the inappropriate behavior? Does the student avoid something unpleasant? Functional assessment, described in Chapter 3, will help to identify the reinforcers that may be maintaining the inappropriate behavior. It is important to remember that reinforcers may not appear to be fun or pleasant. For example, taking a child into the hall for a private talk about her behavior may be reinforcing for the student, even though the teacher gives a firm warning.

Reinforcement can be used with groups or individual students to strengthen or increase all types of behaviors, including academic behaviors. Reinforcement is also important for establishing new behaviors, often through the process of shaping. **Shaping** is the process of reinforcing successive approximations of a desired targeted behavior. In the acquisition stages of learning a new behavior, general approximations of the targeted behavior are reinforced. Gradually, reinforcement is given for increasingly more accurate forms of the targeted behavior. Eventually, only the targeted behavior in its correct form is reinforced. For example, a young child who is learning to write her name is, at first, reinforced if the writing is somewhat legible, even though the letters may be poorly formed and spaced. Each day, however, the teacher tightens the criteria for reinforcement, such as reinforcing only those attempts in which all of the letters are written correctly, then only attempts in which all of the letters are written correctly and spaced correctly in relationship to the line. In another example of shaping, consider Mr. Rolfe, who is teaching young Jonathan to remain in his seat. Jonathan is highly active, is easily distracted, and does not stay in his chair for longer than 1 minute. At first, Jonathan earned reinforcement for staying in his seat for 1 minute. Jonathan's reinforcer was that he could stand up and do 10 jumping jacks. When Jonathan was consistently remaining in his seat for 1-minute periods, Mr. Rolfe raised the criterion for reinforcement to 2 minutes. This shaping process continued until Jonathan was able to remain in his seat for up to 10 minutes.

Positive reinforcement for appropriate behavior is an important feature of positive behavioral supports. As you have seen in Chapter 5, successful schools use positive reinforcement at the schoolwide level (i.e., high levels of positive reinforcement are available for all students) as part of universal-level systems. In addition, many targeted-level interventions include reinforcement as one component. Certainly, reinforcement is an important component in tertiary-level interventions, where individualized reinforcement-based interventions are used to increase desired behaviors in students who exhibit challenging behaviors.

> Reinforcement may explain why inappropriate behaviors continue to be exhibited, despite efforts to mete out consequences for engaging in them.

The Goals of Reinforcement

Reinforcement is a powerful tool that can produce rapid changes in behavior. Despite its effectiveness, some individuals—even educators—are critical of using reinforcement to facilitate behavior change. Most criticisms arise from misconceptions about behavioral interventions, often stemming from the early misuse of "behavior modification" techniques and terminology. For this reason, we encourage educators to use the more current and correct terminology of *applied behavior analysis* or *positive behavioral supports* rather than *behavior modification* and, of course, to always use behavioral interventions correctly. In addition, educators who use behavioral techniques, and who expect other educators to use those techniques (e.g., asking general education teachers to use positive reinforcement strategies), must be able to respond to common misconceptions and criticisms. Some of these are presented in Table 10-1, along with reasoned responses for each.

TABLE 10-1 Common Misconceptions About Reinforcement

Concern: Reinforcement is bribery.

Rebuttal: According to the *Oxford English Dictionary*, a bribe is "a sum of money or something valuable that you give or offer to somebody to persuade them to help you, especially by doing something dishonest." Obviously, this is not how reinforcement is used. Remember, both applied behavior analysis and positive behavioral supports focus on socially significant, socially important behaviors that will increase an individual's success.

Concern: Teachers should not have to use rewards to motivate students; the students should want to learn and should be glad to have the opportunity to come to school.

Rebuttal: We agree! In a perfect world, students would come to school not because laws require them to do so, but because they want to learn and love learning. Unfortunately, we do not live in a perfect world. Many children come to school unprepared for the demands of school, as discussed in Chapter 1. Furthermore, school is not a positive place for many children with chronic learning and/or behavioral problems. These children often do not experience the natural reinforcers that other students enjoy: positive attention from teachers and parents, positive social attention from peers, academic success, or social success in the form of involvement in school and extracurricular activities. If we relied only on these naturally occurring reinforcers for motivation, over time, these students might experience less and less school success and become less and less involved in school. This is a slippery slope that tends to result in serious escalation of minor behavioral problems, as described in Chapter 1. Our best hope for students with a history of learning and behavioral problems is to use external reinforcers as part of a comprehensive intervention to increase the behaviors that will lead to academic and social success. Eventually, our goal is for naturally occurring, intrinsic reinforcers to replace extrinsic reinforcers. But in the meantime, it *is* the teacher's job to teach, which includes motivating students to want to learn.

Concern: If you use reinforcement, children will come to expect it.

Rebuttal: This concern has been widely promulgated by both lay journalists and professional educators (e.g., Deci & Ryan, 1985; Kohn, 1993). The basic assertion is that the use of "rewards" will reduce an individual's intrinsic motivation and will make him or her dependent on extrinsic reinforcers. Of course, the evidence suggests otherwise. In a comprehensive review of the subject, Cameron, Banko, and Pierce (2001) found that the use of positive reinforcement can actually *increase* intrinsic reinforcement. In another thorough review and analysis of studies of the effects of extrinsic reinforcement on motivation, Akin-Little and her colleagues (2004) concluded that concerns that children will become dependent on extrinsic reinforcement are unwarranted. Teachers who are worried that children will demand reinforcement are advised to refer to the problem-solving section earlier in this chapter. Before we leave the issue of concern over students demanding reinforcement, we wish to pose this question: How many adults would go to work without getting paid? To a certain extent, we *all* expect rewards for certain behaviors!

Behavioral interventions, including reinforcement, should usually be considered a means to an end (i.e., tools for achieving target-levels of desired behaviors). Once those targeted behaviors have been attained, the goal should be to gradually withdraw formal positive behavioral supports and allow natural contingencies to maintain the behaviors. For example, a teacher may use a group point system to help teach students to follow the rules and work well together. This point system may be needed for the first few months of school, during which the teacher gradually thins the reinforcement schedule (i.e., reinforcement is gradually available less frequently; see the discussion of reinforcement schedules later in the chapter). Eventually, the teacher should no longer need to use the formal point system; students have learned the targeted skills of following the rules, sharing, and working collaboratively. At this point, natural contingencies should be sufficient to manage behavior: Students follow the rules and do their work, and they then get to participate in desired activities. If they do not follow the rules, finish their work, or work nicely together, they do not get to participate in the desired activities.

For many students who need behavioral interventions in order to learn, including the prompting and reinforcement of appropriate academic and social behaviors, the goal is for the student to reach the point at which intrinsic reinforcement and self-management (see Chapter 11) are sufficient to maintain behavior. **Intrinsic reinforcement** (i.e., internal reinforcement) is the feeling of self-satisfaction, success, or accomplishment that most of us experience when we know that we have done a task well. For many children, extrinsic (i.e., external) reinforcement systems motivate the child to exhibit appropriate behavior, which then produces naturally occurring reinforcers (e.g., praise and recognition from the teacher and parents, good grades, positive social attention from peers, an internal feeling of success). Without positive behavioral supports, students may never exhibit a sufficient level of appropriate behavior to be able to consistently and predictably access those naturally occurring reinforcers.

However, for some students, behavioral interventions may always be needed to maintain appropriate behavior. The presence of biological disorders, negative learning histories, low cognitive functioning, and other conditions may indicate that some children will always need the structure of extrinsic reinforcement strategies and other behavioral interventions. Children with severe emotional/behavioral disorders, mental disorders (e.g., bipolar disorder, anxiety disorder, obsessive compulsive disorder, attention-deficit hyperactivity disorder), or autism, for example, may be successful as long as external positive behavioral supports are present. When those supports are withdrawn or applied incorrectly, students may exhibit higher levels of inappropriate behavior (e.g., aggression, self-injurious behavior, self-stimulatory behavior, noncompliance). For these children, maintaining appropriate behavior through behavioral strategies *is* the goal. It would be unethical to withdraw those positive behavioral supports if those supports are necessary for maintaining appropriate, safe behavior.

TYPES OF REINFORCERS

Primary reinforcers meet basic survival needs.

Reinforcers are categorized as primary reinforcers or secondary reinforcers. **Primary reinforcers,** also called **unlearned reinforcers** or **unconditioned reinforcers,** are those stimuli which we need to survive or which have biological value and are, therefore, naturally reinforcing and very powerful. Primary reinforcers include food, sleep, liquids, sexual stimulation, and shelter. For some individuals with autism or other developmental disabilities, stereotypic behaviors (e.g., rocking, flapping one's hands, spinning) or self-injurious behaviors (e.g., biting, hitting, or scratching oneself; hitting one's head against objects) may function as primary reinforcers (Cowdery, Iwata, & Pace, 1990; Durand & Crimmins, 1988, 1992; National Research Council, 2001).

Secondary reinforcers, also called **conditioned reinforcers**, are those stimuli which we learn to like. They have no intrinsic value for survival and no connection to biological need and, therefore, do not have the unlearned reinforcing qualities of primary reinforcers. We learn to value secondary reinforcers through a process known as **pairing:** associating primary reinforcers with secondary reinforcers. For example, Ms. Gonzalez teaches young children who have autism. Her students are learning to communicate using sign language or picture cards. When a student uses a sign or points to a picture card in order to request a desired activity or object, Ms. Gonzalez simultaneously praises the child, gives him or her a morsel of cereal, and allows the child to have the requested activity or object. Ms. Gonzalez is using pairing by presenting the praise, the cereal, and the requested activity or object simultaneously. Her goal is for her students to eventually learn to value the praise and activities or objects so that she will no longer need to use food to reinforce requests.

Secondary reinforcers can be classified as **social reinforcers**, **activity reinforcers**, **material reinforcers**, and **token reinforcers**. Social reinforcers include praise or other forms of recognition. Activity reinforcers are special privileges, games, or even jobs. Material reinforcers are tangible items and token reinforcers are items that have no intrinsic value but are meaningful because they may be exchanged for other primary or secondary reinforcers. Table 10-2 provides examples of each of these categories of secondary reinforcers. Identifying reinforcers can be a challenging undertaking in which creative thinking can produce highly effective reinforcers. We will discuss how to determine reinforcers in the next section.

Because most students will respond to other types of reinforcers, primary reinforcers should be used only under limited circumstances. Primary reinforcers can have a powerful and immediate effect on behavior. For this reason, it may be necessary to use primary reinforcers for some children who exhibit extremely challenging behaviors, especially very young children, children who have severe cognitive impairments, or children who exhibit particularly severe behaviors (e.g., self-injurious behaviors, self-stimulatory behaviors, aggression). However, primary reinforcers should be considered a means to an end, not a long-term intervention. The goal should be to rely on secondary reinforcers as soon as possible. In order to accomplish this, a primary reinforcer should always be paired with one or more secondary reinforcers, particularly praise.

Previously, we encouraged readers to use correct, current terminology to refer to behavioral interventions. We also urge readers to use correct terminology when discussing positive reinforcement. Correct terminology includes **positive reinforcement** or **reinforcers**, not rewards. The word *rewards* is not a part of professional terminology, and it connotes a less scientific use than does the term *positive reinforcement*. As professionals, teachers should model using correct terminology.

Speak of "reinforcers," not "rewards."

TABLE 10-2 Types of Secondary Reinforcers

Social Reinforcers
- Being in proximity.
- Giving a pat on the back.
- Giving a "high five."
- Offering verbal or written praise.
- Giving public or private recognition, including the following:
  - an award certificate,
  - putting the student's name on the bulletin board or in a newsletter, having it announced over the intercom, or
  - writing a "Good News" note.
- Allowing time for students to talk among themselves at the end of class.

Activity Reinforcers
- Allowing activities in large groups, in small groups, or for individuals, including the following:
  - basketball, flag football, kickball, hopscotch, or jump rope,
  - board games, or
  - computer games.
- Allowing a student to be line leader.
- Offering membership in "First Club" (the students in First Club are the first called to line up, go to lunch, choose a book from the library center, get a drink, etc.).
- Offering classroom jobs such as the following:
  - feeding and caring for class pets,
  - caring for class plants,
  - erasing the chalkboard or dry erase board,
  - writing daily assignments on the board,
  - passing out or collecting papers or materials,
  - acting as a timekeeper for activities, or
  - designing a bulletin board.
- Offering jobs outside of the classroom, such as the following:
  - taking the attendance sheet or correspondence to the office,
  - returning or obtaining materials from another teacher,
  - returning library books,
  - helping to organize books in the library,
  - helping in the school office,
  - helping the P.E., art, or music teacher set up or store materials,
  - reading to younger children, or
  - helping younger children or children with severe disabilities at lunchtime.
- Allowing the use of special materials such as the following:
  - gel pens,

- - dry erase boards,
  - art materials, or
  - musical instruments.
- Allowing the student to sit in the teacher's chair, a beanbag chair, or other special location.
- Allowing the student to bring music to be played during independent work time (of course, the music must meet the teacher's criteria for acceptability: there should be no profanity or violent lyrics).
- Allowing the student to operate the CD player during independent work time.
- Allowing the student to select music for playing during the work time.

Material Reinforcers

- Stickers
- Small toys or trinkets
- School supplies (e.g., pencils, erasers, pens, notebooks, rulers)
- Posters
- Small novelty games
- Books
- Art supplies (e.g., stamps, chalk, finger paints, paint and brushes, modeling clay)

Token Reinforcers

- Stars, stamps, stickers, check marks, or tally marks on a chart
- Bingo chips
- Play money
- Tickets
- Popsicle sticks
- Links added to a paper chain

The use of praise as a reinforcer warrants additional discussion. Giving praise is a relatively simple task that is less intrusive and requires fewer resources than other reinforcement strategies. Most importantly, a number of studies have shown that giving praise can increase the frequency of a desired behavior in a variety of student populations. Contingent teacher praise has been shown to increase task engagement, desired academic response, and compliance, and to reduce off-task, noncompliant, or incorrect responses (Alber, Heward, & Hippler, 1999; Chalk & Bizo, 2004; Gable & Shores, 1980; Gunter & Jack, 1993; Sutherland, Wehby, & Copeland, 2000). Simply put, when teachers give high levels of contingent praise, students tend to exhibit higher levels of appropriate behavior; conversely, disruptive behavior increases when teachers offer less praise (Beaman & Wheldall, 2000; Thomas, Becker, & Armstrong, 1968).

Unfortunately, research has also shown that praise is often used infrequently in both special education and general education classes (Alber et al., 1999; Lewis, Hudson, Richter, & Johnson, 2004; Matheson & Shriver, 2005; Sutherland, 2000;

Sutherland et al., 2000). White (1975) found that the use of praise by teachers decreased with each grade-level; after second-grade, teachers delivered more disapproval statements to students than praise statements. Increasing the use of specific, contingent praise of appropriate behavior may be an appropriate first response to classroom or individual student behavioral problems. Teachers should learn to evaluate their use of praise and use those results to increase the use of praise as a management tool (Bullard, 1998; Keller, Brady, & Taylor, 2005; Sutherland & Wehby, 2001).

Follow the guidelines for giving praise.

A few simple guidelines for delivering praise will help to ensure maximum effectiveness:

1. Deliver praise contingently. Praise should be delivered only following specific, targeted behaviors. Teachers must be alert in order to catch students' exhibiting appropriate behaviors, especially students who exhibit high levels of challenging behaviors.

2. Provide specific, descriptive praise. Martella and his colleagues (1995) recommend that half of the praise statements delivered to students should be specific, with the rest being general statements. Examples of specific praise statements are as follows: "Sean, I am glad that you remembered to put your heading on your paper." "Katy, your work is so neatly done. Great job!" "Ben, what a good job you did paying attention and participating in class today!" Examples of general praise statements are as follows: "Alicia, you had a good day!" "Hunter, you played nicely during centers." "Jose, great work!"

3. Achieve a praise-to-reprimand ratio of 3:1 (Shores, Gunter, & Jack, 1993) to 4:1 or higher (Walker, Ramsey, & Gresham, 2004). The more behavioral difficulty that a student has, the higher the praise-to-reprimand ratio should be.

4. Use a variety of praise statements. If doing this does not come naturally, consider generating a list of phrases that you can incorporate into your vocabulary. There are many ways to say "Good job!" See how many you can generate. (See the "Learning Activities" section at the end of this chapter for this exercise.)

5. Use a positive tone of voice without being overly effusive. For older students especially, too much enthusiasm may actually be embarrassing.

6. Use the student's name when delivering a praise statement to an individual student. This helps to ensure that the student attends to the praise statement and personalizes the praise.

7. If you are concerned that a student may not welcome public praise, deliver the praise privately to the student. This can be done by giving the praise to the student in a voice that is sufficiently quiet to prevent other students from overhearing. You can also provide written praise statements, although it is more difficult to provide high levels of praise in writing. To address this problem, write some "praise notes" on sticky notes ahead of time, using a specific praise statement that targets behaviors that are important in the classroom (e.g., working hard, working accurately, participating in class, helping peers). Then carry the sticky notes during class; when a targeted behavior is observed, a sticky note can be placed on the student's desk.

8. Use a self-monitoring intervention to increase your use of praise in the classroom. Teachers should use brief videotaped or audiotaped samples of teaching

behavior to monitor their use of praise (Keller et al., 2005; Sutherland, 2000). First, teachers should write down their prediction for the average number of praise statements that they will give over a specified period, say, anywhere from 5 minutes (Keller et al., 2005) to 15 minutes (Sutherland & Wehby, 2001). Next, use video or audio recordings to obtain 15-minute samples of teacher behavior collected over 3 or 4 days for baseline data. Then count the number of reprimands and praise statements given during each 15-minute sample, and make the following observations: (a) How does the actual number of praise statements compare against the predicted number? (b) Does the ratio of praise to reprimands meet or exceed the 4:1 standard? Finally, intervention consists of teachers setting goals for the number of praise statements to be delivered per 15-minute period and continuing to self-monitor their behavior to determine whether those goals are being achieved. Of course, teachers should praise themselves when a praise goal is reached!

HOW TO CHOOSE REINFORCERS

Identifying reinforcers is an important task for educators. Choosing effective reinforcers will make a significant difference in classroom and individual behavior management. In fact, as you will see in the problem-solving section at the end of this chapter, ineffective reinforcers can be a major reason why management programs fail. Remember that reinforcers can be determined only by their effect on targeted behaviors. If a particular stimulus results in the maintenance of or an increase in a targeted behavior, we can assume that the stimulus is reinforcing. A stimulus that produces no effect on the behavior is not a reinforcer. School personnel can make educated guesses about activities that will function as reinforcers, but only observation of the effect of those reinforcers on the targeted behavior will confirm whether those guesses are correct. Although it is tempting to provide lists of interesting, creative activities and advise our readers to use them, that would not be a best practice. Rather, best practices direct us to first use assessment strategies to determine potential reinforcers and then observe whether targeted behaviors are maintained or increased because of those reinforcers. Several methods can help to identify potential reinforcers: Use functional assessment data, observe your class, ask your students, or use reinforcer sampling. Each of these is described in the sections that follow.

Use Functional Assessment Data. As you learned in Chapter 3, inappropriate behavior is functional for the student. The hypothesized functions of challenging behavior can be addressed by providing the student with contingent access to activities that address those functions. Table 10-3 lists examples of reinforcers that are categorized by behavioral function. Again, the examples chosen are not intended to serve as a definitive list; they are intended to stimulate creative thinking in choosing function-based reinforcers.

Observe Your Class. Observing can be done informally by noting the materials, activities, and conditions that students prefer. Use the following questions to guide your observations:

- What do students ask to do? Activities or conditions that students request are potential reinforcers. For example, do students ask to play basketball, play

TABLE 10-3   Function-Based Reinforcers

Function: Attention from the Teacher or Another Adult

- Spending time alone with the teacher (e.g., at lunchtime, helping the teacher in the classroom before or after school, going for a walk).
- Spending time alone with the principal (e.g., at lunchtime, a special visit to the principal).
- Being allowed to call the parents. (The teacher or the student can make the call.)
- Receiving a "Good News" note for the parents.
- Helping the teacher (e.g., writing assignments on the board, delivering messages, returning materials to the library, straightening up the lab).
- Helping other teachers (e.g., the librarian, the gym teacher, the art teacher, other primary teachers).

Function: Attention from Peers

- Being a peer tutor.
- Being allowed to choose peers with whom to play games, do tasks, use special materials.
- Telling a joke or reading a story to the class.
- Earning a reinforcer for the entire class (see Chapter 11 for how to design group reinforcement systems).

Function: Escape

- Earning "Get out of work" coupons (i.e., coupons that allow students to be excused from all or part of certain assignments, homework, or quizzes).
- Earning reinforcer dots (developed by Ginger Gates, Director of Special Education for Deer Park Independent School District, Deer Park, Texas): The student earns brightly colored sticky dots (the type used to mark folders) for items completed correctly on independent work (e.g., problems solved, sentences written, questions answered). Each dot may be placed next to an item on the assignment; the student is not required to do that part of the assignment but still gets full credit for that portion. At first, dots are given liberally. Later, dots are given less frequently. One of the authors (BKS) worked with a middle school reading teacher in a rural school. This teacher applied this strategy slightly differently: Her students were reluctant to read during oral reading sessions and often failed to follow along; therefore, the teacher had to prompt them where to begin reading when called on. The teacher began using reinforcer dots to reinforce students who knew where to start reading when called on. Students could apply the dots to the written assignments that followed the oral reading. The teacher reported that her students' attitude toward oral reading changed dramatically: When she implemented the reinforcer dots, students began waving their hands and asking to read! They always knew where to begin reading.

Function: Power, Control

- Assisting the teacher.
- Assisting other teachers.
- Helping peers with academic or social tasks (e.g., peer tutoring).
- Helping younger students with academic or nonacademic tasks (e.g., reading to younger students, listening to students read, teaching students playground games, assisting peers and adults at lunchtime).

- Allowing students to earn a position as the "decision maker." This student gets to choose group activities, music for independent time, or a story that is to be read to the class.
- Operating the class CD player during independent work time.

Function: Status

- Earning reinforcers for the group (see Chapter 11).
- Being allowed to choose other students as partners when using special materials and doing special tasks or projects.
- Working as a "peer buddy" (e.g., helping a peer with social or academic tasks, answering questions about work, reminding others about homework).
- Doing special jobs (e.g., painting a mural, creating sidewalk art, making announcements, designing a class or school newsletter, maintaining a bulletin board).

Function: Attention from the Teacher or Another Adult

- Participating in school or community service tasks.
- Participating in special after-school groups, activities, or performances (e.g., presenting a play, magic show, or talent show for the after-school child care program).

---

with puzzles, use the computer, work together, sit on the floor to do their work, listen to music during work time, eat lunch in the classroom or with the teacher, or have their favorite story read to them? These requested activities indicate student preferences and, therefore, are potential reinforcers.

- What materials do students ask to use? Do they clamor for particular games? Do they ask to use gel pens or colored pens for their work? Do they argue over who gets to operate the DVD player or other equipment? Do they race to see who gets to the basketballs first? Again, high interest in materials suggests possible reinforcers.
- What do students tend to do that is unacceptable to the teacher? Often students' mildly inappropriate behaviors can be offered as reinforcers. For example, teenagers love to talk or write notes, two activities that often get them in trouble. An observant teacher might make these activities contingent upon targeted behaviors, such as work completion, by allowing any student who finishes all assigned work with 80% accuracy or greater to talk quietly or write notes during the last 2 minutes of class. Other examples of mildly inappropriate or unacceptable behaviors that may function as reinforcers include using prohibited items (e.g., headphones, certain classroom equipment), being tardy (e.g., earning a tardy pass after having achieved a predetermined number of on-time arrivals to class), excessive requests to use the restroom or get a drink (e.g., earning an extra restroom or drink pass), sitting in the teacher's chair or at the teacher's desk, or wearing a hat in class. Of course, you must either make sure that you do not allow students to engage in activities that are prohibited by school policy or at least obtain permission in advance.

Ask Your Students. Another approach to identifying potential reinforcers is to ask the students. Although this is certainly the easiest approach, it may not be the most effective (Northup, 2000). Some evidence suggests that having input into determining a reinforcer makes the reinforcer more effective (Thompson, Fisher, & Contrucci, 1998; Wheeler & Richey, 2005). However, children may be unaware of

Check the activities that you would like to earn:

☐ Eating lunch with the teacher.

☐ Being the teacher's helper for a day (e.g., writing the assignments on the chalkboard, passing out papers, taking the attendance sheet to the office).

☐ Playing a game with two friends of your choosing.

☐ Choosing an activity for the class to do (e.g., playing basketball or a trivia game, participating in an academic scavenger hunt).

☐ Doing half of one assignment (selected by you and the teacher).

☐ Being an office helper for 30 minutes after lunch.

☐ Doing a special art project (e.g., using paints, charcoal, colored pencils, clay, papier-mâché, or other materials of your choosing).

☐ Being a library helper for 30 minutes after lunch.

☐ Helping Coach Sims for 30 minutes after lunch.

☐ Calling your parents at home or at work to tell them about your good day.

☐ Having the teacher write a note to your parents to tell them about your good day.

Now put an asterisk (*) next to the items that you like best.

FIGURE 10-1   Reinforcer Survey

potential effective reinforcers (e.g., receiving attention from the teacher, peers, or other adults; escaping from aversive situations) and may simply identify those items or activities which are the most familiar (e.g., food, computer use, extra recess time, access to games). Although student input should be considered, particularly for intermediate and secondary students, teachers should use all available information to make decisions about reinforcers.

> A reinforcer survey can help to identify potential reinforcers.

Using a reinforcer survey addresses the problem of students having a limited perspective with regard to the identification of reinforcers. A **reinforcer survey** or **reinforcer menu**, like a restaurant menu, is a list of potential reinforcers (see Figure 10-1). Students choose the reinforcers that they prefer, possibly by rank ordering their choices. A reinforcer survey allows the teacher to control the choices and avoid the problem of students suggesting reinforcers that the teacher is financially or legally unable to provide. Again, like oral inquiries about reinforcers, teachers should consider the information obtained from a reinforcer survey as only one source of data about potential reinforcers.

Use Reinforcer Sampling.   **Reinforcer sampling** is a technique that is used by many retailers. The practice of offering free product samples through the mail or in stores is essentially reinforcer sampling. Reinforcer sampling involves presenting potential reinforcers to students noncontingently and observing which items or activities the students select. These choices are high-probability reinforcers for those students. Reinforcer sampling is especially useful when, for whatever reason, identification of reinforcers through other means has been unproductive. Reinforcer sampling can be done with both groups and individual students by making a variety of materials, toys, activities, and even foods available to the students and noting the choices that are made. For example, Mr. Ledesma, a new third-grade teacher, has a particularly challenging group of students who have not yet responded to his informal classroom management attempts. He realizes that he needs a strong motivator for these students, so for 2 days, he provides a variety of group games, art supplies, instructional materials, and other activities for his students to use when they finish their work. He notes the most popular activities. The following week, Mr. Ledesma implements a system in which students can earn points for exhibiting rule-following behavior during class. Points may then be exchanged for those small- or large-group activities that were most popular during the reinforcer sampling phase.

In Ms. Sperry's sixth-grade resource class, all of her students are following the rules and completing their assignments except for Joseph. Joseph is new to the school, and Ms. Sperry has limited information on his behavioral and academic needs. Joseph talks tough, saying "I'm gonna kick some ____ if those punks don't leave me alone" and "They're gonna find out they better not mess with me." Joseph also refuses to do almost any work at all. Ms. Sperry knows that she needs to quickly find sufficient motivators for Joseph, so for a few days, she offers Joseph a wide range of activities and materials. For example, she lets him do jobs for her in the classroom and run errands that take him out of the classroom. She lets him choose which games he wants to play, special materials to use, and different places to sit. Throughout this period, she observes those activities and materials that Joseph seems to most enjoy and that he requests or talks about. Then Ms. Sperry begins assessing Joseph's academic skills. She allows Joseph access to those materials and activities that appear to be strong reinforcers, contingent upon his compliance with the assessment procedures. The results of the testing indicate that Joseph is reading at a beginning first-grade level, which may explain his noncompliance with academic tasks. As a result of this academic and reinforcement assessment process, Ms. Sperry now has information with which to plan academic and behavioral interventions for Joseph.

Unless your reinforcer assessment suggests otherwise, we encourage teachers to rely on social reinforcers, particularly activity reinforcers that are free and readily available. We have three reasons for this suggestion: First, we find that teachers who rely on food, pencils, posters, trinkets, toys, and other tangible reinforcers often spend a lot of their own money on these items. Some districts provide a small budget for reinforcement materials, but teachers typically supplement this budget out of their own pocket. Such an approach, however, is potentially very costly for the teacher. A second reason for relying on social reinforcers (perhaps the most important reason) is that activity reinforcers (e.g., games, special privileges, extra recess time, extra credit, get-out-of-work coupons) and social reinforcers (e.g., special recognition certificates, having lunch with the teacher or principal, being a teacher's helper) are typically more powerful than most material reinforcers. Yes, most students like stickers, posters, trinkets, and other material reinforcers; however, in our experience, students who are exposed to social and activity reinforcers prefer those types of reinforcers to material objects. Finally, social and activity reinforcers may be more appropriate when reinforcement systems are to be implemented in a general education environment. Because these types of activities are often used in general education, simply making them contingent upon targeted behaviors is less disruptive than using material or food reinforcers. Therefore, we encourage teachers to be creative in identifying free, easily available social and activity reinforcers for use with students of all ages.

It is important to remember that students will eventually tire of even the most attractive reinforcer. In behavioral terminology, this is referred to as **satiation**. When satiation occurs, the reinforcer loses its motivating power. We discuss how to avoid satiation in the section titled "How to Develop and Implement Reinforcement Systems," but basically, there must be some level of **deprivation** (i.e., students must be able to access the reinforcer only through the reinforcement system and, even then, only for a limited amount of time or in limited quantities). If students can have as much of the reinforcer as they want, they may no longer be motivated to work for the reinforcer in the future. Thus, successful reinforcement programs are a careful balance between deprivation and satiation.

SCHEDULES OF REINFORCEMENT

An important part of any reinforcement program is determining how frequently reinforcement will be given. Will every correct response result in reinforcement? Or, will reinforcement only be given after several correct responses? Or, perhaps reinforcement will be time based (i.e., given only after a certain amount of time has passed). The frequency of reinforcement, referred to as a **reinforcement schedule**, may affect the outcome of the reinforcement program and should be carefully planned as part of the overall reinforcement system. However, in our experience, many educators do not understand the significance of reinforcement schedules, and because of this, reinforcement interventions are often either ineffective or not maximally effective in controlling challenging behavior. In this section, we describe the different schedules of reinforcement and how to use them for classroom or individual behavior management.

There are basically two general types of reinforcement schedules: continuous and intermittent. In a **continuous schedule of reinforcement** (known by the behavioral shorthand **CRF**), every correct response is reinforced. On a CRF schedule, a student will receive reinforcement every time that he or she is in the assigned seat when the bell rings, brings materials to class, shares a toy, waits his or her turn in line, walks down the hall correctly, or whatever the targeted behavior may be. Continuous schedules of reinforcement are appropriate when one is teaching new behaviors to very young children; children with low cognition; or children who have a history of chronic, high-frequency behavioral problems. Even some older students may benefit from a continuous schedule of reinforcement when first learning a new, possibly difficult behavior. For example, a high school student who has a history of acting out may need reinforcement every time that he or she uses a self-control technique to control anger responses, accepts negative feedback, ignores taunts or teasing from peers, or exhibits other targeted behaviors if he or she is to learn to use those new behaviors in place of other unacceptable behaviors.

Although a continuous schedule of reinforcement is a powerful teaching tool, there are reasons that it should usually be considered a means to an end. First, there are few examples of continuous schedules of reinforcement in real life. Such a reinforcement schedule is seldom experienced in general education classrooms, work settings, among friends, or at home. Also, a continuous reinforcement schedule may be difficult or impossible to implement for long periods of time in a busy classroom environment. Finally, the adage "You can sometimes have too much of a good thing" may apply to continuous reinforcement schedules. A student who receives reinforcement for every appropriate behavior may soon experience satiation, rendering the reinforcer ineffective. For these reasons, a continuous schedule of reinforcement, for most students, should be thinned as soon as the student is consistently exhibiting the targeted behavior. **Thinning** the reinforcement schedule refers to gradually moving away from a **dense reinforcement schedule** (e.g., CRF) to an **intermittent schedule of reinforcement** in which some behaviors, but not every correct response, are reinforced. We explain how to thin reinforcement schedules later in the section.

Once the targeted behaviors are mastered through the use of continuous and/or intermittent reinforcement schedules, the goal should be to move to a nonscheduled or naturally occurring reinforcement schedule. The reinforcement is no longer delivered according to a planned schedule but instead is used in an unplanned manner. Most environments rely on nonscheduled reinforcement. Therefore, this should be the goal for most students with mild to moderate behavioral problems. However, because reinforcement in natural environments is typically quite sparse, students with severe cognitive or behavioral challenges may always be more successful with planned schedules of reinforcement.

> Thinning the reinforcement schedule in order to encourage more independent functioning.

There are three categories of intermittent schedules of reinforcement: ratio, interval, and response duration. Each category is appropriate for different types of behaviors or different types of goals, as explained next. These three schedules are also summarized in Table 10-4.

Ratio Schedule of Reinforcement. In **ratio schedules of reinforcement**, reinforcement is contingent upon a certain **number of targeted behaviors**. In a **fixed-ratio schedule (FR),** the student receives reinforcement after a **fixed number of behaviors** have been exhibited. An FR 4 schedule would imply that the student is reinforced after giving four correct responses. In an FR 10 schedule, reinforcement is delivered after every 10th correct response. A continuous schedule of reinforcement, as described previously, refers to an FR 1 schedule. An example of an FR ratio schedule can be seen in Ms. Hernadez's classroom where her students earn class store points for each 10 sight words that they learn. Each Friday, Ms. Hernandez assesses each student's fluency with regard to sight words. Ms. Hernandez or her paraprofessional works individually with the students, presenting each student with sight words (i.e., phonetically irregular words, such as *were, the, have*) that have been previously introduced. Each card that the student reads quickly (e.g., within 5 seconds) and correctly is placed in the "correct" stack. Afterwards, the number of cards in this stack are counted and the student earns 1 point for each 10 cards. The points are added to the other points that the student has earned during the week (e.g., for following the rules or for completing assignments), and points may be used to purchase special activities and privileges from the class store.

A second form of ratio scheduling is a **variable-ratio schedule (VR)**, in which an **average number of responses** is reinforced. A student on a VR 3 schedule would receive reinforcement after an average of every three responses. For example, Michael is on a VR 3 schedule for answering questions during group

TABLE 10-4 Types of Reinforcement Schedules

Schedule	Type of Behaviors	Description	Advantages	Disadvantages	Example
Continuous	Any	All instances of behavior are reinforced	Quickly builds new behaviors	May result in satiation	Ms. Fisher gives Ayesha a small piece of cereal each time that she imitates a sound correctly.
Ratio					
Fixed ratio	Discrete behaviors that are measured using event recording	Reinforcement is delivered following a predetermined number of correct responses	Produces high rates of response	Students may sacrifice accuracy in an effort to respond more quickly; post-reinforcement pause	Anthony earns an extra-credit point for every five assignments that he turns in on time.
Variable ratio	Same as above	An average number of correct responses is reinforced	Avoids the problems of inaccurate responses and post-reinforcement pause	May be difficult to monitor when the teacher is responsible for groups of students with little or no assistance	During oral reading, Mr. Campbell awards a group point for an accurate reading. He determines the reinforcement ratio (e.g., after three sentences read correctly), then reinforces after an average of three sentences (e.g., after two sentences, then after six sentences, then after three sentences).
Interval					
Fixed interval	Either discrete or continuous behaviors	Reinforcement is given for the first instance of the targeted behavior following a set period of time	May be more feasible in certain classrooms than ratio schedules	No rein-forcement is available for behaviors that occur during the "no reinforcement" interval, which may result in lower levels of behavior during those times, followed by an increase in behavior just before the interval ends	Mr. Jacobs is teaching his students to use their newly learned social skills on the playground. He divides the recess period into 5-minute intervals. At the end of each interval, he reinforces the first student whom he observes using one of the class social skills.

Variable interval	Same as above	Intervals average a predetermined number of minutes	Avoids the problems associated with fixed-interval reinforcement	May be difficult to monitor the varying interval lengths	Mr. Jacobs also reinforces the use of appropriate conversational skills during lunch. He has divided the 20-minute lunch period into averaged 4-minute intervals (2 minutes, 8 minutes, 4 minutes, etc.). The first student who uses appropriate conversation at the end of each interval earns a sticker.
Response duration					
Fixed response duration	Continuous behaviors	Reinforcement is delivered following a predetermined amount of time that the targeted behavior is exhibited	Relatively easy to implement in all types of settings	May produce post-reinforcement pause after reinforcement	JP earns a star on his card for every 10 minutes that he is on task during independent work time.
Variable response duration	Same as above	Reinforcement is based on an average duration of the targeted behavior	Avoids post-reinforcement pause	May be difficult to monitor the varying lengths of behavior	Ava is praised at the end of intervals during which she has used only appropriate words for the entire interval. Intervals average 10 minutes in length.
Nonscheduled reinforcement	All	The timing of reinforcement is unplanned	Easy to use, reflects natural environments	Reinforcement may be insufficient to maintain the targeted behaviors	From time to time, when she thinks about it, Ms. Schwartz praises Jia-Li for keeping her hands to herself when she is sitting next to her peers.

instruction. Michael's teacher reinforces him after his second answer, then following his fourth, third, fourth, and second responses, which result in an average of every three responses being reinforced. A variable schedule may be a little more difficult for teachers to implement but avoids one problem associated with fixed schedules of reinforcement: post-reinforcement pause. **Post-reinforcement pause** refers to the tendency of individuals to stop responding immediately following reinforcement when the reinforcement schedule is predictable. The unpredictable nature of a VR schedule should avoid post-reinforcement pause.

Interval Schedule of Reinforcement.   **Interval schedules** are based on the passage of a certain amount of time in order to determine the timing of reinforcement. In a **fixed-interval schedule (FI)**, reinforcement is delivered immediately following the first instance of the targeted behavior after a predetermined amount of time. For example, Hodari's teacher is reinforcing Hodari on an FI 10-minute schedule for playing appropriately with toys. The teacher sets the timer for 10 minutes. When the timer sounds, the teacher immediately observes Hodari and reinforces him as soon as she sees him using a toy correctly. Then the timer is reset for another 10 minutes. Abby is on an FI 30-minute schedule for speaking appropriately to her peers. After the 30-minute interval, Abby receives reinforcement for the first appropriate comment that she directs toward her peers. Then another 30-minute interval begins. Mr. Smith is the assistant coach for a neighborhood football team for 8- to 10-year-olds. He instructed the children to make sportsmanlike comments to teammates on and off the field. He praises the first appropriate comment made after 10-minute intervals.

One interesting problem encountered in using an FI schedule is known as a **fixed-interval scallop**. This refers to the phenomenon whereby the targeted behavior is likely to increase immediately before the end of the interval (hence the "scallop" effect), especially when the student is aware of the time interval. A **variable-interval schedule (VI)** avoids the problem. In a VI schedule, the intervals average a predetermined number of minutes. Consider Ms. Felton's use of a VI schedule to increase on-task behavior in her high school biology class. Ms. Felton began her intervention with a 15-minute schedule. During time spent in the laboratory, Ms. Felton sets the timer to sound an average of every 15 minutes. As soon as she observes that all of the students are on task following the sounding of the timer, she records a point on the class chart and then resets the timer. She has calculated the interval lengths in advance (e.g., 20 minutes, 10 minutes, 15 minutes, 12 minutes, 18 minutes). If the class earns 25 points by Friday, they have reduced homework over the weekend. Ms. Felton justifies this reinforcer to her administrator with data which show that since this system has been in force, her students' on-task time and task completion have increased dramatically.

> Response-duration schedules are designed to increase how long a behavior is exhibited.

Response-Duration Schedules of Reinforcement.   **Response-duration schedules** are designed to increase the duration of a targeted behavior: Reinforcement is contingent upon the targeted behavior being exhibited for a predetermined **amount of time**. A **fixed-response-duration schedule (FRD)** means that a behavior is reinforced following a fixed amount of time. An FRD 5-minute schedule would mean that the student receives reinforcement after exhibiting 5 continuous minutes of the targeted behavior. For example, Mr. Udori reinforced Rana on an FRD 10-minute schedule for wearing her glasses: He set the timer for 10 minutes; if Rana kept her glasses on for the entire 10 minutes, she earned reinforcement when the timer sounded. The timer was then reset for another 10 minutes. If she removed her glasses during the 10-minute interval, Mr. Udori prompted her to put her glasses on, and the timer was reset. Students in Ms. Carroll's class are on an FRD 30-minute schedule: They earn a break after 30 minutes of on-task behavior. The length of the response duration required for reinforcement will depend on the age of the student, the duration goal for the targeted behavior, and the current duration levels of the behavior.

A **variable-response-duration schedule (VRD)** is based on an average length of time for the response duration intervals. A VRD 5-minute schedule means that the student is reinforced when the targeted behavior is exhibited for intervals that average 5 minutes (e.g., 4 minutes, then 7 minutes, then 3 minutes, then 6 minutes).

The goal is for students to be successful under a naturally occurring schedule of reinforcement. For this reason, teachers should carefully plan to move from more dense schedules of reinforcement to gradually thinner schedules. A common error in using reinforcement is to thin the reinforcement schedule too quickly. This causes **ratio strain**, which refers to a phenomenon whereby the behaviors are not maintained under the new, thinner schedules of reinforcement. This may be because teachers or others are excited about the positive changes produced by the initial reinforcement and overestimate their students' ability to maintain the newly learned (or newly strengthened) behaviors. If students stop responding after a newly introduced delay in reinforcement, it may be because the reinforcement schedule was thinned too dramatically (i.e., reinforcement was made too difficult to obtain). To address the problem, return to a more immediate reinforcement schedule for a time and then thin the schedule more gradually in the future.

Thinning the reinforcement schedule is not difficult: Just gradually increase the number of behaviors required before reinforcement, the amount of time to elapse before reinforcement, or the duration of the behavior that must occur before reinforcement. The following examples illustrate thinning for each of the three categories of reinforcement schedules:

- *Fixed ratio and variable ratio.* Mr. Keller reinforces his world history class on an FR 2 schedule for arriving to class on time. That is, every 2 days, if all students are in their seats when the bell rings, the class earns a point toward a Friday group instructional game to review facts and concepts learned during the week. Students have been on time for 6 days in a row, so Mr. Keller now changes to a VR 4 schedule. After 6 consecutive days of on-time arrivals on that schedule, he will further thin the schedule to a VR 8.
- *Fixed interval and variable interval.* Tony is a third-grader who rushes through his work, making many careless mistakes. To teach Tony to work more slowly and carefully, his teacher, Ms. Fawcett, uses an FI 5-minute schedule during independent work time. She sets a timer for 5 minutes and then puts a sticker on Tony's paper for the first correct academic response that he writes on his paper after the timer sounds. Tony has responded well to this system, seldom making mistakes because of rushing, so Ms. Fawcett is now thinning the reinforcement to a VI 10-minute schedule. She has developed a schedule of interval lengths (e.g., 5 minutes, 10 minutes, 8 minutes, 15 minutes, 12 minutes) to follow during his work time.
- *Fixed response duration and variable response duration.* Mr. Rubio teaches middle school students with emotional and behavioral disorders. These students have been experiencing problems at lunchtime, throwing and playing with food. Mr. Rubio knows that if the problems continue, his students will not be allowed to eat in the cafeteria. So, Mr. Rubio implements a reinforcement program based on a fixed-response-duration schedule. Mr. Rubio eats lunch at a separate table from his students, but he can see them clearly. For

the first phase of the program, he sets a timer for 5 minutes (FRD 5-minute schedule). If his students exhibit appropriate cafeteria behavior (which he had taught before beginning the program) for the entire 5-minute interval, he records a point on a class point card. If, during the 5-minute interval, any student breaks the cafeteria rules, he records that student's name and the behavior, and then resets the timer. During the 30-minute lunch period, students can earn a maximum of 6 points, or 30 points for the week. By Friday, if the class has earned 27 points or more (90% of the 30 possible points), they get to play basketball after lunch. If not, they must return to their classroom for afternoon work. His students' cafeteria behavior has improved so significantly (they have earned 27 points or more for 3 consecutive weeks) that he is now thinning the reinforcement to a VRD 15-minute schedule. The timer will be set for intervals that average 15 minutes. Because the intervals will now be longer, the required weekly point total will be reduced.

The reinforcement schedule that you choose depends, in part, on the nature of the behavior being reinforced and, in part, on teacher preference. Discrete behaviors that are counted using event recording may be reinforced on ratio or interval schedules. Ratio schedules allow the teacher to precisely control the number of behaviors that a student must display before reinforcement occurs. However, ratio schedules may be difficult to implement in a busy classroom where the teacher is responsible for teaching small or large groups of students. Under such circumstances, an interval schedule would be more feasible for the teacher. Interval schedules are also more appropriate for ongoing or continuous behaviors that are measured using interval recording or time sampling. When the goal is to increase or decrease the time during which a behavior is exhibited, duration recording is the appropriate measurement system and a response-duration schedule is the appropriate reinforcement schedule. Latency-type behaviors (measured with latency recording) would appropriately be reinforced using ratio schedules. For example, Katy receives reinforcement on a VR 5 schedule for complying with teacher requests within 2 minutes. This means that the teacher records her compliance time and reinforces Katy on an average of every five responses that are within 2 minutes. After several days on a VR 5 schedule for compliance within 2 minutes, the teacher reduces the compliance time to 1 minute. Katy is now reinforced on a VR 5 schedule on an average of every five times that she complies within 1 minute. Because compliance within 1 minute was the goal for Katy, once she exhibits 3 days of compliance within 1 minute on a VR 5 schedule, the teacher begins to thin the reinforcement schedule to VR 10, then VR 15, and then nonscheduled reinforcement.

HOW TO DEVELOP AND IMPLEMENT REINFORCEMENT SYSTEMS

Like any technique, there are certain steps to follow in developing reinforcement systems:

1. Identify the types of problems that need to be addressed. Are the behavioral concerns for a class (i.e., a group) or for one or more individual students? Reinforcement systems can be for groups of students or individual students, or both, depending on the nature of the problems.

TABLE 10-5 Common Classroom Behavioral Problems and Possible Replacement Behaviors

Problem	Replacement Behavior
Group	
• Tardies	• Be in seat when bell rings
• Off-task behavior	• Remain on-task during work time
• Calling out during lessons	• Raise hand and wait for permission to talk
• Making mean or unkind comments to one another	• Make kind, helpful, or encouraging comments
• Not following the rules	• Follow the rules
• Not following directions	• Follow directions within a specified amount of time
• Unruly transitions	• Move from one activity to the next within a specified amount of time, with no loud talking, touching, or playing
• Running, horseplay in the hall	• Walk on the right side of the hall and keep your hands to yourself
Individual	
• Refusing to work	• Complete assignments on time
• Ripping up paper when frustrated	• Ask for help when frustrated
• Leaving class without permission when upset	• Ask for a break or ask to talk to the teacher privately
• Talking about inappropriate topics (e.g., drugs, sexual comments)	• Talk only about appropriate school topics
• Fighting	• Ignore provocations, walk away, or use words to solve problems
• Cursing	• Use appropriate expressions of frustration, excitement, or emphasis

In general, when problems arise, consider taking replacement behaviors from the following areas:

• Classroom and schoolwide rules

• Procedures

• Appropriate social behaviors

• Communicative behaviors (e.g., words, sign language, other forms of communication) to express feelings

• Academic behaviors (e.g., task completion, task accuracy, participation in group activities, participation in lessons)

2. For each of the problems in which you wish to intervene, identify the targeted replacement behavior: What do you want the student(s) to do instead of the problem behavior? Table 10-5 lists common classroom and individual behavioral problems and possible replacement behaviors for each. As discussed in Chapter 3, replacement behaviors should enable students to attain

the same consequences as are currently maintaining the inappropriate behaviors (e.g., attention, escape, status, control). Also, as described in Chapter 2, targeted behaviors should be socially significant for students. That is, the behaviors targeted for intervention should be those behaviors that will increase students' academic and social success in school and in other environments.

3. Select those behaviors which have a high priority for intervention. It is acceptable, even necessary, to have more than one reinforcement system in place in order to address more than one problem area. However, too many different systems, or too many different targeted behaviors within the same system, will be confusing to the students *and* the teacher, which probably means that the reinforcement system will not be used consistently. Also, the ethical use of positive reinforcement requires that we select socially meaningful behaviors for change. This means that behaviors targeted for change should be important for students' success in academic, social, and behavioral contexts. A targeted behavior of "sit in your seat and be quiet" probably does not meet this criterion, whereas a targeted behavior of "finish all of your assignments on time" does. In selecting behaviors for intervention, consider certain broader targets that may encompass more specific behaviors. For example, targeting the rule "follow directions" might address transitions (e.g., follow the teacher's instructions for each transition), hall behavior (e.g., follow the instructions given by the teacher about how to walk in the hall), or work behavior (e.g., "complete all of the exercises on page 47," "use complete sentences," "show your work"). Using one system to reinforce "following directions" is more efficient than using multiple systems to address each of those separate behaviors.

   A final note about selecting a targeted behavior: Remember to describe the targeted behavior in operational terms, as discussed in Chapter 3. For example, if the targeted behavior is "follow directions," the students (and all of the adults who will be implementing the reinforcement plan) should understand exactly what that means.

4. For each behavior that will be addressed by the reinforcement system, collect a few days of baseline data. This is especially important for individual reinforcement systems that target the behaviors listed in the student's individualized educational program or behavior intervention plan. Use one of the data collection systems from Chapter 4 in order to monitor the behavior.

5. Develop one or more reinforcement systems to address the targeted behaviors that have the highest priority. Your reinforcement system(s) might be for the entire group (e.g., reinforcing the group when all of the students arrive to class on time), for individual students, or for a combination of the two. In Chapter 11, we describe how to implement specific reinforcement systems, such as the Premack Principle, token economies, contracts, and group reinforcement systems, and give many examples for each. In general, however, a reinforcement system should be easy to use and fun or interesting for the students.

6. Use one or more of the methods for identifying reinforcers that were discussed previously in this chapter. Depending on the reinforcement system, one reinforcer might be offered for each reinforcement period (e.g., students can earn time in which to play basketball for each week during which all

assignments are turned in on time), or students might be allowed to choose from among multiple reinforcers (e.g., a student who follows the rules every day during recess may choose from among three different reinforcers on Friday). Remember that we encourage teachers to depend primarily on free social and activity reinforcers.

Also, plan to use a variety of reinforcers in your reinforcement system. No matter how much a reinforcer appeals to students, if that reinforcer is overused, the students will eventually become satiated with regard to the reinforcer and it will no longer have motivating power. There are two ways in which to avoid this. One is to offer several different reinforcers for each reinforcement period, and when students earn a reinforcer, allow them to select the one that they prefer. Another way to avoid satiation is to vary the reinforcers from one reinforcement period to the next. This is especially important if only one reinforcer is offered for each reinforcement period.

7. Determine the schedule of reinforcement. Will you use a ratio, interval, or response-duration schedule? Will you begin with a fixed schedule and later move to a variable schedule? Remember to err on the side of reinforcement density: Do not begin with a very thin reinforcement schedule, because it could cause your reinforcement system to fail from the start. It is more effective and efficient to reinforce frequently at first and then thin the schedule to offer less reinforcement as students exhibit higher levels of targeted behaviors.

8. Teach the system to your students. Explain the rationale for why the program is needed, how it works, and what students will earn. Modeling and role-playing the targeted behaviors and subsequent reinforcement are a good idea. For example, the teacher might have the paraprofessional or another adult model make a positive comment to someone (or whatever the targeted behavior might be), which the teacher then reinforces with a token. The adults might also model what happens when the targeted behaviors are *not* exhibited. For example, a paraprofessional might model refusing to work, to which the teacher would respond, "I'm sorry that you do not want to work. I can't give you a ticket for our daily drawing unless you finish your assignment on time."

9. Implement the system. Be sure to use the system regularly and consistently, make access to reinforcers contingent upon targeted behaviors, and always follow through with the delivery of the reinforcers when earned. **Contingent** means that students can only get the reinforcer by exhibiting the targeted behaviors at the specified criterion level, which is critical to the success of reinforcement programs. If students can access the reinforcers without exhibiting the targeted behaviors, those reinforcers will soon lose their motivational value.

10. Monitor the effects of the system on the targeted behaviors. Continue to collect sample data on the targeted behaviors. If those behaviors are changing in the desired direction, determine when to begin thinning the reinforcement schedule. If targeted behaviors are not changing, consider the problems that might be occurring during implementation, which are discussed in the next section, and use the questions for problem solving in order to self-evaluate the implementation.

PROBLEM SOLVING WHEN A REINFORCEMENT SYSTEM DOES NOT PRODUCE THE DESIRED RESULTS

Sometimes reinforcement systems initially do not produce the desired results. This does not mean that reinforcement systems do not work. Typically, it means that one or more common problems have occurred that can be easily addressed. Sometimes there is an initial improvement in behavior and then the system appears to stop working. It is not uncommon for students, either groups or individuals, to experience a "honeymoon period" when first placed on a reinforcement program. For awhile (a week, 2 weeks, or shorter or longer, depending on the students), it seems as though the system has solved all of the behavioral problems that led to the need to use such a system. Then those same problems, or similar problems, begin to reappear. Students no longer are motivated by the reinforcers. Usually, all this means is that the students are beginning to test the system: Do they *really* have to exhibit the targeted behaviors in order to obtain the reinforcer? This is especially true when the targeted behaviors are new to or are challenging for the students. In our experience, teachers who encounter this situation often abandon the reinforcement program as just another idea that does not work. This is a mistake. The most important step to take when the system appears to be ineffective is to keep it in place for awhile while continuing to collect data. The students may need to experience *not* earning reinforcers a few times in order to learn that those reinforcers are, in fact, wholly contingent upon the targeted behaviors. Of course, if the students do not once again begin to demonstrate those targeted behaviors after a few instances of not earning reinforcers then the teacher should follow the steps for problem solving that are described in the next section.

What should you do if a reinforcement plan is not working?

Here are some issues that may arise and the appropriate responses for addressing them:

Students Complain About the Reinforcement Program or State That They Do Not Care About the Reinforcers.   The best advice with regard to this situation is to pay little attention to the students' words and much more attention to the students' behavior. If the data indicate that their behavior is improving, the system is working. Complaining about the system or appearing to dislike or not care about the reinforcers is not unusual, particularly for students with a long history of challenging behavior. This behavior may allow students a certain amount of status with their peers or the feeling of being in control. It is important to rely on objective data in order to make decisions about changing the system.

You Discover the Presence of Unintended Consequences Within the System.   This problem should be easily solved. For example, consider Ms. Long's reinforcement program for her middle school resource class. Her system enabled students to earn tickets for completing their work on time and then exchange those tickets for the privilege of participating in desired activities during the remainder of the class period. But she omitted a critical criterion: the accuracy of their work. She soon learned that students would rush to finish their work, but that their work was sloppy and inaccurate. She easily remedied the problem by adding the rule that the work had to be neat and 80% accurate before a ticket would be given. You should inform your students when teaching the reinforcement system that you, as the teacher, reserve the right to improve the system at any time.

You Discover Loopholes in the System.   This problem is easy to remedy: Close the loopholes! Ms. Montoya learned that sometimes unanticipated problems arise in a reinforcement program. Ms. Montoya allowed Brianna to earn happy face stamps for staying in her seat, completing her assignments, and using appropriate language when talking to peers. If she earned 25 stamps by Friday, she earned a special activity with a friend. Brianna's behavior was almost perfect Monday, Tuesday, and Wednesday. She had earned her 25 stamps by early Thursday afternoon. Things went downhill after that. Brianna refused to stay in her seat, did not do her work, and reverted to her old habit of calling peers by various animal names. But when Friday arrived, Brianna presented her card filled with happy face stamps to Ms. Montoya in order to access her activity. Poor Ms. Montoya! It appeared that Brianna had quickly learned how to "game the system." To her credit, Ms. Montoya made the correct decision: She allowed Brianna to earn the activity despite the intervening inappropriate behavior. Of course, the next week, Ms. Montoya explained the new rules to Brianna: She must earn 35 stamps in order to obtain the activity, *plus* all of her assignments must be completed. Also, for each animal name directed at a peer, Brianna would lose 1 minute of her activity time.

You Realize That the Reinforcement Schedule is Too Dense or Too Thin.   If this occurs, simply change the reinforcement schedule. For example, Mr. Garcia implemented a reinforcement system to encourage his second-grade class to follow the playground rules. If they followed all of the playground rules for a month, they earned a double recess. Unfortunately, he learned that this FI 1-month schedule was too long for his young students to wait for reinforcement. He quickly changed the reinforcement schedule to an FI 1-day schedule: For each day that students followed the playground rules, they earned an extra 5 minutes of recess on Friday. Once his students were successful on that schedule, he planned to move to an FI 2-day schedule, in which students would earn extra recess minutes for every 2 days of appropriate recess behavior. Then he would move to a fixed-interval schedule of 1 week.

Students Begin Asking for or Demanding the Reinforcers.   Teachers often find that students ask for reinforcement. For example, a student might try to negotiate, "If I do this, can I have extra time on the computer?" We do not view this as a bad thing; on the contrary, we like students to solicit reinforcement for a job well done. Most of us have attempted to obtain extra reinforcers: asking our parents to allow us to use the car or asking for a raise in allowance, asking an employer for a raise, or (for a teacher) asking the principal to relax the "no jeans" rule. These are all examples of soliciting reinforcers. Rather than viewing a student who asks for a reinforcer as a challenge, we see it as evidence that the reinforcer is truly motivating for the student. Remember, the teacher is always in charge and can agree to allow the student access to the reinforcer or not.

If a student's request for a reinforcer sounds more like a demand (e.g., "I won't finish my work unless I get to sit next to Sarah"), the teacher should simply remind the student about the consequences of this behavior (e.g., "You may not sit next to Sarah. However, if you choose not to work, you will have to finish your work as homework"). Also, if the demanding behavior continues, a behavior re-duction consequence could be implemented. Behavior reduction consequences will be explained in Chapter 12, but in the example just given, the student might lose 1 minute of recess time for each demand made.

If the reinforcement system still does not produce the desired change in be-havior after attempting to address these problems, or if the problems do not appear to be the source of the ineffectiveness, the following steps for problem solving should help to resolve the issue:

1. Have you described the targeted behaviors in operational terms? This allows the teacher to be consistent in enforcing the rules of the reinforcement sys-tem and in reinforcing the desired behaviors.
2. Have you been consistent in implementing the system and in delivering the reinforcer? Inconsistency in implementing the system is analogous to using an unplanned schedule of reinforcement. Although that will probably be your eventual goal, starting at that point will be unproductive, especially for students or groups exhibiting high levels of challenging behavior.
3. Are the reinforcers contingent upon the targeted behavior? If the reinforcer is available noncontingently (i.e., no targeted behavior need occur in order for the student to get the reinforcer), the entire reinforcement system is under-mined and will probably be ineffective.
4. Are the reinforcers that you have selected truly reinforcing (i.e., truly moti-vating for the students)? How do you know? What process did you use to determine effective reinforcers? One explanation for the failure of a rein-forcement system is that students lose interest in the reinforcer. If you have assessed reinforcers only on the basis of student input, you may need to use another, more objective source in order to obtain reinforcement data, such as observing the students. Also, have you provided a variety of reinforcers in order to avoid satiation? Remember that students will tire of having the same reinforcer used repeatedly.
5. Are one or two students undermining the success of your reinforcement sys-tem? If so, there are specific steps that you can take, which we describe in Chapter 11 when we discuss group reinforcement systems.

NEGATIVE REINFORCEMENT

Negative reinforcement is *not* punishment!

Up to this point, we have focused on the use of positive reinforcement to main-tain, increase, or strengthen behaviors. Another form of reinforcement, negative reinforcement, also maintains or increases behavior but through a different process. **Negative reinforcement (S^{R-})** involves the removal or avoidance of an aversive or negative stimulus once a behavior occurs. That is, there is an aversive or unpleasant condition in place (or even the potential for such a condition). Once a particular behavior occurs, that aversive or unpleasant condition ends or the in-dividual avoids the unpleasant condition. The term *negative reinforcement* is often used erroneously as a synonym for punishment. As you will learn in Chapter 12, punishment occurs when a consequence that follows a behavior reduces the like-lihood that the behavior will be repeated (i.e., punishment reduces the behavior). Despite the use of the adjective *negative* in the term, negative reinforcement is a form of reinforcement, which means that it serves to *maintain* or *increase* a targeted behavior. *Negative* refers to the presence of the aversive, negative, or disliked stimulus that is in place prior to the behavior. The following diagram illustrates the negative reinforcement process:

Negative stimulus ⟶ Behavior ⟶ ~~Negative stimulus~~

Negative reinforcement is considered to be a form of reinforcement because escaping, terminating, or avoiding the negative stimulus increases the likelihood that the individual will exhibit that same behavior the next time that the same negative stimulus is encountered. The scenarios that follow illustrate negative reinforcement. For each scenario, identify the aversive stimulus and the behavior that produces escape, termination, or avoidance of that stimulus.

- Ellie, who is doing quite well on her new diet, goes to the grand opening of an upscale supermarket. As part of the grand opening festivities, numerous free food samples are offered throughout the store. Ellie begins walking through the aisles, but the constant temptation of the free food samples soon becomes aversive, so she quickly leaves the store.
- Marcus recently broke up with his girlfriend. They used to go to the same gym, but Marcus switched gyms soon after the breakup. The possibility of encountering his former girlfriend there was just too painful.
- Caleb hates to write. Each morning, his second-grade teacher poses a question to which the students are to respond during journal writing time (i.e., the first 10 minutes of class). Typically, Caleb complains about the writing task. Sometimes he even cries, saying woefully, "I hate this junk. I'm just no good at writing." His teacher usually responds to his laments with gentle encouragement and a compromise: If Caleb will just write a few sentences in his journal, those sentences are all he will be asked to write that day.
- Tasha is painfully shy and seldom interacts with her peers. She strongly dislikes the crowded school cafeteria because she is the only student who eats alone. Tasha has begun taking her lunch to school and eating outside in the courtyard at a table by herself.
- Dante is loud and disruptive during Mr. Williams' world history class. Several times each week, Mr. Williams sends Dante to the office because of his behavior. Mr. Williams is always relieved when Dante leaves, because then he can finally focus on teaching!

Negative reinforcement can involve the removal of or escape from an existing aversive stimulus or avoidance of a potentially negative stimulus. In our examples, Ellie, Caleb, and Mr. Williams each escaped or terminated a negative stimulus as a result of their behavior. Marcus and Tasha each avoided a potentially aversive stimulus.

Negative reinforcement is often found in school situations in both planned applications (e.g., students may not go to recess until their work is completed; a student must remain in time-out until his tantrum ends) and unplanned, informal situations (e.g., a teacher allows a student to sleep in class because trying to wake him is difficult, and the student is difficult to manage when he is awake; a teacher avoids the teachers' lounge because she does not like how other teachers talk about certain students). We usually advise teachers to avoid planned, systematic use of negative reinforcement. Certainly, negative reinforcement effectively maintains or increases a behavior; however, to achieve that result, the teacher must design a negative situation. We prefer that teachers focus on how to motivate students through the use of positive reinforcement systems.

Summary

In this chapter, we explained basic concepts and practices related to reinforcement. The following are the chapter objectives and a summary of how each objective was addressed:

1. Define reinforcement terminology and give examples of positive reinforcement, primary reinforcer, secondary reinforcer, pairing, negative reinforcement, reinforcement schedules, and thinning.

These are the basic terms used in discussing reinforcement. We defined each term and urged educators to incorporate these terms into their professional vocabulary. These terms describe both the processes (e.g., positive reinforcement, negative reinforcement) and tools (e.g., reinforcers, pairing, reinforcement schedules, thinning) used in reinforcement applications.

2. Provide a rationale for using reinforcement, as well as rebuttals for those who argue against the use of reinforcement in school.

We described a few of the more common arguments that you may encounter. Resistance to reinforcement is usually founded on a lack of understanding of the correct use of reinforcement, misperceptions about reinforcement, or misinformation about reinforcement. None of the arguments commonly used against reinforcement are based on research. On the contrary, much evidence supports the rebuttals that we provided.

Educators must be knowledgeable about the correct, ethical use of reinforcement in order to obtain effective outcomes from reinforcement systems and in order to respond in an articulate, informed manner when encountering resistance to using reinforcement.

3. Describe how to use reinforcement.

Like any tool, reinforcement can be used correctly or incorrectly. The ramifications of incorrect use are, at best, that desired behaviors may not improve and, at worst, that undesirable behaviors may actually be strengthened. Educators should always monitor their use of reinforcement. When reinforcement does not produce the desired results, it is a signal that perhaps some aspect of the design or implementation of the reinforcement program was incorrect or needs to be adjusted.

4. Describe the steps used in problem solving when reinforcement contingencies fail to produce the desired outcomes.

Sometimes a reinforcement plan does not produce the desired results. This does not mean that reinforcement does not work. Rather, this is an indication that one or more of the explanations we provided are at work or that the reinforcement system was not implemented correctly. Addressing the common problems that we described or following our steps for problem solving should remedy the problem.

Dr. ICE Helps Teachers Learn About the Power of Positive Reinforcement

ELEMENTARY SCHOOL

Ms. Hart teaches a class of 10 students who are in grades 1–3. Academically and emotionally, these students function at a prekindergarten to first-grade level.

Ms. Hart uses several instructional activities while teaching. On a recent visit with Dr. ICE, she talked about her concern that her students are taking up too much class time moving from one setting or activity to another. Dr. ICE suggested that she reinforce the students who complete the transition in what she determines to be an appropriate amount of time.

She began to plan by generating a list of possible reinforcers. She used her knowledge of her students to help brainstorm a list of reinforcers that she could realistically use in her classroom. Then she worked with Dr. ICE to determine the appropriate reinforcement schedule to use. Dr. ICE suggested that she use a continuous schedule of reinforcement and then gradually thin the reinforcement to an intermittent schedule of reinforcement. He recommended using an FR 1 schedule first: Students earn a star on a chart each time that they complete a transition in the time allotted by Ms. Hart. After 3 days of successful transitions, Dr. ICE recommended that Ms. Hart move to an FR 3, then an FR 5. At that point, she should use a VR 5 schedule. He recommended these schedules because her students are young. Also, it would not be too difficult for her to implement this plan because she would not have to interrupt a lesson in order to reinforce behavior. Ms. Hart agreed and left feeling very positive about the potential changes in her students' behavior.

MIDDLE SCHOOL

Ms. Marino teaches eighth-grade resource mathematics. She has a policy that students who finish all of their work with 80% accuracy or better do not have homework for that night (negative reinforcement). Most of her students love this policy and work very hard in class.

However, when Dr. ICE visited with Ms. Marino, she told him that a small group of students has begun to act out after a new student enrolled in her class. The new student, she said, does not act out in an aggressive or rude manner. He just talks and socializes as much as possible during independent work time; he acts as though talking to his peers, the paraprofessional, or the teacher is the best thing in the world. She said that, apparently, he pays attention to her direct teaching, because his homework is always of high quality. Dr. ICE made two suggestions: First, he helped Ms. Marino design a reinforcement plan that would help reduce the student's talking and increase on-task behavior during independent work time. Second, he suggested that Ms. Marino learn more about the young man's life outside of school.

Ms. Marino has never been able to contact the parent of this student, so she asked the school social worker to do a family social history. When she received the report, this student's behavior began to make sense.

This student is an only child whose single mother works the 2 to 10 P.M. shift. A neighbor in the next apartment is available to look in on him, but most of the time, he is alone. He told the school social worker that he likes his new school because it has a homework hotline that he can call anytime that he needs help with his work. With a little prodding, he confided to the school social worker that he is lonely at night and that doing his homework helps him pass the time until his mother comes home. He said that he often calls the homework hotline just so he can talk with someone. He also said that he especially enjoys Ms. Marino's class because he has friends that he can laugh and talk with. He said that he doesn't mind the extra homework because he likes mathematics and it is something fun for him to do at home.

Ms. Marino worked with the school social worker to help the student's mother get night supervision for the youngster. In her classroom, she has implemented a system in which any students in the class who finish their work quietly and accurately can earn "talk time" for 3 minutes at the end of each period. This simple system helps to increase on-task behavior for all students and allows the new student the opportunity to socialize with his new friends.

HIGH SCHOOL

Mr. Stead teaches 10th-grade resource history. He has been teaching for almost 30 years. This year, his fifth-period class is almost impossible to teach. The students in this class often refuse to follow his directions and he is seldom able to finish his lesson plan.

Mr. Stead's principal called in Dr. ICE to consult with Mr. Stead. The principal warned Dr. ICE that Mr. Stead is "set in his ways" and believes that students should do what they are told, when they are told to do it. Dr. ICE felt sure that he could convince Mr. Stead to use a reinforcement system in order to change the behavior of his students.

Dr. ICE met with Mr. Stead a few days after the principal's call. Mr. Stead began the conversation by telling Dr. ICE that he does not believe in treating his students like babies, bribing them to be good. They just need to settle down and behave. Dr. ICE asked him to listen as he gave examples of everyday reinforcers. The first was Mr. Stead's paycheck. He agreed that, as much as he loves teaching, he would not work for free. Then Dr. ICE asked him why he attends staff development sessions each year. First, he said that he attends the sessions because he will be written up if he does not go, but then he said that he often gets good

TABLE 10-6   Reinforcement Theory Self-Assessment

Never	Seldom	Sometimes	Often	Always
1	2	3	4	5

Use the numbers from the scale above to rate the following statements:

1. I use reinforcement terminology to describe my reinforcement system to others.   _____
2. I know which reinforcers work well for each of my students.   _____
3. I use functional assessment data in order to select reinforcers.   _____
4. I use high rates of praise with all of my students.   _____
5. I systematically follow reinforcement schedules as part of my reinforcement system.   _____
6. I can describe the steps to use in problem solving when my reinforcement program does   _____
   not produce the desired results.
7. I know how to address the common concerns about reinforcement.   _____
8. I can recognize examples of negative reinforcement in school situations.   _____
9. I systematically thin the reinforcement schedules.   _____
10. I am aware of and can use my personal reinforcers in order to change one of my own   _____
    behaviors.

information from the sessions. Dr. ICE then asked him if he prepares for his history lesson before his classes or if he "wings it." Mr. Stead said that, of course, he prepares and that he likes feeling prepared.

Dr. ICE then pointed out several of the reinforcers that are an important part of Mr. Stead's professional life: his paycheck, the learning opportunities at staff development sessions, and the satisfaction that he feels from being prepared to teach a wonderful history lesson. Then he asked Mr. Stead to imagine that these reinforcers were taken away—that he was expected to continue to do the work, but that he would not be receiving the extrinsic (e.g., his paycheck) and intrinsic (e.g., the feeling of satisfaction) reinforcers that he had come to expect. Would he be as involved? As dedi-

cated? They talked for the remainder of Dr. ICE's visit about natural reinforcers and the difference between what reinforces an adult versus a teenager. By the end of the meeting, Mr. Stead realized that using reinforcement is not bribing, and he and Dr. ICE worked out a simple plan to reinforce rule-following behavior during Mr. Stead's history classes.

In a busy classroom, it is easy to lose sight of important aspects of the correct use of reinforcement. To help ensure that you adhere to best practices in using reinforcement, periodically use the reinforcement self-assessment that we provide in Table 10-6. We recommend that you quickly correct any practices for which you give yourself a rating lower than 4.

Learning Activities

1. Working in small groups, see how many different praise statements you can generate in 1 minute.
2. In small groups, role-play describing a reinforcement system to a parent or administrator. Be sure to use the correct terminology.
3. Describe how you would determine effective, appropriate reinforcers for a student who consistently refuses to work or participate in class activities.
4. Role-play a discussion with a professional peer who does not want to use reinforcers with students.

5. Develop a menu of reinforcers for students whom you will be or are teaching. Discuss why you selected those reinforcers.
6. Working in small groups, brainstorm free, readily available social and activity reinforcers for each of the following age groups: preschool, primary, elementary, middle school, and high school.
7. Discuss how you will educate your principal and others about the importance of reinforcement for students who exhibit challenging behavior.

8. Identify the reinforcement schedules in place for each of the following:
    a. State lotteries
    b. Slot machines
    c. Payment at your place of employment
    d. Obtaining items from vending machines
9. Read the following scenario and identify who is being positively reinforced and how, and who is being negatively reinforced and how.

    Jan took her daughter, Elise, to the toy store in order to purchase a birthday gift for Elise's friend. In the store, Elise spied a toy that she had seen on television. She asked her mother to buy her the toy, but Jan refused. Elise continued to ask and Jan continued to refuse. Each request was a little louder and more forceful until eventually Elise was crying and screaming that her mother was unfair, that she [Elise] never got anything unless Daddy took her to the store. Jan by now had a headache and was embarrassed by the stares from other customers. She gave in to Elise, saying, "I'll get you the toy just this once. But you have to promise me that you will behave during the rest of our errands." Elise happily promised that she would be very, very good.

Resources

WEBSITES

www.eduref.org The Educator's Reference Desk: Provides a variety of materials on all topics related to education.

www.state.ky.us/agencies/behave/homepage.html The Behavior Home Page, hosted by the Kentucky Department of Education and the Department of Special Education and Rehabilitation Counseling at the University of Kentucky: Provides a wide range of behavioral tools, information, and technical assistance for educators, parents, advocates, and anyone who deals with challenging behavior in school and community settings.

http://iris.peabody.vanderbilt.edu The Iris Center for Training Enhancements, Vanderbilt University: Provides a variety of resources, including training modules on various special education topics.

www.behavioradvisor.com Dr. Mac's Behavior Management Site: Provides an array of behavior management interventions. (Tom McIntyre [aka Dr. Mac], a former teacher of students with behavioral disorders and learning disabilities, is now a professor of special education and the coordinator of the Graduate Program in Behavior Disorders at Hunter College of the City University of New York.)

www.LDonline.org LD Online: Provides numerous research and application articles primarily related to the education of students with learning disabilities and related disorders.

After reading this chapter, you will be able to do the following:

1. Define the Premack Principle.
2. Explain how to develop and implement token systems.
3. Explain how to develop and implement contracts.
4. Explain stimulus control and how to establish it.
5. Describe three types of group reinforcement systems and give examples of applications for each.
6. Explain five types of self-management techniques.

Prevention of Challenging Behavior Through Specific Reinforcement Applications

CHAPTER 11

Big ideas in reinforcement systems:

- Examples of reinforcement systems are prevalent in all areas of society.
- Anyone who has signed a lease, participated in a group sport, answered the telephone when it rings, or made a grocery list has experienced a few of the reinforcement systems to be discussed in this chapter.
- Group reinforcement systems can help students learn to work cooperatively toward a common goal.
- The ultimate goal of behavioral interventions is self-management; to achieve this goal, self-management skills may need to be taught.

In the previous chapter, you learned the basic principles of positive reinforcement. You now know that reinforcement is a process that maintains or increases a behavior. All voluntary behavior, both appropriate and inappropriate, can be strengthened through reinforcement. In fact, as explained in Chapter 3, inappropriate behavior continues because it is somehow being reinforced. You have also learned that reinforcement is a powerful tool for use by teachers and, like any tool, it must be applied correctly in order to produce the desired results. Explanations of basic reinforcement principles, types of reinforcers and reinforcement schedules, general guidelines for developing reinforcement programs, and problem-solving strategies were provided in Chapter 10. In this chapter, we describe specific reinforcement applications and how to use these reinforcement systems to increase or improve behaviors for groups or individual students.

Some of the systems that we present in this chapter may be familiar to readers. In fact, some of the systems are widely used in everyday life. For example, any employee has experienced what may be the most widely used reinforcement system: a token economy. Most of us have also been a party to a contract by signing a lease, purchasing a car, signing an agreement for cellular phone service, or agreeing to the terms of a credit card. All of us experience stimulus control on a daily basis. Many readers will have either personal experience with group reinforcement systems or will have heard of certain applications of group reinforcement systems. And almost every person has used self-management techniques to monitor or change a behavior. The fact that all of these

The reinforcement systems described in this chapter can be found in everyday life.

reinforcement systems permeate all aspects of society attests to their power. However, in noneducational settings, reinforcement systems may not be applied as systematically or as precisely as is necessary for use in the classroom, as you will see as you learn more about the various systems presented in this chapter.

THE PREMACK PRINCIPLE

Of all of the reinforcement systems, the easiest to use is the Premack Principle. Most individuals, especially parents, know how to use the Premack Principle, even if they do not know its official name. The **Premack Principle**, known informally as **Grandma's Law**, simply states that a desirable activity is available only after completion of a low-probability behavior (Premack, 1959). "Grandma's Law" states it this way: There will be no dessert unless you eat your vegetables, or there will be no computer games until you finish your homework. These are statements that many children have undoubtedly heard more than once! In the classroom, the Premack Principle is easy to apply. The following are a few examples of the Premack Principle at work:

- Mr. Wheeler tells his students that they may have game time after they complete their vocabulary sentences.
- Ms. Keller has an agreement with David: He must complete all of his assignments before he can work on his art project.
- Ms. Simpson's students dislike the journal writing activity that they have to complete each day. To reduce the number of complaints about this task and to encourage better writing, Ms. Simpson implements a plan whereby she allows 15 minutes for the journal activity; each student who completes the writing task without complaint and who writes a minimum of five complete sentences before the 15 minutes are up may use any remaining time to do a fun extra-credit activity (e.g., a puzzle-type worksheet, practice spelling words with a peer).

Note that in each example a desirable activity reinforcer is contingent upon the completion of a low-probability behavior (e.g., completing an assignment). One of the benefits of the Premack Principle is that it can be implemented without the advance planning that is required for other types of reinforcement systems. For example, if a class is having trouble settling down and focusing on the work, the teacher might devise a Premack Principle type of intervention on the spot, such as "As soon as we all finish our work, we'll play Math Facts Baseball for 5 minutes." For many individual students or groups of students, careful use of the Premack Principle may be sufficient to control inappropriate behavior and maintain appropriate behavior. However, as effective as this technique is, some students may need a more structured type of reinforcement system, such as a token economy or a contract, as described in the next sections.

TOKEN ECONOMY

In Chapter 10, we introduced the concept of tokens as a form of secondary reinforcer. As you recall, tokens have no intrinsic motivational power; their motivational power comes from the fact that they may be exchanged for **backup reinforcers**, such as food, activities, privileges, or material reinforcers. This type of reinforcement system is called a **token economy**. In a token economy, tokens are given as soon as desired behaviors are exhibited. Tokens are later exchanged for other reinforcers. Almost everyone has experienced a token economy. For example, almost every employee works under a token economy: The employee does work (the targeted behavior), gets tokens (money in the form of cash or a paycheck), and exchanges those tokens for backup reinforcers (e.g., food, clothing, gasoline, movies, music). Token systems are widely used in classrooms, in both special education and general education settings, as well as schoolwide (Martella, Nelson, & Marchand-Martella, 2003) to address a variety of behaviors, including academic and social behaviors (Christensen, Young, & Marchant, 2004; Montarello & Martens, 2005; E. L. Phillips, E. A. Phillips, Fixsen, & Montrose, 1971; Sulzer, Hunt, Ashby, Koniarski, & Krams, 1971), and self-management skills (Epstein & Goss, 1978; Self-Brown & Mathews, 2003; Seymour & Stokes, 1976).

Ayllon and Azrin (1968) were the first to describe a token system, used in their work in a hospital for mentally ill patients. The researchers used tokens to reinforce basic grooming tasks; later, tokens could be exchanged for food and other items at the hospital store. Since then, token systems have been extensively researched with populations of all ability levels and ages. Sulzer-Azaroff and Mayer (1991) recommend considering a token system when the following conditions have proven to be ineffective at managing behavior:

> Token economies have a long history of documented effectiveness.

- Natural classroom management techniques (e.g., the Premack Principle, interesting activities) and good teaching techniques
- Matching tasks and materials to the interests and abilities of the students (see Chapter 8 for more information)
- When faced with the possibility of using increasingly negative consequences to respond to behavioral problems

Token systems are an important element in positive behavioral supports. As you learned in Chapter 5, universal systems in schoolwide positive behavioral supports typically include a token system: Students earn some type of token that reflects the school theme or mascot, and those tokens are exchanged for a variety of reinforcers. Token systems are also reflected on the monitoring sheets used in targeted-level interventions such as Check In Check Out. For students who need tertiary-level interventions, token systems are usually a valuable and effective part of an overall intervention plan for increasing appropriate behaviors and reducing challenging behaviors.

A token system consists of two components: the tokens and the backup reinforcers. Of course, to actually design and implement a token system, a few additional decisions must be made, as described in the following steps:

1. Determine whether the token system will be used for group behavior (e.g., for all students in a classroom) or for one or more individual students. We provide more information about developing group reinforcement systems later in this chapter.
2. Identify the targeted behaviors to be addressed by using the token system. Remember our guidelines for choosing targeted behaviors and for using operationally defined targeted behaviors. In using token systems, the targeted behavior will be the replacement behavior that you have identified for

each challenging behavior. Be sure to collect baseline data on the targeted behaviors or the challenging behaviors through an appropriate data collection system, such as one of those described in Chapter 4.

Individual targeted behaviors might include complying with adult requests, completing assigned tasks, asking for permission before leaving the room, and following the playground rules. Targeted group behaviors might include being on time to class, making quick transitions, bringing supplies to class, making nice or supportive comments, or turning in homework.

3. Determine what will be used as tokens. We gave a few examples of tokens in Chapter 10 (e.g., points, stickers, stars, links in a chain, marbles in a jar, tickets, "Caught Being Good" cards). Tokens should be easy for the teacher to make or obtain, but not easy for students to counterfeit or obtain on their own. Paper clips would not make good tokens because students have easy access to them: They could get tokens without exhibiting the targeted behaviors.

4. Determine how often the tokens will be given. This is related to our discussion of reinforcement schedules from Chapter 10. Your baseline data will suggest how frequently the tokens should be given. For example, if a student curses an average of 12 times per hour, you will want to reinforce the desired behavior at a rate equal to or greater than that (e.g., 12 or more tokens per hour for using appropriate language). This concept reflects our discussion of matching law and behavioral efficiency from Chapter 3. You get what you reinforce: The more you reinforce the desired behavior, the more it will be exhibited. One common problem that we see with token systems is insufficient reinforcement: Tokens are not given frequently enough to produce the desired change in the targeted behavior. We encourage teachers to err on the side of too much reinforcement. It is easy to gradually reduce the frequency with which tokens are given once you begin to see an improvement in the targeted behavior.

5. Determine how the students will store the tokens until it is time to exchange them. For example, if your tokens are points or stars on a chart, where will the chart be kept? If your tokens are tickets, where will students keep their tickets? One solution is for each student to have a container (e.g., a manila envelope, small box, zipper bag) in his or her desk for storing tokens. Of course, if students attempt to steal or damage peers' tokens, the teacher will need to address this issue by first establishing and teaching a rule about respecting property and then reinforcing students for following that rule. Another way to manage the problem is through the use of a group contingency, such as the interdependent group contingency described later in this chapter.

6. Determine backup reinforcers. We recommend offering a menu of reinforcers with varying "prices." This provides a range of incentives: The more tokens that students have, the better is the reinforcer that they can purchase. Also, remember to change the reinforcers from time to time in order to avoid satiation. As much as possible, the individual reinforcers offered in your token system should reflect the functions of the inappropriate behaviors (see Table 10-3) and should be primarily social reinforcers.

7. Determine when the tokens will be exchanged (e.g., at the end of each period, daily, or weekly). Remember the discussion of reinforcement schedules when choosing how long to delay the exchange of tokens. When working with young children or children who have severe behavioral problems, we advise more frequent token exchanges (e.g., daily or even multiple times during the day). Of course, as the targeted behaviors become established, the reinforcement schedule will be thinned and students will be required to wait longer before exchanging their tokens. If in doubt, err on the side of frequent reinforcement. It is better to thin the reinforcement schedule than to start with a reinforcement delay that is overly long and then need to move to a more frequent reinforcement schedule.

8. Determine the cost of the backup reinforcers. It is sometimes difficult to determine how many tokens will be required for each reinforcer. Estimate how many tokens you will be giving by determining how often the targeted behaviors will occur and multiplying that by how long the students will be earning the tokens before exchanging them. For example, consider a student who is earning a token for each assignment completed on time and who is working on an FI 5-day schedule (he will be able to exchange his tokens on Friday). His teacher determines that he will have approximately 18 to 20 assignments before he is able to exchange his tokens. Therefore, his reinforcer menu includes several items that range in cost from 12 tokens to 17 tokens. Remember, if you find that your reinforcers are too expensive (i.e., the students seldom earn enough tokens to make purchases), you can always lower the cost.

9. Teach the system to the students. Be very clear on what behaviors will earn tokens, how students will store their tokens, and when and how the tokens will be exchanged.

Once you have developed your system and taught your students how the token system will be operated, you are ready to implement the system. During implementation, continue data collection in order to monitor the effectiveness of the system. Once the data indicate an improvement in the targeted behaviors, begin to thin the reinforcement provided through your token system. This can be done by lengthening the amount of time before the exchange and increasing the cost of the reinforcers because the students will have a longer time in which to earn tokens, or by reducing the frequency with which you give reinforcers.

For example, Mr. Morales used a token system with Rashad, a seventh-grader. Rashad had been exhibiting frequent name-calling and other negative verbalizations directed toward his peers. Mr. Morales implemented a system in which Rashad earned a ticket for making nice, supportive, or encouraging comments to peers. At first, Rashad could exchange his tickets daily for the desired reinforcers. As the frequency of the negative comments began to decrease, Mr. Morales began allowing Rashad to exchange his tickets only every other day, then twice per week, and, eventually, only on Fridays.

Raising the cost of the reinforcers is another way to require students to work for longer periods of time before exchanging their tokens. Our experience is that students typically will not complain about the higher cost of reinforcers if they have been successfully earning the reinforcers before you raise the cost and if you don't increase the cost too much at one time. For example, originally, it might cost

10 tokens to earn a particular reinforcer. As students begin to exhibit the targeted behavior more regularly, that same reinforcer might now cost 12 tokens, then 15, and eventually 20 tokens. If you note an increase in inappropriate behavior soon after raising the price of your reinforcers, you may have raised the price too dramatically.

Another approach is to thin the token delivery schedule by requiring more behaviors (under a ratio schedule) or more time to pass (under an interval schedule) before a token is given. For example, when Ms. Miller first began using a token system with Josh, she reinforced him every time that he complied. She felt that this continual reinforcement schedule was necessary because of Josh's severe noncompliance; baseline compliance data averaged 10%. Now that Josh's compliance has improved to 60%, Ms. Miller has stopped reinforcing every instance of compliance. She now reinforces Josh on an average of every three compliant responses.

Figure 11-1 describes several examples of token systems for all ages. Note the variety of tokens and monitoring systems. As you examine these examples, try to identify the steps described above. Designing token economies can be fun and is a good way for teachers to exercise their creativity!

CONTINGENCY CONTRACTING

Recently, one of the authors (BKS) visited a middle school classroom to observe a student who was frequently in trouble for refusing to follow directions. Staff at the school described the student as "noncompliant" and "oppositional." The student had multiple diagnoses, including oppositional defiant disorder. During the observation, the student was observed to be most compliant when (a) he liked the task, (b) he liked the teacher, and (c) he had some choice in what he was asked to do. Based on the observational data and other indirect data, the author concluded that the student would benefit from an intervention that allowed him to have input and some degree of control regarding the system used. For these reasons, the author recommended that contingency contracting be used as the primary intervention for this student. A **contingency contract** or, simply, a **contract** is an agreement, usually written, between a student and an adult (e.g., parent, teacher, administrator) that delineates what each party will do. Typically, the contract lists the behaviors that the student will perform, how often and when the behaviors will be performed, and what the teacher or other adult will do to support and reinforce those behaviors. Contingency contracts have several advantages as a reinforcement system. First, because contracts are negotiated between the student and adults, the student has input into the system. This may be critical for strong-willed students whose inappropriate behaviors serve a control function. Second, formalizing the contract in writing may increase the likelihood of both parties exhibiting the behaviors specified. Finally, contracts are relatively easy to use.

Contracts, like token systems, are adaptable for many uses. They can be used for many types of targeted behaviors, including academic performance (Martin et al., 2003; Miller & Kelley, 1994; Roberts, White, & McLaughlin, 1997), appropriate classroom behavior (Wilkinson, 2003), and aggression (Ruth, 1996), and can be used for individual students or groups. Contracts can be a one-time event, designed to address a temporary problem, or can be renewed regularly for ongoing use.

Contracts offer many advantages.

Early Childhood: 3- to 4-Year-Olds

- Ms. Spicer uses small pictures of activities that are moved on a felt board from the "To Do" side to the "Finished" side. After the students complete three activities, they earn time at various centers.

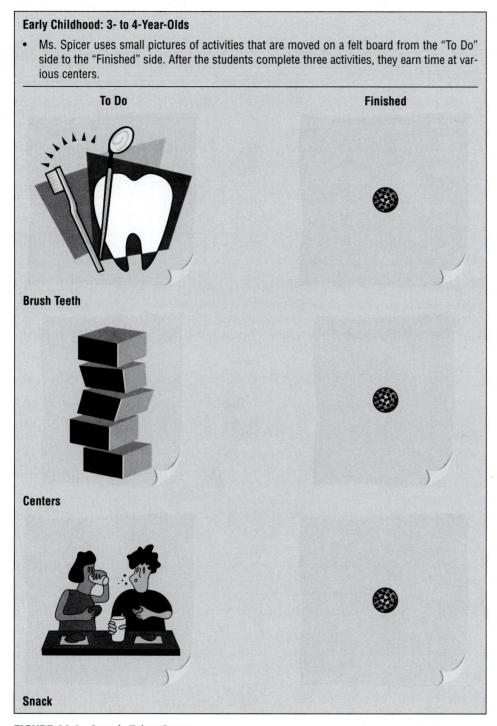

FIGURE 11-1   Sample Token Systems

(*Continued*)

- Mr. Glen gives a craft stick with a picture of a stuffed animal on top to each student who comes when called from the playground after lunch. These students trade their stick for a stuffed animal that stays with them during story time and then during nap time.

Craft Sticks
Early Childhood: craft sticks with pictures of stuffed animals

Elementary—Primary: Kindergarten to Grade 2

- Ms. Jackson gives a small colored stone to each student who has used the line procedure correctly while walking in the hall. The students place these stones in a decorative fishbowl. When the fishbowl is full, the class earns a popcorn party.

Fishbowl
Elementary—Primary: Stones as tokens to fill up a glass fishbowl

FIGURE 11-1 (Continued)

- Mr. James gives round token chips to students who are on task. Students place their chips in zippered plastic bags in their desks. Chips may be traded for classroom activities at the end of the day.

Bag of Chips

Elementary—Intermediate: Grade 3 Through Grade 5

- Mr. Hunt has a student who is a nonreader. This student has such a history of negative learning experiences with regard to reading tasks that he refuses to engage in any reading instruction. After finding out that the student loves baseball, Mr. Hunt arranged for the student to get a special mentor who played baseball for a local university. The mentor met with the student and gradually brought up the subject of reading. After a time, he and the student talked to Mr. Hunt about the student earning baseball time with his mentor. Mr. Hunt suggested that the student could earn baseball stamps for each successful reading lesson. These stamps could then be traded for baseball time with his mentor.

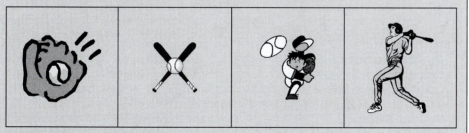

- Ms. Holt taught a social skills lesson on giving and receiving compliments. Ms. Holt made a bulletin board that included steps for giving and receiving compliments. On the lower part of the board, each student's name was posted. Also, a small file box containing note cards was placed next to the bulletin board. Ms. Holt then taught her students to write their name on a small note card whenever they gave or received a compliment. The card was placed under that child's name on the bulletin board. When a student accumulated 20 cards, he or she earned a

FIGURE 11-1 (Continued)

(*Continued*)

special privilege. When the class accumulated 100 cards, the students earned extra recess time on Friday. The students loved seeing the number of cards grow.

Compliment Board:

We Are Great at Giving and Receiving Compliments	
How to give a compliment:	How to receive a compliment:
• Look at the person.	• Listen to what the person is saying to you.
• Think about what you want to say about the person's appearance, behavior, or accomplishments.	• Look at the person.
• Say it in a nice way.	• Say "Thank you."

Kara	Bradley	Anika	Mandy	Jackson
Kara	Bradley	Anika	Mandy	Jackson
Kara	Bradley			
	Bradley			

Middle School: Grade 6 Through Grade 8

- Mr. Adams teaches resource English. His students earn time to do their homework in class by completing class assignments with at least 80% accuracy. Completed homework that is turned in as the students enter the class earns a ticket. Tickets can be traded in on Friday for learning games or for receiving no homework assignment over the weekend.

- Ms. Hatch teaches eighth-grade history in an inclusionary setting. Her students are emotionally younger than their peers in this class; however, they want and need to be treated like other eighth graders. Ms. Hatch worked with the general education teacher to develop a simple point system for the entire class in which students earn points for exhibiting appropriate social and classroom behaviors. The general education students exchange their points for extra-credit points, reduced homework passes, and reduced in-class assignments. Ms. Hatch's students spend their points on activities in Ms. Hatch's room. In addition, when the class as a whole accumulates a predetermined number of points, a class period is spent playing history review games or working on history projects (e.g., making dioramas, building miniature log cabins, making posters). All students participate in these activities together.

FIGURE 11-1 (Continued)

Ms. Hatch's Point Card

You earn 1 point for each behavior. Points will be given twice during class: at the end of the lesson and at the end of the class.

	M	T	W	Th	F
Following directions					
Cooperating with peers					

Weekly Total _____

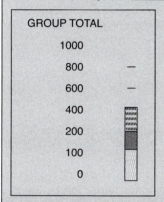

GROUP TOTAL

```
1000

 800    —

 600    —

 400

 200

 100

   0
```

High School

• Mr. Reeder teaches an 11th-grade resource mathematics class. His students chart their assignment grades on the inside cover of their mathematics notebook. Each grade of 80% to 89% earns 5 minutes of social or computer time, and 90% to 100% earns 10 minutes. Mr. Reeder initials each grade that is to be used toward time earned.

High School Grade Chart—Mathematics, Mr. Reeder's Class

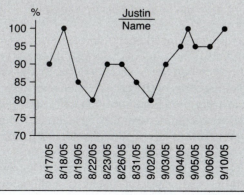

FIGURE 11-1 (Continued)

(Continued)

> • Ms. Sams teaches 10th-grade resource English. Writing reports is a major part of each week's work, but many of her students do not like to write. They also do not want to receive obvious tokens. Ms. Sams decided to use self-inking stamps as tokens. Each report can earn up to three stamps. Stamps are given for content, mechanics, and organization. These stamps, along with the teacher's comments, help the students to learn from their mistakes and to know when they are on target. Stamps are accumulated over the week and totaled. When they receive a predetermined number of stamps, students may use them to purchase the opportunity to choose a report topic and other learning activities. In addition, students earn one link of a paper chain for each stamp that they receive. The paper links are then strung together. When the chain reaches a predetermined length, the class earns time to play an English review game. Ms. Sams keeps a record of how many tokens each student earns for each report so that she can keep track of the total number of stamps earned per student and for the entire class. Ms. Sams' students like this new system. Students seldom complain about writing reports anymore, and the quality and quantity of their writing are improving.

FIGURE 11-1 (Continued)

Cipani (2004), DeRisi and Butz (1975), and Hall and Hall (1982) all suggest the following steps for developing a contract:

1. Determine whether this is a contract for an individual student or a group of students.
2. Select the targeted behaviors to be addressed in the contract. The contract should cover no more than two or three behaviors. The behaviors must be described in operational terms to avoid disagreement later about whether the behavior did or did not occur. The contract should also describe desired behaviors—what the student must *do*—as opposed to focusing on behaviors that are not allowed.
3. You may wish to include the steps that the teacher will take to help the student remember the targeted behavior. These might include offering daily reminders, providing a picture prompt for the student to place on his or her desk, or giving the student a list of assignments to check off after completion.
4. Determine the reinforcers to be earned contingent upon completion of the targeted behaviors.
5. Determine the criteria for receiving a reinforcer (e.g., how often the behavior must occur in order for the student to receive the reinforcer) and the timeline for the contract (i.e., when the contract will begin and end). If the contract is to cover multiple instances of the targeted behavior (e.g., completing in-class assignments, following directions, arriving to class on time, taking turns on the playground), we recommend including a simple behavior monitoring system in the contract. This system will ensure that the terms of the contract are adhered to and will allow both parties to see progress toward the final goal.
6. Put all of the agreed-upon terms of the contract in writing. Use clear language that everyone (i.e., student, teachers, staff, parents) can understand.
7. Have all parties sign the contract. Keep the contract in an easily accessible place, especially if data are to be recorded on the contract.
8. At the specified time, review the contract with all involved parties. Determine whether the criteria noted in the contract have been met. If so, deliver the reinforcer.

9. At this point, the contract can be renewed without change, modified, or terminated.

Contracts can be written in any format, but simple is better. Consider the contract shown in Figure 11-2. This contract is an agreement between John Henry, a fifth-grade student who has problems with noncompliance and anger control, and his teacher, Mr. Jacobs. Note the simple terms of the contract, the daily monitoring via a point sheet, and the data chart. We provide additional examples of contracts in Figure 11-3.

I, John Henry, understand that the following behaviors have been causing me to not do as well in school as I can:

- Not following directions
- Not completing assignments
- Not controlling anger and frustration

To help me be more successful, I agree to do the following:

1. Follow directions: Do what Mr. Jacobs tells me within 1 minute, or ask for clarification or help.
2. Complete assigned work: Do my work, within the time given, with 80% accuracy or better. If I do not understand what to do or if I am having trouble, I will ask for help. If I think that I have been given too much work to be able to finish on time, I will talk to Mr. Jacobs about it.
3. Ask for cool-down time if I start to feel angry or frustrated: I will either raise my hand or hand my "I need a break" card to Mr. Jacobs on the way to the cool-down area.

Mr. Jacobs agrees to help me by doing the following:

1. Giving me private signals to help me remember what I am supposed to do.
2. Allowing me time to talk to him if I feel that something is unfair.
3. Allowing me time to go to the cool-down area when I am feeling angry or frustrated.
4. Giving me points for my appropriate behaviors (e.g., following directions, completing work on time, expressing anger and frustration with words, asking to use the cool-down area).
5. Allowing me to exchange those points for activities or privileges that we both agree on. If I finish my work with 80% accuracy or better, I may use my points to obtain these activities or privileges either on the day that they are earned or on the next day. If I finish my work with less than 80% accuracy, I may not use my points; instead, I will have to correct my work or do other assignments that Mr. Jacobs gives me.
6. I can earn the following:
   - Activities
     - Mathematics, reading, science, or social studies computer activities
     - Academic games with one or two peers who are also finished with their work
     - Special science or mathematics projects
     - Extra-credit work from the extra-credit file
   - Privileges
     - Extra recess time for the class (1 minute for every 3 points, up to 10 minutes)
     - Extra restroom pass
     - Class job (e.g., feed animals, water plants, erase boards, pass out papers)
     - Class game on Friday (1 minute for every 3 points, up to 20 minutes)

I understand that I will earn points for using appropriate behaviors as specified and that I will lose points for engaging in the following inappropriate behaviors:

1. Taking more than 5 minutes to do what I am told to do.
2. Refusing to work (e.g., putting my head on my desk, walking around the classroom during work time).

FIGURE 11-2 John Henry's Contract

(Continued)

3. Yelling, talking back to Mr. Jacobs (e.g., saying "You can't tell me what to do"; "I don't have to do your stupid work"), or using any other inappropriate language ("You're a stupid teacher"; "I hate this d*** class"; "I'm going to rip up this paper and throw it in your face").

Finally, I understand that I can earn bonus points for exceptional behavior, as observed by Mr. Jacobs. These would include behaviors such as staying calm during difficult tasks, being the first person to get started working, and completing assignments with 100% accuracy.

Each day, Mr. Jacobs and I will chart the number of points that I earn. I understand that this system will be in place until Mr. Jacobs and I agree that it can be discontinued. I also understand that Mr. Jacobs and I will renegotiate the terms of this contract every 2 weeks.

_____

John Henry, student

_____

Mr. Jacobs, teacher

John Henry's Daily Point Sheet
Date _____

Appropriate Behavior	Breakfast		Reading		Math		Language Arts		Science		Social Studies		P.E., Music, Art	
Follow	✓	✓	✓	0	✓	✓	✓	✓	✓	✓	0	0	✓	✓
directions	✓	✓	0	0	✓	0	✓	✓	✓	✓	✓	✓	✓	✓
Complete assigned work	N/A		✓		0		✓		✓		0		N/A	
Remain in room unless given permission to leave	✓		✓		✓		✓		✓		0		✓	
TOTAL	5		3		4		6		6		2		5	

= 31 points

BONUS Points for exceptional behaviors	1 Helped Troy		1 Asked to take cool-down time	1 Asked to talk to Mr. Jacobs			

= 3 bonus points

FIGURE 11-2 (Continued)

Inappropriate Behavior							
Refusal		★★★	★★			★	
Name calling			★★★				
Leaving the room							
TOTAL	—	−3	−5	—	—	−1	—

−9 points

DAILY POINT TOTAL	25 points

John Henry's Daily Point Sheet

Date _____

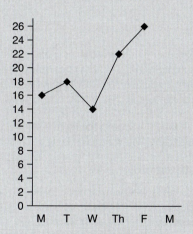

Reinforcer Menu

What You May Do	How Often/How Long	How Many Points Are Needed
Play basketball	15 minutes	35
Go to see the principal	1 trip	25
Have computer time	15 minutes	25
Help Mr. Jacobs	1 day	35
Get a "Good News" note to take home	1 note	22
Call home	1 call	25
Play game with Mr. Jacobs	1 game	23
Practice keyboard program	15 minutes	28

BONUS: Earn 35 points or more for 3 out of 5 days = Double basketball time or computer time on Friday

FIGURE 11-2 (Continued)

Primary

Savannah is a first grader who has been getting into trouble on the playground for pushing her peers off of the swings so that she can play on them. The teacher (Ms. Lindquist) and the playground monitor (Ms. Harrison) have been taking away Savannah's recess as a consequence for pushing her peers off of the swings. Savannah has missed more than 10 recess periods because of this behavior. The teacher and the monitor realize that the punishment is not working and have written this contract for Savannah:

WHO: Savannah

WHAT: I will wait my turn to play on the swings without pushing my friends.

HOW: Ms. Lindquist will remind me before recess. Ms. Harrison will remind me when I'm on the playground.

WHAT I EARN: I will earn a star for each recess that I remember to wait my turn. If I have three stars by Friday, my friends in my class and I will earn an 10 extra minutes of recess.

My Stars for Waiting My Turn

Secondary

Mark is a high school student who has behavioral problems. Mark is having difficulty in biology: He is frequently late to class, he makes inappropriate comments during class, and he is often noncompliant. Mark loves biology labs and is passing the course, but he is in danger of failing because of the classes that he has missed as a result of being sent for office disciplinary referrals. Mr. Long, Mark's biology teacher, has written this contract for Mark:

I, Mark, agree to arrive to biology class on time (I will be in the room when the bell rings). I will refrain from making off-task or inappropriate comments during class and I will follow Mr. Long's instructions.

I, Mr. Long, agree to help Mark by doing the following:

- Recognizing him for exhibiting appropriate behavior, including getting to class on time, participating in class appropriately, and following directions.
- Meeting with Mark after class if Mark has concerns about the class (e.g., if he thinks that I am being unfair).
- Reminding him before class about expectations and using nonverbal signals during class if his behavior is inappropriate.
- Letting Mark know at the end of class how well he met expectations during class that day.

Each day that Mark meets these expectations, he may come to Mr. Long's class after school to help Mr. Long organize the lab materials. In addition, when Mark meets these expectations for 2 weeks, he may come to the lab one day after school (to be scheduled in advance at a time that is mutually agreeable) in order to complete an advanced lab experiment.

This contract will be in place until we meet again to review it.

_____   _____

Mark _____ Date _____   Mr. Long _____ Date _____

FIGURE 11-3 Sample Contracts

STIMULUS CONTROL

When the telephone rings, you pick it up and say "hello," or you check the caller ID and decide whether to answer it or let your voice mail take the call. When you're driving and you come to a red light at an intersection, you stop. A person who has just been introduced to you extends his hand as he says, "Nice to meet you." You respond by shaking his hand and saying, "Nice to meet you, too." When you hear the microwave oven beep, you remove your food. Each of these is an example of stimulus control in daily life. **Stimulus control** refers to the process by which a behavior is governed by a specific antecedent or class of antecedents that precedes it; certain responses are more probable in the presence of these antecedents (Sulzer-Azaroff & Mayer, 1991). Antecedents associated with those behaviors controlled the behaviors in the examples just described: Each behavior occurs only in response to that specific antecedent (or similar enough antecedents). Sulzer-Azaroff and Mayer (1991) describe stimulus control as "a highly predictable relation between a stimulus and a response" (p. 249).

Stimulus control is a powerful technique that, if used correctly, increases appropriate behaviors and reduces challenging behaviors. Effective teachers understand stimulus control and systematically strive to use stimulus control principles in the classroom to increase desired classroom, academic, and social behaviors. Stimulus control has the potential to be both a powerful management tool and an instructional tool. For this reason, we could have discussed stimulus control in previous chapters that examined antecedent interventions (e.g., rules and procedures) and instruction. We include it in this chapter on reinforcement applications because, as you will see, stimulus control is established through reinforcement.

> Stimulus control is easy to use and is a powerful tool for managing behavior.

In order to use stimulus control, you must understand the terminology associated with the process. A stimulus or antecedent that predictably cues a particular response is called a **discriminative stimulus,** or S^D. A ringing telephone is an S^D for answering the phone. A red light at an intersection is an S^D for stopping the car. The teacher giving an instruction should be an S^D for students to follow that instruction. We want the stimulus "4 times 9" or "4×9" to be an S^D for a student to respond "36." We expect that the rule "Bring all required materials to class" will be an S^D for students to remember to bring all of the supplies that they need for that class. As you will see, discriminative stimuli are established through reinforcement. Desired behaviors are repeatedly reinforced in the presence of the S^D, whereas undesirable behaviors are not. In order to learn to respond to specific stimuli as discriminative stimuli, students must learn to differentiate between the S^D and all other stimuli, known as S-**deltas,** or S^Δ. A purple light over an intersection is an S-delta. The beeping of a microwave oven is an S^Δ for picking up the telephone and saying "hello." During oral reading, we want the printed stimulus "where" to be an S^D for student to say "where" and an S^Δ for reading "when" (i.e., an incorrect response). An S^D does not *cause* a response; it simply increases the likelihood that a certain response will occur.

For classroom use of S^Ds, the goal should be to establish a strong connection between the S^D and the desired response. A strong S^D will result in the desired response more often than not. Sulzer-Azaroff and Mayer (1991) refer to this as **complete stimulus control.** Teachers want students to produce high rates of correct responses to academic stimuli. We want students to follow the rules and teacher instructions most of the time. When students encounter social stimuli, we want them to respond with an appropriate social behavior. Weak stimulus control, otherwise known as **incomplete stimulus control**, indicates that the desired response does not predictably or consistently occur when the antecedent stimulus is presented. A common example of incomplete stimulus control is seen in students who consistently exhibit the same academic or behavioral errors. For example, incomplete stimulus control is illustrated when Abby reads: She makes many reading errors because she focuses only on the first part of the printed words. She reads "milk" for "Mike," "wild" for "wide," or "the" for "three." For Abby, many words have not yet been established as S^Ds for the correct response. Another example of a weak S^D can be seen in Justin's noncompliant behavior. When the teacher gives Justin a direction, Justin is more likely to ignore the direction than comply with it. The teacher's instructions are not yet complete S^Ds for compliance.

As we said, stimulus control is established by differentially reinforcing desired behaviors when they occur in the presence of the S^D. Other responses are not reinforced. When the teacher presents a word for a student to read and the student responds correctly, the teacher praises the student. If the student responds incorrectly, the teacher corrects the student. At the beginning of the year, when the teacher is instructing the students about the rules and the procedures, the students are reinforced each time that they follow a rule or procedure. Any student who does not follow the rule is reminded about the rule at first; later, there may be a consequence for failure to follow a rule. When first establishing the S^D, it is important to reinforce the desired response every time that it occurs when the S^D is presented. Eventually, the reinforcement will be given only intermittently.

When it is determined that a weak S^D or incomplete stimulus control explains the challenging behavior (e.g., the noncompliance or reading errors that we described previously), the teacher must take steps to strengthen the stimulus–response relationship. Sulzer-Azaroff and Mayer (1991) recommend examining the following potential explanations for incomplete stimulus control:

1. Does the student know how to perform the desired response? Have you seen the student use the skill previously? Can the student perform the skill when directly instructed to do so? If not, you must assume that the student does not know how to perform the skill. In this case, the skill must be taught. (See Chapter 9 for guidelines on teaching social behaviors.)
2. Does the student respond correctly at certain times and not at others? This may indicate a weak S^D. The intervention for a weak S^D is to clearly explain the S^D, prompt the desired response when the students are first learning the S^D (i.e., give the students a hint about how to respond correctly), and use a continuous schedule of reinforcement in the early stages of establishing the stimulus–response relationship.

3. Are other stimuli interfering with the S^D? Carrie is talking on her cell phone as she drives along the highway and misses her exit; her cell phone conversation interfered with her reading the sign which indicated the exit that she needed. Mr. Keyser is trying to teach a difficult skill in algebra. At the same time, the band begins practicing on the field just outside the classroom windows. The band may be an S^D for attention that competes with Mr. Keyser's instruction on how to perform the skill. When an S^D sometimes fails to control a desired response, an interfering S^D may be to blame. In such situations, the teacher must take steps to increase the power of the desired S^D. Mr. Keyser, for example, might ask more questions and provide more reinforcement when the band is practicing during his lesson. Ms. Meredith was trying to teach one of her preschool children, Jacob, to pay attention during group activities. Jacob was very distractible and tended to watch the other children, look at materials around the room, or play with his shoes. To better establish herself as the S^D for Jacob's attention, Ms. Meredith sat Jacob at her side and reinforced Jacob for paying attention (which she operationally defined as participating or looking at Ms. Meredith) by putting happy face stamps on a card using an FI 30-second ratio. In addition, Ms. Meredith frequently touched Jacob's knee as a reminder to watch her.

4. Are more powerful reinforcers available for competing behaviors? Sometimes students know the correct response but choose not to exhibit it because of more powerful reinforcers from another source. For example, Naveen knows how to answer his teacher's questions correctly and appropriately. However, when he makes smart-aleck comments in response to a teacher's questions, his classmates snicker. His classmates' response is a more powerful reinforcer than the intermittent recognition that he receives from the teacher for an appropriate response. In this case, the teacher must increase the reinforcement for an appropriate response (i.e., use a reinforcer that is more powerful than peers' laughter) and/or control peers reinforcement of Naveen's inappropriate responses.

5. Is the S^D distant in time from the corresponding behavior? Any employee who is expected to be at work at a certain time is responding to a temporally distant S^D: The boss isn't at your side telling you to go to work. A student who completes a major research paper is also responding to a distant S^D (i.e., the teacher's instructions about the assignment). Another good example of this in the classroom is the fact that classroom rules do not directly precede the desired behavior. To encourage compliance with a temporally distant S^D, intervening mediating behaviors may be needed. For this purpose, we recommend one or more of the self-management strategies described later in this chapter.

Stimulus control is a powerful preventive technique that can make the classroom run much more smoothly. The extent to which teachers establish stimulus control over desired behaviors will help to ensure that those behaviors occur more frequently than unacceptable behaviors. An excellent teacher we once observed had established stimulus control over her students' lining up behaviors:

After students were in line, she announced, "Line up rules are now in effect." At that point, the students checked themselves to make sure that they were standing one tile block apart, facing forward, hands at their sides, and mouths quiet. This teacher established the S^D "Line up rules are now in effect" by teaching her students what to do when they heard that statement and then reinforcing them for exhibiting those behaviors. Eventually, she was able to thin the reinforcement schedule while the S^D maintained the desired set of behaviors. Because of this effective S^D, the teacher avoided having to correct her students' line-up behaviors with comments like "We're not leaving until everyone is standing correctly" or "Sarah, go back and try again" or "You're losing recess time the longer I have to wait for you to line up the right way," each of which is a reactive approach to dealing with the problem.

The potential applications of classroom S^Ds are endless. Table 11-1 describes classroom and schoolwide examples of stimulus control. We encourage teachers to be creative in using stimulus control to increase appropriate behaviors and avoid undesirable behaviors.

TABLE 11-1   Examples of Stimulus Control in School Settings

Discriminative Stimuli	Behavior
Primary	
The teacher holds up two fingers.	Students imitate the gesture and stop talking.
When a student encounters teasing, the teacher says, "Remember to be a turtle."	The student uses a self-control procedure that has been previously taught.
Whenever the teacher needs to get the students' attention, she claps as she says "1-2-3, look at me."	Students join in by clapping and, when the rhyme is finished, wait quietly for instructions.
Intermediate	
In response to a student becoming upset, the teacher says, "Do you need a control time?"	The student goes to the area designated for self-control, where he practices the self-control techniques that he learned in the social skills group.
The teacher announces that it is time to work.	Students get out the appropriate work materials.
After giving instructions for independent work and asking if there are any questions, the teacher sets a timer.	Students work quietly when the timer is running. The timer is the S^D for quiet independent work.
Secondary	
The teacher says, "You are dismissed."	Students gather their materials and leave the classroom; students do not leave until the teacher says that they are dismissed, even if the bell rings first.
A student encounters taunting and tells himself to just "Sit it out."	The student reminds himself to "Stop," "Ignore," and "Tell himself, 'It isn't worth it'," a technique that he has learned to help him remember to use self-control.

GROUP REINFORCEMENT SYSTEMS

Up to this point, our discussion of reinforcement applications has focused mainly on the use of reinforcement systems to increase or improve behavior in individual students. However, reinforcement contingencies can also be applied to groups. Group reinforcement systems, also referred to as **group contingencies,** can serve two purposes. First, they can increase one or more targeted behaviors across all students in a group. Second, they can encourage group cohesiveness and teamwork because, in some forms of group contingencies, students work together for a common goal. Group contingencies can be arranged for an entire class, for small groups (e.g., reading groups, cooperative groups), or even for pairs of students (e.g., peer tutoring pairs, peer buddies). Litow and Pumroy (1975) identified three types of group contingencies: independent, interdependent, and dependent. Each of these systems is described next, along with examples of classroom use. When using group contingencies, consideration must be given to the reinforcers that the group will earn. Table 11-2 lists potential reinforcers that may be appropriate for group use with elementary and secondary school students.

TABLE 11-2   Group Reinforcers

Elementary

- Allotting extra recess time.
- Providing time for students to play a group game or engage in a special activity (e.g., nature walk, movie, cooking).
- Giving less homework.
- Giving no homework for a night or over the weekend.
- Giving a grade of 100 to each person in the group as extra credit.
- Giving a reinforcer dot to each student.
- Giving a "Good News" note to each student to take home.
- Posting a special sign that announces the group's accomplishments on the classroom door or on the bulletin board.

Secondary

- Allowing students a few minutes to talk with peers at the end of class.
- Giving less homework.
- Giving no homework for a night or over the weekend.
- Giving a grade of 100 to each person in the group as extra credit.
- Allowing students to leave class 1 minute before the bell rings.
- Giving a free hall pass to each student.
- Providing time for students to play a group game or engage in a special activity (e.g., special project, movie).
- Giving a reinforcer dot to each student (see Chapter 10).
- Allowing students to listen to music during independent work time or during group work time.

Independent Group Contingency. An **independent group contingency** means that although the same reinforcer is available for all students in the group, the attainment of the reinforcer depends on each student's individual performance (Alberto & Troutman, 2006). The criterion for earning the reinforcer can either be the same for each student or can be individually determined (Sulzer-Azaroff & Mayer, 1991). Any student who meets the criterion earns the reinforcer. Students who do not exhibit the targeted behaviors at the expected levels do not earn the reinforcer. Although this type of system may not facilitate group cohesiveness or students working together to achieve a common goal, Shapiro and Goldberg (1986) found that students preferred this type of group contingency over the other two types. Several examples of an independent group contingency are listed in Table 11-3.

Interdependent Group Contingency. In an **interdependent group contingency,** all students work together for a common reinforcer. Every student must exhibit the targeted behavior at the specified criterion level in order for students to receive reinforcement. Interdependent group contingencies have been used to improve academic and social behaviors, and reduce disruptive behaviors (Lo & Cartledge, 2004).

The Good Behavior Game, which we discussed in Chapter 1, uses an interdependent group contingency to manage classroom behavior. The Good Behavior Game is used during specific periods of the day (e.g., mathematics, language arts). During each period, students are divided into two or more teams. Next, the teacher clearly describes what is expected in terms of appropriate behavior and the negative behaviors that will be scored during the game (e.g., talking out, being out of one's seat without permission, disruptive behavior). Every time a student exhibits one of the specified negative behaviors, that student's team receives a check mark on a posted chart. Any team that receives less than the predetermined number of check marks earns a reinforcer.

The original game was implemented first during mathematics and later during language arts class in a fourth-grade class that was experiencing a high number of noncompliant, disruptive behavioral problems (Barrish, Saunders, & Wolf, 1969). Teams were given a check mark for each instance of talking out or out-of-seat behavior that was exhibited by a team member. Any team that earned five or fewer check marks per period that the game was being implemented earned a reinforcer. The reinforcers used in the original game were that the winning team(s) could wear victory badges, put a star next to each team member's name on the chart, line up first for lunch (or if more than one team won, teams could go to lunch early), and enjoy free time at the end of the day to work on special projects. In addition, weekly privileges were given to teams that accumulated 20 or fewer check marks during the week. This relatively simple group contingency resulted in improved classroom behavior during each period that it was in effect. More importantly, as discussed in Chapter 1, large-scale replications of this classroom management system revealed long-term positive effects on children's development in terms of school behavior, mental health, and a lowered risk of engaging in antisocial behavior among the children who participated in the Good Behavior Game.

TABLE 11-3   Examples of Group Contingencies

Independent Group Contingencies

- Ms. Stamper gives a puzzle piece to those students who turn in their "Read with your parent" chart. When the puzzle has been completed, students earn extra time for Ms. Stamper to read to them. Only students who have earned at least two puzzle pieces are allowed to participate in the group reinforcer.

- Students in Mr. Wellborn's high school resource English class earn points for targeted writing skills (e.g., using prewriting strategies, editing and revising their work, using appropriate grammar and mechanics, and developing appropriate ideas in a writing task). Points can be exchanged for extra credit, "no-homework" nights, or dropping the lowest grade on a quiz.

Interdependent Group Contingencies

- If all students in Mr. Kennedy's auto mechanics class turn in their homework every day, the class earns double shop time on Friday.

- Students in Ms. Madison's fourth- and fifth-grade language arts resource class were not nice to one another. Ms. Madison had trouble keeping her students on task because they were constantly making rude or taunting comments to one another, complaining about one another, or refusing to sit next to each other. Ms. Madison implemented a group contingency: When she hears a student make an encouraging or helpful comment to another student, the student earns a ticket. The student writes his or her name on the back of the ticket and stores the ticket in an envelope attached to the side of the student's desk. During the last 10 minutes of class on Thursday, the students pool their tickets. If they have at least 40 tickets, they can vote on a language arts group game to play during class on Friday. In addition, each student has to have at least five tickets for the group to get the activity.

- Mr. Carver has his students do a peer tutoring activity in order to review spelling words during the last 10 minutes of class, 3 days per week. During this time, Mr. Carver walks around, supervising the peer tutoring pairs. Each pair that he observes using appropriate peer tutoring behaviors earns a star on the class "We're a Team" chart, and Mr. Carver puts the initials of the peer tutoring pair on the star. When the class earns 50 stars, the group earns double recess time. Only students who have at least five stars on the chart may participate. In addition, those students who have more than five stars earn a reinforcer dot (see Table 10-3 in Chapter 10 for a description of reinforcer dots) for each extra star. Reinforcer dots may then be used on in-class work.

- Ms. Maxwell needed a strategy to help her preschool students learn to keep their hands to themselves as they walk in line. Each student who walks in line the correct way earns a colored clothespin. The student places the clothespin on his or her name card on the bulletin board in the classroom. At the end of the morning, if every student's name card holds a clothespin, the students earn a sticker to put on their name cards. At the end of the week, the students take their name cards home.

Dependent Group Contingencies

- Sam liked to make animal noises in class. Ms. Robertson arranged a dependent group contingency for Sam: If he made no animal noises during class, he could tell a story or joke the last few minutes of class.

Litow and Pumroy (1975) describe three approaches for determining success in meeting a criterion in an interdependent group contingency:

1. All students must meet a predetermined criterion: If any student does not meet this criterion, no student will receive reinforcement. For example, if every student completes in-class work Monday through Thursday with 80% accuracy or better, the class earns 20 minutes of the Biology Baseball game on Friday.
2. The criterion is based on the average performance for the group: Using this approach, the biology class would earn 20 minutes of the Biology Baseball game on Friday if the daily average is 80% accuracy or better for in-class work.
3. All students must meet a minimum level of performance: For example, if no one scores below 80% on his or her daily biology work, the class earns 20 minutes of the Biology Baseball game on Friday.

Table 11-3 describes examples of interdependent group contingency systems.

Dependent Group Contingency. In a **dependent group contingency,** reinforcement for all students is contingent upon the performance of one or more individual students. If these students perform the targeted behavior, all students receive reinforcement. Examples of dependent group reinforcement systems are provided in Table 11-3.

We offer three recommendations for using dependent group contingencies. First, this system is most likely to be effective if the function of the inappropriate behavior exhibited by the targeted student is peer attention or control. A dependent group system will provide the student access to these reinforcers contingent upon exhibiting appropriate behavior. Second, never punish the group for the behavior of one student. The reinforcers offered should be above and beyond what is normally available to the group. For example, José has a difficult time following the rules on the playground. José's teacher established a dependent group contingency in which José can earn extra minutes of recess time for the class each day that José follows the rules during recess. If José breaks a playground rule, the class does not lose any of their regular recess time; they simply do not earn additional minutes. Finally, teach the other students in the group how to prompt and support the targeted behaviors in the student who is earning the reinforcement for the group. Students should be taught how to remind the student about the expected behaviors, how to praise or compliment the student, and how to respond if the student begins to exhibit an inappropriate behavior. In José's case, José's teacher solicited José to help her teach the class ways in which to help José remember the playground rules. Together, José, his teacher, and the class generated a list of suggestions and then practiced using those reminders; they practiced on the playground during a period when no other students were present.

Hansen and Lignugaris/Kraft (2005) used a dependent group contingency to increase positive verbal statements and reduce negative statements made by middle school students with emotional disturbances. The dependent contingency involved two students being randomly selected each day; if these students exhibited a minimum number of positive statements, the group earned a reinforcer at the end of the day. Prior to implementing the group contingency, the authors first used explanation, modeling, and role-playing to teach the students in the class how to make positive statements. The dependent contingency resulted in students reaching criterion levels for both positive and negative statements; those levels were maintained even after the group contingency was withdrawn.

Of course, when designing a group contingency, teachers must make sure that all students can perform the targeted behavior to the desired level. A good way to determine this is if you have observed each student exhibiting the targeted behavior at times. If you have never observed one or more students engaging in the targeted behavior or exhibiting the behavior to the desired criterion level, you must assume that they may not know how to do the behavior or how to do it sufficiently well for use under all conditions. In this case, you must first teach the behavior and set the initial criterion level low enough for all students to be successful. The criterion level can be raised as the students become more proficient in the targeted behavior.

A potential risk with dependent and interdependent group contingencies is that one or more students may intentionally sabotage the group. There are several possible solutions to this situation. One is that the student who is sabotaging the group can be removed from the larger group contingency and be made a "group of one." In this case, the student's performance affects only himself or herself, not the other students. Another possible solution is to identify a function-based reinforcer for the student who is sabotaging the group effort. Assess the student's behavior to determine a possible function and then provide reinforcement for that student to address that function, contingent upon the group's success. For example, Ms. Craig implemented an interdependent group contingency for her middle school resource mathematics class: Every day that the class had fewer than three inappropriate comments (she clarified to students exactly what this meant) during class, they earned a star on the class chart. When they accumulated 15 stars, they could spend part of the class playing basketball. However, Ernesto continued to make loud, inappropriate comments each day, causing the class total to be well over the maximum of three. Despite the fact that his peers were unhappy with him, Ernesto's comments continued. Ms. Craig determined that Ernesto liked the power that he had over the group because of his inappropriate comments and the status that this power gave him. She modified the reinforcement plan to address this function: First, Ms. Craig made Ernesto a group of his own. If Ernesto made fewer than three inappropriate comments per day, he earned a star on his own chart. When he had 15 stars, he could join the group in basketball the next time that they played. However, in addition, if Ernesto had four stars on his chart by Friday, he was allowed to work in the school office during his advisory period that day. Some of his office aide duties included delivering messages to teachers in other classrooms, answering the telephone, and providing visitors with a name tag. Ernesto's inappropriate comments during resource mathematics class dropped from an average of 12 to less than 2 per day.

SELF-MANAGEMENT

The goal of behavioral interventions is to move the student from external behavioral supports to self-management. External contingency systems are often necessary to establish new behaviors or to improve the fluency of behaviors. Once those behaviors are established, educators should plan how to bring them under students' internal control rather than continuing to rely on external management systems to encourage display of the targeted behaviors. To accomplish this goal, students must be able to use the types of self-management skills that enable any individual to independently initiate, guide, and inhibit behaviors in order to successfully handle academic and social situations in school and in other environments. A substantial body of research has documented the efficacy of teaching self-management skills to increase appropriate behaviors and decrease inappropriate behaviors in children and adolescents with all types of disabilities and behavioral needs (Copeland & Hughes, 2002; Graham & Harris, 2003; Kern, Ringdahl, Hilt, & Sterling-Turner, 2001; Reid, Trout, & Schartz, 2005; Smith & Sugai, 2000; Troia & Graham, 2002). From a behavioral perspective, self-management skills include five skill areas: goal setting, self-monitoring, self-evaluation, self-instruction, and self-reinforcement.

Goal Setting.   Although teachers or individualized educational program (IEP) committees are usually responsible for setting goals for students, there is evidence that having students participate in setting goals for their own academic or behavioral skills can enhance performance (Copeland & Hughes, 2002; Troia & Graham, 2002). **Goal setting** involves having students set goals for their own performance. Most of us use goal setting in some form: We create to-do lists, set goals for weight or athletic performance, and make shopping lists. Students can be taught to use these forms of goal setting or more targeted applications, such as setting specific goals for improving academic performance, exhibiting desired behaviors, or handling social situations appropriately. Alberto and Troutman (2006) recommend teaching students to set goals that are specific, challenging but achievable, and for short-term or immediate accomplishment rather than long-term achievement. For example, each morning, Ms. Kellogg has her students set goals for behavior. Each student sets a goal that is relevant to his or her individual behavioral targets. Justin sets a goal for on-time arrivals to his classes, Marguerite sets a goal for responding appropriately to teachers, Jamail sets a goal for using appropriate language in class, and so forth. Mr. Felton, on the other hand, has his students set goals for weekly academic performance. For example, his students record their daily grades (see the "Self-Monitoring" section) and then set goals for improving their grades during the next week. Students who meet their goals earn reinforcers. Still in another example of goal setting, Ms. Latham has a student, Kendra, who is extremely withdrawn. One of Kendra's IEP goals is to respond appropriately to social initiations by her peers. Each morning, Ms. Latham guides Kendra in setting a goal for how many social responses she will exhibit during the day. To determine this number, they examine Kendra's graph of social response data from the previous day. During various social times throughout the day (e.g., lunchtime, leisure activities, assemblies), Ms. Latham monitors Kendra's social responses using event recording. At the end of the day, Ms. Latham and Kendra graph the data for each daily social period. Ms. Latham encourages Kendra to set goals that are slightly higher for one or more social periods during the day.

Self-Monitoring.   **Self-monitoring** refers to observing and recording one's behaviors (Mace, Belfiore, & Shea, 2001). We all use self-monitoring. Crossing items off of our shopping list is self-monitoring. Recording how many miles we ran and/or our running time is self-monitoring. We self-monitor when we tell ourselves to stand or sit up straight or ask ourselves what we need to take when we leave home. Students self-monitor when they mark off completed homework assignments in their assignment book. Self-monitoring is an important self-control strategy, but it is one that many students do not learn without specific instruction. With instruction, students can learn to use self-monitoring to enhance and improve academic and social performance (Harris, Friedlander, Saddler, Frizzelle, & Graham, 2005; Hughes et al., 2002; Reid et al., 2005).

Self-monitoring increases the awareness of targeted behaviors.

Self-monitoring can be applied to both discrete behaviors (e.g., the number of pages read, assignments completed, or directions followed) and continuous behaviors (e.g., working on an assignment, paying attention during class, maintaining an appropriate social interaction with a peer). To self-monitor discrete behaviors, students record the targeted behavior each time they perform it. For continuous behaviors, students record whether or not the behavior is occurring according to one of the following schedules: (a) at the end of a predetermined interval (e.g., every 15 minutes); (b) in response to an external cue, usually delivered by the teacher; or (c) when the student thinks about it (Rhode, Jenson, & Reavis, 1992). We recommend using external cues, especially when students are first learning self-monitoring skills, because the evidence suggests that externally cued self-monitoring is more effective (Webber, Scheuermann, McCall, & Coleman, 1993). The external cue can be a verbal or nonverbal signal or a recorded signal. Rhode and her colleagues (1992) suggest creating Beeper Tapes for self-monitoring. To make a Beeper Tape, record a tone at random intervals on an audiocassette tape or compact disc. We have used a note played on a piano or on a recorder for this purpose. For use in the early stages of self-management programs, Beeper Tapes should contain frequent tones. For students with more experience in self-management, the tones can occur less frequently. (Therefore, the reinforcement schedule is thinned.) To use the Beeper Tape, have students listen to the tape during a time when the targeted behavior is expected. Headphones may be used if only one student is self-monitoring at any given time. As the Beeper Tape plays, students record occurrences and nonoccurrences of the targeted behavior(s) on their data form (see Figure 11-4 for sample self-monitoring forms).

Ms. Washington has her students self-monitor their grades with the goal of improving academic performance. To do this, she has her students record their daily grade for each subject. (See Figure 11-5 for a sample of the form that Ms. Washington uses for this purpose.) At the end of the week, students record their highest grade and their weekly average for each subject in the appropriate box. The following week, students who meet or exceed their best grade or their weekly average from the previous week earn one to six extra-credit points (depending on the extent of their improvement) for that subject. On our sample form, Tarique exceeded his weekly average in reading, mathematics, and social studies. In addition, he met or exceeded the previous week's high daily grade in reading, writing, mathematics, and social studies. Tarique earned a total of four extra-credit points: two for daily grades and two for weekly averages.

Self-Evaluation.   **Self-evaluation** refers to assessing one's performance against a standard. We use self-evaluation when we evaluate our appearance in a mirror, when mirror, when we examine the results of our housecleaning efforts, or when

Self-Monitoring Forms

Put a ✓ in a box each time you remember to raise your hand before calling out or leaving your seat.

Check your paper before you turn it in!					
Did you remember to do the following	M	T	W	Th	F
Indent each paragraph?	Y N	Y N	Y N	Y N	Y N
Capitalize the first letter of each sentence?	Y N	Y N	Y N	Y N	Y N
Use a punctuation mark at the end of each sentence?	Y N	Y N	Y N	Y N	Y N
Check your spelling?	Y N	Y N	Y N	Y N	Y N
Use the correct heading and margins, and write on one side only?	Y N	Y N	Y N	Y N	Y N

Put a ✓ in a box if you are working when you hear the signal.

Color in a lollipop each time you remember to put away your mat after rest time.

FIGURE 11-4   Sample Self-Monitoring and Self-Evaluation Forms

Self-Evaluation Forms

	How well are you paying attention during social studies? Circle the appropriate number when you hear the tone: 1 = Oops! I haven't been listening very well. 2 = I've been listening well most of the time, but sometimes my mind wanders. 3 = Great! I've been listening the entire time.				
Monday	1 2 3	1 2 3	1 2 3	1 2 3	1 2 3
Tuesday	1 2 3	1 2 3	1 2 3	1 2 3	1 2 3
Wednesday	1 2 3	1 2 3	1 2 3	1 2 3	1 2 3
Thursday	1 2 3	1 2 3	1 2 3	1 2 3	1 2 3
Friday	1 2 3	1 2 3	1 2 3	1 2 3	1 2 3

	How well did you follow the rules? Rate yourself after each class: 3 = Great! I followed every rule all class period. 2 = OK. I followed all of the rules most of the time. 1 = Not so good. I didn't follow some of the rules or didn't follow the rules for the entire class period.				
	M	T	W	Th	F
English	3 2 1	3 2 1	3 2 1	3 2 1	3 2 1
American History	3 2 1	3 2 1	3 2 1	3 2 1	3 2 1
Art	3 2 1	3 2 1	3 2 1	3 2 1	3 2 1
Biology	3 2 1	3 2 1	3 2 1	3 2 1	3 2 1

FIGURE 11-4 (Continued)

Name _____ Date _____

	Last Week's High Grade	Monday	Tuesday	Wednesday	Thursday	Friday	Weekly Average	Last Week's Average
Reading								
Writing								
Math								
Science								
Social Studies								

Extra-Credit (EC) Points for Daily Grades:

Meet or exceed 1–2 daily grades = 1 EC point

Meet or exceed 3–4 daily grades = 2 EC points

Meet or exceed all daily grades = 3 EC points

Extra-Credit (EC) Points for Weekly Average:

Meet or exceed 1–2 weekly averages = 1 EC point

Meet or exceed 3–4 weekly averages = 2 EC points

Meet or exceed all weekly averages = 3 EC points

Name ___Tarique___ Date ___12-05___

	Last Week's High Grade	Monday	Tuesday	Wednesday	Thursday	Friday	Weekly Average	Last Week's Average
Reading	75	73	(78)	77	(78)	72	(75.6)	74.0
Writing	78	70	75	74	(79)	(79)	75.4	76.5
Math	84	89	82	88	(90)	–	(87.25)	84.7
Science	92	85	88	85	84	–	85.5	90.5
Social Studies	95	(100)	95	98	94	96	(96.6)	95.0

FIGURE 11-5 Self-Monitoring Form for Grades

we consider how well we have performed in a job interview. In schools, students might self-evaluate how well they are paying attention during class, how neatly their paper is written, how well they responded to provocation, or how well they followed directions. Self-evaluation is much like self-monitoring in how it is implemented. The difference is that in self-monitoring, students simply record whether the behavior did or did not occur; in self-evaluation, they record how well or to what extent the targeted behavior was exhibited. To teach students to self-evaluate their performance, students must first understand the criteria for behavioral performance. For example, Mr. Dolezal is teaching Charlie to self-evaluate his written work for neatness and format. Before implementing the self-evaluation program, Mr. Dolezal explained to Charlie exactly what constitutes a neat paper and exactly how it should be formatted. During his explanation, he presented Charlie with multiple examples of neat and correctly formatted papers, as well as some nonexamples. When Charlie could consistently identify samples of neat and correctly formatted papers, Mr. Dolezal provided Charlie with a card to keep on his desk that listed the criteria for neatness and formatting. Then Charlie was instructed to compare each written assignment with those criteria and self-evaluate his product using a scale of 1 (i.e., my paper does not meet the standards for neatness or formatting) to 4 (i.e., my paper meets all standards for neatness and formatting).

Both self-monitoring and self-evaluation are appropriate for behaviors that the student knows how to perform (i.e., behaviors that are in the student's behavioral repertoire) but does so inconsistently or insufficiently. The following are the steps for implementing self-monitoring and self-evaluation interventions:

1. Operationally define the targeted behavior.
2. Determine whether you will use self-monitoring or self-evaluation. We recommend self-evaluation when the quality of the performance is important. Otherwise, self-monitoring should be sufficient.
3. Teach students to use the procedure by practicing while performing a behavior that is easy for students to perform. The steps for teaching the procedure include the following:
   a. Explain what the student will do.
   b. Model (demonstrate) how to use the form.
   c. Have students practice using the procedure as the teacher gives feedback.
   d. Introduce the procedure for only one behavior at first. Once students gain proficiency in using the technique, it can be applied to additional behaviors.
4. Reinforce the correct use of the procedure. At first, the teacher may wish to record data on one or more students' behaviors at the same time that the students are self-monitoring or self-evaluating their own behaviors. The teacher could randomly select one or more students by placing each student's name on a craft stick and selecting one or more sticks. Then, as the students use the self-management procedure, the teacher will simultaneously monitor or evaluate the students' behaviors. At the end of the period, each student whose data match the teacher's data with 80% accuracy earns a reinforcer. Teachers may wish to monitor students' data frequently at first, then gradually less often as the students become more skilled at using the procedures and internalize the self-management process.

Table 11-4 provides a sample vignette that illustrates the use of self-monitoring in middle school resource and inclusion classrooms. In addition, Figure 11-4 provides an example of self-evaluation forms.

Self-Instruction. **Self-instruction** is the process of using verbal cues to initiate, guide, or inhibit behavior. Most of us use self-instruction throughout the day. We use self-instruction to guide our performance on difficult tasks, to motivate ourselves to begin disliked tasks, or to control anger or frustration. Most of the time, we self-instruct silently (**covert self-instruction**). However, sometimes our self-instruction is spoken aloud (**overt self-instruction)**, especially when the task is difficult. Students can be taught to use self-instruction for many social and academic purposes. According to Meichenbaum and Goodman (1971), who pioneered much

---

TABLE 11-4   Self-Management Case Study

Self-Management in Mr. Jones's Sixth-Grade Classroom

Mr. Jones is a sixth-grade resource teacher. He also co-teaches an inclusion science class during second period; the students from the inclusion science class are also in his special education fourth-period reading class. In that class, he has taught them to use a self-management system in order to help them remember to raise their hand for help and wait to be called on by a teacher before stating their request. Every 10 minutes, at the sound of a timer, each student self-monitors whether he or she has been doing these behaviors since the time the timer last sounded. Mr. Jones randomly collects data during some of these 10-minute intervals to double-check students' data. Students earn points when their data match Mr. Jones's data with 90% accuracy or better, and when they complete an academic task with 80% accuracy or better. Mr. Jones asked his students if they would like to use this self-management system in their science class; they acknowledged that they thought that it helped them remember the rule about raising their hands and that they would like to use it in science class.

In the science class, the general education students quickly noticed that their peers were on a reinforcement system. They thought it only fair that they get equal treatment. Mr. Jones and Ms. James, the general education teacher, decided that the entire class would use self-monitoring in order to track their on-task behavior during independent work. Independent work time was often problematic for the teachers because students were exhibiting high rates of off-task behavior such as talking and goofing off. A timer with a gentle sound would be set to chime every 5 minutes, and students would note whether they were on task. Each class period usually included 30 minutes of independent work time, meaning that there would be six opportunities for self-monitoring during the period. The two teachers would also monitor randomly selected students each day; students whose data matched the teacher's with at least a 90% correlation rate earned an extra-credit point for the day. The special education students continued to also monitor the two original behaviors; however, they changed from 10-minute intervals to 5-minute intervals during science to enable them to self-monitor using the same timer schedule as was being used for on-task behavior.

This system worked well for the special education students, improving both the hand-raising and on-task behaviors. The system also increased on-task behavior for the general education students as well. The teachers eventually made the self-monitoring intervals longer and selected fewer students to double-check the self-monitoring data.

of the research in self-instruction, the steps for teaching students to self-instruct are as follows:

1. The teacher models the behavior while talking aloud.
2. The teacher talks aloud while the student performs the behavior.
3. The teacher whispers and the student talks aloud while performing the behavior.
4. The teacher mouths the words and the student whispers while performing the behavior.
5. The student performs the behavior while using silent (covert) self-instruction.

Self-Reinforcement. The self-management interventions described thus far are usually more effective when combined with reinforcement. To complete the self-management process, the last step is to teach students to use **self-reinforcement.** Most of us use self-reinforcement to increase our motivation to perform tasks that we dislike or to reinforce a good performance. For example, one of the authors of this text (JAH) used self-reinforcement to encourage her to keep writing and complete the text: She reinforced herself by using a favorite food or activity after writing a predetermined number of pages. In self-reinforcement, students are allowed to award themselves a reinforcer if they determine that they have met the criterion for the targeted behavior (Reid et al., 2005). Reinforcers are usually tokens or points.

Evidence indicates that self-determined contingencies may be more effective than teacher-determined contingencies (Hays et al., 1985). Self-determined contingencies may include having students select their own reinforcers, having students set the criteria for earning reinforcers, or both. As with self-monitoring and self-evaluation, self-reinforcement should be introduced gradually, after the behaviors have been brought under the control of external contingencies (e.g., teacher-managed systems). To implement self-reinforcement, Felixbrod and O'Leary (1974) recommend comparing classroom work with work done on the job: It is important to do good work and then you get paid by your employer. Then allow the students to determine any or all of the following: (a) the criterion for reinforcement, (b) the nature of the reinforcer, and (c) the amount of reinforcement to be earned. Because students tend to set lenient self-reinforcement contingencies (Felixbrod & O'Leary, 1974), students may need to be guided to set higher standards, especially when self-reinforcement is being used for academic performance (Alberto & Troutman, 2006). This can be accomplished by using additional teacher-determined reinforcement for high standards. Remember our example of self-monitoring grades in Ms. Washington's middle school class? During the second-grading period, after her students were familiar with the self-monitoring system, Ms. Washington added a self-reinforcement component. She allowed students to determine their extra-credit point schedule: How many points can they earn and how much improvement will be required? Ms. Washington imposed a limit on the number of extra-credit points that could be earned in a week; however, the students who demonstrated enough improvement that they had exceeded the maximum points allowed could earn other classroom privileges.

Summary

Effective teachers will use a variety of the reinforcement systems described in this chapter. We encourage educators not to be stingy in their use of reinforcement systems. The more challenging the behaviors exhibited by a student or class, the more intensive the reinforcement interventions may need to be. In our work with teachers and administrators, we recommend using layers of reinforcement when there is a need to address multiple problems. For example, a teacher might use one token system to address the problems of work completion and accuracy, a different token system for encouraging rule-following behaviors, and a group contingency for appropriate playground behavior. This is not to say that reinforcement systems need to be complicated. On the contrary, we urge teachers to design simple, easy-to-use systems. An overly intricate system may end up not being used at all.

The objectives for this chapter and how they were addressed are as follows:

1. Define the Premack Principle.

In this chapter, we explained the Premack Principle, the simplest of reinforcement systems. Parents and grandparents know this strategy well, which explains the fact that the principle is commonly called "Grandma's Law." The Premack Principle simply states that access to preferred activities are to be contingent upon the completion of low-preference activities.

2. Explain how to develop and implement token systems.

Token systems are the foundation of most reinforcement programs. Token systems provide a way for teachers to give immediate feedback to students in the form of a token without having to deliver an actual reinforcer that may be disruptive to the learning activity. The tokens are a signal to students that they are earning reinforcement, which will be delivered at a later, more convenient time.

3. Explain how to develop and implement contracts.

A contract is a good tool to use when one student needs more intensive and/or individualized reinforcement. A contract specifies targeted behaviors and criteria, reinforcers to be earned, and supports to be provided by the teacher. Contracts should also include a section for recording data on the targeted behavior. Student input in determining contingency arrangements is allowed, which may help to explain their effectiveness.

4. Explain stimulus control and how to establish it.

Stimulus control is a powerful antecedent intervention. Reinforcement is used to establish stimulus control. Any of the reinforcement systems described in this chapter could be used to establish a specific stimulus as an S^D for stimulus control purposes. Establishing stimulus control over desired behaviors should mean that teachers will spend less time responding to inappropriate behaviors. Stimulus control also streamlines management tasks: When students respond to the S^D for a given behavior, teachers spend less time instructing and prompting students for that behavior.

5. Describe three types of group reinforcement systems and give examples of applications for each.

Group reinforcement systems help to create cohesive, cooperative groups within a classroom. The three types of group reinforcement systems—independent, interdependent, and dependent—each serve different purposes. Interdependent and dependent group contingencies carry the risk of one or more students intentionally sabotaging the group effort. This does not mean that the teacher should abandon the group contingency. Instead, in order to address this problem, the teacher should apply the steps for problem solving that we have described in this chapter.

6. Explain five types of self-management techniques.

The goal of external reinforcement systems should be to bring appropriate behaviors under

TABLE 11-5   Reinforcement Applications Self-Assessment

Never	Seldom	Sometimes	Often	Always
1	2	3	4	5

Use the numbers from the scale above to rate the following statements.

1. I use the Premack Principle in my own life. _____

2. I use the Premack Principle in my classroom. _____

3. I understand how to develop and implement a variety of token systems. _____

4. I use token system(s) to address a variety of behaviors. _____

5. I use student contracts as needed for individual interventions. _____

6. I can explain to other school staff and parents why I choose to use token systems or student contracts. _____

7. I use a variety of group reinforcement systems. _____

8. I know what to do if a student(s) sabotages a group reinforcement system. _____

9. I know how to design and implement self-management systems. _____

10. I am sufficiently comfortable in my knowledge of the preceding reinforcement applications that I can explain their use to my supervisors. _____

external control (i.e., to establish those behaviors within the students' behavioral repertoires). At that point, the next step in responsible reinforcement is to teach students self-management skills to enable them to be successful even when external contingency systems are unavailable. We described five types of self-management techniques: goal setting, self-monitoring, self-evaluation, self-instruction, and self-reinforcement.

Each technique has a slightly different purpose, but all have been shown to improve self-management skills for various ages and all types of populations.

In Table 11–5, we provide a self-assessment for teachers to evaluate their use of reinforcement applications. Effective teachers know and use a variety of reinforcement tools to facilitate appropriate student behavior.

Dr. ICE Helps Teachers Solve Classroom Management Problems Through the Use of Reinforcement

ELEMENTARY SCHOOL

Dr. ICE visited Mr. Vanders, a primary-grade special education resource teacher at Anson Elementary School. Mr. Vanders is an old friend of Dr. ICE and has worked with Dr. ICE many times over the years. Mr. Vanders has 12 students, from grades 1 to 3, in his class. His students have a variety of disabilities that affect not only their academic learning but also their classroom behavior.

Mr. Vanders was happy to see Dr. ICE, and he eagerly told him about the reinforcement program that he wants to implement with his students. He said that he provides liberal praise, but that he feels that he needs something extra in order to help his students learn.

Mr. Vanders has taught his students the rules and procedures for his classroom. He wants to begin a reinforcement system that would help his students continue to experience learning in a positive environment. He had asked his principal if he could be reimbursed for any reinforcers that he bought, but his principal told him that the budget is very lean and that there is no money available for reinforcers. Mr. Vanders has only enough money in his personal budget to buy a few reinforcers, so he knows that he needs to select reinforcers and a reinforcer delivery system that are affordable.

Mr. Vanders wants to reinforce both academic success and social behavior. He has decided to focus on academic grades and following classroom procedures. He will have his students chart their grades. Students will earn one ticket for grades of 80% to 89%, two tickets for 90% to 99%, and three tickets for 100%. He has also decided to randomly pass out tickets for following procedures. Students will sign their name on the back, and a drawing will be held at the end of each academic lesson.

Before asking his students for their input on reinforcers, Mr. Vanders made his own list of possible reinforcers that met his criteria. He knows from past experience that sometimes young children will not or cannot generate ideas for reinforcers when asked. He wanted to give them some ideas. The following are the ideas that Mr. Vanders shared with his students:

- Students can earn track time in 10-minute increments. The P.E. teacher is promoting a walking program for students, and this idea would fit nicely into that program.
- Students would be allowed to draw while the teacher reads.
- Students would be allowed to assist the teacher with certain tasks.
- Students can earn time to work on a class talent show.
- Students can earn time to work on a jigsaw puzzle.
- The class can earn tickets for a Games Day.
- Students can earn the opportunity to have lunch with the teacher.
- Students would be allowed to choose a book for the teacher to read to the class.
- The students in the class can pool their tickets and exchange them for a popcorn/movie party.

Mr. Vanders plans to describe the reinforcement program in detail on Friday. When they get to the part about reinforcers, he will give them his ideas and ask for their ideas, reminding the students about the issue cost as necessary. Then they will role-play how to earn tickets. Implementation of the reinforcement program will begin on the following Monday.

Mr. Vanders has decided to monitor the effectiveness of the reinforcement program by using his students' charts of their grades and by keeping his own graph of the number of tickets earned by each student. He will also monitor the number of office disciplinary referrals. He told Dr. ICE that he plans to find a business that will donate some reinforcers later in the year and that as the reinforcers become more valuable, tickets will be harder to earn.

Dr. ICE liked the reinforcement system that his friend had developed. However, he had a question for Mr. Vanders: What are the problems that can and often do happen in using a reinforcement system? He and Mr. Vanders discussed the following possible problems, as well as some solutions to those problems:

- Students may not buy into the program—a problem that may be resolved by taking the following actions:
  - Talk with and watch the students to find out what they like.
  - Identify additional function-based reinforcers.
- Students may perceive that their environment is so reinforcer rich that they don't have the need to work for more:
  - The teacher may need to make the students work for items that they are taking for granted.
  - Some days, the reinforcement system just does not seem to work—a problem that may be resolved by considering the following questions:
  - Has something happened to alter your class schedule or routine? Students often act out when their routine changes.
  - Do the students feel well? When students—especially young children—are ill, you may see an increase in inappropriate behavior.
  - How do you feel? Teachers who are stressed or sick may behave in ways that negatively impact students more than the teacher realizes.

Mr. Vanders now realizes that he will need to monitor the effects of the program closely. He thanked Dr. ICE for listening to his ideas and for providing him with problem-solving ideas.

MIDDLE SCHOOL

Ms. Grace teaches a self-contained life skills class at Holland Middle School. She has 10 students, ages 11–13 years, who are developmentally at the kindergarten to third-grade levels. Mornings are devoted to academic subjects, and in the afternoon she extends the students' academics into prevocational instruction (i.e., sorting mail by matching names on the mail to names on the mail slots, making copies on the copier, and planting seeds to grow herb plants). She also spends about an hour each day on self-help skills, including hygiene, organization, cooking, leisure skills, and social skills.

Ms. Grace wants to reinforce the skills that her students need to know in order to be successful in school and community settings. She has not had problems with her students acting out, other than an occasional minor tantrum. The primary problem has been attention to task, especially if the task is perceived as being difficult. She has chosen to focus her reinforcement program on following procedures and increasing on-task behavior. Effort Bucks are used for the token economy. These bucks may be used to buy items from the classroom store or may be exchanged for the opportunity to participate in special classroom activities.

Ms. Grace allowed her students free access to all activities during the first week, and then she priced the activities according to their popularity. The classroom store has many items available for purchase, including cards that describe special activities. She knows that many of her students have problems with nutrition and weight, so she does not include junk food as an option. Bottled water has been a hot item. Students have access to the store twice a day at set times after their required academic studies. She also wants the students to work as a group for a reinforcer. She set up a bottle that would hold marbles. The students can buy up to three marbles each time the store is open and put them in the bottle. When the bottle is full, students earn a special cooking class in which they can prepare a special treat to share in class.

Ms. Grace introduced the token economy system during mathematics instruction. She built it into each lesson during the first week. Then she reviewed it as necessary or at least once a week.

As the reinforcement system got underway, she realized that a banking system was needed to help the students keep track of their Effort Bucks. The banking system would also help her to evaluate the effectiveness of the reinforcement system. Students will keep a simple ledger on their desks. As students earn Effort Bucks, they will record them in the ledger. Each time that they make a purchase from the classroom store, they will record the number of Effort Bucks that they spent. At the end of the day, they will use calculators to balance their ledgers. The daily total is then carried over to the next day. Ms. Grace also uses a bar graph of completed work and grades to monitor her students' progress. Gradually, the students' work has became more difficult, so more is expected out of them in order to earn an Effort Buck.

A common problem that occurs is that a student will buy an activity and then want to exchange the activity after a short time. Ms. Grace has turned this problem into a learning experience by allowing the students to trade activities amongst themselves by mutual agreement. However, once an activity has been bought from the store, it cannot be returned during that particular activity period. This rule encourages the students to take time when making their choice and to work together in order to solve a problem.

HIGH SCHOOL

Mr. McNeil teaches a class for students who have academic and behavioral problems that are severe enough to warrant being in a self-contained class. This is a new program and is special in that, although these students have severe problems, they will be allowed to work at jobs in their community each afternoon after their academic classes. Mr. McNeil teaches academic subjects and one vocational class that covers how to handle job stress and other specific job skills that the students need to master.

Mr. McNeil was given very strict guidelines about the work program. Students have to exhibit excellent behavior in order to be allowed to leave campus (e.g., they are not permitted to have any office disciplinary referrals on their record). He wanted to use a reinforcement program to help his students learn to control their own behavior in school and later on at their jobs, so he created a contract for his students with the ultimate goal of helping them keep their jobs. Once they begin working, the students will receive a paycheck. Mr. McNeil knew that, for these teenagers, a paycheck would be a reinforcer that would get their attention.

A contract was developed that focused on the following behaviors:

- Following directions.
- Talking respectfully to authority figures.

- Completing academic tasks.
- Earning grades of 80% or better.
- Following the school dress code.
- Having zero instances of verbal or physical aggression.

Students earn points for each of the preceding behaviors each hour that they spend in school. Students who exhibit no verbal or physical aggression and who earn 80% of their points each week may participate in extra job-training activities on Friday. Students who have had an incidence of verbal or physical aggression are not allowed to participate. The job-training activities include games which address social skills that are needed on the job, movies related to employment and specific job skills, and role-playing activities that pertain to vocationally related social skills. In addition to earning job activities, students are permitted to earn passes that allow them to skip homework when their work in class has been completed with 80% accuracy or better. Finally, students can accumulate points for 6 weeks and earn trips to the mall with the parent specialist. At the mall, they can buy work clothes and other items.

The program has worked very well so far. Students have been successful on their respective jobs. The classroom-based reinforcement system has helped them complete their work and learn to control their inappropriate behavior. Their grades have improved significantly since implementation of the system. Mr. McNeil is very proud of his students. In addition, his students receive many compliments from employers and school administrators. Mr. McNeil credits the reinforcement system for much of this success.

Learning Activities

1. In small groups, discuss examples of the Premack Principle with regard to the following:
   - When you were a child
   - Currently in your life
   - How you would use it in your classroom
     Afterwards, share your discussion with the entire group.
2. Develop a token system in order to change one of your behaviors. Write a short report describing the process.
3. Write a contract for a high school student that you would use to help the student increase the amount of accurate work he or she produces in class. Write a report that describes the contract and how you would implement it. In your report, anticipate possible problems with the contract and how you would address them.
4. In a small group, describe the three types of group reinforcement systems. Be prepared to role-play one of them for the entire group.
5. Identify 15 examples of stimulus control from daily life.
6. Explain how you use each of the following in daily life:
   - Self-monitoring
   - Self-evaluation
   - Self-instruction
   - Self-reinforcement
7. Develop a self-management system for each of the following areas:
   - Studying
   - Following instructions
   - Remembering what needs to be done
   - Using appropriate social skills in the common areas of a school
   - Using appropriate bus-riding behaviors

Resources

BOOKS

Cipani, E. (1998). *Classroom management for all teachers*. Upper Saddle River, NJ: Merrill/Pearson. Offers 11 intervention systems for increasing appropriate behavior and reducing inappropriate behavior.

Jenson, W., Rhode, G., & Reavis, K. (1994). *The tough kid tool box*. Longmont, CO: Sopris West. Provides forms for token systems, contracts, self-management interventions, and other reinforcement-based interventions.

Rhode, G., Jenson, W., & Reavis, K. (1992). *The tough kid book*. Longmont, CO: Sopris West.
Provides classroom and individual student behavioral interventions, including self-management interventions.

WEBSITES

www.vanderbilt.edu/csefel   Center on the Social and Emotional Foundations for Early Learning: Provides guidelines for teaching young children self-management skills.

http://classroommanagement.edreform.net/port al/classroommanagement/studentselfmanage-ment   Part of the Classroom Management section of the Education Reform Website: Provides tools and guidelines for cognitive and behavioral approaches to teaching self-management skills.

http://iris.peabody.vanderbilt.edu/resources.html   The IRIS Resource Locator on the Website of the IRIS Center for Training Enhancements provides a variety of resources on special education topics, including classroom management.

ARTICLES

www.fape.org/pubs/fape-20.pdf   The Families and Advocates Partnership for Education project: Provides a one-page overview on teaching self-management skills. The overview is entitled "Promising Practices: Teaching Students to Self-Manage Their Behavior."

Five

BEHAVIOR REDUCTIVE INTERVENTIONS

Chapter 12
Managing Challenging Behaviors by Using Behavior Reductive Interventions

After reading this chapter, you will be able to do the following:

1. Define nonpunishment and punishment techniques.
2. Describe IDEA's disciplinary provisions and zero-tolerance policies.
3. Define zero tolerance and describe the problems that arise when zero-tolerance policies are applied.
4. Describe the guidelines for judicious and ethical use of behavior reductive interventions.
5. Describe the hierarchy of behavior reductive strategies:
   a. Differential reinforcement
   b. Extinction
   c. Response cost
   d. Time-out
   e. Presentation of aversive stimuli
6. Describe how to implement each strategy correctly and ethically, and explain which strategies conform to a PBIS philosophy and which do not.

Managing Challenging Behaviors by Using Behavior Reductive Interventions

Big ideas in managing challenging behaviors:

- Punishment is often the most common response to challenging behavior, but it is seldom the most effective response for students who exhibit chronic challenging behaviors.

- Taking a positive behavioral interventions and supports (PBIS) approach to challenging behavior means relying on preventive measures, teaching appropriate behaviors, reinforcing appropriate behaviors, using nonpunishment strategies, and only using punishment under certain limited circumstances.

- The Individuals with Disabilities Education Act (IDEA) of 2004 provides parameters for the discipline of students with disabilities.

- Behavioral technology offers several options for reducing the frequency of behaviors by using nonaversive methods, including reinforcement.

It seems that we live in a punishment-oriented society, where reinforcement is usually infrequent and weak. In fact, intrinsic reinforcement is the primary motivational force for most of us: We behave appropriately because we have goals that we wish to accomplish, because we want to do well in school, or because we like the satisfaction of doing a job well. Of course, sometimes we follow rules not because of what we will earn, but in order to avoid penalties, fines, and other negative consequences. That is, negative reinforcement is also a controlling force in our lives. Society relies on punishment as well. When you break a rule or law, you might encounter negative consequences in the form of loss of privileges, fines, penalties, or jail terms.

Generally, our society relies on intrinsic reinforcement, negative reinforcement, and punishment as the primary means of behavioral control. We suspect that you have never been stopped by the police just to be told what a great driver you are, and thanks for following the speed limit. The Internal Revenue Service assesses a penalty if you fail to pay your taxes on time, but we have never heard any government official discuss reinforcing (perhaps through a lower tax assessment?) taxpayers for making timely payments. In fact, even your college or university probably has a well-defined punishment system for failure to pay your tuition on time, for parking in the wrong places, for failing to meet certain minimum grade requirements, or for myriad other targeted behaviors.

Intrinsic reinforcement, negative reinforcement, and punishment are the primary means for controlling behavior in our society.

When faced with serious challenging behavior that continues despite application of the interventions that we have described so far (e.g., clear and predictable environments, good teacher–student relationships, effective instruction, and reinforcement of appropriate behavior), effective teachers will know and be able to use a variety of techniques for reducing challenging behavior. Typically, school personnel have a limited number of strategies for responding to serious misbehavior. These strategies, including office disciplinary referrals, detention, loss of privileges, in-school and out-of-school suspension, and expulsion, are ineffective at improving school safety or preventing severe misbehavior (Skiba & Peterson, 2000) and are also costly in many ways. For example, schools must provide personnel and space for exclusionary disciplinary programs (e.g., in-school suspension, detention); it takes time for the teacher to write office disciplinary referrals and time for the administrator to respond to those referrals; and, perhaps most significantly, the student misses instruction when he or she is sent out of the classroom for disciplinary reasons.

There is good news, however. First, there is a nationwide movement to rethink school discipline from a PBIS framework (see Chapter 5); thus, administrators are beginning to plan school disciplinary systems that rely on positive, preventive, and instructional methods. In addition, behavioral technology provides educators with a range of effective and efficient strategies, many of which are less negative and less costly than the traditional methods of suspension and expulsion. In this chapter, we describe those strategies.

In Chapter 1, we proposed Guiding Principles to help educators establish a positive, proactive mind-set regarding challenging behavior. The sixth Guiding Principle is that positive and preventive strategies are more effective and efficient than punishment for behavior management purposes. A PBIS approach requires relying on antecedent-based interventions, teaching new skills, and giving more attention to appropriate behavior than to inappropriate behavior. However, sometimes a behavior is sufficiently dangerous, disruptive, or chronic and thus warrants an intervention that is intended to reduce or eliminate the challenging behavior while simultaneously replacing it with a more acceptable, functional alternative. For this reason, educators need to know when behavior reductive interventions are needed and how to select appropriate behavior reductive techniques. Behavior reductive techniques are appropriate when there is documented evidence of their effectiveness, they are used correctly as part of a comprehensive array of interventions, and they produce changes in behavior by using the least aversive methods available.

An event can be defined as "punishment" only if it weakens or eliminates a behavior.

At this point, we wish to clarify the terminology used in this chapter. Behavior reductive terminology has been the subject of much debate. We use the term **behavior reductive procedures** as a general term that refers to the entire hierarchy of punishment and nonpunishment interventions. The term **punishment** refers to a stimulus that follows a behavior and reduces future occurrences of the behavior. Like reinforcement, punishment can be defined only by its effect on the behavior: If the behavior is not weakened or eliminated, punishment has not occurred. Understanding this important concept will help teachers and administrators avoid the unpleasant situation of repeatedly applying negative consequences for a student's behavior with no corresponding change in the student's behavior. Consider the case of Sasha, a 13-year-old girl who exhibits high levels of challenging behaviors. Her teachers regularly send her to the office for disruptive and disrespectful behaviors. The principal applies various sanctions, ranging from calling her parents to placing her in in-school suspension, a commonly used disciplinary technique in which students must complete their schoolwork independently during 1 or more days in a specially designated room on campus with no opportunities for socialization. These consequences have been consistently applied, but Sasha continues her problematic behavior. The teachers and the principal intended to punish Sasha, but because her inappropriate behavior has not diminished, punishment has not occurred. Punishment can be a legitimate tool for managing severely challenging behaviors under certain limited circumstances. However, because of the negative connotations associated with the term *punishment* and because other, less negative procedures can be as effective as or more effective than punishment, we use the terms **nonpunishment procedures** to refer to techniques that produce decreases in targeted behaviors through less negative means than punishment. In this chapter, we describe two types of nonpunishment procedures—differential reinforcement and extinction— and two types of punishment—removal of desirable stimuli and presentation of aversive stimuli.

WHAT TYPES OF BEHAVIOR WARRANT THE USE OF BEHAVIOR REDUCTIVE TECHNIQUES?

The strategies and procedures described throughout this text will be sufficient for most students under most circumstances. However, occasionally these methods will not adequately prevent or control extremely challenging behaviors. Some students might need behavior reductive interventions that are specifically designed to reduce or eliminate those challenging behaviors. Generally, students who need these types of interventions are those who exhibit highly disruptive or dangerous behaviors, or for whom challenging behavior is a chronic condition that is unresponsive to the antecedent and reinforcement techniques described thus far (Kauffman, 2005; Kazdin, 1998).

In our three-tiered model of PBIS, traditional disciplinary methods (e.g., calling the parents, loss of privileges, detention) are still applied. In addition, the techniques presented in this chapter can help educators effectively manage challenging behaviors at each level of support. Most of the techniques discussed in this chapter will primarily be used for students at the tertiary level, and will be part of comprehensive, individual, function-based intervention plans. For that reason, we focus on individual applications of the behavior reductive methods presented here. However, positive behavioral interventions and supports (PBIS) teams might also use some of the techniques presented in this chapter to address high-frequency, minor misbehavior at the universal and/or targeted levels. For example, PBIS teams might use one or more of the differential reinforcement techniques described later as part of a comprehensive plan to reduce targeted inappropriate behaviors in common areas (e.g., cafeteria, hallways, playground, bus-loading area, parking lot) (Wheatley, West, Charlton, Sanders, Smith, & Taylor, 2009).

Before implementing most behavior reductive techniques and all punishment, educators should ask the following questions:

1. Are the rules and procedures clear, and have they been taught to students?
2. Does the classroom climate and teacher–student relationship reflect a respectful, positive learning environment?
3. Has a functional behavioral assessment (FBA) been conducted to identify the possible functions of the challenging behavior, and have the resulting hypotheses been used as the basis for designing antecedent and reinforcement interventions?
4. Have dense reinforcement schedules been used to reinforce appropriate behaviors?
5. Are the curricula and instructional methods appropriate for the student's learning needs?
6. Is the student actively and successfully engaged in meaningful learning tasks most of the time?
7. Has the student been directly taught appropriate behavioral skills (e.g., social skills) and communication skills? This is especially important for students with autism and other emotional/behavioral disorders.
8. Have all of these interventions been applied correctly and consistently?

If the answer to any of these questions is "no," the first step should be to address that situation before implementing a behavior reductive procedure. However, if all of these questions are answered affirmatively, it might be appropriate to plan a behavior reductive intervention.

Behaviors that might warrant a behavior reductive intervention include the following:

> Punishment should be reserved for behaviors that are dangerous, highly disruptive, or that persist despite other interventions.

- Chronic inappropriate behaviors that persist despite clear, correct use of antecedent measures (e.g., rules, procedures, climate), reinforcement of appropriate behavior, and natural or logical consequences.
- Behavior that is dangerous to the student or others. Physical aggression, bullying, destruction of property, and, possibly, verbal aggression are examples of the types of behavior that would fall into this category. Marco is a 5-year-old who bites his peers at least once per day. Marco's teacher understands that this behavior must be stopped immediately. Because antecedent and reinforcement interventions have not been effective in stopping the biting, one or more behavior reductive techniques are needed.
- Behaviors that interfere with the student's academic or social success. For example, Charlotte is a ninth-grader who is at or close to grade level in most of her academic subjects. However, Charlotte exhibits a number of behaviors that are highly inappropriate, such as sexual comments, threats, and derogatory comments directed toward peers. Because of these behaviors, Charlotte is shunned by her peers. Charlotte's teachers have decided that a comprehensive behavior plan is needed and that the behavior plan needs to include strategies designed to quickly reduce those inappropriate behaviors.

For students in special education, behaviors that interfere with their learning or their peers' learning need to be addressed in a behavior intervention plan (BIP), as described in Chapter 3. BIPs will typically target for reduction those behaviors that directly or indirectly interfere with learning, including the types of behaviors described previously.

2004 IDEA REQUIREMENTS FOR DISCIPLINING STUDENTS WITH DISABILITIES

The 1997 reauthorization of the Individuals with Disabilities Education Act included a number of new provisions with regard to disciplining students with disabilities. These provisions were the result of hard work on the part of numerous advocacy and professional groups, many of which had conflicting goals and concerns regarding school disciplinary issues. Those provisions were designed primarily to protect students with disabilities from being removed from school for behavioral issues that might be related to the student's disability and to improve procedural protections for students with disabilities with regard to disciplinary actions. At the same time, the provisions of the 1997 IDEA took into account administrators' concerns about school safety and flexibility in decision making. The unique components of the 1997 disciplinary provisions included the following:

IDEA includes provisions to protect students with disabilities with regard to disciplinary actions while allowing administrators the latitude that they need to ensure safe schools.

- *Manifestation determination:* School officials were required to consider whether the misbehavior was a result of the student's disability.
- *"Stay put" provision:* Under most circumstances, a student was required to remain in his or her current placement pending the outcome of a disciplinary process. This meant that a student could not be moved to another, more restrictive placement because of conduct.
- *Placement in an interim alternative educational setting (IAES):* School personnel could either suspend a student or place the student in an IAES or another setting for no more than 10 school days. In the case of a weapons or drug violation, a student could be placed in an IAES for no more than 45 days.

However, once the new disciplinary provisions were being implemented, administrators were unhappy with certain aspects of the law. For this reason, the 1997 IDEA disciplinary provisions were modified in the 2004 reauthorization. Table 12-1 provides an overview of the 2004 IDEA requirements for the disciplining of students with disabilities, particularly with regard to those elements of the 1997 IDEA described previously.

Many current disciplinary practices stem from a particularly troublesome policy known as zero tolerance. **Zero-tolerance policies**, with their roots in the federal drug laws of the 1980s, became required practice for schools with passage of the Gun-Free Schools Act of 1997 (Skiba, 2000). The original law delineated mandatory expulsion for any student in possession of a firearm at school, but subsequent amendments have expanded the language of the bill to include any instrument that might be used as a weapon. Zero-tolerance policies in school districts vary greatly; some apply zero-tolerance punishments (e.g., suspension, placement in an alternative disciplinary setting) equally for a wide range of conduct violations, whereas other districts follow a graduated system of consequences with the severity of the

TABLE 12-1   Highlights of the Disciplinary Provisions of the 2004 IDEA

1. **Authority for school personnel:** School personnel may consider any unique circumstances on a case-by-case basis when determining whether to order a change in placement for a child with a disability who violates a code of student conduct.

   [615(k)(1)(A)]

2. **Manifestation determination:** For students who have been suspended for more than 10 days, the parent(s), school personnel, and relevant members of the individualized educational program (IEP) team must review relevant information in the student's file, including the student's IEP, to determine whether the conduct in question was

   • caused by, or had a direct and substantial relationship to, the child's disability; or

   • the direct result of the local educational agency's failure to implement the IEP.

   This manifestation determination must be done within 10 school days of any decision to change the placement of a child with a disability because of a violation of the code of student conduct.

   [615(k)(1)(E)(i)]

3. **If it is determined that a behavior was a manifestation of the disability,** the IEP team must do the following:

   • Conduct a functional behavioral assessment and implement a behavior intervention plan, if these have not been done.

   • If a BIP is in place, it must be reviewed and modified, if necessary, to address the behavior in question.

   • The student must be returned to the original educational setting, unless the parents and school personnel agree to the change in placement.

   [615(k)(1)(F)]

4. **Special circumstances:** If a student has inflicted serious bodily injury upon another person while at school or at a school function, school personnel may move the student to an IAES for no more than 45 school days without investigating whether the behavior is a manifestation of the child's disability. "Serious bodily injury" is defined as a bodily injury that involves a substantial risk of death, extreme physical pain, protracted and obvious disfigurement, or protracted loss or impairment of the function of a bodily member, organ, or mental faculty.

   [615(k)(7)(D)]

Source: U.S. Department of Education, Office of Special Education and Rehabilitative Services, Topical Brief on Discipline. Available online at www2.ed.gov/policy/speced/guid/idea/tb-discipline.doc

consequence matching the severity of the offense (Skiba, 2000). Unfortunately, in some cases, adherence to zero-tolerance policies has reached the absurd, such as in the case of a 5-year-old student in Deer Lakes, Pennsylvania, who was suspended for wearing a 5-inch plastic ax as part of his firefighter's costume for his class Halloween party. There are many other equally outrageous examples (Advancement Project and the Harvard Civil Rights Project, 2000; Skiba, 2000). Numerous scholarly papers have identified many serious problems with zero-tolerance policies. In 2000, the Advancement Project, in collaboration with the Civil Rights Project at Harvard

University, published a comprehensive review of zero-tolerance research and policies. As stated in the Executive Summary of the report, "The report illustrates that Zero Tolerance is unfair, is contrary to the developmental needs of children, denies children educational opportunities, and often results in the criminalization of children" (Advancement Project and the Harvard Civil Rights Project, 2000, p. v). The report also documents the fact that minority children and students with disabilities are disproportionately affected by zero-tolerance policies (Advancement Project and the Harvard Civil Rights Project, 2000).

Of course, students must experience meaningful consequences for serious behavioral infractions and schools must be safe and orderly. However, the evidence does not indicate that zero-tolerance policies can achieve either of these outcomes. As an alternative to traditional approaches to addressing the breaking of rules (e.g., office disciplinary referrals, detention, suspension), we offer the strategies described in this chapter. In addition, in Chapter 5, we described new approaches to school discipline that are founded on positive, preventive, instructional strategies (i.e., schoolwide PBIS). It is interesting to note that the Harvard Civil Rights Project study mentioned previously included schoolwide PBIS as the first item in a section on promising alternatives to zero tolerance.

> Schoolwide PBIS is an effective approach to school discipline that is founded on positive, proactive, instructional strategies.

ALTERNATIVES FOR BEHAVIOR REDUCTION AND GUIDELINES FOR CHOOSING BEHAVIOR REDUCTIVE TECHNIQUES

Table 12-2 shows a hierarchy of four categories of interventions for reducing challenging behaviors. These interventions range from the least aversive, reinforcement-based techniques (i.e., the differential reinforcement procedures) to the most aversive techniques (i.e., the presentation of an aversive stimulus). Three of the four categories include one or more specific applications.

TABLE 12-2   Hierarchy of Interventions for Reducing Behavior

I. Reinforcement-based strategies
- Differential reinforcement of incompatible behaviors (DRI)
- Differential reinforcement of alternative behaviors (DRA)
- Differential reinforcement of lower rates of behavior (DRL)
- Differential reinforcement of zero levels of behavior or differential reinforcement of other behaviors (DRO)

II. Extinction (withholding reinforcement)

III. Removal of reinforcing stimuli
- Response cost
- Time-out

IV. Presentation of aversive stimuli
- Conditioned aversive stimuli (reprimands)
- Unconditioned aversive stimuli (corporal punishment)
- Overcorrection procedures

To ensure a judicious and ethical response to challenging behavior, the following guidelines should be observed when choosing and implementing behavior reductive strategies:

1. Choose the least aversive intervention that can reasonably be expected to produce the desired results. The reinforcement-based differential reinforcement techniques described in this chapter might be sufficient for most challenging behaviors. Alberto and Troutman (2006) state that differential reinforcement strategies have such a strong history of success, as documented by more than a decade of research, that there is little support for use of aversive procedures in school settings. Should initial interventions fail to control the challenging behavior, move systematically along the behavior reductive continuum only as far as necessary to effectively manage the challenging behavior. That is, first use one or more of the differential reinforcement interventions, perhaps with extinction. If those fail to reduce the challenging behavior sufficiently, you may need to consider removing reinforcing stimuli. Of the three types of intervention in the last category—the presentation of aversive stimuli—we recommend using only the first intervention: reprimands. We discuss concerns about the use of aversive stimuli later in this chapter.

2. Ensure that data are used to make decisions about the need for behavior reductive procedures and to document the effectiveness of nonpunishment techniques before considering punishment strategies.

3. Ensure that a functional assessment has been conducted prior to the implementation of behavior reductive procedures and that previous interventions have been based on functional assessment data. The development of any behavior reductive intervention should take into consideration the results of the functional assessment, particularly the hypothesized functions of the problematic behavior. Remember that the challenging behavior must become less efficient and less effective for the student in terms of producing reinforcement (e.g., attention, control, escape) than appropriate behaviors. Reinforcement for desired behaviors must be more meaningful, more frequent, and more intense than any response to challenging behavior.

Instructional and reinforcement interventions should be used in conjunction with a behavior reductive program.

4. Continue to use instructional and reinforcement strategies in conjunction with behavior reductive methods. Nonpunishment and punishment should never be used in isolation. As you learned in Chapters 2, 3, and 9, challenging behavior is purposeful and often reflects skill deficits in one or more prosocial behaviors. If we simply eliminate a behavior, we are reducing the individual's already limited behavioral repertoire. For severe and resistant challenging behavior, a more effective and more ethical approach is to teach and reinforce desired alternatives to inappropriate behavior at the same time that behavior reductive interventions are being applied.

5. Establish procedural safeguards for the use of any strategy beyond extinction (i.e., for any punishment intervention). Procedures should address, at a minimum, the following:

   a. What punishment intervention will be used? Following our rule about using the least aversive technique first, in most school situations, response cost or time-out should be attempted before the presentation of aversive stimuli is ever discussed.

b. Who will make the decision to use the punishment procedure? Preferably these decisions will be made by the teacher in collaboration with the parents and the instructional supervisor, behavior specialist, school psychologist, or other school personnel who are familiar with the child and with behavior reductive procedures.

c. How will the intervention be implemented? All aspects of the intervention strategy should be described in detail to help ensure that it is used consistently (i.e., always for the same behavior or class of behaviors) and with fidelity (i.e., correctly).

d. How will the fidelity of the implementation be monitored? One of the problems with the use of punishment, as we will discuss later in this chapter, is that the techniques often are not used correctly. When they are not used correctly, the techniques might be ineffective and might even exacerbate the challenging behavior.

e. How will the effects of the intervention be monitored? An objective data system, such as one of those described in Chapter 4, must be used to monitor changes in the targeted behavior.

f. How often will the team meet to evaluate the effects of the intervention? One of the advantages of most punishment techniques is that they produce results relatively quickly. However, the expected time that it takes for an intervention to be effective will vary with the student's age, cognitive level, learning history, frequency of the challenging behavior, and other variables, so no punishment intervention should be applied indefinitely without review. Depending on the variables that are present in the situation, the planning team should meet at least every week or two.

6. Plan for oversight to ensure the correct use of behavior reductive procedures. The more aversive behavior reductive procedures, in particular, are easily misused (Martella, Nelson, & Marchand-Martella, 2003; Zirpoli, 2005). Any behavior reductive procedure must be applied with careful adherence to the guidelines for correct use.

We urge caution in using punishment, and we emphasize the importance of following a decision-making process prior to using punishment, for three reasons. First, punishment is too easy to use. As described earlier, our society generally relies on punishment as a mechanism for controlling behavior. Even schools rely largely on negative consequences for inappropriate behavior rather than relying on positive and proactive strategies (Maag, 2001). Remember that the first Guiding Principle presented in Chapter 1 is that changing inappropriate student behavior requires that we change our own behavior. One of the changes that we might need to make is not to use instinctive responses to inappropriate behavior and to rely instead on systematic, planned interventions.

A second reason for exercising caution when one is considering the use of punishment strategies is that punishment can produce undesirable side effects. According to Azrin and Holz (1966), Bandura (1969), Cooper et al. (2007), and Foxx (1982), punishment has been associated with aggression toward the punisher,

> Caution should be exercised in deciding whether to use punishment.

destruction of nearby property, avoidance of the environments associated with punishment, and modeling negative behaviors. Another potential problem with punishment is the negative reinforcement of the person who is delivering the punishment. For example, when a teacher sends a student to the office for a disciplinary referral, the teacher is temporarily relieved of the student's disruptive or difficult behavior. Unfortunately, this might be reinforcing to the teacher and, as a result, the teacher might fail to examine whether office disciplinary referrals are actually reducing the student's inappropriate behavior.

Last, but not least, IDEA requires the use of PBIS for behaviors that interfere with learning. To that end, hearing officers have ruled that BIPs must include positive behavioral strategies and supports and that BIPs which call for the implementation of only punitive or exclusionary techniques (e.g., sending the student home for misbehaving or moving the student to a more restrictive placement) do not meet this mandate (Etscheidt, 2006a). Table 12-3 summarizes hearing officers' decisions with regard to the use of punishment in BIPs. In these decisions, hearing officers are not saying that punishment cannot be used. Rather, their decisions simply direct IEP teams to include multiple strategies for addressing challenging behaviors, including positive, instructional strategies that teach functional new behaviors and that describe reinforcement interventions for strengthening the desired behaviors.

BEHAVIOR REDUCTIVE TECHNIQUES

In the remaining sections of this chapter, we describe research-based interventions for reducing challenging behaviors. Most of these strategies are appropriately used as part of a comprehensive approach that is founded on PBIS. First, however, we wish to remind readers that certain commonsense responses should be the first intervention implemented for most minor inappropriate behavior. Such responses might include the following:

- Address antecedent conditions that might be contributing to the behavior. For example, two students who continually bicker should be separated. A student who spends too much time off task because he or she watches activity in the hall should be moved away from the door. A student who is easily distracted and is off task during independent work might wear headphones to help block out sound.
- Use physical proximity to the student to stop the inappropriate behavior. Simply standing close to the student, or closely supervising students, will usually stop minor problems.
- Ask the student to stop the behavior. One of the authors (BKS) once experienced a situation that perfectly illustrates this simple advice. She was called to a middle school for consultation about an eighth-grade student with learning disabilities who was experiencing encopresis (i.e., he was having bowel movements in his pants during the day). This behavior was causing the other students to avoid him and to make negative comments about him. The teachers were baffled. They had never experienced a problem like this and were afraid that they were not qualified to handle it. Having never experienced this problem before, the author was equally baffled but had to proceed. On

TABLE 12-3 **Summary of Hearing Officers' Decisions Regarding the Use of Positive Behavioral Supports in Behavior Intervention Plans**

Administrative Hearing or Court Case	Student Data	Issue	Decision
Neosho R-V School District v. Clark (8th Cir. 2003)	12 years old, male, autism/Asperger's Syndrome	SD appealed decision that it failed to provide FAPE. Specifically, P charged BIP had not been adequately developed or implemented.	*For school district:* BIP included positive intervention strategies designed to confer educational benefit to S.
School Town of Highland and Northwest Special Education Cooperative (SEA IN 2005)	10 years old, male, BD	P alleged that BIP lacked specific strategies and social skills instruction and that staff not trained to address student's behavioral needs. SD contended that BIP was appropriate.	*For school district:* SD made "extraordinary efforts" to respond to the extreme disruption by allowing some disruption without consequences, warnings, cooling-off periods, and curricular modifications for his ADHD.
Conroe Independent School District (SEA TX 2002)	15 years old, male, OHI	P claimed the SD failed to individualize and implement the BIP to improve behavior and that student had been punished for behaviors related to his disability (by excessive removals from his classes, placement in the office, suspensions, and police contacts). SD claimed BIP positively addressed his extremely disruptive behavior (e.g., vocal outbursts, walking around the room, lying on floor or desk tops, sexually explicit comments).	*For school district:* S had progressed behaviorally and academically. BIP based on consultation with psychiatrist and psychologist. BIP included classroom aide, cool-off periods in principal's office, more time with special education teacher, and frequent contacts with mother.
Pell City Board of Education (SEAAl 2003)	13 years old, male, MD, ADHD, and conduct disorder	P requested 1:1 behavioral aide due to deteriorating behavior. SD denied aide, asserting student's behavior improved due to BIP.	*For school district:* BIP included a variety of positive behavioral strategies, including crisis intervention, which enabled S to reflect and plan future behavior. Suspensions not resulting in change of placement permitted.

(continued)

TABLE 12-3 **Summary of Hearing Officers' Decisions Regarding the Use of Positive Behavioral Supports in Behavior Intervention Plans (*Continued*)**

Administrative Hearing or Court Case	Student Data	Issue	Decision
Mason City Community School District and Northern Trails AEA 2 (SEA IA 2003)	14 years old, male, ODD and ADHD	P charged that BIP was punitive and that a pattern of suspensions and in-school suspensions denied FAPE. SD argued BIP was appropriate and use of suspensions permissible.	*For parent:* BIP was punitive and resulted in too much time away from the classroom. P was awarded tuition reimbursement for private school.
Lewisville Independent School District (SEA TX 2001)	13 years old, male, LD and autism	Unhappy with the IEP and BIP offered by the school district, parent enrolled S in private school. P claimed SD failed to develop and/or implement a BIP that was individualized or would be reasonably likely to result in successful behavior management.	*For parent:* BIP was punitive in nature and did not teach appropriate behavior. SD failed to consider less restrictive placement. SD ordered to develop appropriate IEP and BIP, and AEA ordered to fund independent evaluation.
Mason City Community School District and Northern Trails AEA 2 (SEA IA 2001)	Not provided	P challenged SD decision to place S in interim setting and charged BIP was ineffective.	*For parent:* SD ordered to design a BIP that did not rely on exclusion from school.
Ingram Independent School District (SEA TX 2001)	13 years old, male, LD	Student's behavior problems (e.g., sleeping in class, defiance of authority, and problems with peers) targeted in BIP, but resulted in excessive removals from class and school.	*For parent:* Use of isolation for inappropriate behavior should be limited to crisis situations, and current behavior strategies in BIP "wholly unsuccessful." SD ordered to hire an educational consultant with expertise in autism to assist in development of revised BIP.
Warren County School District (SEA PA 2001)	11 years old, female, autism and MD	P argued that SD-proposed placement of S in life skills program denied FAPE, and that BIP was inappropriate. SD recommended more restrictive placement following FBA.	*For parent:* SD ordered to include consultant as IEP member to develop appropriate BIP. S awarded compensatory education due to denial of FAPE.

TABLE 12-3 *(Continued)*

Administrative Hearing or Court Case	Student Data	Issue	Decision
Watson Chapel School District (SEA AK 2001)	16 years old, male, MD	P charged the SD failed to provide FAPE by inappropriateness of BIP. Use of disciplinary sanctions violated IDEA.	*For school district (in part):* BIP included level system of positive reinforcement. Student's behavior "cannot be blamed" on inadequate BIP.
School District of Monona Grove (SEA WI 1998)	11 years old, male, ED	P disagreed with SD recommendation for more restrictive placement due to student's violent and disruptive behavior (e.g., punching, kicking, fighting, noncompliance, threatening teacher with scissors).	*For school district:* Consequences to correct misbehavior permissible, even for behaviors that are a manifestation of disability. "Severity clause" did not detract from positive behavioral supports in BIP.
In re: Student with a Disability (SEA WI 2003a)	5th grade, male, autism	P asserted SD failed to draft an appropriate BIP due to "severity clause" that permitted negative sanctions. SD maintained suspensions were a permissible option, even if not in BIP.	*For school district:* Referrals to administrator were not punishment, but "negative reinforcers," which were included in the BIP.
Northeast Independent School District (SEA TX 2001)	14 years old, male, ED and ADHD	P alleged SD failed to use positive behavioral interventions and used punishment inappropriately. SD argued BIP was positive, but did include consequences for inappropriate behavior.	*For school district (in part):* Use of "basket hold" was justified within context of BIP. SD capable of providing FAPE to S.
In re: Student with a disability (SEA VT 2003b)	9 years old, male, autism	P argued that past and present BIPs were inappropriate, particularly the use of "aversives" in form of "basket hold." SD argued that, despite various positive supports, resorting to the "basket hold" was necessary for student's and others' safety.	*For parent:* SD ordered to develop a "structured, in-depth" BIP. Noted that "while the parent should be involved in the behavior plan, the parent should not have the primary responsibility for disciplining her son at school.

(continued)

TABLE 12-3 Summary of Hearing Officers' Decisions Regarding the Use of Positive Behavioral Supports in Behavior Intervention Plans (*Continued*)

Administrative Hearing or Court Case	Student Data	Issue	Decision
Little Rock School District (SEA AK 2002)	15 years old, male, MD	SD proposed a restrictive placement in response to student's behavioral difficulties (e.g., cursing, biting, hitting, spitting, running out of class and around the school, turning over trash cans, and throwing items).	*For parent:* SD ordered to revise BIP. P awarded compensatory education and the cost of privately arranged summer program. The school district's "argument that the abbreviated day schedule was at parent's request and therefore somehow relieves them from any liability is unconvincing."
Augusta School District (SEA ME 2001)	13 years old, male, ED	P disagreed with proposed SD placement in a behavior support room. Student's work completion problems and disruptive behaviors were addressed in the BIP by a shortened school day, a strategy recommended by the P.	*For school district:* BIP included positive intervention strategies designed to confer educational benefit to S. (*For parent:* No cohesive plan in place; only goals and objectives without specific strategies.)

Notes: AEA = Area Education Agency; P = parent; S = student; SD = school district; SEA = State Education Association; FAPE = free appropriate public education; ADHD/ADD = attention-deficit hyperactivity disorder/attention-deficit disorder; EBD = emotional or behavioral disorders; ED = emotional disturbance; LD = learning disability; MD = mental disabilities; ODD = oppositional defiant disorder; OHI = other health impairment; PDD = pervasive developmental disorders; SED = serious emotional disturbance; SLD = specific learning disability; SLI = speech/language impairment.

Cases Cited:

Augusta School District, 36 IDELR 229 (SEA AK 2001).

Conroe Independent School District, 38 IDELR 53 (SEA TX 2002).

Ingram Independent School District, 35 IDELR (SEA TX 2001).

In re: Student with a Disability, 39 IDELR 200 (SEA VT 2003).

In re: Student with a Disability, 41 IDELR 115 (SEA WI 2003).

Lewisville Independent School District, 35 IDELR 236 (SEA TX 2001).

Little Rock School District, 37 IDELR 30 (SEA AK 2002).

Mason City Community School District and Northern Trails Area Education Agency 2, 32 IDELR 216 (SEA IA 2001).

Mason City Community School District and Northern Trails Area Education Agency 2, 39 IDELR 25 (SEA IA 2003).

Neosho R-V School District v. Clark, 38 IDELR 61 (8th Cir. 2003).

Northeast Independent School District, 35 IDELR 229 (SEA TX 2001).

Pell City Board of Education, 38 IDELR 253 (SEA AL 2003).

School District of Monona Grove, 27 IDELR 265 (SEA WI 1998).

School Town of Highland and Northwest Special Education Cooperative, 44 IDELR 21 (SEA IN 2005).

Warren County School District, 35 IDELR 22 (SEA PA 2001).

Watson Chapel School District, 27 IDELR 899 (SEA AK 1998).

Source: From "Behavioral Intervention Plans: Pedagogical and Legal Analysis of Issues," by S. Etscheidt, 2006, *Behavioral Disorders, 31*(2), 223–243. © 2006 Council for Children with Behavioral Disorders. Reproduced by permission.

her first visit to the school, lacking any better ideas, she bought the student a soft drink, took him outside, and talked to him about the problem. She asked whether he knew that his behavior was a problem. He did not. She asked whether he knew that others would prefer that he use the restroom. He did not. The result of this conversation was that the problem ceased: The student never again exhibited the encopretic behavior. Certainly, this was unusually fortuitous, but it nicely illustrates the importance of making students aware of their inappropriate behavior before going to great lengths to stop it.

Reinforcement-Based Strategies

Astute readers will read the heading for this section and ask, "Why is reinforcement—a procedure designed to *increase* behavior—being discussed in a chapter on how to *reduce* behavior?" The answer is that differential reinforcement procedures are effective ways to reduce problem behavior by reinforcing either the absence of that behavior or by reinforcing carefully chosen alternatives. As the periods of absence increase, or as the alternative behaviors increase, the corresponding inappropriate behavior should be reduced.

> Differential reinforcement procedures reduce targeted behaviors through reinforcement of either alternative behaviors or the absence of the targeted behavior.

There are four types of differential reinforcement procedures, each of which is appropriate for different behavioral concerns. The differential reinforcement procedures are as follows:

Differential Reinforcement of Incompatible Behaviors and Differential Reinforcement of Alternative Behaviors. **Differential reinforcement of incompatible behavior (DRI)** is a procedure whereby the challenging behavior is reduced by systematically reinforcing appropriate behaviors that are incompatible with the challenging behavior. Because the alternative behaviors are incompatible with the challenging behavior, both behaviors cannot occur simultaneously. Therefore, as reinforcement increases the incompatible behavior, the challenging behavior should diminish. Ms. Gallegos uses DRI when she records points for students who walk in the hall with their hands at their sides rather than touching the walls or other students. Those two behaviors—hands at side and touching the walls or peers—cannot occur at the same time. Ms. Rogers uses DRI for a young student with autism. The student earns tokens for sitting in group with his hands clasped on his lap, but earns no tokens when he flaps his hands in front of his face (a stereotypic behavior that is a form of **self-stimulation,** a characteristic behavioral trait in individuals with autism). Table 12-4 provides additional examples of challenging behaviors and possible incompatible alternatives.

One limitation of DRI is that it is often difficult to find appropriate behaviors that are incompatible with the challenging behavior. In addition, as Alberto and Troutman (2006) point out, the emphasis should be on identifying replacement behaviors that reflect the functions of the challenging behavior rather than behaviors that are simply physically incompatible with the challenging behavior. For these reasons, **differential reinforcement of alternative behaviors (DRA)** might be a more viable choice for reducing challenging behaviors. DRA allows for the selection of a much broader range of behaviors than does DRI. The criteria for selecting a replacement behavior is that the replacement behavior should serve the same function as the inappropriate behavior (e.g., attention, power, avoidance), should be just as easy to perform as the inappropriate behavior, and should result in

TABLE 12-4 Incompatible Alternatives to Common Inappropriate Classroom Behaviors

Inappropriate Behavior	Incompatible Alternatives
Cursing	Saying "Oh, nuts!" or "phooey."
Sleeping during work time	Completing assignments on time.
Bothering peers during work time	Staying in seat; completing assignments on time.
Talking back	Offering appropriate acknowledgments, such as "OK" or "I will"; appropriate questions about the request, such as "May I tell you my side?" or "May I explain something about that?"
Exhibiting noncompliance	Following directions with no more than one reminder.
Turning in papers that are not neat	Submitting papers that have no obvious erasures, cross-outs, or holes or tears.
Turning in papers that are not legible	Submitting papers that are typed, or papers with writing that is on the lines, with 1/4-inch spacing between words and with letters correctly formed.
Shoving, hitting, spitting, or other forms of aggression	Using words (e.g., "That makes me mad!" or "Please move away from me").
Talking during class	Raising one's hand and waiting to be called on; following the talk/movement rules (see Chapter 6).
Being tardy to class	Being in one's seat when bell rings; being inside the classroom when the bell rings.
Saying rude or unkind comments to peers	Saying nice, polite, or supportive comments to peers.

reinforcement that is just as frequent and intense as the reinforcement that currently exists for the inappropriate behavior (Carr, Robinson, & Palumbo, 1990; Dietz & Repp, 1983; Durand, Berotti, & Weiner, 1993; Horner & Day, 1991; O'Neill et al., 1997). In addition, the alternative behavior should address possible communicative functions of the inappropriate behavior. As we discussed in Chapter 2, inappropriate behavior is often the only, or the most effective, way for some students to communicate. If a student who is exhibiting challenging behavior has no reliable, socially meaningful way to communicate, the alternative behavior for a DRA intervention should be an effective form of communication. Of course, this appropriate means of communication might first have to be taught, a process known as **functional communication training** (Carr & Durand, 1985; Durand, 1990).

To implement DRI or DRA, teachers or planning teams should follow these steps:

1. Operationally define the targeted challenging behavior.
2. Choose and operationally define an appropriate replacement behavior.
3. Teach this new behavior if it is not currently in the student's repertoire.
4. Reinforce the alternative behavior on a continuous reinforcement schedule (CRF) at first, until the alternative behavior is well established.
5. If the inappropriate behavior occurs, it can be placed on extinction (i.e., ignored), or use a mild punisher if the inappropriate behavior continues.

One of the advantages of DRI and DRA is that a socially appropriate and functional replacement behavior is established at the same time that the inappropriate behavior is being reduced. Thus, these procedures strengthen the child's repertoire of prosocial behaviors, unlike most behavior reductive techniques that simply reduce or eliminate the inappropriate behavior with no attention to simultaneously reinforcing appropriate behavior. Of course, remember that we advise that no behavior reductive procedure should be used in isolation: Reinforcement of appropriate behavior should always accompany punishment. DRA and DRI do that as part of the behavior reductive technique.

Differential Reinforcement of Lower Levels of Behavior. Differential reinforcement of lower levels of behavior (DRL) is an excellent choice for reducing mild misbehaviors that are not dangerous or highly disruptive but that are interfering with the student's success. DRL is also appropriate for those behaviors that might be acceptable, or even desirable, at low levels, but are inappropriate when exhibited too much. For example, asking a few questions about an assignment is appropriate and even encouraged, but asking dozens of questions about the same assignment is excessive and unacceptable. We are not concerned about a child who is infrequently noncompliant; however, there is a problem when noncompliance occurs repeatedly throughout the day. Most children will cut in line, say unkind things to one another, turn in an assignment late, or arrive late to class at some time. When those behaviors occur regularly and frequently, however, they become problematic.

Differential reinforcement of lower levels of behavior (DRL) refers to reinforcing the student for meeting a predetermined criterion for the number of behaviors that are allowed. That is, a criterion for acceptable levels of behavior is set, and each session that the amount of challenging behavior is at or less than that criterion, the student is reinforced. After a few successful sessions at one criterion level, the criterion is gradually lowered, or the time between reinforcement opportunities is lengthened. This process continues until the behavior reaches acceptable levels or is eliminated, depending on the goal.

> Differential reinforcement of lower levels of behavior produces gradual reduction of the targeted behavior.

DRL allows the student the opportunity to learn to control the challenging behavior over time. We like this, given that many mildly problematic behaviors are much like bad habits that the student has practiced over time. Anyone who has ever tried to change a bad habit knows how difficult it can be, and the more drastic the change, the more difficult the task. Of course, because DRL is a gradual change process, it is not suitable for dangerous, highly disruptive, or other serious challenging behaviors.

Three types of DRL are commonly used: full-session DRL, interval DRL, and changing criterion DRL. **Full-session DRL** indicates that the criterion which is set for acceptable levels of behavior applies for the duration of the session (e.g., a class period, the entire day, recess, independent work time, time on the bus). If the targeted behavior is at or below this criterion at the end of the session, the student is reinforced. **Interval DRL**, just like interval recording, requires that the session be divided into equal intervals. During each interval, reinforcement is given if occurrences of the behavior are equal to or less than the criterion. For example, Mr. York used interval DRL to reduce Alex's constant requests for affirmation during independent work time. Mr. York wanted Alex to ask for affirmation no more than two times during the 40-minute work period. However, given Alex's high baseline levels of asking for affirmation (he sometimes asked, "Is this right?" more than 30 times per session), Mr. York knew that he needed to use a gradual approach to reach that goal. Mr. York initially divided the 40-minute work session into 2-minute intervals. During each interval, if Alex asked, "Is that right?" two or fewer times, he would earn a token (in this case, a ticket that Alex would keep in a box on his desk) that he could exchange later for one-on-one time with Mr. York. Mr. York used a timer to keep track of the intervals. When Alex was able to meet the criterion of two or fewer questions per 2-minute interval for 2 consecutive days, Mr. York extended the intervals to 5 minutes while maintaining the criterion of two questions. For each 5-minute interval during which Alex asked two or fewer questions, he would earn a ticket. When Alex was successful at this level for 2 days, Mr. York again lengthened the interval, the time to 10 minutes. The process continued until Alex was able to work for the entire 40-minute period and ask no more than two questions about the accuracy of his work.

The final DRL format is **changing criterion**, in which the criterion is gradually lowered across sessions until the target criterion is reached. Ms. Stocks used changing criterion DRL for Dakota, a 10-year-old boy who would rush through his work, making many errors. When coaxed to work more slowly, he could do the work accurately. However, when he worked independently, his error rate was unacceptably high because of his rush to finish. Ms. Stocks first gathered baseline data by counting the number of errors Dakota made during mathematics independent practice work, which was a 15-minute-long session. The number of errors he made during the baseline period was as follows:

Monday = 24

Tuesday = 32

Wednesday = 30

Because Dakota averaged approximately 29 errors per work session, Ms. Stocks set the first criterion at 25 or fewer errors. If Dakota met that criterion, he would earn reinforcement. In addition, Ms. Stocks determined that she wanted Dakota to meet each criterion for 3 consecutive days before she reduced it. Each new criterion would be five fewer than the previous criterion. Figure 12-1 shows Dakota's DRL graph for errors made during independent mathematics practice work. Ms. Stocks kept the DRL plan in place until Dakota reached the final criterion of no more than 2 errors per work session for 5 consecutive days. At that point, natural reinforcers were sufficient to maintain his behavior.

The following steps describe how to implement DRL:

1. Operationally define the challenging behavior.
2. Gather baseline data to determine the current level of the behavior.
3. Determine the final target criterion level for the behavior.
4. Decide what type of DRL would be most suitable: full-session DRL, interval DRL, or changing criterion DRL.
5. For interval DRL, determine the length of the initial interval. For changing criterion DRL, determine the initial criterion level. In setting the length of the

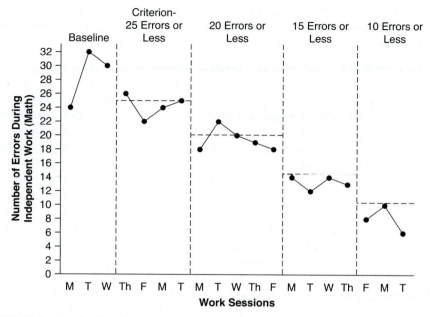

FIGURE 12-1 Sample DRL Changing Criterion Graph

initial interval or the initial criterion level, you should consider how often and to what extent the behavior occurred during the baseline period. One recommendation is that the initial level should be set at the average of the baseline levels (Repp & Dietz, 1979). Be sure to set the initial level high enough (or the interval short enough) for the student to experience success.

6. Decide for how long the initial criterion level must be met before the interval is lengthened or the criterion is lowered. We recommend that each successive interval length or criterion be met for more than one session before a change is made. The nature of DRL is that it is a somewhat slow process, which is an advantage as well. It is better to err on the side of caution with regard to moving the student too slowly toward the desired level. Note that in the examples we described in previous paragraphs, the teachers required students to be successful at the designated criterion level for 2 or 3 consecutive days. There is no absolute guideline for determining how long each criterion level must be met before the criterion is lowered. We recommend basing that decision on the following considerations:
   • The age of the student—The younger the student, the longer you might wish to keep each criterion in place.
   • The history of the behavior—For behaviors that have been exhibited over a long period, you might wish to change the criterion levels more slowly to allow the student more time to learn to control the behavior.

7. Decide how much the intervals will be increased each time or how much the criterion will be lowered. Again, err on the side of caution. Doubling the length of the interval might be too drastic a change. Likewise, reducing the criterion by half might be too much.

8. Implement the DRL procedure while continuing to gather data on the behavior. When the final target criterion level is achieved, gradually thin the reinforcement system even further or switch to naturally occurring reinforcers.

DRO can produce a rapid reduction in challenging behaviors.

Differential Reinforcement of Zero Levels of Behavior or Differential Reinforcement of Other Behaviors.   With this procedure, reinforcement is contingent upon the *absence* of a particular behavior or class of behaviors. The two terms are self-explanatory: **differential reinforcement of zero levels of behavior (DRO)** indicates that reinforcement is given only when zero instances of the targeted behavior are exhibited. Another term for this procedure, **differential reinforcement of other behaviors**, reflects the fact that, technically, reinforcement should be given at the end of a period during which zero instances of the targeted inappropriate behavior are exhibited, *despite other behaviors that did or did not occur during this time.* Because it reinforces the absence of a behavior, DRO is a suitable choice for severely inappropriate, dangerous, or disruptive behaviors. For example, DRO might be an appropriate intervention to reduce biting, tantrums, cursing, sexually explicit behavior, or fighting.

Although DRO has been shown to be an effective way to reduce serious challenging behavior, including aggression (Kahng, Abt, & Schonbachler, 2001), self-injurious behavior (Lindberg, Iwata, & Kahng, 1999), separation anxiety (Flood & Wilder, 2004), and disruptive behavior (Conyers, Miltenberger, & Maki, 2004), two caveats should be considered. First, true DRO requires reinforcement at the end of a predetermined period during which the targeted inappropriate behavior does not occur, regardless of what other behaviors are exhibited. This means that if DRO is used to reduce biting, for example, even if the youngster throws blocks during the interval, as long as he does not bite, he should be reinforced. If DRO is used to reduce tantrums during work time, the student will earn reinforcement if he does not have a tantrum, even if he does no work! Of course, this approach is unacceptable in classrooms. Therefore, for students who exhibit multiple challenging behaviors, DRO might not be the intervention of choice. Alternatively, DRO can be used in conjunction with other procedures (e.g., behavior reductive procedures for challenging behaviors other than the targeted behavior).

Another limitation of true DRO is that it reinforces the *absence* of a behavior. This approach is inconsistent with our emphasis on teaching functional equivalents to replace challenging behaviors. DRO does not teach replacement behaviors.

For these reasons, DRO might be best used in combination with other reinforcement procedures, other differential reinforcement techniques (we discuss variations in differential reinforcement interventions later in this section), or other behavior reductive procedures.

According to Dietz and Repp (1983) and Repp and Dietz (1979), the steps listed next should be followed in implementing DRO:

1. Operationally define the challenging behavior to be eliminated.
2. Gather baseline data to determine how often the behavior occurs (unless the behavior is dangerous or highly disruptive).
3. Determine the length of the DRO interval. It is important to consider the baseline data in determining the length of the initial interval. The interval should be sufficiently brief to allow the student to experience reinforcement.

4. Determine when the interval will be lengthened. Once the student can successfully control the behavior during the initial interval, the interval can be increased slightly.

5. Determine what will happen if the student exhibits the targeted inappropriate behavior during an interval. Consider the following questions:

   a. Will a new interval begin immediately following the misbehavior, or will the current interval continue and a new interval begin at the expected time?

   b. Will the inappropriate behavior receive a consequence, or will the student simply be reminded that the behavior occurred and, therefore, no reinforcement will be earned for that period?

Although we provided guidelines for choosing differential reinforcement interventions, it is often the case that there is no one correct or best system. Rather, it is often a matter of preference and individual student factors that will determine the best system. Table 12-5 lists a variety of challenging behaviors and possible differential reinforcement systems for each.

It is possible and often necessary to combine differential reinforcement procedures. For example, consider Matthew, a 9-year-old boy who hit, kicked, or attempted to bite teachers or peers when frustrated or angry. Matthew's teacher appropriately used a combination of DRO for zero instances of aggression and DRA to reinforce Matthew for using words instead of his behavior to express his feelings. Mr. Anderson provided another example of combining differential reinforcement procedures when he used DRL and DRA to reduce clutter and messiness around Angelica's desk. At the end of each day, Mr. Anderson counted the number of pieces of trash on or in Angelica's desk and the number of items (e.g., books, notebooks, pencils, papers, and supplies) on the floor within a 4-foot-square area around her desk. He used DRL to reduce both the number of items on the floor and the number of pieces of trash in the area. At the same time, he implemented DRA to reinforce Angelica for using the trash can and for keeping the supplies in her desk. Angelica earned tickets if the number of pieces of trash in her area was at or below the target criterion at the end of each day; she earned additional tickets each time that Mr. Anderson observed her throwing trash into the trash can or placing her materials in her desk rather than on the floor. Angelica exchanged her tickets for various privileges and activity reinforcers for both herself and her classmates.

> Differential reinforcement procedures are permitted to be used to reduce problem behaviors in groups of students.

Another variation of differential reinforcement procedures is group application. The following are two examples of group application of differential reinforcement procedures:

- Ms. Dillon's second-grade students have been getting into trouble during lunch in the cafeteria for leaving their table so messy. Ms. Dillon addressed the problem by implementing changing criterion differential reinforcement of lower levels of behavior. Initially, she collected baseline data by counting the number of food items and pieces of trash that were left on the table and on the floor (within a 1-foot perimeter of the table) at the end of the lunch period for 3 consecutive days. Baseline data were 33, 29, and 35. For the first criterion, Ms. Dillon used the baseline average, 32. If no more than 32 items

TABLE 12-5 Differential Reinforcement Systems for Various Challenging Behaviors

Challenging Behavior	Possible Differential Reinforcement Systems
Cursing	DRI: Reinforce appropriate expressions of anger or frustration.
	DRO: Reinforce for increasingly longer periods of time during which no cursing occurs.
Sleeping	DRI: Reinforce work completion or participation in class activity.
	DRO: Reinforce for increasingly longer periods of time during which no sleeping occurs.
Bothering peers	DRI: Reinforce being in seat and/or working or participating appropriately in the activity.
	DRO: Reinforce for increasingly longer periods of time during which no "bothering" occurs.
	DRL: Reinforce for increasingly fewer instances of "bothering" during each designated period.
Talking back	DRI: Reinforce responding appropriately to the teacher's directions.
	DRO: Reinforce for increasingly longer periods of time during which no talking back occurs.
	DRL: Reinforce for increasingly fewer instances of talking back during designated periods.
Noncompliance	DRI: Reinforce compliance.
	DRO: Reinforce for increasingly longer periods during which zero instances of noncompliance occur.
	DRL: Reinforce for increasingly fewer instances of noncompliance during designated periods.
Papers that are not neat	DRI: Reinforce papers that meet specified criteria for neatness.
	DRL: Reinforce for increasingly fewer erasures, cross-outs, or other instances of messiness on papers.
Illegible writing	DRI: Reinforce legible writing (e.g., correctly formed letters, correct spacing).
	DRL: Reinforce for increasingly fewer words written illegibly.
Shoving, hitting, spitting, or other forms of aggression	DRI: Reinforce appropriate expressions of anger, frustration, or other verbal alternatives to aggression.
	DRO: Reinforce for increasingly longer periods of time during which no aggressive behavior occurs.
Talking during class	DRI: Reinforce following the talk/movement rules.
	DRO: Reinforce for increasingly longer periods of time during which no off-task talking occurs.
	DRL: Reinforce for increasingly fewer instances of talking during designated periods.

TABLE 12-5 *(Continued)*

Challenging Behavior	Possible Differential Reinforcement Systems
Tardiness	DRI: Reinforce being on time to class.
	DRO: Reinforce for increasingly longer periods of time (e.g., 1 week) during which no tardies occur.
	DRL: Reinforce for increasingly fewer instances of tardiness during designated periods of time.
Saying rude or unkind comments to peers	DRI: Reinforce nice, polite, or supportive comments to peers.
	DRO: Reinforce for increasingly longer periods of time during which no unkind comments are made.
	DRL: Reinforce for increasingly fewer instances of unkind comments during designated periods.

of food or trash were left on the table or floor at the end of lunch, her students earned 10 extra minutes of recess. After 3 consecutive days of meeting this criterion, Ms. Dillon changed the criterion to 26. After 3 consecutive days at this level, she changed the criterion to 20, and so forth until students reached the target criterion of no food or trash left on the table or floor. At that point, Ms. Dillon moved to a variable-ratio 3-day schedule of reinforcement: Students were reinforced on an average of every 3 days for leaving the table and floor trash- and food-free after lunch. From there, she moved to a random schedule of reinforcement: Once in a while, when she picked her students up after lunch, if the table and floor were clear, she added extra time onto recess.

• Mr. Williams teaches fourth- to sixth-grade resource language arts. His students this year have had a hard time getting along with one another. They taunt each other, say mean things to one another, and, in general, do whatever they can to annoy one another. Mr. Williams is simply not enjoying teaching as much this year because of the negative behaviors exhibited constantly by his students. Mr. Williams knew that he needed to get these behaviors under control quickly. He implemented two differential reinforcement systems: DRO and DRA. At first, he only implemented this plan during the second-period class, which was the most difficult of all of his classes. First, he took baseline data for 3 days, counting the number of put-downs (e.g., "That's so stupid" or "You're the fattest kid in school") and teasing or taunts (e.g., in a sarcastic tone, "Hey, Joey, did you watch TV with *mommy* last night?" or "Your mama!"). During the 55-minute period, baseline data for the class of seven students were 38, 35, and 41, which is an average of approximately 0.7 negative comments per minute. The DRO intervention consisted of the class earning a star on a chart for every 5-minute period (marked by a timer) during which Mr. Williams heard no negative or derogatory comments.

Every star was worth 30 seconds of playing time for a group game on Friday, with the game chosen by the group. If a negative comment was uttered during the 5-minute period, Mr. Williams simply said, "No star," and when that period ended, he reset the timer. In addition, to encourage more positive comments, Mr. Williams implemented DRA in which individual students earned a ticket for each positive, supportive, or encouraging comment made to peers. Tickets could be exchanged for individual reinforcers (including reinforcer dots [see Chapter 10], extra computer time, and phone calls home) or could be pooled for special group activities (e.g., playing vocabulary basketball on the basketball court, working on the class play).

Extinction

Extinction is a procedure that seems simple in theory but is easy to misuse. **Extinction** refers to the withholding of reinforcement for a behavior that has been maintained through reinforcement, usually in the form of attention. Commonly called "ignoring," most of us have used or have been recipients of extinction in one form or another. For example, consider Henry, who has been trying to arrange a date with Elizabeth. Elizabeth is not interested in dating Henry but does not wish to hurt his feelings. When Henry first began calling Elizabeth, she talked to him without committing to a date. After a few calls, he began to attempt to arrange a specific time for them to meet somewhere, but she ended the call without agreeing to anything. After that, she screened Henry's calls and did not answer when his name appeared on her caller identification screen. Elizabeth had begun using extinction to eliminate Henry's calls. Of course, we believe that extinction is *not* a good tool to use in this instance: Elizabeth should have taken a more direct approach and simply asked Henry to stop calling. Remember, a PBIS approach relies on clear communication of expectations as the first step in managing behavior!

In the social environment of the classroom, extinction might be an appropriate technique for eliminating minor inappropriate behaviors that have been maintained through the teacher's attention. Extinction is relatively simple to apply, making it a viable tool for busy classrooms. However, according to Skinner (1953), Sulzer-Azaroff and Mayer (1991), and Cooper, Heron, and Heward (2007), extinction is characterized by the following predictable characteristics that must be taken into consideration:

1. Behaviors placed on extinction reduce slowly. Extinction does not produce immediate or quick effects. How quickly the behavior is reduced depends on how long it has been previously reinforced, the density of the previous reinforcement schedule, and whether the individual has access to equally valued reinforcers during the extinction period. Behaviors that have a long history of frequent reinforcement will persist longer during extinction than behaviors that have a weak history of reinforcement. Behaviors are likely to be eliminated more quickly if concurrent reinforcement for appropriate alternative behaviors is available. Educators must consider the possibility that the targeted behavior will diminish very slowly under extinction. Because of this, extremely disruptive, dangerous, or contagious behaviors (i.e., behaviors that

other students are likely to imitate or respond to, such as name-calling, pushing, or horseplay) might not be appropriate targets for extinction. In our experience, teachers should not use extinction for behaviors that are personally annoying because it might be difficult for the teacher to continue to control the attention given by peers to those behaviors for as long as it might take for extinction to have the desired effect.

2. Behaviors placed on extinction often increase in frequency or intensity before they begin to diminish, a phenomenon sometimes referred to as **extinction burst**. We see examples of this every day. When you push an elevator button, and the elevator does not appear quickly (thus, your button-pushing behavior is placed on extinction), most of us will repeatedly push the elevator button (i.e., our button-pushing behavior increases) until the elevator arrives. Extinction to reduce crying in a child who cries when she does not get her way might result in the child's behavior escalating into full-blown tantrums before the behavior begins to disappear. Teachers must anticipate the potential for extinction burst. For this reason, extinction might not be the intervention of choice for students who have a history of aggression.

3. Behaviors that have been eliminated through extinction might suddenly reappear, an occurrence known as **spontaneous recovery**. Teachers and other personnel must be prepared to continue extinction for that behavior. This is a particularly important aspect of the procedure, for if the behavior produces a response at this point, the behavior might recover and be increasingly resistant to extinction.

> Extinction should be used with caution because of certain undesirable characteristics that are inherent in the process.

The following are steps for implementing extinction:

1. Identify the targeted behavior. Remember that extinction is most appropriate for low-level, minor behavioral problems because of the issues described previously. Extinction might be appropriate for behaviors such as whining, tantrums, low-level disruption (e.g., calling out without permission, making off-task comments), cursing, or minor noncompliance.

2. Ensure that the reinforcers which currently maintain the targeted behavior can be controlled. FBA data should help to identify what that reinforcer is. Teacher attention can be easily controlled; peer attention, under some circumstances, can be controlled, but the teacher must determine that this is possible. For example, peer attention might be controlled through use of a group reinforcement system. However, if the maintaining reinforcer is escape, for example, extinction might not be appropriate. Consider a student who walks out of class when asked to do work that he or she dislikes. Placing the behavior of walking out of class on extinction would probably have no effect because that behavior is maintained by avoidance of the disliked task.

3. Use extinction in conjunction with reinforcement of appropriate behaviors. Ensure that the reinforcement which previously maintained the inappropriate behavior is now available contingent upon the appropriate alternative behavior. For example, every time Austin complained about his work, Ms. Sanchez would talk to him gently, encouraging him to try. Now, Austin's complaining produces no attention from Ms. Sanchez. However, as soon as he starts working, she tells him what a good job he is doing and that she is proud of

him. She continues to praise his work behavior frequently while providing no response to his complaining.

4. Inform the student *in advance* of the procedure. Let the student know that when the targeted behavior occurs, there will be no response. Describe specific other behaviors that will produce teacher (or peer) responses. When the inappropriate behavior occurs, under no circumstances should you say to the student, "I will not pay attention to you as long as you continue doing that."

5. When the targeted behavior occurs, do not respond. Do not look at the student, sigh heavily, roll your eyes, comment about the behavior to your paraprofessional, or show any other form of response.

6. Remember that only the targeted inappropriate behavior is placed on extinction, not the child! One of the authors (BKS) once consulted with a teacher about a highly disruptive young girl. During the first visit, the child displayed a wild tantrum in which she screamed and ran across the tops of the desks. After about 5 minutes, the student quieted down and sat at her desk. She continued to sit quietly with no attention from the teacher or paraprofessional. Later, when the teacher was asked about her strategy for managing the tantrums, she replied, "I have placed them on extinction." Unfortunately, it appeared that she had actually placed the *child* on extinction. For extinction to work, there must be clearly discernable differences between "attention" conditions and "no attention" conditions. The student must be able to discriminate between behaviors that will produce reinforcement (e.g., pay attention) and those which will not.

7. Inform others about the procedure. Anyone who encounters the student should be instructed to use extinction for the same behavior. You do not want to be in a situation such as this: You are walking in the hall with a student, and the student engages in silly behavior that you have begun to place on extinction. The assistant principal sees you and the student and says, "Ms. Scheuermann, look at what Billy is doing! Is that acceptable to you? Billy, you need to stop that and walk the right way." Not only does that put you in an awkward position, but it might inadvertently reinforce the inappropriate behavior.

8. Maintain extinction for as long as is needed to eliminate the behavior, as well as any spontaneous reoccurrences of the behavior.

Removal of Reinforcing Stimuli

Response cost and time-out involve the removal of reinforcement in order to reduce a behavior.

Up to this point, we have described procedures that manipulate reinforcement in order to produce a reduction in targeted behaviors, either through reinforcement for the absence of inappropriate behavior or by withholding reinforcement contingent upon inappropriate behavior. We refer to these procedures as behavior reductive techniques because they do not technically qualify as punishment (i.e., the contingent presentation of a stimulus that results in a decrease in behavior). From this point on, the techniques presented meet the traditional definition of punishment. In this section, we describe two procedures that involve the removal of reinforcers in order to reduce or eliminate a behavior: response cost and time-out.

Response Cost.   **Response cost** is a punishment procedure in which a specified amount of reinforcers is withdrawn or removed, contingent upon a particular behavior. Response cost is a prominent form of punishment in our society, and most of us have experienced response cost in various forms. Consider the following examples:

- You might have to pay library fines for returning books after the due date.
- You have to pay traffic fines as a consequence for violating a traffic rule.
- You might be assessed a penalty for late payment of a bill.
- Employees might be docked pay if they arrive late to work.
- For exhibiting certain behaviors, a football team loses yards for certain penalties and a basketball player earns fouls, which might give the other team a free throw.
- If you are late to the airport, you might miss your flight.
- If you arrive late to class too many times or miss too many classes, your professor might lower your grade.
- A student who wastes time and does not finish his or her work might have to finish that work during activity time.
- A child who throws a toy might have the toy taken away.
- You lose part of your apartment security deposit because of stains on the carpet.

Response cost offers a number of advantages as a behavior reductive procedure: (a) it is an easy procedure to use, (b) it offers versatility for a variety of uses, (c) it might avoid some of the negative side effects associated with other punishment procedures, (d) it tends to produce a rapid reduction in behavior, (e) it might help students learn to discriminate between appropriate and inappropriate behavior, and (f) it has been shown to produce long-term changes in behavior (Alberto & Troutman, 2006; Cooper et al., 2007; Kazdin, 1972; Sulzer-Azaroff & Mayer, 1991). Furthermore, response cost certainly reflects real life and can easily be used in conjunction with a token system.

However, response cost is still a punishment procedure, more aversive than differential reinforcement or extinction. Response cost is easily misused, and for this reason, there are certain caveats that must be considered. The guidelines for using response cost, including the caveats, are as follows:

1. Identify the targeted behavior(s) whose consequences are to be meted out with response cost. As with any procedure, these behaviors should be operationally defined in order to increase the consistency with which the consequences are applied.

2. Make sure that the student has ongoing access to earning reinforcers or tokens. This will probably be most efficiently accomplished by using a token system for reinforcement, such as those described in Chapter 10, in conjunction with response cost for behavior reduction. Under no circumstances should response cost be used when the availability of the reinforcers is fixed. Consider this example: Ms. Carter implemented a response cost system for her elementary students, all of whom are labeled emotionally disturbed. On Monday, Ms. Carter writes, "R" "E" "C" "E" "S" "S" on the board. During the week, whenever she catches a student breaking a rule, she crosses off one

> Response cost should only be used if the student has ongoing access to earning reinforcers.

letter. On Friday, students get 3 minutes of recess for each letter that remains. Unfortunately, her students have been losing all of the letters by Tuesday or Wednesday. They have not had a Friday recess in many weeks. Obviously, the problem with Ms. Carter's system is that students can only lose minutes of recess, but they cannot earn additional minutes. Once the recess minutes are gone, Ms. Carter has no more power to respond to challenging behavior. Equally problematic is that when her students lose all of their recess minutes, their motivation to follow the rules for the rest of the week might disappear. No teacher wants to be in that position!

3. Determine the "cost" for each behavioral infraction (i.e., determine the quantity of the reinforcers or tokens that will be removed contingent upon the targeted inappropriate behavior). This can be a difficult decision. Fines should not be so large that one or two behavioral infractions would result in the student losing all of the reinforcers. On the other hand, the fines need to be meaningful in order to be effective. With regard to parking in an illegal spot on campus, we have overheard our university students say, "I'll probably get a ticket but I don't care—I had to get to class." For these students, the cost of the parking ticket is not sufficient to deter illegal parking, especially when it is compared with the cost of missing class or being late. The cost of each behavioral infraction should be approximately equal to the quantity of the reinforcers that students earn for each appropriate behavior, or slightly more. If more than one behavior is targeted for reduction with response cost, consider developing a hierarchy of fines in which less serious behaviors are fined less than more serious behaviors. Figure 12-2 shows a sample token economy/response cost system for an elementary class. Note the relationship between the amount of reinforcement available for appropriate behavior and the fine for inappropriate behavior. Note also that the system specifies different levels of fines for various challenging behaviors.

4. Ensure that the reinforcers or tokens can be easily removed contingent upon the targeted inappropriate behavior. Response cost requires that reinforcers be removed, which means that the teacher must be able to efficiently remove the reinforcers or subtract tokens. Points, tickets, class currency, and token chips should be easily removed or subtracted. It might be more difficult to take away primary reinforcers, especially if the student consumes them as soon as they are given!

Another potential problem with response cost is that some students might resist giving up their earned tokens, especially students who exhibit high levels of oppositional behavior. Clearly establishing response cost contingencies in advance will help to avoid this problem, as will role-playing the process of returning tokens with the students. Having done this, if you still encounter refusal or other behavioral problems when asking students to return tokens or when you subtract points, you have two options: The first option is to simply use a system other than response cost. The second option is to reinforce response cost compliance by lowering the amount of the fine contingent upon the student promptly and compliantly surrendering the required reinforcers (Sulzer-Azaroff & Mayer, 1991). For example, Mr. McCall uses a token/response cost system for Manvir. Manvir earns tokens for

Take the Tiger Challenge

You can earn Tiger Bucks (TB) by

- Working appropriately when the timer rings:
  - 1 TB each time that the timer rings if you are working
- Completing assignments with 80% or better accuracy:
  - 80%–89% = 1 TB
  - 90%–100% = 2 TBs
- Using Tiger Manners:
  - Making polite, encouraging, or supportive comments = 1 TB (but not every time)
  - Expressing feelings with appropriate words = 1 TB (but not every time)
  - Ignoring teasing, taunts, and distractions = 1 TB (but not every time)

You might lose Tiger Bucks for

- Making unkind comments or teasing = 4 TBs per incident
- Damaging property = 3 TBs per incident
- Leaving class without permission = 3 TBs per incident

Tiger Bucks may be exchanged each Friday for

- Individual privileges:
  - Feeding the animals for a week = 25 TBs
  - Taking care of the plants for a week = 20 TBs
  - Operating equipment for a week = 20 TBs
  - Being first in line for a week = 15 TBs
  - Being allowed to have a water bottle at your desk = 15 TBs
- Group privileges (the group must vote to pool their Tiger Bucks):
  - Playing basketball or baseball outside on Friday = 100 TBs
  - Two extra recesses = 75 TBs
  - Popcorn snack and a video on Friday = 75 TBs
  - Two extra periods to work on hobby projects = 50 TBs

FIGURE 12-2   Sample Token Economy/Response Cost System

following the rules, completing assignments correctly, and playing appropriately. He loses tokens for cursing (4 tokens per cursing event) or throwing materials (10 tokens per thrown item). The first time that Mr. McCall asked Manvir to return 4 tokens for cursing, Manvir said, "These are MINE! You're not getting them" and stuffed the tokens into his pocket. After that incident, Mr. McCall implemented a new contingency: If Manvir curses or throws materials, he still must surrender the tokens; however, if he gives his tokens to Mr. McCall within 1 minute of being asked, without complaining, the fine is cut in half, meaning that he only has to give up 2 tokens for cursing and 5 tokens for throwing something. Although some might question whether this allows the student to "get away with it," we view it as reinforcing the highly desired behavior of compliance. In fact, we consider compliance with a response cost consequence as an operational example of accepting responsibility for one's behavior, something that virtually all teachers want students to do. There is still a consequence for the inappropriate behavior, and this does not (and should not) eliminate that consequence.

> Like any intervention, you should teach the student the response cost procedure before implementation.

5. Ensure that the response cost procedure will be applied only for predetermined targeted behaviors. Response cost is easy to use and, because of this, the potential exists to use it for any minor misbehavior. Care must be taken that adults who use the program remove reinforcers only for predetermined behaviors. It is not appropriate to apply the procedure to other behaviors. For example, Bailey earns points for completing assignments, following directions, and keeping her hands and feet to herself; she loses points for refusing to work and for pushing or pinching. Her teachers should not subtract points for other inappropriate behaviors, such as whining, screaming, running in the hall, or anything else. It is easy to imagine a situation in which an exasperated teacher says, "Bailey, I have told you three times to line up. If you do not line up now, I am going to take away five points!" If other behaviors are interfering with Bailey's success, then interventions should be developed to address those behaviors; of course, at that time, teachers might determine that the response cost procedure should be expanded to include additional behaviors. Without formal advance identification of specific behaviors that will result in the loss of reinforcers, there is a risk that reinforcers will be taken away for behaviors that are not highly problematic (i.e., for behaviors that are momentarily annoying) or that the amount of reinforcers being removed will exceed the amount of reinforcers earned.

6. Explain the program to the student and any adults who will use the program. As with any intervention, strive for consistency in the application of the procedure: Every occurrence of a targeted inappropriate behavior will result in the predetermined amount of reinforcers being removed.

7. Monitor the behaviors targeted for reduction. If those behaviors do not change or do not change significantly as a result of the response cost intervention, reevaluate the intervention or select a different intervention.

Time-Out.   The technical term for this procedure is **time-out from positive reinforcement**, but it is usually called *time-out.* **Time-out** refers to a procedure in which an individual is denied access to reinforcers for a predetermined period of time. Time-out is often referred to incorrectly as a place when, in fact, it is a procedure. As we will explain, time-out can occur in a classroom in the midst of instructional activities; it is not necessary for students to physically move to a time-out area. Used correctly, time-out is effective because the reduced access to reinforcers is contingent upon targeted inappropriate behaviors. Note the difference between time-out and response cost: With response cost, previously earned reinforcers (e.g., points, minutes of reinforcement time, tokens) are removed contingent upon inappropriate behavior; in time-out, by contrast, nothing is removed, but the student may not *earn* points during the time that he or she is in time-out (however, the student is allowed to keep any points that were previously accumulated).

There are several different forms of time-out, ranging from less exclusionary and intrusive to more exclusionary and intrusive. The three basic types of time-out are nonexclusionary, exclusionary, and seclusionary (Cooper et al., 2007; Martella et al., 2003):

1. ***Nonexclusionary time-out.*** Reinforcement is withheld, but the student remains in the instructional setting. Nonexclusionary time-out allows for use of the procedure with a minimal loss of instruction time for both the student and the teacher.

2. ***Exclusionary time-out.*** The student is removed from the instructional activity and taken to another area within the classroom or outside of the classroom. This form of time-out requires more time to implement than nonexclusionary forms and might result in the student missing instruction.

3. ***Seclusionary time-out.*** The student is isolated in a designated time-out room. This form of time-out is the most restrictive and controversial, and possibly the most easily abused form of time-out (Sulzer-Azaroff & Mayer, 1991). Opposition to seclusionary time-out is growing. A number of professional organizations and advocacy groups have taken official positions against it, a number of states have banned the use of seclusionary time-out, and in 2010 Congress introduced legislation that would ban its use (Council for Children with Behavioral Disorders, 2009; Council of Parent Attorneys and Advocates, 2008; National Disability Rights Network, 2009). Because of the severity and intrusiveness of this procedure, it should only be used for dangerous behaviors such as serious physical aggression or destruction of property. (See the guidelines for using time-out that follow shortly.)

We provide examples of nonexclusionary time-out techniques in Table 12-6. Remember that a PBIS approach requires that educators use the least aversive and least intrusive form of time-out, which is the nonexclusionary form.

Like all of the techniques that we have described throughout this text, time-out can be an effective procedure when used correctly. Used incorrectly, time-out will be ineffective at best and will exacerbate a student's behavioral difficulties at worst. The following are guidelines for using time-out correctly and judiciously:

1. Remember that time-out is a punishment technique; thus, teachers and others should adhere to all of the guidelines for using punishment that were described previously in this chapter. These are especially critical when considering exclusionary and seclusionary forms of time-out.

> Nonexclusionary time-out, combined with ongoing reinforcement of appropriate behaviors, is the form of time-out that is most consistent with PBIS.

TABLE 12-6 Examples of Nonexclusionary Time-Out Techniques

- **Head down time-out.** The student places his or her head down on the desk for the designated period.

- **Object removal time-out.** For a designated period, the teacher removes toys, books, or other materials that the student was using when the inappropriate behavior occurred.

- **Observation time-out.** The student's chair is moved a few feet back from the group or activity; this allows the student to observe both the activity and the other students who are continuing to receive reinforcement for appropriate behavior.

- **Time-out card.** Described by Hops and Walker (1988), this form of time-out is used in conjunction with a token system. Students are given cards that are green on the point side and red on the opposite side (i.e., the "time-out" side). As long as the student's behavior is appropriate, the student earns points on the green side. When an inappropriate behavior occurs, the teacher turns the card over; no points can be given while the red side is showing. An alternative to using the time-out card is to use objects as tokens (e.g., plastic chips or tickets) and then briefly remove the container in which the tokens are placed.

- **Active Response Beads Time-out (ARB-TO)** (Grskovic et al., 2004). Active Response Beads are constructed by stringing 10 small wooden beads on a velvet cord with knots at each end to prevent the beads from sliding off. When time-out is needed (as signaled by the teacher), the student picks up the Active Response Beads from the teacher's desk, returns to his or her seat, and puts his or her head down on the desk. While the student's head is down, the student counts backward from 10 to 1 while simultaneously sliding the 10 beads, one at a time, from left to right along the cord. When the student completes the procedure, the teacher praises the student's use of the procedure (e.g., "That was a good job using the ARB. Please return them to my desk"). The student then returns to work.

- **Time-out ribbon.** In this form of time-out, described by Foxx and Shapiro (1978), all students wear a ribbon pinned to their clothing or around their necks. High rates of reinforcement are provided to students who are wearing a ribbon. Contingent upon inappropriate behavior, a student's ribbon is removed for 3 minutes, and the student receives no reinforcement during that period. At the end of time-out, the student resumes wearing the ribbon.

---

2. Always use the least aversive form of time-out that can reasonably be expected to reduce the targeted behavior(s). Although some might consider seclusionary time-out rooms to be warranted for most instances of aggression or other seriously disruptive behavior, research shows that other less aversive forms of time-out, combined with teaching and reinforcing appropriate behavior, can effectively control even the most egregious acting out. For example, Fogt and Piripavel (2002) report dramatic reductions in the use of physical restraints and seclusionary time-outs at a school for students with emotional/behavioral disorders and pervasive developmental disorders/autism. Prior to the interventions described in this study, seclusionary time-out was so prevalent that frequency of use was not even monitored. Furthermore, baseline data during the 1997–1998 school year indicated that, in the same school, there were 1,064

instances of the use of physical restraint and 16 incidents of assault on a teacher. A comprehensive program of schoolwide instruction in social skills, problem-solving skills, and positive reinforcement for appropriate behavior was implemented (see Chapter 5 for more details). Despite increased enrollment, the use of seclusionary time-outs and physical restraints dropped to zero in the second year after the intervention program was implemented. Remember that these encouraging results occurred in a special school for students with the most serious challenging behaviors.

3. Use brief time-out periods. It is not the length of the time-out that determines the effectiveness of the procedure, but rather the distinction between the time-in environment and the time-out condition. In our opinion, even the old adage "1 minute per year of age" might be too long; 7 minutes for a 7-year-old who has severe attention-deficit hyperactivity disorder might seem like an eternity to the child. Even adults overestimate how much time they spend in situations in which they are frustrated and/or anxious to move on to other things (e.g., standing in a busy checkout lane at the supermarket, waiting for a train while on the way to work). To help determine the length of the time-out period, especially for exclusionary or seclusionary time-outs, we encourage teachers to sit in the time-out area for the length of time that they are planning for the student's time-out. If that time-out feels too long for the teacher, it will definitely be too long for the student. Time-outs that are too long might lead to other problems (e.g., the student leaves time-out prematurely, the student exhibits disruptive behavior during time-out). Brief time-outs might help to avoid these problems.

4. Determine how time-out is to end. Gast and Nelson (1977a) describe three procedures for contingent release from time-out:

    a. Release is contingent upon a predetermined duration of appropriate behavior (e.g., the student might exit time-out after 2 minutes of sitting quietly).

    > When using time-out, determine how time-out is to end.

    b. Release is contingent upon a predetermined duration of time-out; if inappropriate behavior is occurring at the end of the time-out period, time-out is extended until the inappropriate behavior ceases. For example, if Charlie is screaming when the timer sounds to signal the end of time-out, say, "Charlie, you are screaming. You must stay in time-out until you are quiet."

    c. Release is contingent upon a predetermined duration of time-out, plus a brief extension during which no inappropriate behaviors are exhibited. For example, if Carly is exhibiting inappropriate behavior when her time-out ends, she will not be allowed to leave time-out until she is sitting appropriately for 30 seconds.

    In most instances, we prefer option a (i.e., release after a predetermined duration of time-out). If the inappropriate behavior continues when the student returns to the time-in environment, another time-out or a different consequence can be applied. In our experience, the other two release options result in too much teacher interaction with the student during time-out, a situation that might provide reinforcement (i.e., attention) to the student during the time-out procedure.

5. Teach the time-out procedure before implementation. Sometimes a student will resist time-out—especially a student who exhibits a high level of oppositional,

noncompliant behavior. This resistance might be a result, at least partially, of a lack of understanding about the time-out procedure. C. Michael Nelson (1997) provides a thorough task-analyzed format for teaching students to take time-out correctly. The steps that he suggests for teaching this procedure are shown in Table 12-7.

6. When the targeted inappropriate behavior occurs, simply say to the student, "That is [state the behavior]. Go to time-out." Because you have taught the procedure, no other explanation is needed. We recommend setting a timer

---

TABLE 12-7   **Technique for Teaching Students to Take Time-Out**

TEACHING STUDENTS TO TAKE A TIME-OUT APPROPRIATELY

Note: You should not assume that students will comply with directions to take a time-out if they have not been taught how to do so. This task analysis is a generic lesson for teaching students to take time-outs. Task steps should be altered according to the characteristics and needs of individual students. Steps should be practiced systematically several times a day until each is mastered. You might use individual or small-group instruction.

Step	Criterion
1. Imitate correct time-out behavior (sitting or standing quietly in designated area) for 10 seconds following demonstration by teacher.	5 consecutive correct trials for 3 consecutive days.
2. Demonstrate correct time-out behavior for 10 seconds following teacher instruction during practice sessions.	Same as above.
3. Demonstrate correct time-out behavior for 30 seconds following teacher instruction during practice sessions.	Same as above.
4. Same as Step 3, but time-out duration is 2 minutes.	Same as above.
5. Take a 5-minute time-out within 10 seconds, when instructed to do so by a teacher in a real time-out situation.	50% of assigned time-outs taken correctly over 5 consecutive days.
6. Same as Step 5.	100% of assigned time-outs taken correctly over 5 consecutive days.
7. Take a 5-minute time-out within 10 seconds, demonstrating appropriate time-out behavior, when instructed to do so by general education teacher.	50% of assigned time-outs taken correctly over 5 consecutive days.
Note: Provide practice steps 1–5 if criterion is not met.	
8. Same as Step 7.	100% of assigned time-outs correctly taken over 5 consecutive days.

Source: From "Effective Use of Time-out" by C. M. Nelson, 1997. Available at www.state.ky.us/agencies/behave/bi/to.pdf. Reproduced by permission.

when the child begins the time-out procedure. This will help to ensure that the teacher does not forget that the student is in time-out! Also, anticipate that students will attempt to engage you in a discussion about why they are being sent to time-out. This is an avoidance behavior that is often very effective: The more you explain why time-out is being given, the longer the student avoids time-out. Remember that you have taught the time-out procedure. No further explanation is needed during implementation.

7. When time-out is over, say, "Time-out is over," and direct the student to return to the activity. Do not engage in conversation with the student while the student is in the time-out area. You do not want to provide attention (i.e., positive reinforcement) while the student is in time-out. Students should be required to complete any work missed during time-out to avoid time-out functioning as an escape tactic.

8. Use one of the data collection techniques from Chapter 4 to monitor the targeted behavior. If the behavior does not improve relatively quickly (e.g., after several applications for most behaviors), reevaluate the time-out procedure and the time-in environment (e.g., the frequency and effectiveness of the reinforcers) or use a different technique.

Presentation of Aversive Stimuli

The most negative and aversive form of punishment is the presentation of aversive stimuli. In this section, we briefly describe aversive stimuli so that readers will understand the nature of these techniques and recognize them when they see them. We will not, however, provide detailed instructions for use because a PBIS approach to behavior management should mean that, for most situations, aversives would not be needed. We present this discussion because educators need to understand the full range of behavioral interventions, including aversive procedures. We *do not*, however, recommend or endorse these procedures! We encourage teachers, administrators, and parents to rely on the powerful antecedent and reinforcement interventions that have been described in previous chapters or the differential reinforcement techniques explained in this chapter.

> The use of aversive procedures is inconsistent with PBIS.

Presentation of Aversive Stimuli.   Aversive stimuli are any stimuli that the individual dislikes and that are presented contingent upon a behavior. **Unconditioned aversive stimuli** are those stimuli which are inherently and naturally distasteful, painful, or annoying to us: We do not have to learn to dislike these stimuli. Unconditioned or **unlearned aversive stimuli**, might include anything that causes pain (e.g., spanking, slapping, burning, shocking) or discomfort (e.g., having to sit or stand in a particular position for a long period of time, applying lemon juice or other distasteful substances to the lips or mouth, the old technique of washing the mouth out with soap). **Conditioned** or **learned aversive stimuli** are stimuli that we learn to dislike as a result of pairing with an unconditioned aversive. The most common conditioned aversive is reprimands, but other stimuli might also take on a punishing nature for some students. For example, some students might dislike being praised in front of their peers. For these students, public praise is a conditioned aversive. Other students might dislike having to read aloud; thus, reading aloud becomes aversive because of the embarrassment or frustration associated with this activity.

It is important to understand that, like any form of punishment, aversives can be determined only by their effect on behavior. A stimulus is aversive only if contingent presentation of the stimulus results in a reduction of the behavior. Likewise, if the targeted behavior is not weakened or reduced following the use of a stimulus, the stimulus was not aversive, despite what you intended. For example, Marcus was a young boy with autism who frequently darted away from his mother and father and did not stop running until he was caught. Marcus's parents had tried many things, but nothing stopped this dangerous behavior. In desperation, they turned to an aversive. When Marcus ran away from a parent, he was given a small squirt of lemon juice in his mouth as a punishment. Unfortunately, after the first time the mother administered this "aversive," the next time Marcus darted away, he headed straight for the lemon juice, grabbed the bottle, and squirted it in his mouth. It turns out that Marcus enjoyed the taste of lemon juice! Of course, perhaps the mother learned something from this mistake: that lemon juice might be a powerful reinforcer for Marcus and could be used in a DRO schedule (i.e., he could earn lemon juice contingent upon increasingly longer periods during which he does not leave the area without permission). Naturally, Marcus should then be taught to value other reinforcers through the process known as pairing, as discussed in Chapter 10.

Sometimes a stimulus might not be liked, but it is less aversive than competing stimuli and, therefore, does not produce a reduction in the targeted behavior. For example, the teacher's reprimands to Manuel regarding his noncompliant behavior are less aversive to Manuel than appearing to be "a school boy" (i.e., being compliant and following the rules) in front of certain peers. In some situations, when those peers are not present, Manuel is more compliant and the teacher's reprimands produce the desired results. However, when those particular peers are present, their opinion of him outweighs anything that the teacher does. A student who has weak skills in mathematics and who strongly dislikes mathematics might find that being sent to the principal's office and even the accompanying consequences, such as detention or in-school suspension, for classroom misbehavior are less aversive than remaining in the difficult, disliked mathematics class.

Incredibly, in this age of advanced behavioral technology, one form of unconditioned aversive stimulus that is still relatively widely used and considered acceptable by many is corporal punishment. **Corporal punishment** is a term that is commonly used synonymously with spanking but that has been defined as any punishment that inflicts bodily pain for disapproved behavior (Robinson, Funk, Beth, & Bush, 2005). In the United States, at least 220,000 children in public schools are paddled each school year (Human Rights Watch and American Civil Rights Union, 2009). As with most school-based punishments, African American students are disproportionately represented in the population of students who are paddled. According to the report from the Human Rights Watch and the ACLU (2009), 17% of all students are African American, but 35.6% of the students who are paddled are African American. Evidence indicates that corporal punishment not only is ineffective as a technique for changing behavior, but also is linked to negative side effects, such as running away, truancy, anxiety, aggression, property destruction, and even animal cruelty (Kennedy, 1995; Robinson et al., 2005).

> Corporal punishment is still used, despite its ineffectiveness and the potential for negative side effects.

As of 2008, 20 states still allow corporal punishment in schools (Center for Effective Discipline, 2008). Virtually every major professional and advocacy organization concerned with children's issues has adopted a position against the use of corporal punishment, particularly in schools. Despite its ineffectiveness, the potential for negative side effects, and behavioral technology that provides far more effective alternatives, many parents, the public, and even many educators support the use of corporal punishment in schools (Evans & Richardson, 1995; Human Rights Watch and ACLU, 2009; Imbrogno, 2000; Kenny, 2004; Robinson et al., 2005). Of course, corporal punishment should not be a part of any intervention plan based on PBIS. Behavioral technology provides sufficient strategies for managing the range of possible behavioral problems; it is not necessary to rely on outdated, ineffective, and potentially dangerous methods like corporal punishment. Fortunately, the tide is beginning to turn. There is a consistent downward trend in the number of students being paddled each year (Center for Effective Discipline, 2008), an increasing number of professional groups and organizations are publicly opposing corporal punishment (Human Rights Watch and ACLU, 2009), and in 2010 a bill was introduced in Congress to ban corporal punishment: H.R. 5628, the Ending Corporal Punishment in Schools Act. Although the bill was not passed, it is one of many encouraging signs that one day, perhaps, corporal punishment, as both a philosophy and a disciplinary tactic, will no longer be a part of our education system.

The only aversive stimulus that we support for behavioral intervention purposes is a mild reprimand. A brief planned reprimand that is systematically, consistently, and privately delivered following a specific behavior and that is accompanied by both a reminder about the expected behavior and corresponding reinforcement of appropriate behavior might be an effective intervention for some mildly inappropriate behaviors. However, reprimands are easily misused. In addition, some students who exhibit high levels of challenging behaviors have received so many reprimands from parents, teachers, and other caregivers that reprimands might have little effect on the targeted behavior.

Overcorrection. Overcorrection was developed as a way to combine a punishing consequence for inappropriate behavior with practice in appropriate behaviors (Azrin & Foxx, 1971). Overcorrection is instructional because it requires students to practice an appropriate behavior that is related to the inappropriate behavior. However, it is also punishing because the student must practice the appropriate behavior multiple times, not just once. Two types of overcorrection procedures are restitutional overcorrection and positive practice overcorrection.

Restitutional overcorrection involves having the student compensate for any damage that is a result of his or her actions. Restitution is required to repair any damage done, restore the environment to its original condition, or make amends to persons who were affected by the behavior. However, "overcorrection" indicates that the compensation is above and beyond the level needed for actual repair or restoration. The following are examples of restitutional overcorrection:

- Manny wrote on his desk. Consequently, he must clean not only his own desk, but also every other desk in the classroom.
- Kayla ripped up all of her papers in frustration. Now she must repair all of those papers with tape, as well as straightening up all of the objects in her desk.

- C.J. made a derogatory comment to a classmate. As a result, he must apologize to that person, as well as every other student in the class.
- Carly threw a stick on the playground. She was required to pick up all the sticks that she could find on the playground during a 10-minute period.

Positive practice overcorrection requires the student to practice the appropriate behavior *repeatedly*.

Positive practice overcorrection involves the student practicing an appropriate alternative to the undesirable behavior. Teachers often use a modified form of positive practice overcorrection: A student who runs in the hall is told to rewalk that portion of the hall, a student who misspells a word on a spelling test must write it correctly five times, or a student who grabs an object from another student is told to return the object and ask politely if she may use it. Correct use of positive practice overcorrection requires multiple practice trials of the desired behavior.

The following are examples of positive practice overcorrection:

- Joshua, a young boy with autism, played with blocks inappropriately, attempting to spin them or bite them. His teacher required Joshua to practice stacking the blocks and knocking them over 10 times.
- Rasheed roughly poked the student sitting next to him. As a result, he was required to practice sitting in his chair with his hands folded in his lap for 5 minutes.
- Lisa, a student with developmental disabilities, licked her fingers during cooking class. The teacher required her to practice spreading peanut butter on 10 crackers without touching her mouth.

Although overcorrection involves practicing an appropriate behavior, we recommend using other less intrusive techniques for most challenging behaviors. Overcorrection can be effective, but it also has potentially negative side effects, including the following:

- Both forms of overcorrection can be very time consuming. Teachers must weigh the disadvantage of the time required to carry out the overcorrection procedure with the potential benefits.
- Overcorrection usually requires the undivided attention of the teacher to ensure that the student completes the procedure. This is a problem for two reasons. First, the teacher's attention is diverted from other students during the procedure. Unless the teacher has a paraprofessional or another teacher present to attend to the other students, overcorrection should not be used. Second, this undivided attention might be reinforcing to students.
- Sometimes the student might become aggressive or noncompliant during the overcorrection procedure. One of the authors (BKS) once used positive practice overcorrection as a consequence for a student who threw rocks on the playground. During the procedure, the student refused to comply with instructions to pick up a rock and place it in a container. The author provided physical guidance in an attempt to get the student to comply, but he responded by letting his entire body go limp, while he laughed giddily. Not only did the overcorrection procedure not work, but it also reinforced undesirable behavior (in this case, noncompliance).
- There is a fine distinction between reinforcing students for compliance during the overcorrection procedure (a desirable behavior) and maintaining the punitive aspects of overcorrection.

For all of these reasons, we recommend that overcorrection be used infrequently and only after all other approaches have proven to be ineffective.

Two techniques that are sometimes erroneously called overcorrection are negative practice and contingent exercise. Negative practice is not overcorrection because it requires the student to repeatedly practice the targeted inappropriate behavior (Dunlap, 1930). Examples of negative practice include having a student spit 50 times into the sink as a consequence for spitting or requiring a child who makes noises during class to make noises continuously for 10 minutes. This is not a technique that we recommend.

> Negative practice and contingent exercise *are not* forms of overcorrection.

Contingent exercise is not overcorrection because it requires the student to perform a motor response that is unrelated to the targeted inappropriate behavior (Luce, Delquadri, & Hall, 1980). Examples of contingent exercise would be having a child do 20 sit-ups as a consequence for hitting or running laps as a consequence for disruptive behavior during physical education class. Again, because of the punitive nature of this technique, and because it lacks any element of teaching or reinforcing a replacement behavior, we do not recommend contingent exercise.

Summary

We expect that using the preventive antecedent techniques described throughout this text, and the reinforcement-based consequence strategies described in Chapters 10 and 11, will solve many behavioral problems that teachers encounter. However, sometimes these approaches are insufficient to prevent or control a particularly challenging behavior. In this chapter, we described how educators should determine when a more direct approach to dealing with a challenging behavior is needed, and we explained specific strategies for reducing or eliminating challenging behaviors. The objectives for this chapter, with a summary of how each objective was addressed, are as follows:

1. Define nonpunishment and punishment techniques.

Not all techniques for reducing challenging behaviors are technically punishment techniques. *Punishment* refers only to those procedures that meet the formal definition of the term: the delivery of a stimulus, following a behavior, that reduces future occurrences of the behavior. Other techniques, such as differential reinforcement and extinction, reduce behavior, but do not meet the definition of punishment.

2. Describe IDEA's disciplinary provisions and zero-tolerance policies.

IDEA describes how educators can respond to students with disabilities who exhibit behaviors that violate school rules and expectations. The goal of the IDEA disciplinary provisions is to ensure safe and effective schools for all students, while protecting the rights of students with disabilities. The 2004 IDEA describes disciplinary responses that are related to manifestation determination, placement in an IAES, the authority of school personnel in dealing with behavioral infractions, and procedures to be followed pending the outcome of a disciplinary inquiry.

3. Define zero tolerance and describe the problems that arise when zero-tolerance policies are applied.

Zero-tolerance policies require administrators to respond to school-based rule violations in a uniform, prescribed manner with no attention to the particulars of each situation. Although the intent of zero-tolerance policies is understandable, implementation of these policies has resulted in harsh penalties for minor misbehavior, even for behavior that is not a problem. As administrators become more aware of and more proficient in using schoolwide PBIS, we hope that zero-tolerance policies become less significant.

4. Describe the guidelines for judicious and ethical use of behavior reductive interventions.

We provided guidelines for selecting and implementing behavior reductive strategies. Not only is there the potential for misuse of many of these strategies, but also some of the strategies have possible negative side effects that must be considered. Great care must be taken when using behavior reductive interventions, especially punishment, to ensure that the interventions are used with fidelity, that side effects are monitored, and that targeted behaviors change in the desired direction.

5. Describe the hierarchy of behavior reductive strategies:
   a. Differential reinforcement

We described four types of differential reinforcement procedures: differential reinforcement of incompatible behaviors (DRI), alternative behaviors (DRA), lower levels of behavior (DRL), and other behaviors (DRO). The differential reinforcement procedures are powerful behavior reductive techniques that provide effective alternatives to punishment.

   b. Extinction

Extinction refers to the withholding of reinforcement for a behavior that was previously reinforced, usually through attention. Extinction is an effective intervention for certain types of behavior, but it must be used carefully in order to avoid inadvertently reinforcing undesirable behaviors. In addition, educators must be aware of the potential side effects of extinction.

   c. Response cost

Response cost is the removal of previously earned reinforcers. Response cost is an effective technique that often produces a rapid reduction in behavior; it is easy to use and versatile, and it can avoid some of the negative side effects associated with other punishment procedures.

   d. Time-out

Time-out from positive reinforcement constitutes the denial of access to reinforcers for a set length of time. The three forms of this strategy are nonexclusionary, exclusionary, and seclusionary. We recommend the nonexclusionary form, which allows students to remain in the instructional environment for time-out. We do not generally recommend seclusionary forms because students are removed from the instructional environment, and it has great potential for escalating the very behavioral problems for which time-out is given.

   e. Presentation of aversive stimuli

We defined unconditioned aversive stimuli (i.e., unlearned, naturally distasteful, or painful) and conditioned aversive stimuli (i.e., learned). Reprimands (i.e., conditioned aversive stimuli) are the only form of aversive stimuli that we recommend for general use. Other techniques that fall into this category include overcorrection. Corporal punishment is perhaps the most well-known aversive stimulus. Corporal punishment is associated with a number of issues, including its disproportionate use with minority students.

6. Describe how to implement each strategy correctly and ethically, and explain which strategies conform to a PBIS philosophy and which do not.

For each technique, we described specific guidelines for correct and ethical use. It is critical that behavior reductive techniques be implemented correctly and that their use be monitored closely. The more negative the technique, the more important it is to use a team approach for monitoring and decision making. A PBIS approach would include the following strategies: differential reinforcement, extinction, and possibly response cost and some forms of time-out.

Given the potential for misuse of the behavior reductive and punishment techniques, we encourage teachers to periodically self-assess their understanding and use of these procedures. We provide a self-assessment tool for this purpose in Table 12-8.

TABLE 12-8   Antecedent and Behavior Reductive Practices Self-Assessments

This chapter includes two self-assessments: The first addresses antecedents that must be in place prior to using behavior reductive strategies; the second addresses the use of behavior reductive practices.

Antecedent Self-Assessment

Never	Seldom	Sometimes	Often	Always
1	2	3	4	5

Use the numbers above to rate the following statements.

1. The rules and procedures in my classroom are clear and have been taught to my students. _____

2. I have a positive relationship with each of my students. _____

3. The climate in my classroom reflects a respectful, positive learning environment. _____

4. I have conducted a functional behavioral assessment that identifies the functions of challenging student behavior. _____

5. I use the resulting hypotheses from the FBA as the basis for designing antecedent and reinforcement interventions. _____

6. I have used dense reinforcement schedules to reinforce appropriate behaviors. _____

7. I use instructional methods that are appropriate for my students' learning needs. _____

8. My students are actively and successfully engaged in meaningful learning tasks most of the time. _____

9. My students have been directly taught appropriate behavior and communication skills. _____

10. All of these interventions have been applied correctly and consistently. _____

Behavior Reductive Practices Self-Assessment

1. I know and follow the criteria for using behavior reductive strategies. _____

2. I can describe the hierarchy of behavior reductive strategies. _____

3. I know how to implement each strategy correctly and ethically. _____

4. I understand and recognize the types of behavior that warrant the use of behavior reductive techniques. _____

5. I choose to use the least aversive intervention that can reasonably be expected to produce the desired results. _____

6. I continue to use instructional and reinforcement strategies in conjunction with behavior reductive techniques. _____

7. I understand how to implement the different types of differential reinforcement and what behaviors are appropriate for each differential reinforcement strategy. _____

8. I understand how to implement extinction as a behavior reductive technique. _____

9. I establish procedural safeguards for the use of any strategy beyond extinction. _____

10. I understand how time-out can be misused and the problems that can occur when time-out is used. _____

Dr. ICE Helps Teachers Manage Challenging Behaviors

Dr. ICE was asked by Dr. Banks, the superintendent of the Iron Fist School District, to speak to the teachers and administrators about how to manage challenging behaviors through the use of PBIS. Dr. ICE had worked with the staff of this district in the past regarding many aspects of positive behavior management techniques. Dr. Banks also asked Dr. ICE to work one-on-one with some of the teachers. The work that Dr. ICE did with those teachers and their students is the subject of the following vignettes. The titles of these vignettes refer to the type of strategy that they describe. The vignettes also include a brief definition of each strategy. In each example, the teacher has met all of the criteria in the Antecedent Self-Assessment before developing a behavior reductive plan.

DIFFERENTIAL REINFORCEMENT OF INCOMPATIBLE BEHAVIOR (DRI)

This is a procedure in which challenging behavior is reduced by systematically reinforcing appropriate behaviors that are incompatible with the challenging behavior.

Mr. Small, a tenth-grade mathematics teacher, asked Dr. ICE to help him with Mark, who is habitually tardy. Mr. Small said that Mark moved into the school district 1 month ago and that he has not yet received Mark's records from his previous school. However, Mark has been placed in resource mathematics because he had been receiving that service in the previous district.

During his observation, Dr. ICE noted that Mr. Small has rules and procedures in place and that his students appear to know what is expected of them. That day, Mark came in 10 minutes late with no excuse. He was sent to the office for a tardy slip. He returned in about 5 minutes with the slip. He sat quietly, but did not participate, during the remainder of the class unless Mr. Smith called on him specifically.

Dr. ICE met with Mr. Small after the observation in order to develop a plan. They defined Mark's targeted behavior as coming in late to class. ("Late" was defined as arriving after the tardy bell.) The replacement behavior is for Mark to be in his seat, ready to work, when the tardy bell rings. The next step that Dr. ICE proposed was to find out why Mark is frequently tardy, because he never has an explanation. Dr. ICE agreed to conduct this FBA; the two men agreed to meet again in 2 days.

Dr. ICE followed Mark for the next 2 days and discovered that Mark's locker is located at the far end of the school from Mr. Small's class. Mark has a group of friends who stand in the hall and talk until just before the tardy bell rings. The friends have classes that are nearby; however, the distance to Mr. Small's class means that Mark will be late in arriving. Dr. ICE discovered that Mark's friends do not receive special education services and that they are in the same history and physical education classes as Mark. The physical education class meets during the period just before Mr. Small's class. Mark leaves that class with his friends and they go to get books from their lockers, which are located in the same area. Dr. ICE also discovered that Mark is tardy only to Mr. Smith's class.

When Dr. ICE met again with Mr. Smith, he shared this information with him. Dr. ICE also told Mr. Smith that because Mark's tardy behavior is limited to this class, it might be caused by more than just the temptation to talk with his friends. However, they would start by determining a reinforcer that would help motivate Mark to arrive to class on time. Dr. ICE suggested to Mr. Small that he conference with Mark to define the problem and to agree on a reinforcer. Then, every day that Mark is in his seat and ready for class when the tardy bell rings, he will earn tokens toward this reinforcer.

Two weeks later, Dr. ICE met with Mr. Smith. Mr. Smith and Mark have agreed to an easy reinforcer. The school office has been calling Mark's parents at work to inform them of his tardiness. They, in turn, have taken privileges away from him because of his chronic tardiness. Mark's reinforcer is that Mr. Smith calls or e-mails Mark's parents every day that Mark is in his seat and ready for work when the tardy bell rings. He also praises Mark's efforts in class. This has made Mark's parents very happy with Mark, and they have allowed him more freedom to be with his friends after school (including his friends from his physical education and history classes). Mark is seldom late these days, and he is becoming a more active learner in Mr. Small's class.

DIFFERENTIAL REINFORCEMENT OF ALTERNATIVE BEHAVIOR (DRA)

This procedure allows for the selection of a much broader range of behaviors than DRI. The criteria for selecting a replacement behavior are that the replacement behavior should serve the same function as the inappropriate behavior, should be just as easy to perform as the inappropriate behavior, and should result in reinforcement that is just as frequent and intense as the reinforcement that currently exists for the inappropriate behavior.

Ms. Jet teaches seventh-grade resource language arts. She asked to work with Dr. ICE concerning a student who acts out repeatedly during class, even after many conferences with the student's parents. This student settles down to work only when Ms. Jet or her teaching assistant gives her one-on-one attention. Ms. Jet is certain that the behavioral problem is not tied to a skill deficit, because the student has always been able to do the work when she is given individual attention.

Dr. ICE observed the class. It was evident that rules and procedures had been taught and were understood by the students. In fact, the student, Marsha, appears to use her knowledge of the rules and procedures in order to get attention. For example, she loudly reminds other students about specific rules or procedures, or she asks multiple questions about the assigned work before actually attempting to do the work (but only when the teacher is busy with other students). When the teachers give her individual assistance, her work is very good and her behavior is appropriate.

Dr. ICE and Ms. Jet had a conference later in the day. They defined Marsha's targeted behavior as any behavior that specifically breaks a rule or fails to follow a procedure. On the basis of the observation and information from Ms. Jet, they hypothesized that the function of the behavior is to get teacher attention. Marsha knows the rules and procedures, and demonstrates this knowledge by following the rules when the teacher is near her. Ms. Jet told Dr. ICE that Marsha's parents often work late and she is left alone after school, sometimes until after she goes to bed. An array of attention-based reinforcers was developed with Marsha's input. The targeted replacement behaviors (i.e., alternative behaviors) are (a) following the class rules and procedures, and (b) completing assignments with no more than one request for assistance. First, Marsha earns points for following the class rules and procedures, as well as completing assignments independently; points may be traded for lunch with the teacher. Next, Ms. Jet spoke with Marsha's parents, and they agreed that for each week in which Marsha earns a predetermined number of points, Marsha may work with Ms. Jet in an after-school drama class the next week. The parents agreed to spend special time with Marsha on the weekend. They also agreed with Ms. Jet that Marsha is still too young to be left alone for such

long periods when they work late. Dr. ICE told Ms. Jet that he will check back with her to see how the procedure is working.

Two weeks later, Dr. ICE checked on Marsha's progress. Although there are still a few times when Marsha is disruptive (usually when Ms. Jet or her paraprofessional are is out of the room for an extended time), the DRA intervention has produced dramatic results. Marsha now follows the rules most of the time, and her rate of independent assignment completion has increased dramatically. Dr. ICE suggested that, as part of the DRA intervention, Marsha be allowed to reserve 10 points per week in the "bank." Whenever Ms. Jet or her paraprofessional is absent, Marsha may use these banked points to purchase special "assistant" privileges, such as helping the teacher or substitute with certain tasks or helping other students with specifically designated tasks (e.g., listening to a student read, reviewing spelling words, giving a spelling test).

DIFFERENTIAL REINFORCEMENT OF LOWER LEVELS OF BEHAVIOR (DRL)

DRL involves reinforcing the student for meeting a predetermined criterion for the number of behaviors that are allowed. Three types of DRL are commonly used:

1. **Full-Session DRL:** Reinforcement is given for the duration of the class, the period, or the day.

Mr. Craft asked to work with Dr. ICE because a student in his fourth-period resource reading class makes a high number of careless errors when he completes independent work. This student, Jim, seems to want to rush through his work so that he can use the computer or go to a learning center.

Dr. ICE met with Mr. Craft and they decided to use DRL during the daily 20-minute independent work time. The targeted behavior would be work errors. First, Mr. Craft gathered baseline data for Jim's work across 3 days. During those 3 days, Jim averaged 15 errors per assignment, most of which were minor (e.g., skipping one or more questions, misspelling words that were provided in a word bank, not using complete sentences to answer questions).

In Phase I of the intervention, Mr. Craft informed Jim that for each day that he makes 12 or fewer errors on his work, he can earn 5 extra minutes of computer or learning center time on Friday. After 4 consecutive days of meeting this criterion, Mr. Craft implemented Phase II, in which Jim can make only 10 or fewer errors in order to earn minutes toward reinforcement time on Friday. Again, after 4 consecutive days of meeting this criterion, the criterion was reduced to 8 or fewer errors. Reduction continued until Jim was making fewer than two errors per assignment.

2. Interval DRL: The session is divided into equal intervals; reinforcement is given if the number of occurrences of the behavior is equal to or less than the criterion for each interval.

Ms. Patty, a first-grade teacher, talked to Dr. ICE about Sarah. Sarah talks out very often during circle time. She seldom allows other students to answer questions without blurting out an answer or comment, which is often off topic. Circle time lasts 20 minutes.

Dr. ICE and Ms. Patty reviewed the data that Ms. Patty had collected. It seems that Sarah begins talking out after 4 minutes and occurrences build up to one time per minute during the last 5 minutes of circle time. Ms. Patty said that Sarah was redirected about every three or four occurrences.

A plan was developed that divided the session into 3-minute intervals. If Sarah has not talked out more than one time during an interval, she is given a token. She can use these tokens to buy special privileges from a list developed by Ms. Patty (e.g., lead the line, erase the board, blow the whistle to signal the end of recess).

When Dr. ICE checked back with Ms. Patty to see how the plan was working, Ms. Patty was pleased to report that Sarah's disruptive talking out during circle time has dropped to almost zero. She now answers questions when she is called on, but does not blurt out answers or make off-task comments. Dr. ICE recommended that Ms. Patty begin to lengthen the intervals, moving first to 4-minute intervals, then 5-minute, and so on.

3. Changing Criterion DRL: The criterion is gradually lowered across sessions until the target criterion is reached.

Ms. Gray, an intermediate-grade resource teacher, has a student who moves his desk and chair so often during science inclusion class that the other students lose instruction time. Ms. Gray asked for help from Dr. ICE because of the importance of her students learning to exhibit appropriate behavior in general education settings.

Dr. ICE asked Ms. Gray to gather baseline data. The student, Mason, moves his desk or chair 11 times, on average, during a 40-minute science class. Ms. Gray

and Dr. ICE set the first criterion at nine desk or chair moves: Mason will be reinforced with 5 minutes of extra computer time if he moves his desk or chair nine or fewer times during a class period. When Mason achieves this criterion for 3 consecutive days, the criterion will be lowered to seven or fewer times. Gradually, the criterion will be lowered until the behavior occurs no more than one time per class. At that point, the amount of computer time will be gradually reduced until it is given only intermittently.

DIFFERENTIAL REINFORCEMENT OF ZERO LEVELS OF BEHAVIOR (DRO)

DRO is reinforcement that occurs only when zero instances of the targeted behavior occur. DRO should be used in conjunction with other procedures.

Ms. Edwards teaches eighth grade in a self-contained behavior class; however, she pairs with the self-contained teacher next door so that their students can have the experience of changing classes. She wanted to work with Dr. ICE because one of her students is becoming more and more verbally aggressive. Each time that the students change to a new activity, Michael curses at her or her teaching assistant, Mr. Brown. Any type of transition provokes a cursing incident that lasts several minutes into the new activity.

Dr. ICE observed Ms. Edwards's class and witnessed the difficulty Michael has with making a transition from one activity to the next. Dr. ICE also observed that once Michael becomes involved in a task, he stops cursing. Dr. ICE met with Ms. Edwards and they developed a plan. They defined the behavior for the DRO procedure as cursing and delineated the types of words or phrases that Michael typically uses during these cursing episodes. From the baseline data, they determined that each lesson has four transitions: arrival, direct teaching to guided practice, guided practice to individual work, and dismissal. Michael will earn a token (a ticket) for each transition during which he does not curse. He will also earn a ticket for every 2-minute interval that he is on task. In addition to the DRO procedure, Dr. ICE recommended that Ms. Edwards provide Michael with specific signals that a transition will be occurring and use precorrection (see Chapter 7) to remind him about the expected transition behavior. He also recommended that Ms. Edwards teach Michael how to express frustration over the end of an activity using appropriate words. Ms. Edwards and Michael generated a list of appropriate words that Michael could use, and they practiced those words in role-play situations. Finally, Michael will earn bonus tickets on an intermittent basis for using those appropriate words instead of cursing (this, of course, is a DRI intervention).

Michael's cursing dropped to zero occurrences by the end of the second week of the intervention. At this point, Ms. Edwards began to thin the reinforcement schedule. She has moved to an intermittent schedule of reinforcement for giving tickets, and the criteria for earning backup reinforcers were increased slightly.

EXTINCTION

Extinction is the withholding of reinforcement for a behavior that has been maintained through reinforcement, often in the form of attention.

Ms. Davis spoke with Dr. ICE about one of her kindergarten students who cries and clings to her mother every morning when it is time to say good-bye. They decided that the targeted behavior is crying. They developed a plan to deal with the undesired behavior.

Ms. Davis met with Ann's mother and told her that each morning, Ms. Davis will meet Ann and her mother at the front door of the school. Ann and her mother will say their good-byes, and then Mom will hug Ann and walk out of the school. Ms. Davis will take Ann's hand and walk with her to the classroom. Along the way, Ms. Davis will tell Ann about all of the fun that they are going to have at school. Any crying will be placed on extinction: Ms. Davis will release Ann's hand and stop talking. As soon as Ann stops crying, Ms. Davis will again take her hand and begin talking to her about the upcoming day. Ms. Davis will walk Ann to her seat in the classroom and begin morning activities. Ann was then brought into the meeting and the preceding steps were explained to her. Ann's mother also told her that they will play a game together at home every day that she walks to class with Ms. Davis.

Dr. ICE met with Ms. Davis 2 weeks later. Ms. Davis said that Ann still cries briefly every morning; however, she does walk to the classroom. Ms. Davis said that Ann's mother initially had a hard time walking away and that she still calls about 30 minutes later to check on Ann. Most of the time, Ann is busy playing in the centers.

Six weeks into the plan, Ann began to have tantrums when her mother left the school. Ms. Davis scheduled a conference and explained to Ann's mother that this type of spontaneous recovery is a common problem with the intervention that they are using. Together, they then reminded Ann about the expectations for walking to class without crying or screaming and what would happen if Ann cried or screamed (Ms. Davis would not hold her hand or talk to her). Ann's mother reminded her about the fun that they had been having during their game time after school.

RESPONSE COST

Response cost is a punishment procedure in which some amount of reinforcers are withdrawn or removed, contingent upon a particular behavior.

Dr. ICE worked with Ms. Tate, who teaches a ninth-grade resource class. Her students earn points for following procedures. Every 15 minutes, she notes the points earned on a preprinted point sheet at each student's desk. The students have been taught the procedures, which are reviewed at least twice a week. When a student has not followed a particular procedure, Ms. Tate writes a dash instead of noting the points earned. Students can spend or save points for classroom activities.

When she began using this technique, a student would sometimes destroy the point sheet in anger if points were not awarded. In the past, Ms. Tate had let students get a new point sheet the next day. Dr. ICE advised her to let her students know that points could be used only if the student had a point sheet that was in one piece. Now if a student destroys a point sheet, Ms. Tate does not respond directly to the behavior other than to calmly remind the student that a point sheet is needed for both earning points and for spending points. She sticks to a strict policy of "no point sheet—no spending." In addition, Ms. Tate sometimes reinforces students who do not earn points, but who accept the loss of the points appropriately, by awarding the student a bonus point for good self-control. Students have learned to refrain from tearing up the point sheets most of the time. However, sometimes a student makes a mistake and destroys the point sheet, but the student knows that he or she must repair the point sheet (Ms. Tate allows the students to use her tape dispenser) in order to continue earning points and to spend the points later. Students who make the mistake of destroying their point sheet now take responsibility for repairing the damage. Ms. Tate has also made this type of angry response a topic for social skills training for the class.

TIME-OUT

Time-out is a procedure in which an individual is denied access to reinforcers for a period of time.

Dr. ICE is very cautious about using time-out and even providing examples of its use. Time-out procedures can and often do cause more problems than the behavior that prompted its use in the first place. However, Dr. ICE agreed to provide examples of the three types of time-out, the problems that he has experienced with each, and what he recommends for addressing those problems:

1. Nonexclusionary Time-out: Reinforcement is withheld; however, the child remains in the instructional setting.

John often disrupts independent work by talking to or about his peers. Ms. Smith uses a 2-minute time-out at his desk. The 2 minutes will start when John is quiet and has his head on his desk. Ms. Smith told Dr. ICE the following problems that she has had with this technique:

- John will remain quiet for about 1 minute and then he will talk out. The time will start over; however, occasionally his peers will laugh, reinforcing the talking-out behavior.
- Sometimes John will refuse to put his head down. Ms. Smith has no control over this because she is not permitted to physically make him put his head down.

Ms. Smith asked Dr. ICE to help her find a way to make John comply with this type of time-out. Instead, Dr. ICE told her that perhaps this is not the correct technique to use, because, instead of being denied access to reinforcers, John seems to have free access to peer reinforcement, the same powerful reinforcer that might be sustaining the talking-out behavior in the first place. Dr. ICE offered to work with Ms. Smith to develop a successful behavioral change plan for John using DRI (making only task-related comments) and allowing John to earn reinforcers that provide peer attention (see Chapters 3 and 9).

2. Exclusionary Time-out: The student is removed from the instructional activity to another area within the classroom or outside of the classroom.

Mr. Adams uses a cubicle desk at the back of the classroom for this type of time-out. The student is required to stay quietly at this desk for 5 minutes. The time does not start until the student is seated quietly; the time will start over if the student is not quiet. Instructional materials are not given to the student. Mr. Adams and Dr. ICE noted the following problems with this technique:

- Some students have a very hard time staying quiet; as a result, the timer is repeatedly reset. The student misses instructional time, and repeatedly resetting the timer results in too much teacher attention during time-out.
- Some students become aggressive or disruptive on the way to the time-out desk. This can result in behaviors that escalate far beyond the original behavior that prompted time-out.
- Some students become so distraught about having to go to time-out that the behavior that sent them to time-out in the first place is lost in the new, more serious behavior.
- Some students refuse to go to the time-out area. These students sometimes escalate to more disruptive types of noncompliant behaviors (yelling, grabbing items from other students' desks).

Dr. ICE recommended the following strategies for Mr. Adams:

- Reevaluate whether this form of time-out is the most appropriate intervention or even whether time-out is an appropriate intervention for these students.
- Teach students how to take time-out, just like any other procedure is taught. Students should practice going to time-out and should receive reinforcement for following the appropriate procedure.
- Implement a contingency for taking time-out correctly. If a student moves immediately (i.e., within 1 minute) to time-out upon being told to do so, time-out is reduced by 1 minute. For each minute that the student remains quiet in the time-out area, time-out is reduced by 1 minute. The result is that time-out can be reduced from 5 minutes to 2 minutes, contingent upon the student taking time-out correctly.

3. Seclusionary Time-out: A designated time-out room is used to isolate the student.

Early in his career, Dr. ICE worked at a school that had a special time-out room. The following are just a few of the problems that he witnessed:

- The student usually had to be physically taken to this time-out room.
- Often the student would exhibit rage upon entering the time-out room, and the time-out period would not start for an extended time or would be lengthened because of the student's behavior.
- Sometimes the student would strip off clothing, urinate in the time-out room, or exhibit other equally disturbing behaviors.
- Some students became aggressive toward staff when the door to the time-out room is opened.
- Some students would go to this time-out room repeatedly for the same behavior.

Because of the problems associated with this form of time-out, the potential risks, and the significant amount of instruction time lost, Dr. ICE does not recommend this type of time-out. His preference is to use more positive behavioral techniques, including less aversive behavior reductive techniques such as differential reinforcement, extinction, other forms of time-out, and response cost.

Learning Activities

1. In small groups, choose three behaviors that might be punished in a classroom. Now discuss positive methods that can be used to change the behaviors.
2. Describe how the reinforcement of appropriate behaviors decreases the need for behavior reductive strategies.
3. Using the hierarchy of behavior reductive strategies, discuss in small groups how you would use the differential reinforcement strategies, extinction, response cost, and time-out in your classroom.
4. Identify one or more of your own bad habits, and describe a differential reinforcement intervention that could be used to reduce or eliminate each bad habit.
5. In small groups, role-play the members of an IEP committee discussing a proposed change in a BIP to include behavior reductive strategies. Include the following roles:
   - A parent, who disagrees with the change because of concern about the use of "punishment"
   - The principal, who is not convinced one way or the other
   - A general education teacher, who argues that something needs to be done because the student's behavior is continuing to interfere with the student's success in this teacher's class
   - The special education teacher, who will need to make a case for the proposed changes, using all of his or her knowledge of the student and the behavioral strategies that have been applied and are being considered

Resources

WEBSITES

www.advancementproject.org/digital-library/ publications/opportunities-suspended-the- devastating-consequences-of-zero-tolerance- *Opportunities Suspended: The Devastating Consequences of Zero-Tolerance and School Discipline*: This Advancement Project report, released in June 2000, was written in collaboration with the Civil Rights Project at Harvard University.

http://www.ccbd.net/advocacy/index.cfm?catego ryID=668947C8-C09F-1D6F-F9375EDC805102B3 The website of the Council for Children with Behavioral Disorders (CCBD), a division of the Council for Exceptional Children. CCBD has published position papers on the use of restraint and seclusion in schools. These papers may be downloaded from the CCBD website.

www.indiana.edu/~safeschl Safe and Responsive Schools: This model demonstration and technical assistance project at Indiana University provides information about school violence, overrepresentation of minority students in special education, disproportionate discipline of minority students, and creating safe schools. Includes links, publications, and overviews of model programs.

www.stophitting.com The Center for Effective Discipline: Provides information about discipline at home and in school. Includes data on the use of corporal punishment, laws related to discipline and corporal punishment, and links to related sites.

www.state.ky.us/agencies/behave/bi/to.pdf *Effec tive Use of Time-Out*: This article is available on the Behavior Home Page, which is hosted by the Kentucky Department of Education and the Department of Special Education and Rehabilitation Counseling at the University of Kentucky.

ARTICLES

Grskovic, J. A., Hall, A. M., Montgomery, D. J., Vargas, A. U., Zentall, S. S., & Belfiore, P. J. (2004). Reducing time-out assignments for students with emotional/behavioral disorders in a self-contained classroom. *Journal of Behavioral Education, 13*(1), 25–36.

Webber, J., & Scheuermann, B. (1991). Accentuate the positive … Eliminate the negative. *Teaching Exceptional Children, 24*(1), 13–19.

REPORTS AND POSITION STATEMENTS

Advancement Project and the Harvard Civil Rights Project. (2000). *Opportunities Suspended: The devastating consequences of zero tolerance and school discipline policies.* Available from www.civilrightsproject.harvard.edu/research/discipline/opport_suspended.hp

Council for Children with Behavioral Disorders (2009). *CCBD'S Position Summary on the use of seclusion in school settings.* Available from http://www.ccbd.net/advocacy/index.cfm?categoryID=668947C8-C09F-1D6F-F9375EDC805102B3#

Council of Parent Attorneys and Advocates (COPAA). (2008). *Declaration of principles opposing the use of restraints, seclusion, and other aversive interventions upon children with disabilities.* Available from http://www.copaa.org/public-policy/copaas-major-legislative-priorities/ending-abuse-through-restraint-and-seclusion/

Human Rights Watch and American Civil Liberties Union (2009). *A Violent Education: Corporal Punishment of Children in U.S. Public Schools.* Available from http://www.aclu.org/human-rights-racial-justice/violent-education-corporal-punishment-children-us-public-schools

National Disability Rights Network. (2009). *School is not supposed to hurt: Investigative report on abusive restraint and seclusion in schools.* Available from http://www.napas.org/en/resources/publications.html

GLOSSARY

A-B-C descriptive analysis—expands on the simple anecdotal format to allow for a grater level of detail in recording the events surrounding the identified behaviors.

A-B-C model—all of the instructional and behavior management strategies of applied behavior analysis can be categorized in this easy to understand model.

Academic learning time (also called successful engaged time)—the amount of engaged time that students are successful in academic responses.

Acknowledgment system—a set of procedures that are used in schoolwide positive behavioral interventions and supports (PBIS) in order to provide feedback to students on rule-following behaviors.

Acquisition deficit—a skill that a student has never learned to use, use correctly, or use in an appropriate context.

Acquisition stage of learning—the first stage in learning a new skill or concept. Some teacher assistance may be needed to help the student complete the skill, and the skill may be performed slowly or awkwardly.

Activity reinforcers—Reinforcers in the form of privileges, games, or special jobs.

Allocated time—the amount of time that a teacher allows for each instructional activity.

Anecdotal report (also called an A-B-C report or A-B-C recording)—a simple data recording method whereby an observer uses an antecedent–behavior–consequence (A-B-C) format to maintain a written description of events that occur during an observation period.

Anoxia—The phenomenon of oxygen deprivation and brain hemorrhaging that occurs during birth.

Antecedent—a stimulus that immediately precedes a particular behavior and that may cue the behavior.

Applied behavior analysis (ABA)—a scientific approach to behavior change that uses interventions based on behavioral principles and that relies on data to verify that behavior change interventions are indeed responsible for the behavior change.

Available time (also called opportunity to learn)—the amount of time that students are in school. Not all available time is spent receiving instruction.

Backward chaining—teaches a task-analyzed skill by starting with the last step in the task and teaching that step to mastery. Then the next to the last step is added and so on until the first step.

Baseline data—the amount of a behavior that occurs before an intervention is implemented. Baseline data are usually gathered for three to five observation periods before an intervention is implemented.

Behavior modification—an outdated term used for behavior change approaches, replaced by the more scientific approach of applied behavior analysis (ABA).

Behavior reductive procedures—techniques that produce a decrease in a targeted behavior through less negative means than punishment.

Behavioral deficit—a condition in which an individual exhibits an insufficient level of a particular behavior that is needed for social or academic success.

Behavioral efficiency—the principle that students will engage in behaviors that most reliably and easily produce the greatest amount of reinforcement.

Behavioral excess—a condition in which an individual exhibits a particular behavior too frequently or to an extreme level.

Behaviorism—the science of behavior and behavior change.

Biofeedback—involves the use of biological measures of muscle tension or brain wave activity as indicators of arousal levels.

Biophysical model (also called a medical model)—a model founded on the assumption that atypical behavior is the result of either biological makeup or some type of organic dysfunction that is inherent in an individual.

Chaining—refers to the process of joining discrete behaviors, or "links," to form a longer, more complex behavior.

Changing criterion DRL—a criterion that is gradually lowered across sessions until the targeted criterion is reached.

Cognitive–behavioral model—a theoretical model that addresses the role of thinking as a contributing factor to overt behavior.

Cognitive–behavioral intervention—an intervention specifically designed to teach a student self-control or self-management skills.

Complete stimulus control—a condition that results when a strong discriminative stimulus (S^D) results in a desired response more often than not.

Computer assisted instruction (CAI)—can provide high levels of response opportunities, immediate feedback, and motivation to improve learning outcomes.

Concept anchoring table—a form of graphic organizer used to help students learn a new concept by comparing it to a known concept.

Conditioned (or learned) aversive stimulus—a stimulus that an individual learns to dislike as a result of pairing it with an unconditioned aversive stimulus.

Consequence—an event that follows a behavior and determines whether the behavior will be repeated (i.e., reinforced) or not (i.e., punished).

Conspicuous strategies—ways of teaching new learners what experts claim makes a task easier to perform or information easier to learn or remember.

Contingent—said of a reinforcer when it is available only to an individual who exhibits a targeted behavior at a specified criterion level. Contingent access to reinforcers is critical to the success of reinforcement programs.

Continuous (schedule of) reinforcement (CRF)—a reinforcement schedule whereby every correct response is reinforced.

Contract—an agreement, usually written, between a student and an adult (e.g., parent, teacher, administrator) that delineates what each party will do.

Cooperative learning (CL)—an instructional activity in which students are placed in heterogeneous groups to complete a group task.

Coping model—in social skills instruction, a model that demonstrates the struggles that may be encountered when the skill is attempted.

Corporal punishment—a term that is commonly used synonymously with spanking but that has been defined as any punishment that inflicts bodily pain for disapproved behavior

Covert self-instruction—self-instruction in which an individual uses silent self-talk to prompt, guide, or evaluate performance.

Curriculum-based measurement (CBM)—a process in which a student's academic performance is systematically and frequently monitored through measurement with the curricular materials that are being used for instruction.

Data points—symbols indicating data from each observation session, plotted on the intersection of the vertical and horizontal lines.

Dense reinforcement schedule—a schedule of reinforcement in which reinforcement is given frequently or continuously.

Dependent group contingency—a system of reinforcement for all students that is contingent upon the performance of one or more individual students.

Dependent variables—behaviors that are the target of interventions.

Deprivation—a state in which reinforcers are only available through the reinforcement system, and even then, only for a limited time or in limited quantities.

Differential reinforcement of alternative behaviors (DRA)—a procedure in which a challenging behavior is reduced by systematically reinforcing alternative behaviors.

Differential reinforcement of incompatible behavior (DRI)—a procedure in which a challenging behavior is reduced by systematically reinforcing appropriate behaviors that are incompatible with the challenging behavior.

Differential reinforcement of lower levels of behavior (DRL)—a procedure in which a student is reinforced for meeting a predetermined criterion for the number of occurrences of a particular behavior that is allowed.

Differential reinforcement of zero levels of behavior or differential reinforcement of other behaviors (DRO)—a procedure in which reinforcement is given at the end of a period during which zero instances of a targeted inappropriate behavior were exhibited, despite the presence or absence of other behaviors during this time.

Direct instruction (di)—refers to a general set of behaviors that teachers engage in to deliver instruction.

Direct instruction (DI)—a highly systematic, organized, comprehensive approach to instruction and curriculum design. Refers to the model developed by Sigfried Engelmann, Douglas Carnine, and others at the University of Oregon in the mid 1960s.

Discrete behaviors—behaviors that have a clearly observable beginning and end.

Discrete trial teaching (also called discrete trial instruction)—a highly structured instructional technique that is founded on applied behavior analysis and data. Includes four components: cue, response, feedback, and inter-trial interval (during which data on student response are recorded).

Discriminative stimulus—a stimulus or antecedent that predictably cues a particular response.

Duration recording—a system for measuring the length of time that a behavior is exhibited. This method is appropriate for behaviors that have a clearly identifiable beginning and end and that occur over a long period.

Ecological assessment—a procedure used to gather information about a child's behaviors and the expectations encountered in the environments in which the child functions.

Ecological model—a theoretical model which posits that deviance stems not solely from the individual but also from the interaction of the individual with his or her environment.

Ecosystem—the environmental system in which an individual functions.

Engaged time (also called academic engaged time [AET] or time on task)—the percentage of allocated time that students actively participate in instructional activities.

Event recording (also called frequency recording)—a data collection system that is used for counting instances of discrete behavior.

Exclusionary time-out—a punishment in which a student is removed from an instructional activity to another area within the classroom or outside of the classroom.

Explicit instruction—clear, unambiguous instruction in which a teacher specifically communicates instructional objectives and content to students.

External locus of control—attributes success and failure to factors beyond the individual's control.

Externalizing disorder—an emotional, behavioral, and/or psychological condition that results in observable, acting-out behaviors.

Extinction—a condition under which a behavior is weakened, reduced, or eliminated because it is no longer reinforced.

Extinction burst—an initial increase in the frequency or intensity of a behavior that has been placed on extinction.

Factual learning—the most common form of learning and is essential to school success.

Fade—gradually reducing a prompt by systematically providing fewer prompts or including less information in the prompt.

Fidelity—the extent to which an intervention is implemented correctly, as originally designed and researched.

Fixed-interval scallop—a phenomenon of reinforcement in which the targeted behavior is likely to increase immediately before the end of the reinforcement interval, especially when the student is aware of the time interval.

Fixed-interval schedule (FI)—a schedule of reinforcement in which the reinforcement is delivered immediately following the first behavior exhibited after a predetermined amount of time.

Fixed-ratio schedule (FR)—a schedule of reinforcement in which a student receives reinforcement after a fixed number of target behaviors have occurred.

Fixed response duration schedule (FRD)—a schedule of reinforcement where reinforcement is delivered following a predetermined duration of the targeted behavior.

Fluency deficit—a situation in which a student knows how to perform a needed skill and is sufficiently motivated to perform the skill, but actual performance of the skill is awkward and ineffective because of insufficient practice.

Fluency (or proficiency) stage of learning—the learning stage in which learners are able to exhibit a skill efficiently, quickly, and accurately.

Forward chaining—the first step of the task analysis is taught until the student can perform it independently, then the second step is added, and so forth until the student can perform all of the steps in order.

Full-session DRL—a procedure in which a student is allowed a predetermined number of targeted behaviors during the entire observation session and earns reinforcement if the number of targeted behaviors is at or less than that criterion.

Functional analysis—the process of manipulating consequence conditions and observing the effects of each condition on a student's behavior for the purpose of identifying function(s) of challenging behavior.

Functional behavioral assessment (FBA)—the process of gathering information about a challenging behavior to determine the environmental influences on the behavior and the function (i.e., purpose) that the behavior may serve for the child.

Functional communication training—the process of teaching new, functional communication skills to a student who is exhibiting challenging behavior and has no reliable, socially meaningful way to communicate.

Function—the purpose of a behavior.

Generalization—the use of a certain skill in different settings, with different people, or with different materials.

Goal setting—the act of determining goals for behavioral improvement.

Graphic organizer—a diagram that helps to organize information and shows hierarchical, sequential, or comparative relationships.

Group contingency—a group reinforcement system in which a small or large group works together to achieve a common reinforcement goal.

Group design—a research design used to evaluate the effectiveness of an intervention on a group of individuals.

Guided practice—the part of a direct instruction lesson during which students practice a new skill or concept under the teacher's supervision and receive immediate feedback.

Guiding principle—fundamental law, doctrine, or assumption.

Homogeneous group—a group of students who possess a similar level of ability in the content area being taught.

Incomplete stimulus control—a condition in which a desired response does not predictably or consistently occur when the antecedent stimulus is presented.

Independent group contingency—a group reinforcement system in which the same reinforcer is available for any student in the group who meets the criterion for reinforcement.

Independent practice—the part of a direct instruction lesson in which students apply one or more newly learned skills or concepts in activities performed with little teacher supervision.

Independent variable—a behavioral intervention that is used to influence a dependent variable (e.g., a targeted behavior).

Individualized instruction—instruction that is appropriate for an individual student; does not necessarily mean one-to-one instruction.

Instructional activity—an activity undertaken by teachers and students in order to promote learning.

Instructional arrangement—the manner in which the instructional environment is organized for the purpose of teaching.

Interdependent group contingency—a group reinforcement system in which all students must meet a criterion in order to attain a common reinforcer.

Intermittent schedule of reinforcement—a reinforcement schedule in which some behaviors, but not all correct responses, are reinforced.

Internal locus of control—assuming responsibility for one's own success or failure.

Internalizing disorder—an emotional, behavioral, or psychological conditions in which symptoms are manifested internally and, therefore, are not readily apparent to observers.

Interval DRL—a form of differential reinforcement of lower levels of behavior in which the session is divided into equal intervals. If the targeted behavior meets a predetermined criterion for each interval, the student earns reinforcement.

Interval recording—data collection system in which the presence or absence of a target behavior is document during brief, regular intervals.

Interval schedule—a reinforcement schedule in which reinforcement is delivered after the passage of a certain amount of time.

Intrinsic reinforcement—internal reinforcement (i.e., a feeling of self-satisfaction, success, or accomplishment).

Latency recording—a data system used to measure the time elapsed between when a stimulus is given and when the response for that stimulus begins.

Learning centers—a form of instructional practice activities consisting of high-motivation activities for students to complete individually or in small groups of two or three students.

Life space interview (LSI)—a cognitive–behavioral intervention that is founded on the assumption that a life event influences behavior and that appropriate verbal mediation (the "life space interview") can turn an otherwise potentially negative life event into a positive, or at least a neutral, event.

Maintenance stage of learning—the learning stage in which previously learned skills are retained over time.

Manifestation determination—a requirement that school officials consider whether a misbehavior was the result of a student's disability before determining the consequences for that behavior.

Matching law—the assumption that the rate of any behavior is determined by the rate of reinforcement for that behavior.

Material reinforcer—a reinforcer in the form of a tangible item.

Mediated scaffolding—providing support during the early stages of learning to assist learners in performing a new task that otherwise might be too difficult or complex.

Modeling—demonstrating a behavior for the purpose of encouraging others to imitate that behavior.

Negative reinforcement (S^R)—a procedure that maintains or increases a behavior because the individual avoids or escapes a negative condition as a result of the behavior.

Nonexclusionary time-out—a punishment in which the child may not earn reinforcement for a fixed amount of time but remains in the instructional setting.

Non-punishment procedures—techniques that produce decreases in targeted behaviors through methods other than punishment; differential reinforcement and extinction are examples.

Non-scheduled reinforcement—the timing of reinforcement is unplanned.

One-to-one instruction—an instructional arrangement in which teachers work individually with students to deliver instruction.

Operational definition—an unambiguous, objective definition of a targeted behavior (often includes examples and nonexamples of the behavior).

Operationally defined and valued outcome—a specific, measurable indicator of a behavior and learning outcome that is selected and evaluated with the use of multiple sources of data.

Opportunity to respond (OTR)—an opportunity that occurs whenever a teacher provides an instructional stimulus.

Overcorrection—punishment procedure in which the individual is required either to repeatedly practice the appropriate behavior (positive practice) or compensate for damage resulting from the behavior (restitutional).

Overt self-instruction—self-instruction that is spoken aloud to prompt, guide, or evaluate performance.

Pairing—the process of teaching one to value secondary reinforcers by presenting them simultaneously with primary reinforcers.

Partial-interval recording—a data measurement system in which a positive occurrence is recorded if the behavior occurs at any time during the interval.

Peer assisted learning strategies (PALS)—a classwide peer tutoring model, used as an instructional practice activity.

Performance deficit—a skill that a student knows how to perform but chooses not to perform because of motivational factors.

Permanent product—a concrete, tangible result or outcome of a behavior.

Positive behavioral interventions and supports (PBIS) (also known as positive behavior supports [PBS], schoolwide PBS [SW-PBS], and response to intervention for behavior [behavior RtI])—a broad range of systematic and individualized strategies for achieving important social and learning outcomes while preventing problem behavior with all students.

Positive practice overcorrection—a punishment in which the student is required to practice an appropriate alternative to the undesired behavior.

Positive psychology—the study of protective factors that enable individuals and communities to succeed. Focuses on positive emotions, positive individual traits, and positive institutions.

Positive reinforcement—a procedure that maintains or increases a behavior as a result of the consequences experienced following the behavior.

Post-reinforcement pause—the tendency of individuals to stop responding immediately following reinforcement when the reinforcement schedule is predictable.

Pragmatics—the use of language for social purposes.

Precorrection—a proactive strategy in which students are reminded of expected behavior, and consequences for that behavior, immediately before activities associated with challenging behaviors.

Premack principle—know informally as Grandma's law, simply states that a desirable activity is available only after completion of a low probability behavior.

Primary-level prevention (also called universal-level prevention)—a component of schoolwide positive behavioral supports in which universal interventions are used to help ensure that all students exhibit appropriate behavior and to reduce the number of new cases of problem behavior and academic difficulties.

Primary reinforcer (also called an unlearned reinforcer or an unconditioned reinforcer)—a stimulus that we need to survive or that has biological value and is, therefore, naturally reinforcing and very powerful.

Priming background knowledge—informing students how new information is related to previously learned material or existing knowledge.

Procedural learning—a form of knowledge that involves the execution of a series of behaviors in a specific sequence.

Procedure—specific steps for performing a classroom task.

Prompt—assistance given to enable a student to correct perform a response; prompts may be verbal, gestural, or physical guidance.

Proximity control—standing next to a student for the purpose of reminding the student to cease unacceptable behavior.

Psychodynamic model—proposes that atypical behavior stems from internal psychological events and motivational forces.

Psychotropic medications—a class of medications used to address behavioral concerns.

Punishment—a process in which a behavior is weakened, reduced, or eliminated because of a consequence that follows the behavior.

Ratio schedule of reinforcement—a reinforcement schedule in which reinforcement is contingent upon the performance of a target behavior a certain number of times.

Ratio strain—a condition in which behaviors are not maintained under a new, diminished schedule of reinforcement.

Redundancy—repeated instruction and/or practice of essential skills.

Reinforcement—a process in which a behavior is strengthened as a result of a consequence that follows the behavior.

Reinforcement schedule—the frequency of reinforcement.

Reinforcer—a consequence that follows a behavior and serves to increase the likelihood that the behavior will be repeated in the future.

Reinforcer sampling—presenting potential reinforcers to students non-contingently and observing which items or activities the students select.

Reinforcer survey (also called a reinforcer menu)—a list of potential reinforcers that is used to identify those items which are preferred by students.

Replacement behavior—a desired behavior that is designed to be part of an intervention plan as a substitute for an unacceptable behavior. A replacement behavior is established through teaching, prompting, and reinforcement.

Research-validated practice—an intervention strategy that has documented evidence of effectiveness, according to the definition of scientific evidence.

Resiliency—the mediating effect of protective factors on risk factors.

Response cards—cards, signs, or items that are simultaneously held up by all students to display their responses to a question or problem presented by the teacher.

Response cost—a punishment procedure in which a specified amount of a reinforcer is withdrawn or removed, contingent upon a particular behavior.

Response duration schedule—a reinforcement schedule that is designed to increase the duration of a targeted behavior. Reinforcement is contingent upon the targeted behavior being exhibited for a predetermined amount of time.

Restitutional overcorrection—a punishment procedure in which the student is required to make amends for his or her inappropriate behavior.

Restricted event (also called a restricted operant)—a behavior that occurs in response to a specific stimulus.

Routines—regularly scheduled classroom activities that occur at the same time each day or week.

Rule learning—a form of knowledge that involves learning connections between two sets of facts or concepts.

Rule matrix—a chart that shows how schoolwide rules are applied in all areas of the school.

S-Delta (S)—any stimulus that does not predictably cue a specific response.

Satiation—a condition in which a reinforcer loses its motivating power.

Scale break—two short slash marks across the y-axis of a graph that indicate the omission of increments on the scale.

Schoolwide positive behavioral interventions and supports (SW-PBIS)—supports that, taken together, constitute a proactive instructional approach to school discipline which emphasizes prevention, environmental clarity and predictability, the teaching of desired behaviors, and a reliance on research-based methods.

Seclusionary time-out—a punishment procedure in which the student is removed to a designated area for the total isolation of the student.

Secondary-level prevention (also called targeted-level prevention)—a component of schoolwide positive behavioral supports that focuses on interventions for targeted students who are considered to be at risk for chronic or serious problem behavior or academic failure, or who continue to exhibit high levels of inappropriate behavior or academic deficits despite exposure to universal interventions.

Secondary reinforcer (also called a conditioned reinforcer)—a stimulus that we learn to like. It has no intrinsic value for survival and no connection to biological need and, therefore, does not have the unlearned reinforcing quality of a primary reinforcer. A secondary reinforcer can be classified as a social reinforcer, an activity reinforcer, a material reinforcer, or a token reinforcer.

Self-evaluation—an individual's assessment of the extent to which he or she exhibited a targeted behavior or how well he or she performed a specific behavior.

Self-instruction—a process in which an individual uses verbal cues in order to initiate, guide, or inhibit his or her behavior.

Self-monitoring—a process in which an individual keeps track of specific personal targeted behaviors for the purpose of changing (i.e., increasing or decreasing) those behaviors.

Self-reinforcement—a process in which an individual learns how to reinforce him- or herself contingent upon targeted behaviors.

Self-stimulation—a characteristic behavioral trait in individuals with autism in which a particular behavior (e.g., flapping hands, rocking, flicking fingers in front of eyes) is displayed repeatedly for no apparent purpose.

Sensory integration therapy—intervention based on the neurobiological theory that postulates that the challenging behaviors associated with autism, ADHD, learning disabilities, and other conditions are a result of the failure of the central nervous system to organize and integrate the sensory feedback that typically occurs as part of the normal development process.

Setting event—an event or condition that may affect behavior, but is not immediately connected in time and place to the behavior in question.

Shaping—teaching a new behavior by reinforcing increasingly more accurate attempts at the behavior.

Single-subject design—a research design that evaluates the effects of the independent variables on individuals rather than groups.

Small group instruction—an instructional arrangement in which the teacher divides the large group into two or more smaller homogeneous groups and teaches each group separately.

Social competence—The overall effectiveness of social skills determined by others' evaluations of an individual's social behavior.

Social reinforcer—praise or another form of attention that functions as a reinforcer.

Social skills—behaviors that facilitate social relationships and school performance and that enable individuals to cope with stressful situations.

Spontaneous recovery—a phenomenon in which a behavior that has been eliminated through extinction may suddenly reappear.

"Stay put" provision—a requirement of the Individuals with Disabilities Education Act (IDEA) whereby, under most circumstances, a student is to remain in his or her current placement pending the outcome of a disciplinary process.

Stereotypic behavior—a repetitive behavior, such as hand-flapping, rocking, twirling objects, or monotone humming, that appears to be for the purpose of self-stimulation.

Stimulant medication—a class of psychotropic medications commonly used to treat ADHD.

Stimulus control—a condition in which a behavior or class of behaviors is likely to occur in the presence of a specific antecedent or class of antecedents.

Systems change—the reshaping of organizational policies, administrative leadership, operational routines, and resources in order to facilitate a sustained reliance on effective, efficient school management practices.

Targeted level—a component of schoolwide positive behavioral supports that focuses on interventions for students who are unresponsive to universal-level systems. Such components are typically programs.

Task analysis—the process of identifying specific, discrete cognitive and manual steps required to perform a task.

Tertiary level—a component of schoolwide positive behavioral supports that focuses on the needs of individual students who require the most intensive and individualized interventions.

Theoretical model of behavior—a philosophical belief system about atypical behavior.

Thinning—the process of gradually moving from a dense reinforcement schedule to an intermittent schedule.

Time delay—an instructional technique, founded on applied behavior analysis, that utilizes prompts for the goal of errorless learning. The two types of time delay are progressive and constant.

Time-out—a procedure in which an individual is denied access to reinforcers for a certain length of time.

Time sampling—a data measurement system in which the data collector indicates whether or not the targeted behavior is occurring at the end of each interval.

Token economy—a reinforcement structure in which tokens are given in close proximity to desired behaviors; tokens are accumulated and later exchanged for back-up reinforcers.

Token reinforcers—stamps, check marks, stars, points, and other items that function as reinforcers because they can be exchanged for other primary or secondary reinforcers.

Total task presentation—a form of chaining in which the individual is expected to perform all steps of a task-analyzed skill each time the task is presented, with assistance or prompts as needed.

Trend—three consecutive data points in the same direction.

Unconditioned aversive stimulus—also known as unlearned aversive stimuli; any stimulus that is inherently and naturally distasteful, painful, or annoying. Includes stimuli intended to cause pain or discomfort, such as corporal punishment.

Unrestricted event (also called a free operant)—a behavior that can occur at any time rather than only in the presence of a particular stimulus.

Variable interval schedule (VI)—a reinforcement schedule in which the reinforcement is delivered for behaviors that occur after a predetermined interval on the basis of an average number of minutes.

Variable ratio schedule (VR)—a reinforcement schedule in which an average number of responses is reinforced.

Variable response duration schedule (VRD)—a reinforcement schedule in which reinforcement is delivered on the basis of the average length of time that the targeted behavior occurs.

Whole-group instruction—an instructional arrangement in which instruction is delivered to the entire class at once (used for teaching new content).

Whole-interval recording—a type of interval recording in which only an occurrence of the targeted behavior that lasts throughout the interval is counted as an occurrence.

Zero-tolerance policy—a disciplinary approach in which predetermined consequences are administered for predetermined behaviors, regardless of the effectiveness of those consequences in reducing the problem or the specific circumstances surrounding the behavior.

REFERENCES

Adams, G. L., & Engelmann, S. (1996). *Research on Direct Instruction: 25 years beyond DISTAR*. Seattle, WA: Educational Achievement Systems.

Advancement Project and the Harvard Civil Rights Project. (2000). *Opportunities suspended: The devastating consequences of zero tolerance and school discipline policies*. Retrieved from www.advancementproject.org/digital-library/publications/opportunities-suspended-the-devastating-consequences-of-zero-tolerance-

Akin-Little, K. A., Eckert, T. L., & Lovett, B. J. (2004). Extrinsic reinforcement in the classroom: Bribery or best practice. *School Psychology Review, 33*(3), 344–362.

Alber, S. R., Heward, W. L., & Hippler, B. J. (1999). Teaching middle school students with learning disabilities to recruit positive teacher attention. *Exceptional Children, 65*(2), 253–270.

Alberto, P. A., & Troutman, A. C. (2006). *Applied behavior analysis for teachers* (7th ed.). Upper Saddle River, NJ: Merrill/Pearson.

Algozzine, R., Serna, L. A., & Patton, J. R. (2001). *Childhood behavior disorders* (2nd ed.). Austin, TX: PRO-ED.

Allen, N. B., Lewinsohn, P. M., & Seeley, J. R. (1998). Prenatal and perinatal influences on risk for psychopathology in childhood and adolescence. *Developmental Psychopathology, 10*(3), 513–529.

American Federation of Teachers. (1998). *Building on what works: Six promising schoolwide reform programs*. Washington, DC: Author.

American Federation of Teachers. (2003). Setting the stage for high standards: Elements of a safe and orderly school. Retrieved from www.aft.org/yourwork/teachers/reports/safeorderly.cfm

Anderson, L., Evertson, C., & Brophy, J. (1979). An experimental study of effective teaching in first-grade reading groups. *Elementary School Journal, 79*(4), 193–223.

Antunez, B. (2000). When everyone is involved: Parents and communities in school reform. In B. Antunez, P. A. DiCerbo, and K. Menken (Eds.), *Framing effective practice: Topics and issues in the education of English language learners*, 53–59. Washington, DC: National Clearinghouse for Bilingual Education.

Association for Positive Behavior Support. (2007). *APBS Standards of Practice: Individual Level*. Retrieved from www.apbs.org/standards_of_practice.html

Ausdemore, K. B., Martella, R. C., & Marchand-Martella, N. E. (n.d.). *School-wide positive behavioral support: A continuum of proactive strategies for all students*. Retrieved from www.newhorizons.org/spneeds/inclusion/teaching/marchand%20martella%20ausdemore%202.htm

Ayers, J. (1972). *Sensory integration and the child*. Los Angeles: Western Psychological Services.

Ayllon, T., & Azrin, N. (1968). *The token economy: A motivational system for therapy and rehabilitation*. New York: Appleton-Century-Crofts.

Azrin, N. H., & Foxx, R. M. (1971). A rapid method for toilet training the institutionalized retarded. *Journal of Applied Behavior Analysis, 4,* 89–99.

Azrin, N. H., & Holz, W. C. (1966). Punishment. In W. K. Honig (Ed.), *Operant behavior: Areas of research and application*. New York: Appleton-Century-Crofts.

Babkie, A. M. (2006). 20 ways to be proactive in managing classroom behavior. *Intervention in School and Clinic, 41*(6), 184–187.

Baer, D. M., Wolf, M. M., & Risley, T. R. (1968). Some current dimensions of applied behavior analysis. *Journal of Applied Behavior Analysis, 1*(1), 91–97.

Bandura, A. (1969). *Principles of behavior modification*. New York: Holt, Rinehart, & Winston.

Bandura, A. (1973). *Aggression: A social learning analysis*. Upper Saddle River, NJ: Prentice Hall.

Bandura, A. (1977). *Social learning theory*. Upper Saddle River, NJ: Prentice Hall.

Barkley, R., Copeland, A., & Savage, C. (1980). A self-control classroom for hyperactive children. *Journal of Autism and Developmental Disabilities, 10*(1), 75–89.

Barlow, D., & Hersen, M. (1984). *Single-case experimental designs: Strategies for studying behavior change*. New York: Pergamon Press.

Baron-Faust, R. (2000, February 21). A new consciousness: Biofeedback trains your brain to treat diseases. Retrieved from www.webmd.com/content/article/13/1668_50191.htm

Barrish, H. H., Saunders, M., & Wolf, M. W. (1969). Good behavior game: Effects of individualized contingencies for group consequences on disruptive behavior in a classroom. *Journal of Applied Behavior Analysis, 2*(2), 119–124.

Baum, W. M. (1994). *Understanding behaviorism*. New York: HarperCollins.

Beaman, R., & Wheldall, K. (2000). Teachers' use of approval and disapproval in the classroom. *Educational Psychology, 20*(4), 431–446.

Bear, G. G., Quinn, M. M., & Burkholder, S. (2001). Interim alternative educational settings for children with disabilities. Bethesda, MD: National Association of School Psychologists.

Becker, W. C., & Gersten, R. (2001). Follow-up of follow-through: The later effects of the direct instruction model on children in fifth and sixth grades. *Journal of Direct Instruction, 1*(1), 57–71.

Beebe-Frankenberger, M., Lane, K. L., Bocian, K. M., Gresham, F. M., & MacMillan, D. L. (2005). Students with or at risk for problem behavior: Betwixt and between teacher and parent expectations. *Preventing School Failure, 49*(2), 10–17.

Berliner, D. (1978). *Changing academic learning time: Clinical interventions in four classrooms.* San Francisco: Far West Laboratory for Educational Research and Development.

Bessellieu, F. B., Kozloff, M. A., & Rice, J. S. (n.d.). *Teachers' perceptions of direct instruction teaching.* Retrieved from people.uncw.edu/kozloffm/teacherperceptdi.html

Beyda, S. D., Zentall, S. S., & Ferko, D. J. K. (2002). The relationship between teacher practices and the task-appropriate and social behavior of students with behavioral disorders. *Behavioral Disorders, 27*, 236–255.

Bijou, S. W., & Baer, D. M. (1961). *Child development I: A systematic and empirical theory.* Upper Saddle River, NJ: Prentice Hall.

Blacher, J. (1984). A dynamic perspective on the impact of a severely handicapped child on the family. In J. Blacher (Ed.), *Severely handicapped children and their families* (pp. 3–50). Orlando, FL: Academic Press.

Bloom, B. (1984). The search for methods of group instruction as effective as one-to-one tutoring. *Educational Leadership, 41*(8), 4–18.

Borich, G. D. (2003). *Observation skills for effective teaching.* Upper Saddle River, NJ: Merrill/Pearson.

Borich, G. D. (2004). *Effective teaching methods* (5th ed.). Upper Saddle River, NJ: Merrill/Pearson.

Bos, C. (1982). Getting past decoding: Using modeled and repeated readings as a remedial method for learning disabled students. *Topics in Learning and Learning Disabilities, 1*, 51–57.

Bostwick, J. M. (2006). Do SSRIs cause suicide in children? The evidence is underwhelming. *Journal of Clinical Psychology: In Session, 62*(2), 235–241.

Bradshaw, C. P., Mitchell, M. M., & Leaf, P. J. (2010). Examining the effects of schoolwide positive behavioral interventions and supports on student outcomes. *Journal of Positive Behavior Interventions, 12*(3), 133–148.

Brandt, R. S. (1988, March). Our students' needs and team learning: A conversation with William Glasser. *Educational Leadership, 45*, 38–45.

Brent, D. (2004). Antidepressants and pediatric depression—The risk of doing nothing. *New England Journal of Medicine, 351*, 1598–1601.

Brophy, J., & Evertson, C. (1976). *Learning from teaching: A developmental perspective.* Boston: Allyn & Bacon.

Brophy, J., & Evertson, C. (1981). *Student characteristics and teaching.* New York: Longman.

Brophy, J., & Good, T. (1986). Teacher behavior and achievement. In M. C. Wittrock (Ed.), *Handbook of research on teaching* (pp. 328–375). Upper Saddle River, NJ: Prentice Hall.

Broussard, C., & Northup, J. (1995). An approach to functional assessment and analysis of disruptive behavior in regular education classrooms. *School Psychology Quarterly, 10*, 151–164.

Bryan, T., & Burstein, K. (2004). Improving homework completion and academic performance: Lessons from special education. *Theory into Practice, 43*(3), 213–219.

Bulgren, J. A., Deschler, D. D., Schumaker, J. B., & Lenz, B. K. (2000). The use and effectiveness of analogical instruction in diverse secondary content classrooms. *Journal of Educational Psychology, 16*, 426–441.

Bullard, B. (1998, November). *Teacher self-evaluation.* Paper presented at the annual meeting of the Mid-South Educational Research Association. (ERIC Document Reproduction Service No. ED428074)

Burke, M. D., Davis, J. D., Lee, Y., Hagan-Burke, S., Kwok, O., & Sugai, G. (in press). Universal screening for behavioral risk in elementary schools using SWPBS expectations. *Journal of Emotional and Behavioral Disorders.*

Callahan, K., & Rademacher, J. (1999). Using self-management strategies to increase the on-task behavior of a student with autism. *Journal of Positive Behavioral Interventions, 1*, 117–122.

Cameron, J., Banko, K. M., & Pierce, W. D. (2001). Pervasive negative effects of rewards on intrinsic motivation: The myth continues. *The Behavior Analyst, 24*, 1–44.

Cameron, J., & Pierce, W. D. (1994). Reinforcement, reward, and intrinsic motivation: A meta-analysis. *Review of Educational Research, 64*, 363–423.

Caprara, G., Barbaranelli, C., Pastorelli, C., Bandura, A., & Zimbardo, P. G. (2000). Prosocial foundations of children's academic achievement. *Psychological Science, 11*(4), 302–306.

Carnine, D. W., Silbert, J., Kame'enui, E., J., & Tarver, S. G. (2010). *Direct instruction reading* (5th ed.). Upper Saddle River, NJ: Merrill/Pearson.

Carr, E. G., & Durand, V. M. (1985). Reducing behavior problems through functional communication training. *Journal of Applied Behavior Analysis, 18*, 111–126.

Carr, E. G., Horner, R. H., Turnbull, A. P., Marquis, J. G., Magito McLaughlin, D., McAtee, M. L., Smith, C. E., Anderson Ryan, K., Ruef, M. B., & Doolabh, A. (1999). *Positive behavior support for people with developmental disabilities: A research synthesis.* Washington, DC: American Association on Mental Retardation.

Carr, E. G., Langdon, N. A., & Yarbrough, S. C. (1999). Hypothesis-based intervention for severe problem behavior. In A. C. Repp, & R. H. Horner (Eds.), *Functional analysis of problem behavior* (pp. 9–31). Belmont, CA: Wadsworth.

Carr, E. G., Levin, L., McConnachie, G., Carlson, J. I., Kemp, D. C., & Smith, C. E. (1994). *Communication-based intervention for problem behavior.* Baltimore: Paul H. Brookes.

Carr, E. G., Newsom, C. D., & Binkoff, J. A. (1980). Escape as a factor in the aggressive behavior of two retarded children. *Journal of Applied Behavior Analysis, 13*, 101–117.

Carr, E. G., Robinson, S., & Palumbo, I. (1990). The wrong issue: Aversive versus nonaversive treatment. The right issue: Functional versus nonfunctional treatment. In A. Repp & N. Singh (Eds.), *Perspectives on the use of nonaversive and aversive interventions for persons with developmental disabilities.* Sycamore, IL: Sycamore Publishing.

Carr, E. G., Taylor, J. C., & Robinson, S. (1991). The effects of severe behavior problems in children on the teaching behavior of adults. *Journal of Applied Behavior Analysis, 3,* 523–535.

Case, L. P., Harris, K. R., & Graham, S. (1992). Improving the mathematical problem-solving skills of students with learning disabilities. *Journal of Special Education, 26*(1), 1–19.

Casey, R. J., & Berman, J. S. (1985). The outcome of psychotherapy with children. *Psychological Bulletin, 98,* 388–400.

Cassel, J., & Reid, R. (1996). Use of a self-regulated strategy intervention to improve word problem-solving skills of students with mild disabilities. *Journal of Behavioral Education, 6,*153–172.

Catalano, R., Loeber, R., & McKinney, K. C. (1999). School and community interventions to prevent serious and violent offending. *Juvenile Justice Bulletin.* Washington, DC: Office of Juvenile Justice and Delinquency Prevention, U.S. Department of Justice.

Center for Effective Collaboration and Practice. (1998). Delinquency: Effective programs from across the nation. *Reclaiming Children and Youth, 7,* 125–126.

Center for Effective Discipline (2008). U.S. Corporal Punishment and Paddling Statistics by State and Race. Retrieved from vistademo.beyond2020.com/ocr2004rv30/xls/2004Projected.html

Center for Innovations in Education. (2005, January). *Teaching social skills.* Columbia, MO: University of Missouri.

Center for Mental Health in Schools. (2002). *A technical assistance sampler on protective factors (resiliency).* Los Angeles: Author.

Center for Mental Health in Schools. (2003). Youngsters' mental health and psychosocial problems: What are the data? Los Angeles: Author. Retrieved from smhp.psych.ucla.edu/pdfdocs/prevalence/youthMH.pdf

Center for Positive Behavioral Support at the University of Missouri–Columbia. (2009, October 22). Getting Started in Missouri Schoolwide PBS. Retrieved from pbismissouri.org/starting.html

Center on Positive Behavioral Interventions and Supports. (2004). *School-wide positive behavior support: Implementation blueprint and self-assessment.* Eugene, OR: Author.

Centers for Disease Control and Prevention. (2006). Brick Township autism investigation. Retrieved from www.atsdr.cdc.gov/hac/pha/pha.asp?docid=380&pg=0

Chalk, K., & Bizo, L. A. (2004). Specific praise improves on-task behaviour and numeracy enjoyment: A study of year four pupils engaged in the numeracy hour. *Educational Psychology in Practice, 20*(4), 335–351.

Chandler, L. K., & Dahlquist, C. M. (2002). *Functional assessment.* Upper Saddle River, NJ: Merrill/Pearson.

Cheney, D., Stage, S. A., Hawken, L. S., Lynass, L., Mielenz, C., & Waugh, M. (2009). A 2-year outcome study of the Check, Connect, and Expect intervention for students at risk for severe behavior problems. *Journal of Emotional and Behavioral Disorders, 17*(4), 226–243.

Cheng, L. (1998). *Enhancing the communication skills of newly-arrived Asian American students.* New York: Columbia University. (ERIC Document Reproduction Service No. ED430726)

Chibnall, S. H., & Abbruzzese, K. (2004). A community approach to reducing risk factors. *Juvenile Justice, 9*(1), 30–31.

Children's Defense Fund. (1975). *School suspensions: Are they helping children?* Cambridge, MA: Washington Research Project.

Christensen, L., Young, K. R., & Marchant, M. (2004). The effects of a peer-mediated positive behavior support program on socially appropriate classroom behavior. *Education and Treatment of Children, 27*(3), 199–234.

Cipani, E. (2004). *Classroom management for all teachers* (2nd ed.). Upper Saddle River, NJ: Merrill/Pearson.

Coie, J., & Krehbiel, G. (1984). Effects of academic tutoring on the social status of low-achieving, socially rejected children. *Child Development, 55,* 1465–1478.

Coie, J., & Kupersmidt, J. (1983). A behavioral analysis of emerging social status in boys' groups. *Child Development, 54,* 1400–1416.

Coleman, M. C., & Webber, J. (2002). *Emotional and behavioral disorders: Theory and practice* (4th ed.). Boston: Allyn & Bacon/Pearson.

Coleman-Martin, M. B., Heller, K. W., Cihak, D. F., & Irvine, K. L. (2005). Using computer-assisted instruction and the nonverbal reading approach to teach word identification. *Focus on Autism and Other Developmental Disabilities, 20*(2), 80–90.

Colvin, G., Sugai, G., & Patching, B. (1993). Precorrection: An instructional approach for managing predictable problem behaviors. *Intervention in School and Clinic, 28,* 143–150.

Conyers, C., Miltenberger, R., & Maki, A. (2004). A comparison of response cost and differential reinforcement of other behaviors to reduce disruptive behavior in a preschool classroom. *Journal of Applied Behavior Analysis, 37*(3), 411–415.

Cooper, H. (1989). Synthesis of research on homework. *Educational Leadership, 47*(3), 85–91.

Cooper, J. P. (1981). *Measurement and analysis of behavioral techniques.* Upper Saddle River, NJ: Merrill/Pearson.

Cooper, J. P., Heron, T. E., & Heward, W. L. (2007). *Applied behavior analysis* (2nd ed.). Upper Saddle River, NJ: Merrill/Pearson.

Copeland, S. R., & Hughes, C. (2002). Effects of goal setting on task performance of persons with mental retardation. *Education and Training in Mental Retardation and Developmental Disabilities, 37*(1), 40–54.

Cosden, M., Gannon, C., & Haring, T. (1995). Teacher-control versus student-control over choice of task and reinforcement for students with severe behavior problems. *Journal of Behavioral Education, 5,* 11–27.

Cotton, K., & Savard, W. G. (1982). *Student discipline and motivation: Research synthesis*. Portland, OR: Northwest Regional Educational Laboratory. (ERIC Document Reproduction Service No. ED224170)

Council for Children with Behavioral Disorders. (2009). *CCBD'S Position Summary on The Use of Seclusion in School Settings*. Reston, VA: Author.

Council for Exceptional Children. (1987). *Academy for effective instruction: working with mildly handicapped students*. Reston, VA: Author.

Council of Parent Attorneys and Advocates (COPAA). (2008). *Declaration of principles opposing the use of restraints, seclusion, and other aversive interventions upon children with disabilities*. Retrieved from http://www.copaa.net/news/Declaration.html

Cowdery, G. E., Iwata, B. A., & Pace, G. M. (1990). Effects and side effects of DRO as treatment for self-injurious behavior. *Journal of Applied Behavior Analysis, 23*, 497–506.

Crone, D. A., Hawken, L. S., & Horner, R. H. (2010). *The behavior education program* (2nd ed.). New York: Guilford Press.

Cullinan, D. (2003). *Students with emotional and behavioral disorders*. Upper Saddle River, NJ: Merrill/Pearson.

Cunningham, E., & O'Neill, R. E. (2000). Comparison of results of functional assessment and analysis methods with young children with autism. *Education and Training in Mental Retardation and Developmental Disabilities, 35*(4), 406–414.

Dalton, T., Martella, R. C., & Marchand-Martella, N. E. (1999). The effects of a self-management program in reducing off-task behavior. *Journal of Behavioral Education, 9*, 157–176.

Darling-Hammond, L. (2005, December). Prepping our teachers for teaching as a profession. *The Education Digest, 71*(4), 22–27.

Darensbourg, A., Perez, E., & Blake, J. J. (2010). Overrepresentation of African American males in exclusionary discipline: The role of school-based mental health professionals in dismantling the school to prison pipeline. *Journal of African American Males in Education, 1*(3), 196–211.

Deci, E. L., & Ryan, R. M. (1985). *Intrinsic motivation and self-determination in human behavior*. New York: Plenum Press.

Delquadri, J., Greenwood, C. R., Whorton, D., Carta, J. J., & Hall, R. V. (1986). Classwide peer tutoring. *Exceptional Children, 52*(6), 535–542.

DePaepe, P. A., Shores, R. E., Jack, S. L., & Denny, R. K. (1996). Effects of task difficulty on disruptive and on-task behavior of students with severe behavior disorders. *Behavioral Disorders, 21*, 216–225.

Derby, K. M., Hagoplian, L., Fisher, W. W., Richman, D., Augustine, M., Fahs, A., & Thompson, R. (2000). Functional analysis of aberrant behavior through measurement of separate response topographies. *Journal of Applied Behavior Analysis, 33*, 113–118.

DeRisi, W. J., & Butz, G. (1975). *Writing behavioral contracts*. Champaign, IL: Research Press.

Deschler, D. D., Schumaker, J. B., Alley, G. R., Warner, M. M., & Clark, F. L. (1982). Learning disabilities in adolescent and young adult populations: Research implications. *Focus on Exceptional Children, 15*(1), 1–12.

Deschler, D. D., Schumaker, J. B., Lenz, B. K., Bulgren, J. A., Hock, M. F., Knight, J., & Ehren, B. J. (2001). Ensuring content-area learning by secondary students with learning disabilities. *Learning Disabilities Research and Practice, 16*, 96–108.

Dietz, D. E. D., & Repp, A. C. (1983). Reducing behavior through reinforcement. *Exceptional Education Quarterly, 3*, 34–46.

Digangi, S. A., Maag, J. W., & Rutherford, R. B. (1991). Self-graphing of on-task behavior: Enhancing the reactive effects of self-monitoring on on-task behavior and academic performance. *Learning Disabilities Quarterly, 14*(3), 221–230.

Dodge, K. (1993). The future of research on conduct disorder. *Development and Psychopathology, 5*(1/2), 311–320.

Dolan, L. J., Kellam, S. G., Brown, C. H., Werthamer-Larsson, L., Rebok, G. W., Mayer, L. S., Laudolff, J., Turkkan, J., Ford, C., & Wheeler, L. (1993). The short-term impact of two classroom-based preventive interventions on aggressive and shy behaviors and poor achievement. *Journal of Applied Developmental Psychology, 14*, 317–345.

Drasgow, E., & Yell, M. L. (2001). Functional behavioral assessments: Legal requirements and challenges. *School Psychology Review, 30*(2), 239–251.

Duchnowski, A. J., Johnson, M. K., Hall, K. S., Kutash, K., & Friedman, R. M. (1993). The alternatives to residential treatment study: Initial findings. *Journal of Emotional and Behavior Disorders, 1*, 17–26.

Dunlap, G., DePerczel, M., Clarke, S., Wilson, D., Wright, S., White, R., & Gomez, A. (1994). Choice making to promote adaptive behavior for students with emotional and behavioral challenges. *Journal of Applied Behavior Analysis, 27*(3), 505–518.

Dunlap, G., & Kern, L. (1993). Assessment and intervention for children within the instructional curriculum. In J. Reichle and D. P. Wacker (Eds.), *Communication alternatives to challenging behavior: Integrating functional assessment and intervention strategies* (pp. 177–204). Baltimore: Paul H. Brookes.

Dunlap, K. (1930). Repetition in the breaking of habits. *The Scientific Monthly, 30*, 66–70.

Durand, V. M. (1990). *Severe behavior problems: A functional communication training approach*. New York: Guilford Press.

Durand, V. M., Berotti, D., & Weiner, J. (1993). Functional communication training: Factors affecting effectiveness, generalization, and maintenance. In J. Reichle and D. Wacker (Eds.), *Communicative alternatives to challenging behavior: Integrating functional assessment and intervention strategies* (pp. 317–340). Baltimore: Paul H. Brookes.

Durand, V. M., & Crimmins, D. B. (1988, 1992). Identifying the variables maintaining self-injurious behavior. *Journal of Autism and Developmental Disorders, 18*, 99–117.

Durand, V. M., & Crimmins, D. B. (1988). *The Motivation Assessment Scale (MAS)*. Topeka, KS: Monaco & Associates.

Dwyer, K., & Osher, D. (2000). *Safeguarding our children: An action guide*. Washington, DC: U.S. Department of Education.

Dwyer, K., Osher, D., & Warger, C. (1998). *Early warning, timely response: A guide to safe schools*. Washington, DC: U.S. Department of Education.

El Paso Independent School District, 39 IDELR 16 (SEA TX 2003).

Elliott, S. N., & Gresham, F. M. (1991). *Social skills intervention guide: Practical strategies for social skills training*. Circle Pines, MN: American Guidance Service.

Ellis, A. (1962). *Reason and emotion in psychotherapy*. New York: Lyle Stuart.

Ellis, E. S. (1992). Perspective on adolescents with learning disabilities. In E. S. Ellis (Ed.), *Teaching the learning disabled adolescent: Strategies and methods*. Denver, CO: Love Publishing Co.

Ellis, E. S., & Worthington, L. A. (1994). *Technical Report No. 5: Research synthesis on effective teaching principles and the design of quality tools for educators*. Eugene, OR: National Center to Improve the Tools of Educators, University of Oregon.

Embregts, P. J. (2000). Effectiveness of video feedback and self-management on appropriate social behavior of youth with mild mental retardation. *Research in Developmental Disabilities, 21*, 409–423.

Emmer, E. T., Evertson, C. M., & Anderson, L. M. (1980). Effective classroom management at the beginning of the school year. *The Elementary School Journal, 80*(5), 219–231.

Emmer, E. T., Evertson, C. M., & Worsham, M. E. (2003). *Classroom management for secondary teachers*. Boston: Allyn & Bacon.

Emmer, E. T., Sanford, I. P., Clements, B. S., & Martin, I. (1983, March). *Improving junior high classroom management*. Paper presented at the annual meeting of the American Educational Research Association, Montreal. (ERIC Document Reproduction Service No. ED234021)

Englemann, S. (2004). Forward. In N. E. Marchand-Martella, T. A. Slocum, & R. C. Martella (Eds.), *Introduction to Direct Instruction* (pp. 19–26). Boston: Allyn & Bacon.

Englemann, S., & Becker, W. C. (1978). Systems for basic instruction: Theory and applications. In A. C. Catania & T. A. Brigham (Eds.), *Handbook of applied behavior analysis* (pp. 325–377). New York: Irvington.

Engelmann, S., & Carnine, D. W. (1991). *Theory of instruction: Principles and applications*. Eugene, OR: Association for Direct Instruction.

Englert, C. S. (1984). Effective direct instruction practices in special education settings. *Remedial and Special Education, 5*, 38–47.

Epstein, M. H. (2001). *Behavioral and Emotional Rating Scale—Second Edition* (BERS-2). Austin, TX: PRO-ED.

Epstein, M. H., & Sharma, J. M. (1998). *Behavioral and Emotional Rating Scale: A strength-based approach to assessment—Examiner's manual*. Austin, TX: PRO-ED.

Epstein, R., & Goss, C. M. (1978). A self-control procedure for the maintenance of nondisruptive behavior in an elementary school child. *Behavior Therapy, 9*, 109–117.

Espin, C. A., Scierka, B. J., Skare, S. S., & Halvorson, N. (1999). Criterion-related validity of curriculum-based measures in writing for secondary students. *Reading and Writing Quarterly, 15*, 5–28.

Etscheidt, S. K. (2006a). Behavioral intervention plans: Pedagogical and legal analysis of issues. *Behavioral Disorders, 31*(2), 223–243.

Etscheidt, S. K. (2006b). Progress monitoring: Legal issues and recommendations for IEP teams. *Teaching Exceptional Children, 38*(3), 56–60.

Evans, E. D., & Richardson, R. C. (1995). Corporal punishment: What teachers should know. *Teaching Exceptional Children, 27*(2), 33–36.

Evans, G., & Lowell, B. (1979). Design modification in an open-plan school. *Journal of Educational Psychology, 71*(1), 41–49.

Everhart, B., Oaks, H., Martin, H., & Sanders, R. (2004). The differences in pre-service lessons taught with pre-packaged and self-designed lesson plans. *International Journal of Physical Education, 41*(3), 104–111.

Evertson, C. (1979). *Teacher behavior, student achievement, and student attitudes: Descriptions of selected classrooms*. Austin, TX: Research and Development Center for Teacher Education, University of Texas (Report No. 4063).

Evertson, C. (1982). Differences in instructional activities in higher- and lower-achieving junior high English and math classes. *Elementary School Journal, 82*, 329–350.

Evertson, C., Anderson, C., Anderson, L., & Brophy, J. (1980). Relationships between classroom behaviors and student outcomes in junior high mathematics and English classes. *American Educational Research Journal, 17*, 43–60.

Evertson, C., Anderson, L., & Brophy, J. (1978). *Texas Junior High School Study: Final report of process–outcome relationships (Vol. 1)*. Austin, TX: Research and Development Center for Teacher Education, University of Texas (Report No. 4061).

Evertson, C., & Poole, I. (n.d.). *Effective room arrangement*. Nashville, TN: The IRIS Center for Training Enhancements. [Online]. Retrieved from iris.peabody.vanderbilt.edu/case_studies/ICS-001.pdf

Evertson, C. M. (1985). Training teachers in classroom management: An experimental study in secondary school classrooms. *Journal of Educational Research, 79*, 51–58.

Evertson, C. M., & Emmer, E. T. (1982). Effective management at the beginning of the school year in junior high classes. *Journal of Educational Psychology, 74*(4), 485–498.

Evertson, C. M., Emmer, E. T., & Worsham, M. E. (2003). *Classroom management for elementary teachers* (6th Ed.). Boston: Allyn & Bacon.

Feingold, B. F. (1975). *Why your child is hyperactive.* New York: Random House.

Feingold, B. F. (1976). Hyperkinesis and learning disabilities linked to ingestion of artificial food colors and flavorings. *Journal of Learning Disabilities, 9,* 551–559.

Felixbrod, J. J., & O'Leary, K. D. (1974). Self-determination of academic standards by children: Toward freedom from external control. *Journal of Educational Psychology, 66,* 845–850.

Ferguson, P. M. (2003). A place in the family: An historical interpretation of research on parental reactions to having a child with a disability. *Journal of Special Education, 36,* 124–130.

Ferguson, R. F. (2002, November). *Closing the achievement gaps. What* doesn't *meet the eye: Understanding and addressing racial disparities in high-achieving suburban schools.* North Central Regional Educational Laboratory. Retrieved from www.ncrel.org/gap/ferg/index.html

Fern Ridge Middle School. (1999). *The High Five Program: A positive approach to school discipline.* Elmira, OR: Author.

Filter, K. J., McKenna, M. K., Benedict, E. A., Horner, R. H., Todd, A. W., & Watson, J. (2007). Check in/check out: A post-hoc evaluation of an efficient, secondary-level targeted intervention for reducing problem behaviors in schools. *Education and Treatment of Children, 30*(1), 69–84.

Fisher, C., Fibly, N., Marliave, R., Cahen, L., Dishaw, M., More, J., & Berliner, D. (1978). *Teaching behaviors: Academic Learning Time and student achievement: Final Report of Phase III-B, Beginning Teacher Evaluation Study.* San Francisco: Far West Laboratory for Educational Research and Development.

Fisher, D. (2009). The use of instructional time in the typical high school classroom. *The Educational Forum, 73,* 168–176.

Flood, W. A., & Wilder, D. A. (2004). The use of differential reinforcement and fading to increase time away from a caregiver in a child with separation anxiety disorder. *Education and Treatment of Children, 27*(1),1–8.

Fogt, J. B., & Piripavel, C. M. D. (2002). Positive schoolwide interventions for eliminating physical restraint and seclusion. *Reclaiming Children and Youth, 10*(4), 227–232.

Forness, S. R., & Kavale, K. A. (2001). Ignoring the odds: Hazards of not adding the new medical model to special education decisions. *Behavioral Disorders, 26*(4), 269–281.

Foxx, R. M. (1982). *Decreasing behaviors of severely retarded and autistic persons.* Champaign, IL: Research Press.

Foxx, R. M., & Shapiro, S. T. (1978). The timeout ribbon: A nonexclusionary timeout procedure. *Journal of Applied Behavior Analysis, 11,* 125–136.

Franklin, M. E. (1992). Culturally sensitive instructional practices for African-American learners with disabilities. *Exceptional Children, 59,* 115–122.

Fuchs, L., Deno, S. L., & Mirkin, P. K. (1984). The effects of frequent curriculum-based measurement and evaluation on pedagogy, student achievement, and student awareness of learning. *American Educational Research Journal, 21*(2), 449–460.

Fuchs, L. S., & Fuchs, D. (2001). Principles for the prevention and intervention of mathematics disabilities. *Learning Disabilities Research and Practice, 16,* 85–95.

Fuchs, L. S., & Fuchs, D. (2004). Determining adequate yearly progress from kindergarten through grade 6 with curriculum-based measurement. *Assessment for Effective Instruction, 29*(4), 25–38.

Fuchs, L. S., Fuchs, D., Hamlett, C. L., & Steecker, P. M. (1991). Effects of curriculum-based measurement and consultation on teacher planning and student achievement in mathematics operations. *American Educational Research Journal, 28,* 617–641.

Gable, R., Hendrickson, J., & Sealander, K. (1998). Ecobehavioral observation: Ecobehavioral assessment to identify classroom correlates of students' learning and behavioral problems. *Beyond Behavior, 8,* 25–27.

Gable, R., Quinn, M. M., Rutherford, R. B., & Howell, K. (1998). Addressing problem behaviors in schools: Use of functional assessments and behavior intervention plans. *Preventing School Failure, 42*(3), 106–119.

Gable, R., & Shores, R. E. (1980). Comparison of procedures for promoting reading proficiency of two children with behavioral and learning disorders. *Behavioral Disorders, 5,* 102–107.

Gardner, R., III. (1990). Life space interviewing: It can be effective, but don't . . . *Behavioral Disorders, 15*(2), 110–126.

Gardner, R., III, Heward, W. L., & Grossi, T. A. (1994). Effects of response cards on student participation and academic achievement: A systematic replication with inner-city students during whole-class science instruction. *Journal of Applied Behavior Analysis, 27,* 63–71.

Gardner, W. I., & Sovner, R. (1994). *Self-injurious behaviors: A functional approach.* Willow Street, PA: Vida Press.

Garmezy, N. (1985). Stress-resistant children: The search for protective factors. In J. E. Stevenson (Ed.), *Recent research in developmental psychopathology* (pp. 213–233). New York: Pergamon Press.

Gast, D. L., & Nelson, C. M. (1977a). Legal and ethical considerations for the use of timeout in special education settings. *Journal of Special Education, 11,* 457–467.

Gast, D. L., & Nelson, C. M. (1977b). Time out in the classroom: Implications for special education. *Exceptional Children, 43,* 461–464.

Gersten, R., Carnine, D. W., & Woodward, J. (1987). Direct instruction research: The third decade. *Remedial and Special Education, 8*(6), 48–56.

Gersten, R., Woodward, J., & Darch, C. (1986). Direct instruction: A research-based approach to curriculum design and teaching. *Exceptional Children, 53,* 17–31.

Gettinger, M. (1988). Methods of proactive classroom management. *School Psychology Review, 17*(2), 227–242.

Gettinger, M., & Seibert, J. K. (2002). Best practices in increasing academic learning time. In A. Thomas (Ed.), *Best practices in school psychology IV: Volume I* (4th ed., pp. 773–787). Bethesda, MD: National Association of School Psychologists.

Getty, L. A., & Summy, S. E. (2006). Language deficits in students with emotional and behavioral disorders: Practical applications for teachers. *Beyond Behavior, 15*(3), 15–22.

Glasser, W. (1965). *Reality therapy: A new approach to psychiatry.* New York: Harper & Row.

Glasser, W. (1998a). *Choice theory.* New York: HarperCollins.

Glasser, W. (1998b). *The quality school: Managing students without coercion.* New York: HarperCollins.

Goldstein, A. (1999). *The prepare curriculum: Teaching prosocial competencies.* Champaign, IL: Research Press.

Goldstein, A., Glick, B., & Gibbs, J. C. (1998). *Aggression replacement training.* Champaign, IL: Research Press.

Goldstein, A., & McGinnis, E. (1988). *The skillstreaming video: How to teach students prosocial skills.* Champaign, IL: Research Press.

Goldstein, A., McGinnis, E., Sprafkin, R., Gershaw, N. J., & Klein, P. (1997). *Skillstreaming the adolescent.* Champaign, IL: Research Press.

Gonzalez, J. E., Nelson, J. R., Gutkin, T. B., Saunders, A., Galloway, A., & Shwery, C. S. (2004). Rational emotive therapy with children and adolescents: A meta-analysis. *Journal of Emotional and Behavioral Disorders, 12*(4), 222–235.

Good, R. H., & Shinn, M. R. (1990). Forecasting accuracy of slope estimates for reading curriculum-based measurement: Empirical evidence. *Behavioral Assessment, 12,* 179–193.

Goodman, R., & Stevenson, J. (1989). A twin study of hyperactivity: II. The aetiological role of genes, family relationships, and perinatal adversity. *Journal of Child Psychology and Psychiatry, 30,* 691–709.

Gordon, C. T. (2002). Pharmacological treatment options, Part 1. *Exceptional Parent, 32*(11), 66–70.

Gordon, C. T. (2003). Pharmacological treatment options, Part 2. *Exceptional Parent, 33*(1), 119–121.

Gordon, T. (1974). *Teacher effectiveness training.* New York: Wyden.

Graham, S., & Harris, K. R. (2003). Students with learning disabilities and the process of writing: A meta-analysis of SRSD studies. In H. L. Swanson, K. R. Harris, & S. Graham (Eds.), *Handbook of learning disabilities* (pp. 323–344). New York: Guilford Press.

Graubard, P. S. (1973). Children with behavioral disabilities. In L. Dunn (Ed.), *Exceptional children in the schools.* New York: Holt, Rinehart, & Winston.

Green, R. L. (1998). Nurturing characteristics in schools related to discipline, attendance, and eighth grade proficiency test scores. *American Secondary Education, 26*(4), 7–14.

Greenwood, C. R., Arreaga-Mayer, C., Utley, C. A., Gavin, K. M., & Terry, B. J. (2001). Classwide peer tutoring learning management system: Applications with elementary-level English language learners. *Remedial and Special Education, 22,* 34–47.

Gresham, F. M. (1981). Social skills training with handicapped children: A review. *Review of Educational Research, 51,* 139–176.

Gresham, F. M. (1995). Best practices in social skills training. In A. Thomas & J. Grimes (Eds.), *Best practices in school psychology* (pp. 1021–1030). Washington, DC: National Association of School Psychologists.

Gresham, F. M., & Elliot, S. (1990). *Social Skills Rating System (SSRS).* Circle Pines, MN: American Guidance Service.

Gresham, F. M., Sugai, G., & Horner, R. H. (2001). Interpreting outcomes of social skills training for students with high-risk disabilities. *Exceptional Children, 67,* 331–344.

Grimes, L. (1981). Learned helplessness and attribution theory: Redefining children's learning problems. *Learning Disability Quarterly, 4,* 92–100.

Grossman, H. (1995). *Special education in a diverse society.* Boston: Allyn & Bacon.

Grskovic, J. A., Hall, A. M., Montgomery, D. J., Vargas, A. U., Zentall, S. S., & Belfiore, P. J. (2004). Reducing time-out assignments for students with emotional/behavioral disorders in a self-contained classroom. *Journal of Behavioral Education, 13*(1), 25–36.

Gunter, P. L., Coutinho, M. J., & Cade, T. (2002). Classroom factors linked with academic gains among students with emotional and behavioral problems. *Preventing School Failure, 46*(3), 126–132.

Gunter, P. L., & Denny, R. K. (1998). Trends, issues, and research needs regarding academic instruction of students with emotional and behavioral disorders. *Behavioral Disorders, 24,* 44–50.

Gunter, P. L., Denny, R. K., Jack, S. L., Shores, S. E., & Nelson, C. M. (1993). Aversive stimuli in academic interactions between students with serious emotional disturbance and their teachers. *Behavioral Disorders, 24,* 44–50.

Gunter, P. L., Denny, R. K., Shores, R. E., Reed, T. M., Jack, S. L., & Nelson, M. (1994). Teacher escape, avoidance, and counter-control behaviors: Potential responses to disruptive and aggressive behaviors of students with severe behavior disorders. *Journal of Child and Family Studies, 3,* 211–223.

Gunter, P. L., Hummel, J. H., & Conroy, M. A. (1998). An effective intervention strategy to decrease behavior problems. *Effective School Practices, 17*(2), 55–62.

Gunter, P. L., Hummel, J. H., & Venn, M. (1998). Are effective academic instructional practices used to teach students with behavior disorders? *Beyond Behavior, 9*(3), 5–11.

Gunter, P. L., & Jack, S. L. (1993). Lag sequential analysis as a tool for functional analysis of student disruptive behavior in classrooms. *Journal of Emotional and Behavioral Disorders, 1,* 138–149.

Gunter, P. L., & Reed, T. M. (1997). Academic instruction of children with emotional and behavioral disorders using scripted lessons. *Preventing School Failure, 42*(1), 33–37.

Gunter, P. L., Shores, R. E., Jack, S. L., Denny, R. K., & DePaepe, P. (1994). A case study of the effects of altering instructional interactions on the disruptive behavior of a child identified with severe behavior disorders. *Education and Treatment of Children, 17,* 435–444.

Gushee, M. (1984). *Student discipline policies*. Eugene, OR: ERIC Clearinghouse on Educational Management, ERIC Digest, Number 12.

Hall, R. V., & Hall, M. C. (1982). *How to negotiate a behavioral contract*. Austin, TX: PRO-ED.

Hallahan, D. P., & Kauffman, J. M. (2006). *Exceptional learners* (10th ed.). Boston: Allyn & Bacon.

Hallahan, D. P., Lloyd, J. M., Kauffman, J. M., Weiss, M. P., & Martinez, E. A. (2005). *Learning disabilities: Foundations, characteristics, and effective teaching* (3rd ed.). Boston: Allyn & Bacon.

Hallahan, D. P., & Reeve, R. E. (1980). Selective attention and distractibility. In B. K. Keogh (Ed.), *Advances in special education (Vol. 1)* (pp. 141–181). Greenwich, CT: JAI Press.

Hanley, G. P., Iwata, B. A., & McCord, B. E. (2003). Functional analysis of problem behavior: A review. *Journal of Applied Behavior Analysis, 36*(2), 147–185.

Hardy, L. (1999). Why teachers leave? *American School Board Journal, 186*(7), 12–17.

Harris, K. R., Friedlander, B. D., Saddler, B., Frizzelle, R., & Graham, S. (2005). Self-monitoring of attention versus self-monitoring of academic performance: Effects among students with ADHD in the general education classroom. *Journal of Special Education, 39*(3), 145–156.

Hawken, L., & Horner, R. (2003). Evaluation of a targeted group intervention within a school-wide system of behavior support, *Journal of Behavioral Education, 12*, 225–240.

Hays, S. C., Rosenfarb I., Wulfert, E., Munt, E., Korn, Z., & Zettle, R. (1985). Self-reinforcement effects: An artifact of social standard setting? *Journal of Applied Behavior Analysis, 18*, 201–214.

Hazel, J. S., Schumaker, J. B., Sherman, J., & Sheldon, J. (1995). *ASSET: A social skills program for adolescents*. Champaign, IL: Research Press.

Healthy Children Project. (n.d.). Retrieved from www.healthychildrenproject.org/welcome.htm

Hernstein, R. J. (1974). Formal properties of the matching law. *Journal of the Experimental Analysis of Behavior, 21*, 486–495.

Hersh, R., & Walker, H. (1983). Great expectations: Making schools effective for all students. *Policy Studies Review, 2*, 147–188.

Heumann, J., & Warlick, K. (2001). Prevention research and the IDEA discipline provisions: A guide for school administrators. U.S. Department of Education, Office of Special Education Programs.

Heward, W. L. (2009). *Exceptional children* (9th ed.). Upper Saddle River, NJ: Merrill/Pearson.

Hiller, J., Fisher, G., & Kaess, W. (1969). A computer investigation of verbal characteristics of effective classroom lecturing. *American Educational Research Journal, 6*, 661–675.

Hobbs, N. (1966). Helping disturbed children: Psychological and ecological strategies. *American Psychologist, 21*, 1105–1115.

Hoffman, L., & Sable, J. (2006). *Public elementary and secondary students, staff, schools, and school districts: School year 2003–04* (NCES 2006-307). Washington, DC: National Center for Education Statistics, U.S. Department of Education. Retrieved from www.nces.ed.gov

Hofmeister, A., & Lubke, M. (1990). *Research into practice: Implementing effective teaching strategies*. Boston: Allyn & Bacon.

Hooper, S. R., Murphy, J., Devaney, A., & Hultman, T. (2000). Ecological outcomes of adolescents in a psychoeducational residential treatment facility. *American Journal of Orthopsychiatry, 70*(4), 491–500.

Hops, H., & Walker, H. M. (1988). *CLASS: Contingencies for learning academic and social skills*. Seattle, WA: Educational Achievement Systems.

Horner, A. C. (1994). Functional assessment: Contributions and future directions. *Journal of Applied Behavior Analysis, 27*, 401–404.

Horner, R., & Day, H. (1991). The effects of response efficiency on functionally equivalent competing behaviors. *Journal of Applied Behavior Analysis, 24*, 719–732.

Horner, R. H., Sugai, G., & Horner, H. F. (2000). A schoolwide approach to student discipline. *The School Administrator, 57*(2), 20–24.

Horner, R. H., Sugai, G., Smolkowski, K., Eber, L., Nakasato, J., Todd, A. W., & Esperanza, J. (2009). A randomized, wait-list controlled effectiveness trial assessing School-wide Positive Behavior Support in elementary schools. *Journal of Positive Behavior Interventions, 11*, 133–145.

Horner, R. H., Todd, A. W., Lewis-Palmer, T., Irvin, L. K., Sugai, G., & Boland, J. B. (2004). The School-Wide Evaluation Tool (SET): A research instrument for assessing school-wide positive behavior support. *Journal of Positive Behavior Interventions, 6*(1), 3–12.

Horton, S. V., Lovitt, T. C., & Bergerud, D. (1990). The effectiveness of graphic organizers for three classifications of secondary students in content area classes. *Journal of Learning Disabilities, 23*, 12–22.

Hosp, M. K., & Hosp, J. L. (2003). Curriculum-based measurement for reading, spelling, and math: How to do it and why. *Preventing School Failure, 48*(1), 10–17.

Howell, K., & Morehead, M. K. (1987). *Curriculum-based evaluation in special and remedial education*. Columbus, OH: Merrill.

Hughes, C., Copeland, S. R., Wehmeyer, M., Agran, M., Rodi, M., & Presley, J. (2002). Using self-monitoring to improve performance in general education high school classes. *Education and Training in Mental Retardation and Developmental Disabilities, 37*(3), 262–272.

Human Genome Project. (n.d.). Retrieved from www.ornl.gov/sci/techresources/Human_Genome/project/about.shtml

Ialongo, N. S., Werthamer, L., Kellam, S., Brown, C. H., Wang, S., & Lin, Y. (1999). Proximal impact of two first-grade preventive interventions on the early risk behaviors for later substance abuse, depression, and antisocial behavior. *American Journal of Community Psychology, 27*, 599–641.

Illinois PBIS Network. (2005). Fiscal Year 2005 PBIS Report. Retrieved from www.pbisillinois.org

Imbrogno, A. R. (2000). Corporal punishment in America's public schools and the U.N. Convention on the Rights of the Child: A case for non-ratification. *Journal of Law and Education, 29*(2), 125–147.

Independent School District No. 2310, 28 IDELR 933 (SEA MN 1998).

Individuals with Disabilities Education Improvement Act, 20 U.S.C. 1400–1482 (2004).

Ingram Independent School District, 35 IDELR (SEA TX 2001).

Ingram, K., Lewis-Palmer, T., & Sugai, G. (2005). Function-based intervention planning: Comparing the effectiveness of FBA function-based and non-function-based intervention plans. *Journal of Positive Behavior Interventions, 7*(4), 224–236.

Institute on Violence and Destructive Behavior. (1999). *Building effective schools together.* Eugene, OR: University of Oregon.

Irvin, L. K., Horner, R. H., Ingram, K., Todd, A. W., Sugai, G., Sampson, N., & Boland, J. (2006). Using office discipline referral data for decision-making about student behavior in elementary and middle schools: An empirical investigation of validity. *Journal of Positive Behavior Interventions, 8*(1), 10–23.

Irvin, L. K., Tobin, T. J., Sprague, J. R., Sugai, G., & Vincent, C. G. (2004). Validity of office discipline referral measures as indices of school-wide behavioral status and effects of school-wide behavioral interventions. *Journal of Positive Behavior Interventions, 6*(3), 131–147.

Ives, B., & Hoy, C. (2003). Graphic organizers applied to higher-level secondary mathematics. *Learning Disabilities Research and Practice, 18,* 36–51.

Iwata, B., & DeLeon, I. (1996). *The functional analysis screening tool.* Gainesville, FL: The Florida Center on Self-Injury, The University of Florida.

Jack, S. L., Shores, R. E., Denny, R. K., Gunter, P. L., DeBriere, T., & DePaepe, P. (1996). An analysis of the relationship of teacher's reported use of classroom management strategies on types of interactions. *Journal of Behavioral Education, 6,* 67–87.

Jerome, A., & Barbetta, P. M. (2005). The effect of active student responding during computer-assisted instruction on social studies learning by students with learning disabilities. *Journal of Special Education Technology, 20*(3), 13–23.

Jolivette, K., Stichter, J. P., McCormick, K., & Tice, K. (2002). Making choices—improving behavior—engaging in learning. *Teaching Exceptional Children, 34*(3), 24–29.

Jolivette, K., Wehby, J., Canale, J., & Massey, N. G. (2001). Effects of choice making opportunities on the behavior of students with emotional and behavioral disorders. *Behavioral Disorders, 26,* 131–145.

Kahng, S., Abt, K. A., & Schonbachler, H. E. (2001). Assessment and treatment of low-rate high-intensity problem behavior. *Journal of Applied Behavior Analysis, 34*(2), 225–228.

Kallman, F., & Roth, B. (1956). Genetic aspects of preadolescent schizophrenia. *American Journal of Psychiatry, 112,* 599–606.

Kame'enui, E. J., & Carnine, D. W. (1998). *Effective teaching strategies that accommodate diverse learners.* Upper Saddle River, NJ: Merrill/Pearson.

Kame'enui, E. J., & Simmons, D. C. (1990). *Designing instructional strategies: The prevention of academic learning problems.* Upper Saddle River, NJ: Merrill/Pearson.

Kame'enui, E. J., & Simmons, D. C. (1999). *Toward successful inclusion of students with disabilities: The architecture of instruction.* Reston, VA: Council for Exceptional Children.

Kansas Institute for Positive Behavior Support. (n.d.). KIPBS Online Library: Toolbox: Functional Behavior Assessment. Retrieved from www.kipbs.org/new_kipbs/fsi/behavassess .html

Kaplan, J. S., & Carter, J. (1995). *Beyond behavior modification: A cognitive-behavioral approach to behavior management in the school.* Austin, TX: PRO-ED.

Kartub, D. T., Taylor-Greene, S., March, R. E., & Horner, R. H. (2000). Reducing hallway noise: A systems approach. *Behavioral Disorders, 9*(3), 161–171.

Kauffman, J. M. (2005). *Characteristics of emotional and behavioral disorders of children and youth* (8th ed.). Upper Saddle River, NJ: Merrill/Pearson.

Kauffman, J. M., Mostert, M. P., Trent, S. C., & Hallahan, D. P. (2002). *Managing classroom behavior: A reflective case-based approach* (3rd ed.). Boston: Allyn & Bacon.

Kazdin, A. E. (1972). Response cost: The removal of conditioned reinforcers for therapeutic change. *Behavior Therapy, 3,* 533–546.

Kazdin, A. E. (1987). Treatment of antisocial behavior in children: Current status and future directions. *Psychological Bulletin, 102,* 187–203.

Kazdin, A. E. (1993). Psychotherapy for children and adolescents: Current progress and future research directions. *American Psychologist, 48,* 644–657.

Kazdin, A. E. (1998). Conduct disorder. In R. J. Morris & T. R. Kratochwill (Eds.), *The practice of child therapy* (3rd ed. pp. 199–230). Boston: Allyn & Bacon.

Keith, T., Keith, P., Quirk, K. J., Sperduto, J., Santillo, S., & Killings, S. (1998). Longitudinal effects of parent involvement on high school grades: Similarities and differences across gender and ethnic groups. *Journal of School Psychology, 36,* 335–363.

Kellam, S. (2002, October). *Prevention science, aggression, and destructive outcomes: Long-term results of a series of prevention trials in school settings.* Presentation to the National Press Club, Washington, DC.

Kellam, S., & Anthony, J. C. (1998). Targeting early adolescents to prevent tobacco smoking: Findings from an epidemiologically based randomized field trial. *American Journal of Public Health, 88*(10), 1490–1495.

Kellam, S. G., Ling, X., Merisca, R., Brown, C. H., & Ialongo, N. (1998). The effect of the level of aggression in the first grade classroom on the course and malleability of aggressive behavior into middle school. *Development and Psychopathology, 10,* 165–185. See also the erratum: Kellam, S. G., Ling, X., Merisca, R., Brown, C. H., & Ialongo, N. (2000). The effect of the level of aggression in the first grade classroom on the course and malleability of aggressive behavior into middle school: Results of a developmental epidemiology-based prevention trial: Erratum. *Development and Psychopathology, 12,* 107.

Kellam, S. G., Rebok, G. W., Mayer, L. S., Ialongo, N., & Kalodner, C. R. (1994). Depressive symptoms over first grade and their response to a developmental epidemiologically based preventive trial aimed at improving achievement. *Development and Psychopathology, 6,* 463–481.

Keller, C., Brady, M. P., & Taylor, R. L. (2005). Using self-evaluation to improve student teacher interns' use of specific praise. *Education and Training in Developmental Disabilities, 40*(4), 368–376.

Kennedy, J. H. (1995). Teachers, student teachers, paraprofessionals, and young adults' judgments about the acceptable use of corporal punishment in the rural south. *Education and Treatment of Children, 18*(1), 53–65.

Kenny, M. C. (2004). Teachers' attitudes toward and knowledge of child maltreatment. *Child Abuse and Neglect, 28,* 1311–1319.

Keogh, B. K. (2003). *Temperament in the classroom: Understanding individual differences.* Baltimore: Paul H. Brooks.

Kern, L., Bambara, L., & Fogt, J. (2002). Class-wide curricular modifications to improve the behavior of students with emotional or behavioral disorders. *Behavioral Disorders, 27,* 317–326.

Kern, L., Dunlap, G., Clarke, S., & Childs, K. E. (1994). Student-assisted functional assessment interview. *Diagnostique, 19,* 29–39.

Kern, L., Ringdahl, E., Hilt, A., & Sterling-Turner, H. E. (2001). Linking self-management procedures to functional analysis results. *Behavior Disorders, 26,* 214–226.

Kern, L., Wacker, D. P., Mace, F. C., Falk, G. D., Dunlap, G., & Kromrey, J. D. (1995). Improving the peer interactions of students with emotional and behavioral disorders through self-evaluation procedures: A component analysis and group application. *Journal of Applied Behavior Analysis, 28,* 47–59.

Kerr, M. M., & Nelson, C. M. (2006). *Strategies for addressing behavior problems in the classroom* (5th ed.). Upper Saddle River, NJ: Merrill/Pearson.

Kerr, M. M., & Zigmond, N. (1986). What do high school teachers want? A study of expectations and standards. *Education and Treatment of Children, 9,* 239–249.

Kessler, J. W. (1966, 1988). *Psychopathology of childhood.* Upper Saddle River, NJ: Prentice Hall.

Kincaid, D., Childs, K., & George, H. (2010). *School-wide benchmarks of quality.* Retrieved from www.flpbs.fmhi.usf.edu/Web_Training_Coaches.asp

Klein, R. G., & Last, C. G. (1989). *Anxiety disorders in children.* Newbury Park, CA: Sage.

Knitzer, J., Steinberg, Z., & Fleisch, B. (1990). *At the schoolhouse door: An examination of programs and policies for children with emotional and behavioral problems.* New York: Bank Street College of Education.

Knoff, H. (2001). *Stop and Think Social Skills Program.* Longmont, CO: Sopris West.

Kohn, A. (1993). *Punished by rewards.* Boston: Houghton Mifflin.

Kube, B. A., & Ratigan, G. (1991). All present and accounted for: A no-nonsense policy on student attendance keeps kids showing up for class—and learning. *The American School Board Journal, 72,* 22–23.

Kupersmidt, J., Coie, J., & Dodge, K. (1990). The role of peer relationships in the development of disorder. In S. Asher & J. Coie (Eds.), *Peer rejection in childhood* (pp. 274–308). New York: Cambridge University Press.

Ladd, G. W., Birch, S. H., & Buhs, E. S. (1999). Children's social and scholastic lives in kindergarten: Related to spheres of influence? *Child Development, 70,* 1373–1400.

Lane, K. L., Givner, C. C., & Pierson, M. R. (2004). Teacher expectations of student behavior: Social skills necessary for success in elementary school classrooms. *Journal of Special Education, 38,* 104–110.

Lane, K. L., Wehby, J., & Barton-Atwood, S. (2005). Students with and at risk for emotional and behavioral disorders: Meeting their social and academic needs. *Preventing School Failure, 49*(2), 6–9.

Langdon, C. A. (1999). The fifth Phi Delta Kappa poll of teachers' attitudes toward the public schools. *Phi Delta Kappan, 80,* 611–618.

Lassen, S. R., Steele, M. M., & Sailor, W. (2006). The relationship of school-wide positive behavior support to academic achievement in an urban middle school. *Psychology in the Schools, 43*(6), 701–712.

Latham, G. I. (1992). *Managing the classroom environment to facilitate effective instruction.* Logan, UT: P&T Ink.

Lembke, E. S., & Stormont, M. (2005). Using research-based practices to support students with diverse needs in general education settings. *Psychology in the Schools, 42*(8), 761–763.

Leone, P. E., Christle, C. A., Nelson, C. M., Skiba, R., Frey, A., & Jolivette, K. (2003). *School failure, race, and disability: Promoting positive outcomes, decreasing vulnerability for involvement with the juvenile delinquency system.* College Park, MD: The National Center on Education, Disability, and Juvenile Justice. Retrieved from www.edjj.org/Publications/list/leone_et_al-2003.pdf

Lewis, T. J., Hudson, S., Richter, M., & Johnson, N. (2004). Scientifically supported practices in emotional and behavioral disorders: A proposed approach and brief review of current practices. *Behavioral Disorders, 29*(3), 247–259.

Lewis, T. J., Powers, L. J., & Kelk, M. J. (2002). Reducing problem behaviors on the playground: An investigation of the application of school-wide positive behavior supports. *Psychology in the Schools, 39*(2), 181–190.

Lewis, T. J., Scott, T., & Sugai, G. (1996). The problem behavior questionnaire: A teacher-based instrument to develop functional hypotheses of problem behavior in general education classrooms. *Diagnostique, 19*(2–3), 103–115.

Lewis, W. W. (1988). The role of ecological variables in residential treatment. *Behavioral Disorders, 13*, 98–107.

Lindberg, J. S., Iwata, B. A., & Kahng, S. W. (1999). DRO contingencies: An analysis of variable-momentary schedules. *Journal of Applied Behavior Analysis, 32*(2), 123–136.

Litow, L., & Pumroy, D. K. (1975). A brief review of classroom group-oriented contingencies. *Journal of Applied Behavior Analysis, 8*, 341–347.

Lo, Y., & Cartledge, G. (2004). Total class peer tutoring and interdependent group oriented contingency: Improving the academic and task related behaviors of fourth-grade urban students. *Education and Treatment of Children, 27*(3), 235–262.

Lovaas, O. I., Koegel, R. L., Simmons, J. Q., & Long, J. S. (1973). Some generalization and follow-up measures on autistic children in behavior therapy. *Journal of Applied Behavior Analysis, 6*, 131–165.

Lovitt, T. C., Fister, S., Freston, J. L., Kemp, K., Moore, R. C., Schroeder, B., & Bauernschmidt, M. (1990). Using precision teaching techniques: Translating research. *Teaching Exceptional Children, 22*(3), 16–19.

Luce, S. C., Delquadri, J., & Hall, R. V. (1980). Contingent exercise: A procedure used with differential reinforcement to reduce bizarre verbal behavior. *Journal of Applied Behavior Analysis, 13*, 583–594.

Luiselli, J. K., Putnam, R. F., Handler, M. W., & Feinberg, A. B. (2005). Whole-school positive behaviour support: Effects on student discipline problems and academic performance. *Educational Psychology, 25*(2–3), 183–198.

Lyon, G. R. (1998). *Overview of NICHD reading and literacy initiatives*. U.S. Senate Committee on Labor and Human Resources. United States Congress. Washington, D.C.: Congressional Printing Office.

Maag, J. W. (2001). Rewarded by punishment: Reflections on the disuse of positive reinforcement in schools. *Exceptional Children, 67*, 173–186.

Mace, F. C., Belfiore, P. J., & Shea, M. (2001). Operant theory and research on self-regulation. In B. Zimmerman and D. Schunk (Eds.), *Learning and academic achievement: Theoretical perspectives* (pp. 39–65). Mahwah, NJ: Lawrence Erlbaum.

Maheady, L., & Gard, J. (2010). Classwide peer tutoring: Practice, theory, research, and personal narrative. *Intervention in School and Clinic, 46*(2), 71–78.

Malecki, C., & Elliot, S. (2002). Children's social behaviors as predictors of academic achievement: A longitudinal analysis. *School Psychology Quarterly, 17*(1), 1–23.

Mancina, C., Tankersley, M., Kamps, D., Kravitz, T., & Parrett, J. (2000). Brief report: Reduction of inappropriate vocalization for a child with autism using a self-management treatment program. *Journal of Autism and Developmental Disabilities, 30*, 599–606.

March, R. E., Horner, R. H., Lewis-Palmer, T., Brown, D., Crone, D. A., Todd, A. W., & Carr, E. G. (2000). *Functional Assessment Checklist for Teachers and Staff (FACTS)*. Eugene, OR: University of Oregon.

Marchand-Martella, N. E., Slocum, T. A., & Martella, R. C. (2004). *Introduction to direct instruction*. Boston: Allyn & Bacon.

Martella, R. C., Marchand-Martella, N. E., Miller, T. L., Young, K. R., & MacFarlane, C. A. (1995). Teaching instructional aides and peer tutors to decrease problem behaviors in the classroom. *Teaching Exceptional Children, 27*, 53–56.

Martella, R. C., & Nelson, J. R. (2003). Managing classroom behavior. *Journal of Direct Instruction, 3*(2), 139–165.

Martella, R. C., Nelson, J. R., & Marchand-Martella, N. E. (2003). *Managing disruptive behaviors in the schools*. Boston: Allyn & Bacon.

Martin, J. E., Mithaug, D. E., Cox, P., Peterson, L. Y., Van Dycke, J. L., & Cash, M. E. (2003). Increasing self-determination: Teaching students to plan, work, evaluate, and adjust. *Exceptional Children, 69*(4), 431–446.

Marzano, R. J. (2003a). *Classroom management that works*. Alexandria, VA: ASCD.

Marzano, R. J. (2003b). *What works in schools*. Alexandria, VA: ASCD.

Mastropieri, M. A., & Scruggs, T. E. (1998). Constructing more meaningful relationships in the classroom: Mnemonic research into practice. *Learning Disabilities Research and Practice, 13*, 138–145.

Mastropieri, M. A., & Scruggs, T. E. (2002). *Effective instruction for special education*. Austin, TX: PRO-ED.

Mastropieri, M. A., Sweda, J., & Scruggs, T. E. (2000). Putting mnemonic strategies to work in inclusive classrooms. *Learning Disabilities Research and Practice, 15*, 69–74.

Matheson, A. S., & Shriver, M. D. (2005). Training teachers to give effective commands: Effects on student compliance and academic behaviors. *School Psychology Review, 34*(2), 202–219.

Mathur, S. R., Kavale, K., Quinn, M. M., Forness, S. R., & Rutherford, R. B., Jr. (1998). Social skills interventions with students with emotional and behavioral problems: A quantitative synthesis of single-subject research. *Behavioral Disorders, 23*, 193–201.

Matson, J. (1994). *Matson evaluation of social skills with youngsters*. Worthington, OH: International Diagnostic Systems.

Matson, J., & Vollmer, T. (1995). *User's guide: Questions about behavioral function (QABF)*. Baton Rouge, LA: Scientific Publishers.

Mayer, R., Sims, V., & Tajika, H. (1995). A comparison of how textbooks test mathematical problem solving in Japan and the United States. *American Educational Research Journal, 32*, 443–460.

McAfee, J. K. (1987). Classroom density and the aggressive behavior of handicapped children. *Education and Treatment of Children, 10*, 134–145.

McClellan, J. M., & Werry, J. S. (2003). Evidence-based treatments in child and adolescent psychiatry: An inventory.

Journal of the American Academy of Child and Adolescent Psychiatry, 42(12), 1388–1400.

McCreight, C. (2000). *Teacher attrition, shortage, and strategies for teacher retention.* College Station, TX: Department of Professional Programs, Texas A & M University. (ERIC Document Reproduction Service No. ED444986)

McFall, R. (1982). A review and reformulation of the concept of social skills. *Behavioral Assessment, 4,* 1–35.

McGinnis, E., & Goldstein, A. (1997a). *Skillstreaming in early childhood.* Champaign, IL: Research Press.

McGinnis, E., & Goldstein, A. (1997b). *Skillstreaming the elementary school child.* Champaign, IL: Research Press.

McKinney, J. D., Mason, J., Clifford, M., & Perkerson, K. (1975). Relationship between classroom behavior and academic achievement. *Journal of Educational Psychology, 67,* 198–203.

McMaster, K. N., & Fuchs, D. (2002). Effects of cooperative learning on the academic achievement of students with learning disabilities: An update of Tateyama-Sniezek's review. *Learning Disability Research and Practice, 17*(2), 107–117.

Medco. (2006). New data: Antipsychotic drug use growing fastest among children. Retrieved from phx.corporate-ir.net/phoenix.zhtml?c=131268&p=irol-newsArticle&ID=850657&highlight=

Meese, R. L. (2001). *Teaching learners with mild disabilities: Integrating research and practice.* Belmont, CA: Wadsworth/Thompson Learning.

Meichenbaum, D. H., & Goodman, J. (1971). Training impulsive children to talk to themselves: A means of developing self-control. *Journal of Abnormal Psychology, 77,* 115–126.

Mercer, C. D., Mercer, A. R., & Bott, D. A. (1984). *Self-correcting learning materials for the classroom.* New York: Merrill/Macmillan.

Merrell, K. (1994). *Preschool and Kindergarten Behavior Scales.* Austin, TX: PRO-ED.

Merrell, K. (2002). *Social Behavior Scales–2.* Austin, TX: PRO-ED.

Merriam-Webster online. (n.d.). www.m-w.com

Merikangas, K. R., He, J., Burstein, M., Swanson, S.A., Avenevoli, S., Cui, L., Benjet, C., Georgiades, K., & Swendsen, J. (2010). Lifetime prevalence of mental disorders in U.S. adolescents: Results from the National Comorbidity Study—Adolescent Supplement (NCS-A). *Journal of the American Academy of Child and Adolescent Psychiatry, 49*(10), 980–989.

Metzker, B. (2003). *Time and learning.* ERIC Digest, ED474260. Eugene, OR: ERIC Clearinghouse on Educational Management.

Meyer, K. (1999). Functional analysis and treatment of problem behavior exhibited by elementary school children. *Journal of Applied Behavior Analysis, 32,* 229–232.

Miller, A. M. (2003/2004). *Violence in U.S. public schools: 2000 school survey on crime and safety, NCES 2004–314 revised.* National Center for Education Statistics, U.S. Department of Education. Washington, DC: U.S. Government Printing Office. Retrieved from nces.ed.gov/pubs2004/2004314.pdf

Miller, D. L., & Kelley, M. L. (1994). The use of goal setting and contingency contracting for improving children's homework performance. *Journal of Applied Behavior Analysis, 27,* 73–84.

Miller, D. N., George, M. P., & Fogt, J. B. (2005). Establishing and sustaining research-based practices at Centennial School: A descriptive case study of systemic change. *Psychology in the Schools, 42*(5), 553–567.

Miller, K. A., Gunter, P. L., Venn, M. J., Hummel, J., & Wiley, L. P. (2003). Effects of curricular and materials modifications on academic performance and task engagement of three students with emotional or behavioral disorders. *Behavioral Disorders, 28,* 130–149.

Miller, M. J., Lane, K. L., & Wehby, J. (2005). Social skills instruction for students with high-incidence disabilities: A school-based intervention to address acquisition deficits. *Preventing School Failure, 49*(2), 27–39.

Montarello, S., & Martens, B. K. (2005). Effects of interspersed brief problems on students' endurance at completing math work. *Journal of Behavioral Education, 14*(4), 249–266.

Morrison, J. A., Olivos, K., Dominguez, G., Gomez, D., & Lena, D. (1993). The application of family systems approaches to school behavior problems on a school-level discipline board: An outcome study. *Elementary School Guidance and Counseling, 27,* 258–272.

Morse, W. (1963). Working paper: Training teachers in LSI. *American Journal of Orthopsychiatry, 33,* 727–730.

MTA Cooperative Group. (1999). A 14-month randomized clinical trial of treatment strategies for attention-deficit hyperactivity disorder (ADHD). *Archives of General Psychiatry, 56,* 1073–1086.

Murdock, S. G., O'Neill, R. E., & Cunningham, E. (2005). A comparison of results and acceptability of functional behavioral assessment procedures with a group of middle school students with emotional/behavioral disorders (E/BD). *Journal of Behavioral Education, 14,* 5–18.

Murray, C., & Greenberg, M. T. (2006). Examining the importance of social relationships and social contexts in the lives of children with high-incidence disabilities. *The Journal of Special Education, 39*(4), 220–233.

Murray, C., & Murray, M. T. (2004). Child level correlates of teacher–student relationships: An examination of demographic characteristics, academic orientations, and behavioral orientations. *Psychology in the Schools, 41,* 751–762.

National Advisory Mental Health Council Workgroup on Child and Adolescent Mental Health Intervention Development and Deployment. (2001). *Blueprint for change: Research on child and adolescent mental health.* Washington, DC: Author.

National Alliance on Mental Illness. (n.d.). About mental illness. Retrieved from www.nami.org/Content/NavigationMenu/Inform_Yourself/About_Mental_Illness/About_Mental_Illness.htm

National Association of School Psychologists. (2001). Zero tolerance and alternative strategies: A fact sheet for educators and policymakers. Retrieved from www.nasponline.org/educators/zero_alternative.pdf

National Center for Educational Statistics. (2005). *The condition of education 2005: Annual report to Congress.* Washington, DC: Author.

National Institute of Child Health and Human Development. (2000). Report of the National Reading Panel. Teaching children to read: An evidence-based assessment of the scientific research literature on reading and its implications for reading instruction: Reports of the subgroups. (NIH Publication No. 00–4754). Washington, DC: U.S. Government Printing Office.

National Institute of Mental Health. (2002). Mental health medications. Retrieved from www.nimh.nih.gov/publicat/medicate.cfm#ptdep10

National Institute of Mental Health. (2003). Attention deficit hyperactivity disorder (ADHD). Retrieved from www.nimh.nih.gov/publicat/adhd.cfm#cause

National Institute of Mental Health. (2008). Autism spectrum disorders. Retrieved from http://www.nimh.nih.gov/health/publications/autism/complete-index.shtml

National Institute of Mental Health. (2009). Bi-polar disorder. Retrieved from www.nimh.nih.gov/health/publications/bipolar-disorder/index.shtml

National Institute of Mental Health. (2009). Schizophrenia. Retrieved from www.nimh.nih.gov/health/publications/schizophrenia/index.shtml

National Longitudinal Transition Study–2. (2006). FACTS from NLTS2: School behavior and disciplinary experiences of youth with disabilities. National Center for Special Education Research, Institute for Education Sciences, U.S. Department of Education. Washington, DC: U.S. Government Printing Office. Retrieved from ies.ed.gov/ncser/pubs.nlts.22000603.asp

National Research Council. (2001). Educating children with autism. Committee on Educational Interventions for Children with Autism. In C. Lord and J. P. McGee (Eds.), *Educating Children with Autism.* Division of Behavioral and Social Sciences and Education. Washington, DC: National Academic Press.

National Research Council and Institute of Medicine (2009). *Preventing Mental, Emotional, and Behavioral Disorders Among Young People: Progress and Possibilities.* Committee on the Prevention of Mental Disorders and Substance Abuse Among Children, Youth, and Young Adults: Research Advances and Promising Interventions. Mary Ellen O'Connell, Thomas Boat, and Kenneth E. Warner (Eds.). Board on Children, Youth, and Families, Division of Behavioral and Social Sciences and Education. Washington, DC: The National Academies Press.

Nelson, C. M. (1997). *Restraint/Seclusion/Effective use of time out.* Retrieved from www.state.ky.us/agencies/behave/bi/TO.html

Nelson, C. M., Sugai, G., & Smith, C. R. (2005). Positive behavior support offered in juvenile corrections. *Counterpoint, 1,* 6–7.

Nelson, J. R. (1996). Designing schools to meet the needs of students who exhibit disruptive behavior. *Journal of Emotional and Behavioral Disorders, 4,* 147–161.

Nelson, J. R., Benner, G. J., Reid, R. C., Epstein, M. H., & Curran, D. (2002). The convergent validity of office discipline referrals with the CBCL-TRF. *Journal of Emotional and Behavioral Disorders, 10*(3), 181–188.

Nelson, J. R., Colvin, G., & Smith, D. J. (1996). The effects of setting clear standards on students' social behavior in common areas of the school. *The Journal of At-Risk Issues, 3*(1), 10–19.

Nelson, J. R., Martella, R. M., & Marchand-Martella, N. (2002). Maximizing student learning: The effects of a comprehensive school-based program for preventing problem behaviors. *Journal of Emotional and Behavioral Disorders, 10*(3), 136–148.

Nelson, J. R., & Roberts, M. L. (2000). Ongoing reciprocal teacher–student interactions involving disruptive behaviors in general education classrooms. *Journal of Emotional and Behavioral Disorders, 8*(4), 27–37.

Nelson, J. R., & Rutherford, R. B. (1983). Time out revisited: Guidelines for its use in special education. *Exceptional Education Quarterly, 3*(4), 56–67.

Newcomb, M. D., & Richardson, M. A. (1995). Substance use disorders. In M. Hersen & R. T. Ammerman (Eds.), *Advanced abnormal child psychology* (pp. 411–431). Hillsdale, NJ: Erlbaum.

Newcomer, L. L., & Lewis, T. J. (2004). Functional behavioral assessment: An investigation of assessment reliability and effectiveness of function-based interventions. *Journal of Emotional and Behavioral Disorders, 12,* 168–181.

Niebuhr, K. E. (1999). An empirical study of student relationships and academic achievement. *Education, 9*(4), 679–681.

Niederhofer, H., & Reiter, A. (2004). Prenatal maternal stress, prenatal fetal movements and perinatal temperament factors influence behavior and school marks at the age of 6 years. *Fetal Diagnosis and Therapy, 19*(2), 160–162.

No Child Left Behind (2004). Retrieved from www.edweek.org/ew/issues/no-child-left-behind/

Northup, J. (2000). Further evaluation of the accuracy of reinforcer surveys: A systematic replication. *Journal of Applied Behavior Analysis, 29,* 201–212.

Northup, J., Wacker, D. P., Berg, W. K., Kelly, L., Sasso, G., & DeRaad, A. (1994). The treatment of severe behavior problems in school settings using a technical assistance model. *Journal of Applied Behavior Analysis, 27*(1), 33–47.

Office of Special Education Programs: Technical Assistance Center on Positive Behavioral Interventions and Supports. (n.d.). What is school-wide PBS? Retrieved from www.pbis.org/school/default.aspx

Office of Special Education Programs. (2003). Use of psychotropic medications by children and youth with disabilities. Washington, DC: Author. Retrieved from www.nlts2.org/fact_sheets/2003_04.html

Office of Special Education Programs: Technical Assistance Center on Positive Behavioral Interventions and Supports. (2010). Wraparound service and positive behavior support. Retrieved from www.pbis.org/school/tertiary_level/wraparound.aspx

Office of Special Education Programs Center on Positive Behavioral Interventions and Supports. (2010). *Schoolwide positive behavioral supports: Implementers' blueprint and self-assessment.* Eugene, OR: Author, University of Oregon. Retrieved from www.pbis.org/pbis_resource_detail_page.aspx?Type=3&PBIS_ResourceID=216

Okun, B. F., Fried, J., & Okun, M. L. (1999). *Understanding diversity: A learning-as-practice primer.* Pacific Grove, CA: Brooks/Cole.

Olds, D., Henderson, C., Kitzman, H., Eckenrode, J., Cole, R., & Tatelbaum, R. (1999). Prenatal and infancy home visitation by nurses: Recent findings. *The Future of Children, 9*(1), 44–65. Monterey, CA: Packard Foundation.

Olson, R., Wise, B., Conners, F., Rack, J., & Fulker, D. (1989). Specific deficits in component reading and language skills: Genetic and environmental influences. *Journal of Learning Disabilities, 22*(6), 339–348.

Olympia, D. E., Sheridan, S. M., & Andrews, D. (1994). Using student-managed interventions to increase homework completion and accuracy. *Journal of Applied Behavior Analysis, 27*, 85–99.

O'Neill, R. E., Horner, R. H., Albin, R. W., Sprague, J. R., Storey, K., & Newton, J. S. (1997). *Functional assessment and program development for problem behavior.* Pacific Grove, CA: Brooks/Cole.

Osguthorpe, R. T., & Scruggs, T. E. (1986). Special education students as tutors: A review and analysis. *Remedial and Special Education, 7*(4), 15–26.

Ostrosky, M., Drasgow, E., & Halle, J. W. (1999). How can I help you get what you want? A communication strategy for students with severe disabilities. *Teaching Exceptional Children, 31*, 56–61.

Oswald, K., Safran, S., & Johanson, G. (2005). Preventing trouble: Making schools safer places using positive behavior supports. *Education and Treatment of Children, 28*(3), 265–278.

Paclawskyj, T., Matson, J., Rush, K, Smalls, Y., & Vollmer, T. (2000). Questions about behavioral function (QABF): A behavioral checklist for functional assessment of aberrant behavior. *Research in Developmental Disabilities, 21*, 223–229.

Panasuk, R. M., & Todd, J. (2005). Effectiveness of lesson planning: Factor analysis. *Journal of Instructional Psychology, 32*(3), 215–232.

Parker, J., & Asher, S. (1987). Peer relations and later personal adjustment: Are low-accepted children at risk? *Psychological Bulletin, 102*, 357–389.

Patterson, G. R., DeBaryshe, B. D., & Ramsey, E. (1989). A developmental perspective on antisocial behavior. *American Psychologist, 44*, 329–335.

Patterson, G. R., Reid, J. B., & Dishion, T. (1992). *Anti-social boys.* Eugene, OR: Castalia.

Pescara-Kovach, L. A., & Alexander, K. (1994). The link between food ingested and problem behavior: Fact or fallacy? *Behavioral Disorders, 19*, 142–148.

Petras, H., Kellam, S. G., Brown, C. H., Muthén, B. O., Ialongo, N. S., & Poduska, J. M. (2008). Developmental epidemiological courses leading to antisocial personality disorder and violent and criminal behavior: Effects by young adulthood of a universal preventive intervention in first- and second-grade classrooms. *Drug and Alcohol Dependence, 95*(Suppl. 1), S45–S59.

Phillips, E. L., Phillips, E. A., Fixsen, D. L., & Montrose, M. W. (1971). Achievement place: Modification of behavior of pre-delinquent boys within a token economy. *Journal of Applied Behavior Analysis, 1*, 45–59.

Pianta, R. C., Hamre, B., & Stuhlman, M. (2003). Relationships between teachers and children. In W. M. Reynolds & G. E. Miller (Eds.), *Handbook of child psychology: Vol. 7. Educational psychology.* Hoboken, NJ: Wiley.

Polloway, E. A., Cronin, M. E., & Patton, J. R. (1986). The efficacy of group versus one-to-one instruction: A review. *Remedial and Special Education, 7*(1), 22–30.

Premack, D. (1959). Toward empirical behavior laws: I. Positive reinforcement. *Psychological Review, 66*, 219–233.

Prizant, B. M., & Wetherby, A. M. (1987). Communicative intent: A framework for understanding social-communicative behavior in autism. *Journal of the American Academy of Child and Adolescent Psychiatry, 26*, 472–479.

Prout, H. T., & DeMartino, R. A. (1986). A meta-analysis of school-based studies of psychotherapy. *Journal of School Psychology, 24*, 285–292.

Public Agenda (2003). Attitudes about teaching. Retrieved from www.publicagenda.org/attitudes-about-teaching

Public Agenda. (2004). Teaching interrupted. Retrieved from www.publicagenda.org/reports/teaching-interrupted

Public Agenda. (2008). *Lessons learned: New teachers talk about their jobs, challenges and long-range plans.* Retrieved from www.publicagenda.org/files/pdf/lessons_learned_2.pdf

Putnam, R. F., Handler, M. W., Ramirez-Platt, C. M., & Luiselli, J. K. (2003). Improving student bus-riding behavior through a whole-school intervention. *Journal of Applied Behavior Analysis, 36*, 583–590.

Randall-David, E. (1989). *Strategies for working with culturally diverse communities and clients.* Rockville, MD: Association for the Care of Children's Health.

Redl, F. (1959a). The concept of a therapeutic milieu. *American Journal of Orthopsychiatry, 29*, 721–736.

Redl, F. (1959b). Strategy and techniques of the life space interview. *American Journal of Orthopsychiatry, 29*, 1–18.

Redl, F., & Wineman, D. (1952). *Controls from within: Techniques for the treatment of the aggressive child*. New York: Free Press.

Reid, R., Trout, A. L., & Schwartz, M. (2005). Self-regulation interventions for children with attention deficit/hyperactivity disorder. *Exceptional Children, 71*(4), 361–376.

Rentz, N. L. (2007). The influence of positive behavior support on collective teacher efficacy (Doctoral dissertation, Baylor University). Retrieved from https://beardocs.baylor.edu/bitstream/2104/5083/2/nan_rentz_phd.pdf

Report on Scientifically Based Research Supported by the U.S. Department of Education. (2002, November 18). Retrieved from www.ed.gov/news/pressreleases/2002/11/11182002b.html

Repp, A. C. (1999). Naturalistic functional assessment in classroom settings. In A. C. Repp & R. H. Horner (Eds.), *Functional analysis of problem behavior* (pp. 238–258). Belmont, CA: Wadsworth.

Repp, A. C., & Dietz, D. E. D. (1979). Reinforcement-based reductive procedures: Training and monitoring performance of institutional staff. *Mental Retardation, 17*, 221–226.

Repp, A. C., & Horner, R. H. (1999). Introduction to functional analysis. In A. C. Repp & R. H. Horner (Eds.), *Functional analysis of problem behavior* (pp. 1–6). Belmont, CA: Wadsworth.

Rezmierski, V., & Kotre, J. (1974). A limited literature review of theory of the psychodynamic model. In W. C. Rhodes & M. L. Tracy (Eds.), *A study of child variance (Vol. 1)*. Ann Arbor, MI: University of Michigan Press.

Rhode, G., Jenson, W. R., & Reavis, H. K. (1992). *The tough kid book*. Longmont, CO: Sopris West.

Rhodes, W. C. (1967). The disturbing child: A problem of ecological management. *Exceptional Children, 33*, 449–455.

Rhodes, W. C. (1970). A community participation analysis of emotional disturbance. *Exceptional Children, 37*, 309–314.

Rhodes, W. C., & Tracy, M. L. (1974). *A study of child variance (Vol. 1): Conceptual Models*. Ann Arbor, MI: University of Michigan Press.

Rice, J., Reich, T., Andreasen, N. C., Endicott, J., Van Eerdewegh, M., Fishman, R., Hirschfeld, R. M. A., & Klerman, G. L. (1987). The familiar transmission of bipolar illness. *Archives of General Psychiatry, 44*, 441–447.

Ripley, X. (1997, July). *Collaboration between general and special education teachers*. Washington, DC: ERIC Clearinghouse on Teaching and Teacher Education.

Rivera, D. P., & Smith, D. D. (1997). *Teaching students with learning and behavior problems*. Boston: Allyn & Bacon.

Roberts, M., White, R., & McLaughlin, T. F. (1997). Useful classroom accommodations for teaching children with ADD and ADHD. *Journal of Special Education, 21*(2), 71–84.

Robinson, D. H., Funk, D. C., Beth, A., & Bush, A. M. (2005). Changing beliefs about corporal punishment: Increasing knowledge about ineffectiveness to build more consistent moral and informational beliefs. *Journal of Behavioral Education, 14*(2), 117–139.

Rose, L. C., & Gallup, A. M. (2002). *The 34th Annual Phi Delta Kappa/Gallup Poll of the public's attitude toward the public schools*. Bloomington, IN: Phi Delta Kappa International.

Rose, L. C., & Gallup, A. M. (2004). *The 36th Annual Phi Delta Kappa/Gallup Poll of the public's attitude toward the public schools*. Bloomington, IN: Phi Delta Kappa International.

Rosenhan, D. L., & Seligman, M. E. P. (1989). *Abnormal psychology*. New York: W. W. Norton.

Rosenshine, B. (1980). How time is spent in elementary classrooms. In C. Denham & A. Lieberman (Eds.), *Time to learn*. Washington, DC: National Institute of Education.

Rosenshine, B. (1983). Teaching functions in instructional programs. *Elementary School Journal, 83*, 335–351.

Rosenshine, B. (1986). Synthesis of research on explicit teaching. *Educational Leadership, 43*(7), 60–69.

Ruth, W. J. (1996). Goal setting and behavior contracting for students with emotional and behavioral difficulties: Analysis of daily, weekly, and total goal attainment. *Psychology in the Schools, 33*, 153–158.

Rutter, M., Maughan, B., Mortimore, J., & Ouston, J. (1979). *Fifteen thousand hours: Secondary schools and their effects on children*. Cambridge, MA: Harvard University Press.

Rylance, B. J. (1997). Predictors of high school graduation or dropping out for youths with severe emotional disturbances. *Behavioral Disorders, 23*, 5–17.

Safran, S. P. (2006). Using the effective behavior supports survey to guide development of schoolwide positive behavior support. *Journal of Positive Behavior Interventions, 8*(1), 3–9.

Sagor, M. (1974). Biological bases of childhood behavior disorders. In W. C. Rhodes, & M. L. Tracey (Eds.), *A study of child variance (Vol. 1): Conceptual models*. Ann Arbor, MI: University of Michigan Press.

Salend, S., & Sylvestre, S. (2005). Understanding and addressing oppositional and defiant classroom behaviors. *Teaching Exceptional Children, 37*(6), 32–39.

Sanger, D., Maag, J., & Shapera, N. R. (1994). Language problems among students with emotional and behavioral disorders. *Intervention in School and Clinic, 30*(2), 103–108.

Scheuermann, B., & Evans, W. (1997). Hippocrates was right: Do no harm. A case for ethics in the selection of interventions. *Beyond Behavior, 8*(3), 18–22.

Scheuermann, B., McCall, C., Jacobs, W. R., & Knies, W. (1994). The personal spelling dictionary: An adaptive approach to reducing the spelling hurdle in written language. *Intervention in School and Clinic, 29*(5), 292–299.

Scheuermann, B., & Webber, J. (2002). *Autism: Teaching does make a difference*. Belmont, CA: Wadsworth.

Schloss, P. J., & Smith, M. A. (1998). *Applied behavior analysis in the classroom*. Boston: Allyn & Bacon.

Schwartz, W. (2001). *School practices for equitable discipline of African American students*. New York: ERIC. Eric

Digest Number 166. Retrieved from www.eric.ed.gov/ERICWebPortal/search/detailmini.jsp?_nfpb=true&_&ERIC ExtSearch_SearchValue_0=ED455343&ERICExtSearch_ SearchType_0=no&accno=ED455343

Scientifically Based Evaluation Methods. (2005, January 25). *Federal Register*, Notices, 70(15), 3586–3589.

Scott, T. M., & Barrett, S. B. (2004). Using staff and student time engaged in disciplinary procedures to evaluate the impact of school-wide PBS. *Journal of Positive Behavior Interventions, 6*(1), 21–27.

Scott, T. M., McIntyre, J., Liaupsin, C., Nelson, C. M., Conroy, M., & Payne, L. D. (2005). An examination of the relation between functional behavior assessment and selected intervention strategies with school-based teams. *Journal of Positive Behavioral Interventions, 7*(4), 205–215.

Scott, T. M., Nelson, C. M., & Liaupsin, C. J. (2001). Effective instruction: The forgotten component in preventing school violence. *Education and Treatment of Children, 24*, 309–322.

Scott, T. M., & Sugai, G. (1994). The Classroom Ecobehavioral Assessment Instrument: A user friendly method of assessing instructional behavioral relationships in the classroom. *Diagnostique, 19*, 59–77.

Scruggs, T. E., & Mastropieri, M. A. (2000). Mnemonic interventions for students with behavior disorders: Memory for learning and behavior. *Beyond Behavior, 10*, 13–17.

Self-Brown, S. R., & Mathews, S. (2003). Effects of classroom structure on student achievement goal orientation. *The Journal of Educational Research, 97*(2), 106–111.

Seymour, F. W., & Stokes, T. F. (1976). Self-recording in training girls to increase work and evoke staff praise in an institution for offenders. *Journal of Applied Behavior Analysis, 9*, 41–54.

Shapiro, E. S., & Goldberg, R. (1986). A comparison of group contingencies for increasing spelling performance among sixth grade students. *School Psychology Review, 15*, 546–557.

Shaw, S. R. (2002). A school psychologist investigates sensory integration therapies: Promise, possibility, and the art of placebo. *NASP Communiqué, 31*(2), 5. Retrieved from www.autismtoday.com/articles/School_Psychologist_ Investigates_Sensory_Integration.htm

Sheridan, S. M. (2000). *The tough kid social skills book.* Longmont, CO: Sopris West.

Shimabukuro, S. M., Prater, M. A., Jenkins, A., & Edelen-Smith, P. (1999). The effects of self-monitoring of academic performance on students with learning disabilities and ADD/ADHD. *Education and Treatment of Children, 22*, 397–414.

Shinn, M., Ramsey, E., Walker, H. M., Stieber, S., & O'Neill, R. E. (1987). Antisocial behavior in school settings: Initial differences in an at risk and normal population. *Journal of Special Education, 21*, 69–84.

Shores, R. E., Gunter, P. L., & Jack, S. (1993). Classroom management strategies: Are they setting events for coercion? *Behavioral Disorders, 18*, 92–102.

Silver-Pacuilla, H., & Fleischman, S. (2006). Technology to help struggling students. *Educational Leadership, 63*(5), 84–85.

Skiba, R. J. (2000). *Zero tolerance, zero evidence: An analysis of school disciplinary practice.* Bloomington, IN: Indiana Education Policy Center. (Policy Research Report #SRS2)

Skiba, R. J., & Knesting, K. (2002). Zero tolerance, zero evidence: An analysis of school disciplinary practice. In R. J. Skiba & G. G. Noam (Eds.), *New directions for youth development (No. 92: Zero tolerance: Can suspension and expulsion keep schools safe?* (pp. 17–43). San Francisco: Jossey-Bass.

Skiba, R. J., Michael, R. S., Nardo, A. C., & Peterson, R. (2000). *The color of discipline.* Bloomington, IN: Indiana Education Policy Center.

Skiba, R. J., & Peterson, R. (2000). School discipline at a crossroads: From zero tolerance to early response. *Exceptional Children, 66*(3), 335–346.

Skinner, B. F. (1953). *Science and human behavior.* New York: Free Press.

Slate, J. R., & Saudargas, R. A. (1986). Differences in the classroom behaviors of behaviorally disordered and regular class children. *Behavioral Disorders, 12*, 45–53.

Slavin, R. E. (1991). Synthesis of research on cooperative learning. *Educational leadership, 48*(5), 71–82.

Slavin, R. E., Stevens, R. J., & Madden, N. A. (1988). Accommodating student diversity in reading and writing instruction: A cooperative learning approach. *Remedial and Special Education, 9*(1), 60–66.

Smith, B. W., & Sugai, G. (2000). A self-management functional assessment-based behavior support plan for middle school students with EBD. *Journal of Positive Behavior Interventions, 2*, 208–217.

Smith, L., & Land, M. (1981). Low-inference verbal behaviors related to teacher clarity. *Journal of Classroom Interaction, 17*, 37–42.

Soar, R. S., & Soar, R. M. (1979). Emotional climate and management. In P. Peterson & H. Wahlberg (Eds.), *Research on teaching: Concepts, findings, and implications.* Berkeley, CA: McCutchan.

Sprague, J. (2002). Getting effective school discipline practices to scale: B.E.S.T. practices staff development. *NASP Communiqué, 30*(6), 28–32.

Sprague, J., Walker, H., Golly, A., White, K., Myers, D. R., & Shannon, T. (2001). Translating research into effective practice: The effects of a universal staff and student intervention on indicators of discipline and school safety. *Education and Treatment of Children, 24*(4), 495–511.

Sprague, J. R., & Horner, R. H. (1999). Low-frequency, high-intensity problem behavior: Toward an applied technology of functional assessment and intervention. In A. C. Repp & R. H. Horner (Eds.), *Functional analysis of problem behavior* (pp. 98–116). Belmont, CA: Wadsworth.

Spring, C., & Sandoval, J. (1976). Food additives and hyperkinesis: A critical evaluation of the evidence. *Journal of Learning Disabilities, 9*, 560–569.

Stallings, J. (1980). Allocated academic learning time revisited, or beyond time on task. *Educational Researcher, 9*(11), 11–16.

Stecker, P. M., Fuchs, L. S., & Fuchs, D. (2005). Using curriculum-based measurement to improve student achievement: Review of research. *Psychology in the Schools, 42*(8), 795–819.

Stephens, T. M., & Arnold, K. D. (1992). *Social skills in the classroom.* Odessa, FL: Psychological Assessment Resources.

Stevens, R. J., & Rosenshine, B. (1981). Advances in research on teaching. *Exceptional Education Quarterly, 2*(1), 1–9.

Stichter, J. P., & Conroy, M. A. (2005). Using structural analysis in natural settings: A responsive functional assessment strategy. *Journal of Behavioral Education, 14*(1),19–34.

Stokes, T. F., & Baer, D. M. (1977). An implicit technology of generalization. *Journal of Applied Behavior Analysis, 10,* 349–369.

Strizek, G. A., Pittsonberger, J. L., Riordan, K. E., Lyter, D. M., & Orlofsky, G. F. (2006). *Characteristics of Schools, Districts, Teachers, Principals, and School Libraries in the United States: 2003–04 Schools and Staffing Survey (NCES 2006–313 Revised).* U.S. Department of Education, National Center for Education Statistics. Washington, DC: U.S. Government Printing Office.

Stronge, J. H. (Ed.). (1997). *Evaluating teachers: A guide to current thinking and best practices.* Thousand Oaks, CA: Sage.

Sugai, G., & Horner, R. H. (2002). Introduction to the special series on positive behavior support in schools. *Journal of Emotional and Behavioral Disorders, 10*(3), 130–135.

Sugai, G., Horner, R., Dunlap, G., Hieneman, M., Lewis, T. J., Nelson, C. M., Scott, T., Liaupsin, C., Sailor, W., Turnbull, A. P., Turnbull, H. R., Wickham, D., Ruef, M., & Wilcox, B. (1999). Applying positive behavioral supports and functional behavioral assessment in schools. *Journal of Positive Behavioral Interventions, 2,* 131–143.

Sugai, G., Horner, R. H., & Lewis-Palmer, T. (2001). Effective behavior support team implementation checklists. Retrieved from www.pbis.org/tools.htm

Sugai, G., Horner, R. H., & Todd, A. (2000). *Effective Behavior Support Self-Assessment Survey.* Retrieved from www.pbis.org/tools.htm

Sugai, G., Sprague, J. R., Horner, R. H., & Walker, H. M. (2000). Preventing school violence: The use of office discipline referrals to assess and monitor schoolwide discipline intervention. *Journal of Emotional and Behavioral Disorders, 8,* 94–112.

Sulzer, B., Hunt, S., Ashby, E., Koniarski, C., & Krams, M. (1971). Increasing rate and percentage correct in reading and spelling in a class of slow readers by means of a token system. In E. A. Ramp & B. L. Hopkins (Eds.), *New directions in education: Behavior analysis* (pp. 5–28). Lawrence, KS: Department of Human Development, University of Kansas.

Sulzer-Azaroff, B., & Mayer, G. R. (1991). *Behavior analysis for lasting change.* Ft. Worth, TX: Holt, Rinehart, and Winston.

Sutherland, K. S. (2000). Promoting positive interactions between teachers and students with emotional/behavioral disorders. *Preventing School Failure, 44,* 110–116.

Sutherland, K. S., & Wehby, J. (2001a). The effect of self-evaluation on teaching behavior in classrooms for students with emotional and behavioral disorders. *Journal of Special Education, 35*(3), 161–172.

Sutherland, K. S., & Wehby, J. (2001b). Exploring the relationship between increased opportunities to respond to academic requests and the academic and behavioral outcomes of students with EBD. *Journal of Emotional and Behavioral Disorders, 22*(2), 113–121.

Sutherland, K. S., Wehby, J., & Copeland, S. (2000). Effect of varying rates of behavior-specific praise on the on-task behavior of students with EBD. *Journal of Applied Behavior Analysis, 8*(1), 2–8.

Swanson, H. L. (1999). Instructional components that predict treatment outcomes for students with learning disabilities: Support for a combined strategy and direct instruction model. *Learning Disabilities Research and Practice, 14*(3), 129–140.

Swift, M. S., & Swift, G. (1968). The assessment of achievement related classroom behavior: Normative, reliability, and validity data. *Journal of Special Education, 2,* 137–153.

Swift, M. S., & Swift, G. (1969a). Achievement related classroom behavior of secondary school normal and disturbed students. *Exceptional Children, 35,* 677–684.

Swift, M. S., & Swift, G. (1969b). Clarifying the relationship between academic success and overt classroom behavior. *Exceptional Children, 36,* 99–104.

Swift, M. S., & Swift, G. (1973). Academic success and classroom behavior in secondary school. *Exceptional Children, 39,* 392–399.

Taylor, M. C., & Foster, G. A. (1986). Bad boys and school suspensions: Public policy implications for black males. *Sociological Inquiry, 56,* 498–506.

Taylor-Greene, S., Brown, D., Nelson, L., Longton, J., Gassman, T., Cohen, J., Swartz, J., Horner, R. H., Sugai, G., & Hall, S. (1997). School-wide behavioral support: Starting the year off right. *Journal of Behavioral Education, 7,* 99–112.

Thomas, A., & Chess, S. (1977). *Temperament and development.* New York: Brunner/Mazel.

Thomas, A., & Chess, S. (1984). Genesis and evolution of behavioral disorders: From infancy to early adult life. *The American Journal of Psychiatry, 141,* 1–9.

Thomas, A., Chess, S., & Birch, H. (1969). *Temperament and behavior disorders in children.* New York: New York University Press.

Thomas, C. P., Conrad, P., Casler, R., & Goodman, E. (2006). Trends in the use of psychotropic medications among adolescents, 1994–2001. *Psychiatric Services, 57,* 63–69.

Thomas, D. R., Becker, W. C., & Armstrong, M. (1968). Production and elimination of disruptive classroom behavior by systematically varying teacher's behavior. *Journal of Applied Behavior Analysis, 1,* 35–45.

Thompson, R., Fisher, W. W., & Contrucci, S. A. (1998). Evaluating the reinforcing effects of choice in comparison to reinforcement rate. *Research in Developmental Disabilities. 19*, 181–187.

Thurlow, M., Graden, J., Greener, J., & Ysseldyke, J. (1983). LD and non-LD students' opportunities to learn. *Learning Disability Quarterly, 6*, 172–183.

Tikunoff, W., Berliner, D., & Rist, R. (1975). *An ethnographic study of the forty classrooms of the beginning teacher evaluation study known sample.* Technical Report No. 75-10-5. San Francisco: Far West Laboratory for Educational Research and Development.

Todd, A., Haugen, L., Anderson, K., & Spriggs, M. (2002). Teaching recess: Low-cost efforts producing effective results. *Journal of Positive Behavior Interventions, 4*(1), 46–52.

Todd. A. W., Campbell, A. L., Meyer, G. G., & Horner. R. H. (2008). The effects of a targeted intervention to reduce problem behaviors. *Journal of Positive Behavior Interventions, 10*, 46–55.

Todd, A. W., Lewis-Palmer, T., Horner, R. H., Sugai, G., Samson, N. K., & Phillips, D. (2005). *The Schoolwide Evaluation Tool implementation manual.* Eugene, OR: University of Oregon.

Torgeson, J. K. (1977). The role of nonspecific factors in the task performance of learning disabled children: A theoretical assessment. *Journal of Learning Disabilities, 10*, 5–17.

Torgeson, J. K. (1980). Conceptual and educational implications of the use of efficient task strategies by learning disabled children. *Journal of Learning Disabilities, 13*, 364–371.

Torgeson, J. K. (1988). Studies of children with learning disabilities who perform poorly on memory span tasks. *Journal of Learning Disabilities, 21*, 605–612.

Townsend, B. (2000). The disproportionate discipline of African American learners: Reducing school suspensions and expulsions. *Exceptional Children, 66*, 381–391.

Troia, G. A., & Graham, S. (2002). The effectiveness of a highly explicit, teacher-directed strategy instruction routine: Changing the writing performance of students with learning disabilities. *Journal of Learning Disabilities, 35*(4), 290–305.

Turnbull, A., Edmonson, H., Griggs, P., Wickham, D., Sailor, W., Freeman, R., Guess, D., Lassen, S., McCart, A., Park, J., Riffel, L., Turnbull, R., & Warren, J. (2002). A blueprint for school-wide positive behavior support: Implementation of three components. *Exceptional Children, 68*, 377–402.

U.S. Department of Education. (2002a). *Guidance for the Reading First program.* Retrieved from www.ed.gov/programs/readingfirst/guidance.doc

U.S. Department of Education. (2002b). *No Child Left Behind Executive Summary.* Washington, DC: Author.

U.S. Department of Education. (2003). *Identifying and implementing educational practices supported by rigorous evidence: A user-friendly guide.* Retrieved from www.ed.gov/rschstat/research/pubs/rigorousevid/rigorousevid.pdf

U.S. Department of Education (2006). Scientifically based research. Retrieved from http://www2.ed.gov/nclb/methods/whatworks/research/index.html

U.S. Department of Education, National Center for Education Statistics. (1998). *Violence and discipline problems in U.S. public schools: 1996–97, NCES 98–030,* by S. Heaviside, C. Rowand, C. Williams, & E. Farris. Project Officers, S. Burns & E. McArthur. Washington, DC. Retrieved from www.nces.ed.gov/pubs98/98030.pdf

U.S. Department of Health and Human Services. (1999). *Mental Health: A Report of the Surgeon General—Executive Summary.* Rockville, MD: Substance Abuse and Mental Health Services Administration, Center for Mental Health Services, National Institute of Mental Health.

U.S. Environmental Protection Agency. (2003). *America's children and the environment.* Washington, DC: Author.

U.S. Food and Drug Administration. (2004). *2004 safety alerts for human medical products.* Retrieved from www.fda.gov/Safety/MedWatch/SafetyInformation/SafetyAlertsforHumanMedicalProducts/ucm152982.htm

U.S. Public Health Service. (2000). *Report of the Surgeon General's Conference on Children's Mental Health: A National Action Agenda.* Washington, DC: Department of Health and Human Services. Retrieved from www.hhs.gov/surgeongeneral/topics/cmh/childreport.htm

University of Vermont. (1999). *Prevention strategies that work.* Center for Effective Collaboration and Practice. Retrieved from http://cecp.air.org/preventionstrategies/

Van Acker, R., Boreson, L., Gable, R. A., & Potterton, T. (2005). Are we on the right course? Lessons learned about current FBA/BIP practices in schools. *Journal of Behavioral Education, 14*(1), 35–56.

Van Acker, R., Grant, S. H., & Henry, D. (1996). Teacher and student behavior as a function of risk for aggression. *Education and Treatment of Children, 19*, 316–334.

Vannest, K. J., Soares, D. A., Harrison, J. R., Brown, L., & Parker, R. I. (2010). Changing teacher time. *Preventing School Failure, 54*(2), 86–98.

Vargas, J. S. (2009). *Behavior analysis for effective teaching.* New York: Routledge.

Vaughn, S., Levy, S., Coleman, M., & Bos, C. S. (2002). Reading instruction for students with LD and EBD: A synthesis of observation studies. *The Journal of Special Education, 36*(1), 2–13.

Vitiello, B., & Swedo, S. (2004). Antidepressant medications in children. *New England Journal of Medicine, 350*, 1489–1491.

Vitiello, B., Zuvekas, S. H., & Norquist, G. S. (2006). National estimates of antidepressant medication use among U.S. children, 1997–2002. *Journal of the American Academy of Child and Adolescent Psychiatry, 45*(3), 271–280.

Waksman, S. (1985). *The Waksman Social Skills Rating Scale.* Portland, OR: ASIEP Education.

Waksman, S., & Waksman, D. (1998). *The Waksman Social Skills Curriculum for Adolescents: An assertive behavior program.* Austin, TX: PRO-ED.

Walker, H. M., (1995). *The acting-out child: Coping with classroom disruption* (2nd ed.). Longmont, CO: Sopris West.

Walker, H. M., Horner, R. H., Sugai, G., Bullis, M., Sprague, J. R. Bricker, D., & Kaufmann, M. J. (1996). Integrated approaches to preventing antisocial behavior patterns among school-age children and youth. *Journal of Emotional and Behavioral Disorders, 4*(4), 194–209.

Walker, H. M., & McConnell, S. (1988). *The Walker-McConnell Scale of Social Competence and School Adjustment: A social skills rating scale for teachers*. Austin, TX: PRO-ED.

Walker, H. M., & McConnell, S. (1995a). *The Walker-McConnell Scale of Social Competence and Social Adjustment: Elementary Version*. Florence, KY: Thompson Learning.

Walker, H. M., & McConnell, S. (1995b). *The Walker-McConnell Scale of Social Competence and School Adjustment: Secondary Version*. Florence, KY: Thomson Learning.

Walker, H. M., McConnell, S., Holmes, D., Todis, B., Walker, J., & Golden, N. (1988). *The Walker Social Skills Curriculum: ACCEPTS*. Austin, TX: PRO-ED.

Walker, H. M., Ramsey, E., & Gresham, F. M. (2004). *Antisocial behavior in schools: Evidence-based practices* (2nd ed.). Belmont, CA: Wadsworth.

Walker, H. M., Schwarz, I. E., Nippold, M. A., Irvin, L. K., & Noell, J. W. (1994). Social skills in school-age children and youth: Issues and best practices in assessment and intervention. *Topics in Language Disorders, 14*(3), 70–82.

Walker, H. M., & Severson, H. H. (1992). *Systematic screening for behavior disorders*. Longmont, CO: Sopris West.

Walker, H. M., Todis, B., Holmes, D., & Horton, G. (1988). *The Walker Social Skills Curriculum: ACCESS*. Austin, TX: PRO-ED.

Wallace, G., & Larsen, S. C. (1978). *Educational assessment of learning problems: Testing for teaching*. Boston: Allyn & Bacon.

Watkins, C. L., & Slocum, T. A. (2004). The components of direct instruction. In N. E. Marchand-Martella, T. A. Slocum, & R. C. Martella (Eds.), *Introduction to direct instruction*. Boston: Allyn & Bacon.

Webber, J., & Scheuermann, B. (1991). Accentuate the positive . . . Eliminate the negative. *Teaching Exceptional Children, 24*(1), 13–19.

Webber, J., Scheuermann, B., McCall, C., & Coleman, M. (1993). Research on self-monitoring as a behavior management technique in special education classrooms: A descriptive review. *Remedial and Special Education, 14*, 38–56.

Wehby, J., Symons, F. J., Canale, J., & Go, F. (1998). Teaching practices in classrooms for students with emotional and behavioral disorders: Discrepancies between recommendations and observations. *Behavioral Disorders, 24*, 52–57.

Wehby, J., Symons, F. J., & Shores, R. E. (1995). A descriptive analysis of aggressive behavior in classrooms for children with emotional and behavioral disorders. *Behavioral Disorders, 20*, 51–56.

Wehlage, G., & Rutter, R. (1986). Dropping out: How much do schools contribute to the problem? *Teachers College Record, 87*, 374–392.

Weinstein, C. (1977). Modifying student behavior in an open classroom through changes in the physical design. *American Educational Research Journal, 14*, 249–262.

Weinstein, L. (1974). *Evaluation of a program for re-educating disturbed children: A follow-up comparison with untreated children*. Washington, DC: Bureau of Education for the Handicapped, U.S. Department of Health, Education, and Welfare.

Weinstein, R. (1979). *Student perceptions of differential teacher treatment*. Final report to the National Institute of Education, Grant NIE-G-79-0078, Berkeley, CA.

Werner, E. (1990). Protective factors and individual resilience. In S. Meisels & J. Shonkoff (Eds.), *Handbook of early childhood intervention*. New York: Cambridge University Press.

Werner, E., & Smith, R. (2001). *Journey from childhood to midlife: Risk, resiliency, and recovery*. New York: Cornell University Press.

Werry, J. S., Scaletti, R., & Mills, F. (1990). Sensory integration and teacher-judged learning problems: A controlled intervention trial. *Journal of Pediatric and Child Health, 26*, 31–35.

WestEd. (1998). *Improving student achievement by extending school: Is it just a matter of time?* Paper presented to the PACE Media/Education Writers Seminar. [Online]. Retrieved from www.wested.org/online_pubs/timeandlearning/TAL_PV.html

WestEd. (2001). *Making time count*. San Francisco: Author. [Online]. Retrieved from www.wested.org/online_pubs/making_time_count.pdf

Wheeler, J. J., & Richey, D. D. (2005). *Behavior management*. Upper Saddle River, NJ: Merrill/Pearson.

Whelan, R. J. (2005). Personal reflections. In J. M. Kauffman (Ed.), *Characteristics of emotional and behavioral disorders of children and youth* (8th ed., pp. 66–70). Upper Saddle River, NJ: Merrill/Pearson.

White, M. A. (1975). Natural rates of teacher approval and disapproval in the classroom. *Journal of Applied Behavior Analysis, 8*, 367–372.

Wicks-Nelson, R., & Israel, A. C. (1984). *Behavior disorders of childhood* (2nd Ed.). Upper Saddle River, NJ: Prentice Hall.

Wilkinson, L. A. (2003). Using behavioral consultation to reduce challenging behavior in the classroom. *Preventing School Failure, 47*(3), 100–105.

Wingert, P. (2010, March 6). Blackboard jungle. *Newsweek*. Retrieved from www.newsweek.com/id/234593

Wolery, M., Holcombe, A., Cybriwsky, C. A., Doyle, P. M., Schuster, J. W., Ault, M. J., & Gast, D. L. (1992). Constant time delay with discrete responses: A review of effectiveness and demographic, procedural, and methodological parameters. *Research in Developmental Disabilities, 13*, 239–266.

Wood, F. H. (1978). Punishment and special education: Some concluding comments. In F. H. Wood & K. C. Lakin (Eds.), *Punishment and aversive stimulation in special education:*

Legal, theoretical and practical issues in their use with emotionally disturbed children and youth (pp. 119–122). Minneapolis, MN: University of Minnesota.

Wyrick, P. A., & Howell, J. C. (2004). Strategic risk-based response to youth gangs. *Juvenile Justice, 9*(1), 20–29.

Xu, C., Reid, R., & Steckelberg, A. (2002). Technology applications for children with ADHD: Assessing the empirical support. *Education and Treatment of Children, 25*(2), 224–248.

Ysseldyke, J. E., Thurlow, M. L., Wotruba, J. W., & Nania, P. A. (1990). Instructional arrangements: Perceptions from general education. *Teaching Exceptional Children, 22*, 4–8.

Zaragoza, N., Vaughn, S., & McIntosh, R. (1991). Social skills interventions and children with behavior problems: A review. *Behavioral Disorders, 16*, 260–275.

Zhang, S. Y., & Carrasquillo, A. L. (1995). Chinese parents' influence on academic performance. *New York State Association for Bilingual Education Journal, 10*, 46–53.

Zionts, L. (2005). Examining student–teacher relationships: A potential case for attachment theory? In K. Kerns & R. Richardson (Eds.), *Attachment theory in middle childhood*. New York: Guilford Press.

Zionts, P. (1996). *Teaching disturbed and disturbing students* (2nd Ed.). Austin, TX: PRO-ED.

Zirpoli, T. J. (2005). *Behavior management: Applications for teachers* (4th ed.). Upper Saddle River, NJ: Merrill/Pearson.

Zito, J. M. (2000). Pharmacoepidemiology of methylphenidate and other medications for the treatment of ADHD. In R. W. Manderscheid & M. J. Henderson (Eds.), *Mental health, United States, 2000. Center for Mental Health Services, DHHS Pub No. (SMA) 01–3537*. Washington, DC: U.S. Government Printing Office, 2001.

Zuvekas, S. H., Vitiello, B., & Norquist, G. S. (2006). Recent trends in stimulant medication use among U.S. children. *American Journal of Psychiatry, 163*, 579–585.

NAME INDEX

SUBJECT INDEX

Page numbers followed by *f, b, t* indicate contents in figures, boxes, and tables respectively.